VORWORT

Work with English 5th edition Revised – Ausgabe Baden-Württemberg bietet einen auf den **aktuellen Bildungsplan** und die **Abschlussprüfung** für Berufsfachschulen in Baden-Württemberg abgestimmten Aufgabenapparat.

In dieser Ausgabe spielen die **interkulturellen kommunikativen Kompetenzen** eine zentrale Rolle und bilden den roten Faden der Units. Außerdem deckt das Lehrwerk kommunikative Kompetenzen, Text- und Medienkompetenzen sowie methodische Kompetenzen ab.

Durch die in jedem Kapitel angebotenen prüfungsrelevanten Aufgabenstellungen bereitet das Lehrwerk darüber hinaus schon von Anfang an auf die **Abschlussprüfung** inklusive der **Kommunikationsprüfung** vor.

Um den individuellen Lernprozess zu unterstützen, enthält das Lehrwerk **Dreifachdifferenzierungsangebote**. Aufgaben mit dem Symbol ●●● sind für leistungsstärkere Lernende gedacht; das Symbol ●●○ verweist auf *Files* mit Hilfestellungen im Anhang (*Files for differentiation*), und dazu befindet sich in den Handreichungen für den Unterricht eine weitere Aufgabe mit dem Symbol ●○○, die um noch eine Stufe nach unten differenziert. Somit eignet sich das Lehrwerk perfekt für das **AVdual Niveau C**.

Aufbau des Lehrwerks:

GETTING STARTED: frischt Grundkenntnisse in Grammatik, Wortschatz sowie Methodenkompetenzen auf.

UNITS 1–14:

- **A – WARM-UP:** bietet einen stark visuellen und kommunikativen Einstieg ins Thema.
- **B – TEXT** und **SITUATION:** führt über eine handlungs- und kompetenzorientierte Lernsituation und einen Lesetext zu einem Handlungsprodukt.
- **C – LISTENING:** beleuchtet durch einen Hörtext das Thema der Unit aus einem anderen Blickwinkel.
- **WORLD OF INTERCULTURAL COMMUNICATION (Units 1–7):** vermittelt Wissen über zielkulturelle Konventionen, führt Lernende durch vertraute Kommunikationssituationen und fördert dabei Interaktion und interkulturelle Handlungskompetenz.
- **TEAMWORK (Units 1–7):** fördert Kommunikation, Kollaboration, Kreativität. Dabei steht das selbstgesteuerte Lernen im Vordergrund.
- **WORLD OF WORK (Units 8–14):** trainiert durch realitätsnahe, handlungsorientierte Aufgaben die Kommunikation im Beruf.
- **EXAM SKILLS (Units 8–14):** bieten Zusatzübungen zur Vorbereitung auf verschiedene Prüfungsformate.
- **REVISION (Units 8–14):** überprüft den Lernfortschritt.

PAGEPLAYER APP

Mit der PagePlayer-App können Sie die Audio- und Videodateien aus dem Lehrwerk auf Ihr Smartphone oder Tablet laden und haben die Inhalte damit überall und jederzeit griffbereit!

Und so geht's:

1. Laden Sie den kostenlosen PagePlayer im App-Store Ihres Smartphones oder Tablets herunter.

2. Öffnen Sie den PagePlayer und laden Sie dort die Inhalte zu **Work with English 5th edition Revised – Ausgabe Baden-Württemberg** herunter.

3. Halten Sie Ihr Smartphone oder Tablet über die Buchseite. Sogleich werden Ihnen alle abspielbereiten Hörtexte und Videoclips in einem Medienmenü angezeigt.

4. Wählen Sie das gewünschte Element aus, drücken Sie *Play* – und los geht's!

Das Team von **Work with English 5th edition Revised – Ausgabe Baden-Württemberg** hofft, dass die Arbeit mit dem Buch Freude bereitet und das Lehrwerk zu einem gelungenen und erfolgreichen Unterricht beiträgt.

CONTENTS

 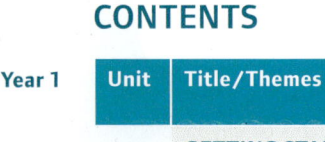

Getting started

Machen Sie sich fit für Ihren neuen Englischkurs. Bearbeiten Sie diese neun Seiten, um die einfachen Grundlagen aufzufrischen. Die Querverweise helfen Ihnen dabei, Ihr Kursbuch besser kennenzulernen.

1 CLASSROOM LANGUAGE

→ Language for speaking: *hintere Umschlagklappe*

Work with a partner. Match the situations (1–8) to the phrases you can use (a–h). Then take turns to practise the situations.

You …

1 are late for class.
2 can't hear what someone says.
3 don't know how to say a word.
4 don't understand a word in the text.
5 don't understand the teacher.
6 know the German word but you don't know the English word.
7 need to go to the toilet.
8 want the speaker to stop talking so fast.

a Can I go to the toilet, please?
b Could you repeat that, please?
c Could you speak up, please?
d How do you pronounce that?
e How do you say … in English?
f Could you please slow down a bit?
g Sorry I'm late.
h What does … mean?

2 PARTS OF SPEECH

A Think: Make a list of five English words you know. Try to find one word for each of the parts of speech. The table below will help you start off. Copy it and add your five words.

parts of speech				
noun	**verb**	**adjective**	**preposition**	**pronoun**
school	live	happy	near	you

Pair: Show your list to the person sitting next to you. Together add five new words, one word for each column.

Share: Work with another pair. Add the words of the other pair to your table. If any of the columns are short on words, try to fill them.

B Use words from your *parts of speech* table above to write six short statements (*Aussagen*). You don't have to use every part of speech in every statement.

EXAMPLE: *I live near the school.*

> **REMEMBER** ❗ *a / an*
>
> Change **a** to **an** before a vowel (a, e, i, o, u).
>
> **a** film   **an** English film

3 THE SIMPLE PRESENT OF THE VERB 'TO BE'

A Look at the photos. Use the information to complete what the people say.

I'm from …

I use English in / at / to …

I'm …

I'm a …

Name	Pat Kruger
From	Cape Town, South Africa
Age	32
Job	waiter

He uses English in the restaurant.

Name	Anika Chopra
From	Delhi, India
Age	23
Job	call centre agent

She uses English to help people from around the world.

Name	Chris Brady
From	Wellington, New Zealand
Age	34
Job	flight attendant

He uses English to explain the safety regulations.

Name	Maria Baumann
From	Stuttgart, Germany
Age	25
Job	hotel receptionist

She uses English to speak to guests.

B Work with a partner. Take turns to ask and answer questions about the people. Ask about their name, where they are from, how old they are, what their job is, and where or when they use English.

C Now take turns to ask and answer personal questions. Use one of the jobs above, or choose another job, to answer the last questions. (You can use a fantasy person if you like.)

1 What's your name?
2 Where are you from?
3 How old are you?
4 What's your job?
5 Where do you use English?
6 When do you use English?

REMEMBER ❗

Where is he/she from?   ~~Where is he/she coming from?~~

He's/She's a/an (+ job).   ~~He/She is (+ job).~~
She's **an** engineer.   ~~She's engineer.~~

D Introduce your partner to another pair.

Start like this:
This is … He's/She's from …

4 PREPOSITIONS OF PLACE

Work with a partner. Look at the picture. Use the prepositions in the box to say where people and things are.

at ▪ behind ▪ between ▪ in ▪ in front of ▪
next to ▪ on ▪ under

REMEMBER ❗

next to   ~~next~~

EXAMPLES: *The teacher is **in front of** the board.*
*The dictionaries are **on** the trolley.*

5 SOME/ANY

→ Quantifiers, S. 280

A **What things do you take to school? Work in groups and brainstorm a list. Here are two things to start you off.**

pencils
mobile

B **Take turns to ask and answer questions about what is in your schoolbag.**

REMEMBER ❗ *some, any*

Use **some** in positive statements.
Use **any** in questions and
negative statements.

EXAMPLES: *Have you got **any** water with you today?*
*No, I haven't got **any** water with me*
*today. I've got **some** iced tea.*

C **Report back to the class.**

EXAMPLE: *Mario has got **some** iced tea, but he hasn't got **any** water.*

6 THERE IS/ISN'T … THERE ARE/AREN'T

A You are going to describe your dream school. Work with a partner. Decide together what rooms and facilities there are. Make a list or a mind map.

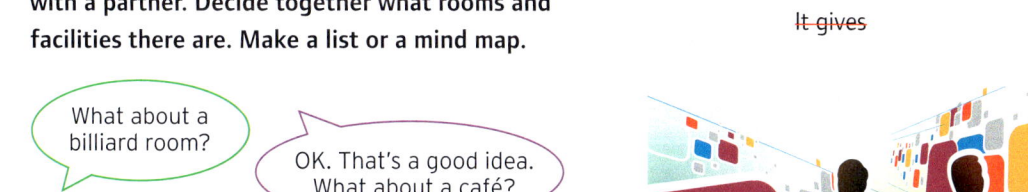

What about a billiard room?

OK. That's a good idea. What about a café?

REMEMBER ❗ *Es gibt*

Es gibt … = There is/are …

~~It gives~~

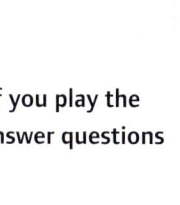

B Work with another pair. Take turns to ask and answer questions about your dream schools. Use *there is/are* and *some/any* when you need to.

EXAMPLES: *Is there a cinema in your dream school?*
Yes, there is. / No, there isn't.
Are there any places where we can sleep?
Yes, there are. / No, there aren't.

C Work in groups of four. Two new students have arrived at your school. Two of you play the new students, while two of you are the old students. Take turns to ask and answer questions about the rooms and facilities.

7 PLURALS

→ Plurals, S. 279

A Copy the table below into your notebook. Complete the 'rules for plural' column and add more examples. Two of the rules have been added for you.

	nouns	rules for plural	examples
1	Most nouns	*add s*	book → books school → schools
2	Most nouns that end in -*ch*, -*sh*, -*s*, -*x* or -*z*	*add -es*	box → boxes church → churches
3	Most nouns that end in a vowel (a, e, i, o, u) followed by *y*	*add --s*	boy → boys day → days
4	Most nouns that end in a consonant followed by *y*	*y becomes -ies*	family → families country → countries
5	Most nouns that end in -*f* or -*fe*	*f/fe becomes -ves*	shelf → shelves knife → knives
6	Nouns that end in -*o*	*add s or es*	piano → pianos hero → heroes

B Not all nouns follow the rules above. Match these exceptions* (1–4) to the rules (a–d).

*exception = *Ausnahme*

1	child → children	a	Certain English nouns change a vowel sound when they become plural.
2	fish → fish sheep → sheep	b	Some nouns are always plural.
3	foot → feet man → men tooth → teeth	c	Some nouns don't change when they become plural.
4	jeans scissors	d	Some nouns have their own special plural form.

8 THE GENITIVE

A Read the sentences and decide if 's is the genitive or the short form of *is*.

EXAMPLE: The student always comes to school by car.
The student's car's in the English teacher's
parking space.

*student's = genitive; car's = car is
(short form of is); teacher's = genitive*

1 Ian's from Edinburgh. Edinburgh's the capital
of Scotland.
2 That's my friend's phone.
3 These are the boy's books.
4 That book's not yours, it's Jane's.
5 The dog's bowl's empty. Its food's in the cupboard in the kitchen.

REMEMBER ❗ it's and its

it's = it is

its = pronoun

This is my cat. **Its** name is Sparky.
It's a big cat.

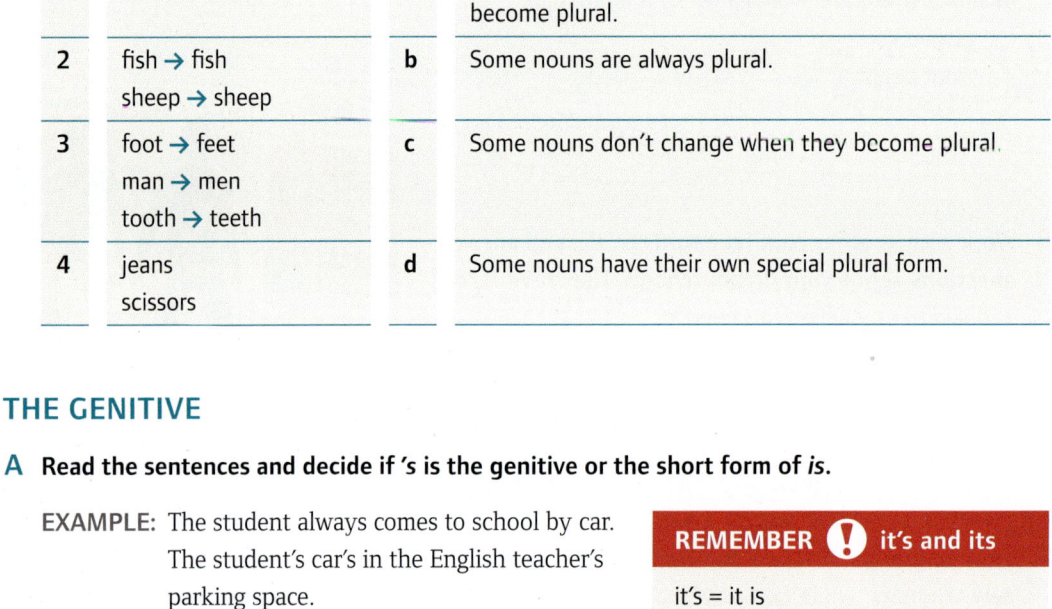

B Add the correct genitive or plural ending to the names and words in brackets.

EXAMPLE: (Peter)[a] (shoe)[b] are dirty.
Peter's shoes are dirty.

1 (Frank) scooter is cool.
2 Are these three (girl)[a] (Lenny)[b] (sister)[c]?
2 All our (name)[a] are on the (English teacher)[b] list.
4 The (teacher) room at school is large.
5 Two of the (boys)[a] books are at home. They are using (Patrick)[b].
6 All of the (teacher)[a] (box)[b] are in the room.

> **REMEMBER** ❗
>
> **genitive singular and plural**
>
> the boy**'s** father =
> the father of the boy
>
> the boy**s'** father =
> the father of the boys

9 PERSONAL PRONOUNS AND POSSESSIVE ADJECTIVES

A Copy and complete the speech bubbles with the correct forms of the pronouns.
The first one has been done for you.

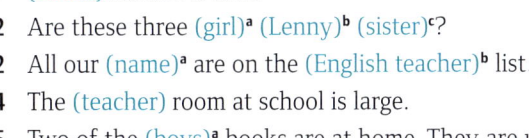

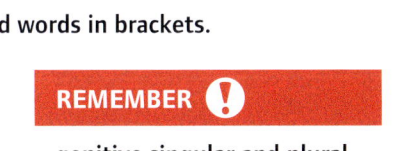

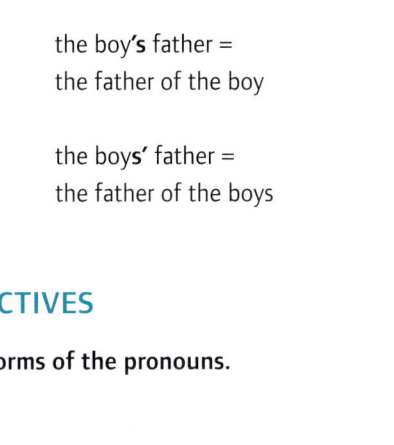

1 I'm Harry. This is *my* bag.

2 Hey Harry! Is this ⬭ bag?

3 No, it's not. It's ⬭ bag.

4 ⬭ 're playing football.

5 ⬭ is very good at maths.

6 ⬭[a] are ⬭[b] friends. ⬭[c] 're coming to ⬭[d] party on Saturday.

B Work with a partner. Decide together if 'Sie/sie' in sentences 1–4 is *she*, *you* or *they*, then translate the sentences. Say what helped you decide.

1 Sie mag Techno.
2 Sind Sie aus England?
3 Sie ist 18 Jahre alt.
4 Sie sind alle Fußballfans.

C Now decide with your partner if 'Ihr/ihr' in the sentences below is *her*, *your* or *their*, then translate the sentences. Say what helped you decide.

1 Shazia ist 16. Ihr Bruder heißt Sadiq.
2 Peter und Laura wohnen in England. Ihre Eltern kommen aus Deutschland.
3 Das ist Joanna. Ihr Freund Luke wohnt zusammen mit ihrem Bruder.
4 Ist das Ihr Handy?

10 OBJECT PRONOUNS

Complete these sentences with the correct pronoun.

EXAMPLE: Emily doesn't like dogs. She's afraid of ▬.
Emily doesn't like dogs. She's afraid of *them*.

1 We're going out tonight. Would you like to come with ▬?
2 Who is that boy? Why's he looking at ▬?
3 Harry left his wallet at home. Can you lend ▬ some money?
4 Your friends are late again. Please call ▬ᵃ and tell ▬ᵇ to hurry up.
5 Did you get your birthday present? I asked your grandad to send ▬ᵃ to ▬ᵇ last week.
6 We're tourists and we're lost. Can you help ▬, please?

11 MUCH / MANY / A LOT OF

→ Quantifiers, S. 280

> **REMEMBER** ❗ much, many, a lot of
>
> **a lot of** is used in positive sentences, especially in spoken language.
>
> **much** is used for things that cannot be counted (e.g. time). 'Time' is an uncountable noun.
> **many** is used for things that can be counted (e.g. book). 'Book' is a countable noun.
> **much** and **many** are usually used in negative sentences and questions.

She likes a lot of milk in her coffee.
I don't drink much milk.

There are a lot of eggs in the fridge.
How many eggs do we need?

Choose *much*, *many* or *a lot of*. Explain your choice. Sometimes you can use two.

EXAMPLE: How ⬭ time do you spend on homework?
How *much* time do you spend on homework?
Reason: time is an uncountable noun

1 There aren't ⬭ good clubs in this city.
2 How ⬭ pocket money do your parents give you every week?
3 I see that you've got ⬭ᵃ shelves but not ⬭ᵇ books.
4 ⬭ᵃ people are coming to my party. I'm a bit worried as I don't have ⬭ᵇ beer.
5 How ⬭ people are coming to the party?
6 Paula couldn't come on holiday with us, as she doesn't have ⬭ money.
7 I want to get bigger muscles so I eat ⬭ chicken.
8 I know ⬭ people in my street but I don't spend ⬭ time with them.

12 TELLING THE TIME

REMEMBER ❗ the time

Use **o'clock** with the full hour only:
It's ten o'clock. ~~It's half past ten o'clock.~~

The twenty-four hour clock (e.g. **sixteen thirty**) is only used for timetables.
Say **in the morning/afternoon/evening** or **a.m./p.m.** when the time is not clear.

Be careful with the half hour. 9:30 (*halb zehn*) is **half past nine**. ~~half ten~~

A Write out the times on the right in full.

EXAMPLE: *It's ten o'clock in the morning.*
It's ten a.m.

B Work in groups. Ask and answer the following questions.

What time …
1 do you go to bed? (on a weekday / at the weekend)
2 do you get up? (on a weekday / at the weekend)
3 does school start?
4 do you get home from school?
5 does your favourite TV show start?
6 is it now?

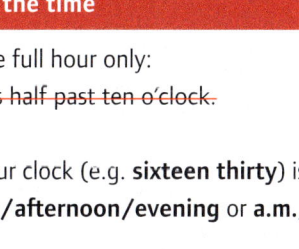
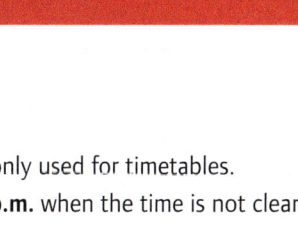

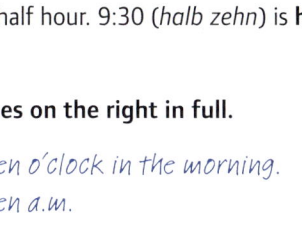

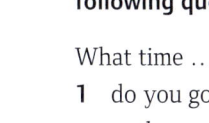
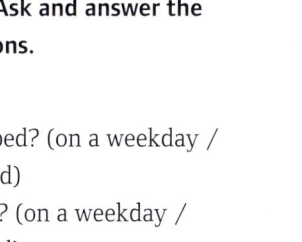

13 COUNTRIES AND NATIONALITIES

A Make sentences by combining things from this chart. Don't use one item more than once.

EXAMPLE: *Saint Basil's Cathedral is a Russian church.*

Antalya		American	church.
California		Australian	city.
Saint Basil's Cathedral		Austrian	holiday resort.
Tasmania	is a/an	German	island.
The Matterhorn		Indian	mountain.
The Rhine		Russian	monument.
The Taj Mahal		Swiss	river.
Vienna		Turkish	state.

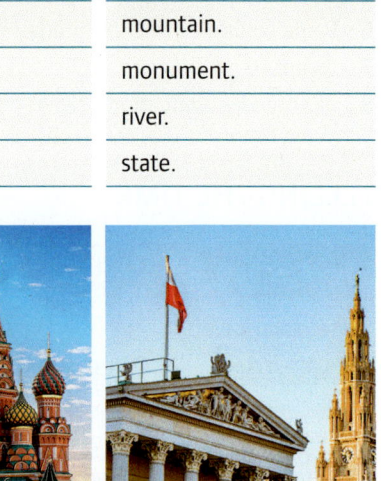

B With a partner, say where you would like to go, and why.

14 COURSEBOOK RALLY

You are going to find out about your coursebook. Work in groups of four. Look through your coursebook and write down ten questions about it like the ones in this table. Swap your questions with another group. Which group can find all the answers first?

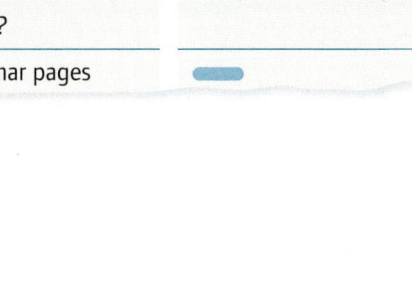

Where can we find …	answer / page number
a photo of Greta Thunberg?	▬
the grammar pages	▬

The food we eat

A WARM-UP: TALKING ABOUT FOOD

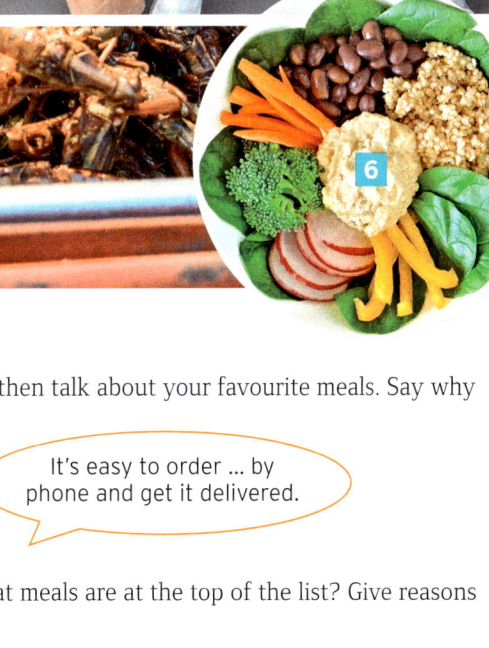

Think: What are your three favourite meals?

Pair: Together identify the food in the photos and then talk about your favourite meals. Say why you like them.

> I like ... because it tastes good.

> It's easy to order ... by phone and get it delivered.

Share: List your favourite foods on the board. What meals are at the top of the list? Give reasons why these are your class favourites. → menti

B EATING HABITS AROUND THE WORLD

SITUATION: Your school is taking part in an Erasmus+ project with a school in Scotland to make people think about global issues. You are working on a blog called 'What foods can we use to feed the world?'. You find a text called 'Feeding the world' (page 17) on a website and want to inform the Scottish school about it (task 5, page 19).

1 PREPARING TO READ

→ Ein Wörterbuch benutzen, S. 240

A The following words are taken from the text. Use your dictionary to find the German translations. Write down some of the translations your dictionary gives for each word. Keep your list for later. You'll need it again in task 2A below.

1	protein	**3**	resources	**5**	lentils	**7**	legumes
2	sustainable	**4**	saturated fat	**6**	flour	**8**	seaweed

••• B Follow the suggestions in the skills box below and make notes. Then answer this question: What is the text going to tell us about food around the world?

> ### TRAIN YOUR SKILLS: Vorbereitung auf das Lesen   vgl. auch S. 242
>
> Versuchen Sie, das Thema eines Textes zu erraten, bevor Sie gründlich lesen. Verwenden Sie dazu alles auf der Seite, das helfen könnte:
>
> - Die Überschrift und Zwischenüberschriften geben Ihnen eine erste Vorstellung vom Inhalt des Textes.
> - Schauen Sie sich die Fotos und Illustrationen zum Text an: Was zeigen sie? Welche Information steckt in den Bildunterschriften?
> - Lesen Sie die Aufgaben zum Text: Was genau müssen Sie machen?

••○ **Go to File 1 on page 186.**

2 READING AND UNDERSTANDING THE TEXT

A Read the text opposite and then look at your list of German translations from task 1A. Which of the words fits the context of the text?

B Match the headings (1–6) to the five paragraphs in the text (A–E). There is one heading more than you need.

EXAM
→ reading comprehension

1	Food from the sea	**4**	Using technology to make food
2	Cooking without water	**5**	Eating new food in order to survive
3	A good source of protein	**6**	Why we need to rethink our food production

02

FEEDING THE WORLD

A ···

Our planet is facing two major problems: Global warming and a population that is growing rapidly. Animal farming contributes to global warming, as more forests are destroyed to provide agricultural land. Scientists argue that a diet that is based on vegetarian options and
5   a small amount of animal protein is better for the planet. We can get ideas about how the diet might look if we study traditional food from around the world.

B ···

In many East Asian countries, people eat insects. Apart from
10 the fact that insects are sustainable and use fewer resources than farm animals, they are generally healthier than meat. One serving of insects has
15 around 60% less saturated fat than the same amount of beef and twice as much vitamin B12. The average insect is about 50% protein.

Insects on sale in a market

20 **C** ···

In many parts of India, people eat vegetarian food due to religious reasons. In the desert areas, lack of water has an influence on what the local people eat. In Rajasthan, for example, where the main ingredients of many of the dishes are beans, dried lentils and flour made from legumes, the inhabitants use dairy products like milk and butter instead of water for cooking.
25 As the planet warms up, we may need to look to the diets of warmer parts of the world to see how they have adapted to the heat.

D ···

Last but not least, some cultures have been eating seaweed for centuries. Seaweed has been eaten in Wales since at least the 17th century, where it is boiled and made into 'laverbread'. On
30 the opposite side of the world, the Japanese also eat seaweed. Seaweed is full of vitamins and healthy minerals, particularly iodine and iron.

E ···

Some types of food may sound strange to us today, but in the future we may be glad to have them on our tables. After all, if other people in different regions can eat this food, so can we!

(328 words)

●●● **C** Finish the sentences using the information from the text.

1 The two biggest problems facing the planet are ▬
2 According to scientists, we should eat ▬
3 Insects are healthier than meat because ▬
4 Because there is not a lot of water in Rajasthan, people use ▬
5 In order to make laverbread, the Welsh ▬
6 Although some food sounds weird to us, one day ▬

●●○ **Go to File 2 on page 186.**

EXAM
→ reading comprehension

→ Gezielt Informationen im Text finden, S. 243

D Talk in small groups. How does global warming affect your diet now?

> It doesn't. I still eat everything, including beef burgers.

> My mum buys less meat than before.

3 **LANGUAGE IN USE: QUESTIONS**

→ Simple present, S. 263

A Form questions using the words in brackets, and then answer them. The first question has been given.

1 ▬ meat? (your family – to eat)
   Does your family eat meat?
2 ▬ beans and lentils? (you – to like)
3 How much ▬ at the market? (the insects – to cost)
4 ▬ seaweed in the supermarket? (you – can – to buy)
5 ▬ a vegetarian? (Martin – to be)

REMEMBER ❗ questions in the simple present

To ask a question in the simple present, you need to add 'do' or 'does' (for he/she/it).

Do you **like** Thai food?	~~You like Thai food?~~
What **does** he **eat** for breakfast?	~~What eats he for breakfast?~~

Questions using a modal auxiliary (e.g. can, should, may) and 'be' do not need 'do'.

Can you give me a slice of pizza?	~~Do you can give me a slice of pizza?~~
Are you in the kitchen?	~~Do you be in the kitchen?~~

●●● **B** Work with a partner. Brainstorm three questions based on information in the text. Write down your questions and give them to another pair. Ask them to answer your questions without looking at the text.

EXAM
→ use of language

EXAMPLES: *How can we feed the world? Why don't we use ... to feed ourselves?*

●●○ **Go to File 3 on page 187.**

4 WORKING WITH WORDS

→ Ein Wörterbuch benutzen, S. 240

●●● **A** Work with a partner. The words below appear in the text. Use an English-German dictionary (print or online) to find words that belong to their families. Write down the German translations of all the words. Two words have been added to start you off.

1	agricultural (adjective) (line 4)		_landwirtschaftlich_
Find	**a** a noun		_Landwirtschaft_
2	scientist (noun) (line 4)		
Find	**a** another noun		
	b an adjective		
	c an adverb		
3	strange (adjective) (line 33)		
Find	**a** an adverb		
	b a noun (describing a person)		

●●○ Go to File 4 on page 187.

B Make six sentences using words you and your partner found while doing task 4A.

5 WRITING AN EMAIL

●●● Now write an email to the students at the Scottish school, in which you tell them about the article on page 17. Include the following points in your email:

EXAM
→ writing

- why we may need to eat different types of food in the future
- what types of food are eaten in different areas of the world, and why they may be interesting for us

Start like this:

Hi, I found an article about feeding the world that I think has some interesting information. The article ... .

●●○ Go to File 5 on page 187.

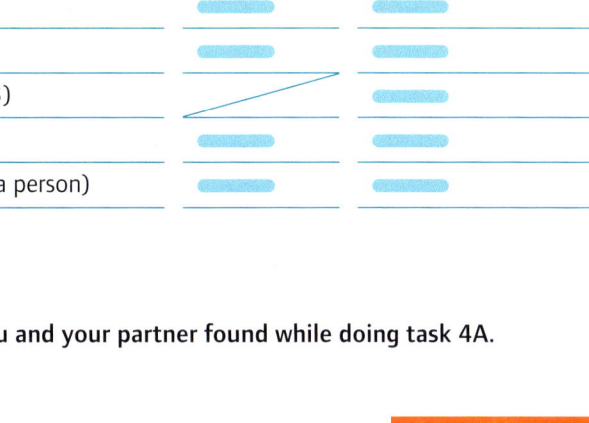

C WHAT I EAT

1 PREPARING TO LISTEN

TRAIN YOUR SKILLS: Vorbereitung auf das Hören   vgl. auch S. 245

- Lesen Sie die Hintergrundinformationen – zum Beispiel eine Situationsbeschreibung oder Angaben, wie viele Personen Sie hören werden.
- Denken Sie daran, dass die Fragen zum Hörtext meist in derselben Reihenfolge gestellt werden, in der die entsprechenden Informationen im Hörtext gegeben werden.

You are going to listen to an interview with Mark and Jane. Before you listen, do the tasks below.

A Read the speech bubbles and answer these questions.

1 What do the speakers eat?
2 Why do they eat their particular diet*?   *diet = *Ernährung* (not *Diät*)

> I eat almost everything, including meat. I believe that you need a variety of food and that includes meat.

> I'm a vegan. Vegans believe that you should never use animals for food.

Jane   Mark

B Match the words and expressions that the speakers use (1–4) to the definitions (a–d). The expressions are in the order they appear in the interview.

1 to survive	**a**	to make something happen
2 to cause something	**b**	to not have enough red blood cells
3 to suffer from anaemia	**c**	to give somebody good reasons to do something
4 to persuade somebody	**d**	to continue to live

2 LISTENING: WHAT I EAT AND WHY

A Read the questions below, then listen to the interview. Which of the questions do you hear?

1 Are you a vegetarian or a vegan?   4 Is your diet healthy?
2 Do you eat meat?   5 Do you have any allergies?
3 Do you suffer from anaemia?   6 Do you have problems with any food?

B Listen to the audio again and match four of the statements (1–6) with either Jane or Mark. Two statements do not match.

EXAM → listening comprehension

	person	statement
1	⬭	Humans don't need food or products made from animals to survive.
2	⬭	I usually eat meat every day.
3	⬭	I suffer from anaemia.
4	⬭	I don't like the taste of pork.
5	⬭	I want to make people change their diet.
6	⬭	As long as it's healthy, people can eat anything they like.

3 LANGUAGE IN USE: ADVERBS OF FREQUENCY

→ Simple present, S. 263

never

usually

always

EXAMPLES: *I never have any problems with food.*
I often eat meat.

often

rarely

sometimes

A Draw a line in your notebook. Complete the line using the words above in the correct order. Two words have been given for you.

– never ————————————————— always +

B Work in groups. Ask and answer questions about your eating habits. It may help you to write down your questions before asking them. Here are some questions to start you off.

EXAM → use of language

- When do you eat your main meal?
- How often do you eat meat?
- Do you ever eat Chinese food?
- How often do you cook?
- Who shops for food when you eat at home?
- How often do you eat in restaurants?

Go to File 6 on page 188.

4 DISCUSSION

→ Interaktion, S. 255

Think: Do you eat like Mark or like Jane?
Pair: Talk about current food trends in Germany. What do you think of diets such as veganism, low-carb diet, keto, vegetarianism, etc.?
Share: Report back to the class.

You are going to visit your exchange partner in the UK for the first time. You check your knowledge of eating and drinking in Britain and prepare for a visit to a restaurant.

1 EATING AND DRINKING QUIZ

Choose a, b or c to complete the sentences.

1 A typical meal in the UK is …
- **a** schnitzel, fried potatoes and salad.
- **b** fish and chips.
- **c** spaghetti bolognese.

2 A quick and traditional British lunch is …
- **a** an apple.
- **b** fast food.
- **c** a sandwich.

3 When students are invited to a party, they usually take …
- **a** a bottle of wine or some cans of beer.
- **b** a salad.
- **c** some snacks like a packet of crisps or pretzels.

4 In pubs it's traditional to have a drink and eat some …
- **a** French fries
- **b** crisps
- **c** chips

5 Before heading to school, most teenagers eat …
- **a** cereal and/or toast.
- **b** porridge and orange juice.
- **c** a fried breakfast with eggs, sausage, bacon, etc.

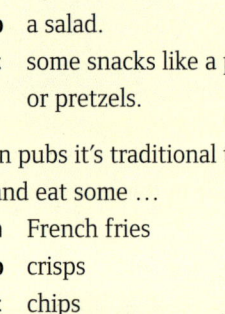

6 If you want to drink alcohol in a pub or buy it from a supermarket, you have to be …
- **a** 16 years old.
- **b** 18 years old.
- **c** 21 years old.

7 Before they start to eat a meal, British people often say …
- **a** 'Cheers!'
- **b** 'Good appetite!'
- **c** 'Enjoy your meal!'

8 Before drinking, British people usually raise their glasses and say …
- **a** 'Cheers!'
- **b** 'Toast!'
- **c** 'Here's to life!'

9 At the end of a meal in a restaurant, it's usual to …
- **a** add 10% to the amount on the credit card bill.
- **b** leave a tip only for good service.
- **c** leave extra coins or notes on the table for the person who served you.

10 Dinner is generally the name used for the meal which
- **a** people in Britain eat in the evening.
- **b** people in southern England eat in the evening and the rest of Britain eats at midday.
- **c** people in Scotland eat at midday and people in England eat in the evening.

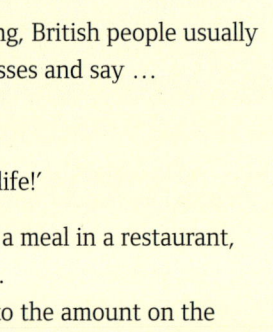

2 ORDERING A MEAL AT A RESTAURANT

A Listen to the dialogue. Use sentences a–g from the list on the right to fill gaps 1–7.

04

Waiter: Hello. Welcome to The Eatwell Restaurant.

Sarah: Thank you. I'd like a table for one, please.

Waiter: Certainly. This way please. … There you go. Can I get you something to drink?

Sarah: Not at the moment, thanks. ● ¹

Waiter: Are you ready to order?

Sarah: I'm not sure. I'm a vegetarian. ● ²

Waiter: Well, the vegetarian pizza is very tasty.

Sarah: That's a good idea. I'll take that and I'd also like a mixed salad.

Waiter: Good. One vegetarian pizza and a mixed salad. Would you like something to drink with your meal?

Sarah: Yes. ● ³

(The waiter brings the meal.)

Waiter: Here you are. ● ⁴

Sarah: Thank you.

Waiter: Shall I bring you the dessert menu?

Sarah: No thanks. I'm quite full actually. ● ⁵

Waiter: How would you like to pay?

Sarah: ● ⁶

(The waiter brings the bill.)

Waiter: I hope you enjoyed your meal.

Sarah: ● ⁷

Waiter: Thank you. Perhaps we'll see you again sometime.

Sarah: Yes, perhaps. Have a nice evening. Bye.

a Can I have the bill, please?

b Can I have the menu?

c Enjoy your meal.

d I'd like a glass of red wine.

e I'd like to pay by credit card.

f It was very nice, thank you.

g What can you recommend?

B How would you say the following in German? Don't just translate word for word.

1 Are you ready to order?	4 Enjoy your meal.	7 I'd like a table for one.
2 Can I get you something to drink?	5 Here you are.	8 Not at the moment.
3 Can I have the bill, please?	6 I hope you enjoyed your meal.	9 There you go.

C Act out the dialogue with a partner. Take turns to play the roles.

3 HANDS ON: EATING AND DRINKING IN GERMANY

A What did you learn from these pages about eating and drinking in the UK that surprised you? Compare and contrast the points with eating and drinking in Germany.

B Use information from these pages to produce a quiz in English for visitors to Germany. Give your quiz to another group and ask them to answer the questions and give you feedback.

Your school wants to improve its canteen. You are going to work in a team and plan and present a menu.

1 NOTICE OF A COMPETITION

Work in groups. Read the notice and answer the questions.

1 Why does the school need to know what you would like to eat?
2 What do you have to do?
3 What do you have to include?
4 What should you remember when you plan your menu?

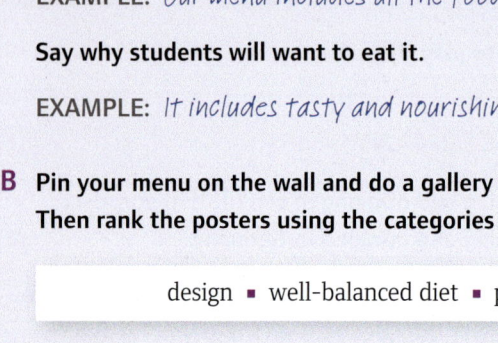

COMPETITION –
MENUS FOR OUR NEW SCHOOL CANTEEN

We need your help to make our new canteen the place where you want to eat. That's why we need you to tell us what you would like to eat.
We would like you to plan a menu.
- Include a starter, a main course and a dessert.
- Remember – we want healthy, balanced meals that everyone can enjoy.
- Please keep the prices low.
It's your canteen. We want you to eat there.
Go and plan the meals!

2 TALKING ABOUT THE TARGET GROUP

Discuss the following questions. Make notes.

a Who eats in your canteen?
b What age groups eat in the canteen?
c Does anyone have a special diet? If so, what do they eat/not eat?

3 PLANNING YOUR MENU

Brainstorm ideas of foods you would like to see in the canteen. Make a list. From your list, choose a starter, a main course and a dessert that will give you a healthy, balanced menu.

4 WRITING AND PRESENTING YOUR MENU FOR THE COMPETITION

A Take a large piece of paper and write up your menu. Illustrate it with drawings or take pictures from the internet if you like. Say why your menu is healthy and well balanced.

EXAMPLE: *Our menu includes all the food types that we need for a well-balanced diet.*

Say why students will want to eat it.

EXAMPLE: *It includes tasty and nourishing food that young people enjoy.*

B Pin your menu on the wall and do a gallery walk. (Walk past all the menus and study them.) Then rank the posters using the categories below. Give points from 1 to 5 for each category.

design ▪ well-balanced diet ▪ prices ▪ attractiveness ▪ overall effect

Sport

2

A Identify the sports in the photos. Then copy and complete the mind map below with as many sports as you can. What do you notice about the sports that are used with 'go'?

jogging   *sport*

GO   **SPORT**   **DO**

PLAY

tennis

B What sports do you enjoy playing or watching? Why?
What sports do not interest you? Say why not.

> I like going to the gym. I meet my friends there.

> I don't like running. It's boring.

REMEMBER ❗

I **do** sport.   I ~~make~~ sport.
It **is** fun.   It ~~makes~~ fun.

25

B THE DIARY OF A WINNER

SITUATION: Your class is taking part in an Erasmus+ project about the importance of sport for young people around the world. Part of the project is a competition to provide one photo with a text which shows why sport is important. The photo will be used on a website photo gallery about sport in Europe (task 5, page 29). The material in this section will help you get some ideas.

1 READING AND UNDERSTANDING THE TEXT

EXAM
→ reading comprehension

TRAIN YOUR SKILLS: Den Sinn eines Textes erfassen   vgl. auch S. 243

Überfliegen Sie den Text und schätzen Sie ein, worum es geht. Gehen Sie anschließend schritt-weise vor:

- Lesen Sie sorgfältig die Überschrift – sie ist meistens eine Inhaltsangabe des Textes.
- Danach lesen Sie den ersten Absatz und sämtliche Zwischenüberschriften.
- Lesen Sie den jeweils ersten Satz der übrigen Absätze – dort finden Sie in der Regel die wichtigsten Gedanken des Textes.
- Lesen Sie den letzten Absatz komplett. Üblicherweise finden Sie hier eine Zusammenfassung des Textes.

Read the text on the opposite page. Then choose the best option for each of the tasks below.

1 Tony's mother wants Tony to do three of the following. Which one does she not mention?
   a She wants Tony to go out more often.
   b She wants him to keep a diary.
   c She wants him to make friends.
   d She wants him to do sport.

2 Going to the gym has helped Tony …
   a become a bodybuilder.
   b know what he wants from life.
   c become a good friend to Paula.
   d feel better and more active.

3 A Park Run is …
   a for everybody, no matter how fit they are.
   b only for fast runners.
   c very competitive.
   d a one-hour run.

4 What does Tony do after the Park Run?
   a Have a meal with friends.
   b Hang out with people from the Park Run.
   c Post photos of the run on his blog.
   d Tell people that he is lonely.

5 To sum up, the text is about …
   a how Tony trains for an important run.
   b Tony's life on Instagram.
   c Tony making an effort to please his mother.
   d steps which Tony takes to improve himself.

THE DIARY OF A WINNER

By BELLA FRY

This month I'm talking to Tony. Tony spends too much time alone at home
on the sofa playing video games. His mum wants him to get out,
meet new friends and get fit – and she thinks sport is the answer.
Tony's keeping an online diary to record his progress.

Tony's Instagram diary

Tony uses Instagram. He scrolls down to his first entry. The photo shows Tony on the sofa. His
mum took the photo. 'My mum is right,' he tells me. 'She says that I'm not really doing much
with my life. I'm very lazy – I just like staying at home listening to music and playing video
games. It's time to get a life!'

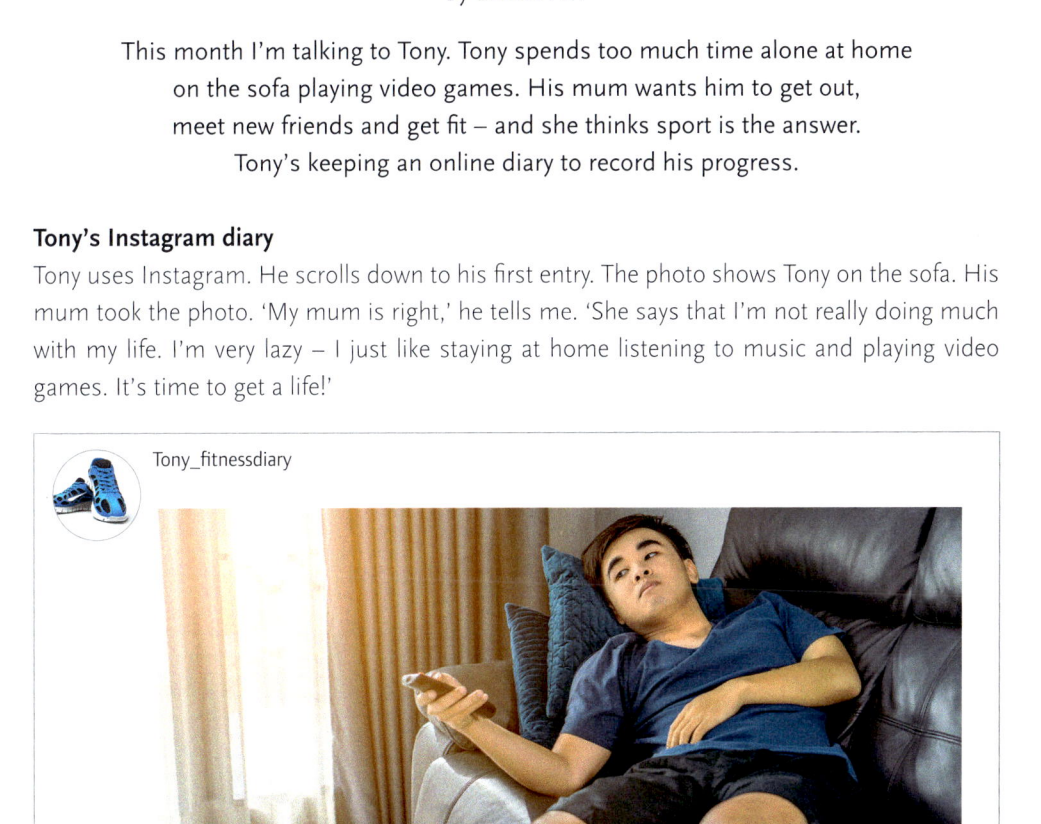

Tony_fitnessdiary

♥ **14 likes**
Time to get a life!
#getalife #fitness #newme #nomoreexcuses #workingonmyself

He's getting his life in order

Like many teenagers, he is finding it difficult to know what he wants from life. But he is getting
his life in order with the help of a personal sports trainer, Paula. 'We train in the gym and we
run together twice a week,' he says. 'Paula's also teaching me mental exercises to improve my
confidence.'

'It's taking time but I'm losing weight and developing muscles. I'm feeling a lot more energetic
now. There are some days when I want to give up, because it is a lot of hard work, but Paula
always helps me to keep me motivated.'

The Saturday Park Run is for everyone

Tony shows me another photo on his account. The tag line reads: *'We're getting ready for the next Park Run.'*

20

Tony_fitnessdiary

'I go to the local Park Run every Saturday morning,' he explains. 'All kinds of people turn up. In this photo you can see Sam and Oliver. We meet there every Saturday. They are faster than me, but it's fun to train with them. Most of the runners are faster than me, but I am getting better at running. We only run 5 kilometres so there's no pressure. You just do what you can and everybody accepts you. After the run, we go to a café and chat. There's a really good atmosphere.'

25

30

♥ **50 likes**
We're getting ready for the next Park Run.
#parkrun #runningmates #getalife #fitness
#newme #nomoreexcuses #workingonmyself

Today's post

Tony shows me his latest photos from a Park Run. In most of them, he's sitting in the café with a lot of other runners. He looks healthy and happy. He posts the photos on his account then types in a tag line: *'We're relaxing after the Park Run.'* The record of his journey online shows his progress from lonely kid to a guy who is making new friends. And he's got a life.   (416 words)

35

2 WORKING WITH WORDS

EXAM
→ use of language

A Find words or expressions in the text which mean more or less the same as the words below.

a development (lines 1–4)   **b** actually (lines 5–9)

B Find the opposites of the following words from the text.

a faster (line 25)   **b** accepts (line 31)

••• **C Explain the following words by completing the sentences or writing your own sentences.**

a Lazy (line 8): If you are lazy, it means that ●

b Pressure (line 30): It is a word that describes the feeling when ●

●●○ **Go to File 7 on page 189.**

3 LANGUAGE IN USE: PRESENT PROGRESSIVE

→ Present progressive, S. 263

EXAMPLES: *Tony is keeping an online diary.*
We are relaxing after the Park Run.

●●● Look at the drawings. Describe what the people
are doing. Use the present progressive form of
the verb.

●●○ Go to File 8 on page 189.

4 DESCRIBING A PICTURE

Sehen Sie sich das Bild genau an und machen Sie sich Notizen zur Vorbereitung:

- ■ Wer oder was spielt die wichtigste Rolle?
- ■ Steht ein Element im Mittelpunkt? Warum?
- ■ Was ist seine „Botschaft"?
- ■ Wir benutzen oft die Zeitform „present progressive", wenn wir Bilder beschreiben, weil Bilder
  (angehaltene) Vorgänge darstellen.

●●● Look at the photo and follow the suggestions in the skills box to describe the picture.

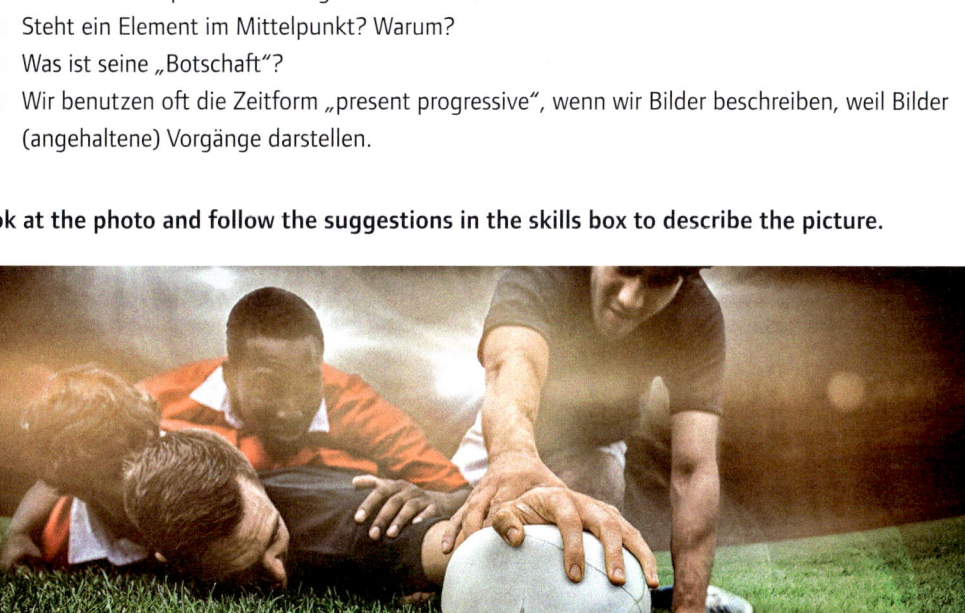

●●○ Go to File 9 on page 189.

5 WRITING ABOUT A PHOTO

Find a photo for the website that you think shows something interesting about sport in Europe.
Write a description of the photo and explain what it shows.

C MY SPORT AND WHY I DO IT

1 PREPARING TO LISTEN

You are going to listen to interviews with two young people, Mia and Fred. They are talking about their favourite sport and why they do it.

Before you listen, check that you know these words from the interviews. Then use them to talk about a sport you like.

coach ▪ draw ▪ exciting ▪ match ▪ pitch ▪ skill ▪ strong ▪ team ▪ train

---

TRAIN YOUR SKILLS: Zuhören und Notizen machen   vgl. auch S. 245

Machen Sie sich beim Hören Notizen auf Englisch. Das ist nicht immer leicht, weil die Sprecher keine Pause machen, während Sie schreiben.

- Konzentrieren Sie sich auf die Aufgabe und notieren Sie Schlüsselwörter und wichtige Ausdrücke.
- Strukturieren Sie Ihre Notizen.

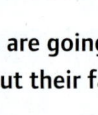

2 LISTENING: MY SPORT AND WHY I DO IT

EXAM
→ listening comprehension

Listen to the interviews with Mia and Fred, and answer the following questions with short answers.

EXAMPLE: What sport does Mia play? *football*

1 How often does Mia train?
2 On which day are Mia's football matches?
3 How many matches has her team won so far?
4 Which team won the Women's World Cup in 2019?
5 Who is Megan Rapinoe?
6 Which sport does Fred's exchange partner play?
7 What's special about his cricket team?
8 Name two countries in which cricket is popular?
9 What does Fred hope to become when he goes back to Germany?

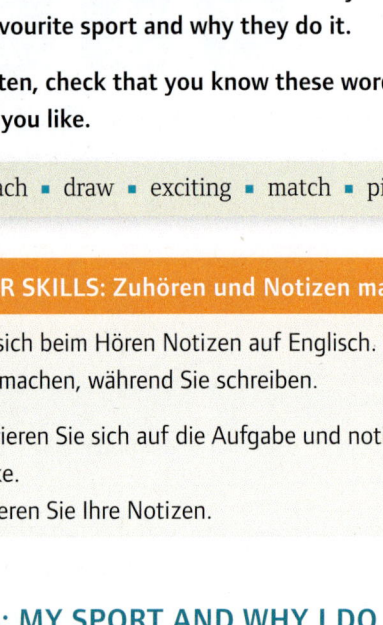

3 LANGUAGE IN USE: SIMPLE PRESENT VS PRESENT PROGRESSIVE

→ Simple present; present progressive, S. 263

A Sort these signal words and expressions into two lists: those that are usually used with the simple present and those that are usually used with the present progressive.

always ▪ at the moment ▪ every day ▪ mostly ▪ never ▪ normally ▪ now ▪ often ▪ rarely ▪ right now ▪ sometimes ▪ this week ▪ today ▪ usually

B It's Sunday morning and Mia is at the gym with her friend Pat. Use the correct form of the verbs in brackets to complete Mia's thoughts. Tip: pay attention to the signal words.

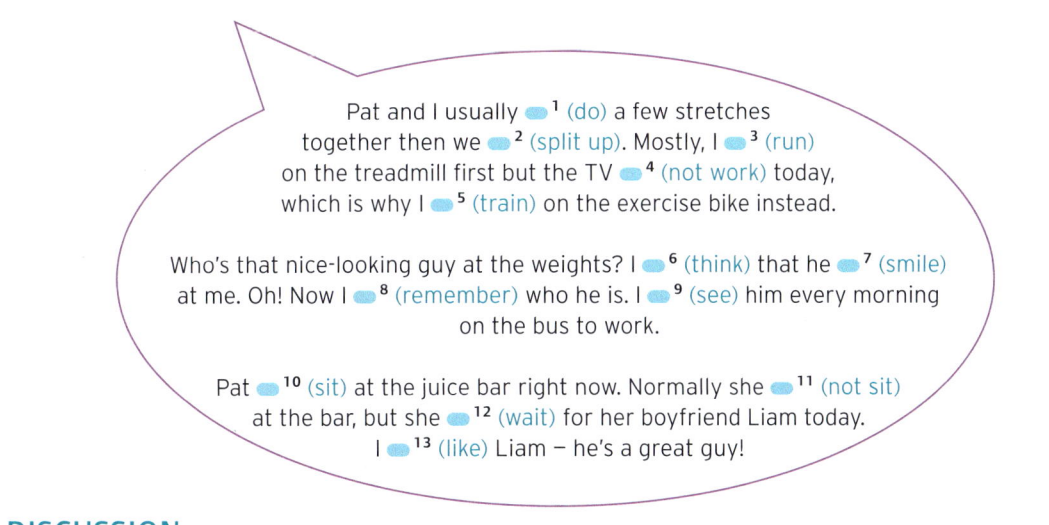

> **TIP** ❗
>
> The following verbs are used mostly in the simple present:
>
> agree – have – hear – know – like – need – remember – see – think – understand – want
>
> | I **like** | ~~I am liking~~ |
> | I **agree** | ~~I am agreeing~~ |

Pat and I usually 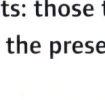¹ (do) a few stretches together then we 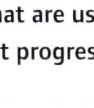² (split up). Mostly, I 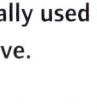³ (run) on the treadmill first but the TV 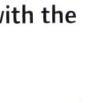⁴ (not work) today, which is why I 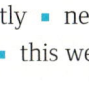⁵ (train) on the exercise bike instead.

Who's that nice-looking guy at the weights? I 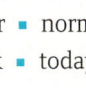⁶ (think) that he ⁷ (smile) at me. Oh! Now I ⁸ (remember) who he is. I ●⁹ (see) him every morning on the bus to work.

Pat ●¹⁰ (sit) at the juice bar right now. Normally she ●¹¹ (not sit) at the bar, but she ●¹² (wait) for her boyfriend Liam today. I ●¹³ (like) Liam – he's a great guy!

4 DISCUSSION

In groups, talk about the importance sport has in the lives of young people in your culture. Cover the following points in your discussion:

- Sports that are popular with young people.
- The reasons why young people play them.
- How popular they are around the world.

WORLD OF INTERCULTURAL COMMUNICATION

You are working at a Youth Centre in Manchester, a city with people from around the world. The Youth Centre wants to introduce a new sport. You find out about different types of sport from around the world.

NATIONAL SPORTS

Which sport is popular in which country? Look at the sports listed below, and match them with the photos of the sports (1–5), the countries where each sport is popular (a–e) and the short texts about the sports in the different countries (I–V).

sport	photo	country	text
capoeira	⬤	⬤	⬤
cricket	⬤	⬤	⬤
ice hockey	⬤	⬤	⬤
rugby union	⬤	⬤	⬤
table tennis	⬤	⬤	⬤

a   Barbados
b   Brazil
c   Canada
d   China
e   New Zealand

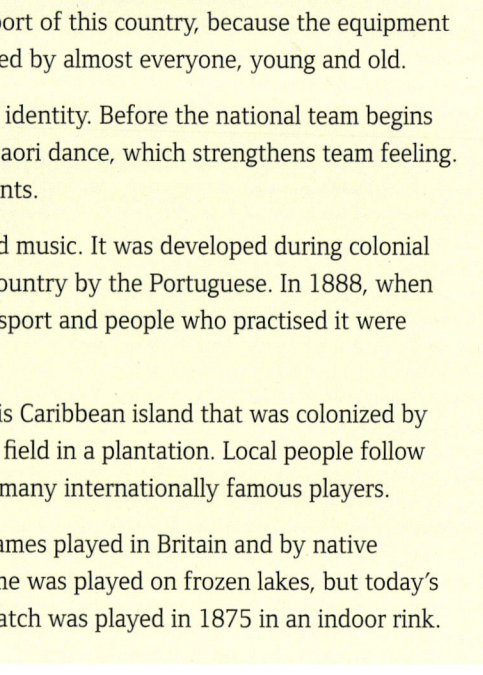

I   Although this sport was invented in England in the 19th century, it soon became popular in East Asia. Around 1952 it was made the national sport of this country, because the equipment could be easily and cheaply made. The game is played by almost everyone, young and old.

II This team game is an important part of the national identity. Before the national team begins a game, team members perform a haka, a type of Maori dance, which strengthens team feeling. The haka is supposed to frighten the team's opponents.

III This is a martial art that is combination of dance and music. It was developed during colonial times by Angolan slaves who were brought to the country by the Portuguese. In 1888, when slavery was abolished, the government banned the sport and people who practised it were sent to prison.

IV This team game is a central part of the culture of this Caribbean island that was colonized by the British. The first club was founded in 1871 on a field in a plantation. Local people follow the game passionately and the island has produced many internationally famous players.

V   This team game has its roots in the stick-and-ball games played in Britain and by native Americans. With the country's cold winters, the game was played on frozen lakes, but today's game was developed in Montreal, where the first match was played in 1875 in an indoor rink.

2 DISCUSSING SPORT

07

A Sports aren't just for big teams – small groups need to organize themselves too. Listen to Karin, who is the manager of the Youth Centre, as she talks to Andy about two new sports for the centre.

As you listen, make notes in English on the advantages of each activity. Then make a table like the one below, listing the information in German.

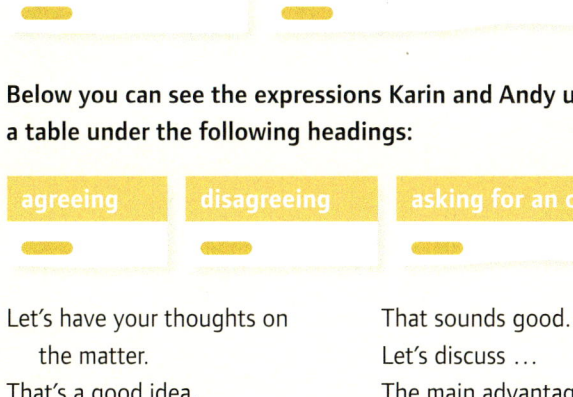

Skateboarding	Boxing
Skaten ist cool.	Die Benutzung des Box-Clubs ist kostenlos.

B Below you can see the expressions Karin and Andy use in their discussion. Put them in a table under the following headings:

agreeing	disagreeing	asking for an opinion	introducing an idea

Let's have your thoughts on
    the matter.
That's a good idea.
I think that … is the best option.
Have you thought about … ?
The problem with that is …

That sounds good.
Let's discuss …
The main advantage is that …
I agree with you that …
I don't think that …
I disagree with you.

Another point I would like
    to make is …
I think you are right that …
Can I suggest that … ?
That's a good idea.

C The Youth Centre wants to add one new sport to its programme. You and the other interns have to choose a sport and present it to the group. Discuss the different sports and make a ranking list to show which ones you should do at the Youth Centre.

1 In small groups choose a sport and make a list of reasons why it would be a good sport to introduce to the Youth Centre.

2 Present your sport in a one-minute speech. Explain why you think it is the best for the Youth Centre.

3 Exchange arguments, try to convince the others that your activity is the best or at least should be second on the list. Be willing to compromise. Make sure you use expressions from task 2B and the list below.

In my opinion, … is the best sport because …
It's so much fun / a team sport / thrilling.
It improves concentration / teaches discipline.
It's a great spectator sport.

I agree. / I think you're absolutely right. /
    I agree with you that …
I don't share your opinion. / I disagree
    (with you).
It's too dangerous/rough. / It promotes violence.

Your school is expecting a group of exchange students. Some of them would like to do sport while they are in your area. You research opportunities for doing sport and produce a flyer in English giving precise information about times and places.

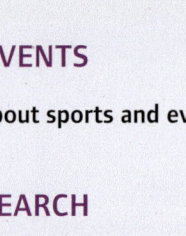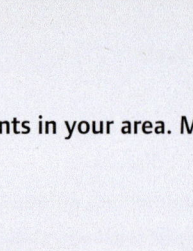

1 SPORTS AND EVENTS

Brainstorm ideas about sports and events in your area. Make a list.

2 INTERNET RESEARCH

Do internet research to find out more about the top three activities in your area. Make notes. Here are some questions to think about. Add your own ideas.

- Where/When does the activity take place?
- Do the exchange students need any special equipment or clothes? (If so, where can they find equipment/clothes?)

3 MAKING A TIMETABLE

Make a list of the activities. Make a timetable showing when they can do the activities. Add information about where the activities take place.

4 MAKING A FLYER

A Use the notes and the timetable you made above to produce a flyer in English for the exchange students. Make the flyer as attractive as possible (e.g. add photos or a map of a running route from the internet).

B Put all the flyers on a table. Choose another group's flyer and comment on the activities. Vote for the best flyer.

Role models

 A WARM-UP: TALKING ABOUT ROLE MODELS

Malala Yousafzai: She is a courageous woman who fights for the rights of women to have education. She has been awarded the Nobel Peace Prize and has been appointed UN Messenger of Peace.

Manuel Neuer: Besides being a member of the German national football team, he donates money to charity and has his own foundation for underprivileged children.

Martin Luther King: He fought so that black people in the USA could be treated equally.

Mum: She always told me I could achieve anything.

Firefighter: She does a dangerous job and saves lives every day.

Grandad: He never stops working, even though he is an old man.

Think: Who are your role models? Could any of the people above be a role model for you?

Pair: Talk to each other about your role models and say why you like them.

Share: List your role models on the board. What makes them role models? How do they behave?

He is a role model because he …

I look up to her because she …

B

AN INFLUENCER AND ACTIVIST

SITUATION: A friend of yours in England is unhappy with his or her body. Everyone on social media seems to have perfect bodies and lead perfect lives. You read an article about a celebrity who has learned to love her body. You write an email (task 5, page 40) to your friend describing the young woman and her ideas.

1 PREPARING TO READ

The following words and phrases (1–8) are used in the text. Match them with the German expressions (a–h).

1	anorexia nervosa	a	angeborene Taubheit
2	congenital hearing loss	b	leicht zu beeindrucken
3	to feel grateful for sth	c	für etw dankbar sein
4	impressionable	d	Gehhilfe/(n)
5	to launch	e	(äußerst) schädlich
6	toxic	f	Magersucht
7	unedited	g	starten, gründen
8	walking aids	h	unbearbeitet

2 READING AND UNDERSTANDING THE TEXT

A **Read the text opposite. Choose the most appropriate sentence (1–6) to fill the gaps in the text (A–E). There is one sentence more than you need.**

1 'Body shaming' is very common on social media.
2 Everything I did was stupid.
3 She hopes that everyone will learn to love their bodies.
4 The community is only open to disabled people.
5 The message Jameela received was that you had to be thin to be attractive.
6 The reason for this was the lack of disabled access at the venues.

B **Read the tasks below and on page 38, and decide which of the options is the correct one.**

EXAM
→ reading comprehension

1 According to the text, which of the following statements about Jameela Jamil is correct?
   a Jameela was born in the UK but lives in the USA.
   b Jameela's parents are from India.
   c Jameela's parents took Jameela to live in the USA.
   d Jameela is a citizen of India, Pakistan and Britain.

BODY POSITIVE

Jameela Jamil was born in London in 1986 to an Indian father and a Pakistani mother, but has lived in the USA since 2016. She is an actress, model, presenter and body positive activist. She has also
5 become an important influencer on social media, as she uses her fame to spread awareness about topics important to her.

Jameela has overcome several health issues in her life. She was born with congenital hearing loss and
10 has had several operations to correct the problem. As a teenager, she suffered from anorexia nervosa. In interviews, she has said that her eating disorder developed due to social pressure. She was overweight, and all the magazines she read in her
15 teens featured weight loss products. 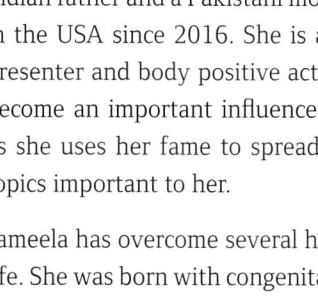 **A**

At the age of 17, she was hit by a car and was told that she might never walk again. Luckily, after steroid treatment and physiotherapy, she slowly recovered. The car accident changed her relation-
20 ship with her body and helped her to recover from her eating disorder.

Jameela started her career in the world of entertainment as a radio presenter and DJ at BBC Radio 1. She was the first Asian female to present
25 a music show on the BBC. Music has always been an important part of her life.

In 2015, she launched a company called *Why Not People?*. While working on various radio and tv shows and visiting concerts and events, she
30 noticed that there were very few people in wheelchairs or with walking aids among the guests. **B** *Why Not People?* has developed a seating system made up of three collapsible seats and a wheelchair space so that wheelchair users
35 can be with their friends during gigs. So that every venue includes an equal proportion of people with disabilities, tickets can only be bought

by members of the *Why Not People?* social network community. **C**

In 2016 Jameela moved to the USA, where she 40 starred in the popular TV show *The Good Place*. In 2018, she launched an Instagram account called 'I Weigh'. The title was inspired by a photo that she came across online of the Kardashian family, which included details of each of the women's 45 weight. The account asks its followers to post genuine, unedited selfies and a text describing the things that they feel grateful for or proud of. **D** She believes that women especially are always shamed by other people, because they are expected 50 to conform to impossible standards of beauty set by society. They are criticized if they are overweight, if they are too skinny, in fact they are criticized no matter what size they are. **E**

Jameela uses her position to get people to talk 55 about this problem and to fight back. In February 2019, she created a petition titled 'Stop celebrities promoting toxic diet products on social media', calling on social media platforms to ban the practice. As she pointed out, this kind of promo- 60 tion sends the wrong message to impressionable young people. (548 words)

2 Jameela has had many roles in her life. Which of the following has she never been?

   a A TV actress   **c** A promoter of slimming products

   b An Instagram influencer   **d** A radio presenter

3 Her car accident helped her …

   a become famous.   **c** lose weight.

   b overcome her eating disorder.   **d** hear clearly again.

4 Who and how does her company *Why Not People?* help?

   a It helps shy people become more self-confident in public.

   b It helps lonely people network with other people.

   c It helps people who love music to get great seats at concerts.

   d It helps disabled people go to concerts with their friends.

5 For which of the following reasons was Jameela angry with the photo of the Kardashians?

   a It was just about the weight of the women.

   b The family came across as proud and arrogant.

   c It was unedited and unfiltered.

   d It encouraged young women to gain weight.

6 Jameela feels that women are body shamed for a lot of reasons. Which of the following reasons is <u>not</u> mentioned?

   a When women are plus sized.   **c** Whatever size women are.

   b When women are too slim.   **d** When women are too beautiful.

7 What does Jameela want social media platforms to do?

   a To promote her account 'I Weigh'.

   b To allow only unedited selfies on their platforms.

   c To ban the advertising of unhealthy diet products.

   d To prevent celebrities from appearing in online adverts.

C **Is Jameela a good role model? Explain why/why not.**

3 LANGUAGE IN USE: SIMPLE PAST VS PRESENT PERFECT

→ Simple past, S. 265; present perfect, S. 267

EXAMPLE: *I read the article yesterday. / I've just read the article.*

A Sort these signal words and expressions into two lists: those that are usually used with the simple past and those that are usually used with the present perfect.

ago ■ already ■ just ■ last month ■ never ■ since ■ when ■ yet

B Look at lines 1–21 and find examples of the simple past and the present perfect. Say why they are in that tense.

C When do we use the simple past? When do we use the present perfect? Complete each of the sentences below with one of the endings, a–d below.

1 Wir verwenden *simple past* für ●

2 Wir verwenden *present perfect* für ●

a abgeschlossene Handlungen, die weiterhin wichtig sind.

b etwas, das sich gerade entwickelt oder verändert.

c etwas, das gerade geschieht

d etwas vollständig Abgeschlossenes

●●● D You have the opportunity to ask Jameela some questions. Ask her the following in English:

EXAM
→ use of language

1 wie lange sie unter Magersucht gelitten hat

2 wann sie mit ihrer Arbeit bei der BBC begonnen hat

3 ob sie nervös war, als sie zum ersten Mal im Radio gesprochen hat

4 ob sie jemals bei öffentlichen Veranstaltungen gesprochen hat

5 ob sie in Amerika viele Freundschaften geschlossen hat

6 wie lange sie in *The Good Place* mitgespielt hat

7 wann sie bemerkt hat, dass *Body Shaming* in den sozialen Medien üblich war

8 wie lange ihre Petition online war

9 ob viele Leute sie wegen „I Weigh" angeschrieben haben

10 wie viele Leute Fotos mit dem Hashtag #iweigh hochgeladen haben

●●○ Go to File 10 on page 190.

E You are talking to a British friend about Jameela. Tell him or her the following in English:

1 dass Jameela viele Gesundheitsprobleme hatte, als sie jung war

2 dass sie mit 17 einen Unfall hatte und seitdem ein anderes Verhältnis zu ihrem Körper hat

3 dass sie seit 2015 in den USA lebt

4 dass sie mehrmals soziale Medien kritisiert hat, weil dort für gefährliche Diätprodukte geworben wird

F Ask your neighbour questions beginning with:

EXAM
→ use of language

When did …? – How long …? – Have you ever …? –
Did you … last year/month? – Where/What … five years ago?

4 WORKING WITH WORDS

A Copy and complete the table. The words in the table are used in the text. The first answer has been given.

verb	noun	adjective	adverb
	positivity[1]	positive	•[2]
•[3]	influencer	•[5]	
	•[4]		
•[6]	•[7]	attractive	•[8]
•[9]	•[10]	popular	•[11]
criticize	•[12]	•[14]	•[15]
	•[13]		

B Complete the reply to a forum comment with the correct form of one of the words from the table in task 4A.

Hi. So, you're going on a diet because you're getting a lot of •[1] about your weight from some of your friends? Don't let them •[2] you in a negative way. Your •[3] doesn't depend on how you look. It's who you are and what you do that counts. Those are the things that •[4] people to you. Get the •[4] out of your life and find some friends who see things •[6].

Go to File 11 on page 190.

5 WRITING AN EMAIL

EXAM
→ writing

After reading the text about Jameela Jamil, you think that it might be interesting for a friend of yours who has been body shamed on social media. Write an email to your friend, in which you inform him or her about Jameela's experiences and explain to him or her how this information might be helpful. Write about 160 words. Mention the following aspects:

- Jameela's problems as a child and young woman.
- What happened to her that changed her life.
- How she is now an activist who both supports and influences other people.

Go to File 12 on page 190.

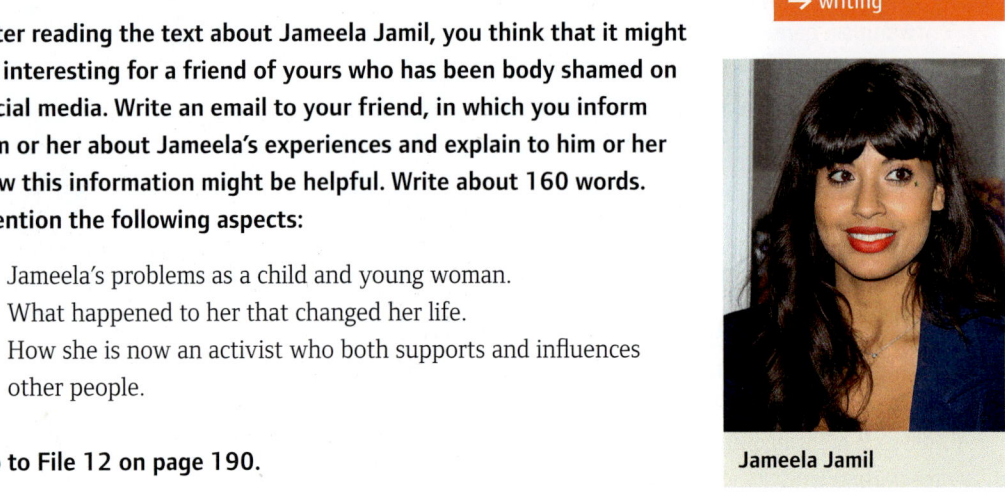

Jameela Jamil

C HOW ROLE MODELS INFLUENCE US

1 PREPARING TO LISTEN

You are going to listen to a podcast on the influence of role models.

A **Before you listen to the podcast, read the introduction below and study the highlighted words and expressions below. Match them to the expressions (1–4).**

Why do we look up to certain people? Why do we choose a certain person as a role model? Sometimes it's because they are famous or successful or <mark>talented</mark>. Role models usually <mark>set an example</mark> that we wish to follow. They can serve as <mark>ambassadors</mark> for certain causes. Today, I'm talking to Marion about role models and how they <mark>influence our lives.</mark>

1 encourage and inspire people to behave in a similar way
2 being naturally able to do well at something
3 the effect role models can have on people
4 person who represents an organization

B **Make sentences using the highlighted expressions from the text.**

> My grandad is a talented teacher.

> She's a great ambassador for the charity.

🎧 2 LISTENING: WHO'S YOUR ROLE MODEL?
09

EXAM
→ listening comprehension

Finish the sentences using words from the podcast.

1 When Greta Thunberg was 15, she started a protest outside ⬬

2 She said that she was striking for ⬬

3 On 15 March 2019 she was joined in her protest by millions of students around ⬬

4 Some politicians and teachers thought that the students should be in school on ⬬

5 A spokesman for OPEC said that the Fridays for Future movement was a great threat to the ⬬

6 Greta doesn't eat meat or travel by plane because she tries to live according to ⬬

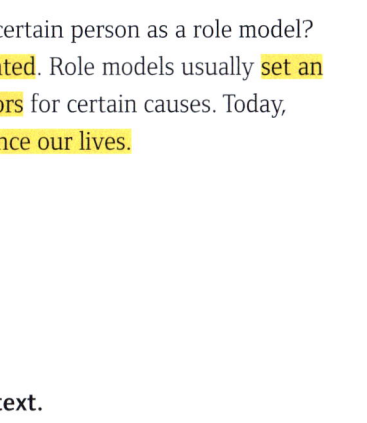

Greta Thunberg speaks on stage during the demonstration Global Strike for Future in Stockholm, 2019.

3 LANGUAGE IN USE: RELATIVE CLAUSES

→ Relative clauses, S. 283

EXAMPLES: *We choose **a person who** is popular among other teenagers.*
*It's one of those **shows which** are shown all over the world.*

A Complete the text using *who* or *which*.

Role models always set an example. That's fine when the role models are people ⬭¹ do good things. Sometimes, however, a role model might encourage us to do things ⬭² are bad. Some of the celebrities ⬭³ we admire do things ⬭⁴ are stupid. Some of them take drugs or get drunk. Doing things like that, ⬭⁵ are against the law, might get you into trouble. The thing is people don't just want role models ⬭⁶ are perfect. They want role models ⬭⁷ used to make mistakes but ⬭⁸ have managed to stand on their own two feet again. Weaknesses are the things ⬭⁹ allow us to identify with role models. Of course, if your role model is someone ⬭¹⁰ was a terrible dictator or a serial murderer, the chances are that you won't turn out to be a great and inspiring person! Choose a role model ⬭¹¹ will make you a better person.

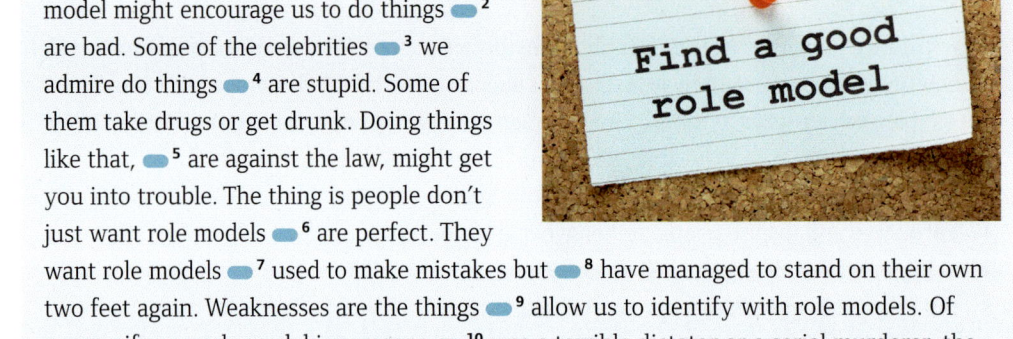

Find a good role model

B Decide whether the following sentences should have *whose* or *who's*.

EXAMPLES:
*Greta Thunberg is a Swedish teenager **who's** now become a famous climate change activist. But it is young people like me **whose** lives will be affected by climate change.*

REMEMBER ❗ *whose* and *who's*

Whose and *who's* sound the same, but they are very different.
Whose = dessen/deren
Who's = who is/has (der/die/das … ist/hat)

1 She's a politician ⬭ going to change the world.
2 She's a politician ⬭ opinions are very popular.
3 Olivia is the actress ⬭ Instagram account I follow.
4 Do you know ⬭ got the most followers on Instagram?
5 Jameela, ⬭ father is Pakistani and ⬭ mother is Indian, was born in London.
6 Harry, ⬭ now Amelia's boyfriend, used to go out with me last year.
7 I heard from a colleague ⬭ visiting Los Angeles that you can buy a SIM card at the airport.
8 ⬭ mobile phone is this on the desk?
9 ⬭ coming to the demonstration with me today?
10 Here's a joke: What do you call someone ⬭ doing an internship at a railway company? – A trainee!

4 LANGUAGE IN USE: TALKING ABOUT THE PAST

EXAMPLES:

I used not to think about the environment, but now I do.
They want role models who used to make mistakes but who have managed to stand on their own two feet again.

> **REMEMBER** *used to*
>
> We use **used to** to talk about how you did something or how you thought about something in the past, but you don't do it any more.
>
> I **used to watch** Kika as a child.
> *Als Kind habe ich Kika geschaut.*
> With negatives we use: **did not use to / used not to** …
> With questions we use: **Did … use to …?**

1 When I was younger I (admire) that singer, but I don't like him now.
2 I (not like) vegetables but I now I'm a vegetarian.
3 He (be) shy, but he has changed.
4 He (not smoke). I wonder why he started.
5   (you – do) sport when you were a child?
6 Germany (be) divided, but now it is one country.
7 When my parents were kids, they (have) a black and white TV.
8 When my grandparents were kids, they (listen) to the radio.
9 In the 18th century people (travel) by horse.
10 In the old days people (get up) at sunrise.

5 VIEWING

→ Videos, S. 211

01

Watch the video called 'Matt Damon calls for action on clean water access' and complete the tasks on page 211.

6 DISCUSSION

→ Interaktion, S. 255

What do you think about role models and the way they influence us? Think about what you know about role models and reflect on what you have learned from the pages in this unit. Discuss in groups, make notes and report to the class.

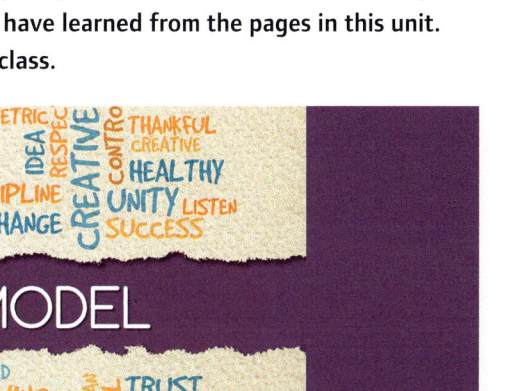

You are interested in meeting people from other cultures. Your teacher points out the following announcement online. You apply for a place to meet and greet visitors from China.

Visitors from our twin town in China

Would you like to be an ambassador for your school? Next month, we are going to welcome a group of people from our twin town in China. They are interested in finding out about our vocational training programmes. We have an exciting programme for our guests, including visits to local factories, workshops and places of further education.

We would like to invite students, who will represent local schools, to take part in a 'Meet and Greet' event. If you are between 17 and 20 and interested in meeting people from other cultures, apply here.

You should have a friendly and open personality. Good spoken English is a must. If your application is accepted, you will be invited to a training session.

🎧 **1** HOW TO BEHAVE WITH CHINESE VISITORS

EXAM
→ listening comprehension

●●● **Your application has been accepted and you go to the training session. The first session is about how to behave when you meet the visitors. Listen to the trainer and complete the table below. Make notes on how the Chinese might behave and how you should behave.**

		Chinese visitors	You
1	Greetings	▬▬▬	▬▬▬
2	Clothes	▬▬▬	▬▬▬
3	Body language	▬▬▬	▬▬▬
4	Being prepared	▬▬▬	▬▬▬
5	Language	▬▬▬	▬▬▬

●●○ **Go to File 13 on page 191.**

2 MAKING SMALL TALK WITH GUESTS

A What is small talk? Choose the best definition.

1 a child's first words
2 using simple language to communicate

3 chatting face to face with someone you don't know

B Work with a partner. Decide together which of the topics in the box you should not talk about with people you do not know well.

> about the journey to the meeting place ▪ food ▪ hobbies ▪ money ▪
> problems at school ▪ religion ▪ sex ▪ sport ▪ the weather ▪ your training

C Your trainer practises small talk with a member of the class who takes the role of one of the Chinese visitors. Read the gapped dialogue and add the questions and statements (a–g) to complete it. The first question has been added for you. When you have finished, listen and check.

Trainer: 🔵¹ *How was your flight to Germany?*
Visitor: Very good, thank you. There weren't any delays. 🔵²
Trainer: That's nice. I'm sorry about the weather here. It's not usually so cold at this time of year.
Visitor: 🔵³ The hotel is warm and the food here is very good. I like German food.
Trainer: 🔵⁴
Visitor: Yes, I have. I visited the Black Forest two years ago. It's a very beautiful region. Now, I'm happy to be here and to meet everyone. 🔵⁵
Trainer: There are 24 students. 🔵⁶
Visitor: Oh, our classes are very big. Sometimes we have as many as 40 students in one class. They are all training for the same profession. What about you? 🔵⁷.

a	Have you been to Germany before?	**e**	I don't mind the cold.
b	How big are the classes in your country?	**f**	It was good weather for flying.
c	How many students are in your class?	**g**	What do you want to do when you have
d	~~How was your flight to Germany?~~		left school?

3 ROLE-PLAY: MEETING AND GREETING A VISITOR

It is time for the Meet and Greet event. With a partner take turns playing the role of the visitor.

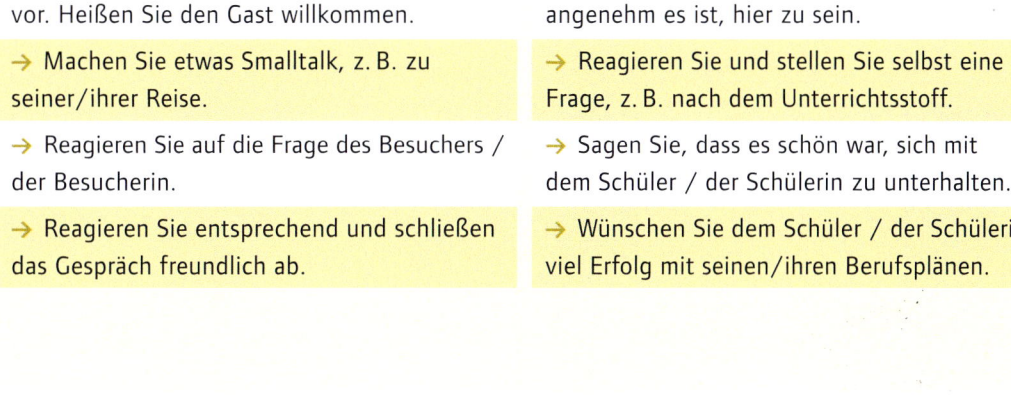

Partner A: You are one of the students	**Partner B: You are one of the visitors**
→ Begrüßen Sie den Gast und stellen sich vor. Heißen Sie den Gast willkommen.	→ Erwidern Sie den Gruß und sagen Sie, wie angenehm es ist, hier zu sein.
→ Machen Sie etwas Smalltalk, z. B. zu seiner/ihrer Reise.	→ Reagieren Sie und stellen Sie selbst eine Frage, z. B. nach dem Unterrichtsstoff.
→ Reagieren Sie auf die Frage des Besuchers / der Besucherin.	→ Sagen Sie, dass es schön war, sich mit dem Schüler / der Schülerin zu unterhalten.
→ Reagieren Sie entsprechend und schließen das Gespräch freundlich ab.	→ Wünschen Sie dem Schüler / der Schülerin viel Erfolg mit seinen/ihren Berufsplänen.

You are going to research and give a presentation about different beauty ideals around the world.

1 CHOOSING A CULTURE

Work in small teams. Decide together which culture you are going to examine. The following examples might help start you off.

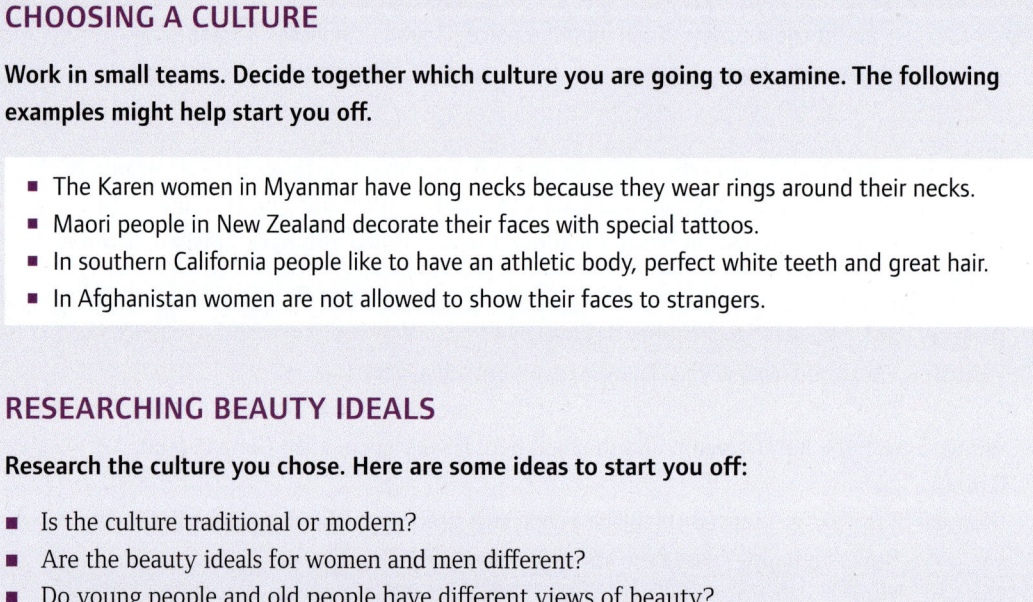

- The Karen women in Myanmar have long necks because they wear rings around their necks.
- Maori people in New Zealand decorate their faces with special tattoos.
- In southern California people like to have an athletic body, perfect white teeth and great hair.
- In Afghanistan women are not allowed to show their faces to strangers.

2 RESEARCHING BEAUTY IDEALS

Research the culture you chose. Here are some ideas to start you off:

- Is the culture traditional or modern?
- Are the beauty ideals for women and men different?
- Do young people and old people have different views of beauty?
- What does their idea of beauty say about their culture?
- Is there something we can learn from their culture?
- How does it compare with German culture?

3 PREPARING YOUR PRESENTATION

A Structure the notes you made above for a presentation. Start by saying why you chose this culture, and conclude by saying what we can learn from this culture.

B Make copies of photos, newspaper articles and anything else that is relevant.

C Make handouts.

4 GIVING YOUR PRESENTATION   → Präsentation, S. 254

A Take turns to present the culture you chose. Answer any questions from the audience. (Remember that your audience will be making notes. See task B below.)

B While you are listening to a presentation, make notes on the categories on the right. Give points from 1 to 5 for each category.

- structure of presentation
- use of language
- body language
- answering of questions
- handouts

C After you have all given your presentation, discuss how German ideas of beauty compare with what you have learned.

Facing life's challenges

4

A WARM-UP: WINDING DOWN

A Modern life is stressful for many people. Look at the photos. What do you think about the different ways in which the people in the photos wind down or switch off?

B What else do people do to relieve stress? What might be the negative results of using some methods to wind down?

B CAFFEINE: THE HIDDEN DANGER

SITUATION: Caffeine drinks are popular at your school kiosk – not just cold coffee drinks but also energy drinks. But how dangerous can they be? You come across a text about the tragic death of a teenager and decide to use it to inform fellow students about the dangers of energy drinks (task 5, page 51).

1 PREPARING TO READ

Work with a partner. You are going to read a newspaper report with the headline: 'Caffeine: The hidden danger'. The notes that the journalist made for his report have got jumbled up. With your partner, put the notes in the correct order. (Look up any words you don't know.)

a   arrived at the hospital in a coma
b   coroner says the young man did not die of a drug overdose
c   doctors put him on a life-support system
d   follow-up with expert: 'Tragic accidents can happen.'
e   paramedics took R. to hospital
f   Richard D. collapsed in his maths class
g   R's parents say that they have started a campaign
h   teacher called an ambulance
i   teen drank too many high-caffeine drinks in a short period of time

2 READING AND UNDERSTANDING THE TEXT

Decide whether the following statements are true or false.

1 A British boy has died, but no-one knows why.
2 He collapsed in the playground during the lunch break.
3 One of his classmates called an ambulance.
4 When the ambulance arrived, the boy was dead.
5 The boy who died didn't drink caffeinated drinks very often.
6 The coroner who examined the boy's body said he didn't appear to have any health problems.
7 The boy's parents are letting other people know about problems with caffeinated drinks.
8 The boy's father said parents must control what their children do.
9 An expert said this was the first time she had heard of an accident like this happening.
10 She suggested people could consume as much caffeine as they wanted to as long as they didn't have heart problems.

EXAM
→ reading comprehension

Caffeine
$C_8H_{10}N_4O_2$

DAILY NEWS

CAFFEINE: THE HIDDEN DANGER

by Aidan Thomas

A British teenager has died because he drank too many high-caffeine drinks in a short period of time. Richard D. (16), of Bristol, drank a café latte and two energy drinks during the 45-minute school lunch break. He collapsed 15 minutes after he took his seat in the maths class, which was his first class of the afternoon. The class teacher called an ambulance and gave the young man first aid until the paramedics arrived. When they got him to hospital, Richard was in a coma. The doctors put him on a life-support system, but they could not save his life.

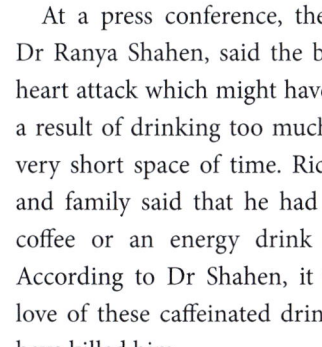

At a press conference, the coroner, Dr Ranya Shahen, said the boy had had a heart attack which might have happened as a result of drinking too much caffeine in a very short space of time. Richard's friends and family said that he had always had a coffee or an energy drink in his hand. According to Dr Shahen, it was Richard's love of these caffeinated drinks that might have killed him.

'Richard was a healthy teenager with no heart conditions. There were no drugs or alcohol in his system when he died,' Dr Shahen said. 'It was not the total amount of caffeine in his system that killed him but the fact that he drank so many caffeinated drinks one after the other. People should cut down on the number of drinks they consume,' she said.

Richard's parents have now started a campaign to let young people know that they have to be careful about drinking too many caffeinated drinks too quickly. Richard's father said, 'You shouldn't drink too many on one day and you have to give your body time to recover between each drink.' He went on, 'Every parent worries about their children's health and safety as they're growing up. At the same time, every young person has to be allowed to do what the other kids do. Richard died because he drank too many drinks with caffeine in them, just like so many of his friends. We must make other parents and their children aware of the possible dangers of these drinks. We hope that our campaign will be able to get that message across.'

An expert said, 'Tragic accidents can happen sometimes. After a report like this, many people might worry that caffeine could put them at risk. My advice is, if you don't have heart problems, you may have two to three cups of coffee a day or, if you prefer to get your caffeine in energy drinks, drinking a couple of them is also all right. As long as you don't drink them all at once, you needn't worry.' (446 words)

WORKING WITH WORDS

A The expressions below are in the text. Use the verbs from column A and the phrases from column B to make other expressions.

- to make people aware of something (lines 50–51)
- to get a message across (line 53)
- to put someone at risk (line 57)

A
make
get
put

B
angry
an appointment
drunk
ill/well
a mistake
someone laugh
someone on a course of treatment
someone on a drip

B Make sentences using six of the expressions.

4 **LANGUAGE IN USE: MODAL AUXILIARIES**

→ Modal auxiliaries, S. 276

A Find all the modal auxiliaries in the text.

EXAMPLE: *they could not save his life (line 15)*

> **REMEMBER** ❗ modal auxiliaries
>
> Modal auxiliaries are used to express permission (**may**), ability (**can**), obligation (**must**), etc. Here is a list of the main modals (and their substitutes in brackets):
> **can (be able to), may (be allowed to), might, must (have to), need not (not have to)**
> Most modals use the substitute form in the future:
> **Can** you come now? → **Will** you **be able to** come tomorrow?

●●● **B** Fill the gaps in the texts below with a modal verb or a suitable substitute.

The opioid abuse crisis

Opioid abuse has been a serious health problem in the United States and Canada for many years. According to statistics, the UK is also heading for an opioid abuse crisis. Abuse of opioids 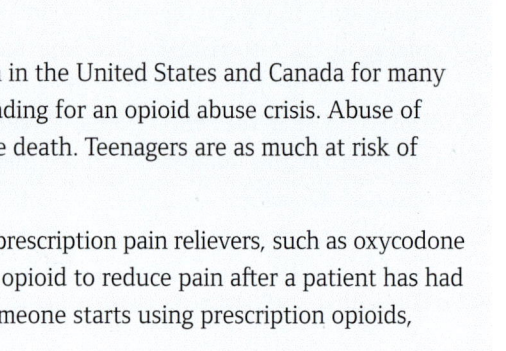¹ lead to addiction and ⬤² also cause death. Teenagers are as much at risk of becoming addicted as older people.

Opioids are a type of drug. They include strong prescription pain relievers, such as oxycodone and fentanyl. A doctor ⬤³ write a prescription opioid to reduce pain after a patient has had surgery or has suffered an injury. As soon as someone starts using prescription opioids, however, there is a risk they 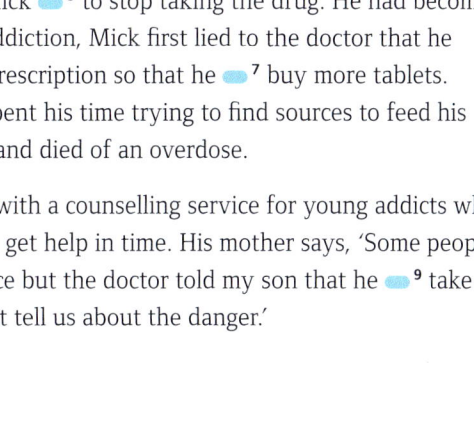⁴ become dependent on the drug. Studies show that 4% to 6% of opioid misusers go on to use heroin.

When Mick R. from Sheffield in the English Midlands was injured playing football at school, his doctor prescribed oxycodone. When Mick's injury was healed, his doctor stopped prescribing the tablets. The problem was, Mick ⁵ to stop taking the drug. He had become dependent on it. Because he ⁶ feed his addiction, Mick first lied to the doctor that he was still in pain, then he said he'd lost his prescription so that he ⁷ buy more tablets. Eventually, he dropped out of school and spent his time trying to find sources to feed his addiction. Finally, Mick switched to heroin and died of an overdose.

Today, Mick's mother works as a volunteer with a counselling service for young addicts who want to come off drugs. Sadly, Mick did not get help in time. His mother says, 'Some people say he ⁸ taken oxycodone in the first place but the doctor told my son that he ⁹ take it. I still ¹⁰ understand why the doctor didn't tell us about the danger.'

●●○ **Go to File 14 on page 192.**

C Choose the correct form of the modal verb to complete the sentences.

1 Opioid abuse needn't / must / could kill more people if the problem isn't dealt with soon.
2 People who take certain types of painkillers are able to / might / should become addicted to them.
3 The government has stated that doctors are able to / ought to / might warn patients of the dangers of taking certain painkillers.
4 Doctors need to / could / mustn't have a good overview of their patient's histories in order not to prescribe opiods incorrectly.
5 Mick is not the only person who must / should / had to buy heroin when he ran out of painkillers.
6 Some young addicts should / may / have to be helped by counselling, but for others it doesn't work.
7 Mick's mother hopes that by doing volunteer work she should / will be able to / will have to help young people get off drugs.
8 You mustn't / couldn't / don't have to blame your friend for her addiction. It isn't her fault.
9 Medication is supposed to / needs to / has to help people, not kill them.

5 WRITING A BLOG ENTRY

EXAM
→ writing

●●● **It will soon be exam time, and you have noticed that many students at your school are drinking energy drinks.**
Write a blog entry for your school's website about the dangers of consuming too much caffeine.
Use information from the text about Richard D. and write about 160 words in English.

●●○ **Go to File 15 on page 192.**

C EXAM STRESS

1 PREPARING TO LISTEN

You are going to listen to a radio interview with Peter Hall, an expert on education in China.

A Before you listen, match the following words and expressions from the text (1–10) to the German translations, (a–j).

1	to commit suicide	6	period	**a**	Aminosäure	**f**	Hauslehrer/in
2	contraceptive pill	7	risk	**b**	Antibabypille	**g**	Infusion
3	extracurricular	8	tough	**c**	außerschulisch	**h**	Menstruation
4	family honour	9	tutor	**d**	Familienehre	**i**	schwer
5	intravenous drip	10	amino acids	**e**	Gefahr	**j**	Selbstmord begehen

B Look at the title of the text and study the words above. Which words do you find odd in the context of education?

C What do you think Peter Hall is going to tell us about the exam and the students who take it?

2 LISTENING: THE GAOKAO – CHINA'S TOUGH EXAM

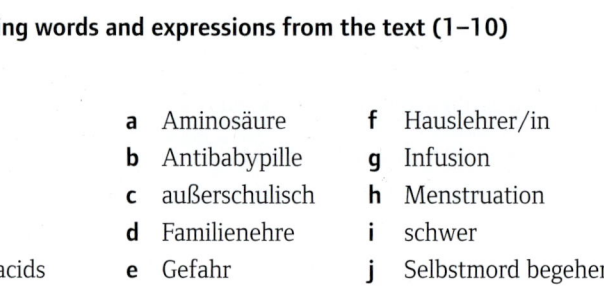

EXAM
→ listening comprehension

Choose the best answer for each of the following questions.

1 Which subjects are in the Gaokao exam?
  a Mathematics, English, Chinese, and one other subject
  b Chinese, English and Mathematics
  c Chinese, English, Mathematics, and either Science or a foreign language
  d English, Chinese, Mathematics and either Science or Geography

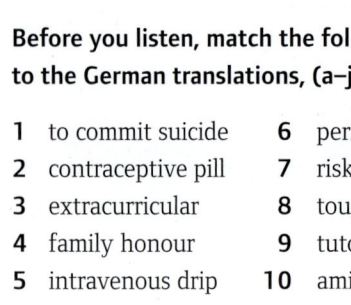

2 Which of the following do the students do in the time before the exam?
  a Hang out with friends.
  b Do more exercise and sport.
  c Use their free time to study more.
  d Ask teachers for more help.

3 Which of the following is <u>not</u> mentioned as a method which students use to deal with exam stress?
  a Taking medicine to help their bodies.
  c Taking drugs to help them relax.
  b Consuming more caffeine.
  d Talking about mental health issues at school.

3 LANGUAGE IN USE: MODAL AUXILIARIES

→ Modal auxiliaries, S. 276

●●● Work with a partner. Decide together where to use *must* or *must not* and where to use *should* or *should not*. Then translate the sentences into German.

EXAMPLES: *... The very tough exam that students* **must** *pass to get into university.*
Students who are putting their mental health in danger **should** *be supported by the school.*

REMEMBER ❗ *must not*
must not = nicht dürfen You **must not** tell anyone. → *Das dürfen Sie niemandem erzählen.*

nicht müssen = not need to
Sie müssen nicht gehen. →
You **don't need to** leave.

1 In order to get into university, Chinese students ⬤ pass a very tough exam.
2 There ⬤ be competition between classmates but there is.
3 Family honour is important in China, so the students feel they ⬤ do well in the exam.
4 Students who suffer from stress ⬤ visit their doctor, but most don't.
5 The teacher told us that we ⬤ study for at least 8 hours a day.
6 You ⬤ take the exam if you are not prepared.
7 You ⬤ cheat in the exam, otherwise you will be removed from the exam hall.

●●○ **Go to File 16 on page 193.**

4 PRESENTATION

You are going to research, prepare and give a presentation on how students in other countries cope with exam stress.

TRAIN YOUR SKILLS: Eine Präsentation vorbereiten	vgl. auch S. 254

Denken Sie immer daran, dass eine Präsentation ein visuelles Medium ist. Überladen Sie die Präsentation nicht mit Text. Verwenden Sie Illustrationen, um Ihre Ideen zu verdeutlichen.

- Erarbeiten Sie sich das Thema und machen Sie sich Notizen.
- Finden Sie online passende Illustrationen zum Thema oder erstellen Sie Ihre eigenen.
- Strukturieren Sie Ihre Notizen unter Überschriften.
- Versehen Sie jede Illustration mit einer Bildunterschrift.

A Do research on the internet and find out about tests in other countries and how students cope with them.

B Before you give your presentation, decide in class, together with your teacher, how you will get feedback on your content and presentation, as well as your way of presenting it.

C Give your presentation to the class.

You are working in a British company. Someone has done some work which you don't think is very good. You have to tell her that it isn't very good.

1 DIFFERENT COMMUNICATION STYLES

A Read the following generalizations about how Germans and British people communicate. Then discuss with a partner if you agree with what it says about how Germans communicate.

German speakers like to know where they stand, so generally they …	British speakers dislike conflict, so generally they …
■ enjoy serious conversations. ■ prefer to avoid small talk with people they don't know well. ■ speak open and honestly. ■ like to get straight to the point.	■ use humour to make a situation more pleasant. ■ use small talk to connect with others. ■ are very polite. ■ are indirect and often avoid saying what they mean.

B Now sort the phrases into stereotypes describing either German or British speakers.

1 They always make silly jokes.
2 They apologize for everything.
3 They can be quite critical.
4 They don't understand a joke.
5 They like to get down to business.
6 They never say directly that something is wrong.
7 It's difficult to know what they really think or mean.
8 They sometimes seem rude.
9 They take everything so seriously.
10 They waste time chatting before they get down to business.

2 BEING POLITE

A The British like to use softening phrases to sound more polite. Notice the use of *could*, *might* and *would* in many of the phrases.

Asking for something politely	Telling someone to do something politely
■ I would be very grateful if I could … ■ I was hoping I could/might … ■ I was wondering if I could/might … ■ Do you think I might be able to …? ■ Would you mind if I …?	■ Would you mind (*verb* + -ing) …? ■ Would it be possible for you to …? ■ Would you be able to …? ■ I was hoping you could/might … ■ I was wondering if you could/might … ■ Do you think you might be able to …? ■ Might I suggest that …?

Saying something negative in a polite way	Using adverbs or adjectives to make something sound less bad
■ I'm afraid (to say this, but) …	■ a little (bit)
■ I'm sorry, but …	■ quite
■ (I'm sorry, but) it looks like / as if …	■ rather
■ There seems to be something wrong with …	■ slightly
■ There seems to be a problem with …	■ short/small
■ I may/might not be able to …	■ somewhat

Use the phrases above to make the following sentences sound more British. The first two have been done for you.

1 This food is cold.
I'm afraid to say this, but this food is a little bit cold.
2 I need to hand my work in late.
I was wondering if I might hand my work in slightly late.
3 Can I borrow your notes?
4 Can you drive me home?
5 I want to book a flight.
6 Open the window.
7 Help me with my presentation.
8 Study harder for the exam.
9 We don't have any vacancies in the hotel.
10 Your credit card isn't working.
11 I'm disappointed by your work.
12 There's a delay in the project.

●●● **B Your boss has written you the following email.**

I'm really disappointed by Sarah's presentation. Tell her that she needs to do it all again. Make sure she uses more colours. Tell her to use different photos. And we need it by Friday. Thanks!

Using phrases from 2A, write an email to Sarah telling her she needs to do things differently. Start like this:

Hi Sarah,
I just want to tell you that …

●●○ **Go to File 17 on page 194.**

Students often complain that school is too stressful. As part of your school's project week on health and medicine today, you discuss ways to make your school less stressful.

1 STRESS AT SCHOOL

The school has put up a notice on the notice board. The aim is to find out what students find stressful at school.

Some students have already added their notes. Brainstorm more ideas of your own. Make a list.

too much noise
other people
no place to do homework

2 HOW WE ALREADY COMBAT STRESS

What can you already do at school to combat stress? What facilities does your school offer? How often do you use them? How do they help?

EXAMPLE: *We can use the library to do our homework.*

3 BRAINSTORMING IDEAS

Copy and complete the mind map with ideas about how to combat stress at your school.

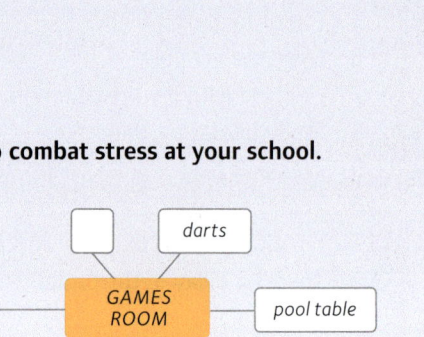

4 CLASS DISCUSSION: REACHING A CONSENSUS

→ Interaktion, S. 255

A In a group, discuss all your suggestions and choose one to present to the class. Be prepared to explain to the class why it is a good suggestion.

B Present your suggestion to the class. Try to reach an agreement on which three suggestions are most suitable. Be prepared to compromise if your suggestion is not accepted.

Sustainable shopping

A WARM-UP: THE SHOPPING EXPERIENCE

A Sort the photos under these four headings. Think of more examples of where to buy or find what we need.

shopping as an experience

giving and sharing

saving the planet

shopping from home

B Discuss these questions in groups.

Where do you shop? Who do you shop with?
What do you share? Who do you share with?
What do you swap? Who do you swap with?

B RUN, RECYCLE, RUN AGAIN

SITUATION: After watching a TED talk online about shopping and sustainability, you find out more about sustainability in order to post a comment (task 6B, page 62) about the topic.

1 PREPARING TO READ

Skim the text opposite to find the expressions below. Look at the expressions in context and explain what they mean. If you are unsure, check your English-German dictionary.

commitment	debris	garbage	to grind	incinerators

landfills	to outperform	to participate	to pollute	pressure

2 READING AND UNDERSTANDING THE TEXT

Read the text on the opposite page. Then choose the best option for each of the tasks below.

1 Which type of companies produced the first recycled shoes?
  a small companies with new ideas
  b international clothing manufacturers
  c local start-ups
  d recycling companies

2 A few years ago, sports' clothing firms made their running shoes …
  a completely out of new plastic.
  b using recycled plastic for a few parts of their shoes.
  c using the same amount of new plastic and recycled plastic.
  d out of natural materials.

3 Today many manufacturers are committed to reducing plastic waste by …
  a making their shoes out of plastic pellets.
  b producing long-lasting shoes.
  c using only recycled plastic in their shoes.
  d using less glue.

4 Some firms encourage their customers to …
  a wash their trainers regularly so that they last longer.
  b wear their trainers for as long as possible before buying new ones.
  c put their old trainers in the recycling bin.
  d give them their old trainers for recycling.

5 For recycling to really work, customers have to …
  a recycle their recycled shoes.
  b be made aware of the problems that plastic pollution causes.
  c buy recycled shoes.
  d purchase fewer trainers.

http://www.therunbetter.blog

RUN, RECYCLE, RUN AGAIN

What happens to your trainers when you're done with them?
They end up in landfills or incinerators which pollute the
atmosphere or they join the other garbage in the oceans.
A lot of the garbage that finds its way into the oceans is made
5 *of plastic. A few pieces of plastic debris sink, but a large*
percentage of it is washed up on the coastlines. Little effort
is made to stop used plastic polluting our environment.
However, under public pressure a few major sportswear firms
have recently started to use recycled plastic to make trainers.

10 As usual, it was small innovative brands that led the way in recycling material. With a commitment to creating clothing and accessories made entirely from recycled material, they created shoes that were expensive and stylish
15 without looking as if they were made from recycled material. They would often team up with organizations that clean the oceans of waste and take the plastic off their hands.

In 2015, several major brands decided to join
20 the ecological trend, as they started to look at ways to produce running shoes from recycled plastic. Plastic water bottles that are collected from the sea are chopped up, melted down and made into material that can be used in
25 shoes. Until now, the major companies used recycled materials for just some parts of their shoes, but most of the shoe was still made from new plastic.

However, things are changing now, and
30 companies are trying to outperform each other in the area of sustainability. As part of their commitment to reduce plastic waste, many of the sportswear companies use only recycled material and no glue in their trainers. Others are making trainers from one sort 35 of plastic, which makes the shoes easy to recycle so that they can be completely remade into another pair of trainers. When customers have got all the wear out of their trainers, they simply return them to the company, 40 which then washes the shoes and grinds them into pellets. These pellets are then melted into the material that's used for the parts of a new pair of shoes. It's zero waste. Few people can complain about that. 45

However, for these programmes to be successful, the customer needs to take part in them. There's little point in the companies offering sustainable models if the consumer does not participate. And we only have a little time 50 to save the planet from plastic!

Comments

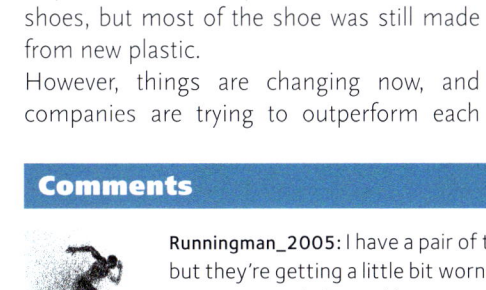

Runningman_2005: I have a pair of trainers that can be recycled. They're great to run in but they're getting a little bit worn out now. I'm definitely going to hand them in and get a new pair made from old pairs. Basically, you're wearing the same shoes over and over again. That's cool. 55

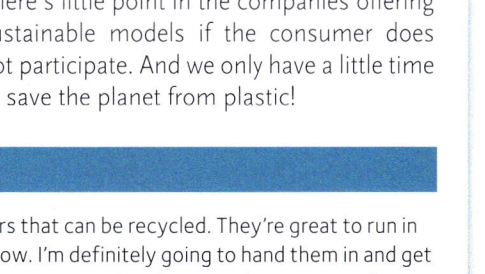

MarciaTNT: I think it's great that all the companies are producing recycled trainers, but to be honest I just care about the price and if they're comfortable.

(475 words)

3 LANGUAGE IN USE: (A) LITTLE, (A) FEW

→ Quantifiers, S. 280

A Translate the expressions from the text into German.

1 a few pieces of plastic debris (line 5)
2 few people can complain (line 45)
3 there's little point (line 48)
4 we only have a little time (line 50)

••• **B Choose (a) little or (a) few to complete the text.**

Today almost the whole beach, except for 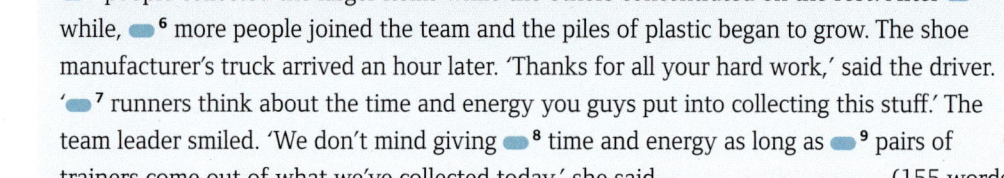¹ areas near the dunes, was littered with plastic. 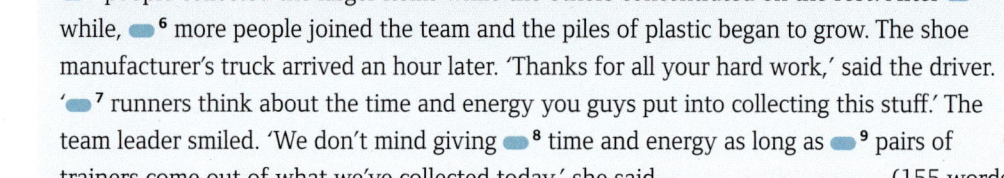² seagulls were picking up pieces of plastic. 'Right. Let's get this mess cleaned up,' said the team leader. 'We've got very 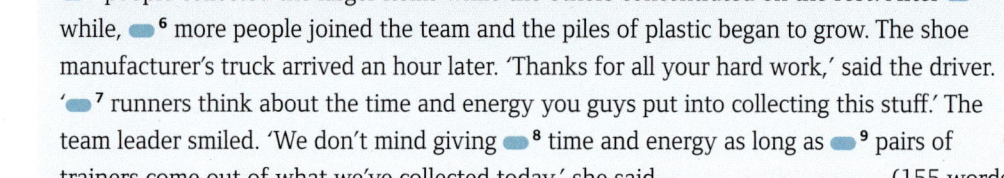³ time, as they'll be sending a truck quite soon.' 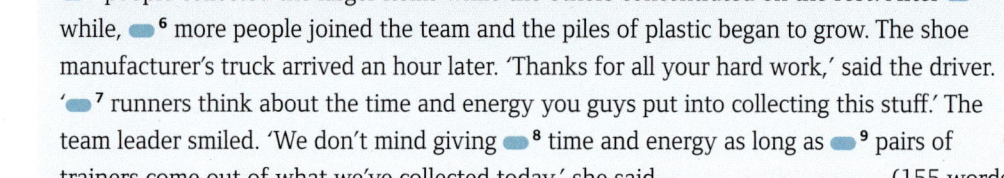⁴ people collected the larger items while the others concentrated on the rest. After 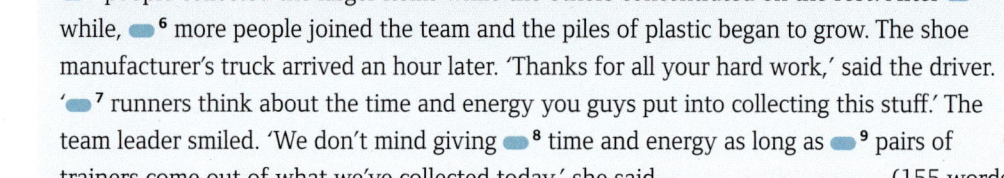⁵ while, 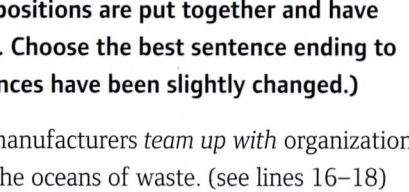⁶ more people joined the team and the piles of plastic began to grow. The shoe manufacturer's truck arrived an hour later. 'Thanks for all your hard work,' said the driver. '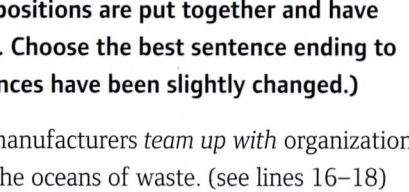⁷ runners think about the time and energy you guys put into collecting this stuff.' The team leader smiled. 'We don't mind giving 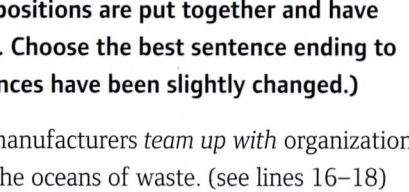⁸ time and energy as long as 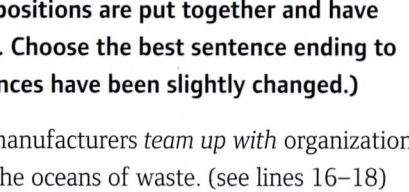⁹ pairs of trainers come out of what we've collected today,' she said. (155 words)

••○ **Go to File 18 on page 194.**

4 WORKING WITH WORDS

A A phrasal verb is when a verb and one or two prepositions are put together and have a meaning that is different from the original verb. Choose the best sentence ending to express the author's ideas in the text. (The sentences have been slightly changed.)

1 What happens to your trainers when you're *done with* them? (see line 1)
What happens to your trainers when …
  a they get old?
  b you no longer want them?
  c you don't use them very often?

2 The trainers *end up* in landfills or incinerators. (see line 2)
They …
  a are dumped in a place where they shouldn't be.
  b become part of the recycling process.
  c are thrown away as rubbish.

3 Shoe manufacturers *team up with* organizations that clean the oceans of waste. (see lines 16–18)
Shoe manufacturers …
  a cooperate with groups that take rubbish from the sea.
  b sign deals with ecological businesses about using recycled plastic.
  c set up companies that collect rubbish from the sea.

4 'I'm going to *hand* my trainers *in* and get a new pair.' (see lines 53–54)
I intend to …
  a sell my old trainers and use the money to buy new ones.
  b give my used trainers to the company that made them and get a new pair back.
  c give away my used trainers in the hope of getting some new ones.

THE PASSIVE

→ The passive, S. 271

The passive is often used when it is not important to say who is doing or has done something.

EXAMPLE: *Plastic water bottles that **are collected** from the sea **are chopped up**, **melted down** and **made** into material that can **be used** in shoes.*

A Change these sentences into the passive. The first one has been done for you.

1 People buy billions of trainers each year.
   Billions of trainers are bought each year.
2 Today firms make most shoes in Asia.
3 People spend over £10 million each year on trainers.
4 Last year consumers threw away 11 million tons of clothes.
5 Firms build more and more factories in Asia.
6 Companies have moved the production of clothes to Asia.
7 You can buy trainers at most sports shops.

**●●● B Copy and complete the flow chart below that shows the life cycle of a recycled shoe.
Use the verbs in the box in the passive. Remember to use the correct tense or the infinitive, and put the adverb in brackets in the correct position.**

> buy ▪ buy ▪ chop ▪ collect ▪ drink ▪ melt ▪ recycle ▪ return ▪
> take ▪ throw ▪ use ▪ use ▪ wear

Plastic bottles ___¹ by people around the world. **1**

Once the contents ___², the plastic bottles ___³ away. **2**

Rivers and seas ___⁴ (often) to dispose of plastic bottles. **3**

The plastic bottles ___⁵ from the sea by ecological companies. **4**

Then they ___⁶ to a recycling plant. **5**

In the plant they ___⁷ up into very small pieces. **6**

The small pieces ___⁸ down. **7**

The material ___⁹ (then) to make shoes. **8**

The recycled shoes ___¹⁰ by customers. **9**

After the shoes ___¹¹ for several years, they can ___¹² to the company to ___¹³. **10**

●●○ Go to File 19 on page 195.

6 WRITING A COMMENT

A You are going to write a comment on shopping and sustainability. Before you begin to write, copy this mind map and add words and expressions from the text on page 59 that you might use in your comment. Add more words of your own.

```
                        ┌──────────────┐
                        │ accessories  │
                        └──────────────┘
                               │
                    ┌────────────────────┐
                    │ TYPES OF CLOTHING  │
                    └────────────────────┘
                               │
┌──────────────┐  ┌────────┐  ┌────────────────┐  ┌──────────┐  ┌──────────────────┐
│ sustainability│─│ VALUES │─│ CLOTHES SHOPPING │─│ FEELINGS │─│ polluting our    │
└──────────────┘  └────────┘  └────────────────┘  └──────────┘  │ environment      │
                               │                                 └──────────────────┘
                    ┌─────────────────────┐
                    │ DESCRIBING PURCHASES │
                    └─────────────────────┘
                               │
                        ┌──────────────┐
                        │  recycled    │
                        └──────────────┘
```

B You watched a TED talk about shopping and sustainability, in which the speaker made the following statement:

'Consumers should stop buying cheap clothes which they throw away after they've worn them a few times.'

Read the suggestions in the skills box below and, using some of the words and phrases you collected in Task 6A, write a comment on the statement in about 100 words.

EXAM
→ writing

TRAIN YOUR SKILLS: Einen *comment* schreiben   vgl. auch S. 246

Bei einem *comment* müssen Sie Argumente sammeln, die die in der Aufgabenstellung enthaltene These stützen und widerlegen.

- Machen Sie zuerst ein Brainstorming, um Argumente und Ideen zu sammeln.
- Es hilft, Argumente in Pro- und Contra-Listen aufzuteilen.
- Es gibt wichtige *connecting words*, die Sie verwenden sollten, um Ihre Argumente einzuleiten und zu unterstützen sowie zum Schluss zu kommen (vgl. hintere Umschlagklappe innen).
- Ordnen Sie Ihr Vokabular systematisch in einer Mindmap.

Go to File 20 on page 195.

C TO SHOP OR NOT TO SHOP?

1 PREPARING TO LISTEN

●●● **These sayings are used in the audio text. Before you listen, talk in groups and decide what they mean. Do you know the same or similar sayings in German or in another language you speak?**

A fool and his money are soon parted.
Money doesn't grow on trees.
You can't take it with you when you go.

●●○ **Go to File 21 on page 196.**

2 LISTENING: SHOPPING HABITS

EXAM
→ listening comprehension

A Decide who says what. There are two statements for each speaker, but there are also two more statements than you need.

speaker	statement
Elias	⬤ ⬤
Kay	⬤ ⬤
Will	⬤ ⬤
Julia	⬤ ⬤

1 I always want the newest version of any tech equipment.

2 I won't buy a new phone until my old one no longer works.

3 I love my friends but they waste money buying stuff they don't need.

4 If it's not a luxury brand, I'm not buying it!

5 I haven't actually worn all the clothes I have.

6 I really love shopping.

7 There's a box of old equipment under my bed.

8 I haven't bought anything new for years.

9 I try to buy as little as possible, as we just don't need so many things.

10 Vintage clothing can be really cool.

B Kay has bought motto T-shirts for herself and her friends. Match one T-shirt (1–4) to each speaker. Give a reason.

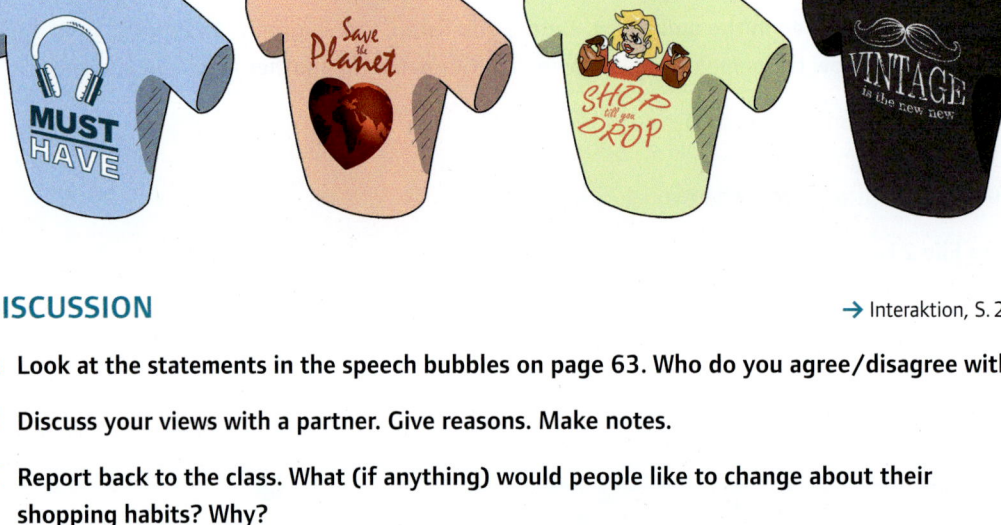

3 DISCUSSION

→ Interaktion, S. 255

A Look at the statements in the speech bubbles on page 63. Who do you agree/disagree with?

B Discuss your views with a partner. Give reasons. Make notes.

C Report back to the class. What (if anything) would people like to change about their shopping habits? Why?

4 LANGUAGE IN USE: (THE) LESS, AT/THE LEAST, FEWER, THE FEWEST

A Look at these examples from the audio text. Explain when we use *less* and when we use *fewer*.

1 These T-shirts cost **less than** the ones in the shopping mall.
2 **The less stuff** you buy, the better.
3 You have **fewer problems** when you have **less stuff**.
4 I have **the fewest T-shirts** of all of us.

B Translate the German phrases in the sentences below with (*the*) *less*, (*at/the*) *least*, *fewer*, *the fewest*. The first phrase has been done for you.

1 My second-hand printer cost *weniger*[a] *less* than a new one. Of all my printers, it's the one that's given me *die wenigsten*[b] problems.
2 Of all the jackets I have, this is the one I wear *am wenigsten*[a]. I like it much *weniger*[b] than the other jackets I own.
3 Shopping is such a waste of time. *Je weniger* time I spend shopping, the more time I have for my hobbies.
4 Boys spend *weniger*[a] money on clothes than girls. That's not because boys buy *weniger*[b] clothes than girls but because boys' clothes cost *mindestens*[c] 25% *weniger*[d] than girls' clothes.

5 LANGUAGE IN USE: RELATIVE CLAUSES

→ Relative clauses, S. 283

Look at these three sentences, all of which contain relative clauses.

EXAMPLES: *They simply return the old trainers to the company,* **which then washes them and grinds them into pellets***.*
You have a ton of stuff **that you've never worn***.*
You can't go on spending everything <u>you've got on things</u> <u>you don't need</u>*.*

●●● Put these sentences together using a relative clause. The first one has been done for you.

1 The trainers are quite expensive. I bought them today.

that ←— *The trainers (*<u>which</u>*) I bought today are quite expensive.*

2 John's new car was damaged in an accident last week. The car cost him all his savings.
3 TTW Company used to be one of the biggest producers of sports clothing. TTW Company went bankrupt last month.
4 The zip on the jacket is already broken. I bought the jacket yesterday.
5 I need to speak to someone. That person must work in the Sales Department.
6 That's the man. He sold me the jacket.
7 My boyfriend spent money on my present. It was all the money which he had.
8 TTW Ltd won the contract. This surprised many people in the industry.

●●○ Go to File 22 on page 197.

 **6** VIEWING

→ Videos, S. 212

Watch the video called 'France ponders opening shops on Sundays despite tradition' and complete the tasks on page 212.

7 COMMUNICATION

Your school has decided to introduce 'Sustainable Fridays' to make students aware of the environmental impact of their lives.

You and a partner discuss ways in which students can change their behaviour.

Agree on two things which you think every student can start or stop doing every Friday to reduce their environmental impact.

You can use the photos in File 1 on page 209 to help you come up with some ideas.

EXAM
→ Kommunikations-
prüfung

You have been offered a part-time job in a clothes store in a small town in the USA. You need to find out more about the shopping experience in the USA.

1 AMERICAN SHOPPING HABITS

A **Paul is on an exchange trip to the USA. His family takes him grocery shopping. Read his exchange diary and note down things that are different from in Germany.**

Today my exchange mum, Mrs Keller, took all of us to the grocery store. There aren't any grocery stores near where we live, so it was a 15-minute drive. The grocery store is situated outside town together with lots of other shops and food chains. As we entered the store, a large sign reminded us that the store would be open on Christmas Day if we needed any
5 groceries. The store is open every day of the year.

I was impressed by how large the store was. Shelves stretched on endlessly, and they were all stocked with five to ten different brands of each product. They didn't just sell food, but also clothes and household items like towels and sheets.

The younger kids loved pushing the trolley up and down the aisles. There was lots of space,
10 so they couldn't hit anyone. Karl and I were more interested in the clothes, and I found a colourful Christmas sweater I liked for $20.

Once Mrs Keller had filled the trolley with all her groceries, we headed to the cash desk, where a cashier stood and greeted us with a big warm smile. The cashier was very chatty and had a long talk with Mrs Keller about lots of things. I wasn't sure if they knew each other.
15 I asked Karl, but he looked puzzled. 'No, of course not! Why do you ask?'

As the cashier scanned our items, she passed them down to a bagger, whose job it is to put our goods into large plastic bags – I recognized him from school, but he was in another class. I was surprised that we didn't have to tip him and that the bags were for free. Normally you tip everyone in the USA. At the end, Mrs Keller paid with her credit card and we left.
20 I gave her $20 for the sweater but she said it actually cost $21.70. Mrs Keller said it was because you always needed to add sales tax. Here it was 8.5%, which was sales and local taxes together. I didn't really understand why the full price wasn't shown in the store, but it was still a good price.

Then we headed home.

B **What will the American students have to get used to when shopping in Germany?**
Make a list and write short descriptions in English for them. The following phrases might be useful:

'Shop Closing Law'	*Ladenschlussgesetz*
Sunday shopping days	*verkaufsoffene Sonntage*
public holidays	*gesetzliche Feiertage*
opening hours	*Öffungszeiten*

2 WORKING IN A STORE

It's your first day working at the clothes store FashMash. You are shadowing Madison, who has worked there for a long time. Listen to the two dialogues.

 A List the expressions from the dialogue (1–9) under the four headings below (some may fit more than one heading).

- Making small talk with a customer
- Showing you remember a customer
- Making a customer feel like a friend
- Offering help to a customer

1 How are you?
2 It's great to see you again!
3 Welcome back.
4 Is it for you or your daughter?
5 Mine is always ruining her clothes.
6 What size is she again?
7 Can I be of assistance to you?
8 How have you been enjoying all the sun we've been having?
9 Just shout if you need any help.

B Now it's your turn. Do a role play with a partner. Decide whether the customer is new or one who visits the store often. Use phrases from Task 2B and/or the lists below.

Making small talk with a customer
- Are you enjoying your afternoon?
- How's your day going?
- We're so lucky with the weather today.

Showing you remember a customer
- It's great to see you again.
- Welcome back! How've you been?
- Did you have a good weekend?
- Coming in for another …?

Making a customer feel like a friend
- I hear the traffic has been terrible. Did you have trouble getting here?
- Are you managing to stay dry with all this rain!?
- Have you been to the new café next door?
- My friend bought this. It looks really great on her.

TIP ! Spelling

UK	USA
colour	color
neighbour	neighbor

Offering help
- Would you like a basket?
- Can I free up your hands?
- Are you finding everything ok?
- Do you need any help?
- Are you looking for a particular size or color?
- If you can't see what you're looking for, we may have it in the back.

Go to File 23 on page 197.

Your discussions about shopping and swapping have made you think about holding a bring-and-swap event. Work together to plan the event.

1 INTERNET RESEARCH

Do internet research to find out about swapping events. Make notes.
Use these search words 'organize swap'.

2 WHAT, WHEN AND HOW

A Decide what you are going to swap.

B Decide where you are going to hold the event.

- Do you need to make any special arrangements, e.g. who do you need to contact for permission?
- Do you need special equipment, e.g. tables, mirrors?

C Decide when you are going to hold the event.

3 RULES

A Set rules for what can be swapped, e.g. only things in good condition.

B Set rules for how to swap, e.g. bring what you can and take what you need.

4 DONATING LEFT-OVER ITEMS

Think about what to do with items that have not been taken. (Do you need to ask people if they want the items back?)

5 ANNOUNCING THE EVENT

Make a poster.

Include:

- an introduction to the event (say why you've decided to hold it).
- date, time, place (mention any important factors, e.g. separate changing rooms for men and women, where people can try on clothes).
- rules (say what can be swapped; say how things can be swapped).
- where the left-over clothes will go.

Screenagers

 WARM-UP: ARE YOU A SCREENAGER?

US teenagers and their screens

Teenagers spend an average of 7½ hours a day using a screen.

The average teenager sends 60 texts a day.

Only 39% of teenagers make or receive voice calls regularly.

Source: www.teensafe.com

A Look at the figures above. How do you compare with the average US teenager? Think about all the kinds of screens that you use.

B What do you think the people in the photos are doing with the devices they are using? Which devices do you use, and what do you use them for? List as many things as you can think of.

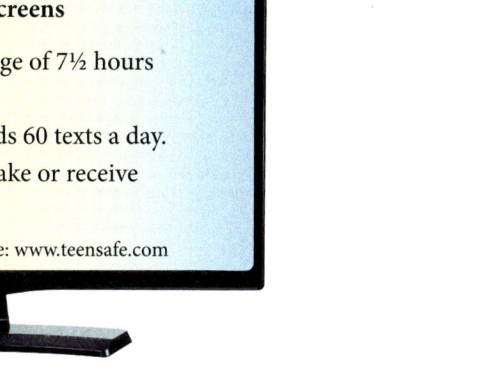

B LIVESTREAMING

SITUATION: You are a member of a leisure group (e.g. fitness, beauty, fashion) on social media. Members around the world share tips and advice. The group language is English. The group is considering using livestreaming and has asked members to write a short statement with their opinions (task 6, page 73).

1 PREPARING TO READ

Work with a partner. Look at the screenshots of livestreaming below. Write a description of livestreaming in one sentence.

Livestreaming is when you … / Internet users can …

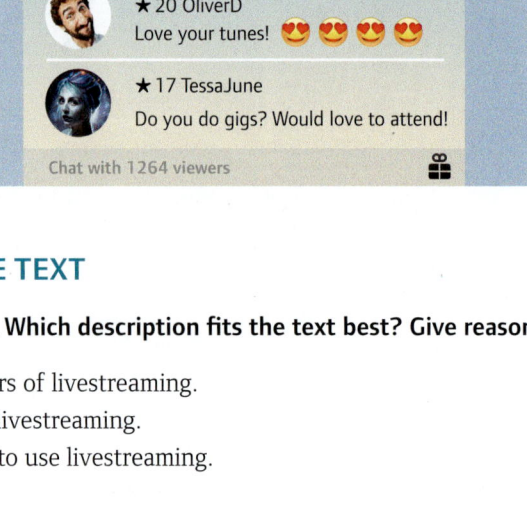

2 READING AND UNDERSTANDING THE TEXT

A Skim the text opposite from an e-magazine. Which description fits the text best? Give reasons.

    a The article warns readers about the dangers of livestreaming.
    b The article gives different opinions about livestreaming.
    c The article gives tips about the best ways to use livestreaming.

B Match the screenshots above to the interviewees. One does not have a screenshot. Why not?

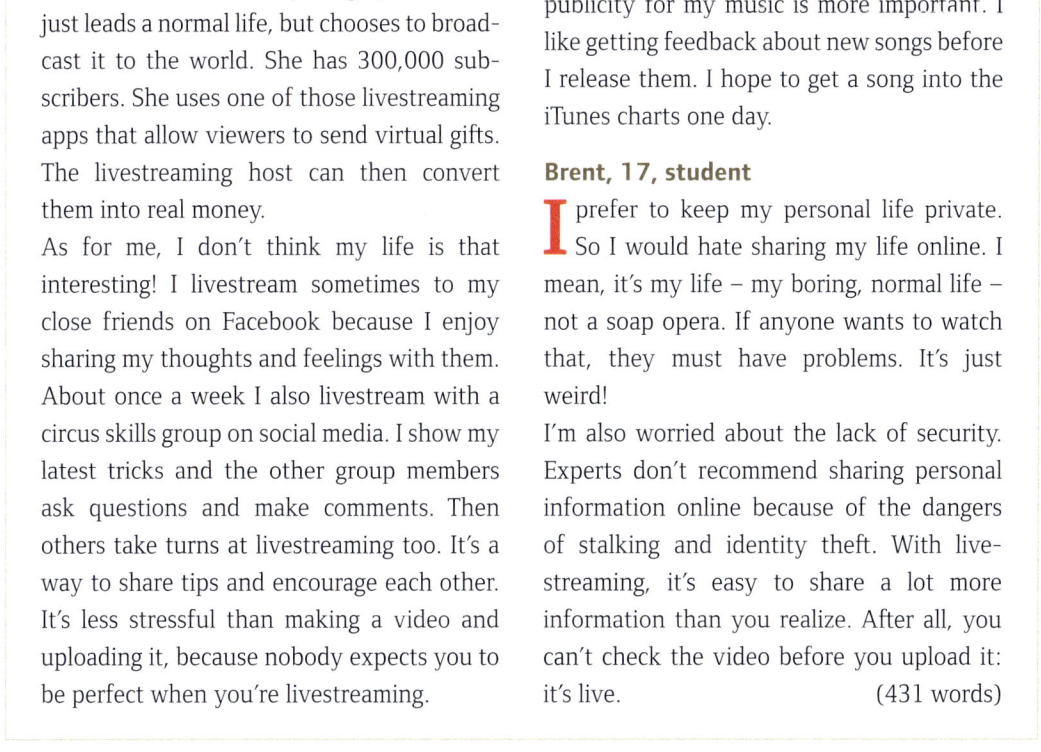

LIVESTREAMING

FUN, GOOD FOR BUSINESS OR JUST WEIRD?

Millions of people around the world use livestreaming to share their lives online. Why do they do it? We asked three of our regular contributors for their thoughts.

Joey, 19, personal trainer

I've heard about people who make a living from livestreaming. There's one girl, Sammie Firth I think her name is, who earns about $200,000 a year as a livestreaming host. She doesn't do anything special – she just leads a normal life, but chooses to broadcast it to the world. She has 300,000 subscribers. She uses one of those livestreaming apps that allow viewers to send virtual gifts. The livestreaming host can then convert them into real money.

As for me, I don't think my life is that interesting! I livestream sometimes to my close friends on Facebook because I enjoy sharing my thoughts and feelings with them. About once a week I also livestream with a circus skills group on social media. I show my latest tricks and the other group members ask questions and make comments. Then others take turns at livestreaming too. It's a way to share tips and encourage each other. It's less stressful than making a video and uploading it, because nobody expects you to be perfect when you're livestreaming.

Alex, 21, musician

I started livestreaming from my studio a couple of years ago as a way to help my music career. It's just like a live concert, only more relaxed. People can chat to me online and ask me questions about my music, or request songs that they like. I love having that personal contact with my audience. It's a great way to connect with other people.

I earn about £100 a month from livestreaming. Viewers can send me virtual money if they like what I'm doing. It isn't much, but it helps to pay my bills. The publicity for my music is more important. I like getting feedback about new songs before I release them. I hope to get a song into the iTunes charts one day.

Brent, 17, student

I prefer to keep my personal life private. So I would hate sharing my life online. I mean, it's my life – my boring, normal life – not a soap opera. If anyone wants to watch that, they must have problems. It's just weird!

I'm also worried about the lack of security. Experts don't recommend sharing personal information online because of the dangers of stalking and identity theft. With livestreaming, it's easy to share a lot more information than you realize. After all, you can't check the video before you upload it: it's live.   (431 words)

C Decide whether the following statements are true or false.

EXAM
→ reading
comprehension

1 Sammie's income comes from advertising.
2 Joey uses livestreaming to share and improve his circus skills.
3 Joey worries a lot about making mistakes when he is livestreaming his tricks.
4 Alex uses livestreaming as a way to connect with other musicians.
5 For Alex, livestreaming is more intimate than a live concert.
6 Alex likes livestreaming because it helps her to find out what her fans want.
7 Brent thinks that his life would make a good soap opera.
8 He thinks that livestreaming is just as safe as making a video.

3 LANGUAGE IN USE: TENSES

EXAM
→ use of language

●●● **You have the opportunity to ask Joey, Alex and Brent some questions.**
Ask them for the following information in English:

1 Joey, wann er das letzte Mal Livestreaming gemacht hat.
2 Joey, wie lange er schon Zirkuskunststücke (*circus tricks*) macht.
3 Alex, wie viele Viewer sie normalerweise hat.
4 Alex, wie viel sie als Musikerin verdient hat, bevor sie mit dem Livestreaming anfing.
5 Brent, weshalb er meint, sein Leben sei langweilig.
6 Brent, ob er schon Erfahrung mit Identitätsdiebstahl gemacht hat.

●●○ **Go to File 24 on page 198.**

4 LANGUAGE IN USE: –ING FORM OR TO-INFINITIVE?

→ Verb + *-ing* Form · Verb + *to*-infinitive, S. 278

A Find verbs in the text which …

1 are followed by *to* + the infinitive.   **EXAMPLE:** *choose to broadcast (line 13)*
2 are followed by *-ing*.   **EXAMPLE:** *enjoy sharing (line 21)*

Write the verbs with the line numbers. Check on page 278 to see which of the verbs can be followed by both forms.

B Copy and complete these sentences with the correct form of the verb in brackets. If both are correct, write both versions.

1 At what age did you start ⬭ (use) social media?
2 Which photo do you recommend ⬭ (put) in my profile?
3 Every morning, Mum enjoys ⬭ (read) what her Facebook friends have written.
4 Matt hopes ⬭ (become) famous through livestreaming.
5 Dan hates ⬭ (read) long posts on Facebook.
6 He only wants ⬭ (follow) celebrities on Twitter.
7 Why does anyone like ⬭ (watch) YouTube videos of cats?

C **Work with a partner and ask each other for the following information in English.**

1 was er/sie gerne in seiner/ihrer Freizeit macht
2 was er/sie hasst, in seiner/ihrer Freizeit zu machen
3 ob er/sie vor kurzem angefangen hat, seine/ihre eigenen Podcasts zu machen
4 ob er/sie vor kurzem zustimmte, einen Blog für die Schule zu schreiben
5 ob er/sie beschlossen hat, nichts mehr auf Facebook zu posten
6 ob er/sie es bevorzugt, keine persönlichen Informationen online zu teilen

5 WORKING WITH WORDS

A **Find these words and expressions relating to social media in the text on page 71.**

1 person who runs a show or social media page (*Joey*)
2 to send information to many people by TV, radio, internet, etc. (*Joey*)
3 person who receives your social media updates (*Joey*)
4 person who watches a TV show, video, etc. (*Joey*)
5 to ask for something (*Alex*)
6 to have a good relationship with somebody (*Alex*)
7 to put something on the internet (*Brent*)

B **Use words from A to complete the text. You will need to change the form of some words.**

Dan Middleton is the ⬤ ¹ of a YouTube video games channel, DanTDM. ⬤ ² of his video clips can see Dan play Minecraft and other games. He ⬤ ³ a new games video almost every day. He also ⬤ ⁴ a vlog about his daily life outside Minecraft. DanTDM is one of the most popular channels on YouTube, perhaps because Dan's sense of fun makes it easy for fans to ⬤ ⁵ with him. He has nearly 15 million ⬤ ⁶ on YouTube and earns about $2 million a year.

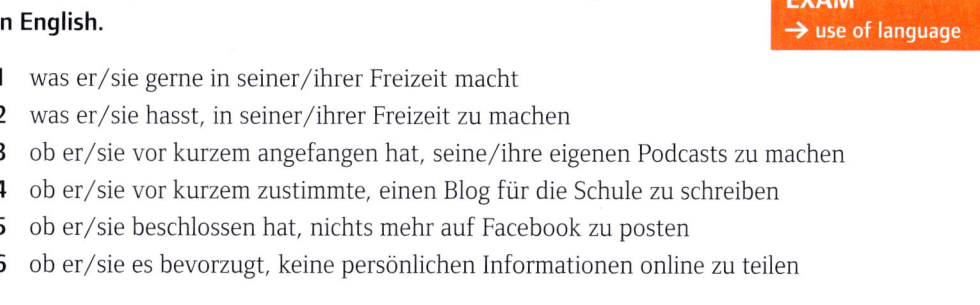

6 WRITING A STATEMENT

●●● **In a statement you are expected to give your own opinion on something.**

Before you start, do a mind map, in which you collect ideas from the text on page 71. Add some of your own ideas.

Give your opinion on livestreaming in about 100 words. You can start like this:

So, you want to hear our views on livestreaming? I personally think that …

●●○ **Go to File 25 on page 198.**

C   USING SOCIAL MEDIA

1 PREPARING TO LISTEN

You are going to listen to a radio chat show about 'sadfishing'. Before you listen, look at the definition, then discuss these questions with a partner. Note down the main points of your discussion.

> **sadfishing**
>
> (noun) The practice of writing about one's unhappiness or emotional problems on social media in order to attract attention and get a sympathetic response.
>
> Source: www.urbandictionary.com

1   Do you think that 'sadfishing' is a problem?
2   Have you seen behaviour which looks like 'sadfishing'?
3   How can you tell whether a person is 'sadfishing' or really unhappy?

2 LISTENING: SADFISHING

18

A   Listen to the recording. Did it make you change your mind about your answers to task 1. Why or why not?

> I already felt / knew that …

> I was surprised to learn that …

> It made me think about …

B   Choose the best answer for each of the following questions.

> **EXAM**
> → listening comprehension

1   What is sadfishing, according to Kylie?
   a   Sadfishing is a way of looking for attention from other people.
   b   Sadfishing is when celebrities complain about the publicity they get.
   c   Sadfishing is when people try to get sympathy from others for their real problems.
   d   Sadfishing is when people lie about their emotional problems to sound more interesting.

2   Why did Ethan talk about suffering from depression online?
   a   He wanted to surprise people with the news.
   b   He was hoping that many people would like his post.
   c   He hoped people would help him overcome his depression.
   d   He was drawing attention to the difference between his outward and inward self.

3   After receiving feedback from others, how did Ethan feel?
   a   He felt even worse than before.
   b   He felt that he had just been sadfishing.

    c He felt good about opening up about his problems.

    d He appreciated the help and support he received from others.

4 What does Kylie say is quite common?

    a That friends on social media are supportive.

    b That people like to remain anonymous on social media.

    c That people use social media to deal with emotional issues.

    d That people who talk about emotional issues on social media receive abuse.

5 Kylie gives advice about how to react when reading about other people's problems online. Which of the following does she <u>not</u> advise?

    a Don't always believe what people write online.

    b Contact the person privately if you know them.

    c Don't react to posts of people you don't know.

    d Never think you know how other people feel.

3 WORKING WITH LANGUAGE

EXAM
→ use of language

A **Find words or expressions in the text on page 76 which mean more or less the same as the words below.**

    a immediate (lines 6–11)   **b** chance (lines 16–23)

B **Find the opposites of the following words from the text on page 76.**

    a negative (line 4)   **b** different (line 18)

C **Explain the following words from the text on page 76 in complete sentences.**

    a central (line 2)   **b** feedback (line 11)

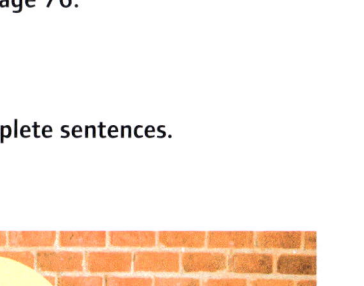

D Complete the text by using suitable forms of the words on the right.

Is social media all bad?

Social media often receives much ^a from different people. But it's such a central element in the lives of youngsters today that it is difficult imagining that it will ever disappear. And we ⬤ ^b just always complain about its negative aspects – social media has its
5   good points too!
    Firstly, it encourages creativity and innovative thinking. Social media sites offer content in a variety of forms. This lets the users display their creativity as writers, photographers and designers. If you're a teen who likes to take and upload photos, social media can
10   help you ⬤ ^c your skills. Social media is an ideal place to share your work and get encouragement and instant feedback from others.
    Social media can be perfect for getting creative. Teenagers can use it to start ⬤ ^d how to solve problems and how to find innovative approaches to different issues. Even when teenagers are making
15   memes and joking around, they're still learning valuable design skills.
    ⬤ ^e social media gives teenagers the opportunity to expand their worldview and get out of the bubble of their own group of friends. It exposes them to different viewpoints, to news from around the world and to people from around the world. It can be ⬤ ^f for teen-
20   agers to find out what's happening outside of their world and to understand big issues. Many teenagers became ⬤ ^g activists after informing themselves of issues on social media. If they're lucky, they ⬤ ^h new friends from different backgrounds. It's a great way for teenagers to connect with other people, and to share their
25   thoughts and feelings.

a	critic
b	couldn't/ mustn't/ shouldn't
c	to improve
d	to learn
e	to use
f	to help
g	to lead
h	to make

E You are talking to two friends about their social media use.
Ask two questions about the role of social media in their lives. Use different question forms or different tenses.

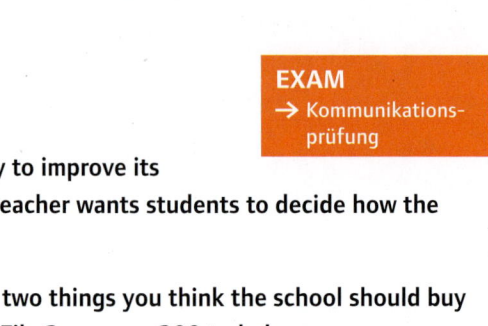

EXAM
➜ Kommunikations-
prüfung

4 COMMUNICATION

Your school has been offered a large sum of money to improve its electronic equipment for classroom use. The headteacher wants students to decide how the money should be spent.

Discuss your ideas with your partner and agree on two things you think the school should buy for the students to use. You can use the photos in File 2 on page 209 to help you come up with some ideas.

5 WORKING WITH DIAGRAMS

TRAIN YOUR SKILLS: Schaubilder beschreiben und analysieren vgl. auch S. 253

Diagramme und Kurven werden verwendet, um Informationen bildlich darzustellen.
Machen Sie sich Notizen zu folgenden Fragen:

- Was sagt die Überschrift aus?
- Welche Zahlen und Einheiten werden verwendet, um die Daten darzustellen?
- Wofür steht die x-Achse? Wofür die y-Achse? Welche Beschriftung liegt vor?
- Welche Muster können Sie in den Daten erkennen?
- Welche Schlüsse können Sie aus diesen Mustern ziehen?

●●● **Look at the bar chart below. Write a short description of the information.**

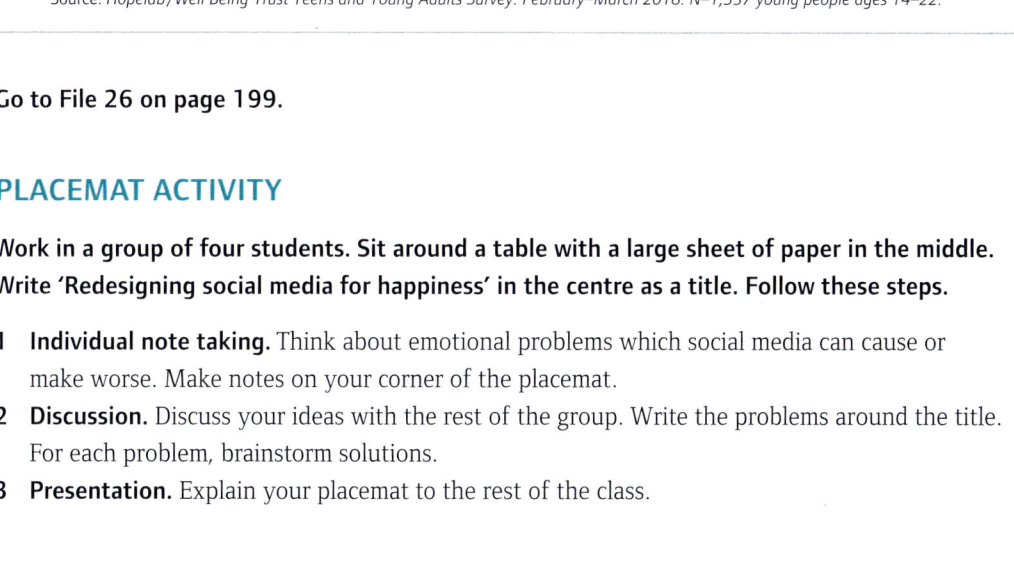

Survey of 14–22-year-old social media users

'Social media is very important to me for getting inspiration from others.'

13%
27%

'I often feel left out when using social media.'

1%
18%

'Social media is very important to me for feeling less alone.'

7%
30%

'I post things but I get few comments or likes.'

7%
29%

■ Among those with no depressive symptoms   ■ Among those with moderate to severe depressive symptoms

Source: *Hopelab/Well Being Trust Teens and Young Adults Survey. February–March 2018. N–1,337 young people ages 14–22.*

●●○ **Go to File 26 on page 199.**

6 PLACEMAT ACTIVITY

Work in a group of four students. Sit around a table with a large sheet of paper in the middle. Write 'Redesigning social media for happiness' in the centre as a title. Follow these steps.

1 **Individual note taking.** Think about emotional problems which social media can cause or make worse. Make notes on your corner of the placemat.
2 **Discussion.** Discuss your ideas with the rest of the group. Write the problems around the title. For each problem, brainstorm solutions.
3 **Presentation.** Explain your placemat to the rest of the class.

WORLD OF INTERCULTURAL COMMUNICATION

1 DO'S AND DON'TS FOR WRITING ACROSS CULTURES

Match the tips (1–4) to the headings (a–e). There is one more heading than you need.

a Learn another language.   **c** Keep it simple.   **e** Watch your style.
b Get times and dates right.   **d** Know how to address people.

1 In Germany and the USA, emails are generally written in a direct manner in order to avoid misunderstandings. In other countries, like Spain and Italy, first emails are written in a more polite formal style that allows a personal relationship to build over time.

2 In many English-speaking countries you can address someone by their first name even if you don't know them. In other countries, like India, you should address someone as Mr or Ms (just as you address people in Germany as *Herr* and *Frau*). If you are uncertain, write 'Dear ...' with just the first name and surname.

3 If you are writing to someone who also uses English as a second language, you should be very careful that you get your message across clearly. Always use simple grammar and easy vocabulary.

4 If you want to avoid misunderstandings when you write dates, times, measurements and figures, you have to know how they are written in the country you are writing to.

2 WRITING DATES

A **Different countries write the date differently. Match the countries with the way of writing the same date: Friday, 4th November 2022.**

1	Canada	a	04.11.2022
2	Hungary	b	11/04/2022
3	Japan	c	2022.11.04
4	the UK	d	2022 11 04 Friday
5	the USA	e	2022. nov. 10

B **Explain the different systems and say which you think is best. Which of them is similar to the German way?**

C **How do you write a date in an email when you are unsure if the reader uses your system?**

3 WRITING NUMBERS

Some countries use commas in numbers, some decimal points. Do research and write the following words in numbers according to the German system and then according to the system in English-speaking countries, adding commas and decimal points where necessary. Then complete the rules below.

1 three thousand and thirty-three
2 one million
3 two and a half per cent
4 four and three-quarters per cent
5 six euros seventy cents
6 one thousand euros and eighty cents

Im Deutschen verwendet man ⬤ᵃ, um große Zahlen zu gliedern, im Englischen verwendet man ⬤ᵇ. Bei Prozentangaben trennt man im Deutschen die Dezimalstelle mit ⬤ᶜ ab, im Englischen mit ⬤ᵈ. Entsprechend werden bei einer Preisangabe die Cents im Deutschen durch ⬤ᵉ, im Englischen durch ⬤ᶠ abgetrennt.

4 STRUCTURING AN EMAIL

A **An email is usually structured as below (a–f). Match the phrases (1–18) to the sections of an email's structure. There are three phrases to each section.**

a *Subject line*
This is above the body of the email and should tell the reader exactly what the email is about.

b *Salutation and greeting*
Here you greet the reader politely and make them feel comfortable.

c *Reason for writing*
Here you describe why you are writing.

d *Details*
Here you give an explanation, apology, information.

e *Request for action*
Here you ask the reader to do something.

f *Concluding and sign-off*
Here you conclude your email in a polite or friendly manner.

1 Best wishes
2 Dear …
3 Flight LF1234
4 I agree with you that this situation could have been dealt with better.
5 I am writing to you in reply to …
6 I hope you are well.
7 I look forward to hearing from you.
8 I was wondering if …
9 I would be very grateful if …
10 I would like to introduce myself: …
11 I'm writing because …
12 If you could …, that would be great.
13 My manager has asked me to …
14 Project XYZ
15 Thanking you in advance.
16 We have decided not to …
17 Our firm is soon going to …
18 Your Order 23456

B **Look at the email below and put the paragraphs (a–e) in the correct order.**

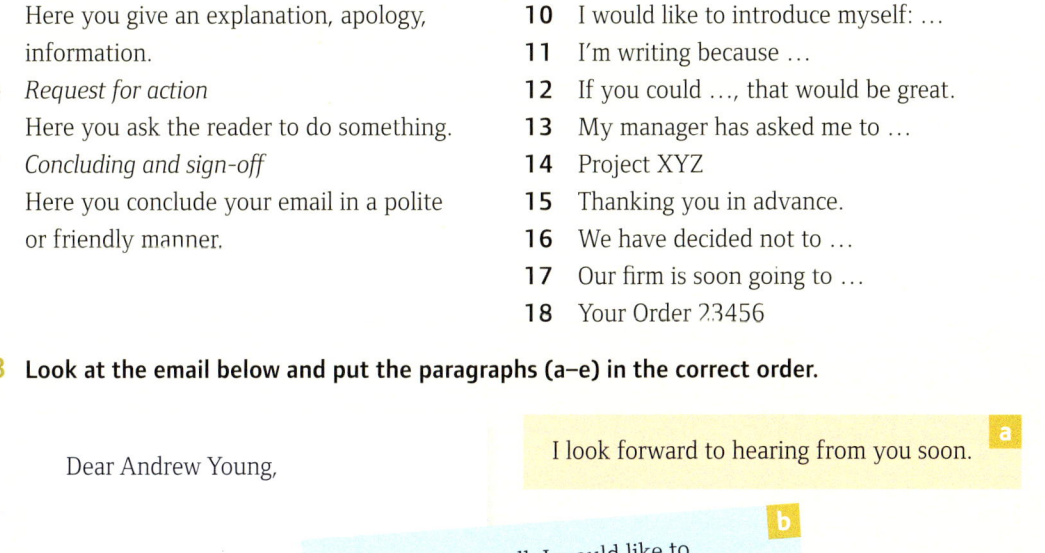

Dear Andrew Young,

a I look forward to hearing from you soon.

b I hope you are well. I would like to introduce myself: I am the new head of sales at the London office of our firm.

c Best wishes

d I would be very grateful if you could send them to me as soon as possible, so that I could get my presentation finished.

e My CEO has asked me to present the sales figures for this year. I understand that we are still missing the figures from your office.

Helen Walker

You design and analyse a questionnaire about how the class uses electronic devices.

1 BRAINSTORMING

In class collect ideas about different electronic devices that you use and how you use them. Here is an example of a mind map:

2 COLLECTING IDEAS

Once the class has gathered ideas on the board, form small groups and decide what sort of information you want to find out.

3 WRITING THE QUESTIONNAIRE

A Write down at least four questions in your questionnaire. Here are two examples:

The three electronic devices I use most are …

a	☐ smartphone	f	☐ smartwatch
b	☐ e-reader	g	☐ laptop
c	☐ games console	h	☐ digital camera
d	☐ (desktop) computer	i	☐ other: _____
e	☐ tablet		

I spend this amount of time on my smartphone each day:

a	☐ 6 hours	d	☐ 2 hours
b	☐ 4 hours	e	☐ 1 hour
c	☐ 3 hours	f	☐ hardly ever

B Hand out the questionnaires. They should be filled in anonymously.

4 ANALYSING THE INFORMATION

A Collect the questionnaires and decide how you wish to present your information, for example as graphs or pie charts.

B Highlight two important findings and present them on an A3 page together with your charts.

5 GALLERY WALK

Everyone walks round and examines the results. In class, decide which was the most interesting finding.

A   WARM-UP: QUIZ

How much do you know about Scotland? Do the quiz to find out.

1 Which of the maps shows Scotland in yellow? (1 point)

a   **b**   **c**   **d**

2 Scotland has 7 cities. Which of the following is not a Scottish city? (1 point)

a	Aberdeen	**e**	Inverness
b	Dundee	**f**	Melbourne
c	Edinburgh	**g**	Stirling
d	Glasgow	**h**	Perth

3 In which year did England and Scotland unite to form the United Kingdom?

a 1603
b 1707
c 1800
d 1921

4 Match the names to the photos of famous attractions. (6 points)

Barras Market, Glasgow ▪ Edinburgh Castle ▪ the Highland Games ▪
the Kelpies ▪ Loch Ness ▪ the V&A Museum, Dundee

B STAYING IN SCOTLAND

SITUATION: You and your friends want to go on a trip to Scotland in the summer. You find a travel blog about various accommodation options. You recommend one of the options in an email to your friends (task 6, page 86).

1 PREPARING TO READ

A Look at the photos of places to stay in Scotland. Match the words in the box to the types of accommodation. There are two items that you do not need.

bed and breakfast ▪ camper van ▪ caravan ▪ hostel ▪ hotel ▪ resort ▪ tent

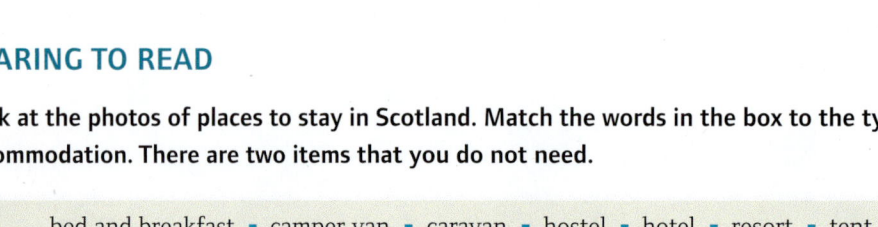

B Work with a partner. Where would you stay? Choose an option from task 1A. Say why.

2 READING AND UNDERSTANDING THE TEXT

A Skim the text opposite. Which types of accommodation in task 1A are mentioned? Does the text mention any others?

B Which option from the text is best for these people? Give reasons.

Annika (18) and Lea (19): It will be our first trip to Edinburgh and we would like to stay with someone who can show us around.

Lukas (16), Jan (17), Fabian (16): We're looking for adventure and wild natural places. Getting to know some young Scots would be nice, too!

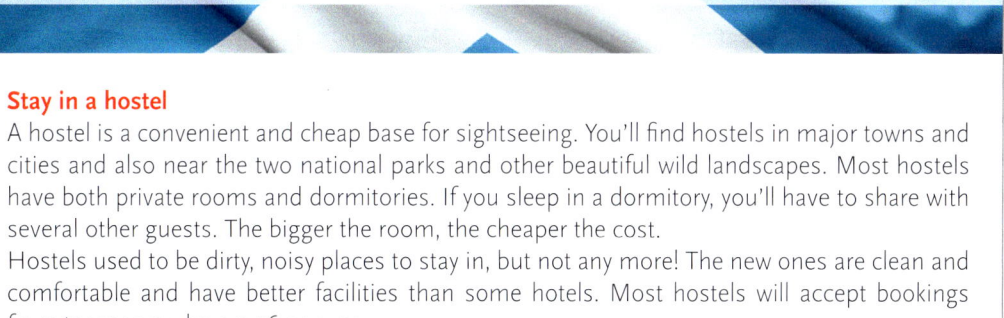

BEN'S TRAVELS

STAYING CHEAPLY IN SCOTLAND – TIPS FOR YOUNG TRAVELLERS

Are you planning your first independent holiday? Do you want to visit Scotland?
There are lots of options.

Stay in a hostel

A hostel is a convenient and cheap base for sightseeing. You'll find hostels in major towns and cities and also near the two national parks and other beautiful wild landscapes. Most hostels have both private rooms and dormitories. If you sleep in a dormitory, you'll have to share with several other guests. The bigger the room, the cheaper the cost.

Hostels used to be dirty, noisy places to stay in, but not any more! The new ones are clean and comfortable and have better facilities than some hotels. Most hostels will accept bookings from teenagers who are 16 or over.

Go camping

Camping is a wonderful way to explore the Scottish countryside and seaside – as long as the weather stays good. If the weather is bad, you'll have a horrible time! In Scotland you are allowed to do wild camping, which means you can camp wherever you like in open land. However, if you want facilities, you'll be better off in a campsite. Finding a campsite which will take a group of young people is a problem. If there are just two or three of you, you'll be fine, but larger groups often have problems. Sadly, campsite managers usually expect groups of teenagers to cause trouble and make a lot of noise.

Volunteer

If you're active, sociable and like to be outdoors, you'll love a volunteering holiday. I go on a volunteering holiday every year and I highly recommend it.

For example, the National Trust for Scotland has a working holiday programme for young people. It's a cheap, fun activity holiday and you'll learn new skills and get to know British teenagers. You might plant trees, repair footpaths or clean up beaches. That might sound more like hard work than a holiday, but you'll also have the chance to participate in exciting activities like kayaking or windsurfing.

The following options are available if you travel with someone who is 18 or older:

Take part in a hospitality exchange

If you stay with a local, you'll learn much more about the culture, language and what to do and see. You won't have to pay any rent – because it's free! Your host will be pleased if you cook a meal or bring a small gift. There are quite a few good websites which match guests and hosts.

Rent a private flat or house

If you rent someone's flat, you'll have all the comforts of home – literally. You'll have a kitchen, so you can cook your own meals. If you don't eat out every day, you'll save a lot of money, as restaurant meals are a big expense. You can find all sorts of homes for rent on various websites.

(438 words)

C **Answer the questions in complete sentences by using the information from the text.**

1 Why are hostels attractive for teenagers?
2 How does wild camping compare with campsites?

D **Beantworten Sie die folgende Frage auf Deutsch.**

Warum wirbt der Autor für freiwillige Arbeits-urlaube, und welchen Personenkreis spricht er an? Nennen Sie stichwortartig

- drei Eigenschaften, die die freiwilligen Helfer und Helferinnen besitzen sollten;
- drei Vorteile, die solche Arbeitsurlaube bieten;
- drei Aktivitäten, an denen die freiwilligen Helfer und Helferinnen teilnehmen werden.

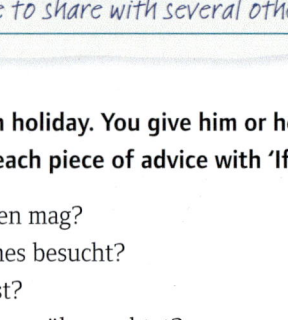

E **Complete the following sentences with information from the text (lines 28–36).**

1 Staying with a local allows you to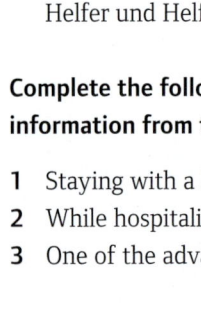
2 While hospitality exchanges are free,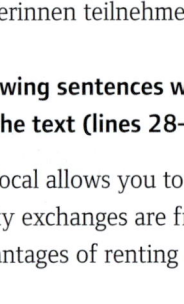
3 One of the advantages of renting a flat while in Scotland is that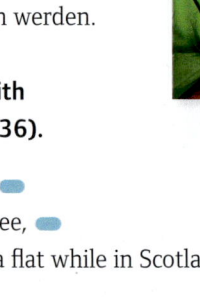

3 **LANGUAGE IN USE: CONDITIONAL SENTENCES TYPE 1** → Conditional sentences, S. 272

A **Find conditional sentences in the text. What is the condition (*Bedingung*) and what is the consequence (*Folge*)? Copy and complete the table.**

REMEMBER ❗ If + will makes me ill!

If you ~~will~~ sleep in a dormitory, you'll have to …

condition	consequence
If you sleep in a dormitory,	you'll have to share with several other guests.
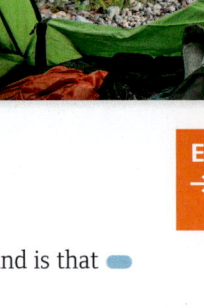	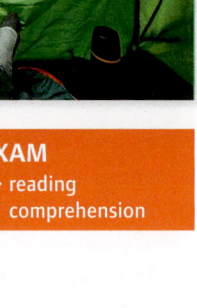

••• B **An American friend of yours wants to go to Scotland on holiday. You give him or her some advice in English, based on the questions below. Start each piece of advice with 'If …'.**

1 Was kann er/sie tun, wenn er/sie Aktivitäten im Freien mag?
2 Was wird er/sie sehen, wenn er/sie die Highland Games besucht?
3 Was kann er/sie machen, wenn das Wetter schlecht ist?
4 Wen wird er/sie treffen, wenn er/sie in Jugendherbergen übernachtet?
5 Welche Informationen wird er/sie finden, wenn er/sie auf die Webseite „Visit Scotland" geht?
6 Wie wird es sein, wenn er/sie mit einer großen Gruppe von Teenagern nach Schottland fährt?

••○ **Go to File 27 on page 200.**

C Work in a small group. Play 'Consequences'. Carry on as long as you can.

EXAMPLES:

A If you go camping, you'll save money on accommodation.

B If you save money on accommodation, you'll spend more on …

C If you spend more on …, you'll …

4 WORKING WITH WORDS

A Find words or expressions in the text which mean more or less the same as the words below.

> **EXAM**
> → use of language

a OK (lines 13–19) **b** friendly (lines 21–27)

B Explain the following words by completing the sentences or writing your own sentences.

> **EXAM**
> → use of language

a facilities (line 16): Facilities are everything that
b participate (line 26): When you participate in something, it means you
c rent (line 31): Rent is

C Find adjectives in the text on page 83 which have the opposite meaning. They are in the same order in the text.

> **EXAM**
> → use of language

1 last	**5** clean	**9** lazy
2 inconvenient	**6** quiet	**10** unfriendly
3 expensive	**7** uncomfortable	**11** boring
4 ugly	**8** enjoyable	

D Hamish himself wrote this review about his own accommodation. Rewrite it with opposites of the highlighted words (most are from 4C) to find out what his guests really think. You may need to change the form of some other words. Decide how many stars to give Hamish.

Hamish's Place, Edinburgh

This is our first[1] time with Flatm8.com. What an experience! 'Hamish's Place' is in a convenient[2] location at the end of a bus route. The surroundings are beautiful[3] and the rent seems very cheap[4] for the location. When we arrived at the flat, we found that it was very clean[5]. We were tired after our long journey and we had a good[6] night's sleep because the beds were large[7] and comfortable[8] and the road outside was very quiet[9]. The next day, we chatted with our host, Hamish. He turned out to be very sociable[10], so we had a very exciting[11] time with him in Edinburgh over the next few days. What a wonderful[12] guy! Our rating: ★★★★☆

5 LANGUAGE IN USE: ADVERBIAL CLAUSES

EXAMPLE: *Camping is a wonderful way to explore the Scottish countryside and seaside,*
__as long as__ the weather stays good.

Use the words below to fill in the gaps.

> although ▪ as soon as ▪ because ▪ by the time ▪ despite ▪
> since ▪ so that ▪ until ▪ while

1 We want to visit Scotland ⬭ everyone has told us how beautiful it is.
2 We met a lot of really nice people ⬭ we were in Edinburgh.
3 ⬭ we arrived at the hostel, we were soaking wet.
4 I called the hostel to tell them we were arriving late ⬭ they wouldn't lock the main door.
5 ⬭ the rain stopped, we started our hike.
6 We didn't stop for a break on the hike ⬭ we reached the lake.
7 ⬭ having a wonderful time, we did regret spending so much money.
8 ⬭ we've got no money, we're going to have to hitchhike.
9 ⬭ the sun was shining in Edinburgh, it wasn't very warm.

6 WRITING A RECOMMENDATION

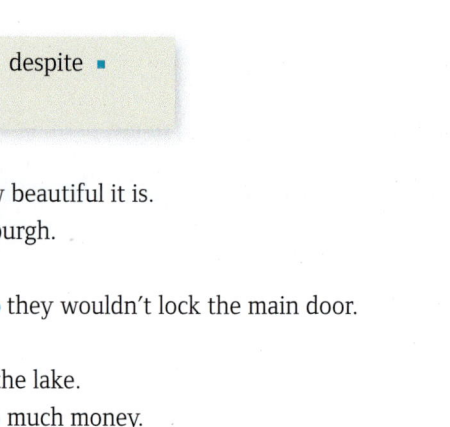

EXAM
→ writing

●●● **You are going with a group of eight friends aged 16 to 17 to Scotland
for two weeks. Four are from your school and four from your partner
school in England. You are in charge of getting information about accommodation. Based on
what you read in the text and your own experience, recommend one type of accommodation for
the group. Write about 100 words in English.**

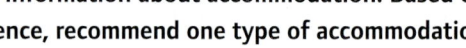

●●○ **Go to File 28
on page 200.**

C A TRIP TO EDINBURGH

1 PREPARING TO LISTEN

Ruby and Lisa from Chicago are on holiday in Edinburgh. You are going to listen to Ruby's voicemail messages to her parents. Before you listen, do the tasks below.

A Match the reviews to the photos. There are two reviews for two of the photos.

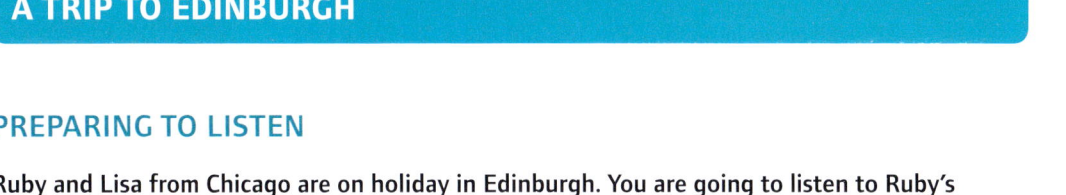

Things to do in Edinburgh – top tips

1 Edinburgh Castle
★★★★★ (15,106 reviews)

2 Escape Room Games
★★★★★ (893 reviews)

3 Camera Obscura & World of Illusions
★★★★★ (1159 reviews)

4 Hop-On Hop-Off Tours
★★★★★ (821 reviews)

5 Edinburgh's Old Town
★★★★★ (3059 reviews)

6 Murder and Mystery Tour
★★★★★ (346 reviews)

Reviews

A The location is great, right next to the castle. Lots of amazing illusions. You won't believe your eyes!

B Great game. The puzzles were quite hard. We got out with only two minutes to spare!

C A lovely part of town to walk around and enjoy the architecture and the atmosphere.

D Very entertaining! Not too scary, lots of fun for the kids.

E It's on top of a very steep hill. The Scottish monarchs used to live there.

F A beautiful old building surrounded by wonderful views over the city. So much history!

G A good way to see the city quickly. The driver was friendly and informative.

H Lots of shops, cafés and restaurants, and such colourful buildings!

B Which of the attractions would you visit if you went to Edinburgh? Why?

2 LISTENING: RUBY'S VOICEMAIL MESSAGES

A Listen to the voicemail messages. Put the sights on the right into the calendar below showing when Ruby and Lisa visited them. Two sights were seen in the same part of the same day.

EXAM
→ listening comprehension

1	Tuesday afternoon	⬤	a	Edinburgh Castle
2	Tuesday evening	⬤	b	Escape Room Games
3	Wednesday morning	⬤	c	Camera Obscura & World of Illusions
4	Wednesday afternoon	⬤	d	Hop-On Hop-Off Tours
5	Thursday morning	⬤	e	Edinburgh's Old Town
			f	Murder and Mystery Tour

B Listen to the messages again and decide whether the following statements are true or false, according to the text.

EXAM
→ listening comprehension

1 The main advantage of the Hop-On Hop-Off Tours is that it you don't get wet when it rains.
2 Lisa found the Murder and Mystery Tour very scary.
3 Ruby and Lisa booked their tickets for Edinburgh Castle online in order to avoid the queues.
4 Ruby and Lisa went to the Camera Obscura because the tickets were quite cheap.
5 Ruby and Lisa were happy to find a café in the Old Town because they were tired of walking.

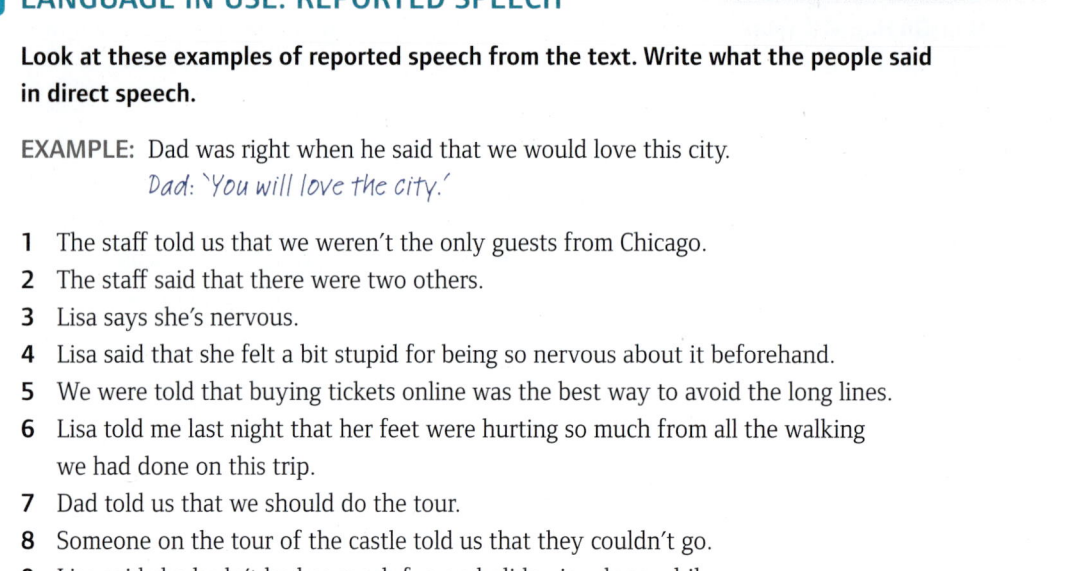

3 LANGUAGE IN USE: REPORTED SPEECH

Look at these examples of reported speech from the text. Write what the people said in direct speech.

EXAMPLE: Dad was right when he said that we would love this city.
Dad: `You will love the city.´

1 The staff told us that we weren't the only guests from Chicago.
2 The staff said that there were two others.
3 Lisa says she's nervous.
4 Lisa said that she felt a bit stupid for being so nervous about it beforehand.
5 We were told that buying tickets online was the best way to avoid the long lines.
6 Lisa told me last night that her feet were hurting so much from all the walking we had done on this trip.
7 Dad told us that we should do the tour.
8 Someone on the tour of the castle told us that they couldn't go.
9 Lisa said she hadn't had so much fun on holiday in a long while.

4 PLANNING A HOLIDAY

A Your class wants to go on a trip to Scotland to celebrate your graduation. You and a partner have been selected to choose two places to visit in Scotland. With your partner discuss advantages and disadvantages of possible places to visit. Agree on two places that you will suggest to your class. You can use the photos on page 81 to help you come up with some ideas.

●●● **B** Work with a partner and role-play an email correspondence in which a hostel is booked for a group of teenagers.

Partner A: You are a German teenager who has decided to stay in a hostel with three of your friends. Decide on your dates and your length of stay. Write an email to the hostel. Find out the price, check-in and check-out times, and what facilities the hostel has. Ask about methods of payment.

Partner B: You are the hostel manager. Think up prices for different rooms. Find out if the teenagers wish to stay in one room together, in two-bed rooms or in a large dormitory. Give any additional information they asked for in their email.

Partner A: After receiving the email from the hostel, decide on your sleeping situation and book the accommodation.

●●○ **Go to File 29 on page 200.**

5 WRITING A SHORT STORY

- Entscheiden Sie, wie die Handlung verlaufen wird. Gibt es Streit, Spannung, Enttäuschung?
- Wer spielt in der Geschichte mit?
- Wie stehen die Figuren zueinander?
- Fügen Sie Dialoge ein.
- Achten Sie darauf, dass sich der Schluss folgerichtig aus der bisherigen Handlung ergibt.

Finish the story below. Before you write the rest of the story, make notes about the following:

- the name of your friend
- what the voice said
- who the voice belonged to
- what happened next
- how you felt

Write about 160 words in English.

My friend and I were on holiday in Oban, Scotland. We knew that wild camping was allowed in most places, so we hiked out of town and set up our tents in a lovely spot. In the middle of the night, we heard an angry, loud voice ...

You are going to call a hostel in Scotland. You are a bit nervous, so you decide to get some tips about making telephone calls.

1 THE NATO SPELLING ALPHABET

A Skim the NATO spelling alphabet on the right, which is used in English-speaking countries. Find the German spelling alphabet and decide what is the main difference between it and the NATO spelling alphabet?

B You are going to practise the NATO spelling alphabet by playing a memory game. Form groups of 6 and sit in a circle. One person begins by saying ALPHA, the next person says ALPHA, BRAVO. Continue round the circle, adding one new word to the list until it is complete. Any player who forgets a word drops out.

2 GIVING CONTACT DETAILS

You are going to practise giving contact details in English and saying telephone numbers in English. Work in pairs.

Partner A: Read the business cards at the bottom of the page, using the NATO alphabet for words that are difficult.
Partner B: Read the business cards at the top of page 91, using the NATO alphabet for words that are difficult.

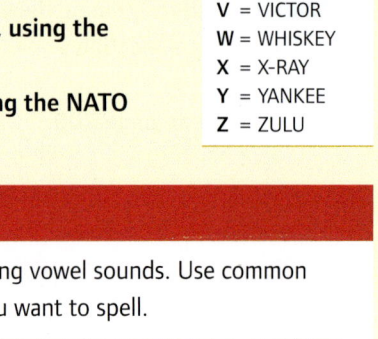

A	= ALPHA
B	= BRAVO
C	= CHARLIE
D	= DELTA
E	= ECHO
F	= FOXTROT
G	= GOLF
H	= HOTEL
I	= INDIA
J	= JULIET
K	= KILO
L	= LIMA
M	= MIKE
N	= NOVEMBER
O	= OSCAR
P	= PAPA
Q	= QUEBEC
R	= ROMEO
S	= SIERRA
T	= TANGO
U	= UNIFORM
V	= VICTOR
W	= WHISKEY
X	= X-RAY
Y	= YANKEE
Z	= ZULU

REMEMBER ❗ Spelling names

When you are spelling a name, the biggest problem is often saying vowel sounds. Use common English words to remind yourself of the sounds of the letters you want to spell.

a as in *may*	*e* as in *he*	*i* as in *eye*	*o* as in *no*	*u* as in *you*

If you are spelling German names with an Umlaut, use the following method:

for *ä* say *a e*	for *ö* say *o e*	for *ü* say *u e*

When saying numbers
In English, each digit is spoken separately, unless it's a double.
0172 56 8933 = Oh-one-seven-two-five-six-eight-nine-double three.

Giving email addresses
@ is pronounced 'at'.
_ is 'underscore'.

Laurence Browne
57318 Wainwright Circle
Leicester, Massachusetts
Telephone +1 21 62 98 54 37
Email address: L_browne@internet.com

Sophia Camilleri
29 Wine Street
Valletta
Telephone: +356 23710400
Email address: soca@net.mt

Anne O'Reilly
18 Joyce Lane
Dublin 4, Ireland
Telephone + 353 1 016 7789
Email address: anne_oreilly@net.ie

Dr Hugh Fyffe
27 Nairn Square
Edinburgh EH1 2BC
Telephone + 44 101 7000 0160
Email address: doctor@net.scot

3 BOOKING A BED AT A HOSTEL

You are backpacking around Scotland and want to reserve a bed in a hostel. Role-play a telephone dialogue with the hostel manager. When you have finished, change roles and role-play the dialogue again.

Partner A: Hostel manager Martin/Mary MacDonald	Partner B: You, trying to reserve a bed in a hostel
→ Begrüßen Sie den Anrufer / die Anruferin.	→ Nennen Sie Ihren Namen und sagen Sie, dass Sie ab morgen ein Bett für sechs Nächte reservieren möchten.
→ Sagen Sie, dass ein Einzelzimmer verfügbar ist oder auch ein Bett in einem gemischten Acht-Bett-Schlafraum.	→ Bitten Sie den Gesprächspartner / die Gesprächspartnerin, alles noch einmal und etwas langsamer zu sagen.
→ Wiederholen Sie, was Sie gesagt haben.	→ Bedanken Sie sich und fragen Sie nach dem jeweiligen Preis pro Nacht.
→ Sagen Sie, dass der Preis für ein Einzel-zimmer bei £22 und für ein Bett im Schlafraum bei £12 pro Nacht liegt.	→ Entscheiden Sie sich und sagen Sie, welches Bett Sie reservieren möchten.
→ Bitten Sie den Anrufer / die Anruferin etwas lauter zu sprechen, da die Verbindung (*connection*) wirklich schlecht ist.	→ Wiederholen Sie ihre Entscheidung und Sagen Sie Ihren Namen.
→ Bitten Sie den Anrufer / die Anruferin, den Namen zu buchstabieren.	→ Buchstabieren Sie Ihren Namen.
→ Wiederholen Sie den Namen. Fragen Sie nach der Telefonnummer des Anrufers / der Anruferin.	→ Nennen Sie Ihre Telefonnummer.
→ Wiederholen Sie die Telefonnummer. Sagen Sie, dass Sie sich auf die Ankunft freuen und dass die Check-in-Zeit ab 14 Uhr ist.	→ Bitten Sie den Gesprächspartner / die Gesprächspartnerin, die Check-in-Zeit zu wiederholen.
→ Wiederholen Sie die Check-in-Zeit. Fragen Sie, ob der Anrufer / die Anruferin sie nun verstanden hat.	→ Bestätigen Sie, dass Sie sie mitbekommen haben. Beenden Sie den Anruf höflich.

Go to File 30 on page 201.

You are working as an intern for an Edinburgh tourist company. You are asked to design and produce a flyer in English for young people showing what there is to do and see in Scotland's capital.

1 A FLYER

Discuss in small groups the questions below, and make notes.

- What is a flyer?
- What size is a typical flyer?
- How does a flyer get its message across?
- What, if anything, should the reader of the flyer do?

2 GATHERING IDEAS

Now talk together about things that could be interesting for young people when visiting a city they don't know.

3 DOING RESEARCH

Search the internet for things to see or do in Edinburgh that young people might find interesting. Make notes.

4 PREPARING THE CONTENT

A Decide on the content you would like to include in your flyer. Use the notes you made for task 1 to help you decide what you need.

B When you have found enough material, write a short text.

C Look for suitable images.

5 DESIGNING THE FLYER

Now take a sheet of A4 paper and sketch in the layout of your flyer.

6 COMPARING FLYERS

A When you are happy with your design, produce your flyer and lay it on a table, so you can look at them all together.

B Which flyer is most eye-catching? Discuss why.

C Which place(s) would you like to visit?

Relationships: families and friends

A WARM-UP: TODAY'S FAMILIES

A Work with a partner. You have three minutes to brainstorm English words that describe family members. Make lists. Which pair has the most words?

father	wife	parents

B Complete the definitions of the types of families (1–5) with the sentence endings (a–e). Then match the definitions to the photos above.

1 A blended family is
2 An extended family is made up of
3 In an intercultural family,
4 In a single-parent family,
5 The nuclear family is made up of

a the parents are from different cultural backgrounds.
b three or more generations in one home.
c a parent brings up his or her children without a partner.
d a mum and dad and their children.
e a family consisting of a couple, the children they have together and their children from earlier relationships.

C Which of the types of families above do you know? What other types of families are you familiar with?

B FAMILIES

SITUATION: Your school is doing a project on relationships around the world. The focus is on families and friends. The school has set up a blog on which to collect interesting material. You read the story below and write a letter to the two girls with questions about them and their families (task 4, page 97).

1 PREPARING TO READ

A Work in small groups. Study the words and expressions below and say which of them you …

   a know and how you know them. (For example, it is like a German word.)
   b can guess the meaning of. (How did you guess?)
   c need to look up in your dictionary. (Look them up now!)

to share   to be an only child   well-off

to adopt

double   lactose intolerant   identical   respective

B Write eight sentences using each of the words above.

2 READING AND UNDERSTANDING THE TEXT

EXAM
→ reading comprehension

A Finish the sentences using the information from the text.

   1 Although Anaïs Bordier was born in South Korea, she ●
   2 It was while Anais was studying fashion in London that ●
   3 It was by doing research that Anaïs discovered that her double ●
   4 Despite the fact that they were brought up far apart from each other, ●
   5 The DNA test confirmed ●

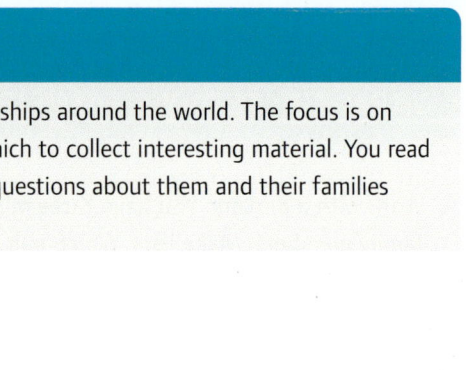

B Beantworten Sie die folgende Frage auf Deutsch.

Welchen Einfluss hat die Kultur auf die persönliche Entwicklung des Einzelnen?
Nennen Sie stichwortartig vier im Text erwähnte Bereiche, in denen sich die Zwillingsschwestern aufgrund der verschiedenen Kulturen, in denen sie aufgewachsen sind, unterscheiden.

DON'T FREAK OUT!

Anaïs Bordier grew up in France. Her parents adopted her from South Korea when she was a baby. After finishing school in Paris, Anaïs studied fashion in London. While she was there, a friend showed her a video on the internet. In the video there was a young American actress who looked exactly like Anaïs. She was Anaïs's double!

5 Anaïs decided to do some research about her double. She found out that the woman in the video, Samantha Futerman, was born on the same day in the same place as she was – Busan, a city in South Korea. She contacted the actress via social media. She introduced herself to Samantha and said: 'Don't freak out!' She went on to describe herself and her family background.

While Anaïs grew up as an only child in Paris, Samantha lived with two older brothers as the only
10 adopted child in a New Jersey family. Like Anaïs, Samantha felt that something or someone was missing in her life. When she received the message from Anaïs, she was surprised but also excited. This stranger looked just like her. The girls began to talk via videochat, and a real friendship soon developed.

As Anaïs and Samantha shared photos and details of their lives, they discovered that they had a
15 lot more in common than just a shared birthday. They both loved the Harry Potter books, they had the same laugh, and both loved cheese – even though they are lactose intolerant.

After a while the two girls decided to take a DNA test together, which confirmed what they had suspected – they are identical twins. Their mother gave them up for adoption when they were babies.

The adoption agency gave them separately to two
20 different sets of parents without mentioning to the adoptive parents that there was a second child.

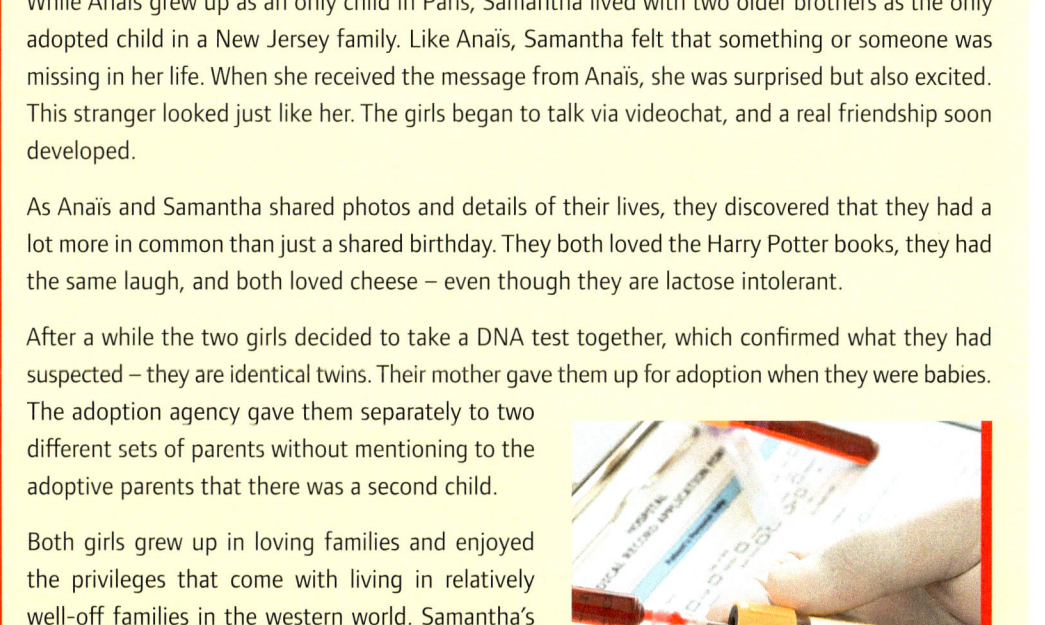

Both girls grew up in loving families and enjoyed the privileges that come with living in relatively well-off families in the western world. Samantha's
25 parents are Jewish while Anaïs's parents are Catholic, and both girls have taken on characteristics of their respective cultures. While Samantha is 'touchy-feely' and open about her emotions, Anaïs is reserved and takes time to warm to people. Anaïs and Samantha have both commented on how
30 European or American their twin is, from the way they eat to the way they dress. Samantha has never had issues with her cultural identity, as the community she lived in accepted her as just another American teenager. Anaïs, on the other hand, had more difficulty identifying as French, but the long journey discovering about her family background has made her feel more French. Anaïs now works as a fashion designer in Paris, while Samantha works as an actress in Los Angeles,
35 so one might say that even their career choices reflect the culture they were brought up in.

In 2015 they produced a film called *Twinsters* about their experience as separated twins.

(482 words)

C Match five of the statements (1–7) with people mentioned in the text. There are two statements that do not match.

EXAM
→ reading comprehension

	person	statement
1	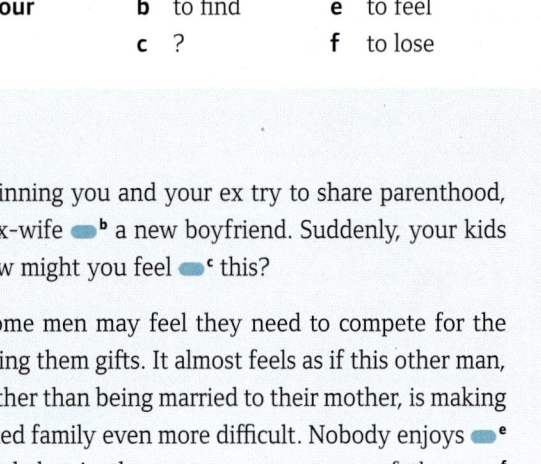	Every baby needs two parents.
2		You must watch this. The main actress looks exactly like you.
3		It was impossible for me to look after two babies.
4		I love her clothes and her style. She's so typically French.
5		She's able to express her feelings much more openly than I am.
6		We wanted to share our story with the world.
7		Skype is a great way to keep in touch.

3 **WORKING WITH WORDS**

EXAM
→ use of language

A Find words or expressions in the text on page 95 which mean more or less the same as the words below.

   a true (lines 9–13)   **b** decisions (lines 29–35)

B Find the opposites of the following words from the text on page 95.

   a older (line 9)   **b** well-off (line 24)

C Explain the following words from the text on page 95 in complete sentences.

   a to adopt (line 1)   **b** identical (line 18)

D Complete the text below by using suitable forms of the words on the right. Find a word of your own to replace the question mark.

  a to divorce   **d** few/less/little
  b to find   **e** to feel
  c ?   **f** to lose

Ex-husbands but still dads

It's not easy being a ___ᵃ dad. At the beginning you and your ex try to share parenthood, but then you might discover that your ex-wife ___ᵇ a new boyfriend. Suddenly, your kids are spending time with another man. How might you feel ___ᶜ this?

Some feelings are completely natural; some men may feel they need to compete for the love of their children for example by buying them gifts. It almost feels as if this other man, who has ___ᵈ connection with your kids other than being married to their mother, is making the already difficult situation of a separated family even more difficult. Nobody enjoys ___ᵉ that they can be replaced. It is estimated that in the next ten years, many fathers ___ᶠ contact with their kids as the mothers move on with their lives with new partners.

E A collocation is when words usually go together, for example 'do sport' (*Sport treiben*) or 'immediate family' (*engste Familie*). Add another word to the words below to make collocations. All the collocations are in the text.

1	adoption ●	4	cultural ●	7	identical ●
2	adoptive ●	5	DNA ●	8	lactose ●
3	career ●	6	finish ●	9	only ●

●●○ Go to File 31 on page 203.

4 WRITING A LETTER

It is time for you to write to the twins as part of your school project about relationships around the world.

EXAM
→ writing

TRAIN YOUR SKILLS: Einen Brief schreiben	vgl. auch S. 248

Die Anrede: Ein Brief beginnt stets mit einer Anrede: *Dear …*
Einführende Worte: Stellen Sie sich vor und beschreiben Sie kurz Ihr Anliegen.
Hauptteil: Hier führen Sie Ihr Anliegen in Einzelnen aus.
Abschließender Satz: Hier nennen Sie freundlich das erhoffte weitere Vorgehen: *I look forward to hearing from you.*
Schlussformel: Der Brief endet mit einer Schlussformel: *Yours sincerely / Best wishes*

Nicht vergessen: Beachten Sie besonders sorgfältig die Zeichensetzungsregeln, um beim Adressaten einen guten Eindruck zu hinterlassen.

A Work in groups. Brainstorm things that you would like to know about the sisters. Make notes. Here are some ideas to start you off.

- how each of them grew up
- how it felt for them to be with their twin sister in their home town
- how they feel about their own culture now that they have learned about the culture in which their twin sister grew up

B Now write the letter with your questions to the twins.

C FRIENDS ACROSS CULTURES

1 PREPARING TO LISTEN

When people meet other people from different cultures, which of the following might make it easy or difficult to make friends? What other issues might present difficulties when making friends across cultures? Explain your views.

gender

social media   family

money   humour

religion   openness

language   texting

cultural background

work

2 LISTENING: MAKING FRIENDS

EXAM
→ listening comprehension

Mark from England and Anna from Germany are at an American high school for a year. One lunchtime they see each other and chat about their experiences in their new school.

A Listen to the dialogue and note down differences in behaviour between Americans and Germans, and Americans and British people, as discussed in the text.

Germans	Americans		British	Americans
3 aspects			*2 aspects*	
▬	▬		▬	▬
▬	▬		▬	▬
▬	▬			

B What is Mark's main piece of advice to Anna?

3 LANGUAGE IN USE: ADJECTIVES AND ADVERBS

→ Comparison of adjectives, S. 282

●●● **Jennifer, from Berlin, and Patience, from Cape Town, both study at university in Stuttgart. Jennifer often invites Patience to visit her family in Berlin. This summer Patience invited Jennifer to Cape Town. After the visit, they talk on videochat.**

Read the videochat on the opposite page and complete the dialogue with the correct form of the word in brackets (adjective or adverb, possibly comparative or superlative).

●●○ Go to File 32 on page 203.

A VIDEOCHAT: Berlin to Cape Town

Patience: What's it like being back home?

Jennifer: It's OK. But I miss you and your family, and I definitely miss the 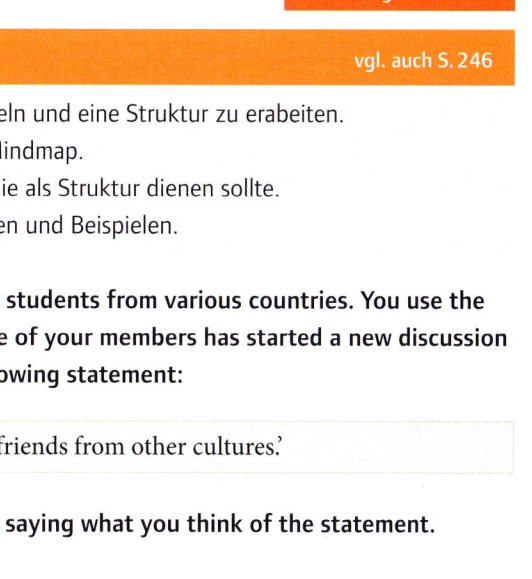 ¹ (good) food I've ever eaten in my life.

Patience: I'll ask my mum to send your dad some recipes. I always meant to say that I found it ² (strange) when I first saw your dad cooking. You know now that my dad never steps foot in the kitchen. He says he works ³ (hard) enough in the office all day.

Jennifer: Yes. I realized that. I enjoyed cooking with your mum and your aunts, though. It was a lot of fun.

Patience: They loved having you here. My family is ⁴ (loud) than any family I know. I was worried it might all be too ⁵ (noisy) for you, so I asked them to talk ⁶ (quiet).

Jennifer: I got used to it ⁷ (quick). Germans are much ⁸ (quiet). By the way, I told my family they have to be a lot ⁹ (careful) with water.

Patience: That's ¹⁰ (great). I remember helping your brothers fill the dishwasher and they were using so much water to rinse the plates. Tell them we had a zero-water day in Cape Town when the government thought we were going to run out of water.

Jennifer: I'll do that. We think we'll always have water in Germany, because it's ¹¹ (continual) raining. How are your brothers, by the way?

Patience: Oh. The same as usual. They're the ¹² (lazy) boys I've ever met. They never help with laying the table or cleaning up in the kitchen like your brothers. They behave so ¹³ (bad). They ¹⁴ (hard) ever help at home.

Jennifer: My mum always says that boys get ¹⁵ (good) as they get ¹⁶ (old) .

Patience: I can only see my brothers getting ¹⁷ (bad).

---

4 **WRITING A COMMENT**

EXAM
→ writing

TRAIN YOUR SKILLS: Bevor Sie schreiben   vgl. auch S. 246

Schreiben Sie nie los, ohne vorher Ideen zu sammeln und eine Struktur zu erarbeiten.

- Ideen sammeln Sie am besten im Form einer Mindmap.
- Listen Sie die Ideen in einer Reihenfolge auf, die als Struktur dienen sollte.
- Untermauern Sie Ihre Aussagen mit Argumenten und Beispielen.

You have started a blog which you share with six students from various countries. You use the blog to exchange your different experiences. One of your members has started a new discussion thread and wants you all to comment on the following statement:

> 'A good way to broaden our horizons is to have friends from other cultures.'

Write a comment in English of about 100 words, saying what you think of the statement.

8 WORLD OF WORK

You are an intern doing work experience in the Frankfurt am Main office of an international insurance company. The main language in the office is English.

1 READING: MOBILE PHONE USE IN THE OFFICE

Read the company policy on mobile phone use, then decide whether the employees in the illustrations are following company policy. Which rules apply?

Global Insurance AG – Mobile Phone Policy

1   Personal mobile phones can cause problems at work. Employees who use their personal mobile phones might:
   a   do less work because they use their phones too much.
   b   disturb their colleagues.
   c   download company documents on their mobiles.

2   We ask our employees to:
   a   use company phones only for work matters.
   b   surf the internet, text and talk on a personal mobile phone only for a few minutes per day.
   c   turn off or silence their phones in meetings.

3   Employees are not allowed to:
   a   use their mobile phone's camera or microphone to record information about the company.
   b   make personal calls at their desk or where they might disturb colleagues.
   c   log on to the company network using a personal mobile phone.

4   Employees are allowed to use their phones:
   a   to receive brief personal calls and messages.
   a   during official breaks or the lunch hour.
   b   if they speak to their manager first.

So I told Mum...

Yes, and then Mum said...

Hi Jack! ... Listen, I've got a break in 15 minutes. I'll call you back then, okay?

1

2

3

🎧 **2** LISTENING: PHONE RULES IN THE OFFICE

EXAM
→ listening comprehension

Listen to the two short dialogues and finish the sentences with information from the text.

1 Bethany wants to know if she can ●

2 Mr Carter tells Bethany she can make her call in ●

3 Darren wants to know if he can ●

4 Mr Carter tells Darren that he can only take photos ●

🎧 **3** LISTENING: NOTING DOWN INFORMATION

24

EXAM
→ listening comprehension

You are an intern in an international company. Your boss has asked you to call the central office in London and ask them about the company's policy on the private use of mobiles in the office and to send him a memo about it. Listen to what your colleague in London says, and copy and fill in the table below with the information.

MEMO (private use of mobiles in the office)		
Colleague's name	●	
Date	23rd February	
Private use of mobile in following situations allowed (3 situations)	● ● ●	
Private use of mobile in following situations not allowed (2 situations)	● ●	
Staff who are allowed to use mobiles (2 groups)	position	reason
	● ●	● ●

4 ROLE-PLAY: ASKING PERMISSION

Use the format below to role-play a dialogue between an intern and his/her supervisor. When you have finished, change roles and role-play the dialogue again.

Praktikant/in	Vorgesetzte/r
→ Entschuldigen Sie sich für die Störung.	→ Fragen Sie, worum es geht.
→ Fragen Sie etwas, z. B. ob Sie einen privaten Anruf im Büro machen dürfen.	→ Reagieren Sie, z. B. indem Sie ihn/sie darum bitten, bis zur Pause zu warten.
→ Erklären Sie, dass es dringlich ist.	→ Reagieren Sie, z. B. dass es in Ordnung geht, er/sie aber Rücksicht auf die Kolleginnen und Kollegen nehmen soll.
→ Reagieren Sie, z. B. indem Sie sich bedanken.	→ Reagieren Sie.

🎧 **1** **MULTIPLE CHOICE: BUY NOTHING DAY**
25

A radio advertisement informs listeners what Buy Nothing Day is all about.

Listen to the recording and choose the best answer for each of the following questions.

1 When is Buy Nothing Day in Europe?
   a Last November it was on a Saturday.
   b It is on the last Saturday in November.
   c It takes place every Saturday in November.
   d It used to be the first Saturday in November.

2 What is Buy Nothing Day?
   a It is when you stay at home on a Saturday.
   b It is when the shops are closed for 24 hours.
   c It's when you are supposed to do no shopping for 24 hours.
   d It is when you are supposed to think about how much money you spend.

3 What is the idea behind Buy Nothing Day?
   a The idea is to destroy consumer culture.
   b The idea is to stop people spending money.
   c The idea is to stop importing products from developing countries.
   d The idea is to think about the ways in which shopping affects the environment.

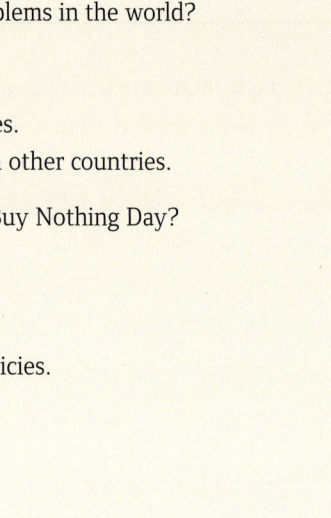

4 Why are rich western countries responsible for many of the problems in the world?
   a The West consumes 80% of the earth's resources.
   b People in western countries don't recycle their products.
   c Western countries don't trade fairly with developing countries.
   d People in western countries love to shop more than people in other countries.

5 What is one thing mentioned that everyone can do to promote Buy Nothing Day?
   a People can stop buying cheap goods.
   b People can sit at home and do nothing.
   c People can talk about it on social media platforms.
   d People can write to companies about their environmental policies.

2 FILLING IN A FORM: A MESSAGE FOR A COLLEAGUE

Someone has left a message on your office answerphone.

Copy and fill in the online form for your colleague. The first field has been done for you.

message for	*Monika Schmidt*
caller's name	
company	
telephone number	
message	
best time to call back	

3 MULTIPLE MATCHING: VOLUNTEERS AT A FESTIVAL

You are going to listen to a broadcast from an outdoor music festival. A reporter is interviewing volunteers. Copy the table below into your exercise book. Then listen to the report and match the statements to the speakers. One person has two statements, and there is one more statement than needed.

Sarah	
Brendan	
Jane	
Lachlan	

Statements

1 People forget that festivals are open-air and often get sunburned.
2 If a performer is late, I have to find out where they are and get them on stage.
3 If someone loses something, it's my job to get it back to them.
4 It's hard to work when everyone else is having fun.
5 I contact musicians and invite them to play at the festival.
6 The best thing about the festival is how happy everyone is.

A Correct these statements using the information in brackets.

EXAMPLE: Sam uses social media every day. (occasionally)
Sam doesn't use social media every day. She uses it occasionally.

1 Sarah texts her mother several times a day. (a few times a week)
2 I'm writing a text message to my dad. (email)
3 My parents work in a hospital. (teach at a school)
4 My girlfriend's having a lot of success with her online business. (not attract customers)
5 My boyfriend makes a living from online tutoring. (personal training)
6 My friends and I are texting each other. (share videos)
7 The text is from his girlfriend. (sister)
8 My boyfriend's trying to lose weight at the gym. (try to gain muscle)
9 We're having fun. (do an English grammar exercise)

B Use the prompts to ask questions which go with the answers.

1 What – you – look at ?   I'm looking at a video my sister sent me.
2 Who – your sister – work for ?   My sister works for a website design company.
3 What – you – do ?   I'm waiting for my parents to pick me up.
4 What – this app – do ?   It helps you to find your friends at a concert.
5 I – disturb – your work ?   Yes, you are disturbing my work.
6 We – be allowed – chat with our friends in class ?   No, we aren't allowed to chat with our friends in class.

C You meet a young Chinese tourist on a bus. What do you say – a or b?

1 a Do you enjoy your stay in Germany?
  b Are you enjoying your stay in Germany?
2 a Do you speak German?
  b Are you speaking German?
3 a What do you do back home in China?
  b What are you doing back home in China?
4 a What part of China are you coming from?
  b What part of China do you come from?
5 a You are speaking very good English.
  b You speak very good English.
6 a Where do you go today?
  b Where are you going today?
7 a What sort of music do you listen to now?
  b What sort of music are you listening to now?
8 a I'm going to a concert this evening. Would you like to come?
  b I go to a concert this evening. Would you like to come?
9 a Lots of my friends are going.
  b Lots of my friends go.
10 a I get off now. Have a great day!
  b I'm getting off now. Have a great day!

D Which sentence could you use the adverbs in the box with?

1 I'm listening to a new band.
2 I listen to music on the bus.

| always ■ at the moment ■ every day ■ never ■ |
| right now ■ sometimes ■ today ■ usually |

Moving out into the world

A WARM-UP: TALKING ABOUT PLANS FOR THE FUTURE

Discuss the following points in small groups.

- What jobs are shown in the photos?
- Where do you see yourself in five years' time?
- How do you think you will use English in your future life or job?
- Can you imagine getting work experience abroad? Why / Why not?
- How are you going to achieve your professional goals?

Report back to the class on what you discussed.

B GETTING EXPERIENCE IN INDIA

SITUATION: You are thinking about your plans for the future but are unsure of what job you would like to do. You read a job advertisement on the website of the Federal Voluntary Service (*Bundesfreiwilligendienst*), which offers links to voluntary service places abroad. You write a covering letter applying for a position (task 5, page 109).

1 PREPARING TO READ

A Work with a partner. Study the words from the text opposite (1–5) and match them to the links (a–f). There is one link more than you need.

d **1** poor families
c **2** support teachers in class and with free-time activities
f **3** speak good English, be able to drive, be good with computers
e **4** enjoy working with children, fit into the local culture, be creative
a **5** small villages and towns throughout India

JOBS	RECRUITERS	ABOUT	COMPANIES	SERVICES	LOGIN

a	where you will work
b	the voluntary organization
c	what you will do
d	who needs your help
e	your character and personal qualities
f	your skills

B Skim the text to check your answers.

2 READING AND UNDERSTANDING THE TEXT

EXAM
→ reading comprehension

A Answer the questions in complete sentences by using the information from the text.

1 Who does the India Charity Foundation aim to help?
2 How does the India Charity Foundation help the people it works with?

B Beantworten Sie die folgende Frage auf Deutsch.

Welche Voraussetzungen erwartet die India Charity Foundation von den jungen Leuten, die sich für einen freiwilligen Hilfseinsatz bewerben? Nennen Sie stichwortartig drei Fähigkeiten bzw. Kompetenzen sowie drei persönliche Eigenschaften.

28

TEACHING UNDER THE INDIAN SUN

| JOBS | RECRUITERS | ABOUT | COMPANIES | SERVICES | LOGIN |

JOB PROFILE:

work with youngsters, education/teaching

The India Charity Foundation supports and helps poor families who live in small villages and towns throughout India. One of our main projects is providing education for young people. Apart from teaching the usual skills like reading, writing and computer skills, we also offer various free-time activities and games for the youngsters.

JOB DESCRIPTION

You will work with our teachers and support them in class and with the free-time activities. Depending on your interests and competences, you will work in creative areas, sport, languages or computer literacy. We also need volunteers who are good with computers or can teach young people to drive or fix machines. Life is a struggle for many poor families. If the young adults in the family can learn skills which will enable them to earn money, this will help families move out of poverty.

But this is not a one-way street: we want you also to learn from the youngsters you will work with. Their lives are very different from yours and we hope that, outside of school, they will give you insight into their lives.

You don't need to worry about your teaching skills. Our pedagogical staff will train and support you.

We are looking for volunteers who ...
- are creative.
- enjoy working in a team.
- enjoy working with teenagers.
- will fit into the local culture.

Good English is a must.
You should be willing to learn the local language, Hindi.
Starting date: September, 20..
Length of service: 9 months

AN IMPORTANT MESSAGE

The communities which you will work with are largely agricultural. The people are religious and conservative. We expect our volunteers to be sensitive towards their religion and to respect the local culture.

Send your CV and covering letter to Mr Kumar at contact@bodhitree.in   (298 words)

3 WORKING WITH WORDS

Complete this short statement using words from the box.

> agricultural ▪ community ▪ culture ▪ dance ▪ pilgrimage ▪ poorest ▪ religion ▪ sensitive

We are happy that the volunteers who work with us know it is important to be ⬮¹ towards our religion and our customs. In my village, for example, there are many ⬮² workers who follow the Buddhist ⬮³. They regularly go on a ⬮⁴ to the nearby village of Bodh Gaya. The surrounding area is one of the ⬮⁵ places in India but our ⬮⁶ is very rich. People make music and ⬮⁷; they practise yoga and meditation. We enjoy sharing our ⬮⁸ life with the volunteers who come here, and hope that they learn something from our way of life.

4 LANGUAGE IN USE: THE WILL-FUTURE

→ The future, S. 270

> **REMEMBER** ❗ **the will-future**
>
> The future with 'will' is formed by using 'will' + infinitive. **He will, we will** ~~he wills~~
>
> The future with 'will' is often used after the following expressions and verbs:
> believe, expect, hope, imagine, suppose, think   **I hope that she will come.**
> It's clear/obvious that …, There's no doubt that …   **There's no doubt that you'll get the job.**

A **Find and write down all the sentences in the text which use the will-future.**

B **Complete the dialogue with** *will* **or** *won't* **and the verb in brackets.**

Mike: When ⬮¹ (we – know) the results of our exams?
Anne: I don't know. All I know is that they ⬮² (not come out) this week.
Mike: ⬮³ (you – apply) for the job in India before the results come out?
Anne: I don't think so. I think I ⬮⁴ (wait) until I know my grades.
Mike: I'm sure you ⬮⁵ (get) good grades and my grades ⬮⁶ (be) bad.
Anne: Don't be so negative. You ⬮⁷ (not fail). Everybody in our class ⬮⁸ (pass) with
good grades.

C **Draw a line in your notebook. Complete the line using the words for prediction in the correct order. Two expressions have been added for you.**

> ~~I don't know~~ ▪ I expect ▪ perhaps ▪ probably ▪ ~~I'm sure~~ ▪ I think

–   **I don't know** ——————————————————————— **I'm sure**   **+**

D Write sentences about yourself. Use expressions from task 4C to answer the questions.

Where will you be …

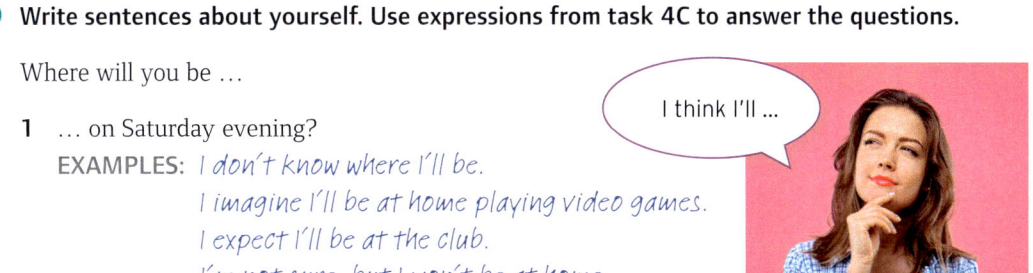

I think I'll …

1 … on Saturday evening?
EXAMPLES: *I don't know where I'll be.*
I imagine I'll be at home playing video games.
I expect I'll be at the club.
I'm not sure, but I won't be at home.

2 … at the weekend?   **5** … this summer?
3 … at 6 a.m. tomorrow?   **6** … next year?
4 … at this time next week?

Go to File 33 on page 204.

5 WRITING A COVERING LETTER

A You are going to write to the Indian Charity Foundation applying for a position. First, complete the covering letter below from another student using the phrases from the box.

advert ▪ languages ▪ mother tongue ▪ people from different cultures ▪ school-leaving
certificate ▪ skills ▪ spoken and written English ▪ voluntary work ▪ volunteer

Dear Mr Kumar

advert
I saw your ⬤ ¹ on your website. I am interested in working as a ⬤ *volunteer* ² at your organization because it will help me develop on a personal basis. I am also keen to work in a country where I can use my practical ⬤ ³. *skills*

I will finish my education this year with a German ⬤ *certificate* ⁴ for year 10. My ⬤ *English* ⁵ is very good as I have studied the language for five years. My ⬤ ⁶ is German. *mother tongue*

In the advert you say you are looking for people who are good with computers. I have excellent computer skills. I believe the experience I am gaining with my ⬤ *voluntary work* ⁷ with the Freiburg refugee programme will be useful to your organization. I get on well with ⬤ ⁸ *people ~~of~~ from other countries* and I learn ⬤ ⁹ quickly and easily. *languages*

I hope that you will consider my application and grant me an interview. Names of referees can be supplied. I look forward to hearing from you soon.

Yours sincerely
Laura Schulze

B Now write your own covering letter to Mr Kumar. Use the structure of Laura's letter but use your own details.

EXAM
→ writing

C **GAINING EXPERIENCE IN AUSTRALIA**

1 PREPARING TO LISTEN

Read the introduction, then choose the best title for the podcast.

a Backpacking in English-speaking countries
b How to get an Australian work permit
c An exciting way to experience life in a foreign country
d How taking a year off can change your life

> Hello. Here's Helen from Home Counties Radio. This week, I'm going to take you on the trip of a lifetime. But first, I'm going to ask you a question. Are you interested in working abroad and earning money? I'm going to talk to Colin, who did just that. Colin took a year off and travelled through all of Australia's states with a visa which allowed him to work in different jobs.

2 LISTENING: WORKING IN AUSTRALIA

29

EXAM
→ listening comprehension

Decide which of the following options is the correct one.

1 Why did Colin decide that he wanted to go to Australia?
  a He wanted to travel all around the world.
  b He wanted to try out lots of different jobs.
  c He had been offered an Australian Working Holiday Visa.
  d He wanted to take time to think about what to do with his life.

2 The Australian Working Holiday Visa …
  a lasts as long as you like.
  b is aimed mostly at teenagers.
  c allows you to work where you want.
  d can be downloaded from the internet.

3 While he was in Australia, Colin …

    a worked all the time.

    b worked only in hotels.

    c stayed mostly in large cities.

    (d) visited every state in Australia.

4 What did Colin not like about the job in the hotel?

    a The other members of staff he worked with.

    (b) The amount of money he earned while working there.

    c The fact that you needed qualifications to work there.

    d The amount of time he spent helping prepare the food.

5 What does Colin want to do with his life now?

    a He wants to stay in Australia.

    b He wants to be a restaurant manager.

    (c) He wants to be a chef in his own restaurant.

    d He wants to continue travelling around the world.

3 LANGUAGE IN USE: THE GOING TO-FUTURE

→ The future, S. 270

REMEMBER ❗ **the going to-future**

The future with *going to* is used when you are making plans:

    What are you going to do?

    I'm going to apply to be a chef.

Or when there is a sign that something is going to happen:

    It's dark and cloudy. It looks like it is going to rain.

A Complete the sentences with *going to*. The first one has been done for you.

    1 What  when he leaves school? (John – do)

    What is John going to do when he leaves school?

    2 We have a class test tomorrow, so ⬤ this evening. (we – study)

    3 ⬤ backpacking with her friends in the summer? (Hannah – go)

    4 My sister is getting married in June. ⬤ her bridesmaid. (I – be)

    5 There's a new series on TV this evening. ⬤ it? (you – watch)

    6 I usually cycle to school but ⬤ ᵃ tomorrow so ⬤ ᵇ the bus. (it – rain; I – take)

    7 My brother never does any homework. ⬤ his exams. (he – fail)

    8 We're all tired. ⬤ ᵃ this evening, ⬤ ᵇ a pizza. (we – not cook; we – order)

●●● **B** Work in small groups. Talk about what you are going to do at the weekend.

●●○   **Go to File 34 on page 204.**

4 WORKING WITH LANGUAGE

EXAM
→ use of language

A **Find words or expressions in the text below which mean more or less the same as the words below.**

   a totally (lines 2–7)   **b** normal (lines 18–23)

B **Find the opposites of the following words from the text below.**

   a stressful (line 14)   **b** cheaper (line 25)

C **Explain the following words from the text in complete sentences.**

   a to miss (line 2)   **b** to shorten (line 19)

D **Complete the text by using suitable forms of the words on the right. Find a word of your own to replace the question mark.**

An email from Australia

Hi Colin,

It's so sad that that you have left Australia. I miss you and our time working together at the hotel! I hope that you get that you job as a chef which you applied for. I 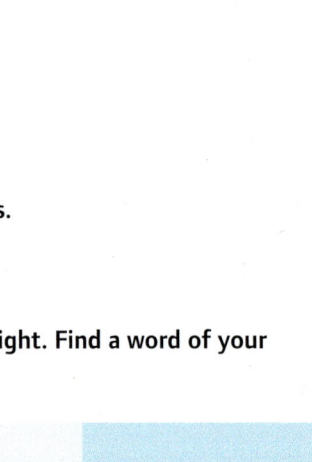ᵃ in Australia for two years now and
5   I absolutely love it here, but I do miss home and there are some things I will never get used to! So, I am a little bit jealous that you are already back home. Perhaps I ᵇ to Germany later this year.

After working with you in Queensland, I moved down to a farm in Victoria. I was not prepared for the weather. I always thought it ᶜ
10   hot in Australia, so I just ᵈ summer clothes with me. It's now winter and it's freezing here! I literally didn't think Australia had seasons. Next weekend I ᵉ down to Melbourne and buy a lot of winter stuff.

I love ᶠ on the farm. It's not as stressful as the hotel where we
15   worked, and the money is much better. However, there are only Australians working here, so I find it difficult to understand what they say. I thought my English was quite good before I arrived, so I didn't expect to have ᵍ problems. But Australians in the outback speak so ʰ and they shorten everything: they
20   don't say 'afternoon', instead they say 'arvo'. And their accent is really strong. In the hotel we were so international that we all spoke good standard English. Here I feel as if I can't speak English at all!

a to be

b to return

c to be
d to bring

e to drive

f to work

g any/some
h quick

25   The Australians here also drink a lot. Most of the people on the farm buy alcohol at bottle shops, as it is much cheaper ▬ ⁱ at the pub. We then all sit around in the evening drinking beer and talking – or in my case just listening, as I have no idea what they are talking about!

i   **?**

Hope to hear from you soon.

Yours Lea

E   Imagine you are Colin. You write back to Lea. In your email you ask her two questions about her life in Australia.

Use different question forms or different tenses.

5 ORGANIZE A TRIP TO AUSTRALIA

You and a friend have organized a Working Holiday Visa for Australia. You don't know yet where you will work, but you want to prepare your trip.

A   You want to visit at least two places while you are there. Discuss your ideas with your partner and agree on two places you want to visit. Look at a map of Australia and at the photos in File 3 on page 210, which may help you come up with some ideas.

EXAM
➔ Kommunikations-
prüfung

B   Search the internet for flights and accommodation. Work out how much money you are going to need for meals, etc.

C   Make a mind map or infographic showing your trip with information about where you plan to go, what you plan to do, and how much you plan to spend.

Pin your mind map or infographic on the wall and do a gallery walk. Whose trip looks most interesting?

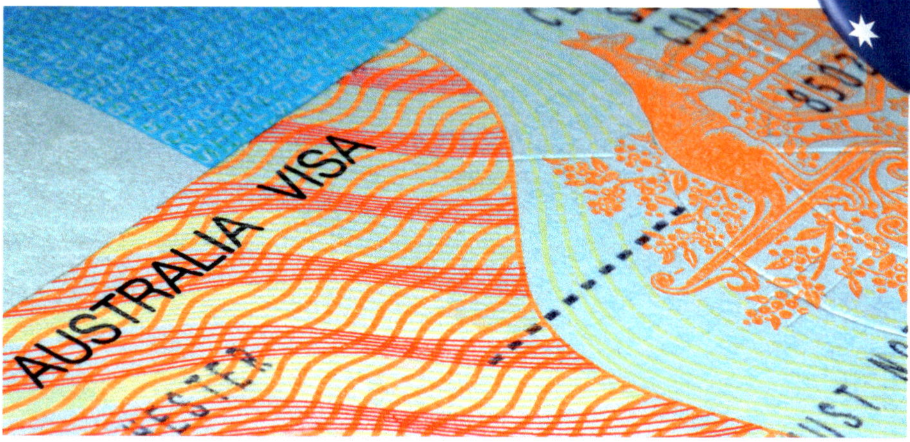

You have applied for a place as a volunteer at the India Charity Foundation. Mr Kumar is coming to Germany to interview applicants, and you are one of them.

1 GET THAT JOB!

You have found these tips online. A friend who is also going to the interview with you asks you to write the tips for him in German. Just tell him the tips but don't translate word for word.

---

http://www.interview-tip-online.comx

Get that job!

You're going to have an interview. Employers want to be sure you will fit into the company so you have to know how to dress and how to behave.

A face-to-face interview is divided into five parts: greetings and introductions; the main part of the interview; your questions; further arrangements; the end of the interview. You need to prepare yourself for each of these parts.

Here are some tips.

On the day of the interview: Get to the interview on time. Wear smart, clean clothes that are appropriate for the job.

Greetings and introductions: Body language is important. Walk into the room as confidently as possible, shake hands and make eye contact with the interviewer.

Making small talk: There are some topics that you should always avoid when you make small talk, for example, religion, politics and illnesses. Don't worry. The interviewer will stick to safe topics like the weather or how bad the traffic is. Just relax and respond appropriately.

The main part of the interview: Answer the interviewer's questions honestly and appropriately.

Your questions: Always do background research into the company before the interview. Use the information to write down one or two questions.

Further arrangements and the end of the interview: Ask when you can expect to hear from the company again. Smile and shake hands again if the interviewer wants to. Say goodbye.

---

2 PLANNING FOR YOUR INTERVIEW

A **Plan for the main part of the interview with a partner. Brainstorm ideas about the questions the interviewer will ask you.**

Here are two ideas:
- Why do you want to work for us?
- What do you know about India?

B In groups, talk about what you would like to know about the India Charity Foundation. Make notes. Then brainstorm a list of questions you can ask.

Here are two ideas:
- How many volunteers work at the foundation?
- What happens to the things the women sew?

3 ROLE-PLAY: A JOB INTERVIEW

Job interview	Job interview

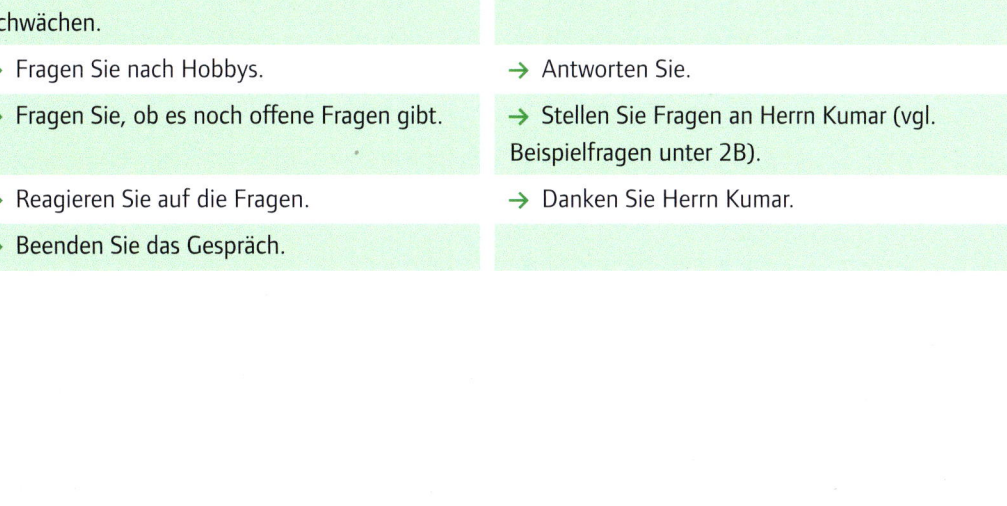

You are **Mr Kumar**, the representative of the Indian Charity Foundation. You interview an applicant for the job as volunteer.
Act out the interview with your partner.

You attend an interview with Mr Kumar of the Indian Charity Foundation. The interview is in English.
Act out the interview with your partner.

→ Begrüßen Sie den/die Bewerber/in und fragen Sie, weshalb er/sie sich als Freiwillige/r bewirbt.

→ Sie begrüßen Herrn Kumar ebenfalls und nennen ihm die Gründe, weshalb Sie sich bewerben.

→ Fragen Sie nach schulischen und beruflichen Erfahrungen.

→ Erzählen Sie ihm von Ihren schulischen und beruflichen Erfahrungen (Schulfächer, Praktika usw.).

→ Fragen Sie nach Stärken und eventuellen Schwächen.

→ Antworten Sie.

→ Fragen Sie nach Hobbys.

→ Antworten Sie.

→ Fragen Sie, ob es noch offene Fragen gibt.

→ Stellen Sie Fragen an Herrn Kumar (vgl. Beispielfragen unter 2B).

→ Reagieren Sie auf die Fragen.

→ Danken Sie Herrn Kumar.

→ Beenden Sie das Gespräch.

Growing up between cultures

Hi, I'm Felix. When I was nine years old, my family moved from Baden-Württemberg in Germany to the Lake District in north England. We moved to follow Mum and Dad's dream: renovating and running an old hotel in the beautiful little town of Keswick (pronounced 'Kezick'). It was hard work at first, but my parents made a success of it, and we have been here for ten years now.

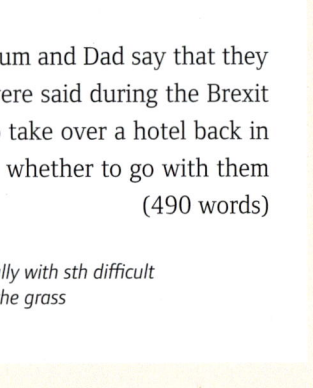

My little brother Lukas was only three years old at the time of the move – not old enough to really know what was going on. Mum and Dad, of course, were over the moon to have the chance to make their dream come true – and busy making it happen.

I, on the other hand, was half-way through primary school in Offenburg in the Rhine Valley, and I didn't appreciate leaving my classmates and friends behind to go to a rainy, cold part of the UK and have to start again with a new school, new classmates – and a whole new language! The first few months were difficult, confusing – and lonely.

I coped though. Fast-forward ten years and I'm as comfortable in the English language as I am in German. I have a great set of friends in Keswick. I also have cousins back in Germany, who we often visit. I've just finished school and am looking for an apprenticeship as an electrician.

I'm sometimes asked if I feel more English or German. It's a difficult one to answer. There are things I love about England, such as the relaxed way of life. English people don't worry too much about what others think of them, and if a rule doesn't make sense to them, they'll ignore it.

I love the English idea of 'common sense'. You can see that in how pedestrians behave on the street. If you judge that it's safe to cross, then you cross the street. You just use your common sense to decide whether it's safe. When I tell my German friends that, most are surprised: 'But it's illegal! And you're setting a bad example for children!' My English friends, on the other hand, can't believe that in Germany pedestrians wait patiently for a green light – even at night or when there are no cars in sight.

There's more. Our Keswick neighbours never complain if we mow the lawn on Sunday. Bus drivers and passengers say goodbye to each other, shopkeepers are ready for a friendly chat if they're not too busy, and people hold the door open for you.

However, since the referendum to leave the European Union, Mum and Dad say that they don't feel welcome in England any more. A lot of horrible things were said during the Brexit campaign about people from the EU. They have the opportunity to take over a hotel back in Germany and have decided to move back to Germany. I'm not sure whether to go with them or not.

(490 words)

---

11 **over the moon:** *very happy*
14 **to appreciate sth:** *to be grateful for sth new*
17 **to cope:** *to deal successfully with sth difficult*
29 **to mow the lawn:** *to cut the grass*

1 TRUE OR FALSE?

Decide whether the following statements are true or false.

1 The family moved to Keswick because of the beauty of the Lake District.
2 Lukas was 13 years old when his brother Felix wrote this text.
3 Renovating and running an old hotel was a dream come true for Felix's parents.
4 The whole family was happy to more to England.

2 SENTENCE COMPLETION

Finish the sentences using the information from the text.

1 His first impression of England was that …
2 Felix doesn't feel lonely in England, because he has …
3 Now that he has finished school, Felix is applying for …

3 MULTIPLE MATCHING

**Who might say what? Match the statements (a–g) to the people (1–5). There is one statement
that doesn't match anyone.**

1 Felix   3 the parents   5 Felix's English friends
2 Lukas   4 Felix's German friends

a I wish I spoke better English.
b Laws are made to help us live
  better lives.
c Settling down in England took
  a long time.
d I don't really remember much
  about moving to England.
e What we really love doing is
  offering hospitality to others.
f If you can think for yourself,
  you can also make your own
  decisions.

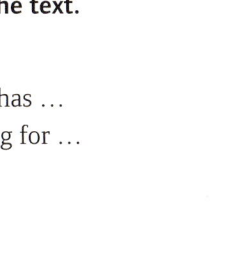

4 INFORMATIONEN AUS DEM TEXT WIEDERGEBEN

Beantworten Sie die folgende Frage auf Deutsch.

Was gefällt Felix an England und den Engländern besonders gut? Nennen Sie stichwortartig fünf
typisch englische Verhaltensweisen, die Felix erwähnt.

A **Correct these statements using the information in brackets.**

EXAMPLE: Anna has been to India three times. (twice)
Anna hasn't been to India three times. She has been there twice.

1 Jude and Lucas went to Sri Lanka for their year abroad. (India)
2 They taught English in a small village near Mumbai. (Mumbai itself)
3 The accommodation was very comfortable. (dirty and noisy)
4 They had a private room in a family's house. (two beds in a dormitory)
5 Their stay in India was expensive. (very cheap)
6 Lucas wanted to spend a lot of money. (spend as little as possible)
7 They have been back to India since then. (stay at home)
8 Jude has booked a flight to India this summer. (not take any decision about his holidays this summer)

B **Complete the dialogue with the most suitable forms of the verbs in brackets (simple past or present perfect). Watch out for signal adverbs.**

Ashley: Hi, Dylan! I (not see)[1] you for a while.
Dylan: No. I (just – return)[2] home after working in Australia for six months.
Ashley: Wow! I (think)[3] you were looking tanned and healthy. Where in Australia (you – go)[4]?
Dylan: I (go)[5] to a place called Mulga in Western Australia. (you ever – be)[6] to Australia?
Ashley: Yes, I (go)[7] once, about two years ago! I (want)[8] to stay and work there but I (not have)[9] a work visa.
Dylan: Actually I (go)[10] there to work. I (apply)[11] for a Working Holiday Visa.
Ashley: I (never – hear)[12] of that? What is it?
Dylan: It's a scheme they (introduce)[13] several years ago to let young non-Australians work in the country for a year. They (have)[14] great success with it.
Ashley: So, what (you – do)[15] down under?
Dylan: I (work)[16] on a large sheep farm. I (never – work)[17] so hard in my life.
Ashley: I can see that! You (become)[18] all muscly and fit. How (you – find)[19] life back in Britain after six months in the sun?
Dylan: I miss the people and the warmth, but since I (be)[20] back here, I (not – have to)[21] work as I (save)[22] up some money from my trip. So, I (have)[23] a great time since my return enjoying my freedom. Next month I'll start applying for jobs again!

C **Complete the sentences by translating the expressions in italics using *for*, *since* or *ago*.**

1 I've been in Mumbai *seit zwei Tagen*.
2 We did volunteering work in India *vor einem Jahr*.
3 Kelly and Dan have been travelling around Australia *seit März*.
4 The Australian government introduced the Working Holiday Visa *vor vielen Jahren*.
5 Large numbers of youngsters people have received Working Holiday Visas *seither*.
6 The farm we worked on in Australia has belonged to the same family *seit langer Zeit*.

Welcome to the Rockies

A WARM-UP: THE ROCKY MOUNTAIN REGION

A Work with a partner. Look at the photos from the Rocky Mountain Region and read the box below. Speculate about …

- the entertainment and leisure activities in the region
- the way of life there

> It looks as if the landscape / cities / people …

> The local people probably …

> I expect it's a good place to …

Rocky Mountain Region

Size	1,608,683 km² (≈ Germany, Austria, Switzerland, France + Spain together)
States	Colorado, Idaho, Montana, Nevada, Utah, Wyoming
Major cities	Denver, Las Vegas, Reno, Salt Lake City
Natural wonders	Mojave Desert, Rocky Mountain National Park, Yellowstone National Park, Bryce Canyon National Park
Activities	nightlife and gambling (e.g. Las Vegas); rock climbing, mountain biking, skiing, hiking, horse riding, extreme sports; spectator sports (e.g. American football, rodeo); Wild West history and culture (e.g. Buffalo Bill Center).

B Discuss in a group.

You are planning a visit to the Rocky Mountain Region. Where will you go there and what will you do?

- Choose a city, a natural wonder and an activity.
- Discuss your choices with the group.
- Make a plan for a two-week trip for your group.

B AN AMERICAN FOOTBALL GAME

SITUATION: You have entered a short story competition in an online youth magazine for English learners. To win the prize of a winter holiday in the Rockies, you have to write a story about a trip you made (task 5, page 123). You find an entry in a blog by Sophie from Münster about an American football game that she attended with her exchange family.

1 PREPARING TO READ

A **Look at the photos from the game.**
Brainstorm ideas about the atmosphere.

B **Discuss these questions with a partner. Then report back to the class.**

- Say what you know about American football.
- Do you think the game should be more popular in Germany? Why (not)?
- Do you think that sports traditions in general are important? Why (not)?

TIP ❗ football
football (BE) = *Fußball*
football (AE) = *Football*
soccer (AE) = *Fußball*

2 READING AND UNDERSTANDING THE TEXT

A GREAT DAY OUT

'It's a great American tradition,' said Mr Duncan mysteriously. 'You'll love it!' The holidays in Colorado with my exchange partner Jess Duncan had been wonderful, but now they were nearly over. It was the start of September, and almost time to fly home and get ready for the start of the new school year. Almost, but not quite. As it turned out, the Duncans had planned one last treat for me.

I was very excited. Then, on the morning of the 'treat', I found out that it was an American football game. 'A really special game: the NFL Kickoff Game,' said Mr Duncan.

Mr Duncan had bought tickets for the first game of the NFL season. The Denver Broncos were playing the Carolina Panthers.

The problem was, I hate sport. All those times when Mr Duncan patiently explained the rules of football to me, and I sat there in front of the TV and looked interested – I just wanted to be polite. Unfortunately, Mr Duncan didn't know that. He thought I was a real sports fan, like him.

So I tried to look pleased, even though I was disappointed. It was too late anyway – he had already bought the tickets. I couldn't disappoint the Duncans, who had been so kind to me. Jess, Mr Duncan and I drove down the Interstate to Denver's Mile High Stadium. It's a huge building – it can hold 76,000 fans, and on the first day of the season, it was full. Our seats were up the back.

It was terrifying. I don't like crowds and I'm scared of heights. As we climbed up the steep steps to our seats high above the playing field, everyone around us started to stamp their feet. It made a deafening sound. Mr Duncan explained that this was the Mile High Thunder. One of the game's 'great traditions', he said.

It was freezing cold, and it started to rain a little bit. Mr Duncan rushed down to the fast food stands to get us something to eat and drink. He came back with three huge buckets of cola and three-foot-long hotdogs. 'Traditional football food,' laughed Jess.

The opening ceremony was amazing. There were fireworks, and brass band music, the American national anthem, and cheerleaders dancing.

Then the game started. I had seen a couple of football games on TV before, but being there in person was different. It was brutal. When two opposing players ran into each other at full speed, we heard the 'crack!' all the way up the back of the stadium.

The game seemed to be three hours of inactivity and discussion with short bursts of violent action. Someone knocked someone down. Stop. Someone came onto the field and kicked the ball. Stop. And so it went on.

And yet ... about halfway through the second quarter, I realized I was enjoying myself. We were next to a bunch of Broncos fans who were cheering wildly for their team. Soon we too cheered loudly each time the Broncos scored. It was actually a great evening out. 'Our' team won, by one point. It was thrilling.

Jess later said to me, 'You know, Dad doesn't really like football. He just wanted to take you to a game, as you're such a fan.'   (545 words)

A Decide which of the following is the correct option.

1 When does the story take place?
- **a** at the beginning of the new school year
- **b** towards the end of Sophie's holidays in the USA
- **c** just as September was about to start
- **d** as she was flying home to Germany

2 How did Sophie react to her surprise present?
- **a** She tried to look happy but had expected something nicer.
- **b** She said she was disappointed.
- **c** She was as excited as any sports fan.
- **d** Her face showed she was not happy.

3 Which of the following do we learn about the stadium?
- **a** It is located just outside Denver.
- **b** It has the largest capacity of any US stadium.
- **c** It is situated a mile above sea level.
- **d** It's an open-air stadium.

4 Which of the following is <u>not</u> considered a tradition at the stadium?
- **a** the spectators stamping their feet on the floor
- **b** eating three hotdogs that are a foot long
- **c** enjoying large portions of fast food
- **d** the playing of the national anthem before the game

5 The game itself could be described in the following way:
- **a** lots of wild cheering by excited fans
- **b** pure brutality from start to finish
- **c** a very boring match
- **d** sudden action between periods of inactivity

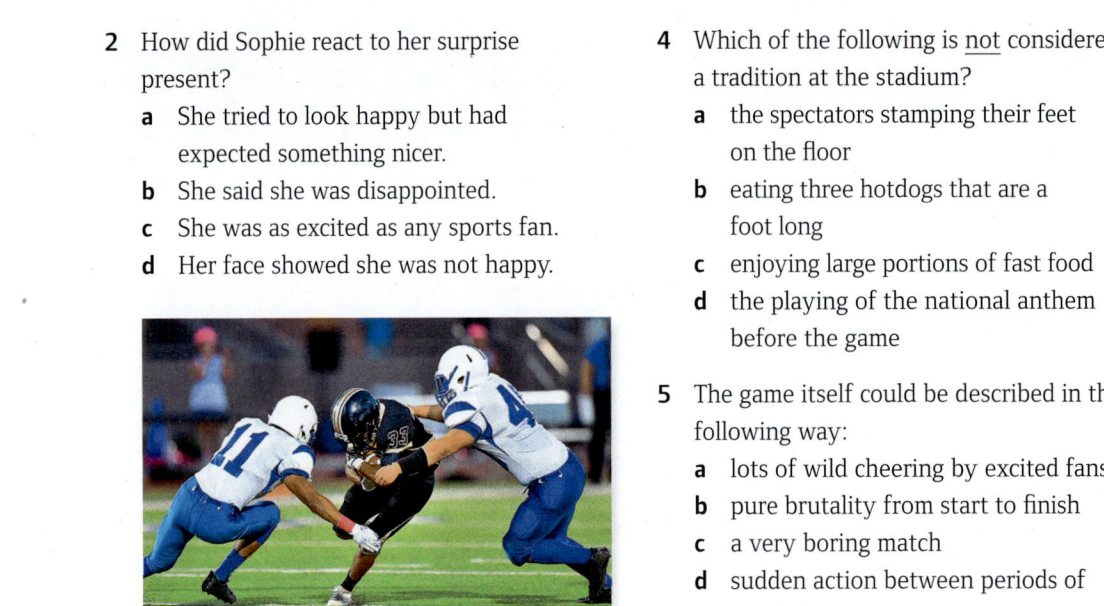

B Ask Sophie three questions about American football or about the match. Use different question forms and different tenses.

EXAMPLE: *Do you want to go to another American football game?*

C Read the text again and make notes on these questions, then discuss your answers with a partner. When you have finished, report back to the class with what you decided.

1 How does Sophie's attitude change during the course of the text, and why?

2 What kind of person is Mr Duncan? Find evidence in the text to support your opinion.

Go to Files 35 and 36 on page 205.

3 LANGUAGE IN USE: PAST PERFECT

→ Past perfect, S. 269

A Find examples of the past perfect in the text. Write them with the line numbers.

EXAMPLE: *the holidays ... had been (lines 2–4)*

B Complete the text with either the simple past or past perfect forms of the verbs in brackets to find out what happened after the game.

After the game *had finished* ¹ (finish), we ⬤ ² (leave) the stadium. The Broncos fans ⬤ ³ (be) very happy because their team ⬤ ⁴ (win). The Panthers fans ⬤ ⁵ (be) sad because their team ⬤ ⁶ (lose). It ⬤ ⁷ (be) still cold and it ⬤ ⁸ (start) to rain again a few minutes before. We ⬤ ⁹ (want) to get in the nice, warm car as soon as possible. Then we ⬤ ¹⁰ (realize) that we ⬤ ¹¹ (forget) where the car was. Before the game it ⬤ ¹² (be) light, but now it ⬤ ¹³ (be) dark and everything ⬤ ¹⁴ (look) different. We ⬤ ¹⁵ (look) for the car for 20 minutes. By the time we ⬤ ¹⁶ (find) it, it ⬤ ¹⁷ (stop) raining, but we ⬤ ¹⁸ (be) very wet. When we finally ⬤ ¹⁹ (arrive) home, we ⬤ ²⁰ (discover) that Mrs Duncan ⬤ ²¹ (cook) a large dinner for us. It ⬤ ²² (be) good to be back home and warm again.

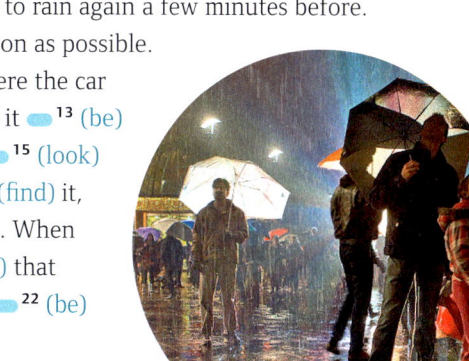

4 WORKING WITH WORDS

A Find words or expressions in the text on page 121 which mean more or less the same.

a final (lines 1–9)
b frightening (lines 33–39)
c commenced (lines 46–55)
d group (lines 61–67)

B Find the opposites of the following words from the text on page 121.

a polite (line 21)
b started (line 50)
c loudly (line 65)

C In groups of four, explain the following words from the text. Two of you find explanations for words a–c, and the other pair find explanations for words d–f.
Read your explanations to the other pair, who have to decide which of your explanations match your three words.

a deafening (line 37)
b disappointed (line 25)
c thrilling (line 67)
d tradition (line 1)
e treat (line 9)
f ceremony (line 46)

5 WRITING A SHORT STORY

Finish the story below about a trip that did not go according to plan.
Before you start to write, make notes on the following and try to include them in the story:

■ what you had planned
■ how and why your trip did not work out as planned
■ what you learned from this experience

I was sure that I had thought of everything: flights, money, accommodation. However, my 'big trip' didn't turn out the way I had expected …

C GOING TO THE RODEO

1 PREPARING TO LISTEN

Leon from Ulm is on a school exchange to Nevada. It's early June and he is going with his hosts, the Jaeger family, to the Reno Rodeo. You are going to listen to Sally Jaeger talking to Leon about the rodeo. Before you listen, read Leon's blog below and do the tasks.

A Note down three things you learned about Nevada, the Jaeger family and farm life.

B Compare information with your partner.

Nevada Life

LEON'S BLOG

Staying with my exchange partner, Ryan, is totally awesome! Nevada is almost exactly how I imagined it – only more so. There are wide open spaces like in a
5 cowboy movie, with snow-covered mountains and colourful deserts, cattle on large ranches – and lots of people actually wearing cowboy hats!
Ryan's parents, Sally and Mike, have
10 normal urban jobs – she works in IT and he's a mechanic – but the family lives on a farm. They call it a 'hobby farm', and

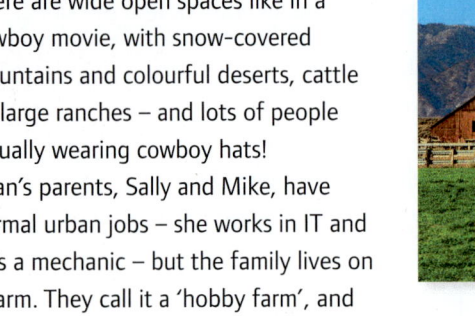

before I came here, I thought that it was just a small patch of land, but it's huge! There are horses, cattle and sheep, as well as some crops.
15 This morning everyone was preparing for the Reno Rodeo. The Jaegers take the whole week off for the rodeo, so they needed to make sure the farm was looked after while they were away. Mike Jaeger was giving the farmhand, Amy, instructions; Sally was showing a neighbour which animals needed special attention, and Ryan was checking the tractor.

🎧 2 LISTENING: GOING TO THE RODEO
31

A **Listen and fill in the gaps with words you hear in the dialogue. There is one word per gap.**

EXAM
→ listening comprehension

1 Leon: We don't have many rodeos back home in Germany, you see, and I've never seen one – except in ●, of course.
2 Sally: It's a sporting competition that involves handling horses and cattle – cows and bulls. The events are based on the skills that a worker needed on a ● ranch.
3 Sally: It kicks off with the arrival of the ● drive on the first day.

B Listen again and finish the sentences using the information from the text.

1 It is said that rodeo is one of the
2 A lot of rodeo riders suffer from injuries like
3 Rodeo riders who do well can win
4 According to Sally, some of the animals in rodeos are treated as
5 Some of the bulls can take part in rodeos for as long as
6 For people in Nevada the rodeo is part of their
7 Rodeos make people think back to the old days of

3 LANGUAGE IN USE: PAST PROGRESSIVE

→ Past progressive, S. 266

A Find examples of the past progressive in Leon's blog on page 124.

B Complete this extract from Leon's blog using the past progressive of the verbs in brackets.

Reno Rodeo – Day 1

LEON'S BLOG

When we got to Reno, the cattle drive ¹ (arrive).
Crowds of people lining the streets ² (cheer)
and a band ³ (play). Afterwards we went back
to the hotel, where we ⁴ (stay) for the week.
We chatted for a while with the owner, Bill.
Like us, he ⁵ (look) forward to the rodeo.

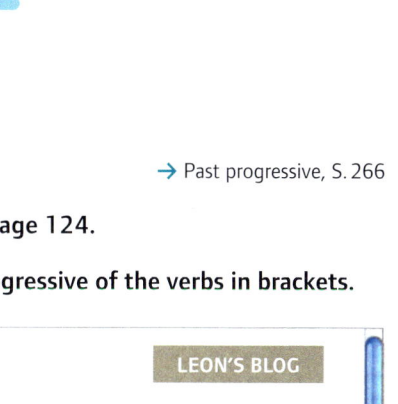

The rodeo arena had a real Wild West appearance,
with the old-fashioned painted signs and all the
people in cowboy clothes. When we arrived,
a cowboy ⁶ (ride) a huge bull – or at least, he ⁷ (try) to. The bull ⁸ (kick) furiously and
threw him off very quickly! Thousands of people ⁹ (watch) the action. The sun ¹⁰ (go)
down and it was all very atmospheric. Later there were fireworks above the arena. I was worried
at first, because cowboys ¹¹ (demonstrate) their riding skills in the arena at the time, but I
soon realized that the horses weren't scared by the flashes and bangs at all.

4 PLANNING A 'WILD WEST' THEME NIGHT

Work in a small group. Exchange students are at your school. You have decided to organize
a party at your school to welcome them and have decided to give it a 'Wild West' or 'rodeo'
theme. Divide up the areas of responsibility amongst your group members. Make individual
notes, then come together and draw up a plan.

- food and drink
- 'ice-breaker' activities and games
- music, decorating the venue
- suggestions for clothes/costumes to wear

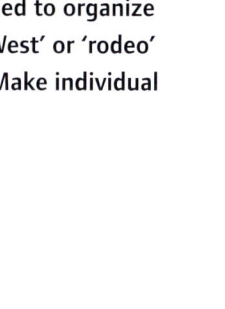

You work for a small car company. Your boss is interested in registering for the US Motor Show in Denver and has asked you to find out some information.

1 A MOTOR SHOW WEBSITE

A Your boss has some questions about the fair. Where is the best place to look for answers on the website? (There may be more than one relevant section.)

1 Wie können wir uns als Aussteller anmelden?

2 Wie sieht das Messegelände aus?

4 Was kostet der Eintritt?

3 Wie können wir uns auf dem Laufenden halten?

Home	Information	Exhibiting	Visiting	Media	Contact us
	About us	Exhibitor list	Tickets	Virtual tour of the exhibition village	Send us a message
	FAQs	Exhibitor registration form	Opening hours		
	Latest news		Getting here	Highlights from last year's show	
	Mailing list		Floor plan		
	Activities		Food and drink	Press registration form	

http://www.automobilefair.comx

B Decide which of the headings on the website the following pieces of information belong to.

> **Over 130 brand new vehicles** **1**
> Over 20 manufacturers and 30 dealerships are represented at this year's show.
> Test drive this year's models.
> See concept cars with the latest automotive designs and technology.
> Special deals for visitors make this the perfect place to buy your next car.

> **Delicious food and drink** **2**
> 20 food trucks cater for all tastes, from freshly made pizza and BBQ sausages to vegetarian Indian food. As well as street food favorites, the show has a sit-down café with a great view of the vehicle displays.

<table>
<tr><td>

Fantastic entertainment   `3`

A full program of talks by motoring
celebrities and industry experts.
Thrilling simulator rides for kids and adults!

</td><td>

State Convention Center   `4`

Ten-minute walk from downtown Denver
30-minute cab ride from airport

</td></tr>
</table>

`2` SHARING INFORMATION

Zur Vorbereitung auf die Handelsmesse möchte Ihre Chefin gern mehr Einzelheiten erfahren. Stellen Sie in einem Memo Informationen aus der Website (Aufgabe 1B) zusammen, die für sie relevant sein könnten. Übersetzen Sie nicht Wort für Wort. Die folgenden Fragen könnten dabei nützlich sein.

1 Was gibt es auf der Messe Interessantes für Fachleute?

2 Was kann man wo essen?

3 Wie kommt man dorthin?

`3` LISTENING: AT THE TRADE FAIR

32

At the trade fair several visitors come to your company's stand. Listen to what they say and choose the best response to each of them (a, b or c).

1 a Yes, we do. Thanks very much.
   b I'm not sure. I'll ask my boss.
   c Yes, of course. Here's our brochure.

2 a Hi, Laura. Are you having fun at the show?
   b Hello, I'm (your name) from (your company). Pleased to meet you.
   c Hi, Laura. I'm (your name). Why don't we go and get a coffee?

3 a Yes, thanks, I'm really enjoying it.
   b No, I'm tired and my head hurts. I'm looking forward to closing time.
   c Yes, thanks. We've had a lot of interest in our new products.

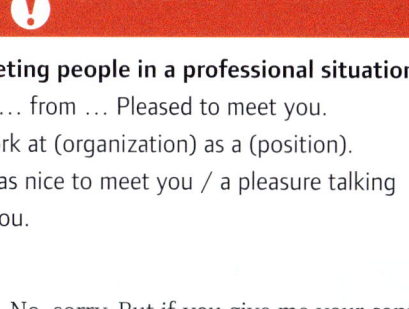

TIP

Meeting people in a professional situation
I'm … from … Pleased to meet you.
I work at (organization) as a (position).
It was nice to meet you / a pleasure talking to you.

4 a No, sorry. But if you give me your contact details, I'll send you one.
   b No, I'm sorry, it's the only one we have on the stand.
   c No. Please download one from our website.

5 a I don't know. Why don't you have a look at the show guide?
   b I recommend the Formula One racing simulator, I'd love to go on that!
   c We're going to present our latest product in about ten minutes. I think you'll find it interesting.

1 WORKING WITH WORDS

A Find words or expressions in the text which mean more or less the same.
   a   adult (adj) (lines 13–17)   b   companies/firms (lines 13–17)

B Find opposites of the following words from the text below.
   a   arrival (line 13)   b   always (line 20)

C Explain one of the following words from the text below in complete sentences.
   a   violent (line 10)   b   employee (line 17)

2 VOCABULARY – GRAMMAR

Complete the text below by using suitable forms of the words on the right or find a word of your own to replace the question mark.

a	tradition	e	origin
b	not understand	f	?
c	many/much	g	to change
d	who/which/what	h	general

Thanksgiving Day

Thanksgiving Day is a public holiday in the USA. It began as a day to give thanks for the harvest. The day usually involves a 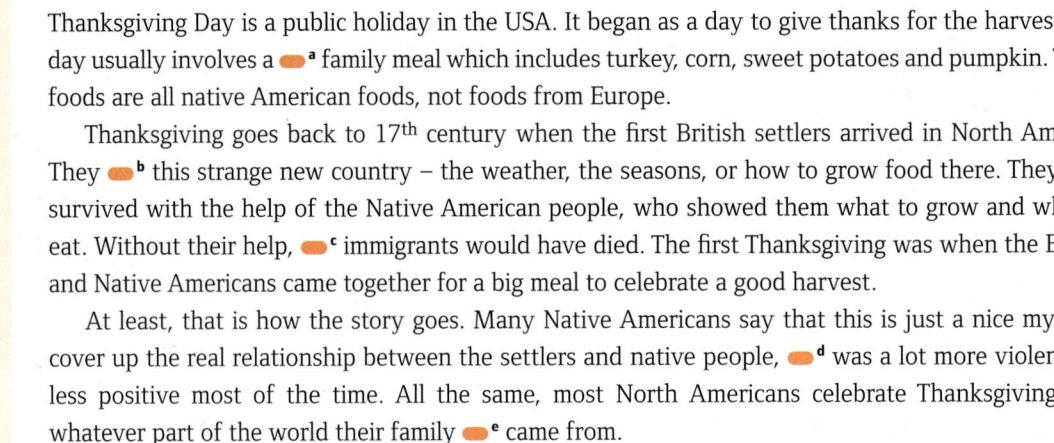 ᵃ family meal which includes turkey, corn, sweet potatoes and pumpkin. These foods are all native American foods, not foods from Europe.

Thanksgiving goes back to 17th century when the first British settlers arrived in North America. They ᵇ this strange new country – the weather, the seasons, or how to grow food there. They only survived with the help of the Native American people, who showed them what to grow and what to eat. Without their help, ᶜ immigrants would have died. The first Thanksgiving was when the British and Native Americans came together for a big meal to celebrate a good harvest.

At least, that is how the story goes. Many Native Americans say that this is just a nice myth, to cover up the real relationship between the settlers and native people, ᵈ was a lot more violent and less positive most of the time. All the same, most North Americans celebrate Thanksgiving Day, whatever part of the world their family ᵉ came from.

ᶠ Thanksgiving has been celebrated in the USA since the arrival of Europeans, it was only in 1941 that the date was legally set as the fourth Thursday in November. Until then, the date ᵍ quite often.

Thanksgiving is a family celebration, and most people take the day off work to be with their family. Grown-up children try to go home for Thanksgiving. Most stores and other businesses are shut for the day so that their employees can stay at home with their families.

People do not ʰ go to work on the day after Thanksgiving Day: they take this day off too, if they can. So they have a four-day weekend. However, all the stores are open, as it is an important shopping day. It is called Black Friday and there are always special deals.   (315 words)

3 ASKING QUESTIONS

You are talking to your American friend about Thanksgiving Day. Ask two questions about Thanksgiving in the USA. Use different question forms or different tenses.

These photos show celebrations that take place in Germany. Discuss why these celebrations are special. Explain which is your favourite festival, and describe how you celebrate it.

Listen to what your partner says about his or her favourite festival and ask questions about it.

Eid al-Fitr

Christmas

New Year's Eve

Reunification Day

October Beer Festival

Carnival

A **Use the comparatives and superlatives of the adjectives and adverbs in brackets to complete the sentences.**

1 The weather in Nevada was ⬤ than usual. (bad)
2 I don't like long flights usually, but the one to Denver went a lot ⬤ than I expected. (well)
3 Soccer is a lot ⬤ than American football in my opinion. (exciting)
4 Mexican food is the ⬤ food that I've ever eaten. (hot)
5 The Broncos fans were a lot ⬤ than the Panthers fans. (noisy)
6 The weather in Colorado was the ⬤ weather I've experienced in September. (cold)
7 Don't queue for tickets at the gate: you can buy tickets ⬤ online. (easily)

B **The Denver Broncos have to decide which football player they should offer a contract to. Compare the players using adjectives from the box. The first one has been done for you.**

EXAMPLE: *Joel is older than Mario but Reuben is the oldest player.*

> fast ▪ heavy ▪ ~~old~~ ▪ successful ▪ tall ▪ young

		Joel Fleischman	Reuben O'Malley	Mario Maretti
1	age	24	25	22
2	time over 100 m	12.14	11.26	11.05
3	height in cm	185	180	182
4	weight in kg	106	93	90
5	points scored (average per season)	158	147	161

C **Leon is uploading photos from his time in Nevada and needs to add captions. Write sentences using relative clauses (with *who*, *which*, *where* or *whose*, or as contact clauses). You may need to change the sentences a little.**

EXAMPLE: These are some photos. I took them on my trip to Nevada.
   These are some photos which I took on my trip to Nevada.

1 Here you can see one of the hosts. We stayed with her in Denver.
2 This is Jane. Her son was riding the bulls in the rodeo.
3 This is Jane's son in the hospital. Many of the rodeo riders ended up there.
4 Reno is a fun place. I would recommend visiting it.
5 This is the guide. He took us kayaking.
6 We visited an island. It had bears on it.
7 Tourists cause a lot of trouble. They feed the bears.
8 Bears become confident around people. They receive food from tourists.
9 There are lots of signs. They say 'Do not feed the bears!'
10 We saw one bear. That bear was fast asleep, so it wasn't dangerous.
11 We then returned to my host's house. I fell asleep immediately there.

Becoming an adult

A   WARM-UP: INFLUENCES

A   Match the expressions from the box to the pictures 1–6.

community ▪ education ▪ family ▪
friends ▪ social media ▪ work

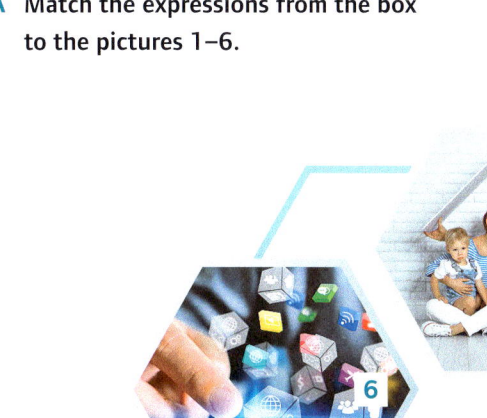

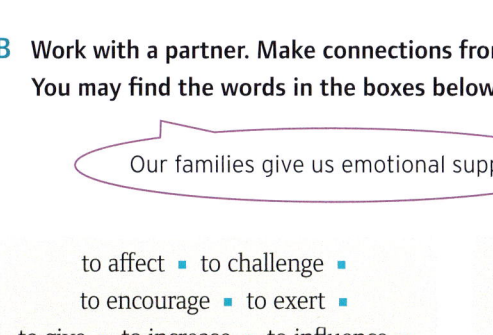

B   Work with a partner. Make connections from each of the pictures to the picture in the centre. You may find the words in the boxes below useful.

> Our friends influence our …

> Our families give us emotional support.

to affect ▪ to challenge ▪
to encourage ▪ to exert ▪
to give ▪ to increase ▪ to influence ▪
to provide ▪ to support

ambitions and aspirations ▪ emotional support ▪
ideas and opinions ▪ moral values ▪
peer pressure ▪ sense of belonging ▪
skills and knowledge

C   Which of the influences mentioned above are most important in your life right now? Why?

B WORLDS APART

SITUATION: You have decided to enter a writing competition in an online youth magazine. The topic of your story should be 'Finding out where I belong' (task 6, page 136). You find an article in a magazine about two Australian youngsters from different indigenous backgrounds.

1 PREPARING TO READ

A Skim the article on pages 133 and 134, then match the images to Mattie or Korben.

B Discuss these questions with a partner. Then report back to the class.

Imagine you are one of the young people in the photos above. You are about to leave your small community and move to the city:

- What challenges will you face in the big city?
- How do you feel about making this move?
- What aspects of the city will you miss when you return home?

2 READING AND UNDERSTANDING THE TEXT

A Mattie's Story

1 My name is **Mattie** and I'm a proud Yorta Yorta woman. My people's traditional lands are on the Murray River – Dungala in our language – in Victoria and New South Wales, Australia. My grandmothers were both members of the Stolen Generations – they were taken from their parents as
5 babies and never saw them again. They were educated in schools which taught them that their culture was inferior. They eventually married European immigrant husbands. Many of our people have similar stories. As a result, a lot of our traditional knowledge has been lost, but some remains.
Because of the things that were done to my ancestors, I feel a big responsibility
10 for keeping our Yorta Yorta customs, knowledge and language alive. I didn't always think this way: when I was a kid, they were just grandma's 'old stories'. I had to leave my community before I could understand.

2 I was given an indigenous scholarship to a private school in Melbourne three years ago. Now I'm about to do my school-leaving exams. I plan to study
15 ecology at TAFE¹, so one day I can work as a conservationist on our traditional lands in the Barmah State Forest.
Going to a mostly white school was a shock. It was as if they were living in a totally different world. My classmates didn't even know that there's a Yorta Yorta language, one of over 200 indigenous languages around Australia. They
20 knew more about traditional cultures on the other side of the world, in the USA or in Africa, than about one in their own state!

3 On the other hand, their questions made me realize how little I knew myself, and how important it was to learn everything I could from elders like my grandma while she's still with us. So, in a way, I had to go away to
25 Melbourne in order to discover my identity as a Yorta Yorta woman.

4 I love Melbourne, but it isn't home. People have a different attitude towards nature: they may go on an annual camping trip to the 'bush', but it plays no part in their daily lives. Even worse, their elders aren't respected – they're put in aged-care homes, where they visit them once a month! That isn't the Yorta
30 Yorta way.

¹TAFE (Technical and Further Education): the Australian system of vocational education colleges

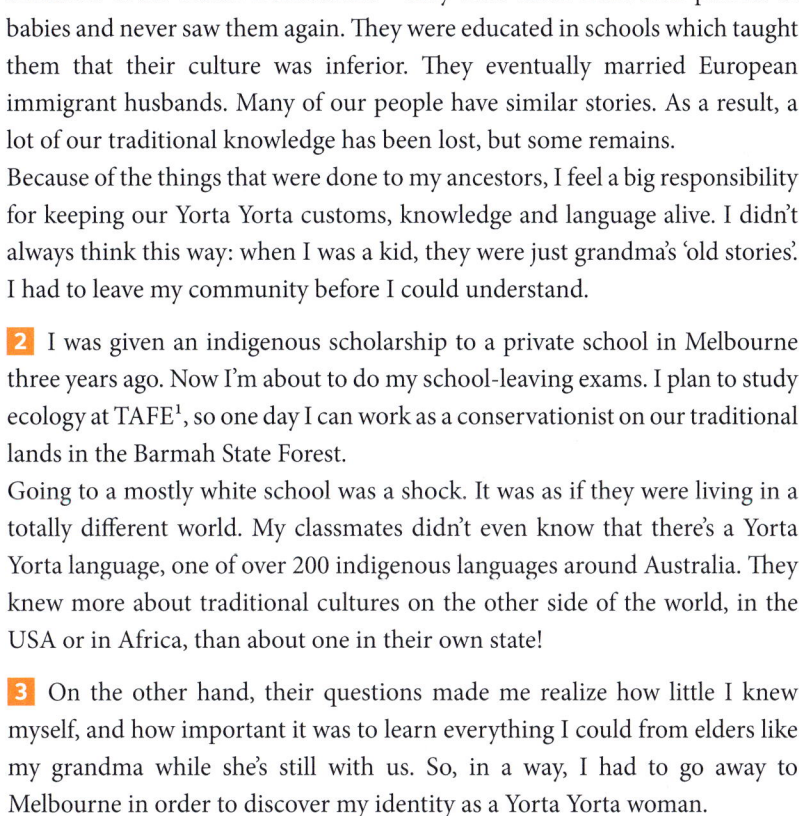

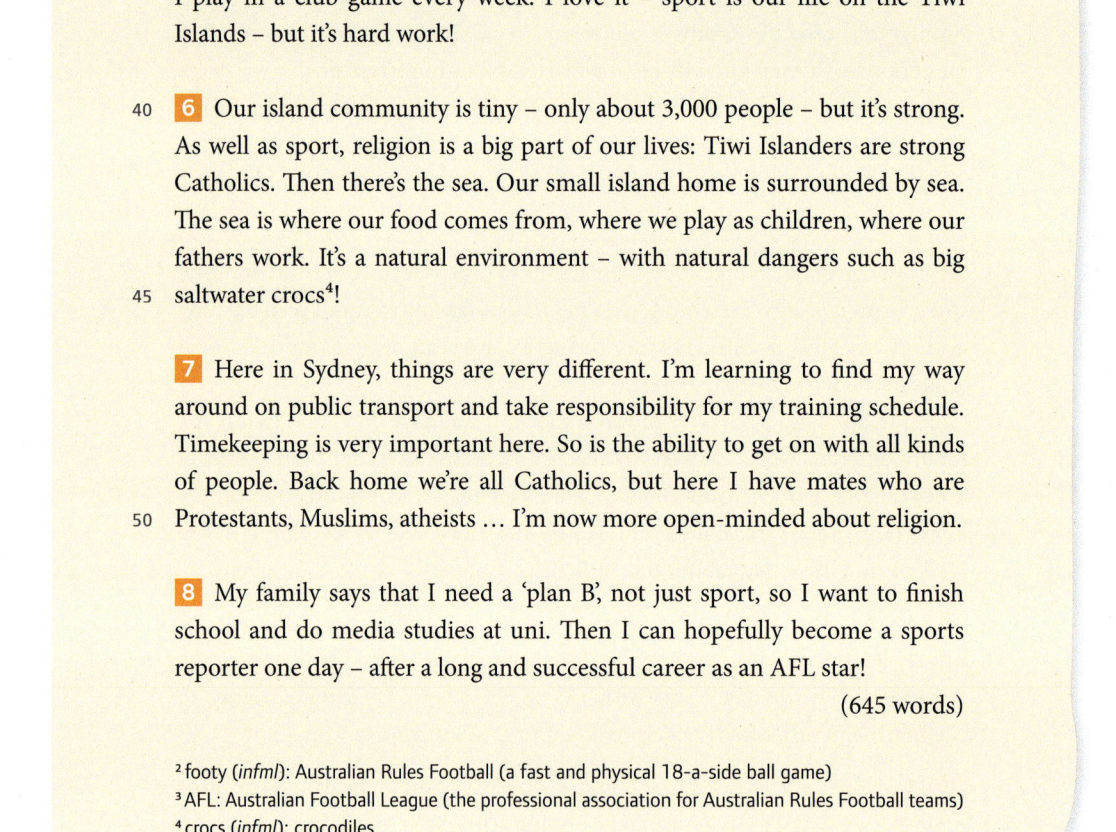

B Korben's Story

5 My name's **Korben**. I'm a Tiwi Islander. The Tiwi Islands are a small group of islands near Darwin in the Northern Territory. I'm 18 and a few years ago I moved to Sydney to live with my uncle and aunt. I go to school, but mainly I'm
35 here to play footy[2]. I've been selected for training with one of the leading teams in Sydney, and my dream is to become a professional AFL[3] player.

It's a busy schedule. I train with the team four times a week. On top of that, I play in a club game every week. I love it – sport is our life on the Tiwi Islands – but it's hard work!

40 **6** Our island community is tiny – only about 3,000 people – but it's strong. As well as sport, religion is a big part of our lives: Tiwi Islanders are strong Catholics. Then there's the sea. Our small island home is surrounded by sea. The sea is where our food comes from, where we play as children, where our fathers work. It's a natural environment – with natural dangers such as big
45 saltwater crocs[4]!

7 Here in Sydney, things are very different. I'm learning to find my way around on public transport and take responsibility for my training schedule. Timekeeping is very important here. So is the ability to get on with all kinds of people. Back home we're all Catholics, but here I have mates who are
50 Protestants, Muslims, atheists … I'm now more open-minded about religion.

8 My family says that I need a 'plan B', not just sport, so I want to finish school and do media studies at uni. Then I can hopefully become a sports reporter one day – after a long and successful career as an AFL star!

(645 words)

[2] footy (*infml*): Australian Rules Football (a fast and physical 18-a-side ball game)
[3] AFL: Australian Football League (the professional association for Australian Rules Football teams)
[4] crocs (*infml*): crocodiles

A Match the headings (a–j) to the numbers 1–8 in the text. There are two more headings than you need.

a	Start of a career	**f**	An alternative career path
b	Missing home	**g**	A close community
c	Culture shock	**h**	Trouble fitting in
d	Learning to value my culture	**i**	Destroying our history
e	Getting on in the big city	**j**	Not my way of life

B **Finish the sentences using the information from the text.**

EXAM
→ reading
   comprehension

1 Mattie is proud that
2 People of the Stolen Generations were
3 Australian schools taught Aborigines
4 When Mattie was a child, she
5 Mattie's dream job is
6 Mattie was surprised that her fellow students
7 In Mattie's opinion, the worst thing about white Australians is that
8 While Mattie is from southern Australia, Korben
9 Korben moved to Sydney, because
10 He spends much of his time
11 When you live on an island,
12 One advantage of a big city like Sydney is that
13 Once he has finished school, Korben
14 After a successful career as an athlete,

3 LANGUAGE IN USE: THE PASSIVE

→ The passive, S. 271

A **Find examples of the passive in the article on pages 133 and 134. Write down the passive form in the text, the infinitives of the verbs and the line numbers.**

passive form	infinitive	line in text
were taken	to take	4

B **Use the passive of the verbs in brackets to tell the story of the Stolen Generations.**

The Stolen Generations were the children of Australian Aboriginal and Torres Strait Islander parents who ¹ (remove) from their families by the Australian authorities. These removals ² (carry out) mostly between 1905 and 1970. In some areas, up to 30% of indigenous Australian children ³ (take) from their families and

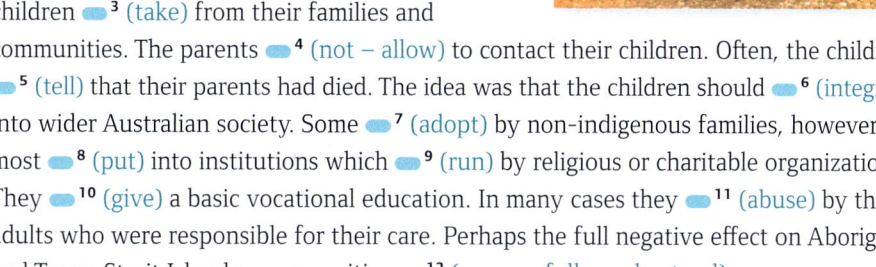

communities. The parents ⁴ (not – allow) to contact their children. Often, the children ⁵ (tell) that their parents had died. The idea was that the children should ⁶ (integrate) into wider Australian society. Some ⁷ (adopt) by non-indigenous families, however most ⁸ (put) into institutions which ⁹ (run) by religious or charitable organizations. They ¹⁰ (give) a basic vocational education. In many cases they ¹¹ (abuse) by the adults who were responsible for their care. Perhaps the full negative effect on Aboriginal and Torres Strait Islander communities ¹² (never – fully understand).

4 WORKING WITH WORDS

●●● **Fill in the gaps with words from the texts on pages 133 and 134.**

1 She was surprised to find that she had African ⬤, as she looked very European. (lines 1–13)
2 Rather than keeping problems within the family, we discuss them with other members of the ⬤ such as friends and neighbours. (lines 1–13)
3 Almost everyone speaks English in Australia, but there are many ⬤ languages. (lines 14–22)
4 Do the local people have a positive ⬤ towards immigrants? (lines 23–31)
5 Compared to a big city like Sydney, towns in the bush are ⬤. (lines 32–45)
6 Both the bush and the city have their own ⬤ – wild animals on the one hand, fast moving vehicles on the other. (lines 32–45)
7 It is the ⬤ of the elders to pass on the tribe's traditional knowledge. (lines 46–53)
8 I used to have strong opinions, but experiencing other cultures has made me more ⬤. (lines 46–53)

●●○ **Go to File 37 on page 205.**

5 VIEWING

→ Videos, S. 213

Watch the video 'Australians celebrate ancient indigenous culture' and complete the tasks on page 213.

6 WRITING A SHORT STORY

EXAM
→ writing

Write a short story with the title 'Finding out where I belong', based on the photo below. Before writing, make notes on the following:

- Who is the main character?
- What is she doing in the photo?
- Where is she going, and why?
- What might she discover?

C RITES OF PASSAGE

1 PREPARING TO LISTEN: COMING OF AGE

A Pick the five most important qualities which, in your view, distinguish adults from adolescents.

emotional maturity ▪ independence ▪ physical strength ▪
responsible money management ▪ sense of responsibility ▪
taking your place in the community ▪ wisdom and understanding

B Now pick your five most significant 'coming of age' events and activities. Explain to your partner how they relate to the qualities in A.

babysit younger siblings for the first time ▪ celebrate a significant birthday ▪
finish school ▪ get a piercing or tattoo ▪ go on a first independent holiday ▪ open a bank
account ▪ pass your driving test / get your first car ▪ start a job / an apprenticeship ▪
undergo a religious or cultural ceremony ▪ vote for the first time in an election

C These photos show events mentioned by the speakers on the recording. How do they relate to 'coming of age'?

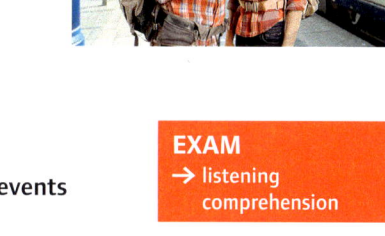

2 LISTENING: 'COMING OF AGE' EVENTS

34

Listen to the radio interview with three young adults about events which made them feel like they had become adults.

EXAM
→ listening comprehension

Then copy and fill in the table with notes from the interviews.

name	country	age	event
Aisling	▭	▭	▭
Ethan	▭	▭	▭
Beth	▭	▭	▭

3 LANGUAGE IN USE: CONDITIONAL SENTENCES TYPE 2

A Find examples of the conditional 2 in the text below. Write down the line numbers.

EXAMPLE: *If I **had** time, I **would see** the film.*

Amish Coming-of-Age Traditions:
RUMSPRINGA

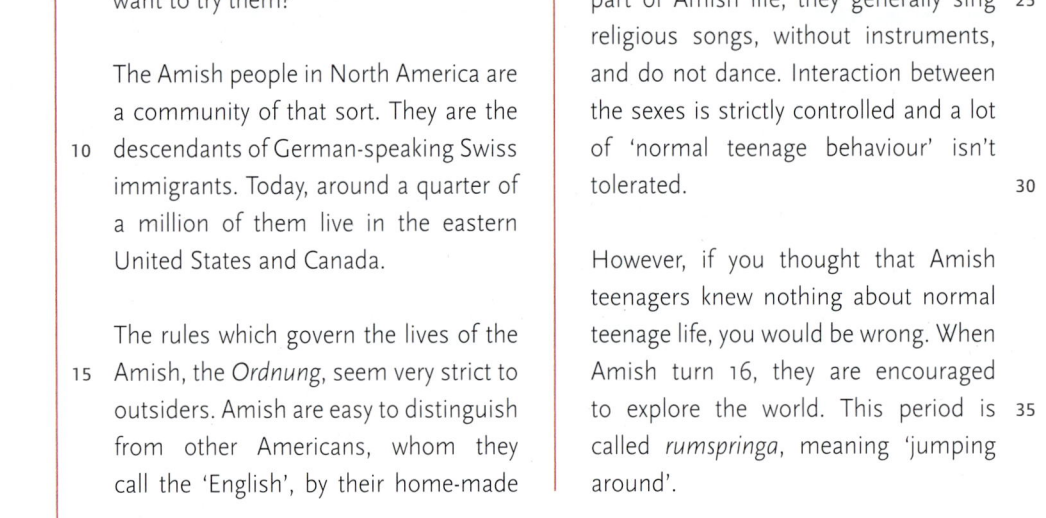

If you lived in a strict religious community without modern technology and consumerism, would you be curious about the outside world? If you lived in
5 a community where smoking, alcohol and dancing were banned, would you want to try them?

The Amish people in North America are a community of that sort. They are the
10 descendants of German-speaking Swiss immigrants. Today, around a quarter of a million of them live in the eastern United States and Canada.

The rules which govern the lives of the
15 Amish, the *Ordnung*, seem very strict to outsiders. Amish are easy to distinguish from other Americans, whom they call the 'English', by their home-made clothes, hairstyles and customs. Most Amish even avoid the use of cars, using 20 horse-drawn vehicles for transport instead. They mostly live from farming, using traditional methods. Although singing and social gatherings are a big part of Amish life, they generally sing 25 religious songs, without instruments, and do not dance. Interaction between the sexes is strictly controlled and a lot of 'normal teenage behaviour' isn't tolerated. 30

However, if you thought that Amish teenagers knew nothing about normal teenage life, you would be wrong. When Amish turn 16, they are encouraged to explore the world. This period is 35 called *rumspringa*, meaning 'jumping around'.

Rumspringa only ends when the individual decides to commit their life
40 to the church and the Amish community. If an Amish person decided not to do that, nobody would force them. However, they would lose their connection with their church and community. Only
45 around 20% decide to leave the Amish community completely after *rumspringa*.

Teenagers who are new to *rumspringa* are called 'simmies', meaning silly and inexperienced. Most want to lose
50 that label as soon as they can. Some interpret *rumspringa* more liberally than others, and participate in binge drinking, drug-taking and sexual relationships. They may live away from their com-
55 munities for a time, or just take weekends away. On the other hand,

most Amish teenagers stay at home and live much less adventurous lives during their *rumspringa* years.

(334 words)

●●● **B Complete the sentences using your own ideas.**

1 If we all lived like the Amish, maybe
2 If I were an Amish teenager doing *rumspringa*, I
3 Fewer young Amish would come back after *rumspringa* if
4 I would / wouldn't miss my mobile phone and social media if
5 If we couldn't dance or listen to music,
6 Maybe the Amish if their religious views were less strict.
7 If I had to live with the Amish for a year,
8 I wonder what young Amish would do if

●●○ **Go to File 38 on page 206.**

4 WRITING A STATEMENT

EXAM
→ writing

You read on the internet that a young politician has the following campaign policy: She wants the government to pay everyone between the ages of 18 and 20 to go wherever they want outside of Germany for six months, in order to find out more about themselves. Her slogan is 'Everybody needs space to become an adult'.

Write a statement in which you either support or oppose the idea.

You have started work in a large hotel in Munich. The housekeeping manager tells you that the hotel has a lot of international guests who are not familiar with German environmental practices and rules.

1 EDITING: CORRECTING SIGNS

The manager has asked you to check these signs before they are printed. Find the two mistakes in each sign and rewrite them correctly so that they can be printed and put up in the hotel.

Guests, please note! a

If you will remove the keycard from the holder by the door when you leave your room, the lights and the air conditioning will be turned off to save electricity. While you are in your room, please leaving the key in its holder to activate the power.

Thank you!
Hotel Manager

Toiletries b

To reduce rubbish, our soap, shampoo and moisturizer are in one dispenser each. We provide not toiletries in individual disposable containers. If you will like the brand, our hotel shop will be happy to sell you toiletries to take with you on your journey.

Mini-bar c

Please turn on the fridge if you will keep things cold. Please turning it off again at the end of your stay in order to save electricity.

Why isn't my towel clean? d

Towels are not wash every day. This helps us saving water and energy. If you require clean towels, please leave your wet towels on the floor and they will be replaced with clean ones.

Thank you!
Housekeeping

Dear Guest e

Welcome at the breakfast buffet. Please understand that jam and butter are being served in large bowls and not individual disposable containers. This is to avoid unnecessary packaging and rubbish.

Enjoy your meal!
Head Chef

2 LISTENING: GUEST COMPLAINTS AND QUESTIONS

35

Guests don't always read the signs in the hotel. Listen and match the complaints and questions to the signs in task 1.

3 DEALING WITH HOTEL GUESTS

An American guest calls the hotel reception and asks for help. You are the hotel receptionist. How would you say your part of the dialogue in English?

Das Telefon klingelt.

You: *1 Melden Sie sich mit „Reception" und Ihrem Namen.*

Guest: Hello, it's Brenda O'Brien here, room 311.

You: *2 Begrüßen Sie Frau O'Brien. Fragen Sie, wie Sie helfen können.*

Guest: We've just moved into our room and the lights and the air conditioning aren't working. Can you send someone to fix them, please?

You: *3 Fragen Sie, ob sie den Schlüssel in den Halter* (holder) *neben der Tür gesteckt hat.*

Guest: Next to the door? No, why?

You: *4 Erklären Sie ihr, dass der Schlüssel den Strom anschaltet, wenn er im Halter steckt. Das ist eine Stromsparmaßnahme.*

Guest: Oh, I see! Thanks for your help … Yes, the lights are working now.

You: *5 Fragen Sie, ob Sie ihr sonst noch behilflich sein können.*

Guest: No, thanks. Bye now!

You: *6 Verabschieden Sie sich und legen Sie auf.*

Frau O'Brien ruft nach kurzer Zeit nochmals an.

Guest: Hello, it's Brenda O'Brien again, room 311.

You: *7 Begrüßen Sie Frau O'Brien. Fragen Sie, wie Sie helfen können.*

Guest: I've just had a look in the bathroom and there aren't any bars of soap or little bottles of shampoo. Just a funny dispenser thing on the wall in the shower and another one next to the basin. Can you ask housekeeping to send up some proper soap and shampoo, please?

You: *8 Erklären Sie ihr, dass die Seifenspender ebenfalls eine Maßnahme zum Umweltschutz sind.*

Guest: Really? Well, that does seem strange. It's not what we're used to back home.

You: *9 Es tut Ihnen leid, aber das ist in deutschen Hotels normal. So werden Seife und Einwegflaschen gespart. Wenn Frau O'Brien möchte, kann sie sich extra Seife und Shampoo im Hotelladen kaufen.*

Guest: No, no. That won't be necessary, thanks. We'll manage.

You: *10 Fragen Sie, ob Sie noch etwas für sie tun können.*

Guest: Yes, perhaps you can explain something else for me. There's a notice here in the bathroom about towels not being washed every day. Does that mean that nobody will come in here to clean the bathroom until we leave? We're staying for three nights, that's too long to wait.

You: *11 Beruhigen Sie Frau O'Brien. Erklären Sie ihr, dass Hotelzimmer und Badezimmer jeden Tag gereinigt werden, die Handtücher aber nur gewechselt werden, wenn der Gast es wünscht. Im Hotel werden täglich Tausende von Handtüchern gewaschen, das verbraucht viel Strom und Wasser.*

Guest: I see. That sounds very sensible. Thank you so much for your help this afternoon.

You: *12 Gern geschehen* (You're welcome). *Wünschen Sie Frau O'Brien einen angenehmen Aufenthalt im Hotel.*

Guest: Thanks again. Goodbye!

1 MULTIPLE CHOICE: EXAM STRESS

Listen to a youth radio phone-in about leisure time and school work.

36

Listen to the recording and choose the best answer for each of the following questions.

1 What do we learn about Jack?
   a He has just finished school at the age of 17.
   b He is worried he might fail his A level exams.
   c He is 17 years old and has failed his A level exams.
   d He will be sitting his A level exams during this school year.

2 Which of the following does Jack say he will be doing this school year?
   a Listening to music.
   b Worrying more about school.
   c Studying much less than last year.
   d Doing fewer extracurricular activities.

3 What do we learn about Lucy?
   a She goes to school in Birmingham.
   b She did her A level exams last year.
   c She is studying at university in Birmingham.
   d She lives in Birmingham and failed her A levels.

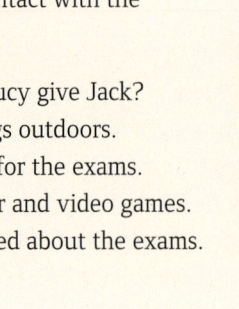

4 How did Lucy deal with the stress before the exams?
   a She did lots of sport.
   b She spent time hiking.
   c She studied harder than ever.
   d She broke off contact with the outside world.

5 What advice does Lucy give Jack?
   a To do more things outdoors.
   b To study harder for the exams.
   c To play computer and video games.
   d To not get stressed about the exams.

2 MULTIPLE MATCHING: YOUNG PEOPLE'S LEISURE TIME

Listen to a radio programme about a report on young people.

37

Decide which of the activities listed below have become more or less popular with young people over the last 10 years.

more popular	▬▬▬▬
less popular	▬▬▬▬

a Doing organized educational activities
b Hanging out with friends
c Going to a youth centre
d Doing voluntary work
e Taking part in organized sport

3 FILLING IN A FORM: PASSING ON A CLIENT'S CALL

You are doing an internship at an energy company. A customer has just left a message on the company's answerphone about a problem he has encountered.

38

Copy and fill in the online form for your colleague.

Customer call	
Caller's name	▬▬▬▬
Description of problem	▬▬▬▬
Caller's address	▬▬▬▬
Caller's telephone number	▬▬▬▬
Action wanted	▬▬▬

A Complete these sentences with a suitable modal auxiliary to replace the German verb.

1 Teenagers *dürfen nicht* buy cigarettes until they reach the age of 18.
2 Health experts say that we *müssen* improve our diet if we want to live longer.
3 Young people *sollten nicht* be allowed to get married until they are 21.
4 We *sollten* talk about cultural differences in order to understand each other better.
5 Indigenous people *können nicht* learn about their culture unless the government supports the community.
6 Nowadays indigenous people *müssen nicht* move to the big cities to earn a living.
7 The elders of the community *könnten* offer language courses to people who never learned the tribal language.
8 Youngsters *sollten* be prepared to move back to their tribal lands to preserve the old way of life.
9 Indigenous people *sollten nicht* rely on the government to solve all their problems.

B Mattie is shocked by how people in Melbourne treat the environment. She is writing down actions that people *could, should, should not* or *must not* take.

EXAMPLE: drop rubbish in the street – *We must not drop rubbish in the street.*

1 use public transport more often
2 stop buying disposable goods
3 waste valuable natural resources
4 use disposable plastic bags
5 have shorter showers to save water
6 leave the lights on when leaving a room
7 replace old appliances with energy-efficient new ones
8 throw away recyclable materials
9 throw plastic in the paper recycling bin
10 turn up the heating instead of putting on warmer clothes

C Rewrite the sentences using the phrases on the right. Change the tense and use substitutes for the modal auxiliaries if necessary.

EXAMPLE: We must find ways to live in harmony with nature. *In the future,* ●
In the future, we will have to find ways to live in harmony with nature.

1 Australians needn't worry about respecting other cultures. *In the 19th century,* ●
2 The government can ignore the demands of indigenous people. *Until now,* ●
3 We can learn Yorta Yorta in our school. *In the last two years,* ●
4 Youngsters must find ways to live successfully between two cultures. *In the future,* ●
5 Volunteers can record the memories of the elders. *Last year,* ●
6 We can't eat kangaroos because they are an endangered species. *In 50 years' time,* ●
7 Schools must teach indigenous languages. *Soon* ●
8 We can see the decline of indigenous culture. *Fifty years ago,* ●
9 We can't prevent the situation from getting worse. *Since then* ●
10 People cannot understand our attitude to the original inhabitants of the country.
Future generations ●

A place for everyone

A WARM-UP: DIFFERENCES AND SIMILARITIES

A Why do people form negative opinions about people they don't know? Make a sentence to go with each photo.

There are many people who

- are intolerant of
- are scared/afraid of
- are suspicious of
- don't like
- don't understand
- don't feel comfortable with
- won't have anything to do with

- alternative lifestyles.
- different attitudes to sex.
- different religious beliefs.
- other races/cultures.
- people who haven't succeeded in life.
- people who dress differently.
- people who just look different.
- people with disabilities.
- younger/older generations.

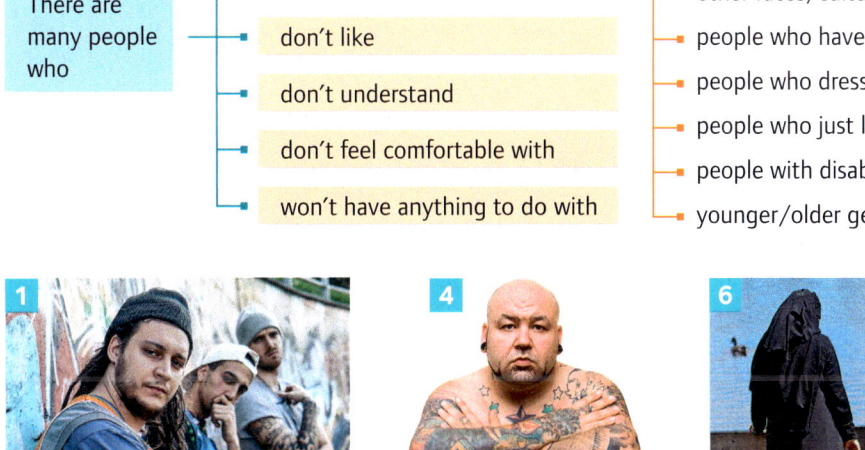

DIFFERENT

B Half the class writes their name on a piece of paper and puts it in the box. The other half draws a name from the box. Sit with the person whose name you have drawn and find five things that you share.

- a fear
- a favourite food or drink
- an ambition
- a place you have been
- a TV show

You have three minutes to complete the task. Report back to the class with what you found out.

B

BLACK LIVES MATTER

SITUATION: You love to travel. You are staying with some friends in a US city. One day an African-American man is shot by the police. Your friends say this is not the first time this has happened. You decide to research about the Black Lives Matter movement, so that you can write a blog entry about the events (task 6, page 149).

1 PREPARING TO READ

Work with a partner.
Look at the images. What do you think happened?
Why do you think it happened?

EXAMPLE:

I'm sure that the police …

#BlackLivesMatter

In the 1950s and 60s, the grandparents of today's US black youths took to the streets to campaign for their civil rights, ending a century of open and legal segregation and discrimination aimed at African Americans, particularly in the southern states of the USA.

For outside observers, it's easy to imagine that this issue has been resolved and that African Americans now have equality. In theory, they have the same legal and demo-cratic rights as the white majority in the USA. After all, in 2009 the USA elected its first African-American president, Barack Obama (2009–2017) and there are many black people in positions of power and responsibility today.

However, statistics show that African Americans as a group still suffer from social and economic disadvantages, and there is also evidence that they are often treated differently by US law enforcement. These days, almost everyone carries a smartphone, and police officers usually wear body cameras on patrol.

As a result, there is often video footage available when the police interact with the public. While a low-quality smartphone video can never tell the whole story, it can provide evidence when these interactions go wrong.

The story that many such videos tell about the treatment of ethnic minority citizens is worrying. All too often, routine police checks, which should have been non-violent, have had fatal outcomes for unarmed civilians. Young black men are particularly at risk.

One particular incident, the shooting of Michael Brown in St. Louis, Missouri, brought a new social justice initiative – Black Lives Matter – to the forefront. Overnight Black Lives Matter turned from being a small movement with an obscure Twitter hashtag to a national and then global movement. Black Lives Matter is a campaign against systemic racism towards black people. It seeks justice for victims of police violence and puts pressure on the government to protect black citizens.

9 August 2014, Ferguson, St Louis, Missouri

Michael Brown, 18, had just graduated from high school and was due to start a business course at college. 'This is a boy who did everything right,' said Cornell Brooks, the president of the National Association for the Advancement of Colored People, 'who never got into a fight, who stayed in school.' His friends describe him as a 'gentle giant' who had no interest in gangs or criminal activity.

On a hot Saturday afternoon, Brown was walking, unarmed, from a convenience store to his grand-mother's apartment in Ferguson, a working-class suburb of St Louis. A police officer encountered Brown and his friend Dorian Johnson while responding to a call about two young men who had just robbed a nearby liquor store. Within minutes, big Mike Brown was shot dead.

The police department later claimed that Brown attacked the police officer and attempted to take his gun. Yet this was denied by Johnson and another eyewitness. They say that Brown answered back when the police officer told the young men to walk on the sidewalk, not the road. Brown's friends say that he was running away with his hands in the air when the police officer opened fire. There was no connection to the liquor store robbery.

The young man's body was left on the hot asphalt for four-and-a-half hours while angry crowds gathered, demanding to know why he had been killed. The police then removed his body without explanation. Protests and riots followed. Perhaps Mike Brown made some poor choices, but what about Eric Garner, John Crawford, Tamir Rice, Walter Scott, Freddie Gray, Sandra Bland, Stephon Clark, Charlie Kinsey and many others? All black, all unarmed, all killed or injured by police. Was that just bad luck – being in the wrong place, at the wrong time – or is there a systemic problem in the police force?

626 words

2 READING AND UNDERSTANDING THE TEXT

EXAM
→ reading comprehension

Decide whether the following statements are true or false.

1 Before the civil rights movement, African Americans had the same rights as white Americans.
2 African Americans are still poorer than other ethnic groups.
3 US police officers are not allowed to video their interactions with the public.
4 The slogan Black Lives Matter did not exist before the death of Michael Brown.
5 Michael Brown had dropped out of school shortly before he died.
6 Brown and Johnson had robbed a liquor store before police stopped them.
7 The police and eyewitnesses gave totally different accounts of what happened.
8 Police immediately gave a public statement about the incident.

3 WORKING WITH WORDS

••• **A** **Fill in the gaps with words from the main part of the text (lines 1–44). Use only one word for each gap. Give the number of the line in which you found the word.**

A: When was the civil ▬¹ movement in the USA?

B: It was a movement that took place during the 1950s and 1960s. Before World War Two, racial ▬² had kept the better jobs for white people. Suddenly in 1941, African Americans were needed to fill many positions in industry which white Americans left when they left to fight in the war. African Americans soon had more ▬³ power and were able to use it to get better social ▬⁴.

A: I've heard about a woman called Rosa Parks. Who was she?

B: She was a black woman who refused to give up her seat on a bus in Alabama to a white man in 1955. Her action became the focus for the fight for racial ▬⁵. Until this point, ▬⁶ of white and black citizens on public transport and in many other areas of life was normal and legal.

A: What did the activists do? Did they attack police or white businesses? Did they start riots?

B: No, the movement was ▬⁷, although controversial figures such as Malcolm X wanted a more aggressive approach. But mostly the leaders of the movement ▬⁸ peacefully for change.

A: What happened to Malcolm X? Wasn't he killed?

B: That's right, like Martin Luther King Jr, he was the victim of a political ▬⁹.

A: Didn't that mean that the white racists had won by using ▬¹⁰?

B: Not at all. The deaths of Malcolm X in 1965 and Martin Luther King Jr. three years later created a lot of public sympathy for the movement and put ▬¹¹ on the government to change the law.

••○ **Go to File 39 on page 206.**

B **Explain the following words in complete sentences.**

EXAM
→ use of language

a unarmed (line 56) **c** riots (line 77)
b witness (line 66) **d** systemic (line 84)

4 **SPEAKING: NEWS REPORT**

You are a news reporter at the scene of Michael Brown's killing (page 147). Before you give your live report, choose your point of view:

A You are a citizen journalist with an online news network that supports Black Lives Matter.
B You are a journalist at an international news organization. You must give a neutral report.
C You are a reporter for a local news network that strongly supports the police.

Give a one-minute report from the scene of the incident.

Think carefully about how you describe the person who was shot: 'a victim', 'a suspect', 'an apparently unarmed man', etc. You can use speculation: 'It seems that …', 'The officer may have believed …', etc.

The class listens and decides whether you are reporter A, B or C.

5 **DISCUSSION**

Discuss these questions in small groups. Note down the main points of your discussion. When you have finished, report back to the class.

- If you were visiting the USA and a police officer stopped you in the street, how would you feel? Why?
- If you were a US police officer, how might you feel when you see a suspect? Why?
- What can be done to reduce tension between police officers and the US public?
- Do you think that police in your country treat people of different ethnic backgrounds differently? What evidence do you have?

6 **WRITING A BLOG ENTRY**

EXAM
→ writing

You write a blog about your travels.

You are in a US city. One day an African-American man is shot by the police. Some of your friends decide to protest and you go with them.

Write a blog entry for the day, describing what you heard about the shooting, what you did with your friends and what you saw on the protest. Say how you think things should change.

Write about 160 words.

C WE ALL GET ALONG

1 PREPARING TO LISTEN

Nagesh, Ryan, Hassan and Ji-hoon share a flat in Wandsworth, south London. They come from different cultures and religious backgrounds, so the flatshare has its challenges. What problems might arise when people of different backgrounds share a flat?

2 LISTENING: A MULTICULTURAL FLATSHARE

EXAM
→ listening comprehension

A Listen to the interview with Nagesh, Ryan, Hassan and Ji-hoon. Copy the table below and make notes about the four men.

name	country	religion	eating habits
Nagesh	▬▬	▬▬	▬▬
Ryan	▬▬	▬▬	▬▬
Hassan	▬▬	▬▬	▬▬
Ji-hoon	▬▬	▬▬	▬▬

B Answer the questions below with short answers in English.

1 How do the flatmates deal with the issues surrounding the following food?
a Ryan's English breakfast
b meat
c food that has a strong smell

2 Which three things do the flatmates like doing together?

3 PLACEMAT ACTIVITY

Work in a group of three or four around a large sheet of paper.

1 **Preparation.** In the centre of the paper, write 'kitchen', 'living room', 'bathroom' and 'bedrooms'. In your corner of the piece of paper write one rule for each room. It should be a rule that you think is important.

2 **Discussion.** Share your ideas about the rules. Discuss any differences of opinion. Try to reach agreement on three rules for each room. Write them in the centre of the paper.

3 **Review.** Walk around the room and discuss the rules drawn up by the other 'flatshares'.

4 LANGUAGE IN USE: REPORTED QUESTIONS

→ Reported questions, S. 274

A **Look at this example of a reported question from the interview.**

EXAMPLE: Dad always asks me when I'm going to cook him another curry.

His father's question to Ryan was: 'When are you going to cook me another curry?'

Write these questions as reported questions. The first one is done for you.

1 Ryan asked Ji-Hoon: 'Do you want to meet me for breakfast on your way back from church?'
Ryan asked Ji-Hoon if he wanted to meet him for breakfast on his way back from church.
2 The reporter asked the flatmates: 'What's the best thing about your flatshare?'
3 Ryan and Nagesh asked Hassan: 'Do you want to come for a run?'
4 Ji-hoon asked Nagesh: 'Did you use my pan to cook curry in?'
5 The reporter asked the flatmates: 'Has living in a multicultural flat changed your attitudes?'
6 Ryan's father asked him: 'When are we going to meet your flatmates?'
7 Ryan's girlfriend asked him: 'Can I move in with you?'

B **Work with a partner.**

Partner A: You are the interviewer from Channel Z. Think of four questions to ask B.
Note them down.
Partner B: You are a new flatmate in the flatshare in Wandsworth. Answer A's questions.
Note down your answers.

When you have finished, report back to the class using reported speech.

> **A**
> I asked B whether he enjoyed living in a shared flat. He said that …

> **B**
> Then A asked me why I … .
> I said that …

5 DESCRIBING A CARTOON

●●● **Describe the cartoon on the right.**

- What can you see?
- What is happening?
- What is the cartoon's message?

●●○ **Go to File 40 on page 207.**

You have started work as a fundraiser for an international refugee charity, **Refugees in Crisis,** which has a small office in Mainz. As it is your first week, you are shadowing an experienced employee, Tobias Werner.

1 LISTENING: TAKING A CALL

Employees take it in turns to do phone duty when the receptionist is on a break. Today it is Tobias Werner's turn.

A Listen to the telephone call. What does the caller want? Copy and fill in the form, using today's date and the present time.

A messsage for you!		EXAM → listening comprehension
Call for:	▬▬	
Caller's name:	▬▬	
Caller's company:	▬▬	
Caller's telephone number:	▬▬	
Message:	▬▬	
Taken by:	▬▬	
Date:	▬	Time: ▬

B Listen again. Which do you hear: a or b?

1 a This is Tobias Werner. How may I help you today?
  b Tobias Werner speaking. What can I do for you?

2 a I'd like to speak to …, please.
  b Please can you put me through to …?

3 a Can I ask who's calling?
  b Who's speaking, please?

4 a It's … from …
  b My name's …. I work at …

5 a I'll connect you straight away. Please wait a moment.
  b I'll put you through. Please hold the line.

6 a I'm afraid there's no answer.
  b I'm sorry, she isn't answering her phone.

7 a Would you like to leave a message?
  b Can I take a message?

8 a Yes, please. Can you let her know that …?
  b Yes, I would. Please tell her that …

9 a Yes, of course, I'll tell her that. Would you mind spelling your surname for me, please?
  b OK, I'll pass that on. Could you spell your surname for me, please?

10 a And what's your phone number, please?
   b May I have your phone number, please?

11 a Let me just repeat that.
   b Can I read that back to you?

12 a That's correct. Thanks for your help.
   b That's right. Thanks very much.

13 a You're welcome. Is there anything else I can do for you?
   b Don't mention it. Can I help you with anything else?

14 a No, that's all, thanks. Bye.
   b No, that's it. Thanks again. Goodbye.

2 ROLE-PLAY: A BUSINESS PHONE CALL

Tobias asks you to take over phone duty for a few minutes. Work with a partner. Use the diagram to role-play a conversation. You will find the expressions you need in task 1B. When you have finished, change roles and play the dialogue again.

Angestellte/r	Anrufer/in
→ Sie melden sich auf Deutsch mit Ihrem Namen und der Abteilung „Spendenaktionen".	→ Sie fragen auf Englisch, ob er/sie Englisch spricht.
→ Sie bejahen die Frage und fragen, wie Sie helfen können.	→ Sie stellen sich und Ihre Organisation vor (*Newark Associated Press*). Es geht um den Marathonlauf in Frankfurt im Oktober.
→ Er/Sie sollte besser mit Ihrer Kollegin Frau Bauer sprechen, da dies ihr Zuständigkeits-bereich (*area of responsibility*) ist.	→ Sie sind damit einverstanden. Kann er/sie Sie mit Frau Bauer verbinden?
→ Sie können es gern versuchen, aber Sie glauben, dass Frau Bauer momentan nicht im Büro ist. Sie werden es trotzdem versuchen.	→ Sie bedanken sich.
→ Sie haben den Namen des Anrufers / der Anruferin leider nicht behalten.	→ Wiederholen Sie Ihren Namen.
→ Frau Bauer geht nicht ans Telefon. Sie fragen, ob der Anrufer / die Anruferin eine Nachricht hinterlassen möchte.	→ Sie hätten gern eine englische Pressemappe (*press kit*) für den Marathon. Sie würden auch gern ein Skype-Interview vereinbaren.
→ Sie versprechen, die Nachricht weiterzulei-ten, und bitten den Anrufer / die Anruferin, seinen / ihren Namen zu buchstabieren.	→ Sie buchstabieren Ihren Namen.
→ Sie bedanken sich und bitten um die Telefonnnummer.	→ 1 für die Vereinigten Staaten, dann 999-406-9150-66. Das ist die Durchwahl (*direct line*).
→ Sie wiederholen die Nummer.	→ Sie bestätigen, dass die Nummer richtig ist (oder korrigieren sie). Sie bedanken sich.
→ Sie reagieren höflich auf den Dank und fra-gen, ob Sie sonst noch behilflich sein können.	→ Sie verneinen und verabschieden sich.
→ Sie verabschieden sich.	

REMEMBER ❗ **telephone numbers**

In English, telephone numbers are read as single digits (except when the same numbers are next to each other): 1234 = 'one two three four' not ~~'twelve thirty-four'~~

44 = double four   444 = triple four

1 WRITING AN EMAIL

Your Australian friend Anna has written you an email. Write an email back to her, in which you answer her questions. Write about 160 words.

Hi!

I'm really looking forward to coming to Germany this summer!
As you know, I'm coming in July. What's the weather like then? Do I need warm clothes, or are shorts and T-shirts enough. Is it likely to rain much?
What is there to do and see in your area? I'm interested in films and music. I'm not very sporty, as you've probably worked out from my emails.
What's the best way to travel if I want to see other parts of Germany, like Berlin for example?
Sorry about all the questions! Please write back soon.

All the best
Anna

2 WRITING A COMMENT

Write a comment in English on the following quote in about 100 words.

> **Education is the most powerful weapon which you can use to change the world.** (Nelson Mandela)

3 WRITING A STATEMENT

Write a statement in English in which you give your opinion on the following phrase. Write about 100 words.

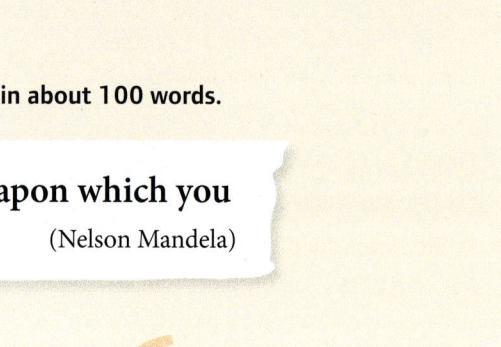

The Customer is King.

4 WRITING A RECOMMENDATION

Your class wants to do something or go somewhere to celebrate the end of the school year. Recommend something or somewhere that you think all of you would like to do or go. Give details and explain why you recommend it. Write about 100 words.

5 WRITING A BLOG ENTRY

You write the blog for your school website. You decide to write an entry for new students who will be starting in the next school year. Give them tips and advice about the school and places near the school that might be interesting for new students. Write 160 words.

6 WRITING A STORY

Finish one of the following stories. Write about 160 words.

I had always wanted to see America. Last summer, my dream finally came true. Unfortunately, our trip didn't get off to a smooth start.

UNITED STATES of AMERICA

It was a cold January afternoon. Jack hurried home from football practice. He was just about to cross the street when he saw a well-dressed, elderly man, who shouted to him, `Help! Something terrible has happened.´

7 WRITING A STORY

Choose one of the two photos below and write a story about it. Write about 160 words.

8 WRITING A NEWSPAPER ARTICLE

Write a newspaper article of about 160 words based on one of the photos in task 7.

A Make the active sentences passive. Use *by* only where you are instructed to do so.

EXAMPLES:

Refugees in Crisis funds the marathon. (by)   *The marathon is funded by Refugees in Crisis.*

They held protests in many cities.   *Protests were held in many cities.*

Simple present

1   We post information packs to the runners a month before the event.
2   We give each competitor a number.
3   They pin the number on their vest before the race.
4   Race officials check the name and number of each runner at registration. (by)
5   We separate the runners into different groups according to their age, sex and ability.

Simple past

6   They didn't inform the police about the protest.
7   The police shot and killed Michael Brown in broad daylight. (by)
8   The family of Michael Brown denied the police's version of events. (by)
9   The police told the young men to stay on the sidewalk. (by)
10   Other people described him as a gentle giant.

Present perfect

11   They have tidied the kitchen.
12   Hassan has asked Ryan not to cook bacon in the flat. (by)
13   Ryan's experience has changed his ideas about different cultures. (by)
14   Channel Z has interviewed the flatmates on several occasions. (by)
15   They haven't washed the dishes yet.

Will-future

16   Our Mainz office will organize the marathon again this year. (by)
17   We will send out press kits in July.
18   We will add more information to our website at a later date.
19   Our volunteers will process your registration forms. (by)
20   We won't pass on your contact details to marketing companies.

B Translate the sentences into English. Think carefully about which tense to use.

1   Michael Brown wurde von einem Polizisten erschossen.
2   Wurde der Polizist von Brown angegriffen?
3   Das Geschäft war nicht von den Jungen ausgeraubt worden.
4   Der Fall Michael Brown wird oft im Zusammenhang mit Black Lives Matter erwähnt.
     (in the context of)
5   Wenig ist seitdem gegen Polizeigewalt unternommen worden.
6   Unbewaffnete Zivilisten werden weiterhin von Polizisten getötet.
7   Wird das Diskriminierungsproblem jemals gelöst werden? (the issue of)
8   In jedem Fall muss eine bessere Lösung gefunden werden.

Communicating around the globe

A   WARM-UP: ENGLISH AROUND THE WORLD

How much do you know about the English language around the world? Do the quiz to find out.

1   What percentage of web pages are in English? (1 point)
    a   More than 90%   **b**   About 60%   **c**   About 50%   **d**   Less than 40%

2   How many countries have English as an official language? (1 point)
    a   5   **b**   17   **c**   56   **d**   127

3   Which country has the largest number of English native speakers? (1 point)
    a   India   **b**   England   **c**   China   **d**   the USA

4   Of which of the following is English the official language? (4 points)
    a   international aviation   **c**   Universal Postal Union
    b   international diplomacy   **d**   international trade

5   Which of the following organizations has English as its only official language?
    a   Asean   **e**   OPEC
    b   Commonwealth of Nations   **f**   United Nations
    c   European Union   **g**   World Bank
    d   FIFA

7   Name the countries. (4 points)
    a   English is just one of 23 official languages in this country. Over a billion people live here.
    b   This country hosts the most websites in the world.
    c   This country has 11 official languages, including English and Afrikaans.
    d   This is the second largest country in the world. It has two official languages: English and French.

8   Match the names of the countries to their shapes. (4 points)

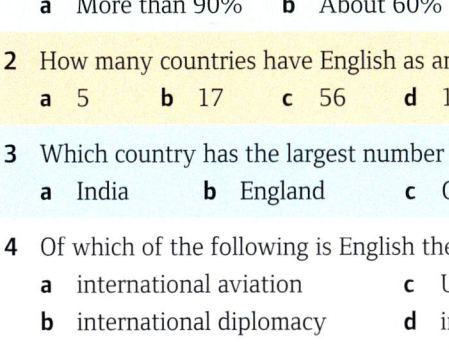
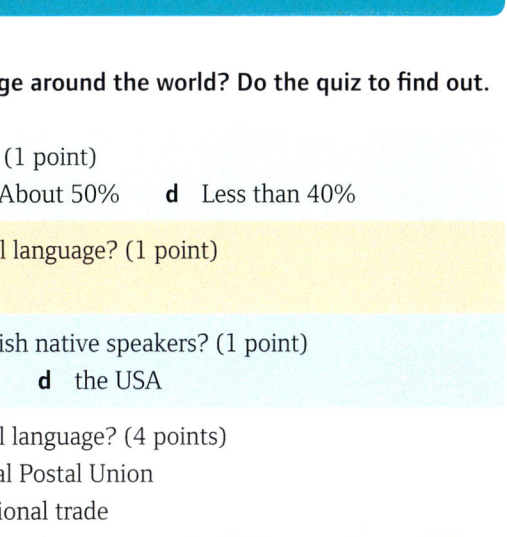
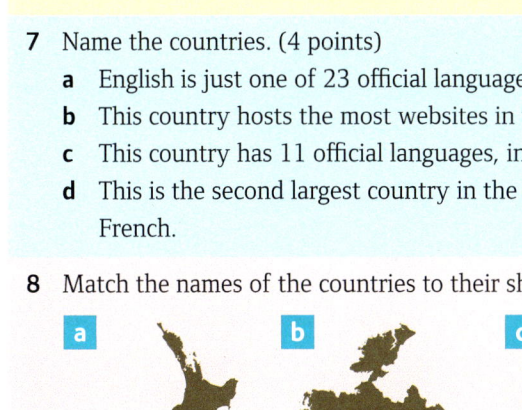
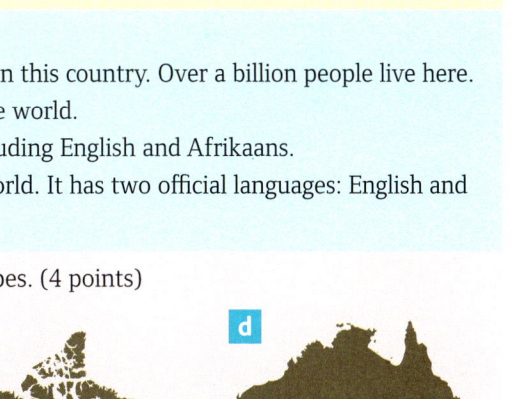

Australia ▪ Canada ▪ India ▪ Republic of Ireland ▪ Jamaica ▪
New Zealand ▪ the USA ▪ Wales

B WHY LEARN ENGLISH?

SITUATION: Your school is holding an open day (*Tag der offenen Tür*) and you have decided to produce a poster explaining why it is important to learn English (task 5, page 161).

1 PREPARING TO READ

A Brainstorm in a group. How many situations can you think of where English is useful? Note down your ideas. (They will be useful for your poster.)

> A tourist stops you in the street and asks you for directions.

B Look at the photos. How do you think these people use English in their daily lives?

> You want to understand the lyrics of your favourite song.

C Match the photos to the interviewees in the article on the opposite page.

> **REMEMBER** !
>
> interviewer – interviewee
> employer – employee

2 READING AND UNDERSTANDING THE TEXT

A Match the statements below with the people in the article. There are two statements that do not match.

> **EXAM**
> → reading comprehension

1 This person needs English for travel. L
2 This person uses English for his/her education. /
3 This person uses English in his/her work and for socializing. E
4 This person speaks English at home. /
5 This person needs English for communicating with colleagues and customers. A
6 This person uses English for his/her hobby. ⌐

42

ENGLISH –
the World Language

This month we profile non-native English speakers from different parts of the world. What do they see as the benefits of speaking English?

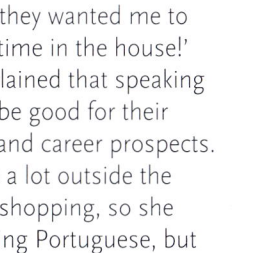

5 **Janek** is an online gamer from Estonia. His great passion is role-playing games (RPGs). The popular stereotype of a gamer is a social misfit who lives alone in a fantasy world. Janek disagrees: 'Non-gamers say 10 that we're unsociable, but that's totally wrong. We spend a lot of our time online discussing strategy, telling stories and swapping tips. It's a social hobby.'
The RPG community is global and gamers 15 need to collaborate with the people in their team (called a 'clan' or 'guild'), so they need a common language. Janek's clan communicates in English. 'We use a lot of game slang and code words,' explains Janek, 20 'but we still need good English to work well together.'

Adeela lives in Bangalore, an important centre for IT. Like most Indians she's multi-lingual: Adeela speaks Tulu at home, 25 Kannada around town and English at work. She can also read Hindi. When she was at school, Adeela showed an aptitude for computer languages and told her teacher that she wanted to work in IT. 'Keep up your 30 English, then!' replied Mrs Sharma. Adeela followed her teacher's good advice and now she works as a software engineer. In her company there are colleagues with several different native languages. This isn't 35 unusual, as there are 23 official languages and over 120 major languages in India. 'English is our company language because it's the only language all of us speak well, even though most of us aren't native 40 speakers,' explains Adeela. 'As a world language, English is also essential for dealing with our customers around the world.'

Luuk is from the Netherlands. For the last three years he's been travelling the world. He's lived in Morocco, Brazil, 45 Mexico, Vietnam and at the moment he's in Malaysia. He doesn't have a lot of savings, so he's working his way around the world. He does casual jobs on building sites and farms, but he says that his best 50 job was as a waiter at a beach bar in Rio de Janeiro.
Luuk would like to speak the local language of every place he visits. Unfortunately, that isn't realistic if you travel a lot. That's why 55 English is so useful for nomads. 'You can always find someone who speaks English,' he explains.

Like almost all Swedes, **Elsa** learned English at school. 'You hear so much English 60 in Sweden, it hardly feels like a foreign language,' she says. After Elsa finished school, she wanted to learn something more exotic, so she spent a summer learning basic Portuguese, in preparation for a job as 65 an au pair in Lisbon.
'And guess what? As soon as I started here, the parents said that they wanted me to speak English all the time in the house!' laughs Elsa. They explained that speaking 70 fluent English would be good for their children's education and career prospects. Elsa uses Portuguese a lot outside the home, for things like shopping, so she feels confident speaking Portuguese, but 75 when she meets up with other au pairs – from Denmark, France, Austria and Poland – English is the language they have in common. 'So we speak English, of course!'

(539 words)

B Answer the questions in complete sentences using the information from the text.

EXAM
→ reading comprehension

1 Why are gamers not antisocial, according to Janek?
2 Where does Adeela use the languages she speaks?
3 What sort of jobs does Luuk find while travelling?
4 Why is Elsa not quite happy with the situation she finds herself in?

C Beantworten Sie die folgende Frage auf Deutsch.

EXAM
→ reading comprehension

Warum sprechen Menschen in unterschiedlichen Teilen der Welt Englisch? Nennen Sie stichwortartig vier Gründe, die im Text angegeben werden.

3 WORKING WITH WORDS

A How many phrases using 'language' can you find in the text?

1 Make a list. Write the German translation next to each phrase.

   EXAMPLE: *common language (l. 17): gemeinsame Sprache*

2 Write down one sentence for each phrase.
3 Compare sentences with a partner, then read out your best sentences to the class.

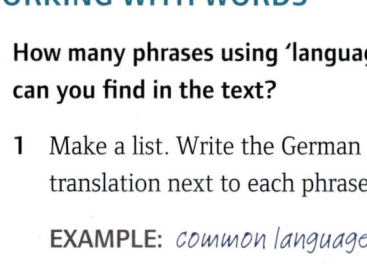

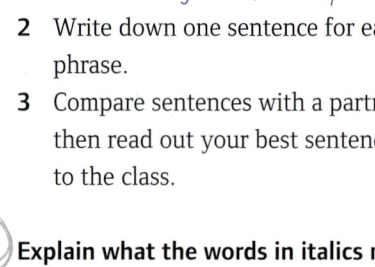
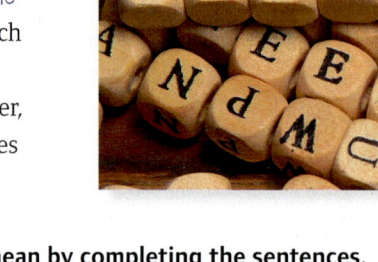

B Explain what the words in italics mean by completing the sentences.

EXAM
→ use of language

1 If a language is *global* (line 14), it means that …
2 A person who is *multilingual* (line 23) is …
3 If you are a *native speaker* (line 39) of German, it means …
4 *Essential* (line 41) is a word used to describe …
5 You can say you are *fluent* (line 71) in English if …
6 *Confident* (line 75) is a word used to describe people who …

C Find words in the section about Janek (lines 5–21) which mean more or less the same as the following words.

EXAM
→ use of language

a completely   b to exchange

D Find the opposites of the following words from the text.

a well (line 38)   b basic (line 65)

4 LANGUAGE IN USE: REPORTED SPEECH

→ Reported speech, S. 274

A **Find examples of reported speech in the text. Write what the people said in direct speech.**

EXAMPLE: *Non-gamers say that we're unsociable.*

B **Report what these people said. Remember to change the pronouns if necessary. The first one has been done for you.**

1 Janek: 'I find it easy to talk about games in English.'
Janek said that he found it easy to talk about games in English.
2 Janek's friends: 'His English has improved very quickly.'
3 Adeela: 'I still make some mistakes in English.'
4 Mrs Sharma: 'Adeela was one of my best students.'
5 Luuk: 'I'm embarrassed by my strong Dutch accent in English.'
6 An American tourist: 'Luuk's Dutch accent is cute!'
7 Elsa: 'I want to practise Portuguese more.'
8 Elsa's employers: 'We'll give you time off to take Portuguese lessons.'

C **Think. Note down your own answers to these questions.**

1 When did you start learning English?
2 What have you enjoyed most about English so far?
3 What do you find most difficult about English?
4 How will you use English in your life?

Pair: Tell your partner your answers and listen to theirs. Make notes on what they said.

Share: Tell the rest of the class the most interesting thing your partner told you. Remember to use reported speech.

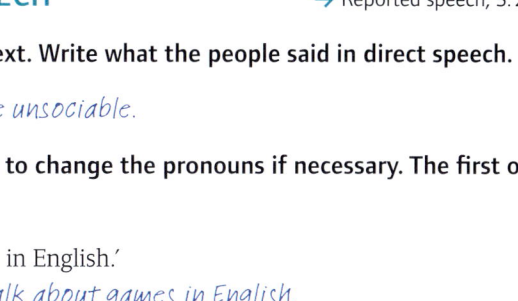
Sven said that he wanted to work in the USA.

5 MAKING A POSTER

Make a poster (one page DIN-A4) for your school's open day to explain to new students why English is important.

1 Draw a mind map to organize your thoughts. You might want to include the following points:
- importance of English as a world language
- training and higher education
- leisure interests (e.g. reading, music, gaming)
- travel

●●● 2 Write a short text. It could be in the form of questions to the reader, or statements, or (invented) quotations from people who have learned English as a foreign language.

●●○ **Go to File 41 on page 207.**

3 Think about pictures to emphasize your message.
4 Give your poster a design that will catch the reader's attention.
5 When you have finished, pin up your poster in the classroom and do a gallery walk.

C INTERCULTURAL (MIS)UNDERSTANDINGS

1 PREPARING TO LISTEN

You are going to listen to a podcast interview with an expert in intercultural communication, Professor Marcus Jones. Before you listen, discuss with a partner and make notes:

- What matters when we communicate, other than choosing the right words?
- How might people from other cultures 'get the wrong idea' when we speak to them?

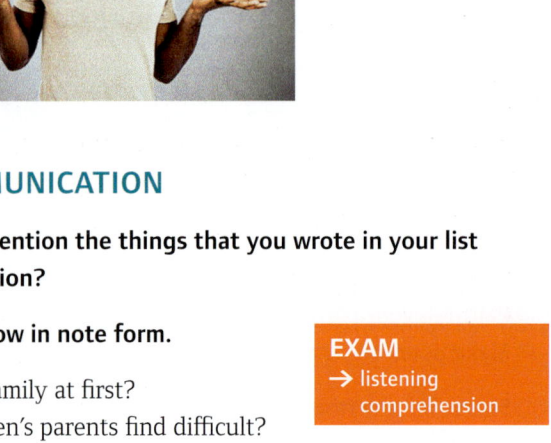

2 LISTENING: INTERCULTURAL COMMUNICATION

43

A **Listen to the recording. Do the speakers mention the things that you wrote in your list in task 1? What other things do they mention?**

B **Listen again and answer the questions below in note form.**

1 How is Emma's relationship with Ben's family at first?
2 What aspects of Emma's behaviour do Ben's parents find difficult?
3 What does Emma do when Ben tells her about her parents' reaction?

EXAM
→ listening comprehension

C **Copy and complete the grid with information from the recording.**

EXAM
→ listening comprehension

	Germany	Australia
General culture	*formal and respectful*	⬭
Authority and age	⬭	⬭
Time	⬭	⬭
Social greetings	⬭	⬭

3 COMMUNICATION

EXAM
→ Kommunikations-prüfung

A new student from India has joined your class. Your teacher asks you to make a list of things which you think foreigners living in Germany should know about the country. With your partner discuss which two things you should put on the list. The photos in File 4 on page 210 may help you come up with ideas.

4 CASE STUDIES: WHAT WENT WRONG

**Read the case studies (1–3), then find the most likely explanation for each one (a–d)
and a way to avoid the problem (i–iv).**

1 Lena from Stuttgart is friends online with Alice from New-
castle upon Tyne, England. Alice posts a video on social
media of herself singing an original song and playing guitar.
Lena doesn't 'like' the post. Instead she responds to Alice
with some suggestions for improving her singing and recom-
mends having some guitar lessons. Alice doesn't respond,
but later 'unfriends' Lena. Lena is confused and hurt.

2 Paul and Lukas from Karlsruhe are on holiday in Morocco.
They have booked a stay with a Moroccan family, Omar and
Zineb and their three teenage children, through a home-
sharing app. Omar is very welcoming and the house is lovely.
However, when Paul tries to shake hands with Zineb and her
daughters, they appear embarrassed. Is it because they don't
like Germans, the boys wonder, or are they just shy?

3 Sophie and David from Tübingen are staying in Madrid. It is
their first time in Spain. They meet a young Spanish couple,
Laura and Dani, while they are out sightseeing. Laura and
Dani invite them to a party that evening at 8 o'clock.
The Germans turn up at 8 p.m., but nobody is home!
Laura eventually responds to Sophie's text message, saying
that she and Dani will be home 'about 9' and the party will
start 'a bit later'. The Germans are annoyed and decide to
go to a bar instead.

Explanation
a Some cultures place more importance on small talk than others.
b Different cultures have different ideas of punctuality.
c In certain cultures physical contact between men and women is not acceptable.
d In some cultures, direct criticism is considered aggressive and hurtful.

Alternative approaches
i Start by saying something positive if you're going to criticize someone's creative efforts.
ii If they had researched the local culture beforehand, they would have known how to behave.
iii If the locals had explained the situation, the visitors wouldn't have been confused.
iv It's important to become part of the local culture when you are on holiday.

5 LANGUAGE IN USE: CONDITIONAL SENTENCES TYPE 3

A Find examples of conditional sentences type 3 in task 3 above.

B Complete the sentences using the key words.

> **REMEMBER**
>
> | past perfect | would have + Partizip Perfekt |
> |---|---|
> | If she **had taken** a taxi, | she **wouldn't have missed** the plane. |
>
> If she ~~would~~ …

1 If you had read a travel guide, 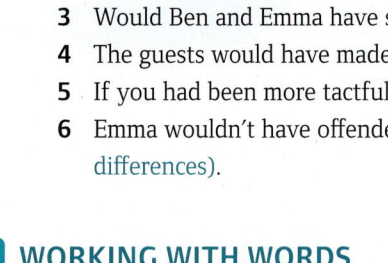 (you – know – what to expect).

2 The host would have been happier if 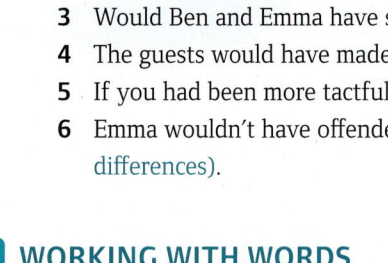 (the guests – take off – their shoes).

3 Would Ben and Emma have stayed together if 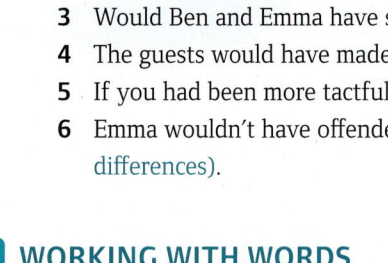 (Ben's family – be – more tolerant)?

4 The guests would have made a better impression if 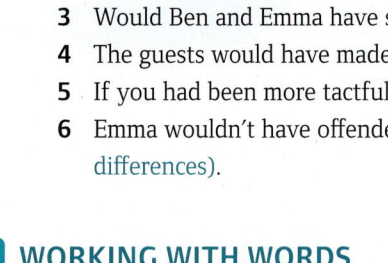 (they – arrive – on time).

5 If you had been more tactful, she 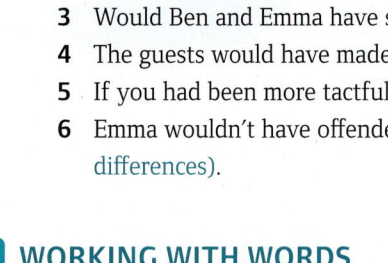 (not – be – hurt – by your criticism).

6 Emma wouldn't have offended Ben's parents if 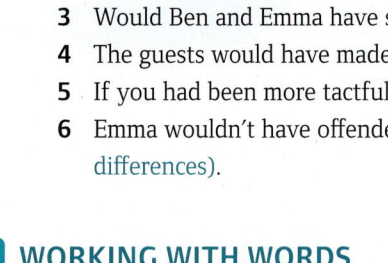 (she – be – more sensitive to cultural differences).

6 WORKING WITH WORDS

A Complete the text by using suitable forms of the words. Find a word of your own to replace the question mark.

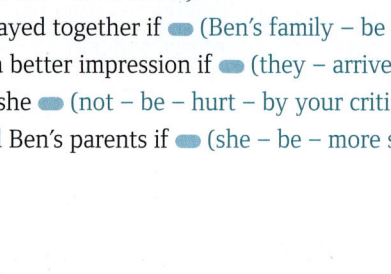

EXAM
→ use of language

An email about an Australian-Japanese trade meeting

Hi Stu,

Here's a few words about the meeting we had today with NPN Company from Japan. As I am the vice-president of our company, I was at the airport to greet them. There were a number of journalists
 5 and photographers present, as we are hoping to sign a big contract with them in the next few days. I was, of course, very excited and ran up the airplane stairs to greet them as they came out.

Mrs Aiko Watanabe, the leader of the delegation, appeared first, so I gave her a big hug. I then  ᵃ welcomed her to Australia, but she
10 didn't seem to understand what I was saying. My first impression of her was not great, I have to say. She seemed very reserved.

a warm

Finally, we got down the stairs, and her translator introduced himself very  ᵇ. He informed me that Mrs Watanabe  ᶜ English very well. I asked him why the Japanese didn't learn English, but he
15 seemed not to understand my question. As you can see, there's a problem with their communication.

b formal

c to not speak

Some of the journalists asked questions. Mrs Watanabe obviously had no idea what the questions were about, so I thought that I would answer them all. Basically, they wanted 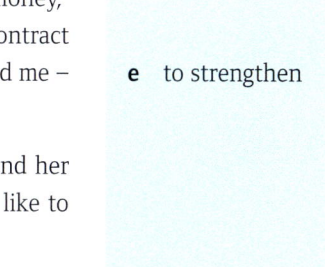 **d** what the Japanese
20 company hoped to gain from a cooperation with us. 'Tons of money,' I laughed! Mrs Watanabe suddenly said that she hoped the contract 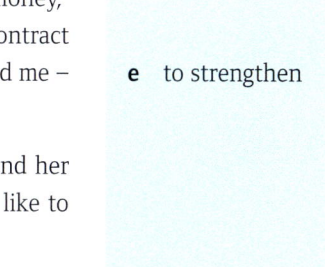 **e** the relationship between our two countries. That surprised me – she does speak English!

d to know

e to strengthen

The photographers asked for a photo, so I put my arm around her
25 and told her to say 'cheese', but I don't think the Japanese like to laugh much.

Then I asked her 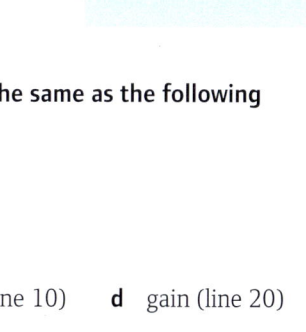 **f** she would drive with me to the firm's offices, but through the translator she informed me that she 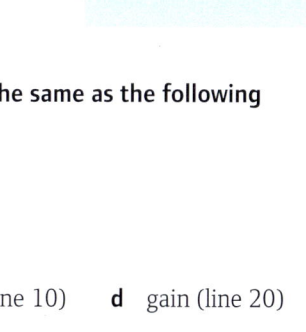 **g** with her team in the second car. She's a bit impolite, I thought. So, anyway, I
30 got into the car and drove off, with them following me.

f ?
g to go

You'll never believe this, but just as I arrived at the firm, the president of our company sent me a message asking me to fly to Brisbane to deal with some trivial problem. I still don't know how they 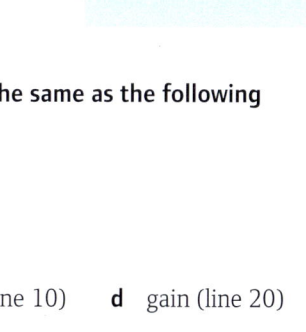 **h** without me …

h to manage

35 Yours Bruce Taylor

B **Find words or expressions in the text which mean more or less the same as the following words.**

   a rude (lines 27–30)   **b** unimportant (lines 31–34)

C **Find the opposites of the following words from the text.**

   a present (line 5)   **b** appeared (line 8)   **c** understand (line 10)   **d** gain (line 20)

7 **WRITING A NEWSPAPER ARTICLE**

EXAM
→ writing

Imagine you are one of the journalists at the airport. Turn the information from the email in task 6A into a short report of 160 words. You can add more information if you wish.

Remember the following points:

- Keep as much as possible to the facts: who, when, where, what.
- Most reports are written in the simple past.
- Use direct quotes where necessary.
- Invent a headline.

You have started work experience at a British printing plant. There are several workplace hazards, so safety procedures are an important part of your induction.

1 WORKING WITH SIGNS

As part of your induction you have to complete a health and safety test. You have to understand the safety signs in your workplace.

A Match the instructions to the signs. There are more instructions than signs.

a You must wear ear protectors in this noisy area.
b You may not enter this area without a helmet.
c You must not operate this machinery without safety glasses.
d You should beware of forklift trucks here.
e This material could catch fire.
f You should beware of getting an electric shock.
g You must wear protective gloves.
h You must pull down the guard before using the machinery.
i This machinery could crush your fingers.
j You must wear protective clothing in this area.

B Your colleague is taking you around the plant. You both do as you are told in the signs. Write down what he/she tells you might/could/would happen if you didn't take notice of the signs.

EXAMPLE: *If you didn't wear safety glasses, your eyes could be damaged.*

C **Which of the signs would you expect to see in these workplaces, and why?**

2 **PLACEMAT: WORKPLACE SAFETY**

Read this case study about an industrial accident at a printing plant, then complete the task below.

Case Study

Jack worked in a magazine printing works. Sometimes there was too much ink on the rollers on the big printing press. Occasionally a whole print run had to be thrown away – thousands of magazines. The company tried to repair the printing press, however the problem always came back. The company couldn't afford a new press: over a million pounds.

The simple solution was to clean the rollers with a cloth every hour. The rules said that the press had to be shut down for this procedure. Jack and his colleagues thought that this wasn't necessary. Besides, it took a lot of time to stop the press and start it again.

One day, Jack was cleaning the rollers on the printing press with a cloth while the press was running. He had done this hundreds of times.

This time, the cloth got stuck between the moving rollers. They pulled the cloth into the press – and Jack didn't have time to let go. His hand was pulled between the rollers. Fortunately his wedding ring got stuck and the rollers didn't pull his whole arm into the press. However his fingers were crushed. Jack spent 13 days in hospital. The doctors took skin from his foot to repair his hand. Unfortunately, they weren't able to save one of his fingers, which had to be removed. Jack spent six months off work.

(Based on a true story, name and details changed.)

Work in a group of four. Sit around a table with a large sheet of paper. Write 'Workplace Safety' in the middle as a title.

You are the members of your company's Youth and Trainee Representation (*Jugend- und Auszu-bildendenvertretung, JAV*). Your task is to write workplace safety recommendations to avoid accidents like the one described above.

Step 1 Make notes on your corner of the sheet.
Step 2 Discuss your ideas with the rest of your group.
Step 3 Take decisions and agree on four workplace safety recommendations.
Write them under the title.
Step 4 Show your recommendations to the class.

Facing discrimination at work

Obesity is one of the few categories where society still appears to find discrimination acceptable. As a result, obese people have a harder time finding work.

After she was made redundant at a media organization, Patricia Simons thought she had finally found a new job last year. The job was at a childcare centre in St Louis, Missouri. When
5 she went for an interview, she met the staff and the children and seemed to get on well. Then she heard nothing.

'I had worked in a childcare centre before, so I was both qualified and experienced,' explains Simons. 'Eventually when I called them, they said that, basically, they weren't going to hire me because I was too big.' Simons is a large woman – 180 cm and more than 180 kg. However,
10 during the interview, she showed that she could easily sit on the floor and play with children.

'I don't understand,' says Simons. 'Discrimination against employees is illegal when it's because of sex, age, ethnicity, sexual orientation, disabilities – almost everything! Yet it still seems okay to refuse to hire obese people.'

Employers often underestimate the abilities of obese people. They tend to assume that
15 they can't do difficult tasks or work for long periods without getting tired. Yet medical data fail to show a simple relationship between a person's body mass index (BMI) and their level of fitness. Some obese people run marathons; some people whose BMI is in the normal range can't climb a flight of steps. It is important to look at each person as an individual, not a number.

20 In the USA, employees who face discrimination because of their large size have little legal protection – unless the court finds that their obesity is a disability. Only the state of Michigan and some cities have laws against discrimination based on body size. The situation in Europe is similar: the European Court of Justice has decided that obese employees are protected only if they are disabled by their weight.

25 Some people have developed their own ways of dealing with obesity discrimination. Physiotherapy assistant Rupert Jones was fired from a clinic in Chicago because of his size – 163 cm and 130 kg. Some of the patients had complained that they felt uncomfortable being treated by him. Rupert complained and the clinic offered him compensation, which he took.

According to Jones: 'Over the years, lots of people I've met have made comments. They
30 assume I'm not as smart as other people because of my weight.' He later went back to college and completed his psychology degree. He now works as a psychiatric counsellor.

'You can teach people how to treat you, to give you respect', says Jones. 'For example, I'll ask questions like, 'Tell me: is something about me bothering you?' when someone treats me disrespectfully. Most of the time, they'll change their behaviour. All the same, I shouldn't have
35 to do this … nobody should.'   (485 words)

| 03 **make sb redundant:** *fire sb from a job*
| 08 **eventually:** *schließlich*

1 MULTIPLE CHOICE

Choose the best answer for each of the following questions.

1 Why did Patricia apply for a job at a childcare center?
  a She had lost her old job.
  b She wanted a new start in life.
  c She got along well with children.
  d It was the only job advert she liked.

2 What did Patricia Simons have to do during her interview?
  a She had to interview the children.
  b She had to show she could sit on the floor.
  c She had to prove she was not too big for the job.
  d She had to show she had experience with children.

3 Which of the following is important to take into consideration when hiring people who are obese?
  a Each individual has different capabilities.
  b Obese people are usually fitter than people think.
  c There is no relationship between BMI and fitness.
  d People with obesity are unable to perform certain tasks.

4 Which of the following sums up Jones's approach to discrimination?
  a You have to get used to it.
  b Teach people what discrimination is like.
  c Challenge people's behaviour so that they change it.
  d You have to prove to others that you are smarter than them.

2 SENTENCE COMPLETION

Finish the sentences using the information from the text.

1 An obese person in the EU can be fired if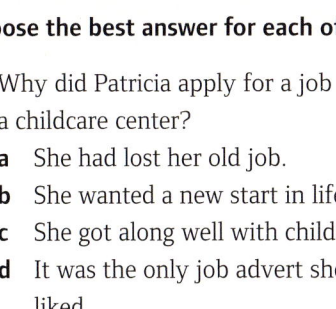
2 Rupert Jones was fired simply because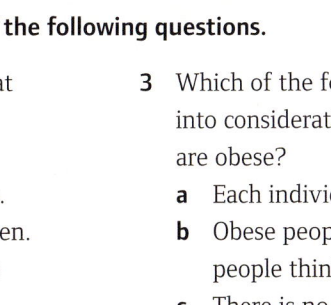

3 OPEN QUESTIONS

Answer the questions in complete sentences by using the information from the text.

1 What happened after Patricia Simons's interview at the childcare centre?
2 What happened after Rupert Jones was fired from his job at a clinic?

4 INFORMATIONEN AUS DEM TEXT WIEDERGEBEN

Beantworten Sie die folgende Frage auf Deutsch.

Wie ist die gesetzliche Lage zur Diskriminierung in den meisten Teilen der USA?

Nennen Sie stichwortartig vier Merkmale, auf deren Basis Diskriminierung verboten ist, und ein Merkmal, auf dessen Basis Diskriminierung nicht explizit verboten ist und weithin geduldet wird.

A *Any* or *some*? Choose the correct alternative.

1 If you could live anywhere / somewhere in the world, where would that be?
2 I love travelling – I can't think of anything / something I'd prefer to do.
3 Think of any / some words which look the same in English and German but have different meanings.
4 Do you speak any / some other foreign languages as well as English?
5 There must be anything / something I can do to learn English faster: don't you have any / some tips?
6 Janek isn't unsociable: he will talk to anybody / somebody.
7 I don't think that any / some of the students in my class speak Hindi.
8 In India it's hard to find anybody / somebody who isn't multilingual – except for tourists.
9 I'd love to live anywhere / somewhere warm – Australia, for example.
10 I can't think of any / some reason to leave Germany.

B Complete the sentences with *many, much, a lot (of), (a) little, (a) few* instead of the German words. There may be more than one possible answer.

1 Luuk speaks very good English, but he still makes *einige wenige* mistakes.
2 Relatively *wenige* web pages are in languages other than English.
3 I've tried to find a good course in Dutch but I've had *wenig* success.
4 Why do so *viele* songs have lyrics in English?
5 Is there *viel* casual work for backpackers in Australia?
6 There are *viele* jobs on farms or in restaurants.
7 *Viele* casual farm jobs are hard work for *wenig* money.
8 *Wenige* local people want to work on farms.
9 English is important for *viele* restaurant jobs.
10 There isn't *viel* work you can do in Australia without good English.

C Translate the sentences into English.

1 Wie viele Amtssprachen (official languages) gibt es in der EU?
2 Wie viel Zeit braucht man für eine Weltreise (trip around the world)?
3 Es gibt nicht viele Restaurants in dieser Stadt.
4 Es gibt viel zu sehen auf der Messe.
5 Es gibt nicht viel Arbeit in dieser Stadt.
6 Es gibt wenige Berufe (professions), in denen Englischkenntnisse nicht nützlich sind.
7 Wenige Messebesucher bleiben mehr als eine Nacht in der Stadt.
8 Weiß hier irgendjemand die richtige Lösung zu dieser Aufgabe?
9 Viele Rucksackreisende reisen jedes Jahr nach Thailand.
10 Einige wenige von ihnen werden dort sesshaft (settle down).

New horizons

A WARM-UP: LOOKING AHEAD

A Look at the photos. Choose one which represents your dreams for the next ten years. Describe the photo to a partner and explain why you chose it.

B What do you want to achieve in the next ten years?

- Use the diagram to organize your ideas.
- Compare ideas with your partner.
- Describe some of your partner's aspirations to the class.

C How will the world be better when your generation is in charge? Brainstorm ideas in a group and write a 'to do' list for 2050.

B GLOBAL NOMADS

SITUATION: Lots of people make use of their time to travel abroad and live for a while in another country. You've been asked by an Australian website to explain to Australian youngsters why they should spend time in Germany (task 5, page 175). Before you do so, you read about some people who have decided to explore other countries.

1 PREPARING TO READ

Skim the blogs on pages 173 and 174. Match each blogger profile below to the correct text.

Hitomi Matsumoto is a chef from Alaska. She loves languages and speaks English, Japanese, German and French. She's now living in Freiburg im Breisgau.

Lukas Petersen is a nurse from Biberach. He's living and working in Durban, South Africa, while he saves to continue his travels.

Anna Lehmann and Fabian Müller are a couple from Munich. Anna is a web designer and Fabian is a motor mechanic. They are currently touring Australia in a converted school bus.

2 READING AND UNDERSTANDING THE BLOGS

Read the blogs on pages 173 and 174, and decide whether the following statements are true or false.

EXAM
→ reading comprehension

Just Jammin'
1 The blogger of 'Just Jammin'' thinks that the world is becoming the same everywhere.
2 He is able to work in most countries because he is a registered nurse.
3 He plays his guitar in the streets for enjoyment.
4 The first time he saw the Victoria Falls he was very emotional.
5 Nothing serious has happened to him on his travels in Africa.

Off Piste
1 The blogger of 'Off Piste' is able to find work easily because she trained as a chef.
2 She works as a ski instructor because it pays better than other jobs.
3 She finds Europeans more unusual than Alaskans.
4 She finds where she lives in Europe is very diverse.
5 She is thinking of settling permanently in Europe in the near future.

Aussie Bush Bus Adventure
1 The blogger of 'Aussie Bush Bus Adventure' is good at repairing engines.
2 The blogger is now pregnant and the baby will be born in Australia.
3 She's having the baby in Australia because its healthcare is the best.
4 She thinks the best thing about Australia is the incredible landscape.
5 The most dangerous thing about Australia are its wild animals.

44

GLOBETROTTING BLOGGERS

JUST JAMMIN'

| HOME | ARCHIVES | GALLERY | **ABOUT ME** |

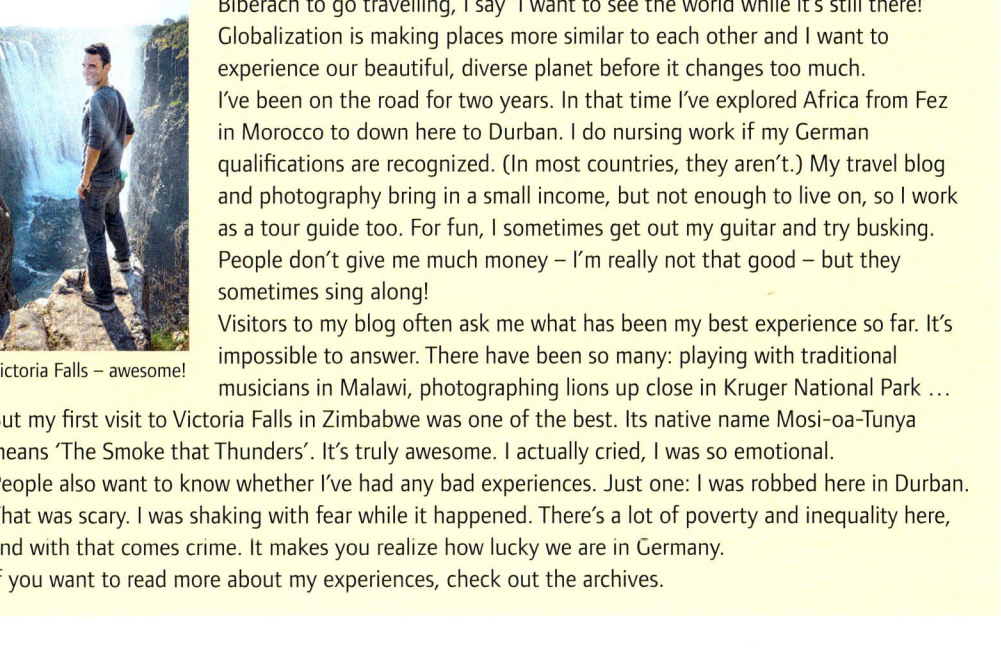

Victoria Falls – awesome!

Whenever people ask me why I gave up my job as a paediatric nurse in Biberach to go travelling, I say 'I want to see the world while it's still there!' Globalization is making places more similar to each other and I want to experience our beautiful, diverse planet before it changes too much.

5   I've been on the road for two years. In that time I've explored Africa from Fez in Morocco to down here to Durban. I do nursing work if my German qualifications are recognized. (In most countries, they aren't.) My travel blog and photography bring in a small income, but not enough to live on, so I work as a tour guide too. For fun, I sometimes get out my guitar and try busking.

10 People don't give me much money – I'm really not that good – but they sometimes sing along!

Visitors to my blog often ask me what has been my best experience so far. It's impossible to answer. There have been so many: playing with traditional musicians in Malawi, photographing lions up close in Kruger National Park …

15 But my first visit to Victoria Falls in Zimbabwe was one of the best. Its native name Mosi-oa-Tunya means 'The Smoke that Thunders'. It's truly awesome. I actually cried, I was so emotional.

People also want to know whether I've had any bad experiences. Just one: I was robbed here in Durban. That was scary. I was shaking with fear while it happened. There's a lot of poverty and inequality here, and with that comes crime. It makes you realize how lucky we are in Germany.

20 If you want to read more about my experiences, check out the archives.

OFF PISTE

March 18

I've been away from home for 18 months. In the summer I work in restaurants and hotels – being a qualified chef means that I can find work quite easily. In the winter, I work as a ski instructor. That's really my dream job. I get a lot of satisfaction from seeing my students' skill and confidence increase.

5   Commenters on my blog often ask me whether I miss Alaska. Well, I don't miss the dark winter nights, that's for sure! I do miss the eccentric characters, though. There's something about our wide-open spaces and harsh climate that attracts unusual people.

What I love about Europe is that everything is so close together. At the moment

10 I'm living near the border between France, Germany and Switzerland. Within a few kilometres there's so much change in language and culture. And so much history! Some of it bloody and violent. I'm glad Europe is peaceful nowadays.

All the same, after 18 months in Europe, I think it's time to leave my comfort zone. I'm not sure where I'll head next. Perhaps east to Kazakhstan and Mongolia. That will be different!

| HOME |
| ABOUT ME |
| MY RECIPES |
| MY SKIING TIPS |
| **MY BLOG** |

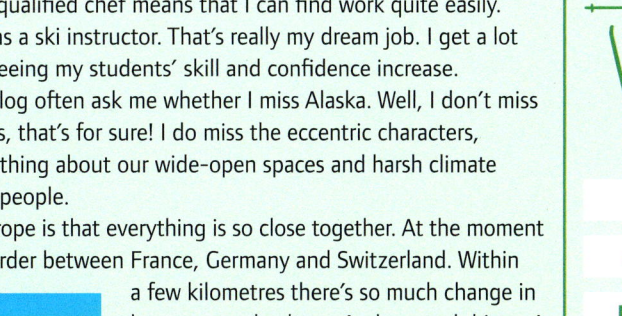

15

Kazakhstan – where I'm heading next!

Aussie Bush Bus Adventure

| HOME | BLOGS | TIPS FOR AUSTRALIA | **ABOUT US** |

Fabian can fix almost any motor, so there's always lots of work for him repairing farm machinery. I write our travel blog, design websites and do any kind of casual work I can find. You have to be flexible on the road. We set off ten months ago, as soon as Fabian had finished his apprenticeship. The plan was to enjoy our freedom and widen our life experience before we settle into a career and start a family.

5 Only it hasn't quite worked out that way.

You guessed it: We're about to start a family! I'm expecting our first baby. She's going to be born here in Australia. They have excellent healthcare, we have health insurance and we aren't ready to go home.

When people ask me what has been my favourite moment here in Australia, I always say: 'Everything!' People are so open and friendly

10 in these little communities in the bush. We're both city kids from Stuttgart, so that's new for us.

Europeans think that Australia is full of dangerous animals: crocodiles, snakes and sharks. Actually the biggest danger, touring the outback in a 1970s school bus, is mechanical failure. If you break down and

15 can't get mobile phone reception, you're in trouble. It's just as well Fabian's good with motors …

Our dear old bus

(682 words)

3 WORKING WITH WORDS

Complete the table. Use a dictionary if necessary.

Adjective	Verb	Noun
global / globalized		globalization
similar		
diverse		
	explore	
		experience
		poverty
		satisfaction
		confidence
violent		
peaceful		
		freedom
		danger

4 LANGUAGE IN USE: TENSE REVISION

A Copy and complete the table. Find at least one example of each of these tenses in the texts on pages 173 and 174.

tense	example	Grund (Deutsch)
simple present	*Whenever people ask me (line 1)*	*sich wiederholende Handlung in der Gegenwart*
present progressive		
present perfect		
simple past		
will-future		
going to-future		
past progressive		
past perfect		

B You are writing an email to a British friend about your friend Lena who is travelling around South-East Asia. You wrote some sentences in German and need to write them in English. The first sentence has been done for you.

1 Nachdem meine Freundin Lena ihre Lehre abgeschlossen hatte, ging sie auf Reisen.
After she had finished her apprenticeship, my friend Lena went travelling.
2 Letzte Woche hat sie mir aus Bali geschrieben.
3 Sie hat einen netten Australier kennengelernt, Lachlan.
4 Sie hat ihn sehr gern.
5 Sie verbringen gerade viel Zeit zusammen.
6 Sie arbeitete in einer Bar, als sie ihn kennenlernte.
7 Sie haben vor kurzem beschlossen, noch ein Jahr auf Bali zu bleiben.
8 Im Sommer fliege ich nach Bali, um mich mit Lena zu besuchen.
9 Es wird interessant sein, Lachlan kennenzulernen.

5 WRITING A BLOG ENTRY

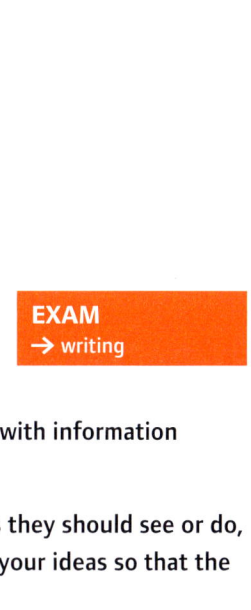

EXAM
→ writing

●●● Just as there is a Working Holiday programme for Germans in Australia (Unit 9, page 110), so too is there one for Australians in Germany.
An Australian website for youngsters has asked you to write a blog entry with information for young Australians.

Do some research about the sort of jobs they could find and about things they should see or do, and explain to them why the experience will be good for them. Structure your ideas so that the information is easy to read.

●●○ Go to File 42 on page 208.

C THE FUTURE OF WORK

1 PREPARING TO READ

Read the introduction and look at the picture. What do you think life will be like in this city?

In the late 21st century the Earth's population reaches 31 billion. Most people live in huge 'mega-cities' and travel in flying pods. Many spend their whole lives in the same apartment complex and get their experience of the outside world from 'proxy broadcasts' – realistic 3D virtual reality experiences which look, feel, smell and even taste like the real thing. Almost all goods and services are provided by robots, so there is little work for humans to do.

2 READING AND UNDERSTANDING THE TEXT

First day at work

'Congratulations!' said the Monitor. 'You're going to work today! Your wage will be 52 Credits an hour.'

Jared's heart missed a beat. Work! Great news!

5 The universal income of 2,500 Credits a month was enough to live on, of course, but it would be good to have some extra money – and real work! What fun!

'What's the job?' he asked the large screen,
10 which took up a whole wall in his small flat.

'You're going to be a proxy,' replied the Monitor. 'You'll have a trial period of one week. If feedback from the audience is positive, it could even become a permanent full-time position.'

'That's amazing,' said Jared, 'and I'm really pleased, but … I've never had a job before. I'm only 25, after all. And I don't really know what a proxy –'

15 'Don't worry! You'll receive the equipment and instructions when the pod arrives to take you to work,' said the Monitor kindly, 'The pod will arrive at 8.37 a.m. – that's in thirty minutes. You can get breakfast at work. Bye now! Have a nice day!'

Forty-five minutes later, Jared was looking out the window of the pod as it approached the mega-city of Frankfurt at 300 kilometres an hour. 'What a city! 27 million residents in skyscrapers
20 80 storeys high,' said the pod. Some pods weren't very talkative, but this was an unusually chatty one. 'How was the induction? Do you know what you have to do now?' it asked.

'Not really,' said Jared. 'The virtual reality lesson was a bit short – and confusing. I guess I've never really thought about what a proxy does before. I mean, I watch the broadcasts, like everyone else, but I didn't realize –' →

25 'I've driven a few proxies to work,' interrupted the pod. 'You'll love it … anyway, we're here: Gruneburg Park. Have a nice day!'

Jared stepped out of the pod, which gave him a cheerful 'Goodbye!', closed its door and zoomed off. As it was identical to the thousands of other small silver robotic vehicles on the street, Jared lost sight of it in seconds. Jared adjusted the Proxy 360° sensor so that it was a
30 comfortable fit in his ear, with a good connection to his brain, and looked around him.

The sun shone down from a clear blue sky and there was a gentle breeze. Jared looked around at the tall trees. He could hear birds singing. In front of him was a footpath, leading between the trees. From his induction, Jared knew that he had to follow this path to get to work. But what exactly was 'work'?

35 He walked along the path eagerly, enjoying the beautiful May morning and the fresh air – so unlike the polluted smog outside the city's protective dome. In Jared's home town, the 'park' was a tiny rooftop garden. Gruneburg Park was the only large park in western Germany and most people had to wait years for permission to visit.

He passed other walkers, alone, in pairs and groups. Three people were jogging, in the old-
40 fashioned way! Jared heard them chatting as they passed, and realized with a shock that he didn't understand them. The universal translator microchip in his brain had been turned off! He tried to pick out different languages as he walked and listened. He thought he heard Chinese, English and possibly even a couple speaking German, just like his grandparents used to.

Jared remembered that he hadn't had any breakfast. Luckily, he could see a food dispenser
45 ahead. As he approached it, Jared realized that it wasn't just an automatic food dispenser, it was a traditional sausage stand – with two real human servers cooking and serving the food! There was even real coffee in paper cups. It all smelled and looked delicious. His heart beating quickly, Jared ordered a currywurst and a black coffee.

Sitting on a bench by the small lake, Jared sighed contentedly. He wondered what to do with
50 the empty cup and paper plate. He asked a young woman who was passing, carrying a strange metal object on her shoulder, like a fork for eating with, only much, much bigger. Jared guessed that it must be some sort of gardening tool, and that the young woman was a park gardener. How exciting to work with your hands, and maybe even get dirty!

'Just throw them on the grass,' explained the woman patiently. 'That's what they used to do,
55 in the old days.'

It seemed a bit strange, but Jared did as he was told. He sat on the bench for a while longer, watching people walking by, and occasionally greeting them if they looked nice. It was such a thrill when they replied in some strange foreign language that he couldn't understand.

Jared blinked twice quickly to call up the virtual reality information screen in his left eye.
60 '10.45 a.m. on Monday, 3 May 2067' read the screen. A quarter to eleven – surely he was late for work? Jared tried to remember what the induction programme in the pod had told him. And what was 'work'?

Just then a middle-aged woman sat down next to Jared. 'Hello, Jared,' she said in a soft voice. 'I'm your boss, Celia Hoffman. How was your first day at work? Feedback from the audience is
65 94% positive. They loved the currywurst! So authentic! It looks like you have a natural talent for proxy work. So – same time tomorrow?'

(904 words)

A It is Jared's first day at work. What will his job involve? How would you feel in Jared's situation? As you read the story, make notes. When you have finished, discuss your notes with a partner and report back to the class.

B Choose the correct option from below.

1 Thanks to his new job Jared will have an income of which of the following?
  a 52 Credits an hour
  b 2,500 Credits per month
  c 2,500 Credits plus 52 Credits per hour
  d 2,500 Credits per month or 52 Credits per hour, whichever is more

2 How does Jared feel when he gets the job as a proxy?
  a Happy because he really needed a job.
  b Amazed that anyone would give him a job.
  c Excited because having a job is a new experience for him.
  d Shocked that he is offered a job without knowing what to do.

3 What do we learn about Frankfurt?
  a It is close to where Jared lives.
  b It is densely populated.
  c It contains most of the inhabitants of Germany.
  d It is heavily industrialized.

4 Which of the following helps Frankfurt retain its clean air?
  a A large park called Gruneberg.
  b The proxies who work there.
  c The proxy 360° sensor.
  d A large dome built over the city.

5 What do we learn about the Gruneberg Park?
  a It isn't very easy to visit.
  b It was named after a green mountain.
  c It is a rooftop garden.
  d It has tall trees, birds and wolves.

6 The people in the park …
  a speak many different languages.
  b are very friendly with one another.
  c are mostly alone and isolated.
  d communicate via an implanted microchip.

7 Which of the following does Jared <u>not</u> do in the park?
  a Eat some food and have a drink.
  b Throw his rubbish on the ground.
  c Get dirty working with his hands.
  d Say hello to people who walk by.

8 What do we learn about Jared's time in the park?
  a He was being watched by people.
  b He was not actually working.
  c He was being tried out for a reality show.
  d It made him late for work.

C What predictions does the story make about life in 2067? Copy and complete the mind map with information from the text.

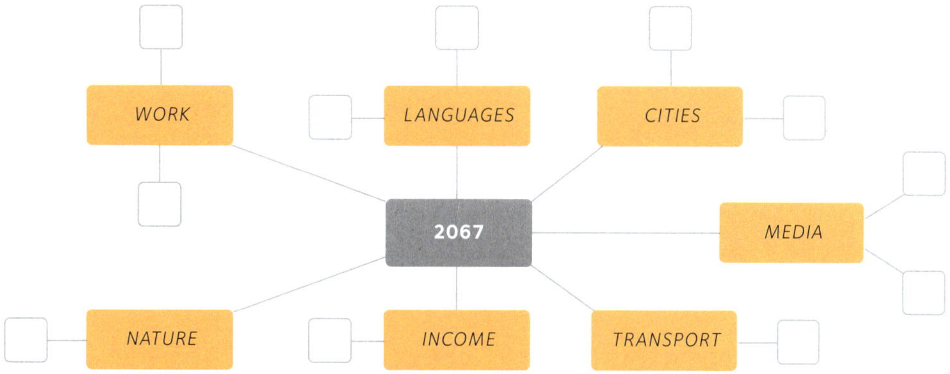

WORK

LANGUAGES

CITIES

2067

MEDIA

NATURE

INCOME

TRANSPORT

D Class discussion. Do you think that these predictions will come true? What other things in 2067 might be different to today? What might be the same?

E Imagine you can communicate with Jared: what do you want to know about his life?

EXAM
→ use of language

1 Write three questions for Jared. Use three different question forms or tenses.
2 Give your questions to a partner. Write answers to your partner's questions as if you are Jared.

3 WRITING A TEXT

EXAM
→ writing

Choose <u>one</u> of the following texts to write.

1 You are a journalist from an international news agency. Write an article about the latest proxy, Jared. Give information about him, about what he did as a proxy and how people have reacted to him. Write about 160 words.
2 These two photos show two other jobs which Jared does as a proxy. Choose one photo and write a story of about 160 words about Jared's workday.

You are doing work experience at an international department store.

1 WHERE CAN I FIND ... ?

A Your supervisor would like you to hang up labels for the various departments in your store. Look at the photos and match them with words from the box.

accessories ▪ children's clothing ▪ cosmetics ▪ food hall ▪ household items ▪ ladies' wear ▪ menswear ▪ sportswear

B Work with a partner. Brainstorm a list of other departments or places in the store. Draw a sketch of 'your' department store and add the names of the departments and places. Do not show your partner your sketch. Take turns to ask and answer questions about where to find goods and places.

> Where can I find the restaurant?

> It's on the fourth floor. The lift is just over there.

2 WORKING ON THE SHOP FLOOR

A Sort the following phrases into what the shop assistant says and what the customer says.

1 Do you have this in a larger size?

2 Would you like to try it on?

3 That will be thirty-nine euros ninety-nine, please.

4 I'm just looking.

5 Could you put this aside for me?

6 Are you looking for anything in particular?

7 Here's your change.

8 Do you have this in a different colour?

9 What style would you like?

10 Can I pay by credit card?

11 How much does it cost?

12 You can exchange it if it's not the right colour.

13 We can order it for you.

14 How many items can I take into the changing room?

B Do a role-play between a customer and a sales assistant. Use phrases from task 2A.

Partner A: You are the sales assistant.
Partner B: You would like to buy a pair of jeans.

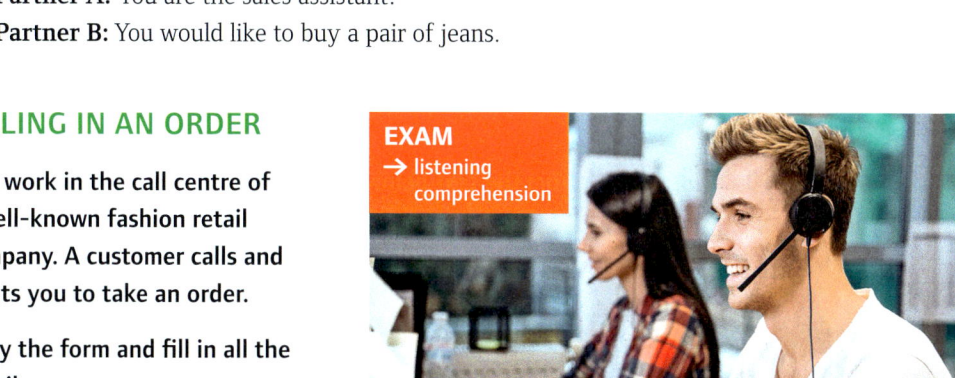

3 FILLING IN AN ORDER

You work in the call centre of a well-known fashion retail company. A customer calls and wants you to take an order.

Copy the form and fill in all the details.

EXAM
→ listening comprehension

Customer details

| Surname: | ▬▬ | First name: | ▬▬ |

Address

Street:	▬▬
Town/city:	▬▬
Post code:	▬▬
Email:	▬▬

Order

Item	Colour	Size	Number	Price
▬▬	▬▬	▬▬	▬▬	▬▬
▬▬	▬▬	▬▬	▬▬	▬▬
▬▬	▬▬	▬▬	▬▬	▬▬
Packaging and postage	express delivery	☐ yes ☐ no	– –	▬▬
Total sum:				▬▬
Method of payment	VISA ☐ MASTERCARD ☐	card number ▬▬	expiry date ▬▬	security code ▬▬

1 WORKING WITH WORDS

A **Find words or expressions in the text below which mean more or less the same.**
  a private (lines 4–11)   **b** worried (lines 4–11)

B **Find opposites of the following words from the text below.**
  a beautiful (line 2)   **b** friends (line 13)

C **Explain one of the following words from the text below in complete sentences.**
  a disagree (line 5)   **b** accommodation (line 17)

2 VOCABULARY – GRAMMAR

Complete the text below by using suitable forms of the words on the right.

a	to make	**e**	that/which/who
b	to educate	**f**	to sail
c	many/much	**g**	to prepare
d	responsible	**h**	to have

Tall ships

'Tall ships' are traditional sailing ships, which 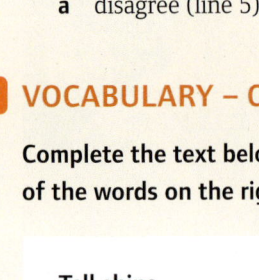 ^a of wood or steel. They have tall masts and huge sails to catch the wind. Many of these beautiful ships are maintained and operated by charities and 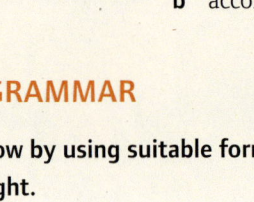 ^b organizations in various countries around the world.

5   Critics may say that tall ships are pure nostalgia in today's high-tech, computerized world. However, the crews that sail them disagree. According to them, sailing a tall ship teaches skills such as problem-solving, communication and teamwork – skills that are important in our careers and personal lives.

    Anna King, 18, joined the British tall ship Lord Nelson for a 14-day trip from Rostock in Germany to Delfzijl in the Netherlands. It was Anna's first time on a sailing ship, so she was nervous and didn't know what to expect. She was one of 40 volunteers from five different European countries. There

10 were 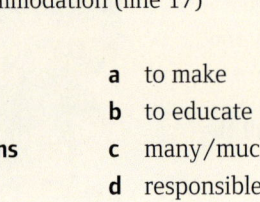 ^c volunteers who had a disability.

    At the beginning of the trip, the ten professional crew members organized the volunteers into four teams, called 'watches'. Each watch was given 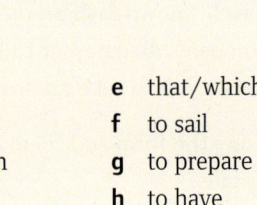 ^d for the whole ship for several hours each day – and night. Anna was put in Blue Watch; she was soon good friends with several of them. All of them were beginners, except for the watch leader, Spike, 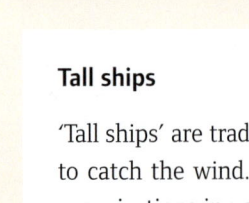 ^e was an experienced crew member and 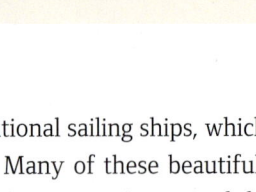 ^f twice around the world.

15   Anna expected life on board to be hard. She was wrong about that, although it was hard work getting out of her nice, warm bed at two o'clock in the morning to go on deck with her watch. The accommodation was comfortable and modern. The food on board was great: three hot meals 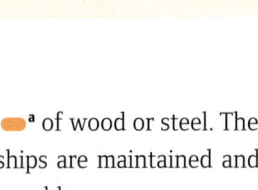 ^g each day by a professional cook. There was fresh fruit and late night snacks for the hungry sailors on deck.

    Anna was sad to leave the ship and her new 'family' after two weeks, but she now 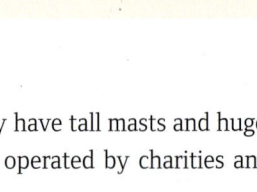 ^h new skills

20 and self-confidence, and new plans for the future.   (331 words)

3 ASKING QUESTIONS

You are talking to Anna King about her trip on the *Lord Nelson*.
Ask two questions about this topic. Use different question forms or different tenses.

Everyone has a different idea of what happiness means.
Discuss with your partner what makes you happy and what you need in life to make you happy.
You can use the photos to help you come up with some ideas.

A Correct these statements using the information in brackets.

EXAMPLE: I'm going to play computer games this evening. (watch TV)
I'm not going to play computer games this evening. I'm going to watch TV.

1 I'm going to travel around Africa. (stay in South Africa)
2 I expect the number of muggings will go up. (go down)
3 I think more people will travel to the Victoria Falls. (go on safari in Botswana)
4 The residents in the ski resorts will be happy about the lack of snow. (very upset)
5 The glaciers will get back to what they used to be. (eventually disappear)
6 Your meal will taste better with some ketchup. (just taste sweeter)
7 It's going to be cold today on the pistes. (warm and sunny)
8 The tourists will obey the warning signs on the beach. (ignore them)
9 We're going to take selfies with the koalas. (make a video)
10 I'm going to share my photo album online. (keep it private)

B Use the prompts to ask questions which go with the answers.

1 Tom – celebrate getting his new job? Yes. He's going to have a big party.
2 who – clean the rubbish off the streets after the parade? The city workers will do it, I expect.
3 the board of directors – sack Marion? No, they've going to offer her a better position.
4 you – work in the same office as June? Yes. I'm going to start working with her tomorrow.
5 the administrators – stop people from smoking inside? Yes. They aren't going to risk another fire in the office.
6 the workers – go on strike tomorrow? No, I'm sure they won't go on strike tomorrow.
7 which text – read next? We're going to read the text on page 102.
8 how – we do in the exams? We'll do very well, hopefully.
9 what – do – when you leave school? I'm going to become a chef.
10 what – do – if you win the lottery? I'll buy a nice car and go on a road trip around the USA.

C Choose the best future form for each context.

1 Do you believe the local newspaper (give) publicity to the opening of the new restaurant?
2 I expect the thieves (get) criminal convictions.
3 It's clear that the problem of drug abuse (get) worse without creative solutions.
4 I hope our town (start) a street art programme.
5 The sky is dark and cloudy: it looks as if it (rain).
6 I imagine my sister (get) a creative job of some kind – she's got a lot of talent.
7 When I leave school, I (start) an apprenticeship.
8 Maria (apply) for a New Zealand work permit when she finishes school.
9 After his accident I'm sure Jack (be) more careful using his tools in future.
10 Jack's family hopes he (look for) a better job.

A **Complete the conditional sentences using the correct forms of the verbs.**

Conditional sentences type 1

1 If it *rains* (rain), I ⬤ (stay) at home today.
2 If our car ⬤ (break down), we ⬤ (call) a motor mechanic.
3 If robots ⬤ (do) most of the work in future, there ⬤ (not be) many jobs for humans.
4 We *will make* (make) your position permanent if you ⬤ (complete) the trial period successfully.
5 I ⬤ (be) happy to help you if you ⬤ (have) any questions.
6 You ⬤ (not make) a good impression if you ⬤ (be) late for work on your first day.

Conditional sentences type 2

7 If I *had* (have) the money to go travelling, I ⬤ (explore) South America.
8 If I ⬤ (try) busking, I ⬤ (earn) lots of money.
9 If there ⬤ (be) a universal income, some people ⬤ (not work) at all.
10 I *wouldn't like* (not like) the long winter nights if I ⬤ (live) in Alaska.
11 Anja ⬤ (want) to see crocodiles and snakes if she ⬤ (go) to Australia.
12 I ⬤ (get) to know all the locals if I ⬤ (live) in a little community in the bush.

Conditional sentences type 3

13 If Anna *had been* (be) pregnant before their trip, she and Fabian ⬤ (stay) at home.
14 If Lukas ⬤ (have) less confidence, he ⬤ (not go) travelling by himself.
15 If Jared ⬤ (listen) carefully during the induction, he ⬤ (know) what to do.
16 Fabian *would have studied* (study) engineering if he ⬤ (be) better at maths.
17 Hitomi ⬤ (have) more difficulty getting a job if she ⬤ (not be) a qualified chef.
18 She ⬤ (become) bored if she ⬤ (stay) in her comfort zone.

B **Translate the sentences into English. (Remember to use 'if', not 'when'.)**

1 Wenn ich ein Visum bekomme, werde ich in Neuseeland arbeiten.
2 Wird Lukas als Krankenpfleger arbeiten, wenn seine Qualifikationen anerkannt werden?
3 Wir werden froh sein, wenn wir eine gute Abschlussnote (final grade) erhalten.
4 Wenn ich Gitarre spielen könnte (be able to play), würde ich mal auf der Straße spielen (try busking).
5 Würdest du nervös sein, wenn heute dein erster Arbeitstag (day at work) wäre?
6 Wenn ich Automechaniker/in wäre, könnte ich mein Auto selber reparieren.
7 Wenn ich Annas Blog nicht gelesen hätte, wäre ich nicht auf die Idee einer Australienreise gekommen (think of a trip to Australia).
8 Ich wäre sofort nach Hause zurückgekehrt, wenn man mich auf meiner Weltreise (while globetrotting) überfallen hätte.
9 Was hättest du gemacht, wenn dir so etwas passiert wäre?
10 Wenn mir so etwas passiert wäre, wäre ich trotzdem weitergereist. (still carry on travelling)

FILE 1 Unit 1, Section B, Task 1B → page 16

Follow the suggestions in the 'Train your skills' box on page 16 and make notes. Then answer this question: What is the text going to tell us about food around the world?

Als erstes sollten Sie die Überschriften und Zwischenüberschriften lesen, da Sie Ihnen eine erste Vorstellung vom Inhalt des Textes geben:

The title of the text is ▭ and the paragraph headings cover the following issues: ▭

Schauen Sie sich dann die Fotos und Illustrationen zum Text an: Was zeigen sie? Welche Information steckt in den Bildunterschriften?

The caption (Bildunterschrift) *under the photo says ▭*

Lesen Sie als Letztes die Aufgaben zum Text: Was wird in der Aufgabe von Ihnen verlangt?

In Task 2B I have to understand the contents of ▭. In Task 2C I have to look for ▭ in the text.
From the title, the headings and the photo, I think the text is probably is about ▭

FILE 2 Unit 1, Section B, Task 2C → page 18

Choose one of the two options to finish the sentences.

1 The two biggest problems facing the planet are ▭
   a global warming and animal farming.
   b a rapidly increasing global population and climate change.

2 According to scientists, we should eat ▭
   a food from other cultures.
   b more vegetables and less meat and dairy.

3 Insects are healthier than meat because ▭
   a they have less saturated fat and more vitamin B12.
   b they have more protein.

4 Because there is not a lot of water in Rajasthan, people use ▭
   a butter and milk to cook.
   b beans and legumes in their recipes.

5 In order to make laverbread, the Welsh ▭
   a follow a Japanese recipe.
   b boil seaweed.

6 Although some food sounds weird to us, one day ▭
   a we may be forced to eat it.
   b we may be happy to eat it.

| **FILE 3** | **Unit 1, Section B, Task 3B** | → page 18 |

Think of three questions to ask your partner. Here are some questions you can ask, but the words have been jumbled up.

1   is / good for / diet / the planet / which
2   you / do / eat / insects
3   do / where / insects / eat / people
4   why / insects / are / healthy
5   than meat / insects / are / better for you
6   is there / protein / in the average insect / how much
7   why / vegetarian food / do / eat / people in India
8   for cooking / what / do / use / people in Rajasthan
9   in Wales / do / people / eat / what
10 people / how many / in the world / eat / vegetarian food
11 don't / we / send / why/ food from Europe to Africa

| **FILE 4** | **Unit 1, Section B, Task 4A** | → page 19 |

Work with a partner. The words below on the left appear in the text. Use an English-German dictionary (print or online) to find words that belong to their families. Write down the German translations of all the words. Some answers have been added to help you.

1		agricultural (adjective) (line 4)		*landwirtschaftlich*
Find	**a**	a noun	*agriculture*	*Landwirtschaft*
2		scientist (noun) (line 4)		▭
Find	**a**	another noun	▭	*[Natur]wissenschaft*
	b	an adjective	*scientific*	▭
	c	an adverb	▭	▭
3		strange (adjective) (line 33)		▭
Find	**a**	an adverb	▭	*merkwürdig, sonderbar*
	b	a noun (describing a person)	*stranger*	▭

| **FILE 5** | **Unit 1, Section B, Task 5** | → page 19 |

Write an email to the students at the Scottish school, in which you tell them about the article on page 17. Include the following points on the next page in your email:

- why we may need to eat different types of food in the future
- what types of food are eaten in different areas of the world, and why they may be interesting for us

Verwenden Sie dabei den Text unten links und ergänzen Sie sie wo notwendig.

Hi,
I found an article about feeding the world that I think has some interesting information. The article describes ¹
In order to save our planet, we need to , as ².
The author examines three unusual types of food that could become part of our diet.
Firstly, the author looks at insects. ³
Next, the author ⁴
Finally, the author ⁵
The author concludes by saying ⁶
Let me know what you think.
All the best

1 Hier beschreiben Sie in einem Satz, worum es im Text geht.
2 Hier erklären Sie aufgrund der Informationen in Absatz A, weshalb wir uns auf neue Arten von Lebensmitteln einlassen sollten.
3 Hier fassen Sie Absatz B kurz zusammen.
4 Hier fassen Sie Absatz C kurz zusammen.
5 Hier fassen Sie Absatz D kurz zusammen.
6 Hier beschreiben Sie die Schlussfolgerung, die der Autor in Absatz E zieht.

FILE 6 | **Unit 1, Section C, Task 3B** | → page 21

Work in groups. Ask and answer questions about your eating habits, using adverbs from Task 3A on page 21 where possible. It may help you to write down your questions before asking them.

Zum Einstieg gibt es hier ein paar Fragen – die Antworten dazu sind allerdings durcheinandergewürfelt. Ordnen Sie die Anworten den richtigen Fragen zu und bringen Sie die Wörter in die korrekte Reihenfolge.

1 When do you eat your main meal?
2 How often do you eat meat?
3 Do you ever eat Chinese food?
4 How often do you cook?
5 Who shops for food when you eat at home?
6 How often do you eat in restaurants?

a Chinese food / sometimes / eat / I
b My parents / always / shop / at home / for food / we / eat / when
c our main meal / we / eat / usually / at 7 p.m.
d never / in restaurants / I / eat
e cook / never / I
f rarely / meat / I / eat

Die Antworten a–f enthalten Häufigkeitsadverbien. Was können Sie zur Stellung dieser Adverbien im Satz sagen?

Ändern Sie nun die Antworten so ab, dass die Aussagen auf Sie persönlich zutreffen. Jetzt formulieren Sie Ihre eigenen Fragen für die Gruppe.

| FILE 7 | Unit 2, Section B, Task 2C | → page 28 |

Decide which of the two options is the best explanation of the words from the text.

a lazy (line 8):
    1 If you are lazy, it means you are not an active person.
    2 If you are lazy, it means you do not work.

b pressure (line 30):
    1 It is a word that describes what you feel when you don't want to be with other people.
    2 It is a word that describes the feeling when people expect you to do too much.

| FILE 8 | Unit 2, Section B, Task 3 | → page 29 |

Look at the drawings on page 29. Describe what the people are doing. Use the present progressive form of the verbs in bracket.

1 He ⬤ weights. (lift)
2 He ⬤ a ball. (kick)
3 He ⬤ gymnastics. (do)
4 She ⬤ a bike. (ride)
5 She ⬤. (ice skate)
6 He ⬤ handball. (play)
7 He ⬤ water polo. (play)
8 They ⬤. (box)

| FILE 9 | Unit 2, Section B, Task 4 | → page 29 |

Follow the suggestions in the skills box to describe the picture on page 29. Here are some expressions you can use.

to fail to do sth	rugby player	to throw yourself
goal line	to lie on sb/sth	to touch the ball down
to hold down the ball	to score a try	to wear a green shirt
in a green/red shirt	to stop sb from doing sth	
rugby ball	team	

Start your description like this:

The picture shows a rugby match. The most important element in the photo is ...

FILE 10 | Unit 3, Section B, Task 3D | → page 39

You have the opportunity to ask Jameela some questions. Use the correct form of the verb (*simple past* or *present perfect*) in the questions below.

1 For how long (you – suffer) from anorexia nervosa?
2 When (you – start) to work for the BBC?
3 Were you nervous the first time (you – speak) on the radio?
4 (you – ever – speak) at a public event?
5 (you – make) a lot of friends in America?
6 For how long (you – act) in *The Good Place*?
7 When (you – first – notice) that body shaming was common in social media?
8 For how long (your petition – be) online?
9 (many people – write) to you because of 'I Weigh'?
10 How many people (upload) photos with the hashtag #iweigh?

FILE 11 | Unit 3, Section B, Task 4B | → page 40

The words in the box below are taken from the text. Using the correct form of the word, complete the reply to a forum comment.

> attractive ▪ criticize ▪ criticize ▪ influencer ▪ popular ▪ positive

Hi. So, you're going on a diet because you're getting a lot of ⬤¹ about your weight from some of your friends? Don't let them ⬤² you in a negative way. Your ⬤³ doesn't depend on how you look. It's who you are and what you do that counts. Those are the things that ⬤⁴ people to you. Get the ⬤⁵ out of your life and find some friends who see things ⬤⁶.

FILE 12 | Unit 3, Section B, Task 5 | → page 40

After reading the text about Jameela Jamil, you think that it might be interesting for a friend of yours who has been body shamed on social media. Write an email to your friend, in which you inform him or her about Jameela's experiences and explain to him or her how this information might be helpful. Write about 160 words, using the structure on the next page to write your email.

Mention the following aspects:

- Jameela's problems as a child and young woman.
- What happened to her that changed her life.
- How she is now an activist who both supports and influences other people.

Hi,

I've just read an article about a British celebrity called Jameela Jamil. Although today she is a successful actress, when she was a child, she ▬ ¹

However, when she was 17, ▬ ²

Since then she has been a body activist. She first got involved with people with disabilities when she ▬ ³

Later, in the USA, she launched ▬ ⁴

Her most recent action was to ▬ ⁵

I hope this information helps you realize that you should not judge yourself by social media. All the best,

(name)

1 Hier fassen Sie die Informationen in Zeilen 8–15 kurz zusammen.
2 Hier fassen Sie die Informationen in Zeilen 16–21 kurz zusammen.
3 Hier beschreiben Sie kurz, was Jameela für Menschen mit Behinderung gemacht hat und warum. Die Informationen entnehmen Sie Zeilen 27–39
4 Hier fassen Sie Zeilen 40–54 kurz zusammen.
5 Hier fassen Sie Zeilen 56–62 kurz zusammen.

FILE 13 **Unit 3, World of intercultural communication, Task 1** → page 44

Your application has been accepted and you go to the training session. The first session is about how to behave when you meet the visitors.

Listen to the trainer and complete the notes below using words from the text. Use one word for each gap. The first gap has been done for you.

		Chinese visitors	You
1	Greetings	shake hands when they meet people	Wait till the other person holds out his/her *hand* ᵃ; look in the other person's ▬ ᵇ as you shake hands.
2	Clothes	dressed in ▬ ᵃ clothes	Wear ▬ ᵇ clothes. Do not wear bright colours, ▬ ᶜ or t-shirts. Women: do not wear low-cut ▬ ᵈ.
3	Body language	do not like ▬ ᵃ ▬ ᵇ	After you have shaken hands, do not ▬ ᶜ the visitors again.
4	Being prepared	it is likely they have done ▬ ᵃ on the places they will visit	Make sure you can give basic details of your ▬ ᵇ and ▬ ᶜ system.
5	Language	might not speak good ▬ ᵃ	Speak ▬ ᵇ and ▬ ᶜ; repeat if necessary.

FILE 14 Unit 4, Section B, Task 4B → page 50

Decide which of the two modal auxiliaries is correct in each case in the text below.

The opioid abuse crisis

Opioid abuse has been a serious health problem in the United States and Canada for many years. According to statistics, the UK is also heading for an opioid abuse crisis. Abuse of opioids must / can [1] lead to addiction and may / ought to [2] also cause death. Teenagers are as much at risk of becoming addicted as older people.

Opioids are a type of drug. They include strong prescription pain relievers, such as oxycodone and fentanyl. A doctor might / needs to [3] write a prescription opioid to reduce pain after a patient has had surgery or has suffered an injury. As soon as someone starts using prescription opioids, however, there is a risk they should / could [4] become dependent on the drug. Studies show that 4% to 6% of opioid misusers go on to use heroin.

When Mick R. from Sheffield in the English Midlands was injured playing football at school, his doctor prescribed oxycodone. When Mick's injury was healed, his doctor stopped prescribing the tablets. The problem was, Mick shouldn't / was not able to [5] stop taking the drug. He had become dependent on it.

Because he needed to / might [6] feed his addiction, Mick first lied to the doctor that he was still in pain, then he said he'd lost his prescription so that he must / could [7] buy more tablets. Eventually, he dropped out of school and spent his time trying to find sources to feed his addiction. Finally, Mick switched to heroin and died of an overdose.

Today, Mick's mother works as a volunteer with a counselling service for young addicts who want to come off drugs. Sadly, Mick did not get help in time. His mother says, 'Some people say he must have / shouldn't have [8] taken oxycodone in the first place but the doctor told my son that he ought to / might [9] take it. I still must / can't [10] understand why the doctor didn't tell us about the danger.'

FILE 15 Unit 4, Section B, Task 5 → page 51

It will soon be exam time, and you have noticed that many students at your school are drinking energy drinks.

Write a blog entry for your school's website about the dangers of consuming too much caffeine.

Use the structure of the text on the opposite page to write your blog. Use information from the text about Richard D. and write about 160 words in English.

Als Erstes sollten Sie Ihrem Beitrag einen Titel geben, damit die Leserinnen und Leser wissen, worum es im Text geht. Dann fangen Sie mit der Einleitung an:

It's time to think about 🔵

In der Einleitung erklären Sie, weshalb Sie über das Thema schreiben, z. B.:

We all know that there are some people who drink 🔵

Dann beschreiben Sie den Fall von Richard D. in England. Fassen Sie die Informationen in Z. 1–25 kurz zusammen.

Recently, 🔵

Erwähnen Sie in einem Satz die Kampagne von Richards Eltern in Z. 35–55:

Richard's parents have now started a campaign to 🔵

Schließen Sie Ihren Text mit dem Rat der Experten in Z. 54–63 und ihren eigenen Rat, z. B.:

The advice of experts is 🔵 . So, my advice is 🔵 !

FILE 16   **Unit 4, Section C, Task 3**   → page 53

Work with a partner. Decide together whether *must* or *must not*, or *should* or *should not* are correct in the sentences below. Then translate the sentences into German.

1   In order to get into university, Chinese students must /should pass a very tough exam.
2   There mustn't / shouldn't really be competition between classmates but there is.
3   Family honour is important in China, so the students feel they must /should do well in the exam.
4   Student who suffer from stress must / should visit their doctor, but most don't.
5   The teacher told us that we must /should study for at least 8 hours a day.
6   You must not / should not take the exam if you are not prepared.
7   You must not / should not cheat in the exam, otherwise you will be removed from the exam hall.

FILE 17 Unit 4, World of intercultural communication, Task 2B   → page 55

Your boss has written you the following email.

> I'm really disappointed in Sarah's presentation. Tell her that she needs to do it all again. Make sure she uses more colours. Tell her to use different photos. And we need it by Friday. Thanks!

Using the words in the box below, fill in the gaps in the email you write to Sarah.

could ▪ might be able to ▪ might I suggest ▪ slightly ▪ were wondering ▪ would it be possible

> Hi Sarah,
> I just want to tell you that we're ●¹ disappointed by your presentation. ●² for you to do it again? ●³ that you use more colours? We ●⁴ if you ●⁵ possibly use different photos? Do you think you ●⁶ finish it by Friday?
> Thanks

FILE 18 Unit 5, Section B, Task 3B   → page 60

Choose the correct option to complete the text.

Today almost the whole beach, except for (a few / few / little)¹ areas near the dunes, was littered with plastic. (A few / Few / A little)² seagulls were picking up pieces of plastic. 'Right. Let's get this mess cleaned up,' said the team leader. 'We've got very (few / a little / little)³ time, as they'll be sending a truck quite soon.' (Few / A few / Little)⁴ people collected the larger items while the others concentrated on the rest. After (few / a little / little)⁵ while, (a few / little / few)⁶ more people joined the team and the piles of plastic began to grow. The shoe manufacturer's truck arrived an hour later. 'Thanks for all your hard work,' said the driver. '(A few / A little / Few)⁷ runners think about the time and energy you guys put into collecting this stuff.' The team leader smiled. 'We don't mind giving (few / little / a little)⁸ time and energy as long as (a few / few / a little)⁹ pairs of trainers come out of what we've collected today,' she said.

FILE 19 | **Unit 5, Section B, Task 5B** | → page 61

Copy and complete the flow chart below that shows the life cycle of a recycled shoe.
Use the verbs in the brackets in the passive. The tenses you must use have been given for you.
Remember to put the adverb in brackets in the correct position.

Plastic bottles ⬭ ¹ by people around the world. (buy; simple present)

1

Once the contents ⬭ ², the plastic bottles ⬭ ³ away. (drink; present perfect – throw; simple present)

2

Rivers and seas ⬭ ⁴ (often) to dispose of plastic bottles. (use; simple present)

3

In the plant they ⬭ ⁷ up into very small pieces. (chop; simple present)

4

Then the bottles ⬭ ⁶ to a recycling plant. (take; simple present)

5

The plastic bottles ⬭ ⁵ from the sea by ecological companies. (collect; simple present)

6

The small pieces ⬭ ⁸ down. (melt; simple present)

7

The material ⬭ ⁹ (then) to make shoes. (use; simple present)

8

The recycled shoes ⬭ ¹⁰ by customers. (buy; simple present)

9

After the shoes ⬭ ¹¹ for several years, the shoes can ⬭ ¹² to the company to ⬭ ¹³. (wear; present perfect – return; infinitive – recycle; infinitive)

10

FILE 20 | **Unit 5, Section B, Task 6B** | → page 62

You watched a TED talk about shopping and sustainability, in which the speaker made the following statement:

'Consumers should stop buying cheap clothes which they throw away after they've worn them a few times.'

Read the suggestions in the skills box on page 62. Then, using some of the words and phrases you collected in task 6A on page 62, write a comment in English on the statement in about 100 words.

Machen Sie zuerst ein Brainstorming, um Argumente und Ideen zu sammeln. Erstellen Sie Liste mit Pro und Contra, zum Beispiel:

PRO	CONTRA
Billions of people throwing away clothes each year means more rubbish.	Not everyone can afford expensive clothes.
weitere Argumente	*weitere Argumente*

Wählen Sie Ihre zwei besten Argumente für Pro und Contra. Entscheiden sie sich, ob Sie eher für oder gegen die Behauptung sind.

Schreiben Sie eine Einleitung; in diese dürfen eigene Erlebnisse, persönliche Einschätzungen oder auch Statistiken einfließen, z. B.:

Today most people can afford to buy lots of stuff without worrying about the price.

Oder:

Today the malls are full of shoppers. But is this a good thing?

Im zweiten Absatz schreiben Sie Ihre Argumente für oder gegen die Aussage. Wenn Sie für die Aussage sind, dann schreiben Sie die Contra-Argumente auf, oder umgekehrt.

Im dritten Absatz schreiben Sie Argumente für die Gegenseite.

Im letzten Absatz ziehen Sie ein Fazit dessen, was Sie geschrieben haben. Oder Sie schreiben hier explizit Ihre Meinung. Sie können auch Ihre Leser zu einem bestimmten Verhalten aufrufen.

To conclude, ━

FILE 21   **Unit 5, Section C, Task 1** → page 63

These sayings are used in the audio text. Before you listen, talk in groups and decide which of the German expressions below they correspond to.

1. A fool and his money are soon parted.
2. Money doesn't grow on trees.
3. You can't take it with you when you go.

a. Zum Leben zu wenig, zum Sterben zu viel.
b. Das letzte Hemd hat keine Taschen.
c. Dem Narren rinnt das Geld zwischen den Fingern hindurch.
d. Ein Narr spricht, der Kluge denkt.
e. Geld kommt immer zu Geld.
f. Das Geld fällt nicht vom Himmel.

FILE 22 — Unit 5, Section C, Task 5 → page 65

Put these sentences together using relative clauses. Some need to be slightly rewritten. The first one has been done for you.

1 The trainers are quite expensive. I bought them today. (defining clause, contact clause)
The trainers (which) I bought today are expensive.

2 John's new car was damaged in an accident last week. The car cost him all his savings. (non-defining clause)

3 TTW Company used to be one of the biggest producers of sports clothing. TTW Company went bankrupt last month. (non-defining clause)

4 The zip on the jacket is already broken. I bought the jacket yesterday. (defining clause, contact clause)

5 I need to speak to someone. That person must work in the Sales Department. (defining clause)

6 That's the man. He sold me the jacket. (defining clause)

7 My boyfriend spent money on my present. It was all the money which he had. (defining clause, contact clause)

8 TTW Ltd won the contract. This surprised many people in the industry. (non-defining clause)

FILE 23 — Unit 5, World of intercultural communication, Task 2C → page 67

Sie arbeiten als Verkäufer/in in einem Sportgeschäft. Sie begrüßen einen Kunden / eine Kundin: Was würden Sie im Dialog jeweils auf Englisch sagen? Versuchen Sie auch, im Dialog Wörter wie *well, certainly, great, no problem* u.ä. zu verwenden.

You: *1 Begrüßen Sie den Kunden / die Kundin und fragen Sie ihn/sie, ob Sie ihm/ihr helfen können.*

Customer: Hi, yes. I'm looking for a pair of trainers.

You: *2 Bemerken Sie humorvoll, dass er/sie am richtigen Ort ist. Fragen Sie anschließend, ob er/sie eine bestimmte Marke sucht.*

Customer: No, just some nice trainers.

You: *3 Zeigen Sie ihm/ihr das beliebteste Modell. Fragen Sie dann nach seiner/ihrer Größe. (Benutzen Sie Might I ask …?)*

Customer: I'm size 42. I like this model. Can I try it on?

You: *4 Während der Kunde / die Kundin die Sportschuhe anprobiert, machen Sie Small Talk: Fragen Sie ihn/sie, ob er/sie es schafft, trotz des regnerischen Wetters trocken zu bleiben.*

Customer: It is miserable. I'll be glad to get home. The trainers fit quite nicely.

You: *5 Sie sagen, dass dies schön zu hören ist. Sie fragen, ob er/sie gerne joggen geht.*

Customer: No, not really. They're just to wear around town.

You: *6 Sie sagen, dass Sie Sportschuhe auch nur zum Herumlaufen tragen und dass Sie das gleiche Modell ebenfalls genau dafür gekauft haben: Sie können sie wirklich empfehlen.*

Customer: Great! They feel comfortable. I'll take them. Now I also need a track suit.

You: *7 Sie zeigen dem Kunden / der Kundin, dass sich die Auswahl vieler verschiedener Trainingsanzüge da drüben (over there) befindet und er/sie sie sich in Ruhe anschauen soll. Er/sie soll Sie rufen, falls er/sie Hilfe benötigt.*

FILE 24   **Unit 6, Section B, Task 3**   → page 72

You have the opportunity to ask Joey, Alex and Brent some questions.
Ask them the questions below in English, using the vocabulary and grammar hints.

1 Fragen Sie Joey, wann er das letzte Mal Livestreaming gemacht hat.
   When – you – last – livestreaming? (use; past tense)

2 Fragen Sie Joey, wie lange er schon Zirkuskunststücke macht.
   How long – you – circus tricks? (do; present perfect continuous)

3 Fragen Sie Alex, wie viele Viewer sie normalerweise hat.
   How many viewers – you – normally? (have; simple present)

4 Fragen Sie Alex, wie viel sie als Musikerin verdient hat, bevor sie mit dem Livestreaming anfing.
   How much – you – as a musician – before you – livestreaming?
   (earn; simple past – start; simple past)

5 Fragen Sie Brent, weshalb er meint, sein Leben sei langweilig.
   Why – you – that – your life – boring? (think; simple present – be; simple present)

6 Fragen Sie Brent, ob er schon Erfahrung mit Identitätsdiebstahl gemacht hat.
   You – any experience of identity theft? (have; present perfect)

FILE 25   **Unit 6, Section B, Task 6**   → page 73

In a statement you are expected to give your own opinion on something.

Before you start, do a mind map, in which you collect ideas from the text on page 71.
Add some of your own ideas.

Give your opinion on livestreaming in about 100 words. You can start like this:

So, you want to hear our views on livestreaming? I personally think that …

Entscheiden Sie, wie Ihre Argumentation weitergehen soll.

Entweder:

I personally think that livestreaming is the future and we need to use it as soon as possible.

Oder:

I personally think that livestreaming is dangerous for us as a group and as individuals.

Vervollständigen Sie einige der Absätze mit Ihren eigenen Ideen.

Entweder:

We can use livestreaming to

There are several advantages to using live streaming. People like it because

The reason why I love livestreaming is because

Oder:

Livestreaming is not secure. What this means is that

Livestreaming is not an effective way to

The main disadvantage of livestreaming is that

FILE 26   **Unit 6, Section C, Task 5**   → page 77

Look at the bar chart on page 77. Write a short description of the information by filling in the gaps below. The first gap has been filled in for you. The gaps contain between one and five words each.

Erklären, wen die Statistik betrifft:

The survey concerns social media users aged *between 14 and 22 years old*[1].

It identifies two groups: [2] and [3].

Allgemeiner Befund:

Social media affects the two groups [4].

Positive Aspekte beschreiben:

On the one hand, social media is very important for [5] of depressed people for inspiration and social contact.

For people who are not depressed, social media seems [6]. [7] consider social media very important for inspiration and social contact.

Negative Aspekte beschreiben:

On the other hand, social media also makes many depressed people feel [8]. [9] feel they get little or no feedback from their social media use.

People without depression generally don't have these negative feelings. [10] feel they don't get enough feedback from their social media use. [11] feel left out when using social media.

Zusammenfassen:

In conclusion, we can see that for people with depression, social media use [12]. Depression may cause people to [13], but it may also [14].

FILE 27 **Unit 7, Section B, Task 3B** → page 84

An American friend of yours wants to go to Scotland on holiday. You give him or her the advice below by matching the parts of the sentences in the box with the beginning of the sentences (1–6).

> can go on a Youth Discovery holiday ▪ can go to museums ▪
> find information about accommodation ▪ have fun but not meet locals ▪
> meet other young tourists ▪ see traditional Scottish sports

1 If you enjoy outdoor activities, ●

2 If you visit the Highland Games, ●

3 If the weather is bad, ●

4 If you stay in a hostel, ●

5 If you visit the homepage of 'Visit Scotland', ●

6 If you go with a big group of youngsters, ●

FILE 28 **Unit 7, Section B, Task 6** → page 86

You are going with a group of eight friends aged 16 to 17 to Scotland for two weeks. Four are from your school and four from your partner school in England. You are in charge of getting information about accommodation. Based on what you read in the text and your own experience, recommend one type of accommodation for the group. Write about 100 words.

> Hi everyone,
> I've just read an article on the internet about accommodation in Scotland, and I would recommend that we stay ●
> There are some reasons why this is the best choice.
> Firstly, ●
> Secondly, ●
> Let me know what you think.

FILE 29 **Unit 7, Section C, Task 4B** → page 89

Work with a partner.

Partner A: You are a German teenager who has decided to book a hostel with three of your friends. Write an email to the hostel, asking for information. Use the email on the opposite page as an example.

Dear Sir or Madam,

I am writing to enquire about the possibility of staying in your hostel.

We are ▬ (Anzahl und Alter).

We would like to stay for ▬ nights from 28 July to 2 August.

Could you please tell us what ▬ (Preis für vier Personen)?

I would also be grateful if you could inform me of ▬ (Check-in- und Check-out-Zeit, Ausstattung).

Finally, you could please inform me of ▬ (Zahlungsweise).

I look forward to hearing from you soon.

Yours

(Name)

Partner B: You are the hostel manager. Reply to the email, using the email below as an example:

Dear (Name),

Many thanks for your email requesting information about our hostel.

Here is the information you require:

We have different prices for different rooms:

If you wish to stay in one room together, ▬ (£40 pro Nacht, also insgesamt £200).

If you wish to book two double rooms, ▬ (£60 pro Nacht, also insgesamt £300).

Our check-in time is ▬, and our check-out time is ▬.

We accept ▬ (Zahlungsweise).

The hostel offers the following facilities: ▬ (Denken Sie sich einige aus, z. B. Fahrradverleih, Waschmaschine, Küche usw.).

I hope this information is of use to you.

(Beenden Sie die E-Mail höflich).

Partner A: On the basis of the response, decide on your sleeping situation and book the accommodation.

| FILE 30 | Unit 7, World of intercultural communication, Task 3 | → page 91 |

You are backpacking around Scotland and want to reserve a bed in a hostel. Role-play a telephone dialogue with the hostel manager. When you have finished, change roles and role-play the dialogue again.

Partner A: Hostel manager Martin/Mary MacDonald	Partner B: You, trying to reserve a bed in a hostel
→ Begrüßen Sie den Anrufer / die Anruferin. *Good morning/afternoon/evening.* *My name's … .* *How can I help you?*	→ Nennen Sie Ihren Namen und sagen Sie, dass Sie ab morgen ein Bett für sechs Nächte reservieren möchten. *Hi, my name's … I'd like to reserve/book …*
→ Sagen Sie, dass ein Einzelzimmer verfügbar ist oder auch ein Bett in einem Acht-Bett- Schlafraum. *Just a moment, please. Let me just check.* *… a single room* *… a bed in an eight-bed dormitory*	→ Bitten Sie den Gesprächspartner / die Gesprächspartnerin, alles noch einmal und etwas langsamer zu sagen. *I'm sorry …* *Could you please …?*
→ Wiederholen Sie, was Sie gesagt haben. *Of course. I said …*	→ Bedanken Sie sich und fragen Sie nach dem jeweiligen Preis pro Nacht. *Thanks. Could you tell me how much they …* *per night?*
→ Sagen Sie, dass der Preis für ein Einzel- zimmer bei £22 und für ein Bett im Schlafraum bei £12 pro Nacht liegt. *… single room … £22 a night* *… bed in dormitory … £12 a night*	→ Entscheiden Sie sich und sagen Sie, welches Bett Sie reservieren möchten. *That's great! I'd like to …*
→ Bitten Sie den Anrufer / die Anruferin lauter zu sprechen, da die Verbindung schlecht ist. *I'm sorry. Would you mind … ?* *The connection is …*	→ Wiederholen Sie ihre Entscheidung und nennen Sie Ihren Namen. *I said that I would like …* *And my name is …*
→ Bitten Sie den Anrufer / die Anruferin, den Namen zu buchstabieren. *That's fine. Could you please … ?*	→ Buchstabieren Sie Ihren Namen. *It's …*
→ Wiederholen Sie den Namen. Fragen Sie nach der Telefonnummer des Anrufers / der Anruferin. *OK. Let me spell that back to you. It's …* *Could you also … ?*	→ Nennen Sie Ihre Telefonnummer. *It's …*
→ Wiederholen Sie die Telefonnummer. Sagen Sie, dass Sie sich auf die Ankunft freuen und dass die Check-in-Zeit ab 14 Uhr ist. *OK, so let me repeat that: It's …*	→ Bitten Sie den Gesprächspartner / die Gesprächspartnerin die Check-in-Zeit zu wiederholen. *I didn't … Could you please … ?*
→ Wiederholen Sie die Check-in-Zeit. Fragen Sie, ob der Anrufer / die Anruferin sie nun verstanden hat.	→ Bestätigen Sie dies. Beenden Sie den Anruf höflich. *Yes, …*

FILE 31 | **Unit 8, Section B, Task 3E** | → page 97

A collocation is when words usually go together, for example 'do sport' (*Sport treiben*) or 'immediate family' (*engste Familie*). Add words from column A to words from column B to make collocations. All the collocations are in the text.

column A					
1	adoption	4	cultural	7	identical
2	adoptive	5	DNA	8	lactose
3	career	6	finish	9	only

column B					
a	agency	d	identity	g	school
b	child	e	intolerant	h	test
c	choice	f	parents	i	twins

FILE 32 | **Unit 8, Section C, Task 3** | → page 98

Jennifer, from Berlin, and Patience, from Cape Town, study at university in Stuttgart. Jennifer often invites Patience to visit her family in Berlin. Last month Jennifer went to stay with Patience in Cape Town for a month. After the visit, they talk on videochat.

Read the videochat below and complete the dialogue with the correct option in brackets (adjective or adverb, comparative or superlative).

A VIDEOCHAT: Berlin to Cape Town

Patience: What's it like being back home?

Jennifer: It's OK. But I miss you and your family, and I definitely miss the ▬ ¹ (good / better / best) food I've ever eaten in my life.

Patience: I'll ask my mum to send your dad some recipes. I always meant to say that I found it ▬ ² (strange / stranger / strangely) when I first saw your dad cooking. You know now that my dad never steps foot in the kitchen. He says he works ▬ ³ (hard / harder / hardly) enough in the office all day.

Jennifer: Yes. I realized that. I enjoyed cooking with your mum and your aunts, though. It was a lot of fun.

Patience: They loved having you here. My family is ▬ ⁴ (louder / more loud / more loudly) than any family I know. I was worried it might all be too ▬ ⁵ (noisy / noisier / noisily) for you, so I asked them to talk ▬ ⁶ (more quietly / more quiet / quietlier).

Jennifer: I got used to it ▬ ⁷ (quick / quicker / quickly). Germans are much ▬ ⁸ (quiet / quieter / quietest). By the way, I told my family they have to be a lot ▬ ⁹ (careful / more careful / more carefully) with water.

Patience: That's ▬ ¹⁰ (great / greater / the greatest). I remember helping your brothers fill the dishwasher and they were using so much water to rinse the plates. Tell them we had a zero-water day in Cape Town when the government thought we were going to run out of water.

Jennifer: I'll do that. We think we'll always have water in Germany, because it's ▬ ¹¹ (continual / more continual / continually) raining. How are your brothers, by the way?

Patience: Oh. The same as usual. They're the ▬ ¹² (lazy / lazier / laziest) boys I've ever met. They never help with laying the table or cleaning up in the kitchen like your brothers. They behave so ▬ ¹³ (bad / worse / badly). They ▬ ¹⁴ (hard / harder / hardly) ever help at home.

Jennifer: My mum always says that boys get ▬ ¹⁵ (good / better / well) as they get ▬ ¹⁶ (old / older / most old).

Patience: I can only see my brothers getting ▬ ¹⁷ (bad / worse / worst).

FILE 33   **Unit 9, Section B, Task 4D**   → page 109

Use the words on the right to answer the following questions.

1 Where will you be on Saturday evening?   I / imagine / I / be / at home / playing video games / on Saturday evening

2 Where will you be at the weekend?   I / probably / meet up / with friends / at the weekend

3 Where will you be at 6 a.m. tomorrow?   I / sure / I / be / in bed / at 6 a.m. tomorrow

4 Where will you be at this time next week?   I / not know / where / I / be / at this time next week

5 Where will you be this summer?   I / expect / I / travel / to Spain / with my family / this summer

6 Where will you be next year?   I / think / I / be doing / an internship / in a firm next year

Now write your own answers to the questions, using any of the expressions in the answers above.

FILE 34   **Unit 9, Section C, Task 3B**   → page 111

Work in small groups. Talk about what you are going to do at the weekend. Use some of the time phrases in the box and some of suggestions below, as well as your own.

> at the weekend ▪ on Saturday morning ▪ on Sunday evening ▪
> early in the morning ▪ all weekend

get up really late / go grocery shopping with my parents / meet up with some friends in town / watch a football match / watch TV and eat pizza / go to a party I've been invited to / go for a long walk

FILE 35	Unit 10, Section B, Task 2C, Question 1	→ page 122

How does Sophie's attitude change during the course of the text, and why?

Hint: These important points in the text tell you what Sophie is thinking:

I was very excited.   *The opening ceremony was amazing.*

I was disappointed.   *I realized I was enjoying myself.*

It was terrifying.   *It was thrilling.*

FILE 36	Unit 10, Section B, Task 2C, Question 2	→ page 122

What kind of person is Mr Duncan? Find evidence in the text to support your opinion.

Hint: These important points in the text tell you what Mr Duncan is like.

Mr Duncan had bought tickets for the first game of the NFL season.

Mr Duncan patiently explained the rules of football to me …

I couldn't disappoint the Duncans, who had been so kind to me.

Mr Duncan rushed down to the fast food stands to get us something to eat and drink.

Dad doesn't really like football. He just wanted to take you to a game, as you're such a fan.

FILE 37	Unit 11, Section B, Task 4	→ page 136

Fill in the gaps with words from the box below. All the words are taken from the texts on pages 133 and 134.

> ancestors ▪ attitude ▪ community ▪ dangers ▪ indigenous ▪
> open-minded ▪ responsibility ▪ tiny

1 She was surprised to find that she had African , as she looked very European. (lines 1–13)
2 Rather than keeping problems within the family, we discuss them with other members of the  such as friends and neighbours. (lines 1–13)
3 Almost everyone speaks English in Australia, but there are many  languages. (lines 14–22)
4 Do the local people have a positive  towards immigrants? (lines 23–31)
5 Compared to a big city like Sydney, towns in the bush are . (lines 32–45)
6 Both the bush and the city have their own  – wild animals on the one hand, fast moving vehicles on the other. (lines 32–45)
7 It is the  of the elders to pass on the tribe's traditional knowledge. (lines 46–53)
8 I used to have strong opinions, but experiencing other cultures has made me more . (lines 46–53)

FILE 38 — Unit 11, Section C, Task 3B — → page 139

Complete the sentences by filling in the gaps with the correct form of the verbs below.

> attract ■ can ■ have ■ not have ■ make ■ meet up ■ produce ■ travel

1 If we all lived like the Amish, maybe we ⬮ less pollution.
2 If I were an Amish teenager doing *rumspringa*, I ⬮ around the world.
3 Fewer young Amish would come back after *rumspringa* if they ⬮ work in the outside world.
4 I wouldn't miss my mobile phone and social media if I ⬮ with my friends all the time.
5 If we couldn't dance or listen to music, we ⬮ so much fun.
6 Maybe the Amish ⬮ more people to their religion if their religious views were less strict.
7 If I had to live with the Amish for a year, it ⬮ me think more about my own lifestyle.
8 I wonder what young Amish would do if they ⬮ more freedom.

FILE 39 — Unit 12, Section B, Task 3 — → page 148

Fill in the gaps with words from the box below. They are all taken from the main part of the text (lines 1–44).

> campaigned ■ discrimination ■ economic ■ equality ■ non-violent ■
> pressure ■ rights ■ segregation ■ shooting ■ treatment ■ violence

A: When was the civil ⬮[1] movement in the USA?
B: It was a movement that took place during the 1950s and 1960s. Before World War Two, racial ⬮[2] had kept the better jobs for white people. Suddenly in 1941, African Americans were needed to fill many positions in industry which white Americans left vacant when they left to fight in the war. African Americans soon had more ⬮[3] power and were able to use it to get better social ⬮[4].
A: I've heard about a woman called Rosa Parks. Who was she?
B: She was a black woman who refused to give up her seat on a bus in Alabama to a white man in 1955. Her action became the focus for the fight for racial ⬮[5]. Until this point, ⬮[6] of white and black citizens on public transport and in many other areas of life was normal and legal.
A: What did the activists do? Did they attack police or white businesses? Did they start riots?
B: No, the movement was ⬮[7], although controversial figures such as Malcolm X wanted a more aggressive approach. But mostly the leaders of the movement ⬮[8] peacefully for change.
A: What happened to Malcolm X? Wasn't he killed?
B: That's right, like Martin Luther King Jr, he was the victim of a political ⬮[9].
A: Didn't that mean that the white racists had won by using ⬮[10]?
B: Not at all. The deaths of Malcolm X in 1965 and Martin Luther King Jr. three years later created a lot of public sympathy for the movement and put ⬮[11] on the government to change the law.

FILE 40 Unit 12, Section C, Task 5 → page 151

Describe the cartoon. What can you see? What is happening? What is the cartoon's message? You can use these sentence beginnings to structure your description.

In the foreground, two …
They are looking …
One of the figures is saying to the other …
In the distance, we can see …

This probably refers to the time when …
The cartoon reflects the fact that …
The cartoonist seems to be suggesting that …

Vocabulary that may be useful:

native people ▪ sailing ship ▪ first contact ▪ colonization ▪ exploration ▪
exploitation ▪ immigrant ▪ negative experience

FILE 41 Unit 13, Section B, Task 5, Part 2 → page 161

Write a short text. It could be in the form of questions to the reader, or statements, or (invented) quotations from people who have learned English as a foreign language. You can use one or more of these ideas in your short text.

Provocative questions:
Do you want to ⬤ ?
Do you enjoy ⬤-ing ⬤ ?
Have you ever dreamed of ⬤-ing ⬤ ?
Do your career goals include ⬤ ?
Then you need to learn English!

Personal testimony (with the name of the person):
When I started learning English, I had no idea that ⬤
Now I know that ⬤
I really enjoy ⬤
I plan to ⬤

Persuasive facts:
Did you know that ⬤ ?
English is spoken ⬤
Companies expect ⬤
⬤ per cent of web pages ⬤
Clearly, it's essential to ⬤ if you want ⬤

FILE 42   **Unit 14, Section B, Task 5**   → page 175

Just as there is a Working Holiday programme for Germans in Australia (Unit 9, page 110), so too is there one for Australians in Germany. An Australian website for youngsters has asked you to write a blog entry with information for young Australians.

Do some research about the sort of jobs they could find and about things they should see or do, and explain to them why the experience will be good for them. Structure your ideas so that the information is easy to read.

To start you off, here a list of four places where Australians might find work and two things they should experience.

Where to find work	What to experience
in a hotel	the nightlife in Berlin
on a farm	the Oktoberfest
in a call centre	▬
in a start-up company	▬
▬	▬

FILE 1 | **Unit 5, Section C, Task 7** → page 65

Your school has decided to introduce 'Sustainable Fridays' to make students aware of the environmental impact of their lives.

You and a partner discuss ways in which students can change their habits.

Agree on two things which you think every student can start or stop doing every Friday to reduce their environmental impact.

You can use these photos to help you come up with some ideas.

PLASTIC BAG

ECO BAG

PAPER BAG

FRIDAYS FOR FUTURE!

100% POLYESTER WARM MACHINE WASH WITH SIMILAR COLOUR DO NOT...

SECOND HAND

FILE 2 | **Unit 6, Section C, Task 4** → page 76

Your school has been offered a large sum of money to improve its electronic equipment for classroom use. The headteacher wants students to decide how the money should be spent.

Discuss your ideas with your partner and agree on two things you think the school should buy for the students to use.

You can use these photos to help you come up with some ideas.

e-book reader

tablet

laptop

whiteboard

multi-function printer

FILE 3   Unit 9, Section C, Task 5A   → page 113

You and a friend have organized a Working Holiday Visa for Australia. You don't know yet where you will work, but you want to prepare your trip. You want to visit at least two places while you are there. Discuss your ideas with your partner and agree on two places you want to visit. The photos on this page may help you come up with some ideas.

Great barrier reef, Queensland

Aboriginal festival, Queensland

Bondi beach, Sydney

Wave Rock, Western Australia

Koala sanctuary, Victoria

Uluru, Northern Territory

FILE 4   Unit 13, Section C, Task 3   → page 162

A new student from India has joined your class. Your teacher asks you to make a list of things which you think foreigners living in Germany should know about the country. With your partner discuss which two things you should put on the list. The photos may help you come up with ideas.

house shoes

coffee and cake

Du?

Sie!   being formal

bureaucracy

following rules

being punctual

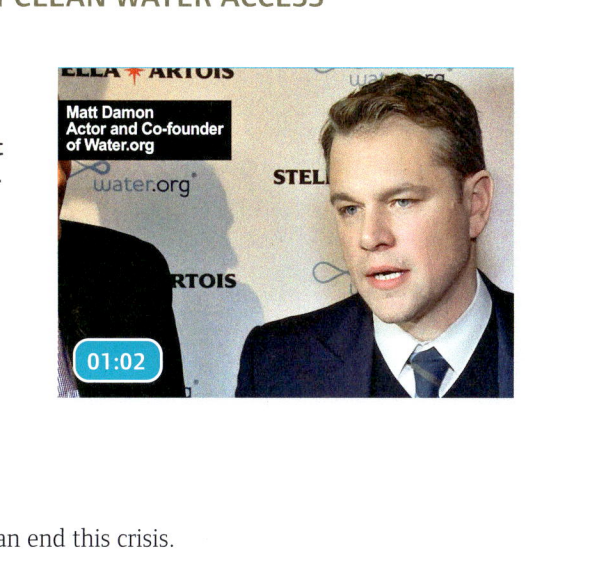

Unit 3, Section C, Task 5 → page 43

MATT DAMON CALLS FOR ACTION ON CLEAN WATER ACCESS

1 **A German journalist at Davos mediated some parts of Matt Damon's speech. Match Matt Damon's soundbites (1–6) to the gist of what he says (a–f). The soundbites are in the order that you hear them in the video.**

1   Water and sanitation undergirded everything.
2   The magnitude of the problem was mind-blowing.
3   The problem is solvable.
4   It animates their entire lives.
5   It's robbing people of their potential.
6   If we make this comprehensive effort, we can end this crisis.

a   Das Problem ist lösbar.
b   Die Größe des Problems war atemberaubend.
c   Es bestimmt ihr ganzes Leben.
d   Es raubt den Menschen Möglichkeiten.
e   Wasser und sanitäre Anlagen unterstützten alles.
f   Wenn wir diese umfangreiche Aufgabe angehen, können wir diese Krise beenden.

2   **Choose one word or phrase from the box to complete the notes. There are two words more than you need. The first answer has been done for you.**

> are thinking about ▪ complex ▪ get educated ▪ in our lifetime ▪
> interested ▪ interesting ▪ learning ▪ shocked ▪ west ▪ USA

1   Some years ago, Matt Damon was *learning* ª and trying to *get educated* ᵇ about issues of poverty.
2   He was 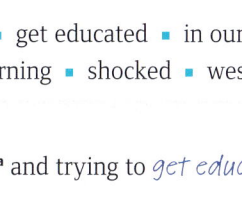 by how water and sanitation problems surrounded everything.
3   Apart from "mind-blowing", he described the problems as endlessly  ª and 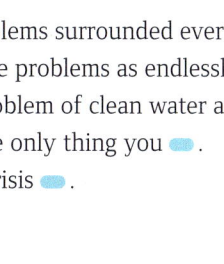 ᵇ.
4   Those of us who live in the 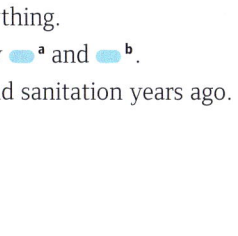 solved the problem of clean water and sanitation years ago.
5   When you don't have access to water, it's the only thing you 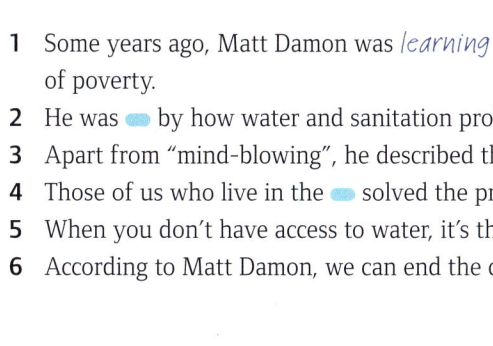.
6   According to Matt Damon, we can end the crisis 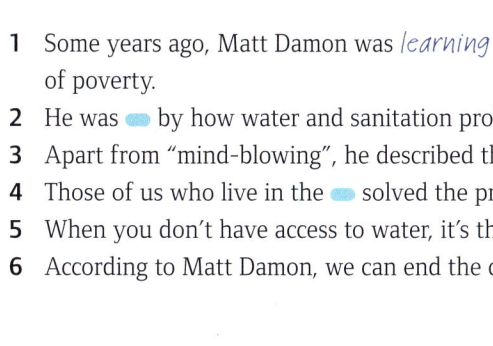.

02

Unit 5, Section C, Task 6 → page 65

FRANCE PONDERS OPENING SHOPS ON SUNDAYS DESPITE TRADITION

The French government wants shops to open on more Sundays to boost consumption in an economy in need of a lift.

1 **Listen to the opinions of the speakers in the video and complete the following statements with words and expressions from the box. There is one word for each gap.**

01:10

> buy something ▪ buyers ▪ convenient ▪
> do your shopping ▪ during the week ▪
> family ▪ need ▪ sacred ▪ shop ▪
> stays open ▪ to shop ▪ walks ▪ work

The shopper from …

1 Belgium says: "This could make people want ⬤ᵃ, even if they didn't plan to. The shop is open, you go in and maybe ⬤ᵇ."

2 the USA says: "I understand why Sunday is so ⬤ᵃ in France and all that, but I think we're at a crossroads now where people ⬤ᵇ to shop and people are busy and Sunday's a great day and it'd be great if the store ⬤ᶜ."

3 Tours (France) says: "It's more ⬤ᵃ for everyone, we're happy to run errands on Sunday because ⬤ᵇ we don't have the time."

4 Portugal says: "I think it's worse for the people who ⬤ᵃ, but for the ⬤ᵇ it's good because during the week it's difficult. On Sunday you can ⬤ᶜ more comfortably."

5 China says: "Sunday is a ⬤ᵃ day, we go out for ⬤ᵇ. Besides I work in a ⬤ᶜ, I wouldn't like it very much if I had to work."

2 **Talk in groups and give your opinion. Use words and expressions from the video if you can. Here are some points to get you started. Report back to the class.**

▪ How often are shops open on Sundays in your area?
▪ How often do you go shopping when the shops are open on Sundays?
▪ What do you usually do on Sundays?

AUSTRALIANS CELEBRATE ANCIENT INDIGENOUS CULTURE

1 **Read the text from a newspaper and list the activities that visitors to the event can experience.**

NAIDOC in the City is here again!

NAIDOC in the City is an annual event that celebrates the indigenous peoples of Australia. Thousands of people will be attending Sydney's popular annual showcase of indigenous culture in Hyde Park on Monday 2 July.

The city of Sydney event will include a whole range of family-friendly activities and performances, including:

- live music
- dance performances
- kids zones
- a Gunya (a structure for living in made from natural materials)
- a marketplace for arts and crafts
- a sports clinic
- food stalls

The theme for **NAIDOC in the City** is "Our Languages Matter". The theme hopes to draw attention to the importance and richness of indigenous Australian languages.

2 **Watch the video. Which of the activities you listed in task 1 do you see in the video?**

3 **Complete this soundbite from the video:**

Matthew Doyle:
"It gives ⬤ ¹ around Australia an opportunity to ⬤ ² our culture, the ⬤ ³ in the world, and to ⬤ ⁴ and indeed with ⬤ ⁵ to our shores."

00:33

4 **Use your answers to task 3 to write one sentence explaining to visitors what the celebrations are about.**

5 **Write a short review in German of the event for a travel website. Include the significance of the event, what you can see and do, and what it feels like to be there.**

UNIT 1

Canned food or fresh food – which is better for your health?

Many people believe that canned foods are less healthy than food that is freshly made. A recent university study compared both types of food and found out that, in a lot of cases,

5   canned foods have similar amounts of vitamins and minerals as the same foods we buy fresh. Food from cans is also often a good source of protein and fibre.

fresh vegetables

The researchers tested dairy products, fish,
10   fruit, vegetables, meat, pasta and soups. Here are some of the results.

Rice pudding: The canned dessert is lower in fat than homemade rice pudding, even when it's made with semi-skimmed milk. Both homemade and canned rice pudding have about the same amount of calcium, but the stuff we buy in cans has three times as much vitamin E and twice as
15   much iodine as the pudding we make at home.

Fish: The researchers found more calcium in canned fish than in fresh fish. This is because the canned fish producers leave some small bones in their products. The bones are soft, so we eat them and take in calcium from them. When they looked at tuna fish canned in salt water, they found it had less saturated fat than fresh tuna. Canned tuna was also a good source of vitamins
20   D, B_{12} and B_6, niacin and phosphorus.

Vegetables: Canned peas give us twice as much beta-carotene as fresh peas and a third more calcium. Even though canned carrots do not have as much beta-carotene, thiamine and folate as fresh carrots, they still give us a similar amount of other vitamins and minerals.

The results of the study showed that you can eat canned foods and get the same amount of
25   goodness as you get from eating fresh foods. As one of the researchers said, 'Canned food takes less time to prepare and cook than fresh foods so people who are too busy to prepare and cook fresh can still have a healthy diet using canned food.'

(326 words)

| 13 | semi-skimmed milk: | 15 | iodine: *Jod* |
| | *Halbfettmilch* | 22 | folate: *Folsäure* |

frozen vegetables

canned vegetables

1 PREPARING TO READ

Study the highlighted words and expressions in the text and say which of them you …

a know and how you know them. (For example, it's like a German word.)
b can guess the meaning of. (How did you guess?)
c need to look up in your dictionary. (Look them up now and add them to your vocabulary notebook.)

2 READING AND UNDERSTANDING THE TEXT

Beantworten Sie folgende Fragen auf Deutsch in ganzen Sätzen.

1 What did the studies compare? (2 items)
2 What was the result?
3 What types of foods did the researchers look at? (7 items)
4 Which is more nutritious, according to the research?
    a canned rice pudding or homemade rice pudding?
    b canned fish or fresh fish?
    c canned peas or fresh peas?
5 Why should no one feel bad about eating canned foods?

3 WORKING WITH WORDS

Find nouns in the text to match the definitions below. The definitions are in the order the words appear in the text.

1 scientists who study things carefully and write reports about them
2 where we get something from
3 business people who make something …
4 … and the things they make
5 a skeleton (*Skelett*) has many of these
6 a large sea fish

4 A SUMMARY OF THE TEXT

Choose the best summary of the text.

1 According to two studies, fresh food always has more vitamins and minerals than canned food. If you have to, you can eat food from a can, but it won't be as good for you as fresh food.
2 Researchers found out that that canned food is just as good for you as fresh food. In some cases canned foods have more nutrients. If you don't have time to buy and prepare fresh food, you can open a can and still eat a healthy meal.
3 Two studies looked at canned food and fresh food. Canned food is quicker to prepare than homemade food. In some cases canned food contains just as many vitamins and minerals. However, it is not as healthy as fresh food.

UNIT 2

How to improve grades while having fun

A recent US survey of 14–18-year-olds shows that high-school students who play a team sport are likely to get better grades than other students.

Academics from two US universities studied data from 9,700 students from schools in urban, suburban and rural areas. All of the students took part in different types of after-school activities,
5   including music, dance and acting societies, clubs that prepared students for jobs, and team sports.

The academics looked for connections between the types of after-school activities and how the teenagers performed in tests and exams at school.

What they discovered was that students who took part in team sports did better than those who took part in other activities. Three of the most interesting results showed that

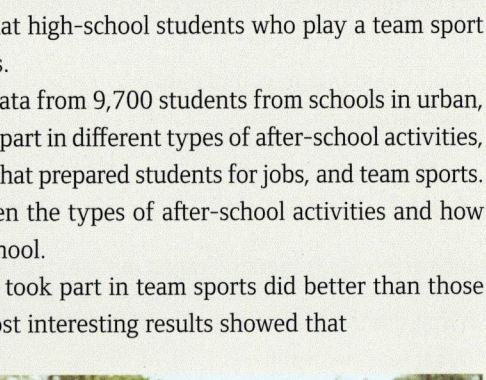

10   ■ students who play team sports are more successful in day-to-day learning in the classroom;

   ■ young people who take part in sport have the self-esteem and
15   determination that makes them more likely to succeed academically than those who prefer other types of activities;

   ■ teenagers who belong to sports
20   clubs are more likely to complete their high-school years and enter higher education than their peers.

One of the academics on the study said: 'Sport allows young people to develop a mentoring relationship with adults and with other students who have a positive feeling about school. These
25   people encourage the others to become more focused on school work. They may also help people develop time-management skills and the ability to deal with problems. Team sports also help young people learn how to work with others.'   (256 words)

03 **academic:** *Wissenschaftler/in*
17 **academically:** *in der Schule, im Studium*

23 **mentoring relationship:** *Mentorverhältnis*
26 **time-management skills:** *Zeitmanagementkompetenz*

1 PREPARING TO READ

Study the headline and the photo. What will the text tell us?

1 After-school activities help students make friends.
2 Doing sports after class helps pupils do better at school.
3 Hanging around with friends makes learning easier.

2 READING AND UNDERSTANDING THE TEXT

Decide whether the following statements are true or false.

Explain your decision in German in full sentences.

1 The report is about a survey of American university students.
2 Only students who do sports activities after school took part in the survey.
3 According to the study, students who play competitive team sports are good learners.
4 Playing in a team helps students to build up their confidence and will-power.
5 Students who play sport often drop out of school.
6 Students who do sports often help other people improve their business and people skills.

3 WORKING WITH WORDS

Decide which word does not belong in the group. Say why.

1	grade	mark	note	score
2	exercise	games	plays	sport
3	college	education	school	university
4	abilities	competences	energy	skills

4 DESCRIBING A PHOTO

Choose the best description of the photo on page 202.

A The photo shows a group of teenagers sitting with an older man on a football pitch. The teenagers are listening carefully to the man. Everyone looks serious. I think the man is asking the teenagers what they think about the game so far. The other teenagers in the background may be waiting for the man to invite them to join the group.

B The photo shows a group of teenage boys sitting with a man on a football pitch. The teenagers are listening carefully to the man. He may be their coach. I think the man is giving the teenagers tips about how to improve their game. The other teenagers in the background may be members of the opposing team.

C The photo shows a group of students sitting outside in the sunshine with a man who may be their sports teacher. The members of the group are talking to the man. They may be asking him questions about how to play football. In the background, we can see goal posts and a net. There are other teenagers in the background. They are probably waiting for the man to stop talking so that they can start playing.

UNIT 3

Why do children worship celebrities?

A recent survey of parents discovered that the average age at which children choose celebrities as their role models is nine years and eight months. Parents said that around that age their child's dreams of being a policeman, a doctor or a farmer changed. Instead, they wanted to be famous.

1 ...

Children and parents disagree about who should be a role model. While youngsters often admire
5 people who look good, are rich and lead lives of luxury, parents worry that such people aren't the best role models.

    Many parents said that their children spend too much time thinking about the person they admire. They check their celebrity's social media accounts before they get out of bed in the morning, all through the day and last thing at night before they go to sleep. Many of them spoke
10 about arguments with their children when they wouldn't allow them to go to a late-night concert.

2 ...

Many parents are also worried about their children's health and spoke about them waiting for hours outside hotels just to get a glimpse of their idol. We've all seen news items on TV showing huge numbers of young women crying, screaming and fainting when their idol finally appears. Young men, who generally begin to follow celebrities at a later age than girls, usually don't
15 express their admiration in the same way.

3 ...

As for the young people themselves, many said that they enjoy sharing their experiences with friends who have the same interests. They talk about what their favourite celebrity has been doing recently, about the latest photos they posted and about their love life. Sharing their experiences helps make their friendships stronger.

4 ...

20 Dr Tim Jameison, a psychologist at the Royal Hospital in London, says that focussing on celebrities is a normal part of growing up. When a young person enters puberty, they often look for role models who are different from their parents and other figures of authority. Admiring a celebrity that their mum and dad do not like is a way for a young person to show they are different to them. It is simply a way of showing their independence. The doctor's advice to parents is: stick it
25 out. Young people develop other interests as they get older. (325 words)

00 to worship: *verehren, vergöttern*	**12 news item:** *(Nachrichten-)Meldung, (TV-)Bericht*
09 last thing: *als letztes*	**13 to faint:** *in Ohnmacht fallen*
10 argument: *Auseinandersetzung, Streit*	**22 figure of authority:** *Autoritätsperson*
12 to get a glimpse: *einen Blick erhaschen*	**24 to stick sth out:** *etwas geduldig ertragen*

1 READING FOR GIST

Match the headings to sections 1–4 in the text. There is one heading more than you need.

a An expert opinion   **c** How young people feel   **e** Things that parents
b Girls and boys   **d** The celebrities' point of view   complain about

2 READING FOR DETAIL

Decide which of these is the correct option according to the text.

1 Before they become interested in
   celebrities, most children want to …
   a follow their parents' profession.
   b have an exciting job.
   c work in traditional jobs.
   d be a famous person.

2 A child's choice of role model often
   results in one of the following:
   a a lack of sleep
   b concern on the part of the parents
   c bad marks at school
   d lots of late nights at concerts

3 When young girls start to become
   obsessed with a celebrity, the following
   may happen:
   a They get into fights with other fans
      to get closer to their idol.
   b They stop telling their parents where
      they are going.
   c They try to appear on TV with their idol.
   d They put their health in danger by
      waiting to see the celebrity.

4 The positive aspect of being a fan of
   a celebrity is that the fan …
   a might fall in love with someone from
      the same fan club.
   b usually becomes interested in fashion
      and music.
   c becomes close friends with other fans.
   d helps the economy by spending money
      on fan items.

5 Celebrity worship is an important phase
   in a young person's live, because …
   a it helps them become individuals.
   b it makes them become a part of society.
   c it stops them from doing more
      dangerous things.
   d it annoys their parents.

3 WORKING WITH WORDS

Find words or expressions in the text which match the gaps.

1 Women in the UK have 1.9 children on ●. (lines 1–3)
2 Many people have ● of becoming rich and famous when they are young. (lines 1–3)
3 There are a few politicians who I really ●. (lines 4–10)
4 In our house we never talk about politics because it always leads to ●. (lines 4–10)
5 A lot of youngsters like ● photos on social media. (lines 16–19)

Dealing with smartphone addiction among teens

Are you interested in the latest news? Do you need to buy some new trainers? Do you want to chat with your best friend? The answer is always: just reach for your smartphone. Smartphones help us to connect
5 with the world, to run our lives and to socialize with the people who are closest to us.

South Korea has one of the highest numbers of smartphone users in the world. More than 98% of South Korean teens use them, but many are now
10 showing signs of addiction. As long ago as 2007, the government started a programme to treat internet addiction and, in 2015, the programme started to include addiction to smartphones. Teenagers who get a place on the programme go to government-run
15 camps to treat their addiction.

Seo-Yun was one of these teenagers. The 15-year-old was on her phone for up to 13 hours a day. Her parents were worried about her. 'If we tried to talk to her about it, she got angry,' her father says. 'Eventually, I asked her to use her phone for only two hours a day, but she couldn't stick to the time limit. She got angry and depressed and cried,' he says. In the end, Seo-Yun
20 agreed that she had a problem. 'I could forget my stress when I was on my phone but as soon as I stopped using it, my mind became full of problems. Even when I knew I should stop using my smartphone, I just kept going,' she says. 'I hated the trouble it caused with my parents, so I decided to go to the camp,' she says. She handed in her phone at the gate and started a 12-day smartphone detox. She's not alone in this. Many teenagers say that they have a lot of stress in their lives and
25 smartphones help them forget their stress.

Accommodation at the camps is free, although there is a €75 fee for food. Boys and girls are sent to separate camps, and each camp takes in no more than 25 teens at a time. The programme includes one-on-one sessions with a psychologist as well as group and family counselling sessions. The teenagers are also encouraged to take part in activities and sports. At the end of
30 each day the campers do meditation. Today, Seo-Yun knows how to use her smartphone sensibly, and she and her family are glad that she has recovered from her addiction.

South Korea is not the only country where teenagers are addicted to their phones. According to a study published by a German health insurance company, 99% of German teenagers have smartphones, and 2.6% of youths aged between 12 and 17 are addicted to their smartphone. The authors
35 of the study suggested that digital education should be taught in schools. In conclusion, they said that smartphones are here to stay, but one needs to be aware of the risks. (449 words)

| 14 **government-run:** *staatlich* | 28 **counselling:** *Beratung, Therapie* |
| 28 **one-on-one session:** *Einzelgespräch* | 33 **health insurance company:** *Krankenkasse* |

1 READING AND UNDERSTANDING THE TEXT

Who might have said what? Match the statements (1–6) to the people (a–d). There are two statements more than you need.

1 I only felt happy when I was on my phone.
2 Now that I am no longer addicted to the internet, my grades have improved.
3 Our daughter refused to obey us.
4 Smartphones are now part of our everyday life.
5 We need to learn to live without smartphones.
6 We work with the government to help teenagers with addiction.

a a psychologist at a South Korean camp
b one of the authors of the German study
c Seo-Yun
d Seo-Yun's mother

2 A SUMMARY OF THE TEXT

Complete the text with words from the box. There are two words more than you need.

addicted ▪ addiction ▪ advice ▪ advise ▪ detox ▪ digital ▪ health ▪ sensibly ▪ sensitively

In South Korea more than 98% of teenagers use mobile phones. Some of them are becoming 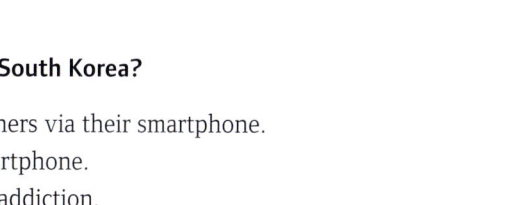¹ to them. The government of the country has set up a programme which helps young people to ●². The teenagers go to free camps where they get help and ●³ from counsellors.
A study carried out by a German ●⁴ insurance company showed that teenagers in Germany also suffer from ●⁵ to their phones. The group that carried out the study proposed that schools should have ●⁶ education classes. They also reminded parents that they should teach their children how to use their smartphones ●⁷.

3 READING FOR DETAIL

Which of the following things did you learn about South Korea?

1 Teenagers in South Korea always buy their trainers via their smartphone.
2 Almost every South Korean teenager has a smartphone.
3 Most South Korean teenagers now suffer from addiction.
4 Over 10 years ago the South Korean government started taking action to fight digital addiction.
5 The South Korean government locks up all addicts in government-run camps.
6 Parents can send their children to camp against their will.
7 Teenagers often use smartphones to avoid stress.
8 Camps for teenagers with smartphone addiction are basically free.
9 It is believed that girls and boys respond better to treatment when they are dealt with separately.
10 The family plays an important role in dealing with addiction.
11 About the same percentage of South Korean and German teenagers have smartphones.
12 All South Korean schools have digital education.

UNIT 5

Dressing in style in Zambia

Chanda Tembo got his first Superman T-shirt at the age of four and his second one at the age of seven. His mother bought these T-shirts at a second-hand clothes market. "When I walked about the village with that big red S on my chest, I felt great," Chanda says. "I believed I could do anything."

5 Today Chanda is the successful owner of a second-hand clothes stall in a market in Lusaka, the capital of Zambia. He sells designer clothes that have been donated to charitable organizations in the USA, Canada and Europe (especially Germany, Belgium and the Netherlands).

In Zambia, almost everyone buys clothes at second-hand market stalls. The country has a fashion-conscious younger generation that follows modern trends in western fashion. Young

10 people use second-hand clothing to create their own style. They want to stand out from the crowd and to produce a "total look" based on trends from across the world.

White-collar workers of both sexes in Lusaka's city centre often spend their lunch hour going through the second-hand clothing stalls looking for something special to wear. Others go to find an accessory to match a particular garment. Some women who make their own clothes go there

15 to find interesting buttons or belts.

Quality and style play a big part in the garments people choose and the designer clothes that Chanda sells are just what his customers are looking for. The clothes are often no longer fashionable in the west, but they are still in very good condition. As a result, even after long use by their original owners, many of these clothes will last for years.

20 Picking through a pile of garments on Chanda's stall, one young man pulls out and tries on a sweatshirt by an Italian fashion house. "I collect this brand," he says. "That's my look."

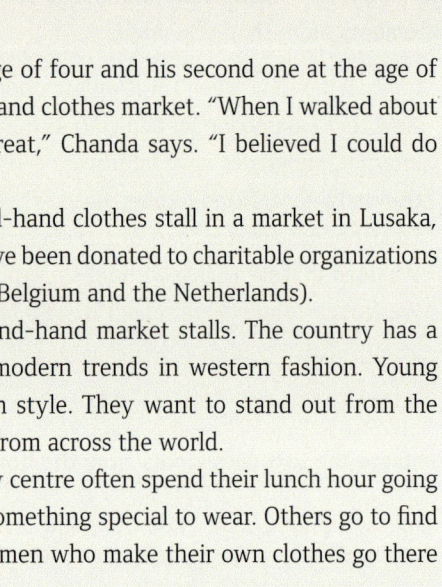

A mother holds up a pretty dress against her teenage daughter while a young Muslim woman wearing a veil hands over $13 for

25 a pair of jeans. She says: "I cover myself in public but when I'm at home I wear nice, modern clothes."

Chanda earns a good living from the clothes he sells. He still wears Superman

30 T-shirts but most of his other clothes carry a designer label. (370 words)

06	charitable organization: *Hilfsorganisation*	15	belt: *Gürtel*
09	fashion-conscious: *modebewusst*	18	fashionable: *in Mode*
14	garment: *Kleidungsstück*	24	veil: *Schleier*
15	button: *Knopf*	25	to cover oneself: *sich bedecken*

1 READING AND UNDERSTANDING THE TEXT

Who said what? Match the statements (1–6) to the people (a–d). There are two statements more than you need.

1 I'm traditional outdoors and modern indoors.
2 I'm happy that stalls like Chanda Tembo's exist.
3 I need something to brighten up this dress.
4 I often wonder why people in the west throw such good clothes away.
5 I don't have much money but I want my kids to look good.
6 I have ten of them already. I'd never be able to afford them new.

a woman looking for accessories
b Italian fashion house fan
c Muslim woman
d Chanda's mother

2 A SUMMARY OF THE ARTICLE

Complete the text with words and phrases from the box.

> accessories ▪ clothing ▪ condition ▪ designer clothes ▪ donated ▪
> garments ▪ market ▪ quality ▪ second-hand ▪ style

When he was a child, Chanda Tembo loved wearing the ⬤ [1] T-shirts his mum bought for him at a ⬤ [2]. Now Chanda has his own business selling used ⬤ [3]. The clothes and ⬤ [4] he offers for sale were once worn by people in the western world. Even though they are in near perfect ⬤ [5], the owners have ⬤ [6] them to charity because they have gone out of ⬤ [7]. Many of them are ⬤ [8] and they are all good ⬤ [9]. Chanda's customers don't mind that someone else has worn the ⬤ [10]. Chanda wears some of the clothes he sells himself.

3 COMPARING CULTURES

Make a list comparing how people do things in Germany and Zambia.

Zambia	Germany
Most people buy clothes at markets.	*Most people buy clothes at big chains.*
People sell designer clothes at the market.	⬤
Young people are very fashion-conscious.	⬤
Young people like to stand out with their fashion style.	⬤
People go clothes shopping at lunchtime.	⬤
Women often make their own clothes.	⬤
Young Zambians will wear clothes that are out of fashion in the west.	⬤
You can pay $13 for a pair of jeans in Zambia.	⬤

UNIT 6

African mobile youth

1 ...

In many parts of rural Africa, computers are rare. Some villages don't even have electricity or telephone lines, so a computer is of little use. This lack of IT infrastructure has held back technological progress and made it difficult for young rural Africans to access education and job opportunities.

2 ...

The spread of mobile phone technology is helping to change this. Around 40% of sub-Saharan Africans now have access to the internet through their mobile phones, creating exciting new possibilities. In general, young people have adopted mobile phone technology more quickly than older adults. In South Africa, for example, 75% of 18- to 29-year-olds use the internet, compared with only 31% aged 50 and older. Teresa Clarke, the head of Africa.com, a news website, told Black Enterprise magazine that for many Africans "the cell phone is their landline, ATM and email in one device. Cell phones are central to life."

3 ...

Getting mobile phone access isn't always easy, however. More than 60% of Africa's unemployed are under 25. Poor people may have to give up other things in order to recharge their phones, maybe even missing out on meals. The phones may be basic models, not smartphones, and data speeds are often slow.

4 ...

Despite all the difficulties, many young Africans are setting up internet- and mobile-phone-based businesses. Young people can be seen running mobile phone kiosks in towns and cities. They offer a variety of services from selling airtime and charging phones to repairing broken screens and replacing batteries. Mostly these are 'micro-businesses' without premises, employees or expensive equipment.

5 ...

Young African software developers are quick to spot practical problems and provide an app to solve them. Kenyan Peter Kariuki is one example. As an 18-year-old he got a job designing a ticket system for a city's bus network in Kigali, Rwanda. While he was working on this, he got the idea for an Uber-style app for a motorcycle taxi service. He and his roommate Barrett Nash, from Canada, left their jobs to develop the app. Today their SafeMotos is the largest motorcycle ride-sharing service in Africa. (340 words)

04	**spread:** *Verbreitung*	16	**kiosk:** *Telefonzelle, Verkaufsstand, Bude*	18	**premises:** *Geschäftsräume*
09	**ATM:** *(hier) Bankkarte*	17	**airtime:** *Sprechzeit*	22	**bus network:** *Busliniennetz*
12	**to recharge sth:** *etwas wiederaufladen*	17	**to charge sth:** *etwas aufladen*	23	**motorcycle:** *Motorrad*
		18	**battery:** *Akku*	25	**ride-sharing:** *Fahrgemeinschaft*

1 READING FOR GIST

Match the headings to sections 1–4 in the text. There is one heading more than you need.

a Innovative software solutions
b Mobile phones and crime
c Mobile phones changing lives
d Online shopping

e Opportunities for small start-ups
f Technological difficulties
g The cost of getting online

2 READING FOR DETAIL

Decide which of these is the correct option, according to the text.

1 There are not many computers in some parts of Africa because …
   a they are too expensive for most people to afford.
   b few people know how to use one.
   c it is difficult to connect one to power and the internet.
   d people do not think that computer technology is important.

2 In sub-Saharan Africa …
   a most young people go online regularly.
   b almost everyone has a mobile.
   c mobile phones are relatively cheap.
   d you cannot have a bank account without a mobile phone.

3 Mobile phone kiosks in African towns and cities …
   a are mostly run by big companies.
   b offer a cheap but poor service.
   c are generally run by individuals.
   d provide a fast internet connection.

4 When Peter Kariuki designed the SafeMotos app, he was …
   a working for a transport company.
   b studying IT.
   c working for Barrett Nash.
   d out of work.

3 WORKING WITH WORDS

Find words or expressions in the text which match the definitions.

1 not often seen (lines 1–3)
2 chance to do or have sth (lines 1–3)
3 extremely important (lines 7–11)

4 simple, uncomplicated (lines 11–14)
5 work which a business does for customers (lines 15–19)
6 to think of and plan sth new (lines 20–24)

4 OVER TO YOU

You plan to spend two months volunteering in a village in Malawi, Africa. While you are away, you want to use your mobile phone to keep in touch with friends and family and write a blog. What do you need to know before you go? Think of at least three questions. Write a short email to the project leader, Jill McKenzie, asking for information.

UNIT 7

Fire festivals in Edinburgh

Edinburgh is a city of festivals: there are music festivals, theatre festivals, comedy festivals, a story-telling festival, an international film festival and the famous Royal Edinburgh Military Tattoo. There is always something going on, and a festival for most interests.

5 Perhaps the most unusual and spectacular are Edinburgh's two fire festivals: Beltane and Samhuinn. They mark the change of the seasons and have their origins in pagan Celtic myth and religion.

These impressive free events both take place on Calton Hill, right in the centre of Edinburgh, a prominent site which is visible across the city.

Beltane

10 Celebrating the arrival of summer, the Beltane Festival at the end of April is one of the most dramatic events in Edinburgh's calendar. It offers an exciting mix of fire, costumes, drums and pagan ritual. Other places celebrate Beltane, but Edinburgh's festival is the largest of its kind. Some may see it as just a wild party, but for others it is an important connection to the cycles of nature.

The word 'Beltane' means 'bright fire' and one of its most important rituals is lighting the 15 Beltane bonfire. This symbolises the darkness of winter giving way to the light of summer. The main characters are the Green Man, who grows and dies each year, and the immortal May Queen, who represents the power of the Earth.

Samhuinn

The Samhuinn Festival takes place on top of Calton Hill on the same night as Halloween. However, 20 it is quite different to the familiar Halloween celebrations. Samhuinn tells the story of the fight between the Summer King and the Winter King. Acrobatics, fire dancing and wild drumming bring this spectacular struggle between the seasons to life. Visitors can wander between the participants, who are dressed in strange costumes to represent mythological creatures.

These are not events for an audience to sit and watch. The idea is to wander around and get 25 involved with the action! (319 words)

02 tattoo: *Zapfenstreich, Musikschau*	**05 Celtic:** *keltisch*	**08 prominent site:** *exponierte Stelle*
05 pagan: *heidnisch*	**05 myth:** *Sage*	**15 bonfire:** *Freudenfeuer*

1 READING FOR GIST

Which of these headings is not relevant for a website about Beltane and Samhuinn? Why?

The myths	Main characters	Things to see	Tickets	Visitor safety

2 READING FOR DETAIL

Copy and complete the table with information from the text.

	type of festival	time of year	cause of celebration	mythological characters	what there is to experience
Beltane	*fire festival*	⬤	⬤	⬤	⬤
Samhuinn	⬤	⬤	⬤	⬤	⬤

3 WORKING WITH WORDS

Which word is the odd one out? Explain why in German.

1 wild ▪ spectacular ▪ famous ▪ dramatic
2 celebration ▪ origin ▪ festival ▪ party
3 season ▪ calendar ▪ site ▪ event
4 creature ▪ audience ▪ visitor ▪ participant
5 fire ▪ bright ▪ darkness ▪ visible

4 OVER TO YOU

Your Scottish friend, Lenny, has sent you a message.

> Hey!!
>
> How's it going over there in Germany? I've just been to the Beltane festival in Edinburgh. It was brilliant! What's your favourite festival or celebration in Germany? When is it? What does it involve? Why is it your favourite? Maybe I can come over next year and celebrate with you!
>
> Cheers
> Lenny

Reply to Lenny, answering his questions.

UNIT 8

Paul's Papas

We've come a long way from the nuclear family – a mum and dad and their children. Today, families come in all different varieties: single-parent families, families in which children are adopted, extended families, blended families, same-sex families. You name it, in some part of the western world, we've got it.

5   Berliners Christof and Florian Müller-Weber are the joint foster parents of eight-year-old Paul. On a typical day, Papa-Chris, who works at a city bank, drops off Paul at school before he goes to work and Papa-Flori, who runs an online company from home, picks him up at the end of the school day.

    Christof and Florian have been Paul's fathers since he was 18 months old. Before they were
10   taken onto the list of possible foster parents, a local children's care agency interviewed both of them together and separately, then they looked very carefully into their lives. It took nine months altogether but, in the end, Christof and Florian passed all the tests. 'They checked everything from our friends to our flat, to our family histories, to our financial situation,' says Florian. 'We had no problems with the investigations. The agency needed to be sure that we were 100% fit to
15   be responsible for a child,' he says.

    Legally, Paul's fathers are only twenty-five percent responsible for him – the remaining seventy-five percent of the responsibility lies with the Youth Welfare Office. 'We have to inform them when we go on holiday and when he has been seen by a doctor. We also had to let them know when and where he was starting school,' says Christof. 'We've never had any trouble with
20   anything but it takes a lot of planning. We have to get the right signatures from the right people every time,' he says.

    'We haven't had any bad experiences,' says Florian. 'We live in a part of town which is full of all types of families and Paul's schoolfriends don't seem to have a problem with Paul having two dads. Of course, if anything nasty comes up in the future, then we'll deal with it,' he says.

25   As different family set-ups become more common, same-sex parenting has as good a chance of finding acceptance as any other.   (369 words)

05 joint: *gemeinsam*	**10 children's care agency:**	**16 legally:** *rechtlich*
05 foster parents: *Pflegeeltern*	*Kinderschutzbehörde*	**17 Youth Welfare Office:** *Jugendamt*

1 READING FOR DETAIL

Decide which of these is the correct option.

1 Family set-ups in the western world today are …
   a changing all the time.
   b difficult to describe.
   c still mainly traditional.
   d very different to what they used to be.

2 Both Christof and Florian …
   a take Paul to school.
   b pick up Paul from school.
   c share the school run.
   d work at schools.

3 They got to know Paul when he was a …
  a baby.
  b young child.
  c schoolchild.
  d teenager.

4 The agency which dealt with Christof and Florian's application to foster …
  a needed to make sure they were fit.
  b checked them out very carefully.
  c made life difficult for the two men.
  d questioned the amount of money they earned.

5 The Youth Welfare Office …
  a needs to be kept informed about Paul's life.
  b makes most of the decisions in Paul's life.
  c reviews the family situation every year.
  d told Christof and Florian they will be able to adopt Paul one day.

6 The family has …
  a experienced some bad reactions to their set-up.
  b heard Paul's schoolfriends being nasty to him.
  c had no problems in their area or at Paul's school.
  d had to deal with criticism from a few people.

2 WORKING WITH WORDS

Find words and expressions in the text to match the definitions 1–6.

1 a couple who take another person's child into their home
2 an organization that looks after children who may be in danger
3 to do with money
4 official examinations of the facts about a situation
5 the job or duty of taking care of somebody
6 events or activities that affect you in some way

3 A SUMMARY OF THE TEXT

Complete the text with expressions from the box.

> deal ▪ family ▪ foster ▪
> foster parents ▪ investigations ▪
> legal ▪ nasty ▪ responsibility ▪
> responsible ▪ same-sex ▪ welfare

Christof and Florian Müller-Weber and their ◗ ¹ son, Paul, live together in what is called a ◗ ² family. The three of them have lived together since Paul was a small child. Before they could become ◗ ³, Christof and Florian had to prove to a children's care agency that they would be able to take ◗ ⁴ for a child. The agency looked into all areas of the men's lives before they were allowed to foster. As the men knew that the agency had the ◗ ⁵ of the child at heart, they accepted the ◗ ⁶. From a ◗ ⁷ point of view, Christof and Florian are 25% ◗ ⁸ for Paul. The Youth Welfare Office has 75% of the responsibility. That department has to be told when the ◗ ⁹ takes a holiday or when Paul has to go to the doctor. His parents have also given the department details about Paul's school. The family set-up has been accepted in the part of town where they live and at Paul's school there have been no ◗ ¹⁰ situations. The parents say they will ◗ ¹¹ with any problems if they ever come up.

The importance of intercultural skills

Are you looking for an interesting job? Do you have good computer skills? Can you speak a second language? While these skills are important, they're only the start. In today's world, employers are also looking for intercultural competence in their employees. It's more than simply being able to speak and understand a foreign language, it's also being aware of cultural differences.

5　　A recent survey asked personnel managers working at international companies how important intercultural skills were in choosing employees. The results of the survey showed that job applicants with intercultural skills are more likely to be taken on than those without. One of the reasons given was that, when they move to a subsidiary in another part of the world, interculturally competent employees adapt well to new work environments. Having previous knowledge of how 10　other people might behave in a foreign land helps people understand their co-workers better. Knowing what to expect in everyday life in a foreign environment also prevents culture shock.

　　The biggest challenge for the companies is being able to find employees who come into the job with intercultural skills in place. On the other hand, the survey also discovered that many international companies do not offer any training in intercultural competence, even though they 15　know that they need people with intercultural skills in the workplace.

　　What does this mean for us? Basically, we have to be proactive and get to grips with intercultural skills ourselves. Many school leavers take a year out and go abroad. Living in a foreign country will help you develop a deeper understanding of how to communicate and work with people from different cultures.

20　　If you can't afford to take a year out, there are plenty of sites on the internet offering advice. Here's a tip from one of them. Be careful with your facial expressions and body language.

Eye contact

Anglo-Americans and Europeans look at each other directly in the eyes when they talk. If they don't do that, the person they are talking to thinks they are hiding something or telling a lie. 25　Japanese and Korean people do just the opposite. Direct eye contact is, to them, considered rude.

Greetings

In Britain, shaking hands is considered very formal. The Brits only shake hands when you meet a business partner for the first time or at a formal occasion like a wedding or a funeral. In Germany, everyone shakes hands, even if they know a person very well. If you're German, don't put your 30　hand out as soon as you meet another person. Wait and see what they are going to do before you offer to shake hands.

Giving approval

In Germany, unlike most countries, people usually don't clap but bang their hands on the table after listening to a speech or presentation. This often surprises British people, who prefer a quiet clap.

(472 words)

03	**competence:** *Befähigung, Kompetenz*	16	**to get to grips with:** *in den Griff bekommen*
13	**in place:** *vorhanden*	32	**approval:** *Zustimmung*

1 READING FOR DETAIL

Answer the following questions in English in complete sentences.

1 What quality do employers want employees to have today?
2 Why do employers want employees to have this quality? (3 aspects)
3 How can school-leavers acquire this quality? (2 aspects)

2 COMPLETING A TABLE

Write down how Germans and British compare in the following aspects.

	Germans	British people
eye contact		
greetings		
giving approval		

3 WORKING WITH WORDS

Without looking back at the text, match the words in column A with the words in column B to make collocations used when discussing intercultural competence.

column A		British people	
1	body	a	contact
2	culture	b	expressions
3	eye	c	hands
4	facial	d	language
5	intercultural	e	shock
6	shaking	f	skills

4 OVER TO YOU

Imagine someone from China is coming to work in Germany. Write down five pieces of advice he or she might need to adjust to life in Germany.

The Wild West – myth meets reality

For 100 years, the Wild West has been the theme of countless comic books, novels, songs, movies and TV series. The romantic image of the 19th century cowboy – strong, independent, ready to use his gun to defend himself and protect the weak – has an attraction for many US Americans. The Wild West is part of the founding mythology of the USA.

5   But the Wild West is mythology, not history. The real Western frontier was rarely violent and lawless. In fact, the Wild West really was not that wild at all. Compared to the chaotic, overcrowded cities of the East, the frontier was a peaceful, if lonely, place.

Law enforcement was quite effective in the frontier states of the 'Old West'. Very few banks were robbed: in the last four decades of the 19th century, there were only four confirmed bank

10   robberies in the 15 Western states. This is hardly surprising when you consider that the bank was generally next door to the sheriff's office. It was difficult to rob a bank without attracting the attention of the local lawman.

On the subject of law enforcement, most people have heard of the famous lawman Wyatt Earp. What Hollywood forgot to mention is that brave Mr Earp spent more time looking for the

15   townspeople's lost pets and putting out house fires than fighting with outlaws.

Of course there were bloody fights – like the famous gunfight at the O. K. Corral – but they became famous precisely because they were rare events. In that 30-second gunfight, three people died. Compare that to the average Western movie, where the number of deaths is usually much higher. There were also outlaw gangs. Some of these gangs, like Jesse James's gang, had their origins after

20   the Civil War, when returning soldiers were unable to fit back into civilian life. Others, like the Dalton Gang, were lawmen who decided to try an alternative career.

However, most of these gangs spent months or years on the run, leading as quiet a life as possible to avoid the attention of law enforcement. The robberies that they planned were often unsuccessful. Mostly it must have been a miserable, boring life.

25   Whenever violent crime threatened to get out of control, local authorities were quick to organise law enforcement and hand out harsh punishments. Organisations such as the Texas Rangers and the Pinkerton Detective Agency made sure that most outlaws had short, unsuccessful careers.

As a result, most crime was minor theft and fraud. After all, it was usually illegal to carry a gun

30   on the streets of towns and cities. Outlaw gangs did not ride into town waving guns around – that would have been suicide.

Out in the countryside, there was occasional armed conflict between ranchers, who needed free access to large areas of land for their cattle, and farmers, who built fences to keep the cattle out of their crops. These were sometimes called 'wars', such as the Sheep Wars. Nevertheless,

35   there were relatively few casualties on either side, and the US army quickly put an end to the violence.

All in all, poor diet, accidents, alcohol and disease killed far more cowboys than guns and violence.

(525 words)

1 READING FOR GIST

Which of these is the best summary of the text?

a The western states were only 'wild' for a few years. They soon became just as safe as the rest of the country.

b The life of a cowboy was a lot easier and less romantic than fictional stories about cowboys suggest. However, many Americans still find the cowboy image attractive.

c Although there was violence and criminal activity in the West, it was not really as wild as popular fiction often shows it to be.

2 READING FOR DETAIL

Decide whether the following statements are true or false. Explain your decision in German.

1 In the 19th century, the eastern states of the USA were wilder than the west.
2 It was very difficult to rob a bank in the Old West.
3 The gunfight at the O. K. Corral was a typical event in the West.
4 Outlaws often had military or police training.
5 Being an outlaw was an exciting way of life.
6 Cowboys usually carried guns when they were in town.
7 Ranchers and farmers worked together to fight the outlaws.
8 The cowboy life was a lot safer than people today imagine.

3 WORKING WITH WORDS

Find words in the text which have the opposite meaning.

1 to attack (lines 1–4)
2 violent (lines 5–8)
3 frequent (lines 16–21)
4 military (lines 16–21)
5 to attract (lines 22–24)
6 enjoyable, pleasant (lines 22–24)
7 mild, gentle (lines 25–28)
8 major (lines 29–31)

4 OVER TO YOU

You are playing one of these characters in a Wild West online game Dodge City. Write a short profile to introduce other players to your character. Include information about your character's personality, motivation and special skills.

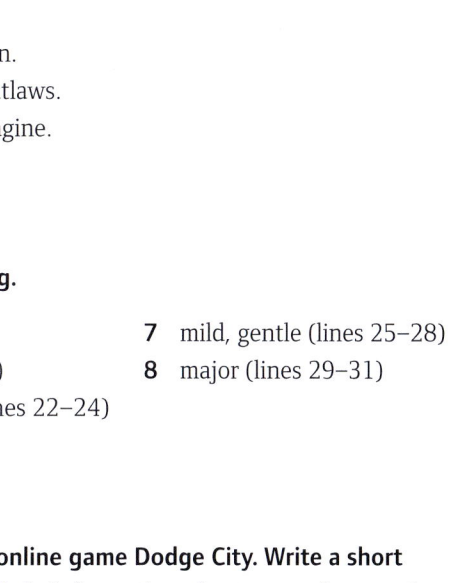

Samuel 'Quick Draw' McGraw

'Lucky' Lucy Fortune

Sheriff Brenton Bridges

Dolores 'Dollars' Gonzales

UNIT 11

For young Inuit, getting an education can mean choosing between cultures

1 ...

Patricia Deveaux was always told she could be anything she wanted to be. When she graduated in June of this year, she won a Governor General's Academic Medal for having the highest grades in her high-school class. Meanwhile, she had long since learned the ropes in the world of work, having talked her way into a job at a local hotel when she was 13.

5   'She was always the one I looked up to,' says her 16-year-old sister, Lissa.

    Lissa was a good student too, but she lived for summers, when she could go camping and fishing. She wanted to stay forever in Nunavik, the far-north Inuit region of Quebec.

2 ...

It was a given, however, that Patricia would leave. Only about a half-dozen students from her home-town of Kuujjuaq move on from high school to Quebec's pre-university colleges each year, and she

10 'always couldn't wait' to be one of them, she says. So she moved to Montreal in August. [...] It took just six weeks for her to change her mind. She quit her business program at John Abbott College and moved back to Kuujjuaq, reoccupying her old bedroom and her job at the local hotel. She entered a local trade school, studying accounting.

3 ...

She had hated living in Montreal, but she had also become sure of something else: she didn't want

15 to adjust to the south. 'It would bother me if I went home and I felt like an outsider,' she says. In fact, she had quietly started to envy her little sister, the 'outside-hunting type Inuk girl.'

    'I haven't had as much time as a kid as I wanted to,' Patricia said during a telephone interview two weeks after she returned home. 'I wasn't much of a person to go outside much. Now that I'm older and I realize that I really like it, I'm going to go for sure with my aunts and uncles whenever

20 they go out hunting and fishing.'

4 ...

Inuit teenagers like Patricia are the source of much hand-wringing in policy circles as decision-makers cope with a range of issues such as food security, economic development and climate change.

    New census numbers released last week showed that her generation is huge, dwarfing their parents' and grandparents' numbers. Many signs of their early experiences are very worrying,

25 particularly when it comes to education. Dropout rates in the northern territories are high, even among the most promising students.

    Police files in Montreal and Ottawa are full of the stories of young Inuit, poorly prepared for the working world, who move south and spiral into poverty and violence. The social dislocation Inuit children face is worsened, policymakers assume, by the way climate change is transforming

30 their land.

5 ...

But some recent statistics might also overturn southern assumptions. Notably, the fluency of young Indigenous people in traditional languages is relatively high, especially in Nunavik. In fact, according to Patricia, southerners understand little about life for the region's young people, especially when it comes to how they choose their schooling.

03 to learn the ropes: *sich einarbeiten*	**23 census:** *Volkszählung*	**28 dislocation:** *Entwurzelung*
21 hand-wringing: *besorgte Absichts-* *erklärungen (ohne Konsequenzen)*	**23 to dwarf sth:** *etwas in den* *Schatten stellen*	**29 to worsen:** *verschlimmern*
21 policy circles: *politische Kreise*	**25 dropout rate:** *Abbrecherquote*	**29 policymaker:** *politische/r* *Entscheidungsträger/in*

6 …

35 For Inuit students, moving south often feels like as much of a sacrifice as it is a benefit, young Inuit say. They know better than anyone that there's a crisis up north, but that's often a reason to stay, not to leave. Climate change isn't necessarily eroding their bond with their land and culture – in fact, for many young people, it provides extra motivation to learn to "be Inuk," even if that's harder now than ever. Torn between two places, two cultures, and two ways of getting educated, each
40 student picks the pieces she needs from each world, in a process that's always unique and often lonely.

Source: Selena Ross, *National Observer*, 1 November 2017; 621 words

1 READING FOR GIST

Match the headings to the sections 1–6 in the text. There are two headings that you do not need.

a There and back

b Worries about young Inuit

c No jobs back home

d Two sisters – different but alike

e The impact of climate change

f A different view of Inuit youth

g Succeeding in a different culture

h Holding on to a traditional way of life

2 READING FOR DETAIL

Decide which of these is the correct option.

1 What was the main reason that Patricia returned home early?
   a She lost interest in doing further study.
   b She found her college course too difficult.
   c She had problems with other students
   d She didn't want to lose her Inuk culture.

2 Which of these is <u>not</u> an official concern about Inuit youth?
   a Too many young Inuit are failing to complete school.
   b There are too few of them because Inuit are having fewer children.
   c They often get involved in crime when they move south.
   d They have difficulty staying in employment.

3 Why might the situation of young Inuit be more positive than these concerns suggest?
   a Many Inuit are doing very well in southern cities.
   b Academic results are improving for those students who remain in Inuit regions.
   c Climate change is forcing young Inuit to create a stronger bond with their region.
   d Inuit are integrating much better into Canadian society than people realize.

3 OVER TO YOU

If you were in Lissa's or Patricia's situation, would you stay in Nunavik or go to Montreal? Give reasons for your decision.

UNIT 12

Mother of four to be deported to Mexico in sign of Trump policy shift

The mother of four American children, the youngest of whom is three years old, has been picked up by federal agents at her home in Fairfield, Ohio, and taken into detention ahead of imminent deportation back to her native Mexico. Maribel Trujillo has been told that her deportation is set for next Tuesday from the US, where she has lived for the past 15 years. […]

5 People who were until recently regarded as of such low priority that it would inflict more harm than good on communities to wrench them from their families are now finding themselves in the deportation pipeline. Trujillo falls firmly into that category. ICE has indicated that she is a priority for removal even though she has no criminal record and last year was granted government permission to work in a local candy factory. Deportation would present Trujillo with a 'Sophie's
10 choice': either she abandons her four US-born, American-citizen children – aged three, 10, 12 and 14 – leaving them to grow up without a mother, or she takes them back to Mexico to an uncertain and potentially perilous future. The children have never set foot outside the US.

In an interview with *The Guardian* conducted before she was detained, she said she was finding the decision extremely painful. 'I don't understand the reason to separate my family. I
15 have no criminal record, I'm here working to support my family, so that my kids can study and have a better life for themselves. Why does President Trump want to divide my family and make me leave my kids behind – what are they going to do without their mama?' […]

A spokesman for ICE told *The Guardian* that Trujillo's case had been reviewed several times by the courts and she was found to have 'no legal basis to remain in the US'. Asked about the
20 dilemma her detention posed with her children, the spokesman said: 'For parents who are ordered removed, it is their decision whether or not to relocate their children with them.' In addition to being the family's main breadwinner, as a result of her husband Gustavo's health problems, Trujillo also cares for two of her children with special medical needs: Gustavo, 10, who has a form of pre-diabetes, and the youngest, Daniela, who has a history of seizures.

25 She told *The Guardian* that she could not conceive of leaving the children behind, though she also struggles with the idea of taking them with her to Michoacán, a state in central Mexico that she abandoned in 2002 in search of a better life. In recent years, Michoacán has been convulsed with violence between drug cartels, vigilante gunmen, police and army, making it one of Mexico's most violent regions. […]

30 The children are also bemused by the idea of going to live in a country that they know scarcely anything about. The elder daughter Alexa, 12, lamented recently: '*Mami*, I can't go to Mexico, I can't go to school there, I don't know how to speak Spanish properly, I have no friends.'

Source: Ed Pilkington, *The Guardian*, 6 April 2017; 504 words

02 federal agent: *FBI-Agent/in*	**09 candy (AE):** *Süßwaren*
06 to wrench sb from sb: *jdn jdm entreißen*	**12 perilous:** *bedrohlich*
07 pipeline: *Warteliste*	**13 to detain sb:** *jdn inhaftieren*
07 ICE = Immigration and Customs Enforcement:	**25 to conceive of sth:** *sich etwas vorstellen*
US-Behörde für Einwanderung und Zoll	**30 bemused:** *verwirrt*

1 READING FOR GIST

Which of these things is Maribel Trujillo <u>not</u> allowed to do?

- **a** Leave her children in the USA and return to Mexico.
- **b** Stay in the USA until her children are old enough to look after themselves.
- **c** Return to Mexico and take her children.

2 READING FOR DETAIL

Decide whether the following statements are true or false.
Explain your decision in German in full sentences.

1 Mrs Trujillo and her children were picked up and put in a detention centre.
2 Immigration and Customs Enforcement believes that Mrs Trujillo has committed a major crime.
3 Mrs Trujillo was working legally in the USA.
4 Mrs Trujillo's children have visited her family in Mexico.
5 She thinks that the decision is just an administrative error.
6 Mrs Trujillo's case will have to go through the US court system before she can be deported.
7 Mr Trujillo doesn't earn as much money as his wife does.
8 Alexa Trujillo is worried about moving to Mexico.

3 WORKING WITH WORDS

Find the (abstract) nouns for the following verbs in the text.

1 choose	3 deport	5 harm	7 permit
2 decide	4 detain	6 live	8 remove

4 OVER TO YOU

As part of an online campaign for the Trujillo family, describe in no more than 100 words what might happen to the family if Maribel is deported.

UNIT 13

International companies switching to English

1 …

Based in Germany, GlobalRobotik AG* has subsidiaries all around the world. One day Peter*, a service representative, gets an urgent call from his boss: a major client's manufacturing robots have stopped working because of a software problem. Peter quickly calls the technical department in Malaysia, but the software team can't help: all the communication between the service
5　engineers is in German – and none of the software team speaks German!

Peter tries running all the highly technical emails through translation software – but the Malaysian team call back to say they can't make sense of the translation. The clients are getting frantic …

A fictitious example, but a real-life problem. This is one reason why companies all around the
10　world are switching to English for all their routine communication – even if there are few native speakers in the company. Communication is faster and more reliable if we all speak the same language.

2 …

English is the fastest-spreading language in human history. Nearly 1.8 billion people around the globe are able to communicate reasonably well in English. That's one in every four people on the
15　planet.

Amongst these people, there are around 400 million native speakers, mostly in countries like the UK, the USA, Canada, Australia and South Africa; about a billion fluent second-language speakers in countries such as India and Nigeria; and millions of people around the world who have studied it as a foreign language. It's estimated that nearly 600 million people use English regularly
20　online. In Europe, nearly 80% of children start to learn English at primary school.

3 …

The German engineering giant Siemens made English its official language many years ago. Airbus, Daimler-Chrysler, Fast Retailing, Nokia, Renault, Samsung, SAP, Technicolor, and Microsoft in Beijing – all of them have English as their official language.

In 2010, Takanobu Ito, the CEO of Honda, criticized Nissan for making a 'stupid' move by
25　making English its official language. There was reported to be widespread approval for this comment amongst the Japanese public. Five years later, however, Honda followed Nissan's lead. As of 2020, English for international communications is official company policy.

Most of these companies, like Honda and Nissan, just want their senior employees around the world to be able to communicate efficiently. For other companies, it's a cultural shift: a recognition
30　that business is organized globally these days, not nationally or even regionally. They expect all employees to be part of that shift.

4 …

Japanese online retailer Rakuten decided in 2010 that English would be its official language of business. CEO Hiroshi Mikitani announced the plan to employees not in Japanese – but in English. From one day to the next, Japanese menus in the company cafeterias were replaced by English
35　ones. Even the signs in elevators were suddenly in English. Employees would have to demonstrate competence in English within two years – or risk losing their jobs.

* The names of the firm and individual have been changed.

■　**02 urgent:** *dringend*　　**09 fictitious:** *fiktiv*

5 …

Fortunately, most companies don't take this radical line, which seems very hard on employees: imagine suddenly having to communicate all the time, about important matters, in a language that isn't your own! 'Bosses and peers alike should realize that others might not fully understand what's 40 being said,' says Keiko Claasen of ITT Motion Technologies, an Italian company where most communications are in English.

An English-only policy might actually be counterproductive, if employees lack the confidence to express themselves freely. Employees facing such policies may worry that the best jobs will be offered only to those with strong English skills, not the person with the best expertise.   (594 words)

■ **42 counterproductive:** *kontraproduktiv*

1 READING FOR GIST

Match the headings to the sections of the text (1–5). There are two headings that you do not need.

a Drawbacks of a single corporate language
b A case study
c Rejecting globalization
d The rise of English
e Taking a hard line
f A sign of things to come?
g Some real-life examples

2 READING FOR DETAIL

Answer the following questions in English in complete sentences.

1 Why have so many companies made English their company language?
2 What negative impact on companies might a change to English have?

3 OVER TO YOU

How would you feel about speaking only English at work? Write a short comment (50–80 words) on the article, discussing the advantages and disadvantages from the employee's point of view.

Skills files

Diese *Skills files* helfen Ihnen, Ihre Sprachfertigkeiten zu trainieren, damit Sie Erfolg in der Prüfung haben. Wenn Sie sich regelmäßig mit dem Lernprozess beschäftigen, fällt Ihnen der Umgang mit der englischen Sprache jeden Tag leichter. Hier bekommen Sie viele hilfreiche Tipps, wie Sie Ihre Fähigkeiten verbessern können.

1 MIT WÖRTERN UMGEHEN

A Ein Wörterbuch benutzen

→ Vokabeln lernen, S. 241

Ein Wörterbuch ist ein hilfreiches Werkzeug. Es hilft Ihnen, einen Text zu verstehen und Ihr Vokabular zu erweitern. Unabhängig von der Art des Wörterbuchs, das Sie nutzen – zwei- oder einsprachig –, ist Folgendes zu beachten:

- Lassen Sie bei Online-Wörterbüchern Vorsicht walten. Wörter haben in verschiedenen Zusammenhängen verschiedene Bedeutungen, und Computer sind nicht schlau genug, um zu erfassen, welchen Zusammenhang Sie brauchen.
- Arabische Zahlen weisen darauf hin, dass es mehrere Bedeutungen gibt. Wählen Sie nicht die erstbeste Bedeutung aus, sondern lesen Sie alle Definitionen und überprüfen Sie sie ein zweites Mal, indem Sie die neu gefundenen Wörter nachschlagen.
- Stellen Sie sicher, dass Sie nach der richtigen Wortart suchen (Verb, Substantiv, Adjektiv, Adverb).

Bevor Sie mit Ihrem Wörterbuch zu arbeiten beginnen:

- Lesen Sie die Inhaltsübersicht, um herauszufinden, was Ihr Wörterbuch neben Definitionen noch alles zu bieten hat. Lesen Sie die Nutzungshinweise sorgfältig durch – sie sind wichtig.
- Sehen Sie sich die Liste der Abkürzungen und Symbole sowie die Legende zur Verbbildung an und stellen Sie sicher, dass Sie deren Bedeutungen verstehen.
- Vergewissern Sie sich, dass Sie die verschiedenen Wortarten kennen. Wenn Sie, zum Beispiel, die Funktion eines Adverbs nicht kennen, wird es Ihnen kaum helfen, ein Adverb nachzuschlagen.

Nutzen Sie ein Wörterbuch, um:

- **mit einem Text zu arbeiten.** Wenn Sie nach Anwendung aller Ihrer Fertigkeiten unbekannte Wörter immer noch nicht verstehen, schlagen Sie sie nach.
- **Ihr Vokabular zu erweitern.** Wenn Sie ein Ihnen unbekanntes Wort nachschlagen, nehmen Sie sich die Zeit, auch verwandte Wörter nachzuschlagen und eine Liste mit Wortfamilien anzulegen.
- *Idioms*/**Redensarten zu erlernen.** In einer Redensart wird ein Wort in einem feststehenden Satz verwendet und ist seiner eigentlichen Bedeutung nur entfernt ähnlich, z. B.: *to get the wrong end of the stick*. Wenn Sie wissen, was *the wrong end* und *stick* bedeuten, verstehen Sie möglicherweise immer noch nicht die Redewendung („etwas in den falschen Hals bekommen").

B Vokabeln lernen

→ Ein Wörterbuch benutzen, S. 240

Das richtige Erlernen und Benutzen von Wörtern einer Fremdsprache macht Spaß, ist aber zeitaufwendig. Es gibt viele Arten, Vokabeln zu lernen. Sie können dies mithilfe von *Work with English* tun und diese Art des Lernens mit englischen Lese- und Hörverständnisübungen außerhalb des Unterrichts ergänzen. Es gibt natürlich auch eine Vielzahl von Onlineprogrammen und -spielen, um Vokabeln zu lernen, doch sie sind nicht so effektiv wie die Lernmethoden, die Sie sich selbst erarbeiten.

Listen und Zettel

- **Vokabellisten (nicht nur in einem Buch)**

  Vokabellisten, die in einem Notizbuch eingetragen werden, stellen einen leichten Weg dar, neue Wörter während des Unterrichts festzuhalten. Zuhause können Sie weitere Listen erstellen, z. B. von Lebensmitteln, die im Kühlschrank aufbewahrt werden, oder Sie schreiben Ihre Einkaufsliste auf Englisch oder Sie listen die Kleidungsstücke in Ihrem Kleiderschrank auf, nach Art, Farbe und Material sortiert.

- **Lernkarten**

  Schreiben Sie die Wörter, die Sie gern lernen möchten, auf Karteikarten. Schreiben Sie das englische Wort auf die eine Seite und die Übersetzung auf die andere. Fügen Sie eine Zeichnung, eine Definition bzw. einen Beispielsatz auf Englisch unter die deutsche Übersetzung hinzu.

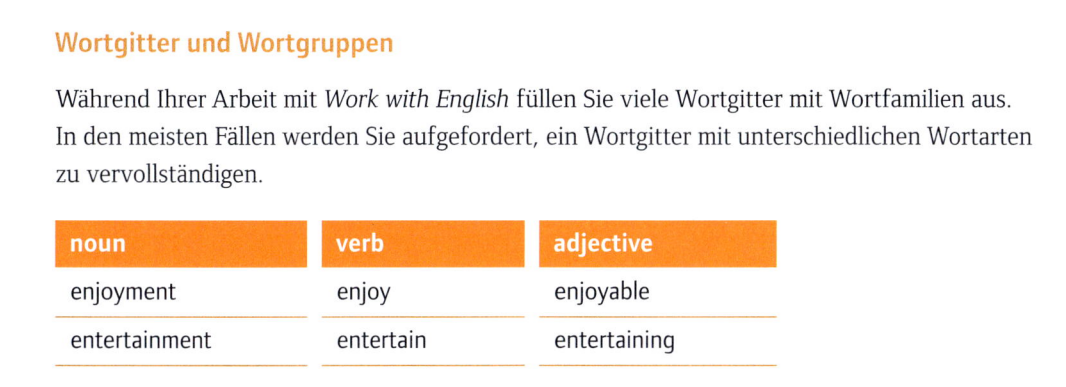

- **Klebezettel**

  Schreiben Sie die Bezeichnung eines Gegenstandes auf einen Notizzettel und kleben Sie ihn an den Gegenstand. Sie können nach Belieben Adjektive hinzufügen, z. B. *pretty picture*, *dirty laundry*.

Wortgitter und Wortgruppen

Während Ihrer Arbeit mit *Work with English* füllen Sie viele Wortgitter mit Wortfamilien aus. In den meisten Fällen werden Sie aufgefordert, ein Wortgitter mit unterschiedlichen Wortarten zu vervollständigen.

noun	verb	adjective
enjoyment	enjoy	enjoyable
entertainment	entertain	entertaining

Wenn Sie sich auf eine Prüfung vorbereiten, können Sie Ihre Wortfamiliengitter um weitere Informationen verändern und ergänzen, z. B. indem Sie Sätze hinzufügen, in denen die Wörter im Kontext benutzt werden.

word	part of speech	opposite(s)	synonym	word in context
large	adjective	small	big	My mum comes from a large family. She has six sisters.
producer	noun	destroyer consumer	manufacturer	Japan is a major producer of cars.

Verknüpfungen herstellen

- **Wortgabeln**

  Wortgabeln eignen sich gut zum Erlernen von Adjektiven und Verben.

delicious			find	
quick			have	
home-made	meal		make	friends
lovely			meet	
tasty			visit	

- **Mindmaps**

  Sie können Mindmaps zum Sammeln und Verknüpfen von Vokabeln wie auch von Ideen benutzen, um sich für eine Präsentation vorzubereiten oder einen Aufsatz und andere Schriftsätze zu planen. Der Vorteil von Mindmaps ist, dass Sie sie in jede beliebige Richtung ergänzen und erweitern können. Heben Sie bestimmte Aspekte farblich hervor. Wenn Sie eine Mindmap erstellen, vergleichen Sie Ihre mit der eines Mitstreiters / einer Mitstreiterin, der/die dasselbe Thema dargestellt hat. Es ist wahrscheinlich, dass Sie beide weitere Wörter zu Ihren Mindmaps hinzufügen können.

2 REZEPTION: LESEVERSTEHEN

A Vorbereitung auf das Lesen

Eine Vorhersage bedeutet, dass Sie versuchen, den Inhalt des Textes zu erraten, bevor Sie ihn lesen. Wenn Sie sich hierzu Zeit nehmen, bevor Sie mit dem Lesen des Texts beginnen, können Sie den Text besser verstehen.

- Sehen Sie sich den Aufbau des Textes genau an und lesen Sie die Überschrift und Unterzeile bzw. die Einleitung, sofern es eine gibt. Das sollte Ihnen Hinweise liefern, worum es in dem Text geht.
- Sehen Sie sich die dazugehörigen Bilder bzw. Zeichnungen an und lesen Sie deren Unterschriften. Dies wird Ihnen helfen, sich vom Text „ein Bild zu machen".

B Den Sinn eines Textes erfassen

Lesen, um den Sinn zu erfassen oder einen Text überfliegen bedeutet, die wichtigsten Punkte schnell zu lesen.

- Lesen Sie den ersten Satz jeden Absatzes (und den letzten Satz, wenn der Absatz lang ist), denn dort können Sie häufig das Wesentliche des Textes entnehmen.
- Konzentrieren Sie sich auf die Schlüsselwörter, die Ihnen den Sinn des Textes vermitteln, z. B. Substantive, Verben und (häufig) die dazugehörigen Adjektive und Adverbien. Wörter, die <u>unterstrichen</u> bzw. **fett** gedruckt oder *kursiv* gestellt sind, sind i.d.R. wichtig.
- Überspringen Sie jene Wörter, die Sie nicht verstehen. Meist wird die Bedeutung dieser Wörter aus dem Zusammenhang heraus klar, und manchmal taucht etwas später ein Synonym auf. Zum Schluss finden Sie wahrscheinlich heraus, dass Sie den Text verstehen, ohne diese Wörter zu kennen.
- Lesen Sie den ganzen letzten Absatz, da dieser häufig eine Zusammenfassung des Textes darstellt.

C Gezielt Informationen im Text finden

Beim Überfliegen eines Textes geht es um das schnelle Finden von bestimmten Informationen. In Texten wie Stellenanzeigen oder Infobroschüren müssen Sie bestimmte Informationen schnell herausfinden. Sie müssen den Text nicht in aller Tiefe lesen, doch Sie müssen sich den gesamten Text ansehen. Hierzu wenden Sie folgende Strategien an:

- Lesen Sie die Aufgaben sorgfältig durch und stellen Sie sicher, dass Sie verstehen, was zu tun ist.
- Lesen Sie den Text schnell durch und halten Sie an, wenn Sie ein Schlüsselwort gefunden haben. Wenn Sie ein Schlüsselwort gefunden haben, lesen Sie um es herum, um die Aufgabe zu lösen.
- Wenn Sie ein Wort oder eine Redewendung nicht verstehen, halten Sie sich nicht damit auf. Lesen Sie den Text weiter, bis Sie am Ende angelangt sind. Sollte sich herausstellen, dass Sie das Wort benötigen, können Sie sich später noch darum kümmern.

Normalerweise werden die Aufgaben zum Text in der Reihenfolge gestellt, in der die Informationen im Text zu finden sind. In einer Prüfung können Sie den Text markieren bzw. sich die benötigten Details notieren, sobald Sie die Informationen finden, die Sie suchen.

D Mit unbekannten Wörtern umgehen
→ Vokabeln lernen, S. 241

Wenn Sie während des Lesens einem Wort begegnen, das Sie nicht kennen, sollten Sie sich fragen, ob es notwendig ist, das Wort zu verstehen. Wenn Sie das Wort tatsächlich benötigen, versuchen Sie, bevor Sie nach dem Wörterbuch greifen (bzw. online nachschlagen), die Bedeutung des Wortes selbst herauszufinden. Manchmal verstehen Sie die Bedeutung eines Wortes, ohne es bewusst zu „kennen". Wenn dem nicht so ist, nutzen Sie folgende Strategien:

- Erarbeiten Sie es sich aus dem Zusammenhang heraus. Sehen Sie sich genau an, wie das Wort im Satz benutzt wird und wie es mit dem Inhalt dieser Textstelle zusammenhängt.
- Nutzen Sie Ihr Wissen über die deutsche Sprache. Viele englische Wörter haben ähnliche deutsche Entsprechungen bzw. stammen sie von derselben Wurzel ab, z. B.: *ten*/zehn, *light*/Licht, *night*/Nacht, *biology*/Biologie, *democracy*/Demokratie.
- Bringen Sie mehr über Wortbildung in Erfahrung (wie man Wörter aus anderen Wörtern bilden kann).

Vorsilben (*prefixes*)

Vorsilben können die Bedeutung eines Wortes verändern.

anti-	'against'	freeze → antifreeze
co-	'together'	operate → cooperate
inter-	'between'	national → international
sub-	'under' / 'below'	standard → substandard
super-	'above' / 'over'	power → superpower
trans-	'across'	form → transform
dis-		agree → disagree
in-		correct → incorrect
im-	'not' / 'opposite'	possible → impossible
ir-		responsible → irresponsible
un-		friendly → unfriendly
mis-	'not correctly'	understand → misunderstand
re-	'again'	discover → rediscover

Nachsilben (*suffixes*)

Nachsilben können die Wortart eines Wortes verändern.

verbs → nouns

verb	suffix	noun
organize	-ation	organization
express	-ion	expression
begin	-ing	beginning
argue	-ment	argument
bake	-er	baker

nouns → adjectives

noun	suffix	adjective
continent	-al	continental
beauty	-ful	beautiful
day	-ly	daily
hunger	-ry	hungry

verbs → adjectives

verb	suffix	adjective
advise	-able	advisable
rain	-y	rainy
care	-ing	caring

adjectives → nouns

adjective	suffix	noun
stupid	-ity	stupidity
happy	-ness	happiness

adjectives → adverbs

adjective	suffix	adverb
awful	-ly	awfully
democratic	-ally	democratically

3 REZEPTION: HÖRVERSTEHEN

A Vorbereitung auf das Hören

Sich auf die Hörübung vorzubereiten, verstärkt das Hörverständnis. Nutzen Sie hierzu alle Informationen, die sich auf der Seite befinden. Bevor Sie zuhören:

- Lesen Sie alle Ihnen zur Verfügung gestellten Hintergrundinformationen, z. B. eine Einleitung, die die Situation beschreibt und Auskunft darüber gibt, wie viele Personen Sie hören werden.
- Lesen Sie die Aufgabenstellung sorgfältig durch. Denken Sie daran, dass die Fragen, die Sie beantworten müssen, häufig der Reihenfolge entsprechen, in der die Informationen auf der Aufzeichnung vorkommen.

B Während des ersten Hörens

Ein Grobverständnis zu erhalten bedeutet, eine Ahnung zu bekommen, worum es in der Aufzeichnung geht. Während des ersten Hörens brauchen Sie nicht jedes Wort zu verstehen. Entwickeln Sie für das Hören möglichst folgende Fertigkeiten:

- Übergehen Sie Wörter, die Sie nicht verstehen.
- Konzentrieren Sie sich auf Schlüsselwörter.
- Machen Sie sich Notizen auf Englisch. Verwenden Sie Abkürzungen. Schreiben Sie so viel wie möglich auf, während Sie zuhören. Sie können Ihre Notizen zu einem späteren Zeitpunkt übersetzen.

Ordnen Sie Ihre Notizen sofort nach dem Ende der Hörübung. Sie können sie später möglicherweise nicht mehr lesen.

Bemühen Sie sich, alle Aufgaben zu lösen. Aufgaben sind chronologisch angeordnet. Wenn Sie einen Teil der Informationen nicht verstanden haben, raten Sie, ausgehend von dem, was Sie verstanden haben.

C Während des zweiten Hörens

Es ist schwierig, während des Zuhörens Notizen zu machen, weil die Aufzeichnung weiterläuft, während Sie schreiben. Daher verpassen Sie möglicherweise wichtige Informationen. Sie haben sich jedoch bereits beim ersten Hören ein Grobverständnis angeeignet und notiert, was Sie verstehen konnten. Beim zweiten Hören versuchen Sie, sich so viel wie möglich an das zu erinnern, was Sie beim ersten Mal gehört haben. Wenn Sie es sich zur Gewohnheit machen, bei jedem Hören Stichpunkte aufzuschreiben, haben Sie bald den Bogen heraus.

4 PRODUKTION: SCHREIBEN

A Eine Stellungnahme schreiben

Einen längeren Text in einer Englischprüfung zu schreiben, stellt Ihr Sprachverständnis und Ihre Schaffenskraft auf die Probe.

Wenn Sie aufgefordert sind, einen *comment* zu schreiben, müssen Sie Argumente sammeln, welche die in der Aufgabenstellung enthaltene These stützen und widerlegen. Es wird erwartet, dass Sie am Schluß Ihre Meinung zum Thema äußern.

Wenn Sie aufgefordert sind, einen *statement* zu schreiben, müssen Sie sich entscheiden, ob Sie für oder gegen die in der Aufgabenstellung enthaltene These sind. Sammeln Sie deshalb nur die Argumente für oder gegen die These. Durch Ihre Argumente und Beispiele müssen Sie versuchen, den Leser/die Leserin zu überzeugen.

Bevor Sie mit dem Schreiben beginnen

- Lesen Sie die Einleitung zu den Aufgaben mehrmals durch und stellen Sie sicher, dass Sie ganz genau verstehen, worüber Sie schreiben sollen.
- Achten Sie auf den genauen Wortlaut der Anweisungen. Suchen Sie nach Schlüsselwörtern in der Aufgabenstellung, die Ihnen sagen, was zu tun ist.
  - Bei einem *comment* können Sie solche Schlüsselwörter erwarten: *comment on*, *discuss*, *explain*, *advantages and disadvantages*, *pros and cons*.
  - Bei einem *statement* können Sie solche Schlüsselwörter erwarten: *give your opinion*, *discuss*, *point of view*, *perspective*.
  - Bei einer *recommendation* können Sie solche Schlüsselwörter erwarten: *write a recommendation*, *recommend*.

Mindmaps zum Inhalt einer Stellungnahme erstellen

Wenn Sie eine Stellungnahme schreiben sollen, ist es sinnvoll, Ihre Ideen in Form einer Mindmap festzuhalten. So könnten die Argumente in einer Mindmap zum Thema „the benefits and dangers of social media" aussehen:

TASK (COMMENT): Comment on the benefits and the dangers of using social media.
TASK (STATEMENT): Give your opinion on the role of social media in today's world.

Bei einer *statement*-Aufgabenstellung verwenden Sie nur die Argumente, die Sie unter *dangers* oder *benefits* gesammelt haben.

Einen Text sinnvoll gliedern

→ *Language for writing*, hintere Umschlagklappe

Wenn Sie etwas schriftlich verfassen, müssen Sie Ihren Text klar und logisch strukturieren.

Jedes längere Schriftstück bedarf eines Anfangs (Einleitung), eines Mittelteils (Hauptteil) und eines Endes (Abschluss).

Einleitung	Stellen Sie das Thema kurz vor und legen Sie dar, wie Sie es angehen wollen.
Hauptteil	Verwenden Sie für jedes Argument einen Absatz. Bei einem *comment* können Sie zunächst alle Argumente dafür und dann alle Argumente dagegen anführen. Verwenden Sie Bindeglieder wie: *However, …*, *That said, …*, um klarzustellen, dass Sie im folgenden Absatz eine gegenteilige Meinung darlegen werden. Bei einem *statement* sollten Sie mindestens zwei Argumente darlegen. Führen Sie Ihr stärkeres Argument an zweiter Stelle an, da es einen größeren Eindruck hinterlassen wird. Verwenden Sie Ausdrücke wie: *In my opinion, …*, *My feeling is that …* usw., wenn Sie Ihre Meinung äußern.
Abschluss	Bei einem *comment* sagen Sie, ob Sie eine der zwei Seiten befürworten. Bei einem *statement* schließen Sie mit einer knappen Zusammenfassung.

Damit der Leser / die Leserin den roten Faden nicht verliert, können Sie die Sprachelemente der hinteren Umschlagklappe dieses Buches nutzen. Hier sind einige Beispiele, wie man mithilfe dieser Elemente einen Aufsatz strukturieren kann.

Argumente gliedern	*In the text we see how three pupils used social media to hurt another pupil.* **First**, *they …* **Secondly / Then**, *they …*
Eine Begründung anführen	**Due to / Because of / As a result of** *this behaviour, the girl became isolated.*

Aspekte ergänzen	*In addition, / Moreover*, the girl didn't get the job she wanted.
Einen Gegensatz ausdrücken	*Although/While* examples like these illustrate the dangers, social media has its benefits, too. Being active on social media can …
Beispiele anführen	A young man, **for example**, who was diagnosed with terminal cancer aged 15, used social media …
Ein Fazit ziehen	*To sum up / To conclude*, social media has its good and its bad sides. **On the one hand, … On the other hand, …**

Wenn Sie mit dem Schreiben fertig sind:

- Überprüfen Sie Ihre Rechtschreibung, Grammatik und Zeichensetzung sowie Ihren Satzbau.
- Lesen Sie sich das, was Sie geschrieben haben, genau durch und verbessern Sie den Aufsatz dort, wo es der Lesefluss erfordert.

Versuchen Sie in einer Prüfung, rechtzeitig mit dem Schreiben aufzuhören, um genau das tun zu können. Fünf bis zehn Minuten sollten hierfür ausreichend sein.

B Eine E-Mail schreiben

Aufbau

- **Anrede**

  Der Stil der Anrede richtet sich danach, wer der Empfänger / die Empfängerin ist. Anbei einige Beispiele:
  – sehr förmlich (unbekannter Empfänger / unbekannte Empfängerin in einem Geschäftsbrief): *Dear Sir or Madam*
  – förmlich (Geschäftsbrief, in dem die Name bekannt ist): *Dear Mr/Mrs/Ms Smith*
  – freundlich (privater Brief): *Dear Paul/Paula*
  – betont locker (privater Brief): *Hi Paul/Paula*

- **Einleitung**

  – Beginnen Sie den ersten Satz nach der Anrede mit einem Großbuchstaben.
  – Danken Sie ggf. dem Empfänger / der Empfängerin für seinen oder ihren letzten Brief.
  – Entschuldigen Sie sich ggf. dafür, nicht schon früher geschrieben zu haben, und nennen Sie die Gründe.
  – Gehen Sie kurz auf den wichtigsten Punkt im vorangegangenen Brief des Empfängers / der Empfängerin ein.

- **Hauptteil**

  – Nennen Sie den Grund oder aktuellen Anlass für Ihren Brief.
  – Erzählen Sie, was Sie mitzuteilen haben, und machen Sie das gegebenenfalls mit Beispielen oder Erläuterungen anschaulich.

- **Ende**

  – Schreiben Sie, dass (und vielleicht auch warum) Sie jetzt zu einem Ende kommen müssen.
  – Schreiben Sie, dass Sie hoffen, bald wieder von dem Empfänger / der Empfängerin zu hören.

- **Abschließender Gruß**

  Der Schlussgruß richtet sich danach, wie gut man den Empfänger kennt, entsprechend der Anrede.

  – sehr förmlich (unbekannter Empfänger in einem Geschäftsbrief): *Yours faithfully*
  – förmlich (Geschäftsbrief, in dem die Name bekannt ist): *Yours sincerely / Sincerely yours*
  – auf üblicherweise freundlich (Geschäftsbrief oder Privatbrief): *Regards / Best regards / Best wishes*
  – Privater Brief: *Yours / All the best / Love*

C Kreatives Schreiben

Kreatives Schreiben ist in vielfältigen Formen möglich: als Blog-Eintrag oder als Vervollständigung des schon bestehenden Anfangs einer Erzählung, oder auch vielleicht werden Sie auch aufgefordert, eine Geschichte zu einem Bild zu verfassen. Auch die Aufgabe, einen Zeitungsbeitrag zu verfassen, kann in den Bereich „Kreatives Schreiben" gehören.

Unabhängig von der genauen Aufgabenstellung gelten beim Kreativen Schreiben grundlegende Regeln.

Planen

Beschließen Sie, wie Sie sich dem Thema nähern wollen, und machen Sie Notizen. Bringen Sie eine Struktur in diese Notizen (Mindmap oder Liste). Schreiben Sie Schlüsselwörter auf, die Sie verwenden wollen.

Schreiben

- Schreiben Sie einen Einführungssatz.
- Verfassen Sie den Hauptteil. Achten Sie auf verbindende Wörter und Satzglieder, die den Leser durch den Text führen.
- Schreiben Sie den abschließenden Satz.

Überprüfen

Beim schnellen Durchlesen entgehen Ihnen leicht ungenaue Wortverwendungen und andere ungeschickte Formulierungen sowie Tippfehler. Wenn die Aufgabe als Hausaufgabe gegeben wurde, können Sie nach Möglichkeit einen Freund oder eine Freundin bitten, Ihren Text zu lesen und Verbesserungsvorschläge zu machen. Sich selbst den Text laut vorzulesen hilft ebenfalls, auf Unstimmigkeiten aufmerksam zu werden.

Drucken Sie Ihren Text nach Möglichkeit aus. Auf Papier entdeckt man oft Dinge, die einem beim Lesen am Bildschirm entgangen sind. Vor allem aber kann man den Text als Ganzes so besser bewerten.

Formen

- **Einen Blog schreiben**

  - Lesen Sie alles, was bereits zum Thema gesagt wurde. Stellen Sie sicher, dass Sie das Thema und seine bisherige Behandlung richtig erfasst haben.
  - Ihr erster Satz sollte sich bereits direkt auf das Thema beziehen.
  - Widmen Sie jedem Aspekt einen eigenen Absatz. Verwenden Sie sinnverbindende Wörter und Satzteile.
  - Betonen Sie Ihre Stellungnahme durch einen prägnanten Schlusssatz.
  - Auch wenn ein Blog-Beitrag weniger förmlich ist als andere schriftliche Kommentare, sollten Sie sich um einen höflichen Ton bemühen. Versuchen Sie nicht, um jeden Preis witzig zu sein.

- **Eine Geschichte fortsetzen**

  - Lesen Sie den Anfangssatz der bestehenden Geschichte. Er gibt oft bereits Auskunft über den Ort der Handlung und enthält Hinweise zum Thema der Geschichte.
  - Studieren Sie dann den Rest der Geschichte sorgfältig.
  - Machen Sie sich mit der Form der Geschichte vertraut. Wird in der Ich-Form erzählt? Wie werden Dialoge eingesetzt? Achten Sie auf Hinweise, die auf den Ausgang der Geschichte hinweisen könnten.
  - Notieren Sie sich die Namen der handelnden Personen. Achten Sie darauf, sie korrekt zu schreiben. Machen Sie Notizen zu den Charakteren, damit Sie wissen, was für Menschen sie sind und wie sie sich in Ihrer Fortsetzung benehmen und agieren werden.
  - Kopieren Sie den bisherigen Schlusssatz. Nutzen Sie dann Ihre Notizen zur Weiterführung der Geschichte.
  - Achten Sie darauf, dass Ihr Schlusssatz die Geschichte zu einem überzeugenden Ende bringt.

- **Eine Geschichte zu einem Bild schreiben**

  - Betrachten Sie das Bild in allen Einzelheiten genau.
  - Notieren Sie alle Ideen, die Ihnen dazu einfallen.
  - Entscheiden Sie, welche Ideen am interessantesten sind.
  - Verbinden Sie diese Ideen nun zu einer zusammenhängenden Geschichte. Achten Sie dabei auch auf eine packende Einleitung und einen überzeugenden Schluss.
  - Möglicherweise verlangt die Aufgabenstellung, einen ganz bestimmten Aspekt des Bildes zu vertiefen, z. B.: „Suchen Sie sich eine der dargestellten Personen aus und schreiben Sie, was diese Person gerade denkt." Konzentrieren Sie sich dann auf diesen Aspekt des Bildes.

■ **Einen Zeitungsartikel schreiben**

– Das Thema und der aktuelle Anlass wird in der Aufgabenstellung vorgegeben. Achten Sie darauf, dieses Thema in Ihrer Überschrift und im Untertitel prägnant herauszuarbeiten.
– Der erste Absatz soll das Interesse am Thema vertiefen. Benennen Sie möglichst schnell die wichtigsten Fakten.
– Im Hauptteil gehen Sie auf Einzelheiten dieser Fakten ein.
– Der letzte Absatz fasst die wichtigsten Ergebnisse noch einmal zusammen.

■ **Eine Bewerbung schreiben**

– Da es sich bei einem Bewerbungsschreiben um einen Brief handelt, müssen die Regeln des Brief- und E-Mail-Schreibens eingehalten werden. → *Eine E-Mail schreiben*, S. 248
– Im ersten Absatz erklären Sie, wo Sie die Stellenausschreibung gesehen haben, oder warum Sie sich bei der Firma bewerben.
– Im zweiten Absatz schreiben Sie etwas über sich selbst.
– Im dritten Absatz erklären Sie, warum Sie der geeigneteste Kandidat / die geeigneteste Kandidatin sind.
– Im letzten Absatz freuen Sie sich auf einen hoffentlich positiven Ausgang.

5 PRODUKTION: BILDER UND CARTOONS BESCHREIBEN UND ANALYSIEREN

A Ein Bild beschreiben und deuten

Bevor Sie mit dem Schreiben beginnen, nehmen Sie Schmierpapier zur Hand, sehen Sie sich das Bild genau an und machen Sie sich Notizen zu den folgenden Fragen:

■ Wer oder was spielt in dem Bild die Hauptrolle?
■ Steht ein Element im Mittelpunkt? Warum?
■ Schafft das Bild eine besondere Atmosphäre, z.B. von Gefahr, Glück?
■ Was ist die „Botschaft" des Bildes?

Folgende Ausdrücke können bei der Bildbeschreibung von Nutzen sein:

The photo shows …
In the photo you can see …
In the centre/foreground/background …
At the top/bottom of the photo …

Als Daumenregel sollten Sie zuerst das Bild beschreiben. Im Anschluss analysieren Sie es, indem Sie sagen, welche Wirkung das Bild auf den Betrachter / die Betrachterin hat und welche Botschaft es vermittelt.

Bei der Beschreibung von was im Bild passiert, nehmen Sie als Zeitform das *present progressive*, z.B. *In the photo two people are standing and talking.*

B Einen Cartoon beschreiben und deuten

Die o.g. Vorschläge zur Vorbereitung auf eine Bildbeschreibung eignen sich auch zur Vorbereitung auf die Beschreibung eines Cartoons. Denken Sie jedoch immer daran, dass ein Cartoonist / eine Cartoonistin auf etwas Besonderes hinweisen will. Die drei wichtigsten Techniken hierfür sind:

- Karikaturen, also ein oder mehrere Merkmale (z. B. körperliche) übertrieben darstellen.
- Symbole, d. h. ein bekanntes Bild verwenden, um eine Idee zu transportieren, z. B. die Freiheitsstatue, um die USA zu verkörpern.
- Bildunterschriften bzw. Sprechblasen, die die Botschaft in wenigen Worten zusammenfassen bzw. den Charakteren als Aussage zugedacht sind.

Bevor Sie über den Cartoon zu schreiben beginnen, stellen Sie sich folgende Fragen:

- Wie sind die Sachen/Personen/Charaktere gezeichnet? Sind die Personen als Karikaturen dargestellt? Stellen sie einen bestimmten „Personentyp" dar?
- Sind Symbole vorhanden? Wenn ja, was repräsentieren sie?
- Sind in der Zeichnung Nummern, Daten oder leicht erkennbare Orte zu sehen? Wenn ja, welche Funktion erfüllen sie? Was teilen sie uns mit?
- Was ist der Standpunkt des Cartoonisten / der Cartoonistin zum ausgewählten Thema?
- Welche Botschaft transportiert der Cartoon? Wie wird diese Botschaft vermittelt?

Folgende Ausdrücke können bei der Cartoonbeschreibung von Nutzen sein:

The caption reads …
The cartoon criticizes the fact that … / the way that …
The message of the cartoon is …
The cartoon conveys the message that …

Sehen Sie sich alles auf dem Cartoon genau an und beschreiben Sie ihn ausführlich. Verwenden Sie hier das *present progressive*, um auszudrücken, was die Personen tun. Denken Sie daran, dass Sie, wenn Sie die Botschaft des Cartoons nicht verstehen, sagen können, dass es *unclear* oder *ambiguous* (mehrdeutig) ist.

6 PRODUKTION: SCHAUBILDER UND STATISTIKEN BESCHREIBEN UND ANALYSIEREN

Diagramme und Kurvenbilder werden verwendet, um Informationen visuell darzustellen.

TYPES OF DIAGRAMS

Table

	Germany	UK
2010	568	261
2018	822	98

Bar chart

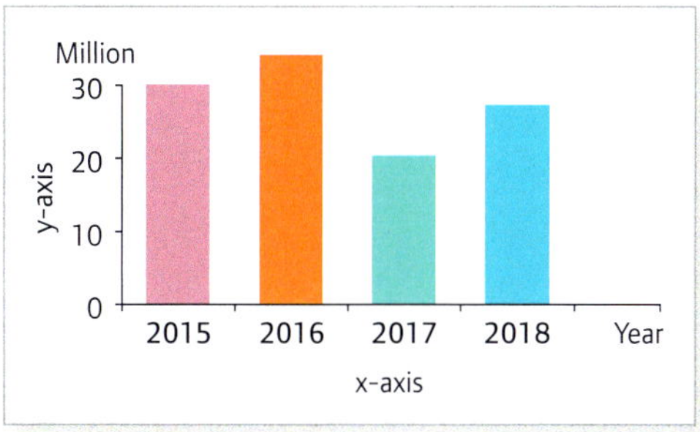

Pie chart

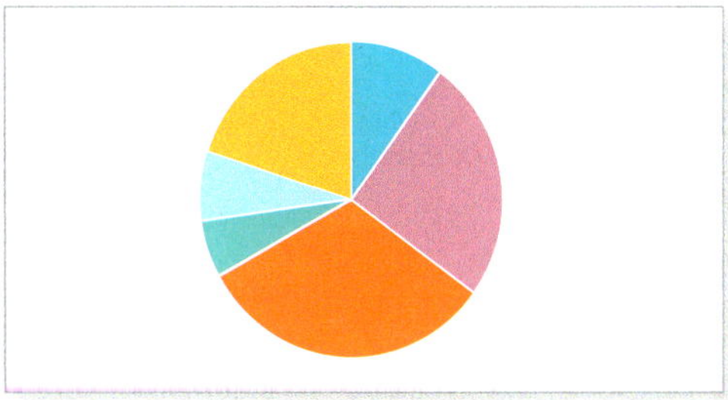

Graph, line graph

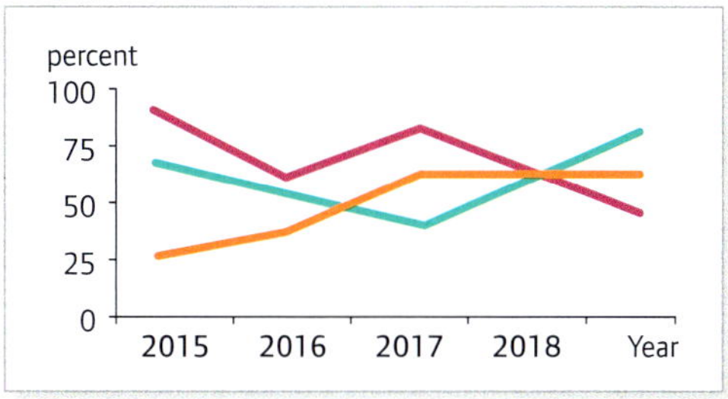

Bevor Sie mit dem Schreiben beginnen, nehmen Sie Schmierpapier zur Hand, sehen sich die Abbildung genau an und machen sich zu folgenden Fragen Notizen:

- Was sagt die Überschrift aus? Welche Beschriftung liegt vor?
- Welche Zahlen und Einheiten werden verwendet, um die Daten darzustellen?
- Wenn ein Balkendiagramm / eine Kurve vorliegt, wofür steht die x-Achse? Wofür die y-Achse?
- Welche Muster können Sie in den Daten erkennen?
- Welche Schlüsse können Sie aus diesen Mustern ziehen?

Um Ihre Beschreibung und Analyse der Abbildung zu ordnen, nutzen Sie Ihre Notizen folgendermaßen:

■ eine Einleitung	*The diagram/graph shows … / refers to …*
■ ein Überblick dessen, was es darstellt	*The figures in the table show …* *The x-axis shows …, the y-axis shows …*
■ eine ausführliche Beschreibung der Informationen	*The graph shows a huge increase in …*
■ die Beziehung zwischen den Kategorien	*Germany produces twice as much … as the UK.*
■ eine Auswertung	*The figures indicate that …*

7 PRÄSENTATION

Im Verlauf Ihres Schuljahres könnten Sie aufgefordert werden, eine Präsentation vorzubereiten und zu geben. Die Fertigkeit des Präsentierens können Sie in der Schule üben; das gibt Ihnen jene Sicherheit, die Sie brauchen, um eine Präsentation auf der Arbeit zu geben.

A Vorbereitung

- Sammeln Sie möglichst viele Informationen und Ideen zu dem Thema, indem Sie im Internet und in Büchern recherchieren, ein Brainstorming machen, usw.
- Wählen Sie jene Ideen aus, die Ihr Thema am sinnvollsten widerspiegeln, und machen Sie sich Notizen.
- Verwenden Sie Ihre Notizen, um Ihre Ideen in logische Einheiten einzuteilen.
- Ordnen Sie diese Einheiten so, dass ein roter Faden klar erkennbar ist.
- Wenn Sie das geschrieben haben, was Sie sagen wollten, lesen Sie Ihre Präsentation durch. Suchen Sie nach Stellen, wo Sie etwas kürzen oder löschen können. Fragen Sie sich immer wieder: Kann ich das noch kürzer, präziser ausdrücken?
- Erstellen Sie sich nun Stichwortkarten als Erinnerungshilfe für die wichtigsten Informationen. Schreiben Sie auf Karteikarten; schreiben Sie deutlich und in Großbuchstaben und möglichst keine ganzen Sätze außer den ersten und den letzten – Sie benötigen nur Stichwörter.
- Es hilft, Ihre Präsentation als Trockenübung zu geben, besonders vor einem Publikum.

B Eine Präsentation halten

- Beginnen Sie mit einer Begrüßung Ihrer Zuhörer/innen und stellen Sie anschließend sich und Ihr Thema vor. Versuchen Sie, das Interesse und die Aufmerksamkeit Ihrer Zuhörerschaft von Anfang an zu wecken. Sagen Sie, wie lang Sie über etwas reden werden, z. B.: *In the next 10 minutes, I will share my ideas about …*
- Teilen Sie Ihrem Hörerkreis mit, wie Sie Ihre Präsentation unterteilt haben bzw. wie viele Punkte Sie abdecken wollen, z. B.: *I've divided my talk into three sections: first … second …*
- Nachdem Sie das Ende Ihrer Präsentation eingeläutet haben, fassen Sie sich kurz und kommen Sie zum Ende. Ermutigen Sie Ihre Zuhörer/innen, Fragen zu stellen.

8 INTERAKTION

Sie werden möglicherweise im Unterricht aufgefordert, an einer Diskussion bzw. einem Rollenspiel mitzuwirken. Beide dieser Aufgaben schließen einen Austausch mit anderen Menschen ein. Folgen Sie den u.s. allgemeinen Tipps.

Tipps für einen guten Austausch

- Verinnerlichen Sie die Ausdrücke auf der hinteren Umschlagklappe und verwenden Sie sie im Unterricht, sooft Sie können.   → *Language for speaking*, hintere Umschlagklappe
- Halten Sie sich an das Thema.
- Bleiben Sie locker und denken Sie, bevor Sie sprechen.
- Bleiben Sie immer höflich und geben Sie anderen die Möglichkeit zu reden. Hören Sie aktiv zu und gehen Sie auf die anderen Teilnehmer/innen ein. Nehmen Sie Augenkontakt auf und zeigen Sie Interesse, Überraschung, usw. Stellen Sie Fragen.
- Werten Sie andere niemals ab. Wenn ein anderer Teilnehmer / eine andere Teilnehmerin Probleme zu haben scheint, helfen Sie ihm/ihr, indem Sie in Worte fassen, was (Sie glauben, was) er/sie ausdrücken möchte, z. B.: *So, you mean that … I think I understand what you're getting at. You're saying that …*

An Diskussionen teilnehmen

In einer Diskussion sollten Sie Ihre Meinung zum Ausdruck bringen.
- Lesen Sie die Anweisungen sorgfältig durch und entscheiden Sie, was Sie sagen möchten.
- Machen Sie sich Notizen und schreiben Sie einige Schlüsselwörter bzw. -ausdrücke auf Englisch auf.
- Versuchen Sie vorauszusehen, was die anderen Teilnehmer/innen sagen könnten. Überlegen Sie sich, wie Sie hierzu reagieren würden, und fügen Sie Ihren Notizen englische Ausdrücke der Zustimmung bzw. Widerrede hinzu.   → *Language for speaking*, hintere Umschlagklappe

9 DIE PRÜFUNG UND PRÜFUNGSSTRATEGIEN

Die Prüfung besteht aus insgesamt vier Teilen und einer mündlichen Kommunikationsprüfung.

Prüfungsteil	Aufgaben	VP
Part I		
Listening Comprehension	- Zielsprache Englisch	**15 VP**
	- drei Teilaufgaben (drei Audiotexte, jeweils mit einem anderen Aufgabentyp)	jeweils 5 VP
	- Aufgabentypen: *multiple choice, multiple matching, true/false, gap filling, table filling, sentence completion, short-answer questions*	

Part II		
Reading Comprehension	Aufgaben 1–3:	**15 VP**
	■ Zielsprache Englisch	10 VP
	■ mehrere Teilaufgaben	
	■ Aufgabentypen:	
	multiple matching, multiple choice, true/false, sentence completion, open questions	
	Aufgabe 4:	
	■ Informationen aus dem Text in Stichpunkte auf Deutsch wiedergeben	5 VP

Part III		
Writing	■ Zielsprache Englisch	**30 VP**
	■ zwei Teilaufgaben:	
	1. Teilaufgabe:	
	■ Stellungnahme: *comment, recommendation, statement*	10 VP
	■ bezieht sich auf den Text oder das Thema des *reading comprehension* Teils	
	■ Textlänge etwa 100 Wörter	
	2. Teilaufgabe:	
	■ Aufgabenformate: *an email, a story, a newspaper article, a job application, a blog entry*	
	■ Eine aus zwei Aufgaben wird ausgewählt.	20 VP
	■ Textlänge etwa 160 Wörter	

Part IV		
Use of language	■ Zielsprache Englisch	**10 VP**
	■ mehrere Teilaufgaben	
	Aufgaben 1–3:	
	■ *synonyms, antonyms, definitions*	
	Aufgabe 4:	
	■ *vocabulary and grammar completion tasks*	
	Aufgabe 5:	
	■ *asking questions*	

mündliche Prüfung		
Kommunikations-prüfung	■ mündliche Prüfung	**30 VP**
	■ findet vor der schriftlichen Prüfung statt	
	■ Zeit: Vorbereitung dauert 10 Minuten, Prüfung dauert 15 Minuten	
	■ Tandemprüfung	
	■ zuerst monologisches Sprechen, dann dialogisches Sprechen	

LISTENING COMPREHENSION

In Part I wird das Hörverstehen geprüft. Der Teil besteht aus drei kurzen Audiotexten. Es gibt jedoch verschiedene Aufgabentypen, aus denen drei verschiedene für die Teilaufgaben ausgewählt werden.

Aufgabentyp	Beschreibung
multiple matching	Dies ist eine (Mehrfach-)Zuordnungsaufgabe.
multiple choice	Dies ist eine Mehrfachwahlaufgabe.
true/false	Hier muss entschieden werden, ob Aussagen richtig oder falsch sind.
gap filling	Hier handelt es sich um Lückentexte.
table filling	Hier müssen Tabellen oder Raster ergänzt werden.
sentence completion	Hier müssen vorgegebene Sätze vervollständigt werden.
short-answer questions	Hier werden sehr kurze Antworten auf Englisch zu Fragen erwartet.

Schritte zum Erfolg:

1 Lesen Sie sich die Aufgaben aufmerksam durch. Markieren Sie Schlüsselbegriffe, auf die Sie beim Hören besonders achten müssen. Auf diese Weise hören Sie zielgerichteter.

2 Hören Sie bereits beim ersten Hören mit dem Stift in der Hand. Nehmen Sie zunächst einen Bleistift, so können Sie falsch gemachte Kreuze/falsche Antworten leicht wieder entfernen.

3 Nutzen Sie die Zeit zwischen dem ersten und dem zweiten Hören, um Ihre bereits gemachten Kreuze/Antworten zu überprüfen oder zu vervollständigen bzw. gegebenenfalls zu korrigieren.

4 Vervollständigen Sie beim zweiten Hören das, was Ihnen noch fehlt. Überprüfen Sie auch Ihre bereits gemachten Kreuze / aufgeschriebenen Antworten.

5 Ersetzen Sie gegebenenfalls alle mit Bleistift verfassten Lösungen nun durch Lösungen mit dem Kugelschreiber/Füller.

READING COMPREHENSION

In Part II wird das Leseverstehen überprüft. Der Teil besteht aus vier Aufgaben zu einem Text.

Aufgaben 1–3: Sie beweisen Ihr Leseverstehen eines englischen Lesetextes mithilfe verschiedener Aufgabenformate.

Aufgabentyp	Beschreibung
multiple matching	Dies ist eine (Mehrfach-)Zuordnungsaufgabe.
multiple choice	Dies ist eine Mehrfachwahlaufgabe.
true/false	Hier muss entschieden werden, ob Aussagen richtig oder falsch sind.
sentence completion	Hier müssen vorgegebene Sätze auf Englisch vervollständigt werden.
open questions	Hier werden Antworten auf Englisch in vollständigen Sätzen zu Fragen erwartet.

Schritte zum Erfolg:

1 Lesen Sie den Text zuerst einmal zügig durch. Lassen Sie sich von schwierigen Passagen oder Wörtern nicht entmutigen. Wenn Sie etwas beim ersten Lesen nicht verstehen, lesen Sie trotzdem weiter. Wenn Sie den gesamten Text gelesen haben, ergibt sich manches aus dem Zusammenhang.

2 Lesen Sie sich die Aufgabenstellungen und die Aufgaben aufmerksam durch, noch bevor Sie den Text durchlesen. Unterstreichen Sie in den Aufgaben die Schlüsselwörter.

3 Legen Sie nun das Aufgabenblatt neben das Blatt mit dem Text, und lesen Sie den Text noch einmal langsam Absatz für Absatz.

4 Bearbeiten Sie nun die Aufgaben. Achten Sie dabei auf die markierten Schlüsselwörter und lesen Sie genau. Geben Sie sich nicht mit schnellen Lösungen zufrieden. Manchmal sind es die „kleinen" Wörter, die für das Finden der richtigen Lösung eine große Bedeutung haben.

5 Wenn Sie alle Aufgaben bearbeitet haben, sollten Sie den Text ein letztes Mal durchlesen und Ihre Lösungen noch einmal am Text überprüfen.

Aufgabentyp	Beschreibung
Informationen aus einem Text wiedergeben	Sie bekommen eine Frage auf Deutsch, die Sie mithilfe von Informationen aus dem Text stichwortartig beantworten müssen. Die Zielsprache ist Deutsch.

Schritte zum Erfolg:

1 Lesen Sie zuerst die Aufgabenstellung genau durch. Unterstreichen Sie die Schlüsselbegriffe der Aufgabenstellung.

2 Sie müssen nun die fünf Aspekte im Text finden, die in der Fragestellung gefordert sind. Lesen Sie den Text sorgfältig durch, und kennzeichnen Sie die in Frage kommenden Informationen, indem Sie Passagen markieren oder unterstreichen.

3 Übertragen Sie nun das Markierte ins Deutsche. Übersetzen Sie dabei nicht Wort für Wort. Sie müssen auch keine vollständigen Sätze schreiben. Stichpunkte genügen.

4 Gleichen Sie Ihre Lösung noch einmal mit den Passagen im englischen Originaltext ab.

WRITING

In Part III wird die Schreibkompetenz überprüft. Der Teil besteht aus zwei Aufgaben.

Aufgabe 1: Sie schreiben eine Stellungnahme zu einem Thema, das mit dem Inhalt oder Thema des Lesetextes zusammenhängen kann.

Der Text soll etwa 100 Wörter umfassen. → *Eine Stellungnahme schreiben*, S. 246

Aufgabentyp	Beschreibung
comment	Ein *comment* fordert eine eher sachliche Erörterung des Für (Pro) und Wider (Kontra). Sie sollten zum Schluss Ihre eigene Meinung darlegen.
statement	Ein *statement* beschränkt sich auf die Darstellung einer Seite einer Argumentation. Diese Form der Erörterung ist deshalb linear, denn sie benennt entweder das Für oder das Wider.
recommendation	Die *recommendation* ist eine sehr persönliche Empfehlung, die der Verfasser/die Verfasserin des Textes ausspricht.

Aufgabe 2: Sie wählen eine Aufgabe aus einem Angebot aus und verfassen einen Text.

Der Text soll etwa 160 Wörter umfassen. → *Eine Stellungnahme schreiben*, S. 246

Aufgabentyp	Beschreibung
writing or answering an email	Sie verfassen oder beantworten eine E-Mail.
writing a blog entry	Sie schreiben einen Blog-Eintrag zu einem bestimmten Thema.
writing the continuation of a story	Sie bekommen den Anfang einer Geschichte, die sie fortführen.
writing a story based on a picture	Sie schreiben eine Geschichte zu einem Bild.
writing a job application	Sie schreiben eine Bewerbung auf eine Stelle.
writing a newspaper article	Sie schreiben eine Zeitungsbericht zu einem bestimmten Ereignis.

Schritte zum Erfolg:

1 Lesen Sie sich die Aufgabenstellung gründlich durch und markieren Sie die Schlüsselbegriffe. Bei Aufgabe 2 entscheiden Sie sich dann zügig, welche der Aufgaben Sie bearbeiten möchten.

2 Nehmen Sie sich Zeit für die Planung, bevor Sie mit dem Schreiben beginnen. Welche Inhalte aus dem Text können Sie für Ihren Text verwenden? Lesen Sie sich den Text dazu erneut durch und schreiben Sie sich passende Inhalte heraus.

3 Überlegen Sie sich, wie Sie Ihren Text aufbauen wollen. Entwerfen Sie eine Gliederung, d. h. bringen Sie die Punkte, die Sie nennen möchten, in eine sinnvolle Reihenfolge. Überlegen Sie sich einen guten Einstieg. Wie wollen Sie Ihren Text beenden?

4 Schreiben Sie nun Ihren Text zuerst auf ein Konzeptblatt.

5 Lesen Sie Ihren Text noch einmal durch und nehmen Sie Korrekturen vor in Bezug auf Grammatik und Rechtschreibung.

6 Verfassen Sie nun Ihre Reinschrift und lesen Sie Ihren Text zum Abschluss noch einmal durch.

USE OF LANGUAGE

In Part IV wird Ihr Wortschatz- und Grammatikwissen überprüft. Der Teil besteht aus fünf Aufgaben.

Wortschatzaufgaben	
Aufgabe 1	Sie müssen zu angegebenen Wörtern die passenden **Synonyme** im *reading comprehension*-Text finden.
Aufgabe 2	Sie müssen zu Wörtern aus dem *reading comprehension*-Text **Antonyme** finden.
Aufgabe 3	Sie müssen die **Bedeutung** von Wörtern aus dem *reading comprehension*-Text erklären.
Grammatik- und Wortschatzaufgabe	
Aufgabe 4	In dieser Aufgabe werden erlernte sprachliche Mittel im Kontext eines Lückentexts überprüft. Es müssen grammatische Strukturen angewendet oder Begriffe aus derselben Wortfamilie angepasst werden. Der Lückentext dieser Aufgabe muss inhaltlich nicht in Zusammenhang mit dem Text der *reading comprehension* stehen.
Fragen bilden	
Aufgabe 5	In dieser abschließenden Aufgabe bilden Sie eigenständig zwei Fragen zu einer vorgegebenen Thematik. Dabei müssen Sie in den beiden Fragen unterschiedlichen Fragewörter sowie Zeitformen benutzen.

Schritte zum Erfolg:

1 Lernen Sie kontinuierlich das ganze Jahr über Vokabeln. Aber nicht nur isoliert die Wörter, sondern auch Synonyme, Antonyme und Definitionen bzw. die Verwendung der Wörter im Kontext von Sätzen. Auch durch das Lernen von Wortfamilien können Sie Ihren Wortschatz effektiv erweitern.

2 Schauen Sie sich während Ihrer Prüfungsvorbereitung die wichtigsten Grammatik-Themen noch einmal an. Welche Tempora gibt es bei den Verben? Was sind die Besonderheiten der verschiedenen Wortarten? Wie bildet man einen Aussagesatz? Wie eine Frage?

3 **Aufgaben 1–2:** Für die Wortschatzaufgaben (Synonyme, Antonyme): Schauen Sie sich ganz genau an, wie das Wort im Satz verwendet wird und was es dort bedeutet. Synonyme und Antonyme passen manchmal in dem einen Kontext, im anderen Kontext aber schon wieder nicht. Achten Sie auch auf die „Suchrichtung":

Aufgabe 1: Hier sollen Sie im Text ein Wort suchen, das dasselbe bedeutet wie das in der Aufgabe abgedruckte Wort. Die Zeilenangaben helfen Ihnen dabei, in welchem Teil des Textes Sie suchen müssen.

Aufgabe 2: Die in der Aufgabe abgedruckten Wörter sind dem Text entnommen – daher die exakte Zeilenangabe. Sie müssen eigenständig aus Ihrem Wortschatz ein passendes Wort finden.

4 **Aufgabe 3:** Auch bei dieser Aufgabe sollten Sie sich zunächst ganz genau anschauen, was das Wort in dem Satz im Text bedeutet, denn das hat Einfluss auf Ihre Definition.
Wenden Sie die KISS-Formel an: *Keep it short and simple*, denn: In der Kürze liegt die Würze. Schreiben Sie einfache Sätze. Je mehr Sie sich in lange Sätze verwickeln, desto fehleranfälliger werden diese Sätze.

5 **Aufgabe 4:** Hier brauchen Sie sowohl Wortschatz- als auch Grammatikwissen.
Schauen Sie sich bei jedem Wort genau an, wie es sich in die Lücke fügen muss. Welche Wortart ist es? Was müssen Sie mit dem Wort tun: konjugieren (Verb), in ein anderes Tempus setzen (Verb), ein *-ly* anhängen (Adverb), usw.?

Manchmal müssen Sie auch komplett eigenständig entscheiden, welches Wort in den Kontext passt, da am Rand nur ein Fragezeichen steht. Auch hier ist Wortart-Wissen hilfreich, denn so wissen Sie, in welche Richtung Sie denken müssen.

Analysieren Sie den Satz, in dem die Lücke ist, genau. Was ist die Aussage des Satzes? Welche Wörter/Wortarten umgeben die Lücke, und welchen Einfluss hat dies auf das Wort, das Sie verwenden müssen? Wie ist der Satzbau? Dies kann Ihnen bei der Frage helfen, ob z. B. durch das Wort, das in die Lücke gehört, ein Haupt- und ein Nebensatz miteinander verbunden werden.

5 **Aufgabe 5:** Für die Bewältigung dieser Aufgabe sollten Sie sich noch einmal bewusst machen, wie man Fragen mit und ohne Fragewörter bildet.

KOMMUNIKATIONSPRÜFUNG

In der Kommunikationsprüfung wird überprüft, wie gut Sie auf Englisch kommunizieren können. Sie absolvieren die Prüfung normalerweise gemeinsam mit einem Mitschüler/einer Mitschülerin als Tandemprüfung. Die Prüfung dauert insgesamt 15 Minuten, inklusive der Notenfindung. Sie besteht aus einem monologischen und einem dialogischen Teil. Der monologische Teil dauert etwa 2–3 Minuten, der dialogische Teil 8–10 Minuten.
Sie dürfen sich vor der Prüfung 10 Minuten vorbereiten.

A Monologisches Sprechen

Dieser Teil ist dazu gedacht, dass Sie sich an die Prüfungssituation gewöhnen und Ihre Nervosität ablegen können. Ihre Lehrkraft/Prüfkraft wird Ihnen Fragen stellen, die Sie schon aus dem Unterricht kennen, z. B. Fragen nach Ihren Hobbys, nach der Schule oder nach Ihren Zukunftsplänen.

Schritte zum Erfolg:

1 Sammeln Sie mögliche Fragen zum Thema „Alltag" und was Sie darauf antworten könnten.
2 Geben Sie die Fragen einer Gesprächspartnerin / einem Gesprächspartner zum Üben.

B Dialogisches Sprechen

Diesen Teil können Sie bereits in der 10-minütigen Vorbereitungszeit schon planen. Sie bekommen Bildimpulse und Leitfragen oder eine Situationsbeschreibung, anhand derer Sie sich vorbereiten können. Sie dürfen sich auch Notizen machen.

Schritte zum Erfolg:

1 Lesen Sie sich die Aufgabenstellung genau durch und markieren Sie die Schlüsselwörter.
2 Schauen Sie sich auch die Bilder genau an. Machen Sie Notizen zu den Bildern. Es ist wichtig, dass Sie ein Bild detailliert beschreiben und die wesentlichen Aussagen eines Bildes wiedergeben können.
3 Schreiben Sie sich je nach Fragestellung Argumente, Ideen, Vorschläge etc. auf.
4 Notieren Sie sich mögliche Redemittel, mit denen Sie Ihre Redebeiträge einleiten können oder auf die Beiträge Ihres Gegenübers angemessen reagieren können. (Idealerweise haben Sie sich diese Redemittel bereits in der Zeit vor der Prüfung gesammelt, gelernt und regelmäßig angewendet). Es ist auch wichtig zu wissen, wie man einer Sache zustimmt, sie ablehnt, kritisch sieht oder widerlegt.
5 Hören Sie Ihrer Mitschülerin / Ihrem Mitschüler gut zu, wenn sie/er die Bilder beschreibt. So können Sie bei Gelegenheit auch eine Rückfrage stellen.
6 Halten Sie sich an die Regeln für eine gelingende Kommunikation. Dazu gehört ein respektvoller Umgang mit der Gesprächspartnerin / dem Gesprächspartner, wie z. B. den anderen ausreden zu lassen und ihm nicht ins Wort zu fallen.
7 Seien Sie in der Prüfung selbst mutig. Trauen Sie sich, etwas zu sagen. Es ist nicht schlimm, wenn Sie mal einen Fehler machen. Das Wichtigste ist, dass die Unterhaltung gelingt. Reißen Sie aber auf der anderen Seite das Gespräch nicht an sich, sondern geben Sie Ihrem Gegenüber auch die Gelegenheit, etwas zu sagen. Ein Gespräch ist dann gut, wenn beide Gesprächspartner gleich viel sagen. Deshalb sollten Sie sowohl Ihren eigenen Standpunkt formulieren können als auch Ihrem Gegenüber Fragen stellen oder die an Sie gestellten Fragen beantworten können.

SIMPLE PRESENT

FORM: Das *simple present* wird so gebildet:

Aussage	*I play football every day.* *He plays football at school.*	*I/we/you/they*: Grundform *he/she/it*: Grundform + *s*
	He goes to school at 8 a.m. *She pushes her bike uphill.*	*he/she/it*: Grundform + *es* (nach einem „o" oder einen Zischlaut wie „sh")
Verneinungen	*They don't play football.* *She doesn't play football.*	*I/we/you/they don't* + Grundform *he/she/it doesn't* + Grundform
Fragen	*Do you play football?* *Does she play football?*	*Do I/we/you/they* + Grundform …? *Does he/she/it* + Grundform …?
Kurzantwort	*Yes, I do.* *Yes, she does.* *No, I don't.* *No, she doesn't.*	*I/we/you/they do* *he/she/it does* *I/we/you/they don't* *he/she/it doesn't*

GEBRAUCH: Das *simple present* wird verwendet für:

gleich bleibende Zustände	*I come from Germany.*
regelmäßige, wiederholte Handlungen	*She eats a lot of fruit.*
was zum Tagesablauf gehört	*I wake up at 7 a.m.*
was man beruflich und in der Freizeit macht	*I work in a hospital.*

SIGNALWÖRTER: Das *simple present* verwendet man häufig mit den folgenden typischen Zeitangaben:

- always, usually, often, sometimes, rarely, never
- every morning/day/year
- at … o'clock, in the morning, at lunchtime, after school
- on Monday(s), at the weekend, in June, in the summer

PRESENT PROGRESSIVE

FORM: Das *present progressive* wird so gebildet:

Aussage	*I'm playing football.* *He is playing football.*	*am/is/are ('m/'s/'re)* + *-ing*-Form des Verbs
	He is taking a photo. *You are sitting in my chair.* *He is running around the house.*	Verben auf *-e*: das *-e* entfällt einsilbige Verben mit Konsonant am Ende, die kurz gesprochen werden: Konsonant verdoppelt

Verneinungen	I'm **not playing** football She **isn't playing** football.	'm not/isn't/'s not/aren't/'re not + -ing-Form des Verbs
Fragen	**Are** you **playing** football? **Is** she **playing** football?	am/is/are wird mit dem Subjekt getauscht
Kurzantwort	**Yes, I am.** **Yes, she is.** **No, I'm not.** **No, she isn't.**	simple present des Verbs „to be"

GEBRAUCH: Das present progressive wird verwendet für:

vorübergehende oder im Moment des Sprechens ablaufende Handlungen und Situationen	I'm **playing** football right now. Shhh! I'm **talking** to my mum.

SIGNALWÖRTER: Das present progressive verwendet man häufig mit den folgenden typischen Zeitangaben:

- at the moment, now
- just, still
- today, this week, this month, this summer

1 Complete the statements in the simple present or the present progressive.

1 Jane ⬤ (eat) meat every day.
2 I ⬤ (eat) meat once or twice a week.
3 Tony ⬤ (train) with Sam and Oliver this morning.
4 They ⬤ (run) around the park.

2 Make the statements negative.

1 Mark likes peanut butter.
2 Chocolate is a good source of fibre.
3 I'm enjoying this meal.
4 We're feeling energetic this morning.

3 Use the keywords to write questions in the simple present or the present progressive.

1 you – speak – German?
2 Alex – like – pizza?
3 they – get – better – at running?
4 she – keep – a diary?

4 Write short answers (e.g. *Yes, I do*) to the questions.

1 Does Tony use Instagram? Yes, ● *he does.*
2 Do they go to the park every day? No, ● *they do not.*
3 Is he training at the moment? Yes, ● *he is.*
4 Are you playing a video game? No, ● *they aren't.*

5 Simple present or present progressive? Use the signal words to decide which tense is correct.

1 Vegans never eat / are never eating animal products.
2 I try / am trying to lose weight at the moment.
3 They relax / are relaxing at home this afternoon.
4 I go / am going running on Mondays.

SIMPLE PAST

FORM: Das *simple past* wird so gebildet:

Aussage	I **played** football yesterday. She **liked** the match.	regelmäßige Verben: Grundform + *-ed* Verben auf *-e*: nur *-d*
	They **stopped** the fight.	einsilbige Verben mit Konsonant am Ende, die kurz gesprochen werden: Konsonant verdoppelt
	She **bought** a bike last week. I **was** at the party.	unregelmäßige Verben: → S. 275
Verneinungen	They **didn't play** football. He **didn't buy** a bike. She **wasn't** at the party.	did not (didn't) + Grundform to be: was not (wasn't) und were not (weren't)
Fragen	**Did** you **play** football? **Did** she **buy** a bike? **Were** you at the party?	did + Grundform to be: was und were
Kurzantwort	Yes, I **did**. No, they **didn't**.	I/you/he/she/it/we/they did I/you/he/she/it/we/they didn't

GEBRAUCH: Das *simple past* wird verwendet für:

abgeschlossene Ereignisse und Zustände	I **saw** him yesterday.

SIGNALWÖRTER: Das *simple past* verwendet man häufig mit den folgenden typischen Zeitangaben:

- yesterday
- last week/year
- three days ago
- in 2010
- When …?

6 Complete the statements in the simple past.

1 I ⬤ (contact) him on Facebook.
2 She ⬤ (grow up) in Germany.
3 I ⬤ (not – watch) the video on YouTube.
4 You ⬤ (not – send) me the link to the video.

7 Use the keywords to write questions in the simple past. Then write short answers (e.g. *Yes, I did*).

1 Anaïs – recognize – her sister on YouTube ? Yes, ⬤
2 the sisters – take – a DNA test ? Yes, ⬤
3 Samantha – grow up – as an only child ? No, ⬤
4 they – meet – their birth mother ? No, ⬤

PAST PROGRESSIVE

FORM: Das *past progressive* wird so gebildet:

Aussage	I **was playing** football. They **were playing** football.	was/were + -ing-Form des Verbs
	He was tak**ing** a photo. You were sit**t**ing in my chair. He was ru**nn**ing around the house.	Verben auf -e: das -e entfällt einsilbige Verben mit Konsonant am Ende, die kurz gesprochen werden: Konsonant verdoppelt
Verneinungen	I **was not playing** football They **weren't playing** football.	was/were not/wasn't/weren't + -ing-Form des Verbs
Fragen	**Were** you **playing** football? **Was** she **playing** football?	was/were wird mit dem Subjekt getauscht
Kurzantwort	Yes, I **was**. Yes, you **were**. No, I **wasn't**. No, you **weren't**.	I/he/she/it was you/we/they were I/he/she/it wasn't you/we/they weren't

GEBRAUCH: Das *past progressive* wird verwendet für:

einen länger andauernden Vorgang, der durch ein Ereignis von kurzer Dauer unterbrochen wird. Dieses kurze Ereignis steht im *simple past*.	I **was doing** my homework <u>when</u> I <u>saw</u> the terrible news on the TV. We **were walking** home <u>when</u> Martina <u>passed</u> us on her moped.
Ereignisse, die in der Vergangenheit zu einem bestimmten Zeitpunkt gerade im Gange waren.	I didn't see my boyfriend last week, as he **was studying** all week.

8 **Complete the sentences with the past progressive of the verbs in brackets.**

1 On Thanksgiving Day it was cold and it ⬤ (rain).
2 Despite the bad weather, the children ⬤ (run) around the garden.
3 When he first saw Mary, Leon ⬤ (eat) in a restaurant.
4 The members of his host family ⬤ (not – talk) to him.

9 **Complete the sentences. In each sentence there is one simple past and one past progressive form.**

1 I ⬤ (watch) TV when Nathan, Sally and their children ⬤ (arrive).
2 We ⬤ (not – mind) the bad weather because we ⬤ (have) a good time.

PRESENT PERFECT

FORM: Das *present perfect* wird so gebildet:

Aussage	*I've played football all my life.* *She's gone to see her friend.*	*have/has ('ve/'s) + Partizip Perfekt* unregelmäßige Verben: → S. 275
Verneinungen	*They haven't played football all day.* *He hasn't bought a bike yet.*	*haven't/hasn't + Partizip Perfekt* unregelmäßige Verben: → S. 275
Fragen	*Have you played football today?* *Has she bought a new bike?* *Have you ever been to China?*	*have/has wird mit dem Subjekt* getauscht
Kurzantwort	*Yes, I have.* *No, he hasn't.*	*I/we/you/they have* *he/she/it has* *I/we/you/they haven't* *he/she/it hasn't*

GEBRAUCH: Das *present perfect* wird verwendet für:

Ereignisse, die in der Vergangenheit begonnen haben und bis in die Gegenwart andauern	*I have lived in this town all my life.* *I've just finished work.*
Ereignisse, die irgendwann einmal – oder noch nie – stattgefunden haben, ohne Angabe des Zeitpunkts	*Have you ever been to London?* *Yes, I've been to London many times.*

SIGNALWÖRTER: Das *present perfect* verwendet man häufig, aber nicht immer, mit den folgenden typischen Zeitangaben:

- already, just, before, (not) yet
- for (*seit*) three weeks/months/years
- since Monday/2010
- How long …?
- ever …?
- lately, recently
- up till now

10 **Complete the statements in the present perfect.**

1 Laura ⬤ (start) school again.
2 Her friends ⬤ (help) her a lot.
3 We ⬤ (apply) for a place at college.
4 Tom ⬤ (fall behind) at school this year.
5 He ⬤ (do) a lot of stupid things.
6 Life ⬤ (be) difficult for both of them.
7 They ⬤ (have) the chance to get back on track.
8 They ⬤ (give) talks about their life on the streets.

11 **Make the statements negative.**

1 I have done my exams.
2 She has turned her life around.
3 We have watched TV all evening.
4 They have met the social worker.

12 **Use the keywords to write questions in the present perfect.**

1 Your sister – learn – anything – from her experience?
2 in what ways – your life – change?
3 how long – you – live in this neighbourhood.
4 your brother – leave – home – yet?

13 **Write short answers (e.g. *Yes, I have*) to the questions.**

1 Has your friend gone back home? Yes, ⬤
2 Has your brother applied for a place at college? No, ⬤
3 Have you ever lived away from home? Yes, ⬤
4 Have you ever worked in a supermarket? No, ⬤

14 **Present perfect or simple present? Use the underlined signal words to decide which tense is correct.**

1 I read / have read a lot of interesting articles recently.
2 We saw / have seen Tom three weeks ago.
3 He has already done / already did his exams.
4 I haven't thought / didn't think about it up till now.
5 Laura phoned / has phoned me yesterday.
6 When did Ben drop / has Ben dropped out of school?
7 Did you apply / Have you applied for a place at college yet?
8 David left / has left home in 2016.

PAST PERFECT

FORM: Das *past perfect* wird so gebildet:

Aussage	I **had** only **visited** London once before I moved there.	*had + Partizip Perfekt*
Verneinungen	I got a bad mark because I **hadn't learned** enough.	*had not (hadn't) + Partizip Perfekt*
Fragen	**Had** you **been** to London before you moved there?	*had wird mit dem Subjekt getauscht*

GEBRAUCH: Das *past perfect* wird verwendet:

wenn etwas beschrieben wird, das bereits vor einem Zeitpunkt in der Vergangenheit geschah	I arrived at the station two minutes late and the train **had** already **left**!

15 Complete the statements in the past perfect.

1 Sophie found out that the Duncans ● (plan) one last treat.
2 Mr Duncan ● (buy) tickets for the football game.
3 The game ● (start) by the time we arrived.
4 We went for a meal after the game ● (finish).
5 I was hungry because I ● (not   have) any breakfast.
6 After I ● (eat) two hotdogs, I wasn't hungry any more.
7 She ● (hear) that football was violent, but it was more brutal than she expected.
8 When Sophie ● (fly) home, the Duncans went to Florida on holiday.

16 Complete the sentences. In each sentence there is one simple past and one past perfect form.

1 They ● (already – eat) before we ● (arrive).
2 The Broncos fans ● (not – realize) that their team ● (win).
3 Although she ● (never – watch) a match before, she really ● (enjoy) it.

THE FUTURE

FORM UND GEBRAUCH:

going to-future	This is **going to** be a great year! **Are** you **going to** move flat?	logische Schlussfolgerungen Pläne und Absichten
will-future	It **won't** rain tomorrow. Your bag looks heavy! I**'ll** carry it for you! Don't worry, I**'ll** do it tomorrow.	Vorhersagen spontane Entscheidungen Versprechen, Angebote
present progressive	Carrie **is travelling** around Australia in July.	konkrete Pläne und Verabredungen (mit Zeitangabe)
simple present	Our plane **leaves** at six o'clock.	Fahrpläne, Programme

Nach den folgenden Verben im *simple present* verwendet man häufig *will-future*:

think, promise, hope, be sure, expect	I promise that I'll come.

---

17 **Complete the statements in the *will* future.**

1 The volunteers ⬭ (support) the teachers in class.
2 We ⬭ (help) families to move out of poverty.
3 You ⬭ (not – be) successful if you don't respect the local customs.
4 The local people ⬭ (not – accept) your help in that case.

18 **Use the keywords to make statements and questions with *going to*.**

1 I – study – for the class test – this evening.
2 they – take – the bus to school – tomorrow
3 we – not watch – TV – this evening
4 it – not rain – today
5 what – you – do – when you leave school?
6 Ben – apply – for a Working Holiday Visa?

19 **Will-future or going to-future? Decide which answer is more suitable.**

1 What are your plans for the summer?
   a I'll go backpacking.
   b I'm going to go backpacking.
2 I don't understand this homework!
   a Don't worry – I'll help you.
   b Don't worry – I'm going to help you.
3 How do you get to school?
   a By bus usually, but tomorrow I'm going to cycle.
   b By bus usually, but tomorrow I'll cycle.

THE PASSIVE

FORM: Das *passive* wird so gebildet:

	Aktiv	Passiv	
		entsprechender Form vom Verb *to be*	+ Partizip Perfekt
simple present	I help	I **am**	help**ed**
present progressive	I am helping	I **am being**	help**ed**
simple past	I helped	I **was**	help**ed**
present perfect	I have helped	I **have been**	help**ed**
will-future	I will help	I **will be**	help**ed**
going to-future	I am going to help	I **am going to be**	help**ed**
modals	I must help	I **must be**	help**ed**

GEBRAUCH: Das *passive* wird verwendet:

wenn es nicht nötig (oder nicht möglich) ist zu sagen, wer etwas tut oder getan hat	*Bikes **are stolen** every day in London.* *My bike **was stolen** yesterday.* *English **is spoken** in many African countries.*
wenn der Schwerpunkt auf dem Objekt liegt (mit *by* können wir sagen, von wem etwas gemacht wird)	*The US president **was welcomed** at the airport.* *Shots **were fired** (by the police).* *This article **was written** by a friend of mine.*

---

20 **Complete the sentences with passive forms of the verbs.**

Simple present:
1 Trees ● (cut down) to make paper.
2 Usually, paper cups ● (not – recycle).

Present continuous:
3 At present, too much rubbish ● (take) to landfill.
4 Recycled materials ● (not – use) enough.

Simple past:
5 Broken furniture ● (fix).
6 Broken things ● (not – throw away).

Present perfect:
7 This furniture ● (make) from broken pallets.
8 The materials ● (not – waste).

Will-future:
9 In future, repair skills ● (teach) to young people.
10 Valuable materials ● (not – throw) away.

21 **Say the same thing in the passive, using the underlined word(s) as the subject.**

1 Someone has opened <u>a second-hand clothes shop</u> in our town.
2 They donated <u>old clothes</u>.
3 They will soon offer <u>workshops on recyling</u>.

Say the same thing in the passive, but include *by* + the words in *italics*.

4 *A local couple* have opened <u>a second-hand clothes shop</u> in our town.
5 *Local people of all ages* have donated <u>old clothes</u>.
6 *Expert volunteers* will soon offer <u>workshops on recycling</u>.

CONDITIONAL SENTENCES

Conditional sentences (*if*-Sätze) drücken Bedingungen aus.

	if-Teil	Hauptsatz
Type 1 für reale Bedingungen	*simple present* If it **rains**,	*will-future* I **will stay** inside today.
Type 2 für unwahrscheinliche Bedingungen	*simple past* If I **had** time,	*would* + **Infinitiv** I **would see** the film.
Type 3 für Situationen, die in der Vergangen- heit geschehen sein könnten, aber nicht geschehen sind	*past perfect* If she **had taken** a taxi,	*would have* + **Partizip Perfekt** she **wouldn't have** **missed** the plane.

ZU BEACHTEN

Anstelle von *will* kann auch ein Modalverb wie *can*, *might* oder *should* im Hauptsatz stehen. Anstelle von *would* kann auch das Modalverb *could* im Hauptsatz stehen.	*If it rains, I* **can** *stay in bed all day.* *If I wanted more money, I* **could** *get a second job.*
Im *If*-Satz stehen nie **will** oder **would**.	*If you ~~will~~ come, …*
Wenn der *if*-Satz am Satzanfang steht, wird er meist mit einem Komma vom Hauptsatz getrennt. Steht der Hauptsatz am Satzanfang, verwendet man meist kein Komma.	*If it rains today, I'll go shopping.* *I'll go shopping if it rains today.*

22 Conditional sentences type 1. Complete the sentences with the correct forms of the verbs.

1 If we ⬮ (stay) in a hostel instead of a hotel, we ⬮ (save) money.
2 If you only ⬮ (speak) German on holiday, your English ⬮ (not – get) better.
3 You ⬮ (enjoy) volunteering if you ⬮ (be) sociable and active.
4 Travellers ⬮ (save) a lot of money if they ⬮ (not eat) out every day.

23 Conditional sentences type 2. Complete the sentences with the correct forms of the verbs.

1 If someone ⬮ (vandalize) our school, I ⬮ (be) shocked.
2 ⬮ (you – spray) graffiti if it ⬮ (not be) illegal?
3 If Nat ⬮ (not – have) artistic skills, he ⬮ (go) law school.
4 We ⬮ (join) a street art programme if there ⬮ (be) one in our area.

24 Conditional sentences type 3. Complete the sentences with the correct forms of the verbs.

1 This photo ⬮ (be) better if you ⬮ (use) natural light.
2 I ⬮ (take) better photos if I ⬮ (not follow) your advice.
3 If the judge ⬮ (not give) the shoplifter another chance, he ⬮ (have) a criminal record.
4 If I ⬮ (take) that photo, I ⬮ (be) proud of it too.

25 Conditional sentences (mixed types). Complete the translations.

1 *Wenn das Wetter schlecht ist, wird Zelten nicht sehr angenehm sein.*
   If the weather ⬮ bad, camping ⬮ very nice.
2 *Wenn ich künstlerisch begabt wäre, könnte ich Mauergemälde malen.*
   If I ⬮ artistic skills, I ⬮ murals.
3 *Wenn der Dieb die zwei Polizisten gesehen hätte, wäre er weggelaufen.*
   If the thief ⬮ the two police officers, he ⬮ away.
4 *Sie können allen von zu Hause gewohnten Komfort haben, wenn Sie eine Wohnung mieten.*
   You ⬮ all the comforts of home if you ⬮ a flat.
5 *Viele Straßen wären interessanter, wenn es mehr Straßenkunst geben würde.*
   Many streets ⬮ more interesting if there ⬮ more street art.

REPORTED SPEECH

Man verwendet die indirekte Rede, um zu berichten, was jemand gesagt hat. Steht das einleitende Verb (*ask*, *say* usw.) in der Vergangenheit, verschieben sich die Zeiten im Satz entsprechend.

direkte Rede	indirekte Rede
simple present Susan: "I often play tennis."	**simple past** Susan said that she often played tennis.
present progressive Susan: "I am playing tennis."	**past progressive** Susan said that she was playing tennis.
simple past Susan: "I played tennis."	**past perfect** (*simple past* auch möglich) Susan said that she had played tennis.
present perfect Susan: "I have played tennis."	**past perfect** Susan said that she had played tennis.
will Susan: "I will play tennis."	**would** Susan said that she would play tennis.
can Susan: "I can play tennis."	**could** Susan said that she could play tennis.

ZU BEACHTEN

Wenn das Berichtete immer oder immer noch gültig ist, muss keine Zeitverschiebung erfolgen.	Susan: "My brother lives with my parents." Susan told us that her brother **lives** with her parents.

REPORTED QUESTIONS

Die Zeitverschiebung bei Fragen findet genauso statt wie bei Aussagen.
Bei Fragen mit Fragewörtern werden die Fragewörter (*where*, *who*, *why* usw.) behalten. Bei Fragen, die mit *do*, *did* usw. anfangen, wird *if/whether* statt *that* (wie bei *reported speech*) verwendet.
Bei Bitten und Befehlen werden *to* + infinitive verwendet.

Fragen	
Susan: "Where is Tom?"	Susan asked where Tom **was**.
Susan: "Do you speak English?"	Susan asked me if I **spoke** English.
Susan: "Are you coming with me?"	Susan asked whether I **was coming** with her.
Susan: "When did you last see Tom?"	Susan asked me when I **had** last **seen** Tom.
Bitten	
Susan: "Can you help me, please?"	Susan asked me **to help** her.
Susan: "Please don't tell anyone."	Susan asked me not **to tell** anyone.
Befehle	
Susan: "Shut up!"	Susan told me **to shut up**.
Susan: "Don't talk!"	Susan told us not **to talk**.

26   Reported speech. Complete the sentences with the correct forms of the verbs.

1   The children: "Elsa, you speak great English!"
    The children told Elsa that she ● great English.

2   Luuk: "I'm learning Portuguese."
    Luuk said that he ● Portuguese.

3   Janek: "I learned English and Russian at school."
    Janek explained that he ● English and Russian at school.

4   Adeela: "I've worked with this company for five years."
    Adeela said that she ● with that company for five years.

5   Adeela to the reporter: "Maybe I'll apply for a job in Germany one day."
    Adeela told the reporter that maybe she ● for a job in Germany one day.

6   Elsa: "I can speak four foreign languages."
    Elsa said that she ● four foreign languages.

27   Reported questions. Complete the sentences with the correct forms of the verbs.

1   Nagesh: "Where do you live?"
    Nagesh asked me where I ● .

2   Vern: "Are you okay, Sly?"
    Vern asked Sly whether he ● okay.

3   Ji-hoon and Ryan: "Are you coming running with us?"
    Ji-hoon and Ryan asked me whether I ● running with them.

4   Hassan: "Ryan, can you help me, please?"
    Hassan asked Ryan ● him.

5   Ryan: "Nagesh, please don't play your music so loud."
    Ryan asked Nagesh ● his music so loud.

6   Hassan's mother: "Phone me more often, Hassan!"
    Hassan's mother told him ● her more often.

28   Write this dialogue in reported speech.

EXAMPLE: *Alexa asked Ryan where he lived. Ryan said that ...*

Alexa: Where do you live?
Ryan: I live in a shared flat in Wandsworth.
Alexa: Are your flatmates nice?
Ryan: Yes, they're very nice.
Alexa: How many flatmates do you have?
Ryan: I have three flatmates, Ji-hoon, Hassan and Nagesh.
Alexa: How long have you lived together?
Ryan: We've lived together for two years.

MODAL AUXILIARIES

Funktion	Modale Hilfsverben	
Fähigkeit	*He **can** speak several languages.* *My dad **could** only speak English.*	
Möglichkeit	*With your qualifications you **could** work abroad.* *The boss **may** come in at any moment.* *He **might** ask you what you are doing.*	
Bitte	***Can** I have a word with Ms Sims, please?* ***Could** I speak to Ms Sims, please?* ***May** I interrupt you?* ***Might** I ask you a personal question?*	(neutral) (höflich) (betont höflich) (äußerst höflich)
Erlaubnis	*You **can** go in now.* *The boss is free. You **may** go in now.*	(neutral) (gefällig)
Verbot	*We **mustn't** be late for work tomorrow.*	
Pflicht	*You **must** wear a hard hat in the factory.*	
Wahl	*Most people **don't have to** work on Sundays.* *You **needn't** come.*	
Empfehlung	*You **should** try harder.* *You **ought to** try harder.* *You **must** try harder.*	(neutral) (betont) (streng)

can, could, be able to

simple present	*I **can** see you.*	Ich kann dich sehen.
simple past	*I **could** swim at the age of six.*	Ich konnte mit sechs schwimmen.
present perfect	*I **haven't been able to** contact Harry yet.*	Ich konnte Harry bislang nicht erreichen.
future	*I **can** pay you tomorrow.* *I'**ll be able to** pay you tomorrow.*	Ich kann dich morgen bezahlen.
conditional	***Could** you give a presentation tomorrow?* ***Would you be able to** give a presentation tomorrow?*	Könnten Sie morgen eine Präsentation halten?

must, mustn't, needn't, don't/doesn't have to, had to

Gegenwart		
Aussage	We **must** meet more often. We **have to** meet more often.	Wir müssen uns öfters treffen.
Verneinung	I **mustn't** forget his birthday.	Ich darf seinen Geburtstag nicht vergessen.
	You really **don't have to** wait for me.	Du musst wirklich nicht auf mich warten.
	You **needn't** come.	Du musst nicht kommen.
Frage	How many tests **do you have to** do?	Wie viele Tests musst du machen?

Vergangenheit		
Aussage	I **had to** work late yesterday evening.	Ich musste gestern abend länger arbeiten.
Verneinung	Nina **didn't have to** pay for the ticket.	Nina musste nicht für die Karte zahlen.
Frage	How much **did** you **have to** pay for the tickets?	Wie viel mussten Sie für die Karte bezahlen?

Zukunft		
Aussage	I'**ll have to** talk to the boss.	Ich werde mit dem Chef sprechen müssen.
Verneinung	He **won't have to** go to prison.	Er wird nicht ins Gefängnis gehen müssen.
Frage	**Will** she **have to** go to hospital?	Wird sie ins Krankenhaus gehen müssen?

29 **Complete the sentences with suitable modal auxiliaries.**

1 He has a heart problem. You ⬤ call an ambulance. (*Pflicht*)
2 James ⬤ take better care of his health. (*neutrale Empfehlung*)
3 We ⬤ put young people in danger. (*Verbot*)
4 I ⬤ take you to the doctor's if you like. (*Möglichkeit*)
5 ⬤ I ask for your advice about something? (*betont höfliche Bitte*)
6 You ⬤ worry as long as you are sensible. (*Wahl / keine Verpflichtung*)
7 They ⬤ do whatever they like. (*Erlaubnis*)
8 ⬤ I make an appointment with the doctor, please? (*neutrale Bitte*)

30 *Can, could, be able to*. Decide which sentence is <u>incorrect</u>: a, b or c. Translate the other <u>two</u> sentences into German.

  1 **a** High-caffeine drinks can be bad for you.
        b High-caffeine drinks could be bad for you.
        c High-caffeine drinks are able to be bad for you.
  2 **a** The doctors cannot save him and so he died.
        b The doctors could not save him and so he died.
        c The doctors were not able to save him and so he died.
  3 **a** The doctor can't see you today, is tomorrow okay?
        b The doctor couldn't see you today, is tomorrow okay?
        c The doctor isn't able to see you today, is tomorrow okay?

31 *Must* or *have to*? Decide which option is correct.

  1 I mustn't / don't have to drink so much caffeine: I have a heart problem.
  2 They mustn't / don't have to follow the doctor's advice, but it's a good idea.
  3 We must / had to call the doctor when Mum was ill.
  4 Must you / Do you have to do a lot of home visits, as a nurse?

VERB + -ING FORM · VERB + TO-INFINITIVE

Auf bestimmte Verben folgt eine *-ing*-Form, während auf andere ein Infinitiv folgt.

Verb + *-ing* Form	Verb + *to*-Infinitiv	Verb + *-ing* Form oder *to*-Infinitiv
*I **enjoy playing** video games.*	*They **wanted to go** on holiday.*	*We **love cooking**.* *We **love to cook**.*
admit, avoid, dislike, enjoy, finish, involve, not mind, recommend, stop, suggest	agree, choose, decide, expect, hope, learn, manage, seem, want, would like	begin, continue, hate, like, love, prefer, start

Einige Verben haben unterschiedliche Bedeutungen, je nachdem, ob ein Gerundium oder ein Infinitiv folgt.

remember	*Do you remember **telling** me about Ashley?* *Please remember **to tell** Ashley.*	sich erinnern, etwas getan zu haben daran denken, etwas zu tun
stop	*I wish you would stop **smoking**.* *On the way we stopped **to pick up** Eric.*	aufhören, etwas zu tun anhalten, um etwas (anderes) zu tun
try	*I tried **to stop** him.* *Why don't you try **jogging** once a week?*	versuchen, etwas zu tun etwas ausprobieren

32 Complete the sentences with *to* + infinitive or the *-ing* form. If both options are correct, use both.

1   My grandmother avoids ⬤ (use) a computer if she can.
2   How old were you when you began ⬤ (use) social media?
3   Dan agreed ⬤ (spend) less time livestreaming.
4   I'm starting ⬤ (get) bored with social media.
5   We hope ⬤ (make) money from livestreaming one day.
6   Don't be angry! I'm trying ⬤ (help) you.
7   Stop ⬤ (worry)! It's completely safe.
8   Remember ⬤ (take) a break from the screen every 30 minutes.
9   I enjoy ⬤ (write) about my life in my blog.
10   I dislike ⬤ (share) personal information online.

PLURALS

Die allermeisten Pluralformen werden mit *-s* gebildet.	computer → computers
Bei Substantiven auf *-y* nach einem Konsonant wird *-y* zu *-ies*.	family → families
Substantive auf *-ch*, *-sh*, *-s* und *-x* bilden die Pluralform meist mit *-es*.	bus → buses beach → beaches
Substantive auf *–f* oder *–fe* bilden die Pluralform mit *-ves*.	thief → thieves
Substantive auf *-o* bilden gelegentlich die Pluralform mit *-es*.	potato → potatoes *aber:* photo → photos
Einige Substantive haben unregelmäßige Pluralformen.	man/woman → men/women tooth → teeth child → children person → people
Einige Substantive werden immer im Plural verwendet.	glasses, jeans, trousers, scissors

COUNTABLE AND UNCOUNTABLE NOUNS

Nicht zählbare Substantive haben keine Mehrzahlform, und man kann weder *a/an* noch eine Zahl davorsetzen.

zählbar	one book, two books, three books
nicht zählbar	weather, money, traffic ~~a weather, two moneys, three traffics~~

Bestimmte Substantive sind im Deutschen zählbar, im Englischen aber nicht.

advice	Rat, Ratschlag, Ratschläge	homework	Hausaufgabe, Hausaufgaben
equipment	Ausrüstung, Geräte	information	Information, Informationen
furniture	Möbel	knowledge	Kenntnis, Kenntnisse
hair	Haar, Haare	paper	Papier, Papiere
help	Hilfe, Hilfen, Hilfestellungen	progress	Fortschritt, Fortschritte

Das Verb steht nach einem nicht zählbaren Substantiv immer im Singular	*This information is interesting.* (Diese Information ist/Diese Informationen sind interessant.)
Nicht zählbare Substantive verwendet man mit *this/that* und *much*.	*There's not much information here.*
Mit Ausdrücken wie *a piece of* oder *a bit of* kann man Ersatzsingular- und Pluralformen bilden:	*Can I have a piece of paper, please?* *Let me give you a piece of advice.* *I need a bit of help.*

QUANTIFIERS

some/any

Some und *any* bezeichnen eine unbestimmte Menge oder Zahl. *Some* wird vor allem in bejahten Aussagesätzen, Angeboten und Bitten verwendet. *Any* steht meist in verneinten Aussagesätzen und in Fragen.

Aussagen	*I downloaded **some** music.* ***Somebody** sent me a message.*
Verneinungen	*I didn't download **any** videos.* *I don't know **anybody** here.*
Fragen	*Have you received **any** emails today?* *Has **anybody** seen Emma today?*
Bitten/Angebote	*Could you send me **some** information?* *Would you like **something** to drink?*

many/much/a lot of/little/a little/few/a few

Das Einsetzen von *many/much/a lot of/little/a little/few/a few* hängt davon ab, ob sie in Zusammenhang mit einem zählbaren oder unzählbaren Substantive verwendet werden.

many	viel	wird mit zählbaren Substantiven verwendet, besonders in Verneinungen und Fragen	*I don't have **many** friends.* *How **many** pets do you have?*

much	viel	wird mit unzählbaren Substantiven verwendet, besonders in Verneinungen und Fragen	*I don't have **much** money.* *How **much** time do you have?*
a lot of	viel	wird statt *many* und *much* in gesprochenem Englisch oft verwendet, besonders in Aussagen.	*I have **a lot of** friends and **a lot of** money!*
few	wenig	wird mit zählbaren Substantiven verwendet	*I have **few** friends.*
little	wenig	wird mit unzählbaren Substantiven verwendet	*We have very **little** time!*
a few	einige / ein paar	wird mit zählbaren Substantiven verwendet	*I spent **a few** days in London.*
a little	etwas / ein wenig	wird mit unzählbaren Substantiven verwendet	*I need **a little** help.*

---

33 *Any* or *some*? **Choose the correct option.**

1 I can't go shopping today – I don't have any / some money.
2 Do you have any / some second-hand clothes in your wardrobe?
3 What can we do to live on less? Any / Some ideas?
4 There are any / some things that Dylan missed when he lived without money.
5 I don't eat any / some mushrooms from the wood. I only eat food from the supermarket.
6 I can't think of anything / something worse than living without money.

34 **Complete the sentences with the correct quantifier.**

1 I've bought ⬤ clothes recently. How about you? *(viele)*
2 How ⬤ time do you spend shopping every week? *(viel)*
3 I have ⬤ time for shopping at the moment. *(wenig)*
4 Here are ⬤ of the clothes that I bought. *(einige)*
5 Are there ⬤ second-hand shops where you live? *(viele)*
6 There isn't ⬤ information online about second-hand shops in my area. *(viel)*
7 ⬤ people know about my favourite second-hand shop. *(wenige)*
8 With ⬤ luck you can find some really good things there. *(etwas)*

COMPARISON OF ADJECTIVES

FORM: Adjektive werden wie folgt gesteigert:

	Adjektiv	Komparativ	Superlativ
einsilbiges Adjektiv	long	long**er**	(the) long**est**
	big	big**ger**	(the) big**gest**
zweisilbiges Adjektiv, das auf -y endet	pretty	prett**ier**	(the) prett**iest**
	lucky	luck**ier**	(the) luck**iest**
Adjektiv mit zwei oder mehr Silben	famous	**more** famous	(the) **most** famous
	important	**more** important	(the) **most** important
unregelmäßige Adjektive	good	better	(the) best
	bad	worse	(the) worst

Wenn zwei Sachen verglichen werden, muss man *than* oder *as … as* verwenden.	*He is taller **than** his brother.* *He is **as** tall **as** his father.*
Wenn man den Superlativ in ein größeres Verhältnis setzen möchte, verwendet man die Präposition *in* oder *of*.	*He is the tallest person **in** the world.* *She is the cleverest student **in** her class.* ***Of** all the people I know he is the tallest.* *She is the cleverest **of** all her friends.*

ADVERBS OF MANNER

Mit Adverbien beschreibt man, wie etwas geschieht.

FORM: Adverbien werden wie folgt gebildet:

	Adjektiv		Adverb	
Adjektiv + *ly*	quick		quick**ly**	
	slow		slow**ly**	
Adjektiv auf -y → -ily	happy		happ**ily**	
	easy		eas**ily**	
Adverb bleibt formgleich mit Adjektiv	fast	early	fast	early
	hard	late	hard	late
unregelmäßige Adverbien	good		well	

FORM: Adverbien werden wie folgt gesteigert:

	Adverb	Komparativ	Superlativ
Adverb formgleich mit Adjektiv: -er/-est anhängen	fast	fast**er**	fast**est**
	hard	hard**er**	hard**est**
Adverb auf -ly: *more/most* voranstellen	carefully	**more** carefully	**most** carefully

35 Complete the sentences with the comparative or superlative form of the adjective.

1 Anaïs's hair is ● (long) than Samantha's.
2 This exercise is ● (easy) than the last one.
3 Which city is the ● (large) – London, New York or Melbourne?
4 Andy's problems are ● (bad) than David's.
5 Are DNA tests ● (expensive) in Germany than in the USA?
6 That's the ● (strange) story I've ever heard.

36 Complete the sentences with the adverbial form of the adjective in brackets.
In 4–6 you also need the comparative form.

1 Dan speaks very ●. (fast)
2 Alex speaks quite ●. (slow)
3 We completed the exercise very ●. (careful)
4 I worked ● on this project – much ● than you! (hard)
5 The twins' story turned out ● in the end – ● than I expected. (good)
6 Sam always gets up ● – an hour ● than me. (early)

RELATIVE CLAUSES

Relativsätze sind Nebensätze, die ein Substantiv näher definieren. Sie werden mit Relativpronomen eingeleitet. Ein Relativpronomen kann weggelassen werden, wenn der Nebensatz ein anderes Subjekt hat (*contact clause*).

Personen	*who* oder (seltener) *that*	*People **who/that** don't eat meat are vegetarians.*
		*That's the girl **(who/that)** I saw at school.*
Dinge	*which* oder *that*	*He bought the bike **which/that** cost 500 euros.*
		*This is the house **(which/that)** I live in.*

ZU BEACHTEN

| Ein bestimmender Relativsatz (*defining relative clause*) enthält nähere Bestimmungen, ohne die der Satz keinen Sinn ergeben würde. Bestimmende Relativsätze werden nicht durch Kommas vom Hauptsatz getrennt. | *Jameela Jamil is one of the people **(who) I follow on social media**.*

 *There are three dogs in the room. I like the one **that's sitting on the sofa best**.* |
| Ein nicht bestimmender Relativsatz (*non-defining relative clause*) enthält Zusatzinformationen, die für das Verständnis des Satzes nicht unbedingt erforderlich sind. Ein nicht bestimmender Relativsatz wird durch Kommata vom Hauptsatz getrennt. | *Jameela Jamil, **who became famous in the TV series The Good Place**, is an influential activist.*

 *I love my dog Scruffy, **who originally belonged to my sister**, very much.* |

Dieses Wörterverzeichnis enthält alle Wörter, die nicht in der Liste des Grundwortschatzes enthalten sind, d. h. die nicht als bekannt vorausgesetzt werden. Wörter aus den *Audiotexten* sind mit einem gelben Balken, Wörter aus den *Videotexten* mit einem orangenen Balken und Wörter aus den *Differentiation files* mit einem blauen Balken gekennzeichnet. Die neuen Wörter aus den *Further reading*-Texten sind am Ende des Verzeichnisses. Vorausgesetzt wird jeweils der Wortschatz aus dem Hauptteil des Buches einschließlich der entsprechenden Unit.

AE = American English	*v* = verb	*phr* = phrase (*festehende Wendung*)
BE = British English	*adj* = adjective	*pl* = plural
AusE = Australian Englisch	*adv* = adverb	*esp* = especially
n = noun (*Substantiv*)	*inf* = informal (*Umgangssprache*)	<> = opposite (*Gegensatz*)

GETTING STARTED

page 6

to **get started**	[get ˈstɑːtɪd]	to begin	loslegen, anfangen
to **match sth (to sth)**	[mætʃ]	to put two things together	etw (einer Sache) zuordnen
to **take turns to do sth**	[ˌteɪk ˈtɜːnz tə duː]	e.g. We took turns to look after the children.	etw abwechselnd tun
to **practise**	[ˈpræktɪs]	*n* practice	üben
to **speak up**	[ˌspiːk ˈʌp]	to say sth louder	lauter sprechen
to **pronounce**	[prəˈnaʊns]	*n* pronunciation	aussprechen
to **slow down**	[ˌsləʊ ˈdaʊn]	to say sth slower	langsamer sprechen
to **mean**	[miːn]	e.g. What does this word mean?	bedeuten
to **start off**	[ˌstɑːt ˈɒf]	<> to finish	anfangen
to **add**	[æd]	*n* addition	hinzufügen
next to	[ˈnekst tə]	beside	neben
column	[ˈkɒləm]	vertical row or list	(*Text:*) Spalte
to **be short on sth**	[bi ˈʃɔːt ɒn]	to not have enough of sth	zu wenig von etw haben
to **fill**	[fɪl]	to make sth full of sth	füllen
statement	[ˈsteɪtmənt]	*v* to state	Aussage, Aussagesatz

page 7

waiter	[ˈweɪtə]	sb who works in a cafe or restaurant	Kellner
call centre agent	[ˈkɔːl sentər eɪdʒənt]	sb who takes/makes phone calls for a business	Telefonagent/in, Callcenteragent/in
flight attendant	[ˌflaɪt əˈtendənt]	sb who works on an aircraft	Flugbegleiter/in
safety regulations *pl*	[ˈseɪfti regjuleɪʃnz]	rules to make a place/thing safe	Sicherheitsvorschriften, -vorkehrungen
receptionist	[rɪˈsepʃənɪst]	sb who welcomes guests, answers phones	Empfangsmitarbeiter/in, Rezeptionist/in
guest	[gest]	*esp* sb staying in a hotel	Gast
personal	[ˈpɜːsənl]	private, about yourself	persönlich, privat
fantasy	[ˈfæntəsi]	*here:* made up	Phantasie-
engineer	[ˌendʒɪˈnɪə]	sb who designs technical/ mechanical things	Ingenieur/in, Techniker/in
to **introduce sb to sb**	[ˌɪntrəˈdjuːs]	e.g. Steve introduced me to Helen.	jdn jdm vorstellen

page 8

in front of	[ɪn ˈfrʌnt əv]	<> behind	vor
board	[bɔːd]	e.g. The teacher wrote the vocabulary on the board.	(Wand-)Tafel
dictionary	[ˈdɪkʃənri]	book with lists of words and their meanings	Wörterbuch
trolley	[ˈtrɒli]	small vehicle with wheels	Wagen
to **brainstorm**	[ˈbreɪnstɔːm]	to think of new ideas	Ideen sammeln
mobile (phone) *BE*	[ˈməʊbaɪl]	e.g. Please turn off your mobile phone in class.	Handy
iced tea	[aɪst ˈtiː]	sweet, cold tea	Eistee
to **report back to sb**	[rɪˌpɔːt ˈbæk tə]	to give sb information	jdm berichten, jdm Bericht erstatten

page 9

dream	[driːm]	images in your mind while you are asleep	Traum
while	[waɪl]	at the same time as sth else	während
facilities *pl*	[fəˈsɪlətiz]	buildings, equipment, services	Einrichtung(en), Ausstattung
cinema	[ˈkæfeɪ]	place to watch films	Kino
to **sleep**	[ˈsɪnəmə]	e.g. I sleep eight hours a night.	schlafen
student	[ˈstjuːdnt]	sb learning at school, college, university	Schüler/in, Student/in
to **arrive**	[əˈraɪv]	<> to leave	eintreffen, ankommen
vowel	[ˈvaʊəl]	e.g. a, e, i, o, u	Vokal
consonant	[ˈkɒnsənənt]	<> vowel (a, e, i, o, u)	Konsonant
church	[tʃɜːtʃ]	building for Christian religion	Kirche
shelf, shelves	[ʃelf, ʃelvz]	sth that you place books on	Regal, Regale
piano	[piˈænəʊ]	large musical instrument with black and white keys	Klavier
hero	[ˈhɪərəʊ]	brave, good person	Held

page 10

exception (to sth)	[ɪkˈsepʃn]	sth that does not follow a rule	Ausnahme (von etw)
certain	[ˈsɜːtn]	special, particular	bestimmte/r/s, gewisse/r/s

sound	[saʊnd]	sth you can hear	Laut, Klang
to **become** (sth)	[bɪˈkʌm]	to later be	(zu etw / etw) werden
sheep, sheep	[ʃiːp]	e.g. one sheep, two sheep	Schaf, Schafe
tooth, teeth	[tuːθ, tiːθ]	e.g. one tooth, two teeth	Zahn, Zähne
scissors *pl*	[ˈsɪzəz]	used for cutting paper, etc.	Schere
sentence	[ˈsentəns]	e.g. Please answer using full sentences.	Satz
to **decide**	[dɪˈsaɪd]	*n* decision	(sich) entscheiden
parking space	[ˈpɑːkɪŋ speɪs]	place to park a car	Parkplatz
capital	[ˈkæpɪtl]	main city in a country or region	Hauptstadt
bowl	[bəʊl]	e.g. a bowl of soup	Schale, Schüssel, Napf
cupboard	[ˈkʌbəd]	e.g. put the plates in tze cupboard	Schrank

page 11

bracket	[ˈbrækɪt]	*phr* in brackets	Klammer
dirty	[ˈdɜːti]	<> clean	schmutzig, dreckig
scooter	[ˈskuːtə]	a light motorcycle with small wheels	Tretroller, Motorroller
speech bubble	[ˈspiːtʃ bʌbl]	circle around words that sb says, especially in a cartoon	Sprechblase
maths	[mæθs]	school subject in which you learn how to calculate	Mathe
to **translate**	[trænsˈleɪt]	to change words into a different language	übersetzen
to **make sb do sth**	[meɪk ˈduː]	e.g. The teacher makes us do our homework.	jdn dazu bringen, etw zu tun

page 12

to **be afraid of sb/sth**	[bi əˈfreɪd əv]	e.g. I am afraid of dogs.	vor jdm/etw Angst haben, sich vor jdm/etw fürchten
wallet	[ˈwɒlɪt]	where you keep your money	Brieftasche, (Herren-)Portemonnaie
to **lend**	[lend]	e.g. The library lends books.	leihen, borgen
to **hurry up**	[ˌhʌri ˈʌp]	to do sth more quickly	sich beeilen
present	[ˈpreznt]	gift	Geschenk
to **send**	[send]	e.g. to send an email/letter/parcel	schicken, senden
to **be lost**	[bi ˈlɒst]	to not know where you are	sich verlaufen haben
to **count**	[kaʊnt]	e.g. He counted all the books on the shelf.	zählen
uncountable	[ˌʌnˈkaʊntəbl]	not able to be counted	unzählbar
countable	[ˈkaʊntəbl]	able to be counted	zählbar
fridge	[frɪdʒ]	refrigerator *AE*	Kühlschrank

page 13

choice	[tʃɔɪs]	*v* to choose	Wahl
to **spend**	[spend]	e.g. I spent a year in Los Angeles learning English.	*(Zeit)* verbringen
homework	[ˈhəʊmwɜːk]	e.g. We have to fill in this worksheet for homework	Hausaufgaben
pocket money	[ˈpɒkɪt mʌni]	money parents give to their children	Taschengeld
worried	[ˈwʌrɪd]	*v* to worry	besorgt, beunruhigt
beer	[bɪə]	e.g. There are many types of beer in Germany.	Bier
muscle	[ˈmʌsl]	e.g. Doing sport helps you build muscles.	Muskel
chicken	[ˈtʃɪkɪn]	bird that is cooked and eaten	Huhn, Hühnchen
timetable	[ˈtaɪmteɪbl]	plan that shows when things happen	Fahrplan, Zeitplan
to **be careful with sth**	[bi ˈkeəfl wɪð]	e.g. Be careful with the glasses!	bei etw aufpassen, vorsichtig bei/ mit etw sein
weekday	[ˈwiːkdeɪ]	e.g. Monday, Tuesday, Wednesday, Thursday, Friday	Wochentag, Werktag

page 14

nationality	[ˌnæʃəˈnæləti]	e.g. German, British, American	Staatsangehörigkeit, Nationalität
to **combine**	[kəmˈbaɪn]	*n* combination	verbinden, kombinieren
item	[ˈaɪtəm]	a thing, a piece	Gegenstand, Artikel, Ding, Sache
once	[wʌns]	one single time	einmal
chart	[tʃɑːt]	e.g. table, bar chart, flow chart, pie chart, etc.	Tabelle
cathedral	[kəˈθiːdrəl]	large church in a city	Dom, Kathedrale
holiday resort	[ˈhɒlədeɪ rɪzɔːt]	place to go on vacation	Urlaubsort, Ferienort
island	[ˈaɪlənd]	land surrounded by water	Insel
monument	[ˈmɒnjumənt]	a statue/place to remember a special person or time	Denkmal
river	[ˈrɪvə]	e.g. Danube, Amazon, Nile, etc.	Fluss
state	[steɪt]	part of a country	Staat
to **fill in**	[ˌfɪl ˈɪn]	e.g. Could you please fill in this form?	eintragen, ausfüllen

UNIT 1

page 15

to **identify**	[aɪˈdentɪfaɪ]	*n* identification	identifizieren, (die Identität) feststellen
to **taste** (of sth)	[teɪst]	*n* taste	(nach etw) schmecken
to **order**	[ˈɔːdə]	e.g. Let's order a pizza	bestellen
to **deliver**	[dɪˈlɪvə]	*n* delivery	liefern
to **give reasons**	[ˌgɪv ˈriːznz]	to say why you do sth	begründen

page 16

habit	['hæbɪt]	sth you do often	Gewohnheit
to **take part in sth**	[teɪk 'pɑːt ɪn]	*n* participant	an etw teilnehmen
exchange	[ɪks'tʃeɪndʒ]	swap, trade	Austausch
global	['gləʊbl]	all around the world	global, weltumspannend
issue	['ɪʃuː]	question, problem	Frage, Streitpunkt, Problem
to **feed**	[fiːd]	*n* food	ernähren
to **inform (sb of sth)**	[ɪn'fɔːm]	to let sb know	(jdn über etw) informieren
to **prepare**	[prɪ'peə]	*n* preparation	(sich) vorbereiten
translation	[trænsˈleɪʃn]	*v* to translate	Übersetzung
task	[tɑːsk]	*phr* to give sb a task	Aufgabe
suggestion	[sə'dʒestʃən]	*v* to suggest	Vorschlag
skill	[skɪl]	*adj* skilled	Fähigkeit, Fertigkeit, Kompetenz
title	[taɪtl]	official name, headline	Titel
paragraph	['pærəgrɑːf]	e.g. Write a paragraph about the environment.	*(Text:)* Absatz
heading	['hedɪŋ]	title	Überschrift
to **deal with sth**	['diːl wɪð]	to think, talk or write about sth	sich mit etw befassen
caption	['kæpʃn]	explanation under a picture or illustration	Bildunterschrift
opposite	['ɒpəzɪt]	on the other side	gegenüber(liegend)
to **fit sth**	[fɪt]	to be right for sth	zu etw passen
context	['kɒntekst]	*phr* in context	Zusammenhang, Kontext
sub-heading	[ˌsʌb 'hedɪŋ]	an extra title after the main title	Zwischenüberschrift
paragraph	['pærəgrɑːf]	e.g. Write a paragraph about the environment.	*(Text:)* Absatz
source	[sɔːs]	where sth comes from	Quelle
protein	['prəʊtiːn]	e.g. You get a lot of protein from meat.	Eiweiß, Protein(e)
technology	[tek'nɒlədʒi]	*adj* technological	Technologie, Technik
in order to	[ɪn 'ɔːdə tə]	e.g. You'll have to do some sport in order to keep fit.	um … zu
to **survive**	[sə'vaɪv]	to live through	überleben
to **rethink sth**	[ˌriː'θɪŋk]	to think again about an issue	etw überdenken
food production	['fuːd prədʌkʃn]	e.g. To feed the world we have to increase food production.	Nahrungsmittelproduktion

page 17

to **face sth**	[feɪs]	e.g. The world is facing big problems at the moment.	einer Sache gegenüberstehen
major	['meɪdʒə]	large, important	groß, bedeutend
global warming	[ˌgləʊbl 'wɔːmɪŋ]	e.g. We have to fight global warming in order to survive.	Erderwärmung
population	[ˌpɒpju'leɪʃn]	all of the people who live in a town or country	Bevölkerung
to **grow**	[grəʊ]	to increase	wachsen, zunehmen
rapid(ly)	['ræpɪd]	quick(ly), fast	schnell, rasch, rapide
forest	['fɒrɪst]	many trees together	Wald
to **destroy**	[dɪ'strɔɪ]	*n* destruction	zerstören
scientist	['saɪəntɪst]	*adj* scientific	(Natur-)Wissenschaftler/in
to **argue**	['ɑːgjuː]	to provide arguments for or against sth	argumentieren
diet	['daɪət]	food, nutrition	Kost, Ernährung
based on	['beɪst ɒn]	e.g. She wrote a story based on her life.	auf Grundlage von
option	['ɒpʃn]	possibilty, choice, alternative	Alternative, Möglichkeit
amount	[ə'maʊnt]	quantity	Menge
to **study sth**	['stʌdi]	to look at sth carefully	sich etw genau ansehen
apart from	[ə'pɑːt frəm]	except for	abgesehen von, außer
sustainable	[sə'steɪnəbl]	*n* sustainability	nachhaltig
resources *pl*	[rɪ'sɔːsɪz]	materials	Rohstoffe, Ressourcen
generally	['dʒenrəli]	in general	normalerweise, im Allgemeinen
healthy	['helθi]	*n* health	gesund
serving	['sɜːvɪŋ]	e.g. Use 50 grams of rice per serving.	Portion
saturated fats *pl*	[ˌsætʃəreɪtɪd 'fæts]	*phr* high/low in saturated fats	gesättigte Fette/Fettsäuren
twice	[twaɪs]	two times	zweimal
average	['ævərɪdʒ]	normal	Durchschnitt(s-), durchschnittlich
due to	['djuː tə]	e.g. The shop is closed due to illness.	aufgrund von
religious	[rɪ'lɪdʒəs]	*n* religion	religiös, Religions-
desert	['dezət]	The Sahara is the world's largest desert.	Wüste
lack (of sth)	[læk]	e.g. lack of food, lack of water, lack of power	Mangel (an etw)
influence (on sb/sth)	['ɪnfluənts]	*v* to influence	Einfluss, Auswirkung(en) (auf jdn/etw)
ingredient	[ɪn'griːdiənt]	e.g. Every recipe has a list of ingredients.	Zutat, Bestandteil
dish	[dɪʃ]	meal	Gericht, Speise
bean	[biːn]	e.g. soya beans	Bohne
dried	[draɪd]	*v* to dry	getrocknet
lentil	['lentl]	e.g. lentil soup	Linse
flour	['flaʊə]	used to make bread, cake, etc.	Mehl
legumes *pl*	['legjuːmz]	e.g. beans, lentils, peas	Hülsenfrüchte
inhabitant	[ɪn'hæbɪtənt]	people living in a city, area, country etc.	Einwohner, Bewohner
dairy products *pl*	['deəri prɒdʌkts]	e.g. milk, butter, cheese	Milchprodukte
instead of	[ɪn'sted əv]	e.g. Mum gave me pieces of fruit instead of biscuits.	anstelle von, anstatt
to **warm up**	[ˌwɔːm 'ʌp]	e.g. When the sun shines the air warms up.	sich erwärmen, sich erhitzen

to **adapt to sth**	[əˈdæpt tə]	to change to fit sth	sich an etw anpassen
heat	[hiːt]	*adj* hot	Wärme, Hitze
last but not least	[ˌlɑːst bət nɒt ˈliːst]	last in order, but not in importance	zu guter Letzt, nicht zu vergessen
culture	[ˈkʌltʃə]	e.g. Every culture has its own traditions.	Kultur
seaweed	[ˈsiːwiːd]	e.g. Seaweed is an important ingredient for sushi.	Seetang
at least	[ət ˈliːst]	e.g. My idea should at least be in second place!	mindestens
century	[ˈsentʃʊri]	period of 100 years	Jahrhundert
to **boil sth**	[bɔil]	e.g. to boil an egg	etw (in Wasser) kochen
mineral	[ˈmɪnərəl]	e.g. calcium, iron, etc.	Mineral(stoff)
particularly	[pəˈtɪkjələli]	especially	besonders, insbesondere
iodine	[ˈaɪədiːn]	chemical element with the symbol I	Jod
iron	[ˈaɪən]	metal, chemical element with the symbol Fe	Eisen
to **sound**	[saʊnd]	e.g. That sounds like a great plan!	klingen
to **be glad**	[bi ˈglæd]	to be happy	froh sein, sich freuen
after all	[ˌɑːftər ˈɔːl]	e.g. I don't want to criticize her – she's my wife after all.	schließlich, immerhin

page 18

weird	[wɪəd]	<> normal	verrückt, schräg, seltsam
one day	[ˌwʌn ˈdeɪ]	e.g. One day you'll realize that I was right all along!	eines Tages
recipe	[ˈresɪpi]	instructions for preparing a meal	(Koch-)Rezept
to **be forced to do sth**	[bi ˈfɔːst tə duː]	<> to be free to do sth	gezwungen sein, etw zu tun
to **affect sb/sth**	[əˈfekt]	to influence sb/sth	sich auf jdn/etw auswirken
slice	[slaɪs]	a piece of sth (e.g. cake)	(Kuchen-)Stück
to **jumble sth up**	[ˌdʒʌmbl ˈʌp]	to mix sth chaotically	etw durcheinanderwerfen

page 19

to **appear**	[əˈpɪə]	*n* appearance	vorkommen, auftauchen
print	[prɪnt]	e.g. I prefer print to sth online.	gedruckt, Druck-
agriculture	[ˈægrɪkʌltʃə]	*adj* agricultural	Landwirtschaft
article	[ˈɑːtɪkl]	*esp* text in a newspaper	Artikel
interesting	[ˈɪntrəstɪŋ]	<> boring	interessant
to **save**	[seɪv]	e.g. He saved my life after the car accident.	retten
to **examine**	[ɪgˈzæmɪn]	*n* examination	untersuchen
finally	[ˈfaɪnli]	<> firstly	schließlich, zuletzt
to **conclude**	[kənˈkluːd]	to finish, to end	schließen

page 20

particular	[pəˈtɪkjələ]	certain	spezielle/r/s, bestimmt
variety	[vəˈraɪəti]	a range of different things	Vielfalt, (große) Auswahl, Abwechslung
never	[ˈnevə]	<> always	nie
order	[ˈɔːdə]	sequence	Reihenfolge
to **cause**	[kɔːz]	*n* cause	verursachen
to **suffer from sth**	[ˈsʌfə frəm]	e.g. to suffer from an illness	an etw *(Krankheit usw.)* leiden
anaemia	[əˈniːmiə]	*adj* anaemic	Blutarmut, Anämie
to **persuade sb**	[pəˈsweɪd]	to talk sb into doing sth	jdn überzeugen, jdn überreden
to **happen**	[ˈhæpən]	to occur	geschehen, passieren, vor sich gehen
to **make sth happen**	[ˌmeɪk ˈhæpən]	e.g. Positive thinking can make good things happen.	dafür sorgen, dass etw geschieht
red blood cells *pl*	[ˌred ˈblʌd selz]	e.g Red blood cells carry oxygen through the body.	rote Blutkörperchen
to **continue to do sth**	[kənˈtɪnjuː tə]	<> to stop doing sth	etw weiterhin tun
allergy	[ˈælədʒi]	e.g. He has an allergy to dogs and nuts.	Allergie
plant	[plɑːnt]	e.g. Our garden is full of exotic plants.	Pflanze
human	[ˈhjuːmən]	e.g. If you wouldn't eat a human, why eat an animal?	Mensch
to **kill**	[kɪl]	e.g. The fire killed 10 people.	töten, umbringen
nutritionist	[njuˈtrɪʃənɪst]	a healthy food expert	Ernährungswissenschaftler/in
health	[helθ]	*adj* healthy	Gesundheit
dietician	[ˌdaɪəˈtɪʃn]	an expert in food and eating	Ernährungswissenschaftler/in
as long as	[əz ˈlɒŋ əz]	e.g. I'll remember that day as long as I live.	solange
soya	[ˈsɔɪə]	protein made from beans	Soja
nutrient	[ˈnjuːtriənt]	*adj* nutritious	Nährstoff
pork	[pɔːk]	a type of meat	Schweinefleisch
taste	[teɪst]	how sth tastes	Geschmack
to **lead**	[liːd]	e.g. to lead sb in the right direction	führen, bringen
final	[ˈfaɪnl]	last	letzte/r/s
to **change one's ways**	[ˌtʃeɪndʒ wʌnz ˈweɪz]	e.g. I'm not going to change my ways – I'm too old!	seine Gewohnheiten ändern
to **agree with sb**	[əˈgriː wɪð]	<> to disagree with sb	jdm zustimmen, jds Meinung sein
in my opinion	[ɪn maɪ əˈpɪnɪən]	I think …, I believe …	meiner Meinung nach

page 21

rarely	[ˈreəli]	*adj* rare	selten, kaum
to **draw**	[drɔː]	e.g. to draw a picture/graph	zeichnen, *(Linie)* ziehen
to **shop for sth**	[ˈʃɒp fə]	to go and buy sth	etw (ein)kaufen
current	[ˈkʌrənt]	<> out-of-date	aktuell

page 22

knowledge	[ˈnɒlɪdʒ]	v to know	Wissen, Kenntnisse
fried	[fraɪd]	v to fry	gebraten, Brat-
can	[kæn]	e.g. a can of beer, a can of Coke	Dose
packet	[ˈpækɪt]	e.g. a packet of crisps	Packung, Tüte
crisps pl	[krɪsps]	a salty snack made from potatoes	Chips
pretzel	[ˈpretsl]	typical southern German salty snack	Brezel
to head for sth	[ˈhed fə]	e.g. As I was heading for the airport, I realized I had forgotten my passport.	sich auf den Weg zum/r … machen
cereal	[ˈsɪərɪəl]	muesli, corn, grains	Müsli, Getreideflocken
juice	[dʒuːs]	e.g. orange juice, apple juice	Saft
bacon	[ˈbeɪkən]	phr bacon and eggs	Speck
pub	[pʌb]	bar	Kneipe, Gasthaus
Cheers!	[tʃɪəz]	muesli, corn, grains	Prost!
appetite	[ˈæpɪtaɪt]	wanting to eat food	Appetit
to raise your glass	[ˌreɪz jɔː ˈɡlɑːs]	e.g. He raised his glass and said "Cheers everyone!"	sein Glas erheben
Here's to …!	[ˈhɪəz tə]	e.g. He raised his glass and said "Here's to you, my darling!"	(Trinkspruch:) Auf …!
amount	[əˈmaʊnt]	sum	(Geld-)Betrag
credit card	[ˈkredɪt kɑːd]	e.g. I used my credit card to pay for some new clothes.	Kreditkarte
bill	[bɪl]	document showing the amount of money to pay	Rechnung
tip	[tɪp]	amount of money you add to the bill for the benefit of the waiter or waitress	Trinkgeld
service	[ˈsɜːvɪs]	e.g. We left the waitress a big tip for her excellent service.	Bedienung, Service
extra	[ˈekstrə]	additional	zusätzliche/r/s
coin	[kɔɪn]	piece of currency	Münze
note	[nəʊt]	e.g. a £10 note, a €50 note	Geldschein, Banknote
to serve sb	[sɜːv]	n service	jdn bedienen
midday	[mɪdˈdeɪ]	noon	Mittag

page 23

gap	[ɡæp]	space left free or open	Lücke
certainly	[ˈsɜːtnli]	e.g. I'd like to book a table. – Certainly, madam.	gern
this way	[ˈðɪs weɪ]	e.g. Let me show me your room. This way, please.	hier entlang
There you go.	[ˌðeə ju ˈɡəʊ]	e.g. A cup of tea, please. – There you go. – Thanks!	Bitte sehr. Bitteschön.
at the moment	[ət ðə ˈməʊmənt]	right now	im Moment, gerade
tasty	[ˈteɪsti]	delicious	schmackhaft, lecker
mixed	[mɪkst]	v to mix	gemischt
Here you are.	[ˌhɪə ju ˈɑː]	e.g. Could you pass the sugar, please? – Here you are.	Bitte sehr. Bitteschön.
dessert	[dɪˈzɜːt]	sweet food you eat at the end of a meal	Nachtisch, Dessert
menu	[ˈmenjuː]	e.g. The restaurant has a big menu.	Speisekarte, Speiseplan
full	[fʊl]	e.g. More ice cream for you? – Oh no, I'm full, thanks.	satt
Did you enjoy your meal?	[dɪd ju ɪnˌdʒɔɪ jɔː ˈmiːl]	e.g. Did you enjoy your meal? – Oh yes, it was absolutely delicious!	Hat es Ihnen geschmeckt?
sometime	[ˈsʌmtaɪm]	in the (near) future	irgendwann, (demnächst) einmal
to recommend	[ˌrekəˈmend]	n recommendation	empfehlen
to act sth out	[ˌækt ˈaʊt]	to play out a scenario	etw (mit verteilten Rollen) spielen
role	[rəʊl]	phr to play a role	Rolle
to contrast sth with sth	[kənˈtrɑːst wɪð]	to compare sth with sth	etw einander gegenüberstellen
to produce sth	[prəˈdjuːs]	n production	etw produzieren, etw erstellen

page 24

canteen	[kænˈtiːn]	place where people eat at work	Kantine, Mensa
to improve	[ɪmˈpruːv]	to make sth better	verbessern, sich bessern
to present (sth to sb)	[prɪˈzent]	n presentation	(etw jdm) vorstellen
notice	[ˈnəʊtɪs]	information on display	Ankündigung, Mitteilung, Aushang
competition	[ˌkɒmpəˈtɪʃn]	v to compete	Wettbewerb
starter	[ˈstɑːtə]	what you eat before your main meal	Vorspeise
course	[kɔːs]	e.g. starter, main course, dessert	(Menü:) Gang
balanced	[ˈbælənst]	v to balance	ausgewogen
price	[praɪs]	how much sth costs	Preis
target group	[ˈtɑːɡɪt ɡruːp]	e.g. Teenagers are one of the main target groups for gaming.	Zielgruppe
to write up sth	[ˌraɪt ˈʌp]	to prepare a text	etw formulieren, etw ausarbeiten
to illustrate	[ˈɪləstreɪt]	to make a picture	illustrieren
drawing	[ˈdrɔːɪŋ]	v to draw	Zeichnung
nourishing	[ˈnʌrɪʃɪŋ]	n nourishment	nahrhaft
to pin	[pɪn]	e.g. pin the photo to the wall	(mit einer Nadel) anheften
past sth	[pɑːst]	e.g. Walk past the traffic lights, then it's the second street to the right.	an etw vorbei
to rank	[ræŋk]	to put in order	einstufen, (nach Rang) ordnen
category	[ˈkætəɡəri]	group of similar things	Rubrik, Kategorie

design	[dɪˈzaɪn]	e.g. Graffiti has interesting designs.	Gestaltung, Entwurf
attractiveness	[əˈtræktɪvnəs]	v to attract	Attraktivität
overall	[əʊvərˈɔːl]	e.g. the overall effect, the overall performance	Gesamt-, insgesamt
effect	[ɪˈfekt]	adj effective	Wirkung, Effekt

UNIT 2

page 25

to do sport	[du ˈspɔːt]	e.g. football, fitness, etc.	Sport treiben
gym	[dʒɪm]	a place to do sport	Fitness-Studio

page 26

diary	[ˈdaɪəri]	journal (esp AE)	Tagebuch
winner	[ˈwɪnə]	v to win	Gewinner/in, Sieger/in
importance	[ɪmˈpɔːtns]	adj important	Bedeutung, Wichtigkeit
to provide	[prəˈvaɪd]	to give	liefen, bieten, zur Verfügung stellen
suitable	[ˈsuːtəbl]	<> unsuitable	geeignet
to suggest	[səˈdʒest]	n suggestion	vorschlagen
to keep a diary	[kiːp ə ˈdaɪəri]	to write about your life every day	ein Tagebuch führen
to make friends	[meɪk ˈfrendz]	to find friends	Freunde finden/gewinnen
active(ly)	[ˈæktɪv]	<> inactive, passive	aktiv
no matter	[ˌnəʊ ˈmætə]	not important	egal, ganz gleich
runner	[ˈrʌnə]	v to run	Läufer/in
run	[rʌn]	e.g. They went on a run in the park every morning.	Lauf
to hang out with sb	[ˌhæŋ ˈaʊt]	e.g. I have nothing to do this afternoon – let's hang out!	mit jdm Zeit verbringen, mit jdm abhängen
lonely	[ˈləʊnli]	alone	einsam
platform	[ˈplætfɔːm]	e.g. social media platforms	Plattform
to sum up	[tə ˌsʌm ˈʌp]	summarizing, to conclude	zusammenfassend
to make an effort	[ˌmeɪk ən ˈefət]	to try hard	sich anstrengen, sich Mühe geben
to please sb	[pliːz]	e.g. I did the washing-up just to please my mum.	jdm einen Gefallen tun, jdm gefallen
step	[step]	phr step by step	Schritt
social	[ˈsəʊʃl]	e.g. I'm not a very social person – I don't particularly like being with people.	gesellig, sozial

page 27

to record	[rɪˈkɔːd]	n record	aufzeichnen, aufnehmen, protokollieren
progress	[ˈprəʊgres]	v to progress	Fortschritt(e), Vorankommen
entry	[ˈentri]	e.g. blog entry	Eintrag, Beitrag
lazy	[ˈleɪzi]	<> hard-working	faul
to get a life	[ˌget ə ˈlaɪf]	e.g. Get off the sofa, turn off the internet and get a life!	mit seinem Leben (endlich) etwas anfangen
to get sth in order	[ˌget ɪn ˈɔːdə]	to get organized, to structure sth	etw ordnen, etw auf die Reihe kriegen
mental	[ˈmentl]	<> physical	geistig, mental
confidence	[ˈkɒnfɪdəns]	adj confident	Selbstvertrauen, Selbstbewusstsein
weight	[weɪt]	v to weigh	Gewicht
to lose weight	[ˌluːz ˈweɪt]	<> to gain weight	abnehmen
to develop	[dɪˈveləp]	n development	(sich) entwickeln
energetic	[ˌenəˈdʒetɪk]	n energy	voller Energie, tatkräftig
to give up	[ˌgɪv ˈʌp]	to stop doing sth	aufgeben
motivated	[ˈməʊtɪveɪtɪd]	n motivation	motiviert

page 28

account	[əˈkaʊnt]	e.g. Facebook account or profile	Konto
tag line	[ˈtæg laɪn]	caption	Bildunterschrift, Slogan
to get ready	[get ˈredi]	to prepare oneself	sich fertigmachen, sich vorbereiten
local	[ˈləʊkl]	<> foreign	örtlich, lokal
kind	[kaɪnd]	type, sort	Art
to turn up	[ˌtɜːn ˈʌp]	to show up	kommen, auftauchen
pressure	[ˈpreʃə]	phr to put sb under pressure	Druck
to accept	[əkˈsept]	n acceptance	akzeptieren, annehmen
atmosphere	[ˈætməsfɪə]	the feeling of a place or situation	Atmosphäre
journey	[ˈdʒɜːni]	trip	Reise, Fahrt
summary	[ˈsʌməri]	v to summarize	Zusammenfassung
record	[ˈrekɔːd]	v to record	Aufzeichnung(en), Protokoll
development	[dɪˈveləpmənt]	v to develop	Entwicklung

page 29

to lift	[lɪft]	to pick sth up, to raise sth	heben, hochheben
to kick the ball	[ˌkɪk ðə ˈbɔːl]	e.g. He kicked the ball over the wall.	den Ball treten/schießen
to do gymnastics	[ˌduː dʒɪmˈnæstɪks]	e.g. I do gymnastics twice a week.	turnen
to ride a bike	[ˌraɪd ə ˈbaɪk]	to cycle	Fahrrad fahren

to **ice skate**	[ˈaɪs skeɪt]	*n* ice skating	eislaufen
water polo	[ˈwɔːtə pəʊləʊ]	e.g. to play water polo	Wasserball
to **box**	[bɒks]	*n* boxer	boxen
to **fail to do sth**	[ˈfeɪl tə duː]	to not do sth; to not manage to do sth	etw nicht schaffen
goal line	[ˌɡəʊl laɪn]	end line	Tor(aus)linie
to **score a try**	[ˌskɔːr ə ˈtraɪ]	e.g. I scored two tries in my rugby match.	(Rugby:) einen Versuch erzielen
to **stop sb from doing sth**	[stɒp]	to prevent sb from doing sth	jdn daran hindern, etw zu tun
to **touch down the ball**	[tʌtʃ ˌdaʊn ðə ˈbɔːl]	*n* touchdown	(Rugby:) den Ball niederlegen
match	[mætʃ]	e.g. A football match lasts 90 minutes.	Spiel, Partie

page 30

coach	[kəʊtʃ]	team trainer	Trainer/in
to **draw**	[drɔː]	e.g. If we don't win, we usually draw – but we never lose!	unentschieden spielen
exciting	[ɪkˈsaɪtɪŋ]	*n* excitement	aufregend, spannend
match	[mætʃ]	e.g. A football match lasts 90 minutes.	Spiel, Partie
pitch	[pɪtʃ]	playing field for football, rugby etc.	(Spiel-)Feld, (Fußball-)Platz
member	[ˈmembə]	*phr* to become a member of sth	Mitglied
Congratulations on …!	[kənˌɡrætʃʊˈleɪʃnz]	*v* to congratulate	Herzlichen Glückwunsch zu …!
win	[wɪn]	*v* to win	Sieg
motivating	[ˈməʊtɪveɪtɪŋ]	*v* to motivate	motivierend
interested in sth	[ˈɪntrəstɪd ɪn]	*adj* interesting	an etw interessiert
world cup	[ˌwɜːld ˈkʌp]	to win the world cup	Weltpokal, Weltmeisterschaft
semi-final	[ˈsemi faɪnl]	to play in the semi final	Halbfinale
on and off the pitch	[ɒn ən ˌɒf ðə ˈpɪtʃ]	when playing the sport and when not	auf und neben dem Spielfeld
especially	[ɪˈspeʃəli]	specifically	besonders, insbesondere
captain	[ˈkæptɪn]	team leader	Kapitän/in
skillful	[ˈskɪlfl]	good at doing sth	geschickt, erfahren, gut
brilliant	[ˈbrɪliənt]	fantastic, great	genial
to **speak out against sb**	[ˌspiːk ˈaʊt əɡenst]	to criticise sb publicly	sich (öffentlich) gegen jdn aussprechen, jdn kritisieren
school exchange	[ˈskuːl ɪkstʃeɪndʒ]	foreign exchange	Schüleraustausch
to **join sth**	[dʒɔɪn]	to become part of sth	bei etw mitmachen
to **go along with sb**	[ˌɡəʊ əˈlɒŋ wɪð]	to accompany sb	mit jdm mitkommen/mitgehen
sex	[seks]	gender	Geschlecht
separate(ly)	[ˈseprət]	<> together	getrennt, separat, einzeln
nowadays	[ˈnaʊədeɪz]	these days, now, today	heute, heutzutage
to **involve**	[ɪnˈvɒlv]	to contain sth, to consist of	beinhalten, erfordern
skill	[skɪl]	ability	Geschicklichkeit
to **bowl**	[bəʊl]	to throw the ball (in cricket)	(Cricket:) werfen
to **bat**	[bæt]	to hit the ball with a bat	(den Ball) schlagen
to **catch**	[kætʃ]	to grab, to get hold of	fangen
motor skills *pl*	[ˈməʊtə skɪlz]	to have good motor skills	Motorik
considerably	[kənˈsɪdərəbli]	noticeably, significantly	beträchtlich, erheblich
brain	[breɪn]	e.g. Walking is good for the brain.	Gehirn
popular	[ˈpɒpjələ]	<> unpopular	beliebt
empire	[ˈempaɪə]	e.g. The British Empire	(Welt-)Reich
at all	[ət ˈɔːl]	e.g. That was no fun at all.	überhaupt
however	[haʊˈevə]	but, on the other hand	allerdings, aber, doch, jedoch
team mate	[ˈtiːm meɪt]	a member of the same team	Mannschaftskamerad
to **be sb's turn**	[bi ˌsʌmbədiz ˈtɜːn]	e.g. It's your turn to wash the dishes, darling.	an der Reihe sein, dran sein
so far	[səʊ ˈfɑː]	yet, up to now, until now	bislang
to **name**	[neɪm]	to identify	nennen

page 31

mostly	[ˈməʊstli]	generally, mainly	hauptsächlich, meistens, überwiegend
normally	[ˈnɔːməli]	e.g. I normally eat breakfast before going to work.	normalerweise
right now	[raɪt ˈnaʊ]	in this moment	gerade (jetzt)
thought	[θɔːt]	*v* to think	Gedanke
attention	[əˈtenʃn]	*adj* attentive	Aufmerksamkeit
to **pay attention to sth**	[ˌpeɪ əˈtenʃn tə]	to notice sth	auf etw achten, etw beachten
to **agree**	[əˈɡriː]	e.g. I agree with you.	zustimmen, einverstanden sein
to **split up**	[ˌsplɪt ˈʌp]	to go separate ways	sich trennen
treadmill	[ˈtredmɪl]	a machine at a gym that you run on	Laufband
exercise bike	[ˈeksəsaɪz baɪk]	stationary bike	Trainingsfahrrad, Heimtrainer
instead	[ɪnˈsted]	e.g. We didn't want to go out and stayed at home instead.	stattdessen
guy	[ɡaɪ]	man	Typ, Kerl
to **cover sth**	[ˈkʌvə]	to discuss sth, to mention sth	etw (Thema) behandeln

page 32

youth centre	[ˈjuːθ sentə]	place for young people	Jugendzentrum
to introduce	[ˌɪntrəˈdjuːs]	n introduction	einführen, vorstellen
although	[ɔːlˈðəʊ]	even though, though	obwohl
to invent	[ɪnˈvent]	n invention	erfinden
equipment	[ɪˈkwɪpmənt]	things you need to do a certain sport	Ausrüstung, Ausstattung, Geräte
identity	[aɪˈdentəti]	e.g. national identity, social identity	Identität
to perform sth	[pəˈfɔːm]	n performance	etw aufführen, etw spielen
to strengthen	[ˈstreŋθn]	n strength	stärken
to be supposed to do sth	[bi səˈpəʊzd tə du]	e.g. I'm sorry, but don't understand what I am supposed to do.	etw (eigentlich) tun sollen
to frighten sb	[ˈfraɪtn]	to scare sb	jdm Angst einjagen
opponent	[əˈpəʊnənt]	opposition, rival	Gegner/in
martial art	[ˌmɑːʃl ˈɑːt]	e.g. Karate is a martial art.	Kampfsport, Kampfkunst
combination	[ˌkɒmbɪˈneɪʃn]	v to combine	Verbindung
during	[ˈdjʊərɪŋ]	while sth else is happening	während
slave	[sleɪv]	e.g. The Slave Trade	Sklave/Sklavin
slavery	[ˈsleɪvəri]	e.g. to be sold into slavery	Sklaverei
to abolish sth	[əˈbɒlɪʃ]	n abolition	etw abschaffen
government	[ˈɡʌvənmnt]	officials and ministers running a state or country	Regierung
to ban sth	[bæn]	to not allow sth	etw verbieten
to practise sth	[ˈpræktɪs]	to repeat regularly	etw ausüben
prison	[ˈprɪzn]	jail	Gefängnis
to colonize	[ˈkɒlənaɪz]	e.g. Britain colonized large areas of North America.	kolonisieren
to found	[faʊnd]	to establish, to set up, to create	gründen
plantation	[ˌplænˈteɪʃn]	e.g. a sugar plantation	Plantage
passionate(ly)	[ˈpæʃənət]	n passion	leidenschaftlich
root	[ruːt]	e.g. roots of a tree	Wurzel
stick	[stɪk]	small branch	Stock
native American	[ˌneɪtɪv əˈmerɪkən]	original American people before the Europeans arrived	amerikanische/r Ureinwohner/in
frozen lake	[ˌfrəʊzn ˈleɪk]	v to freeze	zugefrorener See
ice rink	[ˈaɪs rɪŋk]	skating rink	Eisbahn

page 33

manager	[ˈmænɪdʒə]	leader	Leiter/in
advantage	[ədˈvɑːntɪdʒ]	<> disadvantage	Vorteil
activity	[ækˈtɪvəti]	adj active	Tätigkeit, Beschäftigung, Äktivität
ramp	[ræmp]	sloping surface	Rampe
jump	[dʒʌmp]	obstacle	Sprunghindernis
matter	[ˈmætə]	subject, business	Sache, Angelegenheit
to join in	[ˌdʒɔɪn ˈɪn]	to be part of sth	mitmachen
youngster	[ˈjʌŋstə]	young person	Jugendliche/r
basics pl	[ˈbeɪsɪks]	most important information	Grundlagen
pound	[paʊnd]	British currency	Pfund
to offer	[ˈɒfə]	n offer	bieten, anbieten
free of charge	[ˌfriː əf ˈtʃɑːdʒ]	at no cost	gebührenfrei, kostenlos
glove	[ɡlʌv]	sth to keep your hands warm	Handschuh
anger	[ˈæŋɡə]	adj angry	Wut
beauty	[ˈbjuːti]	adj beautiful	Schönheit
to hit	[hɪt]	to punch	schlagen, treffen
to disagree (with sb)	[ˌdɪsəˈɡriː]	n disagreement	(jdm) widersprechen
violence	[ˈvaɪələns]	adj violent	Gewalt
control	[kənˈtrəʊl]	phr to keep things under control	Kontrolle
to make a point	[ˌmeɪk ə ˈpɔɪnt]	to present an argument	ein Argument vorbringen
community	[kəˈmjuːnəti]	people in a place	Gemeinschaft, Gemeinde
role model	[ˈrəʊl mɒdl]	sb you want to be like	Vorbild
to respect	[rɪˈspekt]	to think a lot of	respektieren, achten
intern	[ˈɪntɜːn]	sb doing a work experience	Praktikant/In
ranking list	[ˈræŋkɪŋ lɪst]	a list organized by level	Rangliste
speech	[spiːtʃ]	v to speak	Vortrag, Rede
to exchange	[ɪksˈtʃeɪndʒ]	n exchange	austauschen
to convince	[kənˈvɪns]	e.g. We convinced them to join us.	überzeugen
to be willing to do sth	[bi ˈwɪlɪŋ tə]	to be happy to do sth	bereit/willens sein, etw zu tun
to compromise	[ˈkɒmprəmaɪz]	to find a compromise	einen Kompromiss eingehen
to make sure	[ˌmeɪk ˈʃʊə]	to ensure	dafür sorgen, sicherstellen
thrilling	[ˈθrɪlɪŋ]	very exciting	aufregend, spannend, mitreißend
discipline	[ˈdɪsəplɪn]	self control	Disziplin
spectator sport	[spekˈteɪtə spɔːt]	e.g. Football is a spectator sport.	Publikumssport
absolutely	[ˌæbsəˈluːtli]	completely, totally	völlig, absolut, total
to share	[ʃeə]	to divide into parts	teilen
rough	[rʌf]	forceful, aggressive	grob, rau
to promote sth	[prəˈməʊt]	to encourage sth, to support sth	etw begünstigen, etw fördern

page 34

flyer	['flaɪə]	advertising brochure	Handzettel, Broschüre
exchange student	[ɪks'tʃeɪndʒ stjuːdnt]	a student from another country	Austauschschüler/in
area	['eərɪə]	district, region	Gegend, Gebiet, Bereich
to **research** sth	[rɪ'sɜːtʃ]	to look for information about sth	etw recherchieren, Nachforschungen über etw anstellen
opportunity	[ˌɒpə'tjuːnəti]	possibility	Möglichkeit, Gelegenheit
precise	[prɪ'saɪs]	exact	genau, präzise
event	[ɪ'vent]	happening	Veranstaltung
research	[rɪ'sɜːtʃ]	*v* to research	Recherche, Nachforschungen
attractive	[ə'træktɪv]	nice to look at	ansprechend, attraktiv
map	[mæp]	atlas	Landkarte, Karte
to **comment on** sth	['kɒment ɒn]	to say sth about sth	etw kommentieren, zu etw Stellung nehmen
to **vote**	[vəʊt]	*n* vote	abstimmen, wählen

UNIT 3

page 35

courageous	[kə'reɪdʒəs]	*n* courage	mutig
rights *pl*	[raɪts]	e.g. the right to vote	Rechte
education	[ˌedʒu'keɪʃn]	*adj* educational	Schulbildung, Ausbildung
to **award**	[ə'wɔːd]	*n* award	(Preis) verleihen
peace	[piːs]	*phr* peace and quiet	Frieden
Nobel Peace Prize	[nəʊˌbel 'piːs praɪz]	an award for outstanding achievement in promoting peace	Friedensnobelpreis
to **appoint** sb sth	[ə'pɔɪnt]	to give sb an official position	jdn zu etw ernennen
messenger	['mesɪndʒə]	sb who brings news	Botschafter/in
besides	[bɪ'saɪdz]	except	außer
to **donate**	[dəʊ'neɪt]	to give money	spenden
charity	['tʃærəti]	non-profit organization that helps people	Hilfsorganisation(en), wohltätige Zwecke
foundation	[faʊn'deɪʃn]	an organization that gives money to projects	Stiftung
underprivileged	[ˌʌndə'prɪvəlɪdʒd]	e.g. We want to make sure all underprivileged children can go to school.	benachteiligt, unterprivilegiert
to **treat**	[triːt]	to deal with	behandeln
equal(ly)	['iːkwəl]	e.g. All men are created equal.	gleich
firefighter *AE*	['faɪəfaɪtə]	*BE* fireman	Feuerwehrmann
to **save**	[seɪv]	e.g. He saved my life after the car accident.	retten
to **achieve** sth	[ə'tʃiːv]	*n* achievement	etw erreichen
even though	['iːvn ðəʊ]	although	obwohl
to **behave**	[bɪ'heɪv]	*n* behaviour	sich verhalten, sich benehmen
to **look up to** sb	[ˌlʊk 'ʌp tə]	to have respect for sb	zu jdm aufsehen, jdn bewundern

page 36

celebrity	[sə'lebrəti]	famous person	Prominente/r, Promi
appropriate	[ə'prəʊprɪət]	suitable	passend
to **shame**	[ʃeɪm]	e.g. She was shamed for wearing a short dress.	beschämen
common	['kɒmən]	popular	verbreitet
disabled	[dɪ'seɪbld]	*v* to be disabled, to have a disability	behindert
to **receive**	[rɪ'siːv]	*n* receipt	erhalten, bekommen
disabled access	[dɪˌseɪbld 'ækses]	*adj* accessible	behindertengerechter Zugang
venue	['venjuː]	place where an event takes place	Veranstaltungsort
citizen	['sɪtɪzn]	*n* citizenship	(Staats-)Bürger/in

page 37

amazing	[ə'meɪzɪŋ]	fantastic	toll, super, erstaunlich
fashion	['fæʃn]	*adj* fashionable	Mode
bubbly	['bʌbli]	e.g. She has a bubbly personality.	quirlig, lebendig
personality	[ˌpɜːsə'næləti]	a person's character	Persönlichkeit
actress	['æktrəs]	a woman who acts in films, TV, theatre	Schauspielerin
presenter	[prɪ'zentə]	TV host	Moderator/in
activist	['æktɪvɪst]	e.g. animal rights activist	Aktivist/in
fame	[feɪm]	*adj* famous	Ruhm
to **spread awareness on** sth	[ˌspred ə'weənəs]	to be aware of sth	Bewusstsein für etw schaffen
to **overcome** sth	[ˌəʊvə'kʌm]	to get over sth	etw überwinden
health issue	['helθ ɪʃuː]	e.g. illness, injury	Gesundheitsproblem
congenital	[kən'dʒenɪtl]	inherited, hereditary	angeboren
hearing loss	['hɪərɪŋ lɒs]	hearing impairment	Schwerhörigkeit, Gehörverlust
anorexia nervosa	[ˌænə'reksɪə nɜː'vəʊzə]	to suffer from anorexia, to have anorexia	Magersucht
eating disorder	['iːtɪŋ dɪsɔːdə]	to have an eating disorder	Essstörung
overweight	[ˌəʊvə'weɪt]	*underweight*	übergewichtig

to **feature sth**	[ˈfiːtʃə]	e.g. The newspaper featured a story on missing children.	über etw berichten, (Story) bringen
weight loss	[ˈweɪt lɒs]	v to lose weight	Abnehmen
to **hit sb**	[hɪt]	to run sb over	jdn anfahren
luckily	[ˈlʌkɪli]	thankfully	glücklicherweise
treatment	[ˈtriːtmənt]	v to treat	Behandlung
to **recover**	[rɪˈkʌvə]	to get well again	sich erholen
accident	[ˈæksɪdənt]	e.g. a traffic accident	Unfall
relationship	[rɪˈleɪʃnʃɪp]	connection you have with sb	Beziehung, Verhältnis
entertainment	[ˌentəˈteɪnmənt]	v to entertain	Unterhaltung
show	[ʃəʊ]	e.g. What is your favourite TV show?	(Radio-, TV-)Sendung, (TV-)Serie
to **present sth**	[prɪˈzent]	e.g. He presents a TV talent show.	etw (Sendung usw.) moderieren
to **launch sth**	[lɒntʃ]	phr to launch a business	etw (Unternehmen usw.) gründen
various	[ˈveəriəs]	different types of	verschiedene/r/s
walking aids pl	[ˈwɔːkɪŋ eɪdz]	e.g. walker, walking stick	Gehhilfe(n)
among	[əˈmʌŋ]	in the middle of	unter, bei
seating	[ˈsiːtɪŋ]	number and type of seats	Bestuhlung
to **be made up of sth**	[bi ˌmeɪd ˈʌp əv]	to consist of	aus etw bestehen
collapsible seat	[kəˈlæpsəbl ˈsiːt]	foldable seat	Klappsitz
gig	[ɡɪɡ]	concert	(Rock-, Pop-, Jazz-)Konzert
so that	[ˌsəʊ ˈðæt]	e.g. He worse suncream so that he didn't get burned.	damit
proportion	[prəˈpɔːʃn]	amount, fraction, ratio	Anteil
disability	[ˌdɪsəˈbɪləti]	adj disabled	Behinderung
to **star in a show**	[ˌstɑːr ɪn ə ˈʃəʊ]	to be the main character in a show	in einer Serie mitspielen
to **launch sth**	[lɒntʃ]	e.g. to launch an app	etw starten
to **weigh**	[weɪ]	e.g. Tom weighs 69 kilograms.	wiegen
title	[taɪtl]	official name, headline	Titel
to **inspire**	[ɪnˈspaɪə]	adj inspirational	anregen, inspirieren
to **come across sth**	[ˌkʌm əˈkrɒs]	to find sth	auf etw stoßen, etw (zufällig) finden
details pl	[ˈdiːteɪlz]	phr contact details	Angaben, Daten, Einzelheiten
genuine	[ˈdʒenjuɪn]	real	echt, authentisch
unedited	[ʌnˈedɪtɪd]	not manipulated	unbearbeitet
grateful	[ˈɡreɪtfl]	n gratitude	dankbar
proud (of sb/sth)	[praʊd]	e.g. He was proud of his work.	stolz (auf jdn/etw)
to **conform to sth**	[kənˈfɔːm tə]	phr to conform to rules	einer Sache entsprechen
impossible	[ɪmˈpɒsəbl]	<> possible	unmöglich
impossible standards pl	[ɪmˌpɒsəbl ˈstændədz]	unachievable targets	unerreichbare Maßstäbe
society	[səˈsaɪəti]	adj social	Gesellschaft
to **criticize**	[ˈkrɪtɪsaɪz]	n critcism	kritisieren
skinny	[ˈskɪni]	very thin	mager, dürr
to **fight back**	[ˌfaɪt ˈbæk]	to oppose sth	sich verteidigen, zurückschlagen
to **create sth**	[kriˈeɪt]	produce, make, invent	etw entwerfen, etw verfassen
petition	[pəˈtɪʃn]	e.g. Please sign this petition to allow 16 year olds to vote.	Petition
titled	[ˈtaɪtld]	n title	mit dem Titel
to **stop sth**	[stɒp]	to end sth	etw verhindern
to **promote sth**	[prəˈməʊt]	to advertise sth	für etw werben
toxic	[ˈtɒksɪk]	poisonous	giftig, (äußerst) schädlich
diet	[ˈdaɪət]	e.g. a healthy diet	Diät
to **call on sb to do sth**	[ˈkɒl ɒn]	to ask sb to do sth, to urge sb to do sth	jdn dazu auffordern, etw zu tun
to **point out sth**	[ˌpɔɪnt ˈaʊt]	to make sb see sth	auf etw hinweisen
promotion	[prəˈməʊʃn]	e.g. promotional material, advertising	Werbung
impressionable	[ɪmˈpreʃnəbl]	easy to influence	leicht zu beeinflucken

page 38

role	[rəʊl]	job, function	Rolle, Funktion
advocate	[ˈædvəkət]	n advocacy	Befürworter/in, Verfechter/in
slimming product	[ˈslɪmɪŋ prɒdʌkt]	weightloss product	Schlankheitsmittel
shy	[ʃaɪ]	<> confident	schüchtern
self-confident	[ˌself ˈkɒnfɪdənt]	self-assured	selbstbewusst
in public	[ɪn ˈpʌblɪk]	e.g. You must wear clothes in public.	in der Öffentlichkeit
seat	[siːt]	a place to sit	Sitz, Platz
to **come across as ...**	[ˌkʌm əˈkrɒs əz]	to seem to be (like)	... wirken
unfiltered	[ʌnˈfɪltəd]	without limits	ungefiltert
to **encourage sb to do sth**	[ɪnˈkʌrɪdʒ]	to urge sb to do sth, to motivate sb to do sth	jdn dazu ermuntern, etw zu tun; jdm dazu raten, etw zu tun
slim	[slɪm]	<> fat, wide	schlank
advertising (of sth)	[ˈædvətaɪzɪŋ]	v to advertise	Werbung (für etw), Bewerben (von etw)
unhealthy	[ʌnˈhelθi]	<> healthy	ungesund
to **appear**	[əˈpɪə]	to be on a TV program or in an advertisement	(TV, Werbung:) auftreten
advert	[ˈædvɜːt]	short for 'advertisement'	Anzeige, Werbespot

page 39

| to **sort sth into sth** | [ˈsɔːt ɪntə] | e.g. Sort the class into groups of 3. | etw in etw einsortieren |

page 40

positivity	[pɒzəˈtɪvəti]	<> negativity	positive Einstellung
reply	[rɪˈplaɪ]	answer, response	Antwort, Erwiderung
comment	[ˈkɒment ɒn]	v to comment	Kommentar, Stellungnahme
to **go on a diet**	[gəʊ ɒn ə ˈdaɪət]	to diet	eine Diät machen
to **depend on sth**	[dɪˈpend ɒn]	adj dependent	von etw abhängen
to **get involved with sb**	[ˌget ɪnˈvɒlvd wɪð]	to spend time with sb, so associate with sb	mit jdm zu tun haben
most recent	[ˌməʊst ˈriːsnt]	current, newest	jüngste/r/s
sb realizes sth	[ˈrɪəlaɪzɪz]	e.g. I realized that he was talking to me.	jdm wird/ist etw bewusst
to **judge sb/sth**	[dʒʌdʒ]	e.g. Don't judge me by my appearance.	jdn/etw bewerten, jdn/etw beurteilen
experience	[ɪkˈspɪəriəns]	v to experience sth	Erlebnis, Erfahrung
helpful	[ˈhelpfl]	useful	nützlich, hilfreich
to **support sb**	[səˈpɔːt]	n support	jdm helfen, jdn unterstützen
to **influence**	[ˈɪnfluəns]	n influence	beeinflussen

page 41

introduction	[ˌɪntrəˈdʌkʃn]	the beginning of a text	(Text:) Einleitung
to **highlight**	[ˈhaɪlaɪt]	to show that sth is important	hervorheben
successful	[səkˈsesfl]	<> unsuccessful	erfolgreich
talented	[ˈtæləntɪd]	n talent	begabt, talentiert
to **set an example**	[ˈset ən ɪgˈzɑːmpl]	e.g. Smoking sets a bad example for children.	ein Beispiel geben
to **serve as sth**	[ˈsɜːv əz]	e.g. This situation serves as an example of the bigger issue.	als etw dienen
ambassador	[æmˈbæsədə]	sb who represents a country	Botschafter/in
similar (to sb/sth)	[ˈsɪmələ]	nearly the same	(jdm/einer Sache) ähnlich
to **represent**	[ˌreprɪˈzent]	n representation	vertreten, repräsentieren
to **educate**	[ˈedʒukeɪt]	to teach	unterrichten, informieren, (aus)bilden
public	[ˈpʌblɪk]	e.g. the general public	Öffentlichkeit
in case	[ɪn ˈkeɪs]	if/when sth happens	falls; für den Fall, dass
climate	[ˈklaɪmət]	phr climate change	Klima
climate change	[ˈklaɪmət tʃeɪndʒ]	e.g. Scientists met to discuss climate change.	Klimawandel
strike	[straɪk]	v to strike, to go on strike	Streik
movement	[ˈmuːvmənt]	campaign	Bewegung
to **protest**	[prəˈtest]	n protest	protestieren, demonstrieren
parliament	[ˈpɑːləmənt]	e.g. the Houses of Parliament in London	Parlament
politician	[ˌpɒləˈtɪʃn]	sb who made politics their career	Politiker/in
hand-painted	[ˌhændˈpeɪntɪd]	e.g. I bought a hand-painted bowl from the market.	handgemalt
banner	[ˈbænə]	e.g. They put up a banner saying "Stop the war".	Transparent
to **strike**	[straɪk]	to refuse to work in protest	streiken
determined	[dɪˈtɜːmɪnd]	purposeful, decided, intent	entschlossen, willensstark
to **admire**	[ədˈmaɪə]	n admiration	bewundern
to **make up one's mind**	[ˌmeɪk ˈʌp wʌnz maɪnd]	to decide	beschließen, (sich) entscheiden
to **report on sth**	[rɪˈpɔːt ɒn]	to tell others about sth, to describe sth	über etw berichten
protest	[ˈprəʊtest]	demonstration	Protest, Demonstration
big break	[bɪg ˈbreɪk]	a chance for success, a moment of good luck	großer Durchbruch
to **go viral**	[ˌgəʊ ˈvaɪrəl]	to become popular on the internet very quickly	sich rasant (im Internet) verbreiten
to **join sb in doing sth**	[dʒɔɪn]	to start doing sth that sb else is already doing	sich jdm bei etw anschließen
to **involve sb in sth**	[ɪnˈvɒlv ɪn]	to make sb a part in sth	jdn an etw beteiligen
complaint	[kəmˈpleɪnt]	v to complain	Klage, Beschwerde
to **join sth**	[dʒɔɪn]	to take part in sth, to become a member of sth	sich einer Sache anschließen
to **support sth**	[səˈpɔːt]	n support	etw unterstützen
from all walks of life	[frəm ˌɔːl wɔːks əv ˈlaɪf]	from a variety of backgrounds	aus allen Gesellschaftsschichten
to **fix sth**	[fɪks]	to solve, to repair	etw reparieren
spokesperson	[ˈspəʊkspɜːsn]	sb who speaks for a group	Sprecher/in
threat (to sb/sth)	[θret]	v to threaten	Gefahr, Bedrohung (für jdn/etw)
fossil fuel	[ˈfɒsl fjuːəl]	e.g. to burn fossil fuels	fossiler Brennstoff
to **get sth across**	[ˌget sth əˈkrɒs]	phr to get the message across	etw vermitteln
satisfaction	[ˌsætɪsˈfækʃn]	when sb is happy with what they have or have achieved	Zufriedenheit, Genugtuung
audience	[ˈɔːdiəns]	the people who watch sth	Publikum, Zuschauer, Zuhörer
to **matter**	[ˈmætə]	to be important	wichtig sein, von Belang sein
crowd	[kraʊd]	a large number of people in one place	Menschenmenge
to **make an impact (on sth)**	[ˌmeɪk ən ˈɪmpækt]	to have an effect on sth, to make a difference to sth	Wirkung haben
value	[ˈvæljuː]	worth	Wert
abroad	[əˈbrɔːd]	in/to another country	im/ins Ausland
responsible	[rɪˈspɒnsəbl]	aware of one's responsibility	verantwortungsbewusst
on a personal level	[ɒn ə ˌpɜːsənl ˈlevl]	adv personally	persönlich, selbst
to **affect sb/sth**	[əˈfekt]	e.g. Our decisions today will affect our grandchildren.	jdn/etw betreffen, jdn/etw beeinflussen
sb becomes aware of sth	[bɪˌkʌmz əˈweər əv]	to realize sth	jdm wird etw bewusst

to **share** sth	[ʃeə]	to talk about sth in public	über etw *(vor Publikum)* sprechen
spokesman	[ˈspəʊksmən]	a man who speaks for a group	Sprecher
stage	[steɪdʒ]	e.g. The stage is very large in this theatre.	Bühne

page 42

to **get drunk**	[ˌget ˈdrʌŋk]	to drink too much alcohol	sich betrinken
law	[lɔː]	*adj* legal	Gesetz(e), Recht
to **manage to do** sh	[ˈmænɪdʒ]	e.g. Did you manage to finish your homework?	es schaffen, etw zu tun
weakness	[ˈwiːknəs]	*adj* weak	Schwäche
to **identify with** sb/sth	[aɪˈdentɪfaɪ wɪð]	to feel similar to sb	sich mit jdm/etw identifizieren
terrible	[ˈterəbl]	bad, awful	furchtbar
dictator	[dɪkˈteɪtə]	all-powerful leader	Diktator/in
chances are that …	[ˈtʃɑːnsɪz ɑː ðət]	most probably	aller Wahrscheinlichkeit nach …
serial murderer	[ˌsɪəriəl ˈmɜːdərə]	serial killer	Serienmörder/in
to **turn out to be** sb/sth	[ˌtɜːn ˈaʊt tə bi]	to become sb/sth	zu jdm/etw werden, sich als jd/etw herausstellen
internship	[ˈɪntɜːnʃɪp]	*phr* unpaid internship	Praktikum
railway	[ˈreɪlweɪ]	*phr* railway station	Eisenbahn

page 43

action	[ˈækʃn]	e.g. In a crisis you need immediate action.	Handeln, Maßnahme(n), Aktion(en)
access (to sth)	[ˈækses]	e.g. I need high-speed internet access to watch films online.	Zugang (zu etw), Zugriff (auf etw)
poverty	[ˈpɒvəti]	*adj* poor	Armut
shocked	[ʃɒkt]	surprised in a bad way	schockiert
sanitation	[ˌsænɪˈteɪʃn]	canalization, drinking water system	Abwasserkanalisation
to **undergird**	[ʌndəˈgɜːd]	to reinforce	untermauern
magnitude	[ˈmægnɪtjuːd]	e.g. the magnitude of the tsunami	Größe
mind-blowing	[ˈmaɪnd bləʊɪŋ]	unbelievable	irre, überwältigend
kind of	[ˈkaɪnd əv]	somehow	irgendwie
endless(ly)	[ˈendləs]	without an end	unendlich
complex	[ˈkɒmpleks]	complicated	komplex, kompliziert
solvable	[ˈsɒlvəbl]	*v* to solve	lösbar
to **solve**	[sɒlv]	*n* solution	lösen
to **animate**	[ˈænɪmeɪt]	to bring to life	antreiben, mit Leben erfüllen
to **mean**	[miːn]	to have the opinion/idea	meinen
to **rob** sb **of** sth	[ˈrɒb əv]	to take sth away from sb	jdn einer Sache berauben
comprehensive	[ˌkɒmprɪˈhensɪv]	<> simple, partial	umfassend
crisis	[ˈkraɪsɪs]	big emergency	Krise
in our lifetime	[ɪn aʊə ˈlaɪftaɪm]	during the time we are alive	zu unseren Lebzeiten

page 44

announcement	[əˈnaʊnsmənt]	*v* to announce	Ankündigung, Mitteilung
to **apply for** sth	[əˈplaɪ fə]	*n* application	sich um etw bewerben
to **greet**	[griːt]	e.g. by saying 'Hello!'	begrüßen
visitor	[ˈvɪzɪtə]	<> host/hostess	Besucher/in
twin town	[ˌtwɪn ˈtaʊn]	partner city in another country	Partnerstadt
vocational training	[vəʊˌkeɪʃənl ˈtreɪnɪŋ]	job training	Berufsausbildung
workshop	[ˈwɜːkʃɒp]	place where things are made	Werkstatt
further education	[ˌfɜːðə edʒuˈkeɪʃn]	e.g. college, university, etc.	Weiterbildung
to **invite** sb **to do** sth	[ɪnˈvaɪt]	to give sb the opportunity to do sth	jdn auffordern, etw zu tun
a must	[ə ˈmʌst]	sth you have to do	ein Muss
application	[ˌæplɪˈkeɪʃn]	*v* to apply	Bewerbung
training session	[ˈtreɪnɪŋ seʃn]	a short class in which you learn new skills	Schulungseinheit
trainer	[ˈtreɪnə]	teacher, leader	Dozent/in, Ausbilder/in
to **settle down**	[ˌsetl ˈdaʊn]	to get calm, to become quiet	die Plätze einnehmen, zur Ruhe kommen
consultant	[kənˈsʌltənt]	sb who gives advice	Berater/in
affairs *pl*	[əˈfeəz]	business	Geschäfte, geschäftliche Angelegenheiten
town council	[ˌtaʊn ˈkaʊnsl]	local government	Stadtrat, Stadtverwaltung
dos and don'ts	[ˌduːz ən ˈdəʊnts]	what you should and shouldn't to	Dinge, die man tun und lassen sollte
smooth(ly)	[smuːð]	<> rough	reibungslos, glatt
to **be aware of** sth	[bi əˈweər əv]	to know about sth	sich einer Sache bewusst sein
to **have** sth **in common**	[həv ɪn ˈkɒmən]	to like the same things as sb	etw gemeinsam haben
to **shake hands**	[ʃeɪk ˈhændz]	e.g. It's polite to shake hands when you meet somebody for the first time.	die Hand geben, die Hände schütteln
to **hold** sth **out**	[ˌhəʊld ˈaʊt]	e.g. He held out his hand for a handshake.	etw ausstrecken
to **go on**	[ˌgəʊ ˈɒn]	to continue	weitermachen, fortfahren
smart(ly)	[smɑːt]	stylish, chic	*(Kleidung:)* schick, elegant
bright	[braɪt]	colourful	*(Farbe:)* kräftig, bunt
low-cut top	[ˌləʊ kʌt ˈtɒp]	She was wearing a very low-cut top.	tief ausgeschnittenes Oberteil
to **move on (to** sth**)**	[ˌmuːv ˈɒn]	e.g. shake hands, then move on to the next person	(mit etw) weitermachen
body language	[ˈbɒdi læŋgwɪdʒ]	communication using the body	Körpersprache

body contact	[ˈbɒdi kɒntækt]	physical contact with another person	Körperkontakt
to **touch**	[tʌtʃ]	*n* touch	berühren
to **be prepared to do sth**	[bi prɪˈpeəd tə duː]	*n* preparation	bereit sein, etw zu tun
likely	[ˈlaɪkli]	probably	wahrscheinlich
basic	[ˈbeɪsɪk]	simple	einfach, grundlegend, elementar
to **deal with sb**	[ˈdiːl wɪð]	to handle sb	mit jdm zu tun haben
customer	[ˈkʌstəmə]	person who buys sth	Kunde/-in
colleague	[ˈkɒliːg]	sb you work with	Kollege/-in
gentleman	[ˈdʒentlmən]	<> lady	Herr
greeting	[ˈgriːtɪŋ]	*v* to greet	Begrüßung
face to face	[ˌfeɪs tə ˈfeɪs]	<> via email, telephone, etc.	persönlich

page 45

flight	[flaɪt]	*v* to fly	Flug
delay	[dɪˈleɪ]	e.g. The train had a delay of one hour.	Verzögerung, Verspätung
to **train for sth**	[ˈtreɪn fə]	e.g. to train for a profession	eine Ausbildung zu etw machen
profession	[prəˈfeʃn]	job	Beruf

page 46

to **examine**	[ɪgˈzæmɪn]	*n* examination	untersuchen
neck	[nek]	part of the body between the head and shoulders	Hals
to **decorate sth**	[ˈdekəreɪt]	*n* decorations (pl)	etw schmücken
athletic	[æθˈletɪk]	sporty, muscly	sportlich, athletisch
stranger	[ˈstreɪndʒə]	e.g. Don't talk to strangers.	Fremde/r, Unbekannte/r
view	[vjuː]	*phr* point of view	Ansicht, Meinung
idea (of sth)	[aɪˈdɪə]	conception (of sth), (image of sth)	Auffassung (von etw)
to **compare with sth**	[kəmˈpeə wɪð]	*n* comparison	sich mit etw vergleichen lassen
to **conclude**	[kənˈkluːd]	to finish, to end	schließen
handout	[ˈhændaʊt]	e.g. The woman prepared a handout for the meeting.	Arbeitsblatt, Handzettel
structure	[ˈstrʌktʃə]	form, organization	Aufbau

UNIT 4

page 47

challenge	[ˈtʃælɪndʒ]	*adj* challenging	Herausforderung, (schwierige) Aufgabe
to **wind down**	[ˌwaɪnd ˈdaʊn]	to relax, to calm down	abspannen, sich entspannen
stressful	[ˈstresfl]	hard, difficult	anstrengend, stressig
to **switch off**	[ˌswɪtʃ ˈɒf]	<> to switch on	abschalten
to **relieve stress**	[rɪˌliːv ˈstres]	to de-stress	Stress abbauen

page 48

caffeine	[ˈkæfiːn]	e.g. Caffeine can be found in drinks like coffee.	Koffein
hidden	[ˈhɪdn]	*v* to hide	verborgen, versteckt
danger	[ˈdeɪndʒə]	*adj* dangerous	Gefahr
fellow student	[ˌfeləʊ ˈstjuːdnt]	sb in your class	Mitschüler/in
report	[rɪˈpɔːt]	e.g. a sports report	Reportage, Bericht
headline	[ˈhedlaɪn]	large title of a paragraph or newspaper article	Überschrift
to **jumble sth up**	[ˌdʒʌmbl ˈʌp]	to mix sth chaotically	etw durcheinanderwerfen
coma	[ˈkəʊmə]	*phr* to fall into a coma	Koma
coroner	[ˈkɒrənə]	a doctor who explains why/how sb died	Gerichtsmediziner/in
overdose	[ˈəʊvədəʊs]	too many drugs taken at the same time	Überdosis
life-support system	[ˈlaɪf səpɔːt sɪstəm]	a machine to keep sb alive	Lebenserhaltungssystem
follow-up	[ˈfɒləʊ ʌp]	e.g. After the operation, I had a follow-up meeting with my doctor.	Nachfassen
expert	[ˈekspɜːt]	sb with special knowledge	Fachmann/-frau, Experte/-in
paramedic	[ˌpærəˈmedɪk]	healthcare worker for emergencies	Rettungssanitäter/in
to **collapse**	[kəˈlæps]	e.g. The old man collapsed in the heat.	zusammenbrechen, zusammenklappen
campaign	[kæmˈpeɪn]	movement, action	Kampagne, Aktion
ambulance	[ˈæmbjələns]	used for transporting sb to hospital	Rettungswagen
period (of time)	[ˈpɪəriəd]	length of time	Zeitabschnitt, Zeit, Phase
playground	[ˈpleɪgraʊnd]	play area	Spielplatz
lunch break	[ˈlʌntʃ breɪk]	time to have lunch	Mittagspause
caffeinated	[ˈkæfiːneɪtɪd]	with caffeine	koffeinhaltig
body	[ˈbɒdi]	a dead person's body	Leichnam
to **appear**	[əˈpɪə]	*n* appearance	scheinen
to **consume**	[kənˈsjuːm]	*n* consumption	zu sich nehmen, konsumieren

page 49

to **take one's seat**	[ˌteɪk wʌnz ˈsiːt]	to sit down	seinen Platz einnehmen
first aid	[ˌfɜːst ˈeɪd]	help you give sb who has had an accident	Erste Hilfe
heart attack	[ˈhɑːt ətæk]	*phr* to suffer from a heart attack	Herzinfarkt
space of time	[ˌspeɪs əf ˈtaɪm]	e.g. an hour, a day, etc.	Zeitspanne

condition	[kən'dɪʃn]	illness, sickness	(chronische) Krankheit, Leiden
system	['sɪstəm]	organism	Organismus
total	['təʊtl]	e.g. the total amount	Gesamt-, Gesamtmenge/-betrag
to cut down on sth	[ˌkʌt 'daʊn ɒn]	to have less of sth	etw reduzieren
to worry about sth	['wʌri əbaʊt]	adj worrying	sich um etw Sorgen machen
safety	['seɪfti]	adj safe	Sicherheit
as	[əz]	during, while	während
at the same time	[ət ðə seɪm 'taɪm]	simultaneously	gleichzeitig
to make sb aware of sth	[ˌmeɪk ə'weər əv]	to bring sth to sb's attention	jdm etw vor Augen führen
to put sb at risk	[ˌpʊt ət 'rɪsk]	to put sb in danger	jdn gefährden, jdn in Gefahr bringen
advice	[əd'vaɪs]	v to advise	Rat, Ratschlag
at once	[ət 'wʌns]	immediately	auf einmal

page 50

appointment	[ə'pɔɪntmənt]	e.g. an appointment with the doctor	Termin
course of treatment	[ˌkɔːs əf 'triːtmənt]	medicine/therapy	Therapie, Behandlung
(intravenous) drip	[ɪntrəˌviːnəs 'drɪp]	phr to be on a drip	Infusion
to express	[ɪk'spres]	n expression	ausdrücken, äußern
permission	[pə'mɪʃn]	e.g. My parents gave me permission to stay out late.	Erlaubnis
ability	[ə'bɪləti]	<> inability	Fähigkeit, Möglichkeit
obligation	[ˌɒblɪ'geɪʃn]	sth you must do	Verpflichtung
substitute	['sʌbstɪtjuːt]	replacement	Ersatz, Ersetzung
abuse	[ə'bjuːs]	e.g. alcohol abuse, drug abuse	Missbrauch
serious(ly)	['sɪəriəs]	e.g. Why are you laughing? Please take what I say seriously!	ernst, ernsthaft
statistics	[stə'tɪstɪks]	sets of figures recording results, events, etc.	Statistik(en)
to be heading for sth	[bi 'hedɪŋ fə]	to be on the way toward sth	auf dem (besten) Weg zu etw sein
addiction	[ə'dɪkʃn]	adj addictive	Sucht
to be at risk	[bi ət 'rɪsk]	to be in danger (of sth)	gefährdet sein
to be addicted to sth	[bi ə'dɪktɪd tə]	e.g. The rock star was addicted to drugs.	nach etw süchtig sein, von etw abhängig sein
prescription	[prɪ'skrɪpʃn]	a piece of paper the doctor gives you to get medicine	(ärztliches) Rezept; rezeptpflichtig
pain reliever	['peɪn rɪliːvə]	pain killer	Schmerzmittel
surgery	['sɜːdʒəri]	operation	Operation
to suffer sth	['sʌfə]	phr to suffer an injury	etw erleiden
injury	['ɪndʒəri]	v to injure	Verletzung

page 51

dependent (on sth)	[dɪ'pendənt]	<> independent	abhängig (von etw)
study	['stʌdi]	investigation, research	Untersuchung, Studie
(drug) misuser	[mɪs'juːzə]	sb who abuses drugs	(Drogen-)Konsument/in
to injure	['ɪndʒə]	n injury	verletzen
to prescribe sth	[prɪ'skraɪb]	e.g. The doctor prescribed some pills	etw verschreiben
to heal	[hiːl]	to make/get well again	heilen, abheilen
tablet	['tæblɪt]	pill	Tablette
to feed one's addiction	[ˌfiːd wʌnz ə'dɪkʃn]	e.g. He needed money to feed his alcohol addiction	sich Stoff besorgen
to be in pain	[bi ˌɪn 'peɪn]	to feel pain	Schmerzen haben
to drop out of school	[ˌdrɒp aʊt əf 'skuːl]	to leave school suddenly	die Schule abbrechen
to switch to sth	['swɪtʃ tə]	e.g. I don't enjoy volleyball any more. I'm going to switch to handball.	auf etw umsteigen
volunteer	[ˌvɒlən'tɪə]	adj voluntary	(freiwillige/r) Helfer/in
counselling service	[ˌkaʊnsəlɪŋ 'sɜːvɪs]	institution where you get professional advice	Beratungsdienst
addict	['ædɪkt]	sb who is addicted to sth	Süchtige/r
sadly	['sædli]	unfortunately	leider
in time	[ɪn 'taɪm]	at or before an agreed point in time	rechtzeitig
in the first place	[ɪn ðə 'fɜːst pleɪs]	to begin with	überhaupt, von vornherein
case	[keɪs]	e.g. There have been several cases of flu in our class this week.	Fall
to deal with sth	['diːl wɪð]	to overcome sth	etw angehen, etw bewältigen
painkiller	['peɪnkɪlə]	pain medication	Schmerzmittel
to state sth	[steɪt]	to say sth, to claim sth	etw erklären, etw sagen, etw feststellen
to warn sb of sth	[wɔːn]	n warning	jdn vor etw warnen
overview	['əʊvəvjuː]	summary	Überblick
incorrectly	[ˌɪnkə'rektli]	falsely	unsachgemäß, falsch
sb runs out of sth	[ˌrʌnz 'aʊt əv]	sb has none of sth left	jdm wird etw knapp
counselling	['kaʊnsəlɪŋ]	therapy	Therapie, Beratung
volunteer work	[vɒlən'tɪə 'wɜːk]	adj voluntary	ehrenamtliche Tätigkeit
to blame sb	[bleɪm]	to say sb is guilty	jdm die Schuld geben
sth is sb's fault	[ˌsʌmθɪŋ ɪz ˌsʌmbədiz 'fɔːlt]	sth was caused by sb	jd ist schuld an etw
medication	[ˌmedɪ'keɪʃn]	medicine	Arzneimittel

page 52

tough	[tʌf]	very difficult	hart
to **do exercise**	[duː ˈeksəsaɪz]	to do healthy physical activity	trainieren, sich fit halten
to **study**	[ˈstʌdi]	to spend time learning sth	lernen
method	[ˈmeθəd]	technique	Methode, Verfahren
medicine	[ˈmedsn]	adj medicinal	Medizin
mental health	[ˌmentl ˈhelθ]	condition of sb's mind	geistige Gesundheit
to **get into university**	[ˌget ɪntə juːnɪˈvɜːsəti]	e.g. I got into Cambridge University!	einen Studienplatz erhalten
score	[skɔː]	e.g. to get a good score in a test	Punktzahl, Ergebnis
to **set the course of sth**	[ˌset ðə ˈkɔːs əv]	to determine the future of sth	die Weichen für etw stellen
studies pl	[ˈstʌdiz]	e.g. I need to focus on my studies if I want to pass my exams.	Studium, hier: Schule
competition	[ˌkɒmpəˈtɪʃn]	rivalry	Konkurrenz
extracurricular	[ekstrəkəˈrɪkjʊlə]	outside school	außerschulisch
to **care about sth**	[ˈkeər əbaʊt]	e.g. You only care about your work!	sich (nur) für etw interessieren
grade	[greɪd]	result from a test or an exam	Note
to **waste**	[weɪst]	e.g. to waste money, time	verschwenden, vergeuden
physical	[ˈfɪzɪkl]	bodily	körperlich, physisch
well-being	[ˈwel biːɪŋ]	health, happiness, safety	Wohlbefinden
to **increase sth**	[ɪnˈkriːs]	to improve	etw steigern, etw erhöhen
isolation	[ˌaɪsəˈleɪʃn]	separation from others	Vereinsamung
acid	[ˈæsɪd]	e.g. hydrochloric acid	Säure
to **concentrate (on sth)**	[ˈkɒnsntreɪt]	n concentration	sich (auf etw) konzentrieren
to **focus (on sth)**	[ˈfəʊkəs]	n focus	sich (auf etw) konzentrieren
mark	[mɑːk]	e.g. to get good marks	Note
tutor	[ˈtjuːtə]	teacher outside of school	Nachhilfelehrer/in
honour	[ˈɒnə]	glory	Ehre
to **perform**	[pəˈfɔːm]	e.g. to perform well under pressure	(in einer Prüfung usw.) abschneiden
intense	[ɪnˈtens]	extreme, very strong	heftig, intensiv
psychological	[ˌsaɪkəˈlɒdʒɪkl]	related to the mind	psychologisch
support	[səˈpɔːt]	help, assistance	Hilfe, Unterstützung
to **struggle with sth**	[ˈstʌgl wɪð]	to have difficulty with sth	mit etw zu kämpfen haben
taboo	[təˈbuː]	e.g. Talking about sex ia a taboo in many cultures.	Tabu
to **commit sth**	[kəˈmɪt]	to do sth, to undertake sth	etw (Tat, Verbrechen usw.) begehen
suicide	[ˈsuːɪsaɪd]	killing yourself	Selbstmord
quantity	[ˈkwɒntəti]	amount	Menge
awake	[əˈweɪk]	not sleeping/asleep	wach
to **pass**	[pɑːs]	e.g. Do you think you've passed?	(Prüfung) bestehen
entire	[ɪnˈtaɪə]	whole	ganze/r/s, vollständig
on the other hand	[ɒn ði ˈʌðə hænd]	introducing a contrary aspect	andererseits, allerdings
privileged	[ˈprɪvəlɪdʒd]	advantaged	priviligiert
success	[səkˈses]	v to succeed	Erfolg

page 53

to **cheat**	[tʃiːt]	to break the rules in order to win	schummeln, abschreiben, spicken
otherwise	[ˈʌðəwaɪz]	e.g. Open the door, otherwise I can't get in.	sonst
to **remove sth**	[rɪˈmuːv]	to take sth/sb away	etw entfernen
to **cope with sth**	[ˈkəʊp wɪð]	to deal with sth, to tolerate sth	etw bewältigen
content	[ˈkɒntent]	v to contain	Inhalt

page 54

style	[staɪl]	adj stylish	Stil, Art
generalization	[ˌdʒenrəlaɪˈzeɪʃn]	statement about a group of people	Verallgemeinerung
to **avoid**	[əˈvɔɪd]	to try not to do sth	vermeiden, meiden
honest(ly)	[ˈɒnɪst]	truthful(ly)	ehrlich, aufrichtig
to **connect with sb**	[kəˈnekt wɪð]	n connection	sich mit jdm (intensiv) austauschen
humour	[ˈhjuːmə]	e.g. Sb with a sense of humour finds life amusing.	Humor
pleasant	[ˈpleznt]	nice, good	angenehm
polite	[pəˈlaɪt]	n politeness	höflich
to **apologize**	[əˈpɒlədʒaɪz]	to say sorry	sich entschuldigen
critical	[ˈkrɪtɪkl]	harsh, always pointing out problems	kritisch
to **get down to business**	[get ˌdaʊn tə ˈbɪznəs]	to start talking aboout the important topic	zur Sache kommen
rude	[ruːd]	very impolite	unverschämt, unhöflich
to **take sb/sth seriously**	[teɪk ˈsɪəriəsli]	e.g. What's he talking about? – Don't take him too seriously, darling.	jdn/etw ernst nehmen
to **soften**	[ˈsɒfn]	to weaken, to lessen	mildern, abschwächen
to **wonder**	[ˈwʌndə]	to question	sich fragen
to **mind**	[maɪnd]	not to be okay	etw dagegen haben

page 55

I'm afraid …	[aɪm əˈfreɪd]	e.g. I'm afraid I can't come tomorrow.	leider …
as if	[əz ˈɪf]	e.g. He ran as if dogs were chasing him.	als ob
slightly	[ˈslaɪtli]	a little	leicht, ein wenig
somewhat	[ˈsʌmwɒt]	to some degree, a little	etwas, irgendwie
to hand sth in	[ˌhænd ˈɪn]	e.g. You have three days left to hand in your work.	etw abgeben
to borrow sth	[ˈbɒrəʊ]	to take sth temporarily	sich etw ausleihen
vacancy	[ˈveɪkənsi]	free/empty room or position	(Hotel:) freies Zimmer
disappointed (in sb/sth)	[ˌdɪsəˈpɔɪntɪd]	n disappointment	enttäuscht (von jdm/etw)

page 56

to combat sth	[ˈkɒmbæt]	to fight sth and win	etw bekämpfen
notice board	[ˈnəʊtɪsbɔːd]	place for advertisements, information, etc.	Schwarzes Brett
aim	[eɪm]	goal, purpose	Ziel
library	[ˈlaɪbrəri]	place where you can borrow books for a short time	Bibliothek
to chill	[tʃɪl]	to relax, to do nothing	chillen, relaxen
pool table	[ˈpuːl teɪbl]	table to play billiards	Billardtisch
to reach	[riːtʃ]	phr to reach a decision	erreichen
consensus	[kənˈsensəs]	everyone has the same opinion	Übereinstimmung, Konsens
agreement	[əˈɡriːmənt]	v to agree	Übereinkunft, Übereinstimmung

UNIT 5

page 57

to swap	[swɒp]	to exchange	tauschen, austauschen

page 58

talk	[tɔːk]	speech, presentation	Vortrag
sustainability	[səˌsteɪnəˈbɪləti]	adj sustainable	Nachhaltigkeit
to skim	[skɪm]	to read something quickly	(Text) überfliegen
unsure	[ˌʌnˈʃʊə]	not certain	unsicher
clothing	[ˈkləʊðɪŋ]	what people wear	Kleidung, Bekleidung
manufacturer	[ˌmænjuˈfæktʃərə]	producer	Hersteller/in
to be committed to sth	[bi kəˈmɪtɪd tə]	to do things actively and in a serious and motivated way	sich für etw engagieren, sich zu etw verpflichten
waste	[weɪst]	rubbish	Müll, Abfall
long-lasting	[ˌlɒŋ ˈlaːstɪŋ]	to last	langlebig
glue	[ɡluː]	adhesive	Klebstoff
to last long	[ˌlaːst ˈlɒŋ]	<> to be short-lived	lang halten
bin	[bɪn]	box, basket, etc. for rubbish	Mülltonne, Mülleimer
trainers pl BE	[ˈtreɪnəz]	sneakers pl AE	Turnschuhe, Sportschuhe
regularly	[ˈreɡjələli]	often	regelmäßig
to commit to sth	[kəˈmɪt tə]	to promise to do sth	sich für etw engagieren
pollution	[pəˈluːʃn]	v to pollute	(Umwelt-)Verschmutzung
to purchase	[ˈpɜːtʃəs]	to buy	kaufen

page 59

to be done with sth	[bi ˌdʌn wɪð]	to have finished using sth	mit etw fertig sein
to end up somewhere	[ˌend ˈʌp]	to reach a final place or situation	irgendwo landen
landfill	[ˈlændfɪl]	place where rubbish is buried between layers of dirt	Mülldeponie
incinerator	[ɪnˈsɪnəreɪtə]	a plant for burning waste	Müllverbrennungsanlage
to pollute	[pəˈluːt]	to make sth dirty	verschmutzen
to join	[dʒɔɪn]	to become a part of	sich dazugesellen, dazukommen
garbage	[ˈɡaːbɪdʒ]	rubbish BE, trash AE	Müll, Abfall
to find one's way somewhere	[ˌfaɪnd wʌnz ˈweɪ]	to arrive somewhere by chance	wohin gelangen
debris	[ˈdebriː]	broken pieces of sth	Rückstände, (Trümmer-)Teile
percentage	[pəˈsentɪdʒ]	parts out of one hundred	Anteil, Prozentsatz
to wash up sth	[ˌwɒʃ ˈʌp]	e.g. The wood was washed up on the beach.	etw anspülen
coastline	[ˈkəʊstlaɪn]	coast, seashore	Küste
used plastic	[ˌjuːzd ˈplæstɪk]	old plastic	Altplastik
recently	[ˈriːsntli]	lately	in letzter Zeit, neulich
as usual	[əz ˈjuːʒuəl]	as normal	wie üblich
brand	[brænd]	e.g. a brand name	Marke
to lead the way	[ˌliːd ðə ˈweɪ]	to be the best	führend sein, wegweisend sein
commitment (to sth)	[kəˈmɪtmənt]	dedication (to sth)	Engagement (für etw)
accessory	[əkˈsesəri]	e.g. earrings, scarves, etc.	Accessoire
entirely	[ɪnˈtaɪəli]	totally	völlig, vollständig
to team up with sb	[ˌtiːm ˈʌp wɪð]	to work with sb	sich mit jdm zusammentun
to take sth off sb's hands	[teɪk sʌmθɪŋ ˌɒf sʌmbədiz ˈhændz]	to take over sth from sb	jdm etw abnehmen
to chop sth up	[ˌtʃɒp ˈʌp]	to cut sth into (small) pieces	etw zerkleinern, etw schreddern

to **melt sth down**	[ˌmelt ˈdaʊn]	to turn a solid into a liquid	etw einschmelzen
to **outperform sb**	[ˌaʊtpəˈfɔːm]	to do better than sb	jdn übertreffen
sportswear	[ˈspɔːtsweə]	clothes for sports	Sportbekleidung
wear	[weə]	damage from continued use	Abnutzung, Verschleiß
to **get all the wear out of sth**	[get ˌɔːl ðe ˈweər aʊt əv]	e.g. You really got all the wear out of those shoes. There are holes in them!	etw benutzen, bis es nicht mehr geht
to **grind sth**	[graɪnd]	to make sth into a powder	etw zermahlen
there's no/little point in doing sth	[ðeəz ˌnəʊ/ˌlɪtl ˈpɔɪnt ɪn duːɪŋ]	e.g. There's no point talking to him, he never listens.	es hat keinen/wenig Sinn, etw zu tun
to **participate (in sth)**	[pɑːˈtɪsɪpeɪt]	to take part (in sth)	(an etw) teilnehmen
to **save sb/sth from sth**	[ˈseɪv frəm]	to rescue sb/sth from sth	jdn/etw vor etw bewahren
worn out	[ˌwɔːn ˈaʊt]	with holes in it, overused	abgenutzt, (Schuhe:) ausgelatscht
definitely	[ˈdefɪnətli]	absolutely	(ganz) bestimmt, auf jeden Fall
to be honest, …	[tə bi ˈɒnɪst]	e.g. To be honest, I don't really want to go.	ehrlich gesagt …
comfortable(-ly)	[ˈkʌmftəbl]	n comfort	bequem, komfortabel

page 60

except for	[ɪkˈsept fə]	apart from	außer, abgesehen von
to **be littered with sth**	[bi ˈlɪtəd wɪð]	e.g. The street was littered with beer cans.	mit etw übersät sein
seagull	[ˈsiːgʌl]	e.g. That seagull stole my sandwich!	Möwe
to **pick sth up**	[ˌpɪk ˈʌp]	e.g. to pick up litter	etw aufheben
mess	[mes]	rubbish, disorder, chaos	Chaos, Sauerei
team leader	[ˈtiːm liːdə]	sb who organizes the work of a team	Teamleiter/in
truck	[trʌk]	lorry	Lastwagen
pile	[paɪl]	e.g. a big pile of rubbish	Stapel, Haufen
driver	[ˈdraɪvə]	sb who makes music	Fahrer/in
to **put in sth**	[ˌpʊt ˈɪn]	e.g. We put lots of time and energy into this project.	etw (Zeit, Energie usw.) investieren
stuff	[stʌf]	things	Sachen, Zeug
meaning	[ˈmiːnɪŋ]	v to mean	Bedeutung
author	[ˈɔːθə]	sb who writes a book, article, etc.	Verfasser/in, Autor/in
to **dump**	[dʌmp]	to dispose of waste illegally	(Müll) (wild) abkippen
to **cooperate**	[kəʊˈɒpəreɪt]	to work with sb/sth	zusammenarbeiten
deal	[diːl]	agreement, business transaction	Geschäft, Abkommen
to **intend to do sth**	[ɪnˈtend tə duː]	n intention	die Absicht haben, etw zu tun; vorhaben, etw zu tun
to **give sth away**	[ˌgɪv əˈweɪ]	to gift sth to sb	etw verschenken

page 61

billion	[ˈbɪliən]	one thousand million	Milliarde
to **spend**	[spend]	e.g. to spend a lot of money	(Geld) ausgeben
ton	[tʌn]	1,000 kg	Tonne
goods pl	[gʊdz]	items manufactured and traded	Güter, Waren
to **close sth down**	[ˌkləʊz ˈdaʊn]	to shut sth down	etw schließen, etw zumachen
flow chart	[ˈfləʊ tʃɑːt]	e.g. She had to made a flow chart for her homework.	Flussdiagramm
once	[wʌns]	as soon as	sobald
contents	[ˈkɒntents]	e.g. On page three you find the table of contents.	Inhalt
to **dispose of sth**	[dɪˈspəʊz əv]	to get rid of sth, to throw sth away	etw entsorgen, sich einer Sache entledigen
plant	[plɑːnt]	factory	Werk, Fabrik
▪ to **contain**	[kənˈteɪn]	e.g. Wine contains alcohol.	enthalten

page 62

feeling	[ˈfiːlɪŋ]	opinion, view, impression	Gefühl, Ansicht, Meinung
purchase	[ˈpɜːtʃəs]	act of buying, things bought	Kauf, Einkauf
▪ to **afford sth**	[əˈfɔːd]	to be able to buy sth	sich etw leisten

page 63

saying	[ˈseɪɪŋ]	a short expression that offers advice or wisdom	Sprichwort
fool	[fuːl]	idiot, joker	Narr
to **part**	[pɑːt]	to break, to separate	auseinandergehen, (sich) trennen
▪ to **correspond to sth**	[ˌkɒrɪˈspɒnd tə]	to match sth	einer Sache entsprechen
luxury	[ˈlʌkʃəri]	things that are unnecessary but enjoyable	Luxus
catalogue	[ˈkætəlɒg]	a book with a list of products you can buy	Katalog
technological	[ˌteknəˈlɒdʒɪkl]	n technology	technologisch, technisch
piece of equipment	[ˌpiːs əv ɪˈkwɪpmənt]	a device, part of a machine	Gerät
to **get by with sth**	[ˌget ˈbaɪ wɪð]	e.g. I get by with the little money I earn.	mit etw auskommen
to **break down**	[ˌbreɪk ˈdaʊn]	to stop working	kaputtgehen
to **admit**	[ədˈmɪt]	e.g He admitted the truth in the end.	zugeben, eingestehen
a ton of	[ə ˈtʌn əv]	a lot of	jede Menge
to **earn**	[ɜːn]	to get money for doing work	verdienen
to **save**	[seɪv]	<> to spend (money)	(Geld usw.) sparen
store	[stɔː]	shop	Laden, Geschäft
to **fall in love with sb/sth**	[ˌfɔːl ɪn ˈlʌv wɪð]	e.g. I can't help falling in love with you!	sich in jdn/etw verlieben

unlikely	[ʌnˈlaɪkli]	e.g. It is unlikely to snow in summer.	unwahrscheinlich
dust	[dʌst]	*adj* dusty	Staub
to change one's mind	[ˌtʃeɪndʒ wʌnz ˈmaɪnd]	e.g. I liked it at first, but then changed my mind.	seine Meinung ändern

page 64

to drop	[drɒp]	to die exhausted	(tot) umfallen
printer	[ˈprɪntə]	*v* to print	Drucker
jacket	[ˈdʒækɪt]	light coat	Jacke, Jackett
to own	[əʊn]	to have sth which is yours	besitzen
waste of time	[ˌweɪst əf ˈtaɪm]	e.g. Watching that film was a waste of time.	Zeitverschwendung

page 65

to contain	[kənˈteɪn]	e.g. Wine contains alcohol.	enthalten
savings *pl*	[ˈseɪvɪŋz]	money that is saved rather than spent	Ersparnisse
to go bankrupt	[gəʊ ˈbæŋkrʌpt]	to be unable to pay debts	Pleite gehen, in Konkurs gehen
zip	[zɪp]	e.g. You can close the bag using the zip.	Reißverschluss
department	[dɪˈpɑːtmənt]	part of a business	Abteilung
contract	[ˈkɒntrækt]	(written) agreement	Vertrag
to win a contract	[ˌwɪn ə ˈkɒntrækt]	to get a client to agree to work with you	einen Auftrag erhalten, den Zuschlag erhalten
industry	[ˈɪndəstri]	e.g. I work in the fashion industry.	Branche
to ponder sth	[ˈpɒndə]	to think about sth	über etw nachdenken, etw erwägen
despite	[dɪˈspaɪt]	e.g. Despite the many problems, the project was a big success!	trotz
sacred	[ˈseɪkrɪd]	holy, from God	heilig
to be at a crossroads	[bi ət ə ˈkrɒsrəʊdz]	e.g. I'm at a crossroads in my life.	an einem Scheideweg stehen, an einem Wendepunkt stehen
convenient	[kənˈviːniənt]	easy, practical	praktisch, bequem
to run errands	[ˌrʌn ˈerəndz]	e.g. I need to run some errands for my dad.	Besorgungen machen
to go for walks	[ˌgəʊ fə ˈwɔːks]	e.g. I like to go for long walks.	spazieren gehen
besides	[bɪˈsaɪdz]	apart from that	außerdem
attempt	[əˈtempt]	*v* to attempt	Versuch
to raise awareness	[ˌreɪz əˈweənəs]	to make people aware of sth	Bewusstsein schaffen
impact	[ˈɪmpækt]	influence	Auswirkung(en), Einfluss
behaviour	[bɪˈheɪvjə]	*v* to behave	Verhalten

page 66

grocery store	[ˈgrəʊsəri stɔː]	food shop	Lebensmittelladen
drive	[draɪv]	journey by car	Fahrt *(mit dem Auto)*
to be situated	[bi ˈsɪtʃueɪtɪd]	to be located	liegen
chain	[tʃeɪn]	e.g. Most people by their food from supermarket chains.	Kette
to enter	[ˈentə]	to go inside	betreten
to remind sb that ...	[rɪˈmaɪnd ðət]	e.g. Please remind me later that I need to buy milk.	jdn daran erinnern, dass ...
groceries *pl*	[ˈgrəʊsəriːz]	food and supplies	Lebensmittel
impressed	[ɪmˈprest]	*v* to impress	beeindruckt
to stretch	[stretʃ]	to reach, to cover	sich erstrecken
to stock a shelf	[ˌstɒk ə ˈʃelf]	to fill a shelf with products	eine Regal befüllen
household items *pl*	[ˈhaʊshəʊld aɪtəmz]	things for your home	Haushaltsartikel
towel	[ˈtaʊəl]	used to dry your body/hands/face after washing	Handtuch
sheet	[ʃiːt]	bedsheet	Bettlaken
trolley	[ˈtrɒli]	shopping cart *AE*	Einkaufswagen
aisle	[aɪl]	walkway	Gang
sweater	[ˈswetə]	jumper *BE*	Pullover
cash desk	[ˈkæʃ desk]	place in a shop where you pay	Kasse
chatty	[ˈtʃæti]	always happy to chat	geschwätzig
to pass sth down to sb	[ˌpɑːs ˈdaʊn tə]	to pass sth along to sb	etw an jdn weiterreichen
to bag sth	[bæg]	to put sth in a bag	etw einpacken, etw eintüten
surprised	[səˈpraɪzd]	shocked, amazed	überrascht, erstaunt
to tip sb	[tɪp]	to give sb a tip	jdm ein Trinkgeld geben
tax	[tæks]	money that must be paid to the state	Steuer
sales tax *AE*	[ˈseɪlz tæks]	Value Added Tax (VAT) *BE*	Mehrwertsteuer

page 67

to shadow sb	[ˈʃædəʊ]	to follow sb around and learn from them	mit jdm *(zur Einarbeitung)* mitlaufen
to ruin	[ˈruːɪn]	to destroy	ruinieren
selection	[sɪˈlekʃn]	range, choice	Auswahl, Angebot
to be of assistance to sb	[ˌbi əv əˈsɪstəns tə]	to help sb	jdm behilflich sein
to be lucky	[bi ˈlʌki]	to have good fortune	Glück haben
basket	[ˈbɑːskɪt]	e.g. a shopping basket	Korb
to free up sth	[ˌfriː ˈʌp]	to make sth available to use	etw freimachen, etw entlasten
miserable	[ˈmɪzrəbl]	e.g. The weather was really miserable – it was raining for days on end!	*(Wetter:)* mies, grässlich

page 68

arrangements *pl*	[əˈreɪndʒmənts]	preparations	Vorbereitungen
mirror	[ˈmɪrə]	e.g. Look at yourself in the mirror.	Spiegel
condition	[kənˈdɪʃn]	*phr* in good/bad condition	Zustand
left over	[left ˈəʊvə]	sth not used	übrig (geblieben)
to **announce**	[əˈnaʊns]	to tell people about sth (officially)	ankündigen
factor	[ˈfæktə]	sth to think about	Faktor
changing room	[ˈtʃeɪndʒɪŋ ruːm]	place to try on clothes in a shop	Umkleidekabine
to **try sth on**	[ˌtraɪ ˈɒn]	to put on clothes to see if you like them	etw anprobieren

UNIT 6

page 69

screen	[skriːn]	display of an electronic device	Bildschirm
text (message)	[tekst]	short message sent on a mobile phone	SMS
voice call	[ˈvɔɪs kɔːl]	speaking to sb on the phone	Sprachanruf
figure	[ˈfɪgəz]	number	Zahl

page 70

leisure	[ˈleʒə]	free time	Freizeit
to **consider sth**	[kənˈsɪdə]	to think about sth	etw in Betracht/Erwägung ziehen
tune	[tjuːn]	song	Lied, Song
to **warn**	[wɔːn]	*n* warning	(auf etw) hinweisen, warnen
interviewee	[ˌɪntəvjuˈiː]	<> interviewer	*Person, die interviewt wird*

page 71

contributor	[kənˈtrɪbjuːtə]	author of a magazine article	Autor/in (eines Magazins)
to **make a living from sth**	[ˌmeɪk ə ˈlɪvɪŋ frəm]	to earn money doing sth	seinen Lebensunterhalt mit etw verdienen
host	[həʊst]	e.g. a TV show host	Moderator/in (einer Sendung usw.)
to **broadcast**	[ˈbrɔːdkɑːst]	*n* broadcasting	senden, verbreiten, ausstrahlen
subscriber	[səbˈskraɪbə]	sb who pays to receive a regular service	Abonnent/in
virtual	[ˈvɜːtʃuəl]	<> real	virtuell
to **convert**	[kənˈvɜːt]	to change	umwandeln
circus skills *pl*	[ˈsɜːkəs skɪlz]	e.g. He learnt his circus skills from a famous clown.	Zirkuskünste, Akrobatik
musician	[mjuːˈzɪʃn]	sb who makes music	Musiker/in
relaxed	[rɪˈlækst]	<> stressed	locker, entspannt
to **request sth**	[rɪˈkwest]	to ask for sth	um etw bitten, sich etw wünschen
publicity	[pʌbˈlɪsəti]	public attention	öffentliche Aufmerksamkeit, Werbung
to **release**	[rɪˈliːs]	to bring out	veröffentlichen
soap opera	[ˈsəʊp ɒprə]	*informal* soap	Seifenoper
identity theft	[aɪˈdentəti θeft]	to steal sb's details	Identitätsdiebstahl

page 72

sb realizes sth	[ˈrɪəlaɪzɪz]	e.g. I realized that he was talking to me.	jdm wird/ist etw bewusst
income	[ˈɪnkʌm]	money you get from work	Einkommen
to **advertise**	[ˈædvətaɪz]	*n* advertisement	werben, Werbung machen
safe(ly)	[seɪf]	<> dangerous(ly)	sicher, unbedenklich, ungefährlich
intimate	[ˈɪntɪmət]	very personal	intim

page 73

to **run sth**	[rʌn]	to manage sth, to operate sth	etw betreiben, etw führen
disadvantage	[ˌdɪsədˈvɑːntɪdʒ]	<> advantage	Nachteil
secure	[sɪˈkjʊə]	e.g. This internet connection is not secure.	sicher
effective	[ɪˈfektɪv]	e.g. Your system isn't effective – it doesn't work!	effektiv, wirkungsvoll

page 74

to **seek**	[siːk]	to look for sth	suchen
practice	[ˈpræktɪs]	*phr* to put sth into practice	Praxis
unhappiness	[ʌnˈhæpinəs]	sadness	Elend, Traurigkeit, Unglücklichsein
sympathetic	[ˌsɪmpəˈθetɪk]	being understanding of others' feelings	mitfühlend, verständnisvoll
response	[rɪˈspɒns]	answer, reaction	Reaktion, Antwort
growing	[ˈgrəʊɪŋ]	increasing	zunehmend, steigend
exaggerated	[ɪgˈzædʒəreɪtɪd]	e.g. You're the very best! – That's exaggerated, I'm not that good.	übertrieben
claim	[kleɪm]	stating sth as a fact	Behauptung
emotional	[ɪˈməʊʃənl]	related to sb's emotions	emotional
sympathy	[ˈsɪmpəθi]	understanding of others' feelings	Mitgefühl, Verständnis, Mitleid
attention-seeking	[əˈtenʃn siːkɪŋ]	wanting attention from others	Aufmerksamkeitsbedürfnis
term	[tɜːm]	specific name for something	Begriff
to **grow out of sth**	[ˈgrəʊ aʊt əv]	to come from sth, to originate in sth	aus etw entstehen
criticism	[ˈkrɪtɪsɪzəm]	*v* to criticize	Kritik
skin	[skɪn]	e.g. The doctors took skin from his foot.	Haut

up to a point	[ˌʌp tu ə ˈpɔɪnt]	to a certain degree	bis zu einem gewissen Grad
to **turn sth into sth**	[ˈtɜːn ɪntə]	to make sth into sth	etw aus etw machen
increasing(ly)	[ɪnˈkriːsɪŋ]	getting more and more	zunehmend
ordinary	[ˈɔːdnri]	normal	gewöhnlich, normal
unfair	[ˌʌnˈfeə]	unjust	ungerecht, unfair
to **accuse sb of sth**	[əˈkjuːz əv]	to make an accusation	jdm etw vorwerfen
to **experience sth**	[ɪkˈspɪəriəns]	*n* experience	etw erleben, etw erfahren
depression	[dɪˈpreʃn]	*adj* depressed	Depression(en)
easy-going	[ˌiːzi ˈɡəʊɪŋ]	relaxed, uncomplicated	gelassen, unkompliziert
sb is embarrassed by sth	[ɪz ɪmˈbærəst baɪ]	*n* embarrassment	jdm ist etw peinlich
to **cover sth up**	[ˌkʌvər ˈʌp]	to hide sth	etw überspielen, etw verbergen
to **open up**	[ˌəʊpən ˈʌp]	e.g. to open up about your feelings	sich öffnen
at first	[ət ˈfɜːst]	to begin with, at the start	zunächst
disappointing	[ˌdɪsəˈpɔɪntɪŋ]	*n* disappointment	enttäuschend
take (on sth)	[teɪk]	opinion, view, perspective	Sicht (auf etw), Meinung (zu etw)
abuse	[əˈbjuːs]	insult, violence, harm	Beschimpfung(en)
to **deal with sth**	[ˈdiːl wɪð]	to handle sth	mit etw zurechtkommen
to **advise sb to do sth**	[ədˈvaɪz]	to recommend that sb does sth	jdm empfehlen, etw zu tun
to **respond to sth**	[rɪˈspɒnd tə]	to react to sth	auf etw reagieren
to **jump to conclusions**	[dʒʌmp tə kənˈkluːʒnz]	to come to an opinion too quickly	voreilige Schlüsse ziehen
concerned	[kənˈsɜːnd]	worried	besorgt, beunruhigt
face-to-face	[ˌfeɪs tə ˈfeɪs]	in person	persönlich, unter vier Augen
to **assume**	[əˈsjuːm]	to believe, to think	davon ausgehen, annehmen
to **draw attention to sth**	[ˌdrɔː əˈtenʃn tə]	to highlight sth	Aufmerksamkeit auf etw lenken
outward	[ˈaʊtwəd]	on the outside	äußere/r/s
inward	[ˈɪnwəd]	on the inside	innere/r/s
self	[self]	e.g. my true self	Selbst

page 75

supportive	[səˈpɔːtɪv]	*n* support	hilfsbereit, unterstützend
to **remain**	[rɪˈmeɪn]	to stay	bleiben
anonymous(ly)	[əˈnɒnɪməs]	not identified by name	anonym
to **appreciate**	[əˈpriːʃieɪt]	to admire, to value	schätzen, zu schätzen wissen

page 76

critic	[ˈkrɪtɪk]	sb voicing criticism	Kritiker/in
to **imagine sth**	[ɪˈmædʒɪn]	*adj* imaginary	sich etw vorstellen
to **disappear**	[ˌdɪsəˈpɪə]	e.g. I tried to find the man again, but he had disappeared.	verschwinden
aspect	[ˈæspekt]	side	Gesichtspunkt, Aspekt
to **encourage sth**	[ɪnˈkʌrɪdʒ]	*n* encouragement	etw begünstigen, etw fördern
thinking	[ˈθɪŋkɪŋ]	the way sb thinks	Denkweise, Denken
to **display sth**	[dɪˈspleɪ]	to show sth	etw zur Schau stellen
writer	[ˈraɪtə]	*v* to write	Schriftsteller/in
to **upload**	[ˌʌpˈləʊd]	<> to download	hochladen
encouragement	[ɪnˈkʌrɪdʒmənt]	*v* to encourage	Ermutigung, Zuspruch
instant	[ˈɪnstənt]	immediate	sofortig, unmittelbar
creative	[kriˈeɪtɪv]	*v* to create	schöpferisch, kreativ
approach	[əˈprəʊtʃ]	way of doing sth	Herangehensweise, Ansatz
valuable	[ˈvæljuəbl]	worth a lot of money, very important	wertvoll
to **expand sth**	[ɪkˈspænd]	to make sth larger	etw erweitern, etw ausweiten
worldview	[ˈwɜːldvjuː]	the way sb sees the world	Weltsicht, Weltbild
bubble	[ˈbʌbl]	e.g. He lives in his own little bubble.	Blase
background	[ˈbækɡraʊnd]	origin	Herkunft, Milieu, Hintergrund
to **come up with sth**	[ˌkʌm ˈʌp wɪð]	to think of sth	sich etw ausdenken

page 77

bar chart	[ˈbɑː tʃɑːt]	type of graph with columns	Säulendiagramm
survey	[ˈsɜːveɪ]	researching public opinion by a series of questions	Umfrage
inspiration	[ˌɪnspəˈreɪʃn]	sth that gives sb an idea	Anregung(en), Inspiration
to **feel left out**	[fiːl ˌleft ˈaʊt]	to not feel included in sth	sich übergangen/ausgeschlossen fühlen
depressive	[dɪˈpresɪv]	related to depression	depressiv
symptom	[ˈsɪmptəm]	sign of an illness	Symptom, Anzeichen
moderate	[ˈmɒdərət]	average, medium	gemäßigt, leicht
severe	[sɪˈvɪə]	serious, strong	schwer, ernst
trust	[trʌst]	foundation	Stiftung
adult	[ˈædʌlt]	<> child	Erwachsene/r
to **concern sb/sth**	[kənˈsɜːn]	to affect sb	jdn/etw betreffen
to **identify**	[aɪˈdentɪfaɪ]	to recognize, to determine	ermitteln, bestimmen
depressed	[dɪˈprest]	suffering from depression	niedergeschlagen, deprimiert
to **consider sth sth**	[kənˈsɪdə]	to think sth is sth	etw für etw halten
in conclusion	[ɪn kənˈkluːʒn]	To conclude, …	abschließend
to **cause sb to do sth**	[kɔːz]	to prompt sb to do sth	jdn dazu veranlassen, etw zu tun

placemat	[ˈpleɪsmæt]	a small mat	Tischset
sheet (of paper)	[ʃiːt]	piece of paper	Blatt (Papier)
to redesign	[ˌriːdɪˈzaɪn]	to reorganize, to rethink	umgestalten, neu konzipieren
individual	[ˌɪndɪˈvɪdʒuəl]	single	einzeln, individuell
corner	[ˈkɔːnə]	e.g. There is a bird in the corner of the photo.	Ecke
solution	[səˈluːʃn]	answer	Lösung

page 78

gender	[ˈdʒendə]	e.g. male, female, diverse	Geschlecht
manner	[ˈmænə]	way	Art, Weise
misunderstanding	[ˌmɪsʌndəˈstændɪŋ]	failure to understand correctly	Missverständnis
to address sb	[əˈdres]	to talk to sb, to name sb	jdn anreden
measurement	[ˈmeʒəmənt]	v to measure	Maß
comma	[ˈkɒmə]	e.g. Items in a list are separated by a comma.	Komma
decimal point	[ˌdesɪml ˈpɔɪnt]	e.g. 3.14 has two numbers after the decimal point.	Dezimalpunkt

page 79

salutation	[ˌsæljuˈteɪʃn]	greeting in a letter	(Brief:) Anrede
to feel comfortable	[ˌfiːl ˈkʌmftəbl]	to feel good, to be at ease	sich wohlfühlen
explanation	[ˌekspləˈneɪʃn]	v to explain	Erklärung, Erläuterung
apology	[əˈpɒlədʒi]	v to apologize	Entschuldigung
request (for sth)	[rɪˈkwest]	v to request sth	Bitte (um etw)
sign-off	[ˈsaɪn ɒf]	end of a letter, phone call etc	(Brief, Telefonat usw.:) Schluss, Verabschiedung
in advance	[ɪn ədˈvɑːns]	beforehand, ahead of time	im Voraus
order	[ˈɔːdə]	e.g Your order no. 275814 has been delivered to your home.	Bestellung, Auftrag
head of sales	[ˌhed əf ˈseɪlz]	sales director	Verkaufsleiter/in
sales figures pl	[ˈseɪlz fɪɡəz]	turnover	Verkaufszahlen, Umsatzzahlen
sb is missing sth	[ɪz ˈmɪsɪŋ]	sb is lacking sth, sb doesn't have sth	jdm fehlt etw

page 80

to design	[dɪˈzaɪn]	to create, to construct	gestalten, entwerfern
questionnaire	[ˌkwestʃəˈneə]	list of questions for a survey	Fragebogen
to gather sth	[ˈɡæðə]	to collect sth	etw sammeln, etw zusammentragen
device	[dɪˈvaɪs]	machine, electronic gadget	(elektronisches) Gerät
graph	[ɡrɑːf]	diagram showing figures	Diagramm, Grafik
pie chart	[ˈpaɪ tʃɑːt]	type of graph in the shape of a circle	Tortendiagramm
finding	[ˈfaɪndɪŋ]	result	Ergebnis

UNIT 7

page 81

to unite	[juːˈnaɪt]	to join together	sich vereinigen
to form	[fɔːm]	to build, to shape	bilden
attraction	[əˈtrækʃn]	famous building or place that many people visit	Sehenswürdigkeit
castle	[ˈkɑːsl]	where kings and queens live	Burg, Schloss

page 82

accommodation	[əˌkɒməˈdeɪʃn]	place to stay	Unterkunft
to summarize	[ˈsʌməraɪz]	to sum up	zusammenfassen
bed and breakfast	[ˌbed ən ˈbrekfəst]	a place to stay (often a family home) that offers breakfast	Frühstückspension, Übernachtung mit Frühstück
camper van	[ˈkæmpə væn]	motor home	Wohnmobil
caravan	[ˈkærəvæn]	mobile home	Wohnwagen
resort	[rɪˈzɔːt]	e.g. holiday resort	Ferienort
tent	[tent]	e.g. When we go camping we sleep in a tent.	Zelt
to show sb around	[ˌʃəʊ əˈraʊnd]	to give sb a tour	jdn herumführen
adventure	[ədˈventʃə]	exciting experience or journey	Abenteuer
to get to know sb	[ɡet tə ˈnəʊ]	to learn about sb new in your life	jdn kennenlernen

page 83

(travel) guide	[ɡaɪd]	a book with information about a place for tourists	Reiseführer
traveller	[ˈtrævələ]	sb who goes on a trip or journey	Reisende/r
independent	[ˌɪndɪˈpendənt]	<> dependent	unabhängig
stay	[steɪ]	time spent somewhere	Aufenthalt
base	[beɪs]	starting point	Ausgangspunkt, Basis
landscape	[ˈlændskeɪp]	scenery	Landschaft
booking	[ˈbʊkɪŋ]	reservation	Reservierung, Buchung
countryside	[ˈkʌntrisaɪd]	area outside of the city with large fields	Land, Landschaft
seaside	[ˈsiːsaɪd]	coast (beside the sea)	Küste
horrible	[ˈhɒrəbl]	awful	schrecklich
dormitory	[ˈdɔːmɪtri]	a large room (often in a hostel) where many people can sleep	Schlafsaal

to explore	[ɪkˈsplɔː]	to investigate	erkunden
to camp	[kæmp]	to live outdoors	kampieren
to be well/better off	[bi ˌwel/ˌbetər ˈɒf]	to be in a beter position	gut/besser dran sein
campsite	[ˈkæmpsaɪt]	a place where sb goes camping	Campingplatz
to cause trouble	[kɔːz ˈtrʌbl]	to cause problems	Ärger machen
sociable	[ˈsəʊʃəbl]	friendly, likes people	gesellig, umgänglich
highly	[ˈhaɪli]	very	sehr
National Trust	[ˌnæʃnl ˈtrʌst]	an organization that aims to protect monuments and nature	brit. Organisation für Denkmalpflege und Naturschutz
working holiday	[ˌwɜːkɪŋ ˈhɒlədeɪ]	holiday internship	Ferienpraktikum, Arbeitsurlaub
to plant	[plɑːnt]	to put seeds in the ground	pflanzen
to repair	[rɪˈpeə]	to fix	reparieren
footpath	[ˈfʊtpɑːθ]	a path for people to walk on (often beside a road)	(Wander-)Weg, Pfad
hospitality	[ˌhɒspɪˈtæləti]	treating guests in a friendly way	Bewirtung, Gastfreundschaft
hospitality exchange	[ˌhɒspɪˈtæləti ɪksˈtʃeɪndʒ]	home stay	Aufenthalt bei einer Gastfamilie
rent	[rent]	e.g. The rent in London has risen a lot.	Miete
host	[həʊst]	<> guest	Gastgeber/in
to rent	[rent]	to pay money every month to live somewhere	mieten
flat BE	[flæt]	AE: apartment	Wohnung
comforts pl	[ˈkʌmfəts]	luxuries	Annehmlichkeiten
expense	[ɪkˈspens]	costs	Kosten, Ausgabe(n), Aufwendung(en)

page 85

consequence	[ˈkɒnsɪkwəns]	result	Konsequenz, Folge
opposite	[ˈɒpəzɪt]	<> the same	gegenteilig, entgegengesetzt
inconvenient	[ˌɪnkənˈviːniənt]	difficult (to reach)	ungünstig gelegen, unpraktisch
ugly	[ˈʌgli]	<> pretty	hässlich
uncomfortable	[ʌnˈkʌmftəbl]	<> comfortable	unbequem, unkomfortabel
enjoyable	[ɪnˈdʒɔɪəbl]	fun, pleasant	angenehm, erfreulich
unfriendly	[ʌnˈfrendli]	<> friendly	unfreundlich
review	[rɪˈvjuː]	a critical article or report (about food, hotels, etc.)	Rezension, Kritik
to rewrite	[ˌriːˈraɪt]	to write again in a different way	umformulieren, neu schreiben
star	[stɑː]	e.g. We stayed in a 3-star hotel.	Stern
flatmate	[ˈflætmeɪt]	sb with whom sb lives with in a flat	Mitbewohner/in
convenient	[kənˈviːniənt]	<> inconvenient	günstig gelegen
location	[ləʊˈkeɪʃn]	place, situation	Standort, Lage
bus route	[ˈbʌs ruːt]	bus line	Buslinie
surroundings pl	[səˈraʊndɪŋz]	the area around a place	Umgebung
rating	[ˈreɪtɪŋ]	evaluation	Bewertung

page 86

as soon as	[əz ˈsuːn əz]	e.g. Call me as soon as you get home.	sobald
by the time	[baɪ ðə ˈtaɪm]	e.g. By the time we arrived, the show had already begun.	wenn, als
since	[sɪns]	because	weil
soaking wet	[ˌsəʊkɪŋ ˈwet]	dripping wet, full of water	klatschnass
to lock	[lɒk]	to secure, to close sth so that others can't open it	verschließen, abschließen
hike	[haɪk]	v to go on a hike	Wanderung
to regret	[rɪˈgret]	to feel sad about sth that happened or that you did	bedauern, bereuen
to hitchhike	[ˈhɪtʃhaɪk]	to hitch a ride	per Anhalter fahren/reisen
to shine	[ʃaɪn]	to glow	scheinen
recommendation	[ˌrekəmenˈdeɪʃn]	v to recommend	Empfehlung
to be in charge of sth	[bi ɪn ˈtʃɑːdʒ əv]	to be responsible for sth	für etw zuständig sein
firstly	[ˈfɜːstli]	There are three reasons for this: firstly, …	erstens

page 87

voicemail	[ˈvɔɪsmeɪl]	e.g. He left me a voicemail message yesterday.	Mailbox
illusion	[ɪˈluːʒn]	sth that is not what it seems	Täuschung, Illusion
to hop on/off	[ˌhɒp ˈɒn/ˈɒf]	to jump on/off	ein-/aussteigen
old town	[ˈəʊld taʊn]	historic district	Altstadt
murder	[ˈmɜːdə]	v to murder	Mord
mystery	[ˈmɪstri]	His death remains a mystery.	Rätsel, Geheimnis
puzzle	[ˈpʌzl]	a game with problems to be solved	Rätsel
to spare sth	[speə]	phr to have time to spare	etw übrig haben
entertaining	[ˌentəˈteɪnɪŋ]	enjoyable, amusing	unterhaltsam
scary	[ˈskeəri]	frightening	gruselig, unheimlich
steep	[stiːp]	e.g. Castles were often built on top of really steep hills.	steil
hill	[hɪl]	e.g. She ran down the hill.	Hügel, Berg
monarch	[ˈmɒnək]	ruler of a country, e.g. king or queen	Herrscher/in, Monarch/in
surrounded	[səˈraʊndɪd]	e.g. The village is surrounded by trees.	umgeben
view	[vjuː]	sight	Aussicht, Ausblick
informative	[ɪnˈfɔːmətɪv]	educational, explanatory	aufschlussreich, informativ
colourful	[ˈkʌləfl]	e.g. This picture is very colourful.	bunt, farbenfroh

Chronological word list

page 88

sight	[saɪt]	place of interest that tourists visit	Sehenswürdigkeit
to **suppose**	[sə'pəʊz]	to think	annehmen, glauben
lunchtime	['lʌntʃtaɪm]	a time in the middle of the day when lunch is eaten	Mittag
to **let sb know**	[ˌlet 'nəʊ]	to inform sb	jdm Bescheid sagen
staff	[stɑːf]	the people who work in a company	Personal
out and about	[ˌaʊt ənd ə'baʊt]	on the road, on your way someplace	unterwegs
I can't wait!	[aɪ ˌkɑːnt 'weɪt]	I'm looking forward to it!	Ich kann es kaum erwarten!
to **pick up the phone**	[ˌpɪk ˌʌp ðə fəʊn]	to answer a call	ans Telefon gehen
beforehand	[bɪ'fɔːhænd]	earlier	vorher
to **climb**	[klaɪm]	e.g. to climb a mountain	steigen, klettern
entrance	['entrəns]	<> exit	Eintritt, Einlass
line *AE*	[laɪn]	queue *BE*	Warteschlange
to **hurt**	[hɜːt]	to be painful	wehtun, schmerzen, verletzen
to **turn bad**	[ˌtɜːn 'bæd]	to get worse, to deteriorate	sich verschlechtern, (*Wetter:*) umschlagen
to **work sth out**	[ˌwɜːk 'aʊt]	to find sth out, to calculate sth	etw herausfinden
limit	['lɪmɪt]	e.g. age limit	Beschränkung
guided tour	[ˌgaɪdɪd 'tʊə]	e.g. The guided tour in the History Museum is fantastic.	Führung
while	[waɪl]	e.g. While I was in Paris, I visited the museums.	Weile
to **catch the train**	[ˌkætʃ ðə 'treɪn]	e.g. He caught the train just in time!	den Zug erwischen
queue *BE*	[kjuː]	people lining up to wait	Warteschlange
relieved	[rɪ'liːvd]	glad, no longer worried	erleichtert

page 89

to **celebrate**	['selɪbreɪt]	*n* celebration	feiern
graduation	[ˌgrædʒu'eɪʃn]	the end of your time at school	Abschluss, Schulabschluss
to **select**	[sɪ'lekt]	*n* selection	auswählen
correspondence	[ˌkɒrɪ'spɒndəns]	exchange of letters or emails between two people	Briefwechsel, Korrespondenz
length of stay	[ˌleŋθ əf 'steɪ]	number of days/nights spent somewhere	Aufenthaltsdauer
to **reserve**	[rɪ'zɜːv]	to keep aside, to save	reservieren
to **enquire about sth**	[ɪn'kwaɪər əbaʊt]	to ask for information about sth	sich nach etw erkundigen
method of payment	[ˌmeθəd əf 'peɪmənt]	e.g. Methods of payment include cash, credit/debit card, bank transfer	Zahlungsart, Zahlungsweise
possibility	[ˌpɒsə'bɪləti]	chance	Möglichkeit
to **require sth**	[rɪ'kwaɪə]	to need sth	etw benötigen, etw wünschen
to **hike**	[haɪk]	*n* hiking	wandern
to **set up a tent**	[set ˌʌp ə 'tent]	e.g. As soon as we got to the camping site we started to set up our tent.	ein Zelt aufschlagen

page 90

spelling alphabet	['spelɪŋ ælfəbet]	(NATO) phonetic alphabet	Buchstabieralphabet
memory	['meməri]	images of past events in your mind	Gedächtnis, Erinnerung
digit	['dɪdʒɪt]	figure, number from 0–9	Ziffer
unless	[ən'les]	e.g. She can't go to the disco unless an adult is with her.	außer wenn, es sei denn
underscore	['ʌndəskɔː]	_	Unterstrich

page 91

to **backpack**	['bækpæk]	travel with only a rucksack	mit dem Rucksack reisen

page 92

to **sketch**	[sketʃ]	to draw quickly	skizzieren
to **lay**	[rɪ'spektɪv]	to put sth down (gently)	legen
eye-catching	['aɪkætʃɪŋ]	immediately noticeable	prägnant, auffallend

UNIT 8

page 93

blended family	[ˌblendɪd 'fæmli]	a family made from two or more families	Patchworkfamilie
extended	[ɪk'stendɪd]	e.g. My extended family includes my aunts, uncles and cousins.	erweitert
single parent	[ˌsɪŋgl 'peərənt]	parent without a partner	Alleinerziehende/r
single-parent family	[ˌsɪŋgl peərənt 'fæməli]	family with one parent	Einelternfamilie
nuclear family	[ˌnjuːkliə 'fæməli]	family with two parents and children	Kernfamilie, Kleinfamilie
generation	[ˌdʒenə'reɪʃn]	people born around the same time	Generation
to **bring sb up**	[ˌbrɪŋ 'ʌp]	e.g. They are bringing up three children.	jdn großziehen, jdn aufziehen
to **consist of sb/sth**	[kən'sɪst əv]	e.g. Their family consists of one child, one parent and a dog.	aus jdm/etw bestehen
to **be familiar with sth**	[bi fə'mɪliə wɪð]	to know about sth	mit etw vertraut sein, etw kennen
focus	['fəʊkəs]	*v* to focus	Schwerpunkt, Hauptaugenmerk

page 94

to **set up sth**	[ˌset ˈʌp]	to start sth	etw einrichten, etw gründen
to **look sth up**	[ˌlʊk ˈʌp]	to look in a dictionary	etw (in einem Wörterbuch) nachschlagen
to **discover**	[dɪˈskʌvə]	n discovery	entdecken, herausfinden
apart (from)	[əˈpɑːt]	distant (from), separate, not together	(voneinander) entfernt, getrennt
to **confirm**	[kənˈfɜːm]	n confirmation	bestätigen

page 95

to **freak out**	[ˌfriːk ˈaʊt]	to become emotional, to lose control	ausrasten, durchdrehen
to **grow up**	[ˌgrəʊ ˈʌp]	to get older, to become an adult	aufwachsen
to **adopt sb**	[əˈdɒpt]	n adoption	jdn adoptieren
double	[ˈdʌbl]	sb who looks exactly the same as another	Double, Doppelgänger/in
via	[ˈvaɪə]	e.g. to fly to London via Hamburg	mittels, über
only child	[ˈəʊnlɪ tʃaɪld]	child without brothers or sisters	Einzelkind
shared	[ʃeəd]	common	gemeinsam
laugh	[lɑːf]	e.g. She has a very loud laugh.	Lachen
to **suspect**	[səˈspekt]	to guess, to have a feeling	vermuten
twin	[twɪn]	one of two children from the same birth	Zwilling
identical twins pl	[aɪˌdentɪkl ˈtwɪnz]	two babies that grew from one egg	eineiige Zwillinge
adoption	[əˈdɒpʃn]	e.g. She gave her child up for adoption	Adoption
to **give sb up for adoption**	[gɪv ˌʌp fər əˈdɒpʃn]	to give a child to another family	jdn zur Adoption freigeben
agency	[ˈeɪdʒənsi]	business or organization	Agentur, Behörde
set of parents	[ˌset əf ˈpɜːrənts]	mother and father	Elternpaar
adoptive parents pl	[əˌdɒptɪv ˈpeərənts]	people who adopt a child and raise it as theirs	Adoptiveltern
privilege	[ˈprɪvəlɪdʒ]	advantage	Privileg
relatively	[ˈrelətɪvli]	in comparison	vergleichsweise, relativ
well-off	[ˌwel ˈɒf]	wealthy, rich	wohlhabend
Jewish	[ˈdʒuːɪʃ]	related to the Jews or Judaism	jüdisch
to **take sth on**	[ˌteɪk ˈɒn]	to accept sth e.g. a new task	etw übernehmen, etw annehmen
characteristic	[ˌkærəktəˈrɪstɪk]	feature	Merkmal, Eigenschaft
respective	[rɪˈspektɪv]	e.g. After the school trip we all went back to our respective houses.	jeweilige/r/s
touchy-feely	[ˌtʌtʃi ˈfiːli]	emotional, sentimental	körperbetont, emotional
reserved	[rɪˈzɜːvd]	slow to share feelings or opinions	zurückhaltend, reserviert
to **warm to sb**	[ˈwɔːm tə]	to start to like sb	sich für jdn erwärmen
to **reflect**	[rɪˈflekt]	e.g. Her friendly expression reflected her positive attitude.	widerspiegeln, wiedergeben
to **separate**	[ˈsepəreɪt]	to divide	trennen

page 96

to **keep in touch**	[ˌkiːp ɪn ˈtʌtʃ]	e.g. We promised to keep in touch after we split up. But we didn't.	in Verbindung bleiben
question mark	[ˈkwestʃən mɑːk]	symbol showing that the sentence is a question	Fragezeichen
to **divorce sb**	[dɪˈvɔːs]	n divorce	sich von jdm scheiden lassen
to **share sth**	[ʃeə]	to exchange sth	sich etw teilen
parenthood	[ˈpeərənthʊd]	the state of being a parent	Elternschaft
to **compete for sth**	[kəmˈpiːt fə]	adj competitive	um etw konkurrieren
connection (to sb/sth)	[kəˈnekʃn]	v to connect	Verbindung (mit jdm/etw), Bezug (zu jdm/etw)
to **estimate**	[ˈestɪmeɪt]	e.g. It is estimated that he has $10 million.	schätzen
to **move on with one's life**	[muːv ˌɒn wɪð wʌnz ˈlaɪf]	e.g. Forget about him! It's time to move on with your life!	seinen eigenen Weg gehen, das Vergangene hinter sich lassen

page 98

to **present difficulties**	[prɪˌzent ˈdɪfɪkəltiz]	to be difficult to deal with	Schwierigkeiten darstellen, mit Schwierigkeiten verbunden sein
openness	[ˈəʊpənnəs]	acceptance of new ideas	Offenheit
to **text**	[tekst]	to send a message on a mobile phone	eine SMS senden, simsen
to **settle into sth**	[ˈsetl ɪntə]	to become comfortable in/with sth	sich an etw gewöhnen
intention (of doing sth)	[ɪnˈtenʃn]	plan (to do sth), aim	Absicht (etw zu tun)
to **act as if**	[ˌækt əz ˈɪf]	e.g. He acts as if he's smarter than everyone, but he isn't.	so tun, als ob
to **get upset**	[ˌget ʌpˈset]	get annoyed	sich aufregen, sich ärgern
mate	[meɪt]	friend, informal buddy, pal	Kumpel, Freund
to **tend to do sth**	[ˈtend tə]	to often be a certain way	dazu neigen, etw zu tun
irony	[ˈaɪrəni]	saying the opposite of what you mean for humour	Ironie
to **watch out**	[ˌwɒtʃ ˈaʊt]	to be careful	vorsichtig sein, aufpassen
swear word	[ˈsweə wɜːd]	e.g. When he hurt his foot, he shouted a swear word.	Schimpfwort
horrified	[ˈhɒrɪfaɪd]	very shocked	entsetzt
to **swear**	[sweə]	e.g. If you swear in school, you'll get in trouble.	fluchen
piece of advice	[piːs əv ədˈvaɪs]	e.g. Let me give you a piece of advice: never give up.	Rat

page 99

recipe	[ˈresɪpi]	instructions for preparing a meal	(Koch-)Rezept
to **mean to do sth**	[miːn]	to intend to do sth	beabsichtigen, etw zu tun
to **step foot in sth**	[ˌstep ˈfʊt ɪn]	to enter sth	etw betreten
aunt	[ɑːnt]	<> uncle	Tante
by the way	[baɪ ðə ˈweɪ]	e.g. Oh, by the way, I saw your teacher in the supermarket today.	übrigens
dishwasher	[ˈdɪʃwɒʃə]	e.g. Please put your dirty plates in the dishwasher.	Spülmaschine
to **rinse sth**	[rɪns]	to wash sth with water	etw (mit Wasser) abspülen
plate	[pleɪt]	a flat dish from which food is eaten	Teller
to **run out of sth**	[ˌrʌn ˈaʊt əv]	to not have any more of sth	etw nicht mehr haben
to **lay the table**	[leɪ ðə ˈteɪbl]	to set the table	den Tisch decken
hardly ever	[ˌhɑːdli ˈevə]	very rarely	kaum, so gut wie nie
to **broaden one's horizons**	[ˌbrɔːdn wʌnz həˈraɪznz]	to give oneself more opportunities	den eigenen Horizont erweitern

page 100

work experience	[ˈwɜːk ɪkspɪəriəns]	phr to do work experience	Praktikum
insurance	[ɪnˈʃʊərəns]	financial protection against loss or damage	Versicherung
policy (on sth)	[ˈpɒləsi]	way a company or institution does sth	Richtlinie(n) (für etw), Politik
to **apply (to sb/sth)**	[əˈplaɪ]	e.g. Club rules apply to all members.	(für jdn/etw) gelten
employee	[ɪmˈplɔɪiː]	<> employer	Beschäftigte/r, Mitarbeiter/in
to **disturb**	[dɪˈstɜːb]	to interrupt	stören
to **download**	[ˌdaʊnˈləʊd]	<> to upload	herunterladen
to **turn sth off**	[ˌtɜːn ˈɒf]	<> to turn sth on	etw ausschalten
to **silence**	[ˈsaɪləns]	to make quiet	(Handy) stummschalten
to **log on (to sth)**	[ˌlɒg ˈɒn]	<> to log out (of sth)	sich (in etw) einloggen
brief	[briːf]	short and to the point	knapp, kurz
official	[əˈfɪʃl]	<> inofficial	offiziell

page 101

to **bother sb**	[ˈbɒðə]	to annoy sb	jdn stören
corridor	[ˈkɒrɪdɔː]	hallway	Flur
reception	[rɪˈsepʃn]	front desk	Empfang(sbereich), Rezeption
memo	[ˈmeməʊ]	note, short message	Notiz, Vermerk, Kurzmitteilung
to **gather**	[ˈgæðə]	e.g. Did you know she left him? – I've gathered as much.	vermuten, sich etw denken
to **regulate**	[ˈregjəleɪt]	e.g. The use of private emails is strictly regulated.	regeln
to **turn a blind eye to sth**	[ˌtɜːn ə ˌblaɪnd ˈaɪ tə]	not to be too strict with sth	bei etw ein Auge zudrücken
nevertheless	[ˌnevəðəˈles]	all the same, anyway	trotzdem, dennoch
to **guide**	[gaɪd]	e.g. In his decisions, he was guided by instinct rather than reason.	leiten
to **restrict**	[rɪˈstrɪkt]	n restriction	einschränken, beschränken
emergency	[ɪˈmɜːdʒənsi]	e.g. In an emergency, call 999.	Notfall
to **enforce sth**	[ɪnˈfɔːs]	to make sure a rule etc. is respected	etw durchsetzen
strict(ly)	[strɪkt]	e.g. My parents are very strict – I have to be home by 9 o'clock.	streng
warning	[ˈwɔːnɪŋ]	e.g. The judge gave him a warning.	Verwarnung, Abmahnung
participant	[pɑːˈtɪsɪpənt]	v to participate	Teilnehmer/in
open-plan office	[ˌəʊpən ˌplæn ˈɒfɪs]	office with lots of desks in one large space	Großraumbüro
to **insist**	[ɪnˈsɪst]	to not accept no for an answer	darauf bestehen
on silent	[ɒn ˈsaɪlənt]	e.g. I didn't hear you calling, my mobile was on silent.	stummgeschaltet
to **prevent**	[prɪˈvent]	to stop happening	verhindern
furthermore	[ˌfɜːðəˈmɔː]	moreover	außerdem, darüber hinaus
drawer	[drɔː]	e.g. Where are my socks? – In the sock drawer, darling.	Schublade
to **distract sb**	[dɪˈstrækt]	to move sb's attention away from sth	jdn ablenken
unnecessary	[ʌnˈnesəsəri]	<> necessary	unnötig
landline	[ˈlændlaɪn]	<> mobile	Festnetzanschluss
management	[ˈmænɪdʒmənt]	people at the top of a company	Geschäftsleitung, Führungskräfte
obviously	[ˈɒbviəsli]	clearly	natürlich, selbstverständlich
flexible	[ˈfleksəbl]	happy to change	flexibel
to **hesitate**	[ˈhezɪteɪt]	e.g. Don't hesitate to call me if you have any questions.	zögern
to **get back to sb**	[ˌget ˈbæk tə]	to call sb again	sich bei jdm melden
supervisor	[ˈsuːpəvaɪzə]	boss	(direkte/r) Vorgesetzte/r

page 102

radio advertisement	[ˈreɪdiəʊ ədvɜːtɪsmənt]	e.g. the radio advertisement was annoying	Werbespot (im Radio)
across	[əˈkrɒs]	all over	in ganz
What's the point?	[ˌwɒts ðə ˈpɔɪnt]	What's this all about?	Was soll das? Was hat das für einen Sinn?
to **switch off**	[ˌswɪtʃ ˈɒf]	to turn off	ausschalten, ausmachen

consumer	[kən'sjuːmə]	v to consume	Verbraucher/in, Konsument/in
consumer culture	[kən'sjuːmə kʌltʃə]	society that values people based on their consumption of goods	Konsumkultur
provided	[prə'vaɪdɪd]	under the condition that	vorausgesetzt, dass
spending	['spendɪŋ]	money spent	Ausgabe(n), Geldausgaben
developing country	[dɪˌveləpɪŋ 'kʌntri]	a country with poor industry and economy	Entwicklungsland
in itself	[ɪn ɪt'self]	e.g. In itself, this change was not so bad.	an sich
harmful	['hɑːmfl]	dangerous	schädlich, nachteilig
distribution of wealth	[dɪstrɪˌbjuːʃn əv 'welθ]	how money or materials are spread across the population	Wohlstandsverteilung
to put out the word	[pʊt ˈaʊt ðə ˈwɜːd]	to spread a piece of information	die Nachricht verbreiten
convinced	[kən'vɪnst]	v to convince	überzeugt
to make a difference	[ˌmeɪk ə 'dɪfrəns]	to change sth	etw bewirken
lasting	['lɑːstɪŋ]	with permanent effect	dauerhaft
to consider sth	[kən'sɪdə]	to think about sth	Rücksicht auf etw nehmen
Count me in!	[ˌkaʊnt miː 'ɪn]	being enthusiastic about taking part in sth	Ich bin dabei!
to import	[ɪm'pɔːt]	<> to export	importieren, einführen
to consume	[kən'sjuːm]	n consumer	verbrauchen
to trade	[treɪd]	n trade	Handel treiben, handeln

page 103

answerphone	['ɑːnsəfəʊn]	telephone answering machine	Anrufbeantworter
broadcast	['brɔːdkɑːst]	a radio or television programme	Sendung, Übertragung, Ausstrahlung
sensible(-ly)	['sensəbl]	<> silly	vernünftig
varied	['veərɪd]	n variety	abwechslungsreich
behind the scenes	[bɪˌhaɪnd ðə 'siːnz]	things that are not seen	hinter den Kulissen
to make sth happen	[ˌmeɪk 'hæpən]	to put sth into effect	etw verwirklichen, etw ermöglichen
organizing committee	['ɔːgənaɪzɪŋ kəmɪti]	group that organizes an event	Organisationskomitee
cancellation	[ˌkænsə'leɪʃn]	v to cancel	Absage
running order	['rʌnɪŋ ɔːdə]	time schedule	Ablaufplan
responsibility	[rɪˌspɒnsə'bɪləti]	adj responsible	Verantwortung
rewarding	[rɪ'wɔːdɪŋ]	satisfying	erfüllend, befriedigend
to put one's hand up for sth	[pʊt wʌnz ˌhænd 'ʌp fə]	to volunteer for sth	sich für etw melden
pleasure	['pleʒə]	enjoyment	Vergnügen
in good spirits	[ɪn ˌgʊd 'spɪrɪts]	in a good mood	guter Dinge, gut gelaunt
common sense	[ˌkɒmən 'sens]	good judgement	gesunder Menschenverstand
to apply sth to sth	[ə'plaɪ tə]	to use sth on/for sth	etw auf etw anwenden
to get badly burned	[get ˌbædli 'bɜːnd]	to have a bad sunburn	einen schweren Sonnenbrand bekommen
to look after sb/sth	['lʊk ɑːftə]	e.g. The babysitter looked after the children.	sich um jdn/etw kümmern
steward	[stjuːəd]	sb who takes care of audience members at a festival	Ordner/in
to give directions	[ˌgɪv də'rekʃnz]	to tell sb the way	den Weg erklären
to reunite sb/sth with sb	[ˌriːjuː'naɪt wɪð]	to bring sb/sth back together with sb	jdn/etw mit jdm wieder zusammenbringen
lost property	[lɒst prɒpəti]	belongings that have been lost	Fundsachen
owner	['əʊnə]	sb who possesses sth	Besitzer/in, Inhaber/in
you name it	[juː 'neɪm ɪt]	anything	alles Mögliche
runner at large	[ˌrʌnər ət 'lɑːdʒ]	messenger dealing with all sorts of tasks at a festival	etwa: Laufbursche für besondere Aufgaben
performer	[pə'fɔːmə]	anyone who performs on a stage, e.g. actor, musician	Künstler/in, Darsteller/in
to sort out sth	[ˌsɔːt 'aʊt]	to make sth clear, to organize sth	etw klären, etw regeln
unexpected	[ˌʌnɪk'spektɪd]	sudden	unvorhergesehen
event	[ɪ'vent]	sth that is happening	Ereignis
to get sunburned	[get 'sʌnbɜːnd]	e.g. I was at the beach all day and got sunburned.	sich einen Sonnenbrand holen

page 104

occasionally	[ə'keɪʒənəli]	from time to time	gelegentlich, ab und zu
to attract customers	[əˌtrækt 'kʌstəməz]	to bring in business	Kunden gewinnen
tutoring	['tjuːtərɪŋ]	extra teaching outside of school	Nachhilfe
to gain muscle	[ˌgeɪn 'mʌsl]	to build muscle	Muskeln aufbauen
prompt	[prɒmpt]	cue, key word(s)	Stichwort

UNIT 9

page 105

professional	[prə'feʃnl]	related to your job	beruflich

page 106

job advertisement	['dʒɒb ədvɜːtɪsmənt]	text a company writes when they are looking for employees	Stellenanzeige
federal	['fedərəl]	governmental	Bundes-
voluntary service	[ˌvɒləntri 'sɜːvɪs]	civil work without pay	Freiwilligendienst

covering letter	[ˈkʌvərɪŋ letə]	letter you send with a job application	Anschreiben, Begleitschreiben
position	[pəˈzɪʃn]	place, job	Stelle, Stellung, Position
to fit into sth	[ˈfɪt ɪntə]	e.g. It took me a long time to fit into my new school.	sich in etw einfügen
throughout …	[θruːˈaʊt]	the whole way	in ganz …
recruiter	[rɪˈkruːtə]	sb who finds jobs for people	Personalvermittler/in
character	[ˈkærəktə]	personality	Charakter
quality	[ˈkwɒləti]	e.g. Punctuality is a quality employers are looking for in an employee.	Eigenschaft
to aim to do sth	[eɪm]	to intend to do sth	beabsichtigen, etw zu tun

page 107

job description	[ˈdʒɒb dɪskrɪpʃn]	job specification	Stellenbeschreibung
depending on	[dɪˈpendɪŋ ɒn]	e.g. Depending on the weather, we could go to the park.	je nach
competence	[ˈkɒmpɪtəns]	skill	Kompetenz
computer literacy	[kəmˌpjuːtə ˈlɪtərəsi]	ability to use a computer	Computerkenntnisse
to fix	[fɪks]	to repair	reparieren, flicken
struggle	[ˈstrʌgl]	difficulty	Kampf
to enable sb to do sth	[ɪˈneɪbl]	to make it possible for sb to do sth	jdm ermöglichen, etw zu tun
one-way street	[ˌwʌnweɪ ˈstriːt]	for a relationship: where only one person is benefitting	Einbahnstraße
insight (into sth)	[ˈɪnsaɪt]	deeper understanding of sb/sth	Einblick(e) (in etw)
pedagogical staff	[pedəˌgɒdʒɪkl ˈstɑːf]	teachers in a company	Lehrpersonal
length of service	[leŋθ əv ˈsɜːvɪs]	how long sb has worked for a company	Dienstzeit, Beschäftigungsdauer
largely	[ˈlɑːdʒli]	mostly	überwiegend, größtenteils
agricultural	[ˌægrɪˈkʌltʃərəl]	n agriculture	landwirtschaftlich
conservative	[kənˈsɜːvətɪv]	<> liberal	konservativ
to be sensitive towards sb/sth	[bi ˈsensətɪv təwɔːdz]	to be understanding about sb/sth	für jdn/etw Verständnis haben, verständnisvoll mit jdm/etw umgehen
CV BE	[ˌsiː ˈviː]	AE résumé	Lebenslauf

page 108

pilgrimage	[ˈpɪlgrɪmɪdʒ]	a journey to an area of significance	Pilgerreise
custom	[ˈkʌstəm]	a traditional way of doing sth	Sitte, Brauch
surrounding area	[səˌraʊndɪŋ ˈeərɪə]	e.g. The surrounding area is beautiful countryside.	Umland, Umgebung
way of life	[weɪ əv ˈlaɪf]	culture, traditions, lifestyle	Lebensweise, Lebensart
obvious	[ˈɒbvɪəs]	clear	klar (erkennbar), offensichtlich
doubt	[daʊt]	e.g. I have my doubts that this is a good idea.	Zweifel
to fail	[feɪl]	e.g. She failed three exams because she didn't study.	(Prüfung) nicht bestehen, durchfallen
prediction	[prɪˈdɪkʃn]	v to predict	Voraussage, Vorhersage

page 109

mother tongue	[ˈmʌðə tʌŋ]	native language	Muttersprache
school leaving certificate	[ˌskuːl liːvɪŋ səˈtɪfɪkət]	qualification you get at the end of school	Schulabgangszeugnis
voluntary work	[ˈvɒləntri wɜːk]	e.g. I do voluntary work with old people.	Freiwilligenarbeit
to be keen to do sth	[bɪ ˈkiːn tə]	to really want to do sth	etw unbedingt tun wollen
to gain	[geɪn]	to get	erwerben, erlangen
refugee	[ˌrefjuˈdʒiː]	sb who had to leave his/her country	Flüchtling
to get on well with sb	[ˌget ɒn ˈwel wɪð]	e.g. I get on well with all my classmates.	gut mit jdm auskommen
to grant	[grɑːnt]	to give sb sth they want	gewähren
referee	[ˌrefəˈriː]	sb who recommends you for a job	Referenzgeber/in
to supply sth	[səˈplaɪ]	to give sb sth they need	etw zur Verfügung stellen
Yours sincerely	[ˌjɔːz sɪnˈsɪəli]	what you write at the end of a formal letter	Mit freundlichen Grüßen

page 110

work permit	[ˌwɜːk ˈpɜːmɪt]	document which allows you to work	Arbeitserlaubnis
foreign	[ˈfɒrən]	from another country	ausländisch, fremd
to take time off	[teɪk ˌtaɪm ˈɒf]	not go to school/work for a period of time	sich freinehmen
of a lifetime	[əv ə ˈlaɪftaɪm]	phr chance of a lifetime	einmalig
visa	[ˈviːzə]	travel document	Visum
to fasten one's seat belt	[ˌfɑːsn wʌnz ˈsiːt belt]	e.g. In a car, you must fasten your seat belt.	sich anschnallen
Off we go.	[ˈɒf wi gəʊ]	Let's begin.	Los geht's!
temporary	[ˈtemprəri]	<> permanent	befristet
to apply for sth	[əˈplaɪ fə]	to officially ask for sth e.g. job or a place at a university	etw beantragen
backpacker	[ˈbækpækə]	traveller	Rucksackreisende/r
qualification	[ˌkwɒlɪfɪˈkeɪʃn]	sth you get at the end of a course of study	Abschluss, Ausbildung
towards the end	[təˌwɔːdz ði ˈend]	e.g. The film was boring so I fell asleep towards the end.	gegen Ende
pay	[peɪ]	money from a job	Lohn, Bezahlung
chef	[ʃef]	sb who cooks food professionally	(Chef-)Koch/Köchin
to fulfil	[fʊlˈfɪl]	e.g. He fulfilled the requirements and got the job.	erfüllen
to be aimed at sb/sth	[bi ˈeɪmd ət]	to be meant for sb/sth, to be targeted at sb/sth	sich an jdn/etw wenden, sich an jdn/etw richten

page 111

member of staff	[ˌmembər əf ˈstɑːf]	employee	Mitarbeiter/in
cloudy	[ˈklaʊdi]	with clouds in the sky	bewölkt
to **get married**	[ˌget ˈmærid]	<> to get divorced	heiraten
bridesmaid	[ˈbraɪdzmeɪd]	friend or sister of the woman getting married	Brautjungfer
to **cycle**	[ˈsaɪkl]	to ride a bike	Fahrrad fahren, radeln

page 112

to **get used to sth**	[get ˈjuːst tə]	e.g. I'll never get used to living in the city.	sich an etw gewöhnen
jealous	[ˈdʒeləs]	e.g. What a beautiful coat! I'm so jealous!	neidisch
freezing	[ˈfriːzɪŋ]	e.g. In Alaska, it was freezing even in April.	eiskalt
not literally	[ˌnɒt ˈlɪtərəli]	not really	nicht wirklich
season	[ˈsiːzn]	e.g. There are four seasons in the year.	Jahreszeit
outback *AusE*	[ˈaʊtbæk]	e.g. Tough Australians live in the outback.	HInterland, Busch, Outback
to **shorten**	[ˈʃɔːtn]	e.g. Thomas prefers to shorten his name to Tom.	verkürzen, abkürzen
standard English	[ˌstændəd ˈɪŋglɪʃ]	e.g. At school you learn standard English.	hochsprachliches Englisch

page 113

bottle shop *AusE*	[ˈbɒtl ʃɒp]	e.g. In Australia you buy alcohol at bottle shops.	(konzessionierter) Spirituosenladen
festival	[ˈfestɪvl]	celebration	Fest, Festtag
sanctuary	[ˈsæŋtjʊəri]	place where animals are looked after	Schutzgebiet, (Tier-)Pflegestation
infographic	[ˈɪnfəʊgræfɪk]	diagram showing or explaining information	Infografik

page 114

(job) interview	[ˈɪntəvjuː]	e.g. I was invited for a job interview at the London office.	Vorstellungsgespräch
to **interview sb**	[ˈɪntəvjuː]	*n* interviewer, interviewee	mit jdm ein Vorstellungsgespräch führen
applicant	[ˈæplɪkənt]	*n* application	Bewerber/in
employer	[ɪmˈplɔɪə]	<> employee	Arbeitgeber/in
to **divide**	[dɪˈvaɪd]	to share, to split	teilen
introductions *pl*	[ˌɪntrəˈdʌkʃnz]	*v* to introduce	Vorstellung, Bekanntmachen
further	[ˈfɜːðə]	e.g. We can make further arrangements via email.	weiter, weitergehend
on time	[ɒn ˈtaɪm]	punctual	pünktlich
confident(ly)	[ˈkɒnfɪdənt]	*n* confidence	selbstbewusst
eye contact	[ˈaɪ kɒntækt]	when you look sb in the eye	Blickkontakt
illness	[ˈɪlnəs]	*adj* ill	Krankheit
to **stick to sth**	[ˈstɪk tə]	to stay with sth	sich an etw halten
to **respond**	[rɪˈspɒnd]	to answer	antworten
appropriate(ly)	[əˈprəʊpriətl]	suitable(-ly)	angemessen
interviewer	[ˈɪntəvjuːə]	<> interviewee	*Person, die ein Vorstellungsgespräch führt*

page 115

to **sew**	[səʊ]	to join material together	nähen
representative	[ˌrepriˈzentətɪv]	*v* to represent	Vertreter/in, Repräsentant/in
to **attend sth**	[əˈtend]	to take part in sth	an etw teilnehmen

page 116

to **renovate**	[ˈrenəveɪt]	to restore to a better condition	renovieren
to **make a success** of sth	[ˌmeɪk ə səkˈses əv]	to achieve a good result from sth	etw zum Erfolg führen, etw gelingt
to **make a dream come true**	[meɪk ə ˌdriːm kʌm ˈtruː]	to make sth that you really wanted happen	sich einen Traum erfüllen
half-way	[ˌhɑːf ˈweɪ]	at the middle point	auf halbem Wege, halbwegs
primary school	[ˈpraɪməri skuːl]	the school you go to between the age of 6 and 10	Grundschule
valley	[ˈvæli]	low land between hills or mountains	Tal
rainy	[ˈreɪni]	raining a lot	regnerisch
confusing	[kənˈfjuːzɪŋ]	*n* confusion	verwirrend
to **fast-forward**	[ˌfɑːst ˈfɔːwəd]	<> to rewind	vorspulen, springen
cousin	[ˈkʌzn]	e.g. I went to the cinema with my aunt and cousins.	Cousin/Cousine
apprenticeship	[əˈprentɪʃɪp]	traineeship	Lehre, Ausbildung, Lehrstelle
electrician	[ɪˌlekˈtrɪʃn]	sb who works with electrical equipment	Elektriker/in
to **make sense**	[meɪk ˈsens]	to be clear	vernünftig sein, einleuchten
to **ignore sth**	[ɪgˈnɔː]	to not pay attention to sth	etw ignorieren
pedestrian	[pɪˈdestriən]	sb who is on foot	Fußgänger/in
to **judge**	[dʒʌdʒ]	to form an opinion about sth	zum Urteil kommen, der (begründeten) Meinung sein
to **cross**	[krɒs]	to go across a street	überqueren
patient(ly)	[ˈpeɪʃnt]	*n* patience	geduldig
in sight	[ɪn ˈsaɪt]	visible	in Sicht
passenger	[ˈpæsɪndʒə]	sb who travels in a car, on a train, bus, plane, boat, etc.	Fahrgast
shopkeeper	[ˈʃɒp kiːpə]	person who owns a shop	Ladenbesitzer/in

page 117

completion	[kəmˈpliːʃn]	*v* to complete	Vervollständigung
impression	[ɪmˈpreʃn]	e.g. She made a good impression.	Eindruck
to **settle down**	[ˌsetl ˈdaʊn]	to get comfortable somewhere	Fuß fassen, sich eingewöhnen

311

page 118

work visa	[wɜːk ˈviːzə]	document which allows you to work in another country	Arbeitsvisum
tanned	[tænd]	brown from being in the sun	sonnengebräunt, braun
scheme	[skiːm]	programme	Programm, Maßnahmen
down under	[daʊn ˈʌndə]	in/to Australia	in Australien
muscly	[ˈmʌsli]	muscular	muskulös
warmth	[wɔːmθ]	*adj* warm	Wärme
in italics	[ɪn ɪˈtælɪks]	e.g. *This sentence is set in italics.*	kursiv (gesetzt)

UNIT 10

page 119

to **speculate**	[ˈspekjuleɪt]	to form an opinion about sth without all the information	mutmaßen, spekulieren
natural wonder	[ˌnætʃrəl ˈwʌndə]	e.g. The Seven Natural Wonders of the World	Naturwunder
gambling	[ˈgæmblɪŋ]	betting, playing games of chance for money	Glücksspiel
rock climbing	[ˈrɒk klaɪmɪŋ]	*v* to rock-climb	Klettern
skiing	[ˈskiːɪŋ]	e.g. I went skiing in Italy with my family.	Skifahren
horse riding	[ˈhɔːsraɪdɪŋ]	e.g. I don't like horse riding. I'm always scared I will fall off.	Reiten

page 120

to **enter sth**	[ˈentə]	to take part in sth	(Wettbewerb usw.:) an etw teilnehmen
prize	[praɪz]	e.g. I won a prize for my photograph.	Preis, Gewinn
to **open the mind**	[ˌəʊpən ðə ˈmaɪnd]	to offer new ideas and fresh perspectives	den Geist öffnen
to **attend sth**	[əˈtend]	to go to sth	etw (Veranstaltung usw.) besuchen
stadium	[ˈsteɪdiəm]	e.g. The football stadium was huge!	Stadion

page 121

day out	[ˌdeɪ ˈaʊt]	trip away for a day	freier Tag, Ausflug
mysterious(ly)	[mɪˈstɪəriəs]	*n* mystery	geheimnisvoll, rätselhaft
not quite	[nɒt ˈkwaɪt]	not completely	nicht ganz
to **turn out**	[ˌtɜːn ˈaʊt]	e.g. He turned out to be a liar – he didn't tell the truth.	sich herausstellen
treat	[triːt]	e.g. Dad took me to the cinema as a treat.	Vergnügen, Leckerbissen
kickoff	[ˈkɪkɒf]	start, beginning (often of a sports activity)	Start, Anfang, Anstoß
season	[ˈsiːzn]	e.g. The football season kicks off in September	Saison
unfortunately	[ʌnˈfɔːtʃənətli]	<> fortunately	leider, unglücklicherweise
to **disappoint sb**	[ˌdɪsəˈpɔɪnt]	to let sb down	jdn enttäuschen
kind(ly)	[kaɪnd]	nice, friendly	nett, freundlich, liebenswürdig
interstate *AE*	[ˌɪntəˈsteɪt]	motorway *BE*	Autobahn, Fernstraße
terrifying	[ˈterɪfaɪɪŋ]	very scary	entsetzlich, furchteinflößend
to **be scared of heights**	[bi ˌskeəd əv ˈhaɪts]	I won't climb this mountain – I'm scared of heights!	Höhenangst haben
to **stamp one's feet**	[ˌstæmp wʌnz ˈfiːt]	e.g. Everybody stamped their feet at the stadium.	mit den Füßen trampeln
deafening	[ˈdefnɪŋ]	really loud	ohrenbetäubend
thunder	[ˈθʌndə]	e.g. Did you hear the thunder last night?	Donner
to **rush**	[rʌʃ]	to go somewhere very quickly	eilen
bucket	[ˈbʌkɪt]	e.g. a bucket of water	Eimer
foot	[fʊt]	e.g. He is six feet tall.	Fuß (ca. 30,5 cm)
opening ceremony	[ˌəʊpnɪŋ ˈserəməni]	a small show at the beginning of an event	Eröffnungszeremonie
brass band	[ˌbrɑːs ˈbænd]	a musical group with brass and percussion instruments	Blasorchester
national anthem	[ˌnæʃnəl ˈænθəm]	a song officially accepted as a country's song	Nationalhymne
in person	[ɪn ˈpɜːsn]	face to face	persönlich, selbst
opposing	[əˈpəʊzɪŋ]	competing	gegnerisch
speed	[spiːd]	how fast sth moves	Geschwindigkeit
crack	[kræk]	a sudden sharp noise	Knall, Krachen
inactivity	[ˌɪnækˈtɪvəti]	<> activity	Untätigkeit
burst	[bɜːst]	*phr* burst of action	Ausbruch, Explosion
violent	[ˈvaɪələnt]	*n* violence	brutal, gewalttätig
to **knock sb down**	[ˌnɒk ˈdaʊn]	e.g. The players knocked each other down.	jdn niederschlagen, jdn umhauen
to **kick a ball**	[ˌkɪk ə ˈbɔːl]	e.g. She kicked the ball hard.	einen Ball schießen
halfway though sth	[ˌhɑːfweɪ ˈθruː]	midway through sth	mitten in etw, während etw
to **enjoy oneself**	[ɪnˈdʒɔɪ wʌnself]	to have fun	sich gut amüsieren
a bunch of people	[ə ˌbʌntʃ əf ˈpiːpl]	a group of people	ein Haufen Leute, ein paar Leute
to **cheer**	[tʃɪə]	to shout encouragingly	jubeln, anfeuern
to **score**	[skɔː]	to win or get a point	einen Punkt machen, ein Tor erzielen

page 122

to **be about to do sth**	[bi əˈbaʊt tə]	e.g. The game was about to start when it started to rain.	etw gleich tun; im Begriff sein, etw zu tun
capacity	[kəˈpæsəti]	e.g. The capacity of this water bottle is 1 litre.	Fassungsvermögen
sea level	[ˈsiː levl]	e.g. Innsbruck is located 574 metres above sea level.	Meereshöhe
to **be considered sth**	[bi kənˈsɪdəd]	to be seen as sth	als etw angesehen werden
spectator	[spekˈteɪtə]	viewer	Zuschauer/in

pure	[pjʊə]	not mixed with anything else	pur, rein
brutality	[bruːˈtæləti]	violence, cruelty	Brutalität
sudden	[ˈsʌdn]	unexpected	plötzlich, jäh, überraschend
attitude	[ˈætɪtjuːd]	belief, view	Einstellung, Haltung
during the course of sth	[ˌdjʊərɪŋ ðə ˈkɔːs əv]	while sth is happening, thoughout sth	im Verlauf von etw
evidence	[ˈevɪdəns]	proof	Indizien, Hinweise
to support	[səˈpɔːt]	e.g. Give reasons to support your argument.	(Argument) untermauern, stützen

page 123

hint	[hɪnt]	extra information to help sb find an answer	Hinweis, Tipp
light	[laɪt]	<> dark	hell
to commence	[kəˈmens]	to start	beginnen, anfangen
frightening	[ˈfraɪtnɪŋ]	scary	beängstigend, erschreckend
to work out	[ˌwɜːk ˈaʊt]	e.g. Don't worry! Everything will work out.	sich entwickeln, laufen
to turn out	[ˌtɜːn ˈaʊt]	e.g. Things turned out well in the end.	sich entwickeln, laufen

page 124

awesome	[ˈɔːsəm]	great	beeindruckend, toll
wide open spaces pl	[waɪd ˌəʊpən ˈspeɪsɪz]	large areas not covered by housing, etc.	weites Land, Weiten
cattle	[ˈkætl]	cows and bulls	Vieh, Rinder; Stück Vieh, Rind
urban	[ˈɜːbən]	in a town or city	städtisch, Stadt-
mechanic	[mɪˈkænɪk]	sb who repairs vehicles	Mechaniker/in
patch of land	[ˌpætʃ əv ˈlænd]	small area of land	(kleines) Stück Land
crop	[krɒp]	plants grown on a large scale, especially cereals	Ackerpflanze, Getreide
farmhand	[ˈfɑːmhænd]	sb who works on a farm	Landarbeiter/in
instruction	[ɪnˈstrʌkʃn]	v to instruct	Anleitung, Anweisung
to handle horses	[ˌhændl ˈhɔːsɪz]	to work with horses, to look after horses	mit Pferden arbeiten
cow	[kaʊ]	e.g. The farmer bought a cow so that we could have fresh milk.	Kuh
bull	[bʊl]	e.g. The bull put its head down and attacked the man.	Stier
social occasion	[ˌsəʊʃl əˈkeɪʒn]	social event e.g. a birthday party	gesellschaftlicher Anlass
carnival	[ˈkɑːnɪvl]	e.g. Carnival in Rio de Janeiro	Karneval
procession	[prəˈseʃn]	parade	Festzug, Umzug
stall	[stɔːl]	e.g. I sold thirty jars of jam at the market stall today.	(Markt-)Stand
to kick off	[ˈkɪk ɒf]	to start	starten, anfangen
cattle drive	[ˈkætl draɪv]	process of moving cattle from one place to another	Viehtrieb
to ride on horseback	[ˌraɪd ɒn ˈhɔːsbæk]	to ride a horse	reiten
campfire	[ˈkæmpfaɪə]	a fire in the middle of a campsite	Lagerfeuer
city folk	[ˈsɪti fəʊk]	people who live in a city	Stadtmenschen, Städter
taste	[teɪst]	a short experience of sth	Kostprobe, Vorgeschmack
to keep sb safe	[ˌkiːp ˈseɪf]	to protect sb	auf jdn aufpassen, jdn beschützen
arrival	[əˈraɪvl]	the moment sb/sth arrives	Ankunft
rider	[ˈraɪdə]	sb who travels by bike or horse	Reiter/in
grounds pl	[graʊndz]	an area of land used for a certain purpose	Anlage, Gelände
spectacular	[spekˈtækjələ]	impressive, very exciting	eindrucksvoll, spektakulär
You bet!	[ˌjuː ˈbet]	Certainly!	Und ob!
apparently	[əˈpærəntli]	supposedly	anscheinend
broken bone	[ˌbrəʊkən ˈbəʊn]	e.g. The accident left me with two broken bones.	Knochenbruch
to step on sb/sth	[ˌstep ˈɒn]	to place or press one's foot on sb/sth	auf jdn/etw treten
contest	[ˈkɒntest]	competition	Wettbewerb
to prove (sth to sb)	[pruːv]	n proof	(jdm etw) beweisen
to compete	[kəmˈpiːt]	to take part (in a competition)	(bei einem Wettbewerb) antreten
to make money	[meɪk ˈmʌni]	to earn money	Geld verdienen
professional	[prəˈfeʃnl]	e.g. Don't try to fix it by yourself, speak to a professional.	Profi
prize money	[ˈpraɪz mʌni]	reward	Preisgeld
amateur	[ˈæmətə]	sb who takes part in a sport/hobby and isn't paid	Amateur(-)
unpredictable	[ˌʌnprɪˈdɪktəbl]	can't be planned for	unberechenbar
organizational	[ˌɔːgənaɪˈzeɪʃənl]	e.g. I have excellent organizational skills.	organisatorisch, Organisations-
to rely on sb	[rɪˈlaɪ ɒn]	to be dependent on sb	auf jdn angewiesen sein
cruel	[kruːəl]	horrible, brutal	grausam
campaigner	[kæmˈpeɪnə]	activist	Wahlkämpfer/in, Aktivist/in
at the end of the day	[ət ði end əv ðə ˈdeɪ]	ultimately, in the end	letzten Endes, letztlich
romantic	[rəʊˈmæntɪk]	e.g. He bought me roses, how romantic!	romantisch
You're welcome.	[jɔː ˈwelkəm]	e.g. Thank you for your help! – You're welcome!	Bitte (sehr). Gern geschehen.

page 125

extract	[ˈekstrækt]	short text taken from a longer article or book	Auszug, Ausschnitt
to line the streets	[ˌlaɪn ðə ˈstriːts]	to stand in lines along the streets	die Straße säumen, Spalier stehen
appearance	[əˈpɪərəns]	how sb or sth looks	Erscheinung(sbild), Aussehen
old-fashioned	[ˌəʊldˈfæʃənd]	<> modern	altmodisch
painted sign	[ˌpeɪntɪd ˈsaɪn]	e.g. The village pub still has its original painted sign above the door.	handgemaltes Schild

furious(ly)	[ˈfjʊəriəs]	angry, angrily	wild, heftig
to **throw sb off**	[ˌθrəʊ ˈɒf]	e.g. The horse threw me off its back.	jdn abwerfen
atmospheric	[ˌætməsˈferɪk]	having a certain atmosphere or mood	stimmungsvoll
fireworks *pl*	[ˈfaɪəwɜːks]	e.g. The fireworks this year were very loud.	Feuerwerk
to **demonstrate sth**	[ˈdemənstreɪt]	to show others how to do sth or how sth works	etw vorführen
to **scare sb**	[skeə]	to shock sb, to make sb scared	jdn erschrecken, jdm Angst einjagen
flash	[flæʃ]	bright light on a camera	Blitz(licht)
bang	[bæŋ]	a sudden loud noise	Knall
to **divide sth up**	[dɪˈvaɪd ʌp]	to separate sth into smaller parts	etw aufteilen
responsibility	[rɪˌspɒnsəˈbɪləti]	*adj* responsible	Zuständigkeit, Aufgabe
to **draw sth up**	[ˌdrɔː ˈʌp]	to prepare sth in writing, to write a draft of sth	etw entwerfen
to **break the ice**	[ˌbreɪk ði ˈaɪs]	to do/say sth to start a conversation between people who have just met	das Eis brechen, einander kennenlernen, miteinander ins Gespräch kommen
costume	[ˈkɒstjuːm]	an outfit of a particular style or period	Kostüm

page 126

trade fair	[ˈtreɪd feə]	exhibition	(Branchen-/Handels-)Messe
to **register**	[ˈredʒɪstə]	to sign up	sich anmelden
motor show	[ˈməʊtə ʃəʊ]	exhibition of cars and other vehicles	Automobilmesse
to **exhibit**	[ɪgˈzɪbɪt]	*n* exhibition	ausstellen
exhibitor	[ɪgˈzɪbɪtə]	sb who owns something shown in an exhibition	Aussteller/in
registration	[ˌredʒɪˈstreɪʃn]	e.g. Registration closes at 5 p.m.	Anmeldung
floor plan	[ˈflɔː plæn]	drawing of a floor of a building	Grundriss, Übersichtsplan
exhibition	[ˌeksɪˈbɪʃn]	show, trade fair	Ausstellung, Messe
highlight	[ˈhaɪlaɪt]	the best moment	Höhepunkt
press	[pres]	the media and their journalists and reporters	Presse
brand new	[ˌbrænd ˈnjuː]	e.g. a brand new car	brandneu, nagelneu
vehicle	[ˈviːəkl]	automobile	Fahrzeug
car dealership	[ˈkɑː diːləʃɪp]	business that sells new or used cars	Autohaus, Autohändler/in
to **test drive**	[ˈtest draɪv]	to drive a vehicle to see if it is worth buying	probefahren
model	[ˈmɒdl]	e.g. I want to buy a new car, but don't know which model to choose.	Modell
concept car	[ˈkɒnsept kɑː]	car made to show new style or design	Konzeptauto
automotive	[ˌɔːtəˈməʊtɪv]	e.g. automotive company	Automobil-, Auto-
special deal	[ˌspeʃl ˈdiːl]	bargain offer	Sonderangebot
to **cater for all tastes**	[ˌkeɪtə fər ˌɔːl ˈteɪsts]	to offer something for everybody	für jeden Geschmack etw bieten
display	[dɪˈspleɪ]	presentation of sth	Ausstellung, (Messe-)Stand, Display

page 127

motoring	[ˈməʊtərɪŋ]	driving a car	Autofahren, Automobil-
ride	[raɪd]	journey	Fahrt
convention	[kənˈvenʃn]	conference	Konferenz, Tagung, Versammlung
cab	[kæb]	taxi	Taxi
brochure	[ˈbrəʊʃə]	small book with product information	Prospekt, Broschüre
Formula One	[ˌfɔːmjələ ˈwʌn]	e.g. She loves watching Formula One on TV.	Formel 1
racing	[ˈreɪsɪŋ]	e.g. Terry likes watching horse racing.	Rennen, Renn-

page 128

origin	[ˈɒrɪdʒɪn]	*adj* original	Ursprung
public holiday	[ˌpʌblɪk ˈhɒlədeɪ]	e.g. Christmas is a public holiday.	gesetzlicher Feiertag
harvest	[ˈhɑːvɪst]	time when agricultural crops are collected	Ernte
turkey	[ˈtɜːki]	e.g. Turkey for Christmas dinner is a UK tradition.	Truthahn
corn *AE*	[kɔːn]	e.g. Corn was first grown in Mexico.	Mais
pumpkin	[ˈpʌmpkɪn]	vegetable often eaten at Thanksgiving	Kürbis
native	[ˈneɪtɪv]	existing naturally in a place	einheimisch
settler	[ˈsetlə]	sb who comes to a new region to live there	Siedler/in, Kolonist/in
to **grow sth**	[grəʊ]	e.g. I like to grow herbs on my balcony.	etw (Pflanzen usw.) anbauen
immigrant	[ˈɪmɪgrənt]	*v* to immigrate	Einwanderer/-in
legal(ly)	[liːgl]	regulated by law	gesetzlich, legal, rechtmäßig
celebration	[ˌselɪˈbreɪʃn]	*v* to celebrate	Feier, Fest
shut	[ʃʌt]	closed	geschlossen

page 129

festival	[ˈfestɪvl]	celebration	Fest, Festtag
New Year's Eve	[ˌnjuː jɪəz ˈiːv]	e.g. In Germany people celebrate New Year's Eve with fireworks.	Silvester
reunification	[ˌriːjuːnɪfɪˈkeɪʃn]	e.g. On 3rd October Germans celebrate Reunification Day.	Wiedervereinigung

page 130

to **queue**	[kjuː]	to stand in line	sich (in einer Warteschlange) anstellen
gate	[geɪt]	entrance	Tor, Pforte
height	[haɪt]	how tall someone is	Höhe, Körpergröße
to **score a point**	[ˌskɔːr ə ˈpɔɪnt]	e.g. How do you score points in cricket?	einen Punkt erzielen

caption	['kæpʃn]	explanation under a picture or illustration	Bildunterschrift
bear	[beə]	e.g. Bears are dangerous animals.	Bär
to **feed**	[fiːd]	to give food to an animal	füttern
sign	[saɪn]	notice	Hinweisschild
to **be fast asleep**	[bi ˌfɑːst əˈsliːp]	Don't wake the baby. She's fast asleep.	(tief und) fest schlafen
immediately	[ɪˈmiːdiətli]	right away	sofort, unverzüglich

UNIT 11

page 131

to **challenge sb**	[ˈtʃælɪndʒ]	to test sb	jdn herausfordern
to **exert**	[ɪgˈzɜːt]	e.g. He's popular and he likes to exert his influence on everyone.	(Einfluss usw.) ausüben
ambition	[æmˈbɪʃn]	aim, goal	Ziel, Wunschtraum, Ehrgeiz
aspiration	[ˌæspəˈreɪʃn]	aim, goal	Bestreben, Ziel
peer pressure	[ˈpɪə preʃə]	influence from members of the same social group	sozialer Druck
sense of belonging	[sens əv bɪˈlɒŋɪŋ]	feeling that one is part of a group	Zugehörigkeitsgefühl

page 132

indigenous	[ɪnˈdɪdʒənəs]	native	einheimisch, eingeboren; Ureinwohner/in, Eingeborene/r

page 133

stolen	[ˈstəʊlən]	taken without asking	geraubt, gestohlen
inferior	[ɪnˈfɪəriə]	worse, of less worth	minderwertig
eventually	[ɪˈventʃuəli]	in the end	schließlich, am Ende
ancestor	[ˈænsestə]	forefather, older relative	Vorfahre/-in, Ahne/-in
scholarship	[ˈskɒləʃɪp]	financial help for a sb who wants to continue education	Stipendium
school-leaving exam	[ˌskuːl liːvɪŋ ɪgˈzæm]	exam sat at the end of secondary school	Abschlussprüfung
conservationist	[ˌkɒnsəˈveɪʃənɪst]	sb who works to protect nature	Naturschützer/in
elder	[ˈeldə]	elderly person	Ältere/r, Älteste/r
in a way	[ɪn ə ˈweɪ]	so to speak	sozusagen, in gewisser Weise
bush	[bʊʃ]	Australian term for land outside main towns	Busch
aged care home AusE	[ˌeɪdʒd ˈkeə həʊm]	nursing home, care home BE	Altenpflegenheim
vocational education	[vəʊˌkeɪʃənl edʒuˈkeɪʃn]	training to work in a certain trade	berufliche Bildung

page 134

islander	[ˈaɪləndə]	sb who lives on an island	Insulaner/in, Inselbewohner/in
territory	[ˈterətri]	area owned by sb/a group	Gebiet, Territorium
professional	[prəˈfeʃnl]	<> amateur	professionell
association	[əˌsəʊsiˈeɪʃn]	organization	Verband, Vereinigung
on top of sth	[ɒn ˈtɒp əv]	extra	zusätzlich zu etw
tiny	[ˈtaɪni]	very small	klein, winzig
saltwater	[ˈsɔːltwɔːtə]	e.g. The water in the ocean is saltwater.	Salzwasser
to **find one's way around**	[faɪnd wʌnz ˌweɪ əˈraʊnd]	to find the right way to go to reach a location	sich zurechtfinden
public transport	[ˌpʌblɪk ˈtrænspɔːt]	buses, trains, trams, etc.	öffentliche Verkehrsmittel
timekeeping	[ˈtaɪmkiːpɪŋ]	punctuality	Pünktlichkeit
to **get on (with sb)**	[ˌget ˈɒn]	to be friendly with sb, to have a good relationship with sb	(mit jdm) zurechtkommen
open-minded	[ˌəʊpən ˈmaɪndɪd]	willing to learn about new ideas without prejudice	aufgeschlossen, unvoreingenommen
media studies pl	[miːdiə ˈstʌdiz]	academic study of mass media	Publizistik, Medienwissenschaft
hopefully	[ˈhəʊpfli]	e.g. Jermaine is hopefully away next weekend	hoffentlich
to **value**	[ˈvæljuː]	to consider sb/sth to be important	schätzen, wertschätzen
career path	[kəˈrɪə pɑːθ]	the way sb progresses in a profession	(beruflicher) Werdegang, Laufbahn

page 135

athlete	[ˈæθliːt]	adj athletic	Sportler/in
aboriginal	[ˌæbəˈrɪdʒənl]	original inhabitants of Australia	australische/r Ureinwohner/in
strait	[streɪt]	a narrow strip of water that connects two seas/oceans	Meerenge, Straße
to **remove sb from sb**	[rɪˈmuːv]	to take sb away from sb	jdn jdm wegnehmen
authority	[ɔːˈθɒrəti]	a person or organization that has power	Behörde
to **carry sth out**	[ˌkæri ˈaʊt]	to do, to enforce	etw (Tätigkeit) ausführen
to **integrate**	[ˈɪntɪgreɪt]	to bring people into a wider social group	eingliedern, integrieren
charitable	[ˈtʃærətəbl]	related to helping people in need	wohltätig
to **abuse sb**	[əˈbjuːz]	to treat sb very badly	jdn missbrauchen
responsible	[rɪˈspɒnsəbl]	in charge	verantwortlich, zuständig
care	[keə]	protection and support of sb/sth	Betreuung, Obhut, Fürsorge

page 136

rather than	[ˈrɑːðə ðən]	as opposed to	anstatt
to **pass sth on**	[ˌpɑːs ˈɒn]	to share	etw weitergeben
tribe	[traɪb]	a group of people who share the same culture	Stamm

shore; shores *pl*	[ʃɔː; ʃɔːz]	coast	Küste, Ufer; Land
unity	[ˈjuːnəti]	togetherness	Einheit, Zusammengehörigkeit
character	[ˈkærəktə]	person in a film or novel	*(Roman, Film usw.:)* Figur

page 137

rite of passage	[ˌraɪt əf ˈpæsɪdʒ]	sth that sb does to make them an adult	Initiation(sritus), Erwachsenwerden
coming of age	[ˌkʌmɪŋ əv ˈeɪdʒ]	the process of becoming an adult	Erwachsenwerden
to **distinguish sb/sth** from sb/sth	[dɪˈstɪŋgwɪʃ frəm]	to tell the difference between sb/sth and sb/sth	jdn/etw von jdm/etw unterscheiden
adolescent	[ˌædəˈlesnt]	sb who is developing from a child into an adult	Heranwachsende/r, Jugendliche/r
maturity	[məˈtʃʊərəti]	e.g. She dealt with the problem calmly, which showed emotional maturity.	Reife
independence	[ˌɪndɪˈpendəns]	*adj* independent	Unabhängigkeit
strength	[streŋθ]	*adj* strong	Stärke, Kraft
money management	[ˈmʌni mænɪdʒmənt]	dealing with (one's own) money	Umgang mit Geld
sense of responsibility	[ˌsens əv rɪˌsppnsəˈbɪləti]	awareness of one's duties	Verantwortungsgefühl
wisdom	[ˈwɪzdəm]	knowledge and good judgement gained from experience of the world	Weisheit, Klugheit, Lebenserfahrung
understanding	[ˌʌndəˈstændɪŋ]	ability to understand others/situations	Verständnis
to **relate to sth**	[rɪˈleɪt tə]	to have a relationship with sth	mit etw in einem Verhältnis stehen
siblings *pl*	[ˈsɪblɪŋz]	brothers and/or sisters	Geschwister
significant	[sɪgˈnɪfɪkənt]	important	bedeutend
bank account	[ˈbæŋk əkaʊnt]	e.g. My wages are paid into my bank account.	Bankkonto
driving test	[ˈdraɪvɪŋ test]	test to prove that one is able to drive safely	Fahrprüfung
to **undergo sth**	[ˌʌndəˈgəʊ]	to experience sth, to take part in sth	sich einer Sache unterziehen
to **vote**	[vəʊt]	to choose an option e.g. a political candidate	abstimmen, wählen
election	[ɪˈlekʃn]	official choosing of a person for a position	Wahl
county	[ˈkaʊnti]	e.g. I live in Surrey, a county in southern England.	Grafschaft
overseas	[ˌəʊvəˈsiːz]	abroad	im/ins Ausland, in/nach Übersee
rail	[reɪl]	e.g. I work at a rail company. I repair trains.	Bahn, Eisenbahn
pass	[pɑːs]	ticket (usually for more than one use)	Monatskarte, Zeitkarte
tall tales *pl*	[ˌtɔːl ˈteɪlz]	lies, stories that are made up	abenteuerliche Geschichten
to **pay one's own way**	[ˌpeɪ wʌnz ˌəʊn ˈweɪ]	to live without financial help from others	alles selbst bezahlen
casual job	[ˌkæʒuəl ˈdʒɒb]	temporary work	Gelegenheitsarbeit
to **cover sth**	[ˈkʌvə]	to put sth over or on top of sth	etw bcedecken
senior	[ˈsiːniə]	older or more experienced (at a job)	älter, höherrangig
wearer	[ˈweərə]	person who wears sth	Träger/in
unique	[juˈniːk]	different to everything else	einzigartig
tattoo artist	[təˈtuː ɑːtɪst]	sb who creates tattoos	Tätowierer/in
achievement	[əˈtʃiːvmənt]	sth that was done successfully	Leistung, Errungenschaft
a big deal	[ə ˌbɪg ˈdiːl]	sth that is important, sth that matters a lot	eine große Sache
to **go crazy**	[ˌgəʊ ˈkreɪzi]	to go insane (usually exaggerated)	durchdrehen
to **hire sth**	[ˈhaɪə]	to pay to use sth for a limited time	etw mieten
ballroom	[ˈbɔːlruːm]	a large room used for dancing and events	Festsaal
gown	[gaʊn]	long formal dress	Abendkleid
make-up artist	[ˌmeɪkʌp ˈɑːtɪst]	sb who puts makeup on others as their job	Visagist/in
grown up	[ˈgrəʊn ʌp]	adult	erwachsen

page 138

curious	[ˈkjʊəriəs]	*eager to learn more*	*neugierig*
descendant	[dɪˈsendənt]	offspring, younger relative	Nachkomme
to **govern**	[ˈgʌvn]	to regulate, to be in charge	regeln, bestimmen
outsider	[ˌaʊtˈsaɪdə]	sb who does not belong to a group	Außenstehende/r
hairstyle	[ˈheəstaɪl]	haircut, hairdo *BE*	Frisur
horse-drawn vehicle	[ˌhɔːs drɔːn ˈviːəkl]	a vehicle that is pulled by horses	Pferdefuhrwerk
farming	[ˈfɑːmɪŋ]	growing crops and raising animals	Landwirtschaft
social gathering	[ˌsəʊʃl ˈgæðərɪŋ]	a small party	geselliges Beisammensein
interaction	[ˌɪntərˈækʃn]	communication	Miteinander, Austausch, Interaktion
to **tolerate**	[ˈtɒləreɪt]	to allow sth to continue without resisting	dulden, tolerieren
to **turn 16**	[tɜːn]	to have one's 16th birthday	16 werden

page 139

to **commit sth to sth**	[kəˈmɪt tə]	e.g. David Hockney dedicated his whole life to being an artist.	etw (voll und ganz) einer Sache widmen, etw einer Sache anvertrauen
to **force**	[fɔːs]	to make sb do sth or sth happen	zwingen
inexperienced	[ˌɪnɪkˈspɪəriənst]	having little experience	unerfahren
label	[ˈleɪbl]	a small note that gives information about an item	Etikett, Bezeichnung
to **interpret**	[ɪnˈtɜːprɪt]	to understand sth as having a certain meaning	auslegen, interpretieren
liberal(ly)	[ˈlɪbərəl]	loose(ly), not precise(ly)	freizügig, liberal
binge drinking	[ˈbɪndʒ drɪŋkɪŋ]	drinking a large amount of alcohol	Komasaufen
drug-taking	[ˈdrʌg teɪkɪŋ]	using drugs	Drogenkonsum
sexual	[ˈsekʃuəl]	related to sex	sexuell
adventurous	[ədˈventʃərəs]	willing to take risks and try new things	abenteuerlustig
freedom	[ˈfriːdəm]	*adj* free	Freiheit
to **oppose sth**	[əˈpəʊz]	<> to support sth	gegen etw sein, etw ablehnen

page 140

housekeeping	[ˈhaʊskiːpɪŋ]	managing duties that need to be done in a home e.g. cleaning	Hauswirtschaft
practice	[ˈpræktɪs]	e.g. It is common practice for interns to work for free.	Praktik, Verhaltensweise, Maßnahme
to print	[prɪnt]	n printer	drucken
to put sth up	[ˌpʊt ˈʌp]	to hang sth up	etw aufhängen
to remove sth from sth	[rɪˈmuːv frəm]	to take sth out of sth	etw aus etw nehmen
keycard	[ˈkiːkɑːd]	card required to get into a building or hotel room	Schlüsselkarte
holder	[ˈhəʊldə]	e.g. keycard holder	Halter
air conditioning	[ˈeə kəndɪʃnɪŋ]	system to control air temperature in a building	Klimaanlage
electricity	[ɪˌlekˈtrɪsəti]	adj electric, electrical	Strom
to activate	[ˈæktɪveɪt]	to turn on	aktivieren, einschalten
power	[ˈpaʊə]	energy	Strom
toiletries pl	[ˈtɔɪlətriz]	hygiene products normally used in a bathroom	Hygieneartikel, Kosmetikartikel
conditioner	[kənˈdɪʃənə]	product used to improve the condition of hair	Haarspülung
moisturizer	[ˈmɔɪstʃəraɪzə]	product used to stop skin from becoming dry	Feuchtigkeitscreme
dispenser	[dɪˈspensə]	e.g. soap dispenser	Spender
disposable	[dɪˈspəʊzəbl]	designed to be thrown away	Einweg-, Wegwerf-
container	[kənˈteɪnə]	used to hold a product	Behälter
to require	[rɪˈkwaɪə]	to want, to need	wünschen, benötigen
wet	[wet]	<> dry	feucht, nass
breakfast buffet	[ˈbrekfəst bʊfeɪ]	a self-service hotel breakfast	Frühstücksbüfett
jam	[dʒæm]	e.g. toast with strawberry jam	Marmelade
packaging	[ˈpækɪdʒɪŋ]	wrapping	Verpackung
complaint	[kəmˈpleɪnt]	v to complain	Klage, Beschwerde, Reklamation
hygienic	[haɪˈdʒiːnɪk]	n hygiene	hygienisch
proper(ly)	[ˈprɒpə]	correct(ly), as it should be	richtig, ordentlich
to smell	[smel]	n smell	riechen, stinken
heating	[ˈhiːtɪŋ]	v to heat	Heizung
liquid	[ˈlɪkwɪd]	<> solid	flüssig

page 141

bar of soap	[ˌbɑːr əf ˈsəʊp]	a block of soap	Stück Seife
basin	[ˈbeɪsn]	sink	Waschbecken
to be used to sth	[bi ˈjuːst tə]	to be familiar with sth	etw gewohnt sein
to manage	[ˈmænɪdʒ]	to cope with sth	zurechtkommen

page 142

phone-in	[ˈfəʊn ɪn]	TV or radio show where you get the chance to call in on the phone	Sendung mit Hörerbeteiligung per Telefon
A levels pl BE	[ˈeɪ levlz]	AE high school exams	Abitur
exhausted	[ɪgˈzɔːstɪd]	n exhaustion	erschöpft
balance	[ˈbæləns]	phr to keep your balance	Gleichgewicht, Ausgleich
to take time out	[teɪk ˌtaɪm ˈaʊt]	e.g. I'm completely stressed out, I have to take some time out.	sich freinehmen
walking holiday	[ˈwɔːkɪŋ hɒlədeɪ]	e.g. I went on a walking holiday in the Lake District last summer.	Wanderurlaub

page 143

to make use of sth	[ˌmeɪk ˈjuːs əv]	to use sth	etw verwenden, etw nutzen
economic	[iːkəˈnɒmɪk]	e.g. Economic research showed that the poor had become poorer.	wirtschaftlich, Wirtschafts-
based in	[ˈbeɪst ɪn]	being located in	mit Sitz in, ansässig in
to find	[faɪnd]	to show, to identify	feststellen
electronics	[ɪˌlekˈtrɒnɪks]	e.g. the electronics company was doing well	Elektronik
educational	[edʒuˈkeɪʃənl]	related to education	Bildungs-, schulisch
to go out of fashion	[gəʊ ˌaʊt əf ˈfæʃn]	to become unpopular	aus der Mode kommen
to encounter sb/sth	[ɪnˈkaʊntə]	to be faced with sb/sth	auf jdn/etw stoßen, jdm/einer Sache begegnen
technician	[tekˈnɪʃn]	sb who makes sure machines are working	Techniker/in

page 144

not unless	[nɒt ənˈles]	except if	nur (dann), wenn
tribal	[ˈtraɪbl]	belonging or related to a tribe	Stammes-
to preserve	[prɪˈzɜːv]	to maintain sth in its original state	bewahren
to drop sth	[drɒp]	to let sth fall	etw fallen lassen, etw (auf den Boden) werfen
appliance	[əˈplaɪəns]	a machine that is used in the home	Elektrogerät, Haushaltsgerät
demand	[dɪˈmɑːnd]	a very strong request	Forderung
decline	[dɪˈklaɪn]	decrease, fall	Niedergang
original(ly)	[əˈrɪdʒənəl]	existing at the beginning	ursprünglich

UNIT 12

page 145

similarity	[ˌsɪməˈlærəti]	<> difference	Ähnlichkeit
to **be intolerant of** sb/sth	[bi ɪnˈtɒlərənt əv]	<> to tolerate sb	intolerant gegenüber jdm/etw sein
to **be suspicious of** sb	[bi səˈspɪʃəs əv]	*n* suspicion	jdm gegenüber misstrauisch sein
race	[reɪs]	*adj* racist	Rasse
to **succeed**	[səkˈsiːd]	*n* success	Erfolg haben, erfolgreich sein
to **draw**	[drɔː]	to pull	ziehen
fear	[fɪə]	feeling sb has when they are scared	Angst
interethnic tension	[ɪntərˌeθnɪk ˈtenʃn]	arguments and fights between ethnic groups	Spannung(en) zwischen ethnischen Gruppen

page 146

to **shoot** sb	[ʃuːt]	to hit sb with a bullet	jdn anschießen, jdn erschießen

page 147

to **take to the streets**	[ˌteɪk tə ðe ˈstriːts]	to protest, to go on a protest march	auf die Straße gehen *(um zu demonstrieren)*
segregation	[ˌsegrɪˈɡeɪʃn]	separation of different races	Rassentrennung
discrimination	[dɪˌskrɪmɪˈneɪʃn]	unfair treatment of people based on race, gender, age etc.	Diskriminierung
African American	[ˌæfrɪkən əˈmerɪkən]	Americans whose ancestors are from Africa	afroamerikanisch; Afroamerikaner/in
observer	[əbˈzɜːvə]	sb who watches sth	Beobachter/in
to **resolve**	[rɪˈzɒlv]	e.g. to resolve an issue	*(Problem usw.:)* lösen
equality	[ɪˈkwɒləti]	state of being equal	Gleichheit, Gleichbehandlung
democratic	[ˌdeməˈkrætɪk]	related to democracy, where leaders are chosen by vote	demokratisch
in theory	[ɪn ˈθɪəri]	e.g. The plan is great in theory, but will it really work?	theoretisch
majority	[məˈdʒɒrəti]	the largest part of sth	Mehrheit
to **elect**	[ɪˈlekt]	to choose sb via a vote	wählen
president	[ˈprezɪdənt]	elected head of state	Präsident
power	[ˈpaʊə]	*adj* powerful	Macht, Einfluss
law enforcement	[ˌlɔː ɪnˈfɔːsmənt]	organizations that make sure citizens follow the law	Polizei (und Justiz), Exekutive
these days	[ðiːz ˈdeɪz]	nowadays	heutzutage
to **carry** sth	[ˈkæri]	to keep sth with you at all times	etw mit sich führen, etw bei sich tragen
police officer	[pəˈliːs ɒfɪsə]	sb who enforces the law	Polizist/in, Polizeibeamter/-in
on patrol	[ɒn pəˈtrəʊl]	keeping watch over an area by walking around it	auf Streife
footage	[ˈfʊtɪdʒ]	video recording(s)	Aufnahme(n), Filmmaterial
to **interact with** sb	[ˌɪntərˈækt wɪð]	to have contact with sb	mit jdm zu tun haben
to **provide evidence**	[prəˌvaɪd ˈevɪdəns]	to give proof	Beweise liefern
to **go wrong**	[ˌɡəʊ ˈrɒŋ]	to turn bad, to run into problems	schiefgehen, aus dem Ruder laufen
minority	[maɪˈnɒrəti]	the smaller part of sth	Minderheit
worrying	[ˈwariɪŋ]	causing concern and worry	beunruhigend, besorgniserregend
routine	[ruːˈtiːn]	a sequence of actions that are regularly performed	routinemäßig, Routine-
non-violent	[ˌnɒn ˈvaɪələnt]	peaceful, not using violence	gewaltlos, gewaltfrei
fatal outcome	[ˌfeɪtl ˈaʊtkʌm]	when sth results in death	tödlicher Ausgang
unarmed	[ʌnˈɑːmd]	not carrying a weapon	unbewaffnet
civilian	[səˈvɪliən]	sb who is not in the police force or army	Zivilist/in
shooting	[ˈʃuːtɪŋ]	an incident where sb is shot with a gun	Erschießung
incident	[ˈɪnsɪdənt]	sth that happened/is happening	Vorfall
justice	[ˈdʒʌstɪs]	fairness in the way people are treated	Gerechtigkeit
to **bring** sth **to the forefront**	[ˌbrɪŋ tə ðə ˈfɔːfrʌnt]	to highlight the importance of sth in public	etw öffentlich machen, etw in den Vordergrund stellen
overnight	[ˌəʊvəˈnaɪt]	during the night	über Nacht
to **turn to** sth	[ˈtɜːn tə]	to develop into sth	zu etw werden, sich zu etw entwickeln
obscure	[əbˈskjʊə]	not well known	(völlig) unbekannt
systemic	[sɪˈstemɪk]	affecting a whole system	systemimmanent, systembedingt
racism	[ˈreɪsɪzəm]	discrimination against sb based on their race	Rassismus
victim	[ˈvɪktɪm]	sb who is harmed or killed by sb else	Opfer
to **graduate**	[ˈɡrædʒueɪt]	to successfully complete an academic course	den (Schul-/Universitäts-)Abschluss machen
to **be due to do** sth	[bi ˈdjuː]	to be expected to do sth	etw *(laut Plan)* machen sollen
business course	[ˈbɪznəs kɔːs]	a program of study for a business qualification	kaufmännische Ausbildung
advancement	[ədˈvɑːnsmənt]	development	Entwicklung, Förderung
colored *AE*	[ˈkʌləd]	non-white skin	farbig
gentle	[dʒentl]	kind, good-natured	sanft
giant	[ˈdʒaɪənt]	a supersized human	Riese
criminal	[ˈkrɪmɪnl]	illegal	kriminell
convenience store	[kənˈviːniəns stɔː]	corner shop *BE*	Laden um die Ecke, Spätkauf
working class	[ˌwɜːkɪŋ ˈklɑːs]	people who work for wages, often in manual work	Arbeiterklasse
suburb	[ˈsʌbɜːb]	residential area on the outside of a city	Vorort
to **rob**	[rɒb]	to steal money or possessions	ausrauben, überfallen
liquor store *AE*	[ˈlɪkə stɔː]	government-regulated shop that sells alcohol	(konzessionierter) Spirituosenladen

to **shoot sb dead**	[ˌʃuːt ˈded]	to kill sb by shooting them	jdm erschießen
police department *AE*	[pəˈliːs dɪpɑːtmənt]	local branch of the police force	Polizeibehörde
to **claim**	[kleɪm]	to state sth as a fact	behaupten
to **attack**	[əˈtæk]	to try to hurt sb using violence	angreifen, attackieren
to **attempt to do sth**	[əˈtempt]	to try to do sth	versuchen, etw zu tun
gun	[ɡʌn]	weapon used to shoot someone	(Schuss-)Waffe
to **deny sth**	[dɪˈnaɪ]	to say that sth is not true	etw bestreiten, etw leugnen
eyewitness	[ˈaɪwɪtnəs]	sb who saw an incident occur	Augenzeuge/-in
to **answer back**	[ˌɑːnsə ˈbæk]	to reply to sb (usually rudely)	Widerworte geben, frech werden
sidewalk *AE*	[ˈsaɪdwɔːk]	pavement *BE*	Bürgersteig, Gehweg
robbery	[ˈrɒbəri]	the action of stealing things from sb/somewhere	Überfall, Raub
to **gather**	[ˈɡæðə]	to form a group	sich versammeln
to **demand**	[dɪˈmɑːnd]	to ask for sth forcefully	fordern
to **remove sth**	[rɪˈmuːv]	to take sth away	etw wegbringen
riot	[ˈraɪət]	violence and disturbance by a crowd	Aufstand, Aufruhr, Unruhe
poor choices *pl*	[ˌpʊə ˈtʃɔɪsɪz]	bad decisions	falsche Entscheidungen
bad luck	[ˌbæd ˈlʌk]	<> good luck	Pech
police force	[pəˈliːs fɔːs]	an organization of police officers	Polizei, Polizeiapparat

page 148

civil rights *pl*	[ˌsɪvl ˈraɪts]	rights that civilians have to freedom	Bürgerrechte
racial	[ˈreɪʃl]	related to race	Rassen-
industry	[ˈɪndəstri]	work involving manufacturing goods	Industrie
to **refuse to do sth**	[rɪˈfjuːz tə duː]	to say you will not do sth	sich weigern, etw zu tun
to **give sth up to sb**	[ˌɡɪv ˈʌp tə]	to give sth that is yours to sb	jdm etw überlassen
act	[ækt]	a thing that is done	Handlung, Tat, Akt
focus	[ˈfəʊkəs]	the centre of interest	Brennpunkt, Mittelpunkt
controversial	[ˌkɒntrəˈvɜːʃl]	causing diagreements	umstritten
figure	[ˈfɪɡə]	person, character	Persönlichkeit, Gestalt
aggressive	[əˈɡresɪv]	ready to attack, violent	aggressiv
peaceful(ly)	[ˈpiːsfl]	calm(ly), not violent(ly)	friedlich
racist	[ˈreɪsɪst]	sb who discriminates against people based on their race	Rassist/in
to **create sth**	[kriˈeɪt]	to cause sth	etw hervorrufen

page 149

scene	[siːn]	place where sth happened	Ort, Tatort
killing	[ˈkɪlɪŋ]	murder	Ermordung, Tötung
point of view	[ˌpɔɪnt əv ˈvjuː]	perspective	Perspektive, Blickwinkel
suspect	[ˈsʌspekt]	sb who may have committed a crime	Verdächtige/r
speculation	[ˌspekjuˈleɪʃn]	making guesses, forming theories without evidence	Mutmaßung(en), Vermutung(en)

page 150

flatshare	[ˈflætʃeə]	to live with other people in a flat	Wohngemeinschaft
to **arise**	[əˈraɪz]	to develop, to appear	*(Probleme usw.:)* entstehen
mining	[ˈmaɪnɪŋ]	e.g. The Ruhrgebiet used to be a vast mining region.	Bergbau
engineering	[ˌendʒɪˈnɪərɪŋ]	construction and design of machinery	Maschinenbau
mushroom	[ˈmʌʃrʊm]	fungus you can eat	Pilz
pan	[pæn]	e.g. She burnt the pan cooking.	Topf, Pfanne
spicy	[ˈspaɪsi]	with lots of spices	würzig, scharf
smell	[smel]	odour	Geruch, Gestank
mint	[mɪnt]	e.g. mint sauce	Minze
pickled	[ˈpɪkld]	preserved in vinegar	(sauer) eingelegt
preparation	[ˌprepəˈreɪʃn]	*v* to prepare	Vorbereitung

page 151

cartoon	[kɑːˈtuːn]	comic	Karikatur, Zeichnung
cynical	[ˈsɪnɪkl]	e.g. My brother's comments are always cynical, never friendly.	zynisch
foreground	[ˈfɔːɡraʊnd]	the closest area in a picture	Vordergrund
figure	[ˈfɪɡə]	character	Figur
distance	[ˈdɪstəns]	e.g. On a clear day in Potsdam, it is possible to see the Berlin TV tower in the distance.	Ferne
to **refer to sth**	[rɪˈfɜː tə]	*n* reference	sich auf etw beziehen, auf etw verweisen
to **suggest**	[səˈdʒest]	e.g. Survey results suggest an improvement in public health.	andeuten, nahelegen
sailing ship	[ˈseɪlɪŋ ʃɪp]	large boat with sails	Segelschiff
exploration	[ˌekspləˈreɪʃn]	travelling around a place in order to learn about it	Erforschung, Entdeckung
exploitation	[ˌeksplɔɪˈteɪʃn]	using sb or sth for one's own benefit	Ausbeutung

page 152

fundraiser	[ˈfʌndreɪzə]	sb who collects money for a charity	Spendensammler/in
phone duty	[ˈfəʊn djuːti]	e.g. Over 100 clients called while I was on phone duty!	Telefondienst
to **be on a break**	[bi ɒn ə ˈbreɪk]	e.g. The receptionist was on a 15-minute break.	Pause machen

to **put sb through**	[ˌpʊt ˈθruː]	to pass sb to sb else on the phone	*(Telefon:)* jdn durchstellen
to **catch sth**	[kætʃ]	to understand sth	etw verstehen, etw mitbekommen
to **hold the line**	[ˌhəʊld ðə ˈlaɪn]	to stay on the phone	*(Telefon:)* am Apparat bleiben
to **answer the phone**	[ˌɑːnsə ðə ˈfəʊn]	e.g. John never answers the phone!	ans Telefon gehen
to **leave a message**	[ˌliːv ə ˈmesɪdʒ]	e.g. She left a message for him.	eine Nachricht hinterlassen
Speaking.	[ˈspiːkɪŋ]	That's me.	*(Telefon:)* Am Apparat.
to **connect sb**	[kəˈnekt]	to put sb through	*(Telefon:)* jdn durchstellen
to **take a message**	[ˌteɪk ə ˈmesɪdʒ]	<> to leave a message	*(Telefon:)* jdm etw ausrichten
Don't mention it.	[dəʊnt ˈmenʃn ɪt]	No problem.	Nichts zu danken.

page 154

sporty	[ˈspɔːti]	e.g. My sister's very sporty – she plays tennis and football.	sportlich
happiness	[ˈhæpinəs]	*adj* happy	Zufriedenheit, Glück

page 155

to **hurry**	[ˈhʌri]	to go quickly	eilen
football practice	[ˈfʊtbɔːl præktɪs]	e.g. Susan goes to football practice once a week.	Fußballtraining
elderly	[ˈeldəli]	older	ältere/r/s
to **keep to sth**	[ˈkiːp tə]	to write only about sth	sich an etw halten, bei etw bleiben
quote	[kwəʊt]	v to quote	Zitat

page 156

to **instruct sb to do sth**	[ɪnˈstrʌkt]	to tell sb to do sth	jdn anweisen, etw zu tun
to **fund**	[fʌnd]	to pay for sth	finanzieren
competitor	[kəmˈpetɪtə]	sb who takes part in a competition	Teilnehmer/in *(an einem Wettbewerb)*
vest	[vest]	t-shirt without sleeves that runners wear	Laufshirt
race	[reɪs]	e.g. I finished first in the race.	Rennen
official	[əˈfɪʃl]	sb who is in charge of the rules of a competition	*(Sport:)* Kampfrichter/in
in broad daylight	[ɪn ˌbrɔːd ˈdaɪlaɪt]	when everyone can see what's happening	am hellichten Tag, vor aller Augen
to **tidy (up)**	[ˈtaɪdi]	to clear up	aufräumen, saubermachen
on several occasions	[ɒn ˌsevrəl əˈkeɪʒn]	more than once	mehrfach
to **wash the dishes**	[ˌwɒʃ ðə ˈdɪʃɪz]	to do the washing up	*(Geschirr)* spülen
press kit	[ˈpres kɪt]	information material given to journalists	Pressemappe
to **process sth**	[ˈprəʊses]	to deal with sth, to work on sth	etw bearbeiten

UNIT 13

page 157

globe	[gləʊb]	world, the Earth	Welt, Erde, Globus
official language	[əˌfɪʃl ˈlæŋgwɪdʒ]	e.g. English is the official language of the UK.	Amtssprache
native speaker	[ˌneɪtɪv ˈspiːkə]	sb who has spoken a language since they were a baby	Muttersprachler/in
aviation	[ˌeɪviˈeɪʃn]	related to aircrafts	Luftfahrt, Luftverkehr
diplomacy	[dɪˈpləʊməsi]	managing international relations	Diplomatie
Universal Postal Union	[ˌjuːnɪˌvɜːsl ˈpəʊstl juːnɪən]	agency that controls mail worldwide	Weltpostverein
trade	[treɪd]	buying and selling goods or services	Handel
United Nations *pl*	[juːˌnaɪtɪd ˈneɪʃnz]	an international peace organization	Vereinte Nationen
to **host sth**	[həʊst]	to organize an event	etw *(Veranstaltung usw.)* ausrichten

page 158

open day	[ˈəʊpən deɪ]	day on which an organization allows the public to visit	Tag der offenen Tür
to **ask for directions**	[ˌɑːsk fə dəˈrekʃnz]	to ask the way	nach dem Weg fragen
socializing	[ˈsəʊʃəlaɪzɪŋ]	to meet other people socially, e.g. at a party	Geselligkeit

page 159

to **profile**	[ˈprəʊfaɪl]	to describe sb in a short article	porträtieren
passion	[ˈpæʃn]	powerful emotion, enthusiasm	Leidenschaft
role-playing game	[ˈrəʊl pleɪɪŋ geɪm]	game where the players pretend to be sb else	Rollenspiel
stereotype	[ˈsteriətaɪp]	cliché	Klischee
social misfit	[ˌsəʊʃl ˈmɪsfɪt]	sb who does not fit in, outsider	Außenseiter, Sonderling
fantasy world	[ˈfæntəsi wɜːld]	world that does not actually exist	Traumwelt, Phantasiewelt
unsociable	[ʌnˈsəʊʃəbl]	sb who avoids contact with others	kontaktarm, menschenscheu
strategy	[ˈstrætədʒi]	*adj* strategic	Strategie
to **collaborate**	[kəˈlæbəreɪt]	to work together	zusammenarbeiten
guild	[gɪld]	professional organization of a single trade	Zunft, Gilde
common	[ˈkɒmən]	shared	gemeinsam
multilingual	[ˌmʌltiˈlɪŋgwəl]	able to speak more than one language	mehrsprachig
aptitude	[ˈæptɪtjuːd]	natural talent	Talent, Befähigung
to **keep up sth**	[ˌkiːp ˈʌp]	to carry on with sth	mit etw weitermachen
native language	[ˌneɪtɪv ˈlæŋgwɪdʒ]	mother tongue	Muttersprache
essential	[ɪˈsenʃl]	absolutely important	wesentlich, unerlässlich

building site	[ˈbɪldɪŋ saɪt]	place where building work takes place	Baustelle
realistic	[ˌriːəˈlɪstɪk]	likely to happen	realistisch
nomad	[ˈnəʊmæd]	sb who has no permanent home	Nomade/-in
hardly	[ˈhɑːdli]	e.g. Is that true? I can hardly believe it!	kaum
Guess what!	[ges ˈwɒt]	e.g. 'Guess what!' – 'What?' – 'I won the competition!'	Stell Dir vor! Wissen Sie was?
fluent	[ˈfluːənt]	*adv* fluently	*(Sprache:)* fließend
career prospects *pl*	[kəˈrɪə prɒspekts]	chances regarding work	Berufsaussichten
to **feel confident**	[ˌfiːl ˈkɒnfɪdənt]	to feel self-assured	sich sicher fühlen

page 160

antisocial	[ˌæntiˈsəʊʃl]	not wanting to spend time with other people	ungesellig, unsozial

page 161

cute	[kjuːt]	sweet	süß, niedlich
accent	[ˈæksent]	the way sb speaks	Akzent
higher education	[ˌhaɪə edʒuˈkeɪʃn]	university education	Hochschulbildung
quotation	[kwəʊˈteɪʃn]	*v* to quote	Zitat
provocative	[prəˈvɒkətɪv]	*v* to provoke	provokant, provozierend
career goal	[kəˈrɪə gəʊl]	aim regarding work	berufliches Ziel
testimony	[ˈtestɪməni]	statement	Aussage, Erfahrungsbericht
persuasive	[pəˈsweɪsɪv]	convincing	überzeugend, schlagkräftig

page 162

to **get the wrong idea** (about sth)	[get ðə ˌrɒŋ aɪˈdɪə]	to misunderstand sth	etw falsch verstehen
politeness	[pəˈlaɪtnəs]	respectfulness, manners	Höflichkeit
complicated	[ˈkɒmplɪkeɪtɪd]	<> simple	kompliziert
theoretical	[ˌθɪəˈretɪkl]	based on a theory rather than experience	theoretisch, spekulativ
fortunately	[ˈfɔːtʃənətli]	<> unfortunately	glücklicherweise, zum Glück
to **offend sb**	[əˈfend]	to insult sb	jdn beleidigen, jdn verletzen
disrespectful(ly)	[ˌdɪsrɪˈspektfl]	rude(ly)	unhöflich, respektlos
constantly	[ˈkɒnstəntli]	continuously	ständig, andauernd
to **interrupt**	[ˌɪntəˈrʌpt]	e.g. It's rude to interrupt someone when they're speaking.	unterbrechen
inappropriate(ly)	[ˌɪnəˈprəʊpriət]	not suitable for the situation	unangemessen
flirty	[ˈflɜːti]	showing romantic interest	kokett
to **hug sb**	[hʌg]	e.g. He hugged her tightly.	jdn umarmen
upset	[ˌʌpˈset]	annoyed	aufgebracht, verärgert
unwelcoming	[ʌnˈwelkəmɪŋ]	not friendly towards guests	abweisend
to **be to blame**	[bi tə ˈbleɪm]	to be the reason that sth happened	schuld sein
to **come down to sth**	[ˌkʌm ˈdaʊn tə]	to be explained by sth	auf etw hinauslaufen
individualist	[ˌɪndɪˈvɪdʒuəlɪst]	related to the idea of people being independent	individualistisch
respectful	[rɪˈspektfl]	showing respect for sth	respektvoll
automatic(ally)	[ˌɔːtəˈmætɪk]	by itself	automatisch
authority	[ɔːˈθɒrəti]	power	Autorität, Obrigkeit
to **say what's on your mind**	[ˌsaɪ wɒts ɒn jɔː ˈmaɪnd]	to say what you're thinking	sagen, was man denkt
punctuality	[ˌpʌŋktʃuˈæləti]	being on time	Pünktlichkeit
to **visit**	[ˈvɪzɪt]	e.g. When my parents visit, they expect my flat to be super-tidy.	zu Besuch sein
cheek	[tʃiːk]	e.g. In Spain, people greet each other by kissing both cheeks.	Wange
to **add up**	[ˌæd ˈʌp]	to mount up to	sich summieren
convincing	[kənˈvɪnsɪŋ]	persuasive	überzeugend
norm	[nɔːm]	sth that is normal/typical	Norm
guideline	[ˈgaɪdlaɪn]	rule, recommendation	Richtlinie, Empfehlung
niece	[niːs]	the daughter of one's sibling	Nichte
bureaucracy	[bjʊəˈrɒkrəsi]	*adj* bureaucratic	Bürokratie
punctual	[ˈpʌŋktʃuəl]	being on time	pünktlich

page 163

original	[əˈrɪdʒənl]	created by the artist	eigene/r/s
singing	[ˈsɪŋɪŋ]	e.g. I've always liked Pavarotti's singing.	Gesang
to **unfriend sb**	[ʌnˈfrend]	to delete sb as a friend on social media	*(soziale Medien:)* jdn als Freund löschen
confused	[kənˈfjuːzd]	*n* confusion	verwirrt
welcoming	[ˈwelkəmɪŋ]	friendly (especially to guests)	freundlich, gastfreundlich
embarrassed	[ɪmˈbærəst]	ashamed	verlegen, peinlich berührt
annoyed	[əˈnɔɪd]	angry, disappointed	verärgert, sauer
to **place importance on sth**	[ˌpleɪs ɪmˈpɔːtns ɒn]	to value sth	einer Sache Bedeutung beimessen, auf etw Wert legen
hurtful	[ˈhɜːtfl]	upsetting, mean	verletzend

page 164

to **make an impression**	[meɪk ən ɪmˈpreʃn]	e.g. I hope I make a good impression in my job interview.	einen Eindruck hinterlassen
tactful	[ˈtæktfl]	being sensitive to others when dealing with issues	taktvoll
present	[ˈpreznt]	<> absent	anwesend
to **give sb a hug**	[ˌgɪv ə ˈhʌg]	e.g. I gave my friend a big hug.	jdn umarmen

page 165

to **gain sth from sth**	[geɪn]	<> to lose sth	sich etw von etw versprechen, etw mit etw erreichen
tons of …	[ˈtʌnz əv]	e.g. I've got tons of work.	jede Menge …, tonnenweise …
impolite	[ˌɪmpəˈlaɪt]	<> polite	unhöflich
trivial	[ˈtrɪviəl]	unimportant	banal, belanglos

page 166

printing plant	[ˈprɪntɪŋ plɑːnt]	large factory where books and magazines are printed	Großdruckerei
workplace	[ˈwɜːkpleɪs]	e.g. Women face discrimination in the workplace.	Arbeitsplatz
hazard	[ˈhæzəd]	danger	Gefahr
safety procedures pl	[ˈseɪfti prəsiːdʒəz]	e.g. You have to follow safety procedures to avoid injury at the workplace.	Sicherheitsmaßnahmen, Sicherheitsbestimmungen
health and safety	[ˌhelθ ənd ˈseɪfti]	measures against accidents	Arbeitsschutz, Arbeitssicherheit
safety sign	[ˈseɪfti saɪn]	warning sign	Sicherzeitszeichen, Warnzeichen
ear protectors pl	[ɪə prˈtektəz]	e.g. Ear protectors must be worn in the factory at all times.	Gehörschutz
helmet	[ˈhelmɪt]	protection for the head	Helm
to **operate**	[ˈɒpəreɪt]	e.g. It's my job to operate printing machinery.	(Geräte) bedienen
machinery	[məˈʃiːnəri]	different machines	Maschinen, Geräte
safety glasses pl	[ˈseɪfti glɑːsɪz]	e.g. Wear safety glasses for eye protection!	Schutzbrille
to **beware of sth**	[bɪˈweər əv]	to be careful so that sth doesn't happen	sich vor etw in Acht nehmen
forklift truck	[ˌfɔːklɪft ˈtrʌk]	vehicle used to lift lots of pallets at once	Gabelstapler
to **catch fire**	[ˌkætʃ ˈfaɪə]	to start burning	Feuer fangen, in Brand geraten
electric shock	[ɪˌlektrɪk ˈʃɒk]	e.g. The broken hairdryer gave him an electric shock.	Stromschlag
protective gloves pl	[prəˌtektɪv ˈglʌvz]	gloves that stop sb's hands from being hurt, burnt, etc.	Schutzhandschuhe
to **pull sth down**	[ˌpʊl ˈdaʊn]	hold and move sth down firmly	etw herunterziehen
guard	[gɑːd]	safety cover	Schutzhaube
to **crush**	[krʌʃ]	to squash, to squeeze heavily	zerquetschen
protective clothing	[prəˌtektɪv ˈkləʊðɪŋ]	clothes that stop sb from being hurt, burnt, etc.	Schutzkleidung
to **take notice of sth**	[ˌteɪk ˈnəʊtɪs əv]	e.g. Please take notice of the safety regulations.	etw beachten

page 167

workplace safety	[ˈwɜːkpleɪs seɪfti]	e.g. The company is strict about workplace safety.	Sicherheit am Arbeitsplatz
case study	[ˈkeɪs stʌdi]	example	Fallstudie
industrial accident	[ɪnˌdʌstriəl ˈæksɪdənt]	e.g. He got hurt in an industrial accident.	Arbeitsunfall
printing works	[ˈprɪntɪŋ wɜːks]	factory in which things are printed	Druckerei
ink	[ɪŋk]	e.g. The printing press uses four different inks.	Druckfarbe
roller	[ˈrəʊlə]	e.g. The paper is squeezed dry between rollers.	Walze
printing press	[ˈprɪntɪŋ pres]	machine used for printing, especially books or newspapers	Druckmaschine
print run	[ˈprɪnt rʌn]	number of copies that are printed at one time	Auflage
to **afford sth**	[əˈfɔːd]	to be able to buy sth	sich etw leisten
cloth	[klɒθ]	piece of fabric for cleaning	Lappen, Tuch
to **shut down**	[ˌʃʌt ˈdaʊn]	to turn off	abschalten
procedure	[prəˈsiːdʒə]	process, measure	Vorgang
to **get stuck**	[get ˈstʌk]	to get caught	hängen bleiben, sich verfangen
to **pull**	[pʊl]	<> to push	ziehen
to **let go (of sth)**	[ˌlet ˈgəʊ]	to release sth	(etw) loslassen
wedding ring	[ˈwedɪŋ rɪŋ]	ring worn as a symbol of marriage	Ehering

page 168

obesity	[əʊˈbiːsəti]	adj obese	Fettleibigkeit
obese	[əʊˈbiːs]	heavily overweight	fettleibig
sb has a hard time doing sth	[hæz ə ˌhɑːd ˈtaɪm]	sb struggles with doing sth	jdm fällt es schwer, etw zu tun
childcare center AE	[ˈtʃaɪldkeə sentə]	nursery BE	Kindertagesstätte
to **be qualified**	[bi ˈkwɒlɪfaɪd]	to have a qualification	eine Ausbildung haben, einen Abschluss haben
ethnicity	[eθˈnɪsəti]	ethnic background	ethnische Zugehörigkeit
to **hire sb**	[ˈhaɪə]	to employ sb, to give sb a job	jdn einstellen
to **underestimate**	[ˌʌndərˈestɪmeɪt]	e.g. I underestimated the weight of these boxes. I can't lift them.	unterschätzen
to **fail to do sth**	[feɪl]	to not be able to do sth	nicht in der Lage sein, etw zu tun
level	[ˈlevl]	degree	Niveau
range	[reɪndʒ]	e.g. Most customers are in the 18–25 age range.	Bereich
flight of steps	[ˌflaɪt əf ˈsteps]	stairs	Treppe

individual	[ˌɪndɪˈvɪdʒʊəl]	single person, unique personality	(selbständige) Persönlichkeit, Individuum
protection	[prəˈtekʃn]	*v* to protect	Schutz
to **find**	[faɪnd]	e.g. The court found him guilty of murder.	befinden, festellen, entscheiden
court of justice	[ˌkɔːt əv ˈdʒʌstɪs]	the highest court of the European Union	Gerichtshof
to **fire sb**	[ˈfaɪə]	informal to let sb go	jdn entlassen, jdn feuern
clinic	[ˈklɪnɪk]	e.g. dental health clinic	Klinik
compensation	[ˌkɒmpənˈseɪʃn]	sth (usually money) given to sb to make up for loss	Abfindung
counsellor	[ˈkaʊnsələ]	sb who listens and gives advice	Berater/in

page 169

to **take sth into consideration**	[ˌteɪk ɪntə kənˌsɪdəˈreɪʃn]	to think about sth before making a decision	etw berücksichtigen, etw beachten
to **perform sth**	[pəˈfɔːm]	e.g. In this job you must perform a variety of tasks.	etw (Tätigkeit usw.) ausführen, etw durchführen
to **challenge sth**	[ˈtʃælɪndʒ]	to test sth	etw infrage stellen

UNIT 14

page 171

horizon	[həˈraɪzn]	*phr* on the horizon	Horizont
to **look ahead**	[ˌlʊk əˈhed]	to think about the future	nach vorne schauen
to **be in charge of sth**	[bi ɪn ˈtʃɑːdʒ əv]	to be in control of sth	das Sagen haben, am Drücker sein

page 172

(registered) nurse	[nɜːs]	sb qualified to take care of the ill or injured	(examinierte/r) Krankenpfleger/ -schwester
motor mechanic	[ˈməʊtə mɪkænɪk]	sb who repairs cars	Automechaniker/in
currently	[ˈkʌrəntli]	at the moment	zur Zeit, momentan
to **tour**	[tʊə]	to travel around	(Land usw.) bereisen
to **convert**	[kənˈvɜːt]	to change, to transform	umbauen
to **jam**	[dʒæm]	to casually play an instrument	eine Jamsession machen, jammen
enjoyment	[ɪnˈdʒɔɪmənt]	fun, entertainment	Vergnügen
sb is/gets emotional	[ɪz/gets ɪˈməʊʃənl]	e.g. Looking at old family photos always makes me emotional.	jdm kommen die Tränen
off piste	[ˌɒf ˈpiːst]	away from conventional paths	abseits der Piste
ski instructor	[ˈskiː ɪnstrʌktə]	sb who teaches people how to ski	Skilehrer/in
diverse	[daɪˈvɜːs]	varied	vielfältig
permanent(ly)	[ˈpɜːmənənt]	<> temporary	dauerhaft
engine	[ˈendʒɪn]	motor	Motor
pregnant	[ˈpregnənt]	*n* pregnancy	schwanger
healthcare	[ˈhelθkeə]	medical care	Gesundheitswesen, Krankenversorgung
incredible	[ɪnˈkredəbl]	unbelievable	unglaublich

page 173

globetrotting	[ˈgləʊbtrɒtɪŋ]	travelling around the world	weltreisend
archive	[ˈɑːkaɪv]	a collection of records and documents	Archiv
whenever	[wenˈevə]	e.g. I go running whenever I can.	immer wenn, wann immer
paediatric nurse	[piːdiˌætrɪk ˈnɜːs]	nurse who cares for children	Kinderkrankenpfleger/-schwester
while	[waɪl]	e.g. I'm working part-time while I'm living abroad.	solange
on the road	[ɒn ðə ˈrəʊd]	travelling	unterwegs
nursing	[ˈnɜːsɪŋ]	the job performed by nurses	Krankenpflege
to **busk**	[bʌsk]	to perform music on the street for money	Straßenmusik machen
to **sing along**	[ˌsɪŋ əˈlɒŋ]	to sing with others	mitsingen
up close	[ˌʌp ˈkləʊs]	near sth	aus nächster Nähe
truly	[ˈtruːli]	really	wirklich, echt
to **thunder**	[ˈθʌndə]	e.g. The storm came and it started to thunder.	donnern
to **cry**	[kraɪ]	e.g. Don't cry, it will be all right!	weinen
to **rob sb**	[rɒb]	to steal sth from sb	jdn bestehlen
robber	[ˈrɒbə]	sb who steals things	Räuber/in
to **shake**	[ʃeɪk]	e.g. He was so upset he was shaking with anger.	zittern
inequality	[ɪnɪˈkwɒləti]	<> equality	Ungleichheit
crime	[kraɪm]	*phr* to commit a crime	Verbrechen, Kriminalität
to **check sth out**	[ˌtʃek ˈaʊt]	to see what sth is like	sich etw ansehen
to **increase**	[ɪnˈkriːs]	to get higher	zunehmen, sich steigern
That's for sure.	[ðæts fə ˈʃʊə]	e.g. We can't find the dog, but he'll come back when he's hungry, that's for sure.	Na klar! So viel steht fest.
eccentric	[ɪkˈsentrɪk]	unusual and slightly crazy	exzentrisch
harsh	[hɑːʃ]	*phr* harsh climate	rau
border	[ˈbɔːdə]	e.g. There are no border controls between France and Germany.	Grenze
bloody	[ˈblʌdi]	e.g. 'Why is your face all bloody?' – 'Jason punched me in the nose.'	blutig
to **head east**	[ˌhed ˈiːst]	to go east	gen Osten aufbrechen

page 174

motor	['məʊtə]	car, engine	Auto, Motor
farm machinery	['fɑːm məʃiːnəri]	e.g. Farm machinery helps to make farming easier and faster.	Landmaschinen
to **set off**	[ˌset 'ɒf]	to start a journey	losfahren
freedom	['friːdəm]	*adj* free	Freiheit
to **widen**	['waɪdn]	to extend	erweitern
to **start a family**	[ˌstɑːt ə 'fæmli]	to decide to have children	eine Familie gründen
health insurance	['helθ ɪnʃʊərəns]	type of insurance one needs to get medical care	Krankenversicherung
snake	[sneɪk]	a long thin reptile with no legs	Schlange
shark	[ʃɑːk]	a large fish with sharp teeth	Hai
mechanical failure	[mɪˌkænɪkl 'feɪljə]	when sth stops working	technisches Versagen, Motorschaden
to **break down**	[ˌbreɪk 'daʊn]	e.g. Our car broke down right on the motorway.	eine Panne haben
It's just as well that …	[ɪts ˌdʒʌst əz 'wel ðət]	it's good that …	Da ist es gut, dass …

page 176

pod	[pɒd]	cabin on an observation wheel	Gondel, Kapsel
proxy	['prɒksi]	representative	Stellvertreter/in, stellvertretend
services *pl*	['sɜːvɪsɪz]	e.g. He bought a sign to advertise his services.	Dienstleistungen
robot	['rəʊbɒt]	e.g. The robot could talk and walk.	Roboter
wage	[weɪdʒ]	pay	Lohn
credit	['kredɪt]	point you get instead of money	Guthabenpunkt
His heart missed a beat.	[hɪz ˌhɑːt mɪst ə 'biːt]	He was very excited.	Dies ließ sein Herz höher schlagen.
universal	[ˌjuːnɪ'vɜːsl]	general	allgemein, universell
to **take up**	[ˌteɪk 'ʌp]	*phr* to take up a lot of space	*(Platz, Raum)* einnehmen
to **reply**	[rɪ'plaɪ]	to answer	antworten, entgegnen
trial period	[ˌtraɪəl 'pɪəriəd]	*phr* to be on a trial period	Probezeit
permanent	['pɜːmənənt]	<> temporary	unbefristet
full-time	[ˌfʊl 'taɪm]	<> part-time	Vollzeit-
resident	['rezɪdənt]	inhabitant	Bewohner, Einwohner
skyscraper	['skaɪskreɪpə]	tall building	Wolkenkratzer
storey	['stɔːri]	floor	Stockwerk
talkative	['tɔːkətɪv]	chatty	gesprächig
induction	[ɪn'dʌkʃn]	session organized to introduce sb to a new job	Einarbeitung

page 177

to **step out of sth**	[ˌstep 'aʊt əv]	to get out of sth	aus etw steigen, aus etw treten
cheerful	['tʃɪəfl]	<> sad	fröhlich
to **zoom off**	[ˌzuːm 'ɒf]	to leave quickly	davonsausen
identical (to sb/sth)	[aɪ'dentɪkl]	the same	identisch (mit jdm/etw)
robotic	[rəʊ'bɒtɪk]	*n* robot	Roboter-
to **lose sight of sth**	[ˌluːz 'saɪt əv]	to forget about sth	etw aus den Augen verlieren
to **adjust**	[ə'dʒʌst]	*adj* adjustable	einstellen, justieren
sth is a comfortable fit	[ɪz ə ˌkʌmftəbl 'fɪt]	e.g. Make sure that the shoes are a comfortable fit.	etw sitzt bequem
breeze	[briːz]	light wind	Brise, (leichter) Wind
eager(ly)	['iːgə]	wanting to do or have sth	eifrig, ungeduldig
unlike sth	[ˌʌn'laɪk]	different from sth	anders als etw
protective	[prə'tektɪv]	e.g. Wear protective goggles when working with chemicals.	schützend, Schutz-
dome	[dəʊm]	a spherical roof of a building	Kuppel
home town	[ˌhəʊm 'taʊn]	the town sb is from or lives in	Heimatstadt
rooftop garden	[ˌruːftɒp 'gɑːdn]	garden on the roof of a building	Dachgarten
to **pass sb**	[pɑːs]	to go past sb	jdn überholen, an jdm vorbeigehen
translator	[træns'leɪtə]	*v* to translate	Übersetzer/in
to **pick sth out**	[ˌpɪk 'aʊt]	to choose sth	etw aussuchen, etw auswählen
server	['sɜːvə]	e.g. The server brought our food over to us.	Servierer/in
to **beat**	[biːt]	*n* heartbeat	schlagen, pochen
bench	[bentʃ]	e.g. We sat on a bench in the park.	Bank
contented(ly)	[kən'tentɪd]	happy (happily)	zufrieden, wunschlos glücklich
paper plate	['peɪpə pleɪt]	plate made of cardboard	Pappteller
fork	[fɔːk]	*phr* knives and forks	Gabel
gardening tool	['gɑːdnɪŋ tuːl]	tools for garden work	Gartengerät
gardener	['gɑːdnə]	sb who works in a garden	Gärtner/in
grass	[grɑːs]	e.g. Lawn tennis is played on grass.	Gras
to **walk by**	[ˌwɔːk 'baɪ]	to pass by	vorbeilaufen, vorübergehen
thrill	[θrɪl]	feeling of excitement	Nervenkitzel, Kick
to **blink**	[blɪŋk]	to close one's eyes for a fraction of a second	blinzeln, zwinkern
middle-aged	[ˌmɪdl'eɪdʒd]	neither young nor old	mittleren Alters
authentic	[ɔː'θentɪk]	real	echt, authentisch

page 178

amazed	[əˈmeɪzd]	pleasantly surprised	erstaunt, verblüfft
to **entail sth**	[ɪnˈteɪl]	e.g. The trip will entail two train journeys.	etw mit sich bringen
densely populated	[ˌdensli ˈpɒpjuleɪtɪd]	e.g. The city of Mumbai is very densely populated. Lots of people live there.	dicht besiedelt
to **industrialize**	[ɪnˈdʌstrɪəlaɪz]	to develop more industries	industrialisieren
to **retain sth**	[rɪˈteɪn]	to keep sth	etw behalten
wolf, wolves	[wʊlf, wʊlvz]	e.g. Be careful. There are wolves in that forest.	Wolf, Wölfe
isolated	[ˈaɪsəleɪtɪd]	alone, not close to anyone/anything else	einzeln, vereinsamt
to **implant**	[ɪmˈplɑːnt]	e.g. We found our cat very quickly because she has an implanted microchip.	einpflanzen

page 179

news agency	[ˈnjuːz eɪdʒənsi]	organization that sells news stories	Nachrichtenagentur

page 180

department store	[dɪˈpɑːtmənt stɔː]	a large shop that sells many different things	Kaufhaus
cosmetics *pl*	[kɒzˈmetɪks]	e.g. mascara, lipstick, etc.	Kosmetik
food hall	[ˈfuːd hɔːl]	department for food	Lebensmittelabteilung
ladies' wear	[ˈleɪdiz weə]	clothes for women	Damenbekleidung
menswear	[ˈmenzweə]	clothes for men	Herrenbekleidung
sketch	[sketʃ]	drawing of sth	Skizze
shop floor	[ˌʃɒp ˈflɔː]	where things are sold	Verkaufsfläche
shop assistant	[ˈʃɒp əsɪstənt]	sb who works in a shop	Verkäufer/in
to **put sth aside**	[ˌpʊt əˈsaɪd]	to keep/save sth for sb	etw zurücklegen
sth in particular	[ɪn pəˈtɪkjələ]	sth special	etw Spezielles
change	[tʃeɪndʒ]	money you get back	Wechselgeld
to **exchange**	[ɪksˈtʃeɪndʒ]	to replace sth	umtauschen

page 181

retail	[ˈriːteɪl]	*phr* to work in retail	Einzelhandel
post code	[ˈpəʊst kəʊd]	series of numbers and letters that identify an area	Postleitzahl
postage	[ˈpəʊstɪdʒ]	the money you pay to send sth by post	Porto, Versandkosten
total sum	[ˌtəʊtl ˈsʌm]	total amount	Gesamtbetrag
delivery	[dɪˈlɪvəri]	*v* to deliver	Lieferung, Zustellung
expiry date	[ɪkˈspaɪri deɪt]	e.g. I wasn't able to use my credit card – it was past its expiry date!	Ablaufdatum
to **update**	[ˌʌpˈdeɪt]	*n* update	auf den neuesten Stand bringen
to **amount to sth**	[əˈmaʊnt tə]	to make the total sum of sth	*(Kosten:)* sich auf etw belaufen

page 182

sailing ship	[ˈʃeɪlɪŋ ʃɪp]	a ship that uses wind to move	Segelschiff
sail	[seɪl]	*v* to sail	Segel
to **maintain sth**	[meɪnˈteɪn]	*n* maintenance	etw instand halten, etw unterhalten
to **operate sth**	[ˈɒpəreɪt]	*n* operation	etw betreiben
computerized	[kəmˈpjuːtəraɪzd]	*n* computer	computergesteuert
crew	[kruː]	staff that works on a ship	Mannschaft
to **sail**	[seɪl]	to travel in a ship	segeln
watch	[wɒtʃ]	to watch	Wache, Wachmannschaft
sailor	[ˈseɪlə]	person who works on a ship	Matrose/-in, Segler/in

page 184

mugging	[ˈmʌɡɪŋ]	robbery on the street	Raubüberfall *(auf der Straße)*
glacier	[ˈɡlæsiə]	large area of ice	Gletscher
piste	[piːst]	ski run	Skipiste
to **obey sth**	[əˈbeɪ]	to do what sth requires you to do	etw befolgen
board of directors	[ˌbɔːd əv dəˈrektəz]	group of leaders of a company	Vorstand, Geschäftsführung
administrator	[ədˈmɪnɪstreɪtə]	sb who works in administration	Verwalter/in
to **win the lottery**	[ˌwɪn ðə ˈlɒtəri]	e.g. If I win the lottery, I'll buy myself a house.	im Lotto gewinnen
road trip	[ˈrəʊd trɪp]	(long) car journey	Autoreise
thief, thieves	[θiːf, θiːvz]	sb who steals things	Dieb, Diebe
criminal conviction	[ˌkrɪmɪnl kənˈvɪkʃn]	e.g. We didn't hire her as she had a criminal conviction for stealing.	strafrechtliche Verurteilung

Dieses Wörterverzeichnis enthält alle Wörter aus **Work with English 5ᵗʰ Edition** in alphabetischer Reihenfolge. Nicht aufgeführt sind internationale Wörter wie *hotel*, *email* usw. Wörter, die in den Audio- und Videotexten vorkommen, sind mit einem T bzw. einem V, und Wörter, die in den *Differentiation files* vorkommen, mit einem F hinter der Seitenzahl gekennzeichnet.

A

A levels *pl BE* 142T Abitur
ability 50 Fähigkeit, Möglichkeit
to **abolish sth** 32 etw abschaffen
aboriginal 135 australische/r Ureinwohner/in
about, out and ~ 88T unterwegs; to **be ~ to do sth** 122 etw gleich tun; im Begriff sein, etw zu tun
abroad 41T im/ins Ausland
absolutely 33 völlig, absolut, total
abuse 50 Missbrauch; 74T Beschimpfung(en)
to **abuse sb** 135 jdn missbrauchen
to **accept** 28 akzeptieren, annehmen
access: ~ (to sth) 43 Zugang (zu etw), Zugriff (auf etw); **disabled ~** 36 behindertengerechter Zugang
accessory 59 Accessoire
accident 37 Unfall; **industrial ~** 167 Arbeitsunfall
accommodation 82, 220 Unterkunft
account 28 Konto; 148 Schilderung, Bericht; **bank ~** 137, 225 Bankkonto
to **accuse sb of sth** 74T jdm etw vorwerfen
to **achieve sth** 35 etw erreichen
achievement 137T Leistung, Errungenschaft
acid 52T Säure
across 102T in ganz
act 148 Handlung, Tat, Akt
to **act: ~ sth out** 23 etw (mit verteilten Rollen) spielen; **~ as if** 98T so tun, als ob
action 43 Handeln, Maßnahme(n), Aktion(en)
to **activate** 140 aktivieren, einschalten
active(ly) 26 aktiv
activist 37 Aktivist/in
activity 33 Tätigkeit, Beschäftigung, Äktivität
actress 37 Schauspielerin
to **adapt to sth** 17 sich an etw anpassen
to **add** 6 hinzufügen; **~ up** 162T sich summieren
addict 51 Süchtige/r
addicted, to be ~ to sth 50 nach etw süchtig sein, von etw abhängig sein
addiction 50 Sucht; to **feed one's ~** 51 sich Stoff besorgen
to **address sb** 78 jdn anreden
adequate 77F angemessen
to **adjust** 177 einstellen, justieren
administrator 184 Verwalter/in
to **admire** 41T bewundern
to **admit** 63T zugeben, eingestehen
adolescent 137 Heranwachsende/r, Jugendliche/r
to **adopt: ~ sb** 95 adoptieren
adoption 95 Adoption; to **give sb up for ~** 95 jdn zur Adoption freigeben
adoptive parents *pl* 95 Adoptiveltern
adult 77 Erwachsene/r
advance, in ~ 79 im Voraus
advancement 147 Entwicklung, Förderung
advantage 33 Vorteil
adventure 82 Abenteuer
adventurous 139 abenteuerlustig
advert 38 Anzeige, Werbespot
to **advertise** 72 werben, Werbung machen
advertising (of sth) 38 Werbung (für etw), Bewerben (von etw)

advertisment, job ~ 106 Stellenanzeige; **radio ~** 102T Werbespot (im Radio)
advice 49 Rat, Ratschlag; **piece of ~** 98 Rat
to **advise sb to do sth** 74T jdm raten, etw zu tun; jdm empfehlen, etw zu tun
advocate 38 Befürworter/in, Verfechter/in
affairs *pl* 44T Geschäfte, geschäftliche Angelegenheiten
to **affect sb/sth** 18 jdn/etw beeinflussen, sich auf jdn/etw auswirken; 41T jdn/etw betreffen
to **afford sth** 62F, 167 sich etw leisten
afraid, to be ~ of sb/sth 12 vor jdm/etw Angst haben, sich vor jdm/etw fürchten; **I'm ~ ...** 55 leider ...
African American 147 afroamerikanisch; Afroamerikaner/in
after all 17 schließlich, immerhin
age, coming of ~ 137 Erwachsenwerden
aged care home *AusE* 133 Altenpflegeheim
agency 95 Agentur, Behörde; **news ~** 179 Nachrichtenagentur
agent, call centre ~ 7 Telefonagent/in, Callcenteragent/in
aggressive 148 aggressiv
to **agree** 31 zustimmen, einverstanden sein; **~ with sb** 20T jdm zustimmen, jds Meinung sein
agreement 56 Übereinkunft, Übereinstimmung
agricultural 107 landwirtschaftlich
agriculture 19 Landwirtschaft
aid, first ~ 49 Erste Hilfe; **walking ~s** *pl* 37 Gehhilfe(n)
aim 56 Ziel
to **aim to do sth** 106 beabsichtigen, etw zu tun
aimed, to be ~ at sb/sth 110 sich an jdn/etw wenden, sich an jdn/etw richten
air conditioning 140 Klimaanlage
aisle 66 Gang
all, after ~ 17 schließlich, immerhin; **at ~** 30T überhaupt
allergy 20 Allergie
although 32 obwohl
amateur 124T Amateur(-)
amazed 178 erstaunt, verblüfft
amazing 37 toll, super, erstaunlich
ambassador 41 Botschafter/in
ambition 131 Ziel, Wunschtraum, Ehrgeiz
ambulance 48 Rettungswagen
among 17 unter, bei
amount 17 Menge; 22 (Geld-)Betrag
to **amount to sth** 181T *(Kosten:)* sich auf etw belaufen
anaemia 20 Blutarmut, Anämie
ancestor 133 Vorfahre/-in, Ahne/-in
anger 33T Wut
to **animate** 43V antreiben, mit Leben erfüllen
to **announce** 68 ankündigen
announcement 44 Ankündigung, Mitteilung
annoyed 163 verärgert, sauer
anonymous(ly) 75 anonym
anorexia nervosa 37 Magersucht
to **answer: ~ back** 147 Widerworte geben, frech werden; **~ the phone** 152T ans Telefon gehen

answerphone 103 Anrufbeantworter
anthem, national ~ 121 Nationalhymne
antisocial 160 ungesellig, unsozial
apart 94 (voneinander) entfernt, getrennt, auseinander; **~ from** 17 abgesehen von, außer
to **apologize** 54 sich entschuldigen
apology 79 Entschuldigung
apparently 124T anscheinend
to **appear** 19 vorkommen, auftauchen; 38 *(TV, Werbung:)* auftreten; 48 scheinen
appearance 125 Erscheinung(sbild), Aussehen
appetite 22 Appetit
appliance 144 Elektrogerät, Haushaltsgerät
applicant 114 Bewerber/in
application 44 Bewerbung
to **apply: ~ (to sb/sth)** 100 (für jdn/etw) gelten; **~ for sth** 44 sich um etw bewerben; 110T etw beantragen; **~ sth to sth** 103T etw auf etw anwenden
to **appoint sb sth** 35 jdn zu etw ernennen
appointment 50 Termin
to **appreciate** 75 schätzen, zu schätzen wissen
apprenticeship 116 Lehre, Ausbildung, Lehrstelle
to **approach** 51 sich nähern, näherrücken, näherkommen; **~ sb** 149 sich jdm nähern, an jdn herantreten
approach 76 Herangehensweise, Ansatz
appropriate(ly) 36 passend; 114 angemessen
aptitude 159 Talent, Befähigung
archive 173 Archiv
area 34 Gegend, Gebiet, Bereich; **surrounding ~** 108 Umland, Umgebung
to **argue** 17 argumentieren
to **arise** 150 *(Probleme usw.:)* entstehen
arrangements *pl* 68 Vorbereitungen
article 19 Artikel
as 49 während; **~ if** 55 als ob; **~ long as** 20T solange; **~ soon as** 86 sobald; **~ usual** 59 wie üblich
to **ask for directions** 158 nach dem Weg fragen
asleep, to be fast ~ 130 (tief und) fest schlafen
aspect 76 Gesichtspunkt, Aspekt
aspiration 131 Bestreben, Ziel
assistance, to be of ~ to sb 67T jdm behilflich sein
assistant, shop ~ 180 Verkäufer/in
association 134 Verband, Vereinigung
to **assume** 74T davon ausgehen, annehmen
assumption 75 Vermutung, Annahme
athlete 135 Sportler/in
athletic 46 sportlich, athletisch
atmosphere 28 Atmosphäre
atmospheric 125 stimmungsvoll
to **attack** 147 angreifen, attackieren
attack, heart ~ 49 Herzinfarkt
attempt 65 Versuch
to **attempt to do sth** 147 versuchen, etw zu tun
to **attend sth** 115 an etw teilnehmen; 120 etw *(Veranstaltung usw.)* besuchen
attendant, flight ~ 7 Flugbegleiter/in

category 24 Rubrik, Kategorie
to cater for all tastes 126 für jeden Geschmack etw bieten
cathedral 14 Dom, Kathedrale
cattle 124 Vieh, Rinder; Stück Vieh, Rind; ~ drive 124T Viehtrieb
to cause 20 verursachen
to cause: ~ sb to do sth 77F jdn dazu veranlassen, etw zu tun; ~ trouble 83 Ärger machen
to celebrate 89 feiern
celebration 128 Feier, Fest
celebrity 36 Prominente/r, Promi
century 17 Jahrhundert
cereal 22 Müsli, Getreideflocken
ceremony, opening ~ 121 Eröffnungszeremonie
certain 10 bestimmte/r/s, gewisse/r/s
certainly 23 gern
certificate, school leaving ~ 109 Schulabgangszeugnis
chain 66 Kette
challenge 47 Herausforderung, (schwierige) Aufgabe
to challenge: ~ sb 131 jdn herausfordern; ~ sth 169 etw infrage stellen
chances are that … 42 aller Wahrscheinlichkeit nach …
change 180 Wechselgeld; climate ~ 41T Klimawandel
to change: ~ one's mind 63T seine Meinung ändern; ~ one's ways 20T seine Gewohnheiten ändern,
changing room 68 Umkleidekabine
character 106 Charakter; 136 (Roman, Film usw.:) Figur
characteristic 95 Merkmal, Eigenschaft
to characterize 122 etw beschreiben, etw charakterisieren
charge, free of ~ 33T gebührenfrei, kostenlos; to be in ~ of sth 86 für etw zuständig sein; 171 das Sagen haben, am Drücker sein
charitable 135 wohltätig
charity 35 Hilfsorganisation(en), wohltätige Zwecke
chart 14 Tabelle; bar ~ 77 Säulendiagramm; flow ~ 61 Flussdiagramm; pie ~ 80 Tortendiagramm
chatty 66 geschwätzig
to cheat 53 schummeln, betrügen, abschreiben, spicken
to check sth out 173 sich etw ansehen
cheek 162T Wange
to cheer 121 jubeln, anfeuern
cheerful 177 fröhlich
Cheers! 22 Prost!
chef 110T (Chef-)Koch/Köchin
chicken 13 Huhn, Hühnchen
child, only ~ 95 Einzelkind
childcare center AE 168 Kindertagesstätte
to chill 56 chillen, relaxen
choice 13 Wahl; poor ~s pl 147 falsche Entscheidungen
to chop sth up 59 etw zerkleinern, etw schreddern
to chuck 178 schmeißen
church 9 Kirche
cinema 9 Kino
circus skills pl 71 Zirkuskünste, Akrobatik
citizen 36 (Staats-)Bürger/in
city folk 124T Stadtmenschen, Städter
civil: ~ rights pl 148 Bürgerrechte
civilian 147 zivil; Zivilist/in

claim 74T Behauptung
to claim 147 behaupten
class, working ~ 147 Arbeiterklasse
climate 41 Klima; ~ change 41T Klimawandel
to climb 88T steigen, klettern
climbing, rock ~ 119 Klettern
clinic 168 Klinik
close, up ~ 173 aus nächster Nähe
to close sth down 61 etw schließen, etw zumachen
cloth 167 Lappen, Tuch
clothing 58 Kleidung, Bekleidung; protective ~ 166 Schutzkleidung
cloudy 111 bewölkt
coach 30 Trainer/in
coastline 59 Küste
code, post ~ 181 Postleitzahl
coin 22 Münze
to collaborate 159 zusammenarbeiten
to collapse 48 zusammenbrechen, zusammenklappen
collapsible seat 37 Klappsitz
collar, white-~ worker 222 Büroangestellte/r
colleague 44T Kollege/-in
to colonize 32 kolonisieren
colored AE 147 farbig
colourful 87 bunt, farbenfroh
column 6 (Text:) Spalte
coma 48 Koma
to combat sth 56 etw bekämpfen
combination 32 Verbindung
to combine 14 verbinden, kombinieren
to come: ~ across as … 38 … wirken; ~ across sth 37 auf etw stoßen, etw (zufällig) finden; ~ down to sth 162T auf etw hinauslaufen; ~ up with sth 76 sich etw ausdenken, sich etw einfallen lassen
comfortable 59 bequem, komfortabel; to feel ~ 79 sich wohlfühlen; sth is a ~ fit 177 etw sitzt bequem
comforts pl 83 Annehmlichkeiten
coming of age 137 Erwachsenwerden
comma 78 Komma
to commence 123 beginnen, anfangen
comment 40 Kommentar, Stellungnahme
to comment on sth 34 etw kommentieren, zu etw Stellung nehmen
to commit: ~ sth 52T etw (Tat, Verbrechen usw.) begehen; ~ sth to sth 139 etw (voll und ganz) einer Sache widmen, etw einer Sache anvertrauen; ~ to sth 58 sich für etw engagieren, sich zu etw verpflichten
commited, to be ~ to sth 58 sich für etw engagieren, sich zu etw verpflichten
commitment (to sth) 59 Engagement (für etw), Verpflichtung (zu etw)
committee, organizing ~ 103T Organisationskomitee
common 36 verbreitet; 159 gemeinsam; to have sth in ~ 44T etw gemeinsam haben; ~ sense 103T gesunder Menschenverstand
community 33T Gemeinschaft, Gemeinde
to compare with sth 46 sich mit etw vergleichen lassen, Unterschiede zu etw haben
compensation 168 Abfindung
to compete 124T (bei einem Wettbewerb) antreten; ~ for sth 96 um etw konkurrieren
competition 24 Wettbewerb; 52T Konkurrenz; 107, 217 Kompetenz
competitor 156 Teilnehmer/in (an einem Wettbewerb)

complaint 41T, 140 Klage, Beschwerde, Reklamation
completion 117 Vervollständigung
complex 43V komplex, kompliziert
complicated 162T kompliziert
comprehensive 43V umfassend
to compromise 33 einen Kompromiss eingehen
computer literacy 107 Computerkenntnisse
computerized 182 computergesteuert
to concentrate (on sth) 52T sich (auf etw) konzentrieren
concept car 126 Konzeptauto
to concern sb/sth 77F jdn/etw betreffen
concerned 74T besorgt, beunruhigt
to conclude 19F, 46 schließen
conclusion, to jump to ~s 74T voreilige Schlüsse ziehen; in ~ 77F abschließend
condition 49 (chronische) Krankheit, Leiden; 68 Zustand
conditioner 140 Haarspülung
confidence 27 Selbstvertrauen, Selbstbewusstsein
confident 114 selbstbewusst; self-~ 38 selbstbewusst; to feel ~ 159 sich sicher fühlen
to confirm 94 bestätigen
conflict, armed ~ 232 bewaffnete Auseinandersetzung
to conform to sth 37 einer Sache entsprechen
confused 163 verwirrt
confusing 116 verwirrend
congenital 37 angeboren
Congratulations on …! 30T Herzlichen Glückwunsch zu …!
to connect, ~ sb 152 (Telefon:) jdn durchstellen; ~ with sb 54 sich mit jdm (intensiv) austauschen, mit jdm in Kontakt kommen
connection (to sb/sth) 96 Verbindung (mit jdm/etw), Bezug (zu jdm/etw)
conscious, fashion-~ 222 modebewusst
consensus 56 Übereinstimmung, Konsens
consequence 85 Konsequenz, Folge
conservationist 133 Naturschützer/in
conservative 107 konservativ
to consider: ~ sth 70 etw in Betracht/ Erwägung ziehen; 102T Rücksicht auf etw nehmen; ~ sth sth 77F etw für etw halten; to be ~ed sth 122 als etw gelten, als etw angesehen werden
considerably 30T beträchtlich, erheblich
consideration, to take sth into ~ 169 etw berücksichtigen, etw beachten
to consist of sb/sth 93 aus jdm/ etw bestehen
consonant 9 Konsonant
constantly 162T ständig, andauernd
consultant 44T Berater/in
to consume 48 zu sich nehmen, konsumieren; 102 verbrauchen
consumer 102T Verbraucher/in, Konsument/in; ~ culture 102T Konsumkultur
consumerism 62F Konsumdenken
contact, body ~ 44T Körperkontakt; eye ~ 114 Blickkontakt
to contain 61F, 65 enthalten
container 140 Behälter
content 53 Inhalt
contented(ly) 177 zufrieden, wunschlos glücklich
contents 61 Inhalt
contest 124T Wettbewerb
context 16 Zusammenhang, Kontext

to **continue to do sth** 20 etw weiterhin tun
contract 65 Vertrag; to **win a ~** 65 einen
Auftrag erhalten, den Zuschlag erhalten
to **contrast sth with sth** 23 etw einander ge-
genüberstellen, etw miteinander vergleichen
contributor 71 Autor/in *(eines Magazins)*
control 33T Kontrolle
controversial 148 umstritten
convenience store 147 Laden um die Ecke,
Spätkauf
convenient 65V praktisch, bequem;
85 günstig gelegen
convention 127 Konferenz, Tagung,
Versammlung
to **convert** 71 umwandeln; 172 umbauen
conviction, criminal ~ 184 strafrechtliche
Verurteilung
to **convince** 33 überzeugen
convinced 102T überzeugt
convincing 162T überzeugend
to **cooperate** 60 zusammenarbeiten
to **cope with sth** 28F, 53 etw bewältigen,
mit etw zurechtkommen
corn *AE* 128 Mais
corner 77 Ecke
coroner 48 Gerichtsmediziner/in
to **correspond to sth** 63F einer Sache
entsprechen
correspondence 89 Briefwechsel,
Korrespondenz
corridor 101T Flur
cosmetics *pl* 180 Kosmetik
costume 125 Kostüm
council, town ~ 44T Stadtrat, Stadtverwaltung
counselling 51 Therapie, Beratung;
~ service 51 Beratungsdienst
counsellor 168 Berater/in
to **count** 12 zählen; **C~ me in!** 102T Ich
bin dabei!
countable 12 zählbar
countless 232 zahllos
country, developing ~ 102T Entwicklungsland
countryside 83 Land, Landschaft; **in the ~**
232 auf dem Land
county 137T Grafschaft
courageous 35 mutig
course 24 *(Menü:)* Gang; **~ of treatment**
50 Therapie, Behandlung; **business ~** 147
kaufmännische Ausbildung; to **set the ~ of**
sth 52T die Weichen für etw stellen; **during**
the ~ of sth 122 im Verlauf von etw
court, ~ of justice 168 Gerichtshof
cousin 116 Cousin/Cousine
to **cover: ~ sth** 31 etw *(Thema)* behandeln,
sich mit etw befassen; 137T etw bedecken;
~ sth up 74T etw überspielen, etw verbergen
covering letter 106 Anschreiben, Begleitschreiben
cow 124T Kuh
crack 121 Knall, Krachen
crazy, to go ~ 137T durchdrehen
to **create sth** 37 etw entwerfen, etw verfassen; 148 etw hervorrufen
creative 76 schöpferisch, kreativ
creature, mythological ~ 226 Sagengestalt
credit 176 Guthabenpunkt; **~ card** 22
Kreditkarte
crew 182 Mannschaft
crime 173 Verbrechen, Kriminalität
criminal 147 kriminell; **~ conviction** 184
strafrechtliche Verurteilung

crisis 43V Krise
crisps *pl* 22 Chips
critic 76 Kritiker/in
critical 54 kritisch
criticism 74T Kritik
to **criticize** 37 kritisieren
crop 124 Ackerpflanze, Getreide
to **cross** 116 überqueren
crossroads, to be at a ~ 65V an einem
Scheideweg stehen, an einem Wendepunkt
stehen
crowd 41T Menschenmenge
cruel 124T grausam
to **crush** 166 zerquetschen
to **cry** 173 weinen
culture 17 Kultur; **consumer ~** 102T
Konsumkultur
cup, world ~ 30T Weltpokal, Weltmeisterschaft
cupboard 10 Schrank
curious 138 *neugierig*
current 21 aktuell
currently 172 zur Zeit, momentan
custom 108 Sitte, Brauch
customer 44T Kunde/-in
to **cut down on sth** 49 etw reduzieren
cute 161 süß, niedlich
CV *BE* 107 Lebenslauf
to **cycle** 111 Fahrrad fahren, radeln
cynical 151 zynisch

D

dairy products *pl* 17 Milchprodukte
danger 48 Gefahr
date, expiry ~ 181 Ablaufdatum
day: open ~ 158 Tag der offenen Tür; **~ out**
121 freier Tag, Ausflug; **at the end of the ~**
124T letzten Endes, letztlich; **one ~** 18
eines Tages; **these ~s** 147 heutzutage
daylight, in broad ~ 156 am hellichten Tag,
vor aller Augen
dead, to shoot sb ~ 147 jdm erschießen
deafening 121 ohrenbetäubend
deal 60 Geschäft, Abkommen; **a big ~** 137T
eine große Sache; **special ~** 126 Sonderangebot
to **deal: ~ with sb** 44T mit jdm zu tun haben;
~ with sth 16F sich mit etw befassen;
51 etw angehen, mit etw fertig werden;
74T mit etw zurechtkommen, etw bewältigen
dealership, car ~ 126 Autohaus, Auto-
händler/in
debris 59 Rückstände, (Trümmer-)Teile
to **decide** 10 (sich) entscheiden
decimal point 78 Dezimalpunkt
decline 144 Niedergang
to **decorate sth** 46 etw schmücken
definitely 59 (ganz) bestimmt, auf jeden Fall
delay 45 Verzögerung, Verspätung
to **deliver** 15 liefern
delivery 181 Lieferung, Zustellung
demand 144 Forderung
to **demand** 147 fordern
democratic 147 demokratisch
to **demonstrate sth** 125 etw vorführen
densely populated 178 dicht besiedelt
to **deny sth** 147 etw bestreiten,
etw leugnen
department 65 Abteilung; **police ~** *AE* 147
Polizeibehörde; **~ store** 180 Kaufhaus
to **depend on sth** 40 von etw abhängen
dependent (on sth) 51 abhängig (von etw)
depending on 107 je nach

depressed 77F, 220 niedergeschlagen,
deprimiert
depression 74T Depression(en)
depressive 77 depressiv
descendant 138 Nachkomme
description, job ~ 107 Stellenbeschreibung
desert 17 Wüste
design 24 Gestaltung, Entwurf
to **design** 80 gestalten, entwerfern
desk, cash ~ 66 Kasse
desperate(ly) 178 verzweifelt
despite 65 trotz
dessert 23 Nachtisch, Dessert
to **destroy** 17 zerstören
details *pl* 37 Angaben, Daten, Einzelheiten
determined 41T entschlossen, willensstark
to **develop** 27 (sich) entwickeln
developing country 102T Entwicklungsland
development 28 Entwicklung
device 80 (elektronisches) Gerät
diary 26 Tagebuch; to **keep a ~** 26 ein
Tagebuch führen
dictator 42 Diktator/in
dictionary 8 Wörterbuch
diet 17 Kost, Ernährung; 37 Diät; to **go on**
a ~ 40 eine Diät machen
dietician 20T Ernährungswissenschaftler/in
difference, to make a ~ 102T etw bewirken
difficulty, to present ~ies 98 Schwierigkeiten
darstellen, mit Schwierigkeiten verbunden sein
digit 90 Ziffer
diplomacy 157 Diplomatie
directions *pl*, to **ask for ~** 158 nach dem Weg
fragen; to **give ~** 103T den Weg erklären
director, board of ~s 184 Vorstand,
Geschäftsführung
dirty 11 schmutzig, dreckig
disability 37 Behinderung
disabled 36 behindert; **~ access** 36 behindertengerechter Zugang
disadvantage 73 Nachteil
to **disagree (with sb)** 33T (jdm) widerspre-
chen, anderer Meinung (als jd) sein
to **disappear** 76 verschwinden
to **disappoint sb** 121 jdn enttäuschen
disappointed (in sb/sth) 55 enttäuscht
(von jdm/etw)
disappointing 74T enttäuschend
disappointment 122 Enttäuschung
discipline 33 Disziplin
to **discover** 94 entdecken, herausfinden
discrimination 147 Diskriminierung
dish 17 Gericht, Speise; to **wash the ~es**
156 (Geschirr) spülen
dishwasher 99 Spülmaschine
disorder, eating ~ 37 Essstörung
dispenser 140 Spender
display 126 Ausstellung, (Messe-)Stand,
Display
to **display sth** 76 etw zur Schau stellen
disposable 140 Einweg-, Wegwerf-
to **dispose of sth** 61 etw entsorgen, sich
einer Sache entledigen
disrespectful(ly) 162T unhöflich,
respektlos
distance 151F Ferne
to **distinguish sb/sth from sb/sth** 137
jdn/etw von jdm/etw unterscheiden
to **distract sb** 101T jdn ablenken
distribution of wealth 102T Wohlstandsverteilung
to **disturb** 100 stören
diverse 172 vielfältig

to **divide** 114 teilen; **~ sth up** 125 etw
aufteilen
to **divorce sb** 96 sich von jdm scheiden
lassen
do: ~s and don'ts 44T Dinge, die man tun
und lassen sollte
to **do: to be done with sth** 59 mit etw fertig
sein
dome 177 Kuppel
to **donate** 35 spenden
dormitory 83 Schlafsaal
double 95 Double, Doppelgänger/in
doubt 108 Zweifel
down under 118 in Australien
to **download** 100 herunterladen
to **draw** 21 zeichnen, *(Linie)* ziehen; 30
unentschieden spielen; 145 ziehen; **~ sth
up** 125 etw entwerfen; **~ attention to
sth** 74 Aufmerksamkeit auf etw lenken
drawer 101T Schublade
drawing 24 Zeichnung
dream 9 Traum; to **make a ~ come
true** 116 sich einen Traum erfüllen
dried 17 getrocknet
drip 50 Infusion
drive 66 Fahrt *(mit dem Auto)*; **cattle ~**
124T Viehtrieb
to **drive: to test ~** 126 probefahren
driven, to be ~ by sth 62F von etw
getrieben sein
driver 60 Fahrer/in
driving test 137 Fahrprüfung
to **drop** 64 (tot) umfallen; **~ sth** 144 etw
fallen lassen, etw (auf den Boden) werfen;
~ out of school 51 die Schule abbrechen
drug: ~ misuser 51 (Drogen-)Konsument/
in; **~-taking** 139 Drogenkonsum
due, to be ~ to do sth 147 etw *(laut Plan)*
machen sollen
drunk, to get ~ 42 sich betrinken
due to 17 aufgrund von
to **dump** 60 *(Müll)* (wild) abkippen
during 32 während; **~ the course of sth**
122 im Verlauf von etw
dust 63T Staub
duty, phone ~ 152 Telefondienst

E

eager(ly) 177 eifrig, ungeduldig
ear protectors *pl* 166 Gehörschutz
to **earn** 63T verdienen
easy-going 74T gelassen, unkompliziert
eating disorder 37 Essstörung
eccentric 173 exzentrisch
economic 143T wirtschaftlich, Wirtschafts-
economy 62F Wirtschaft
to **educate** 41 unterrichten, informieren,
(aus)bilden
education 35 Schulbildung, Ausbildung;
further ~ 44 Weiterbildung; **higher ~** 161
Hochschulbildung; **vocational ~** 133 berufliche Bildung; to **enter higher ~** 216 ein
Studium beginnen
educational 143T Bildungs-, schulisch
effect 24 Wirkung, Effekt
effective 73F effektiv, wirkungsvoll
effort, to make an ~ 26 sich anstrengen,
sich Mühe geben
elder 133 Ältere/r, Älteste/r
elderly 155 ältere/r/s
to **elect** 147 wählen
election 137 Wahl
electric shock 166 Stromschlag

electrician 116 Elektriker/in
electricity 140 Strom
electronics 143T Elektronik
embarrassed 163 verlegen, peinlich berührt;
sb is ~ by sth 74T jdm ist etw peinlich
emergency 101T Notfall
emotional 74T emotional; **sb is/gets ~**
172 jdm kommen die Tränen
emphasis, to put ~ on sth 38 etw hervorheben, etw betonen
empire 30T (Welt-)Reich
employee 100 Beschäftigte/r, Mitarbeiter/in
employer 114 Arbeitgeber/in
to **enable sb to do sth** 107 jdm ermöglichen, etw zu tun; jdn befähigen, etw zu tun
encounter 148 Begegnung, Zusammenstoß
to **encounter sb/sth** 143 auf jdn/etw
stoßen, jdm/einer Sache begegnen
to **encourage: ~ sb to do sth** 38 jdn dazu er-
muntern, etw zu tun; jdm dazu raten, etw zu
tun; **~ sth** 76 etw begünstigen, etw fördern
encouragement 76 Ermutigung, Zuspruch
to **end up somewhere** 59 irgendwo landen
end, towards the ~ 110T gegen Ende
endless(ly) 43V unendlich
energetic 27 voller Energie, tatkräftig
to **enforce sth** 101T etw durchsetzen
to **engage in small talk with sb** 67 mit jdm
ins Plaudern kommen
engine 172 Motor
engineer 7 Ingenieur/in, Techniker/in;
service ~ 238 Servicetechniker/in
engineering 150T Maschinenbau
to **enjoy: ~ oneself** 121 sich gut amüsieren;
Did you ~ your meal? 23 Hat es Ihnen
geschmeckt?
enjoyable 85 angenehm, erfreulich
enjoyment 172 Vergnügen
to **enquire about sth** 89 sich nach etw
erkundigen
to **entail sth** 178 etw mit sich bringen
to **enter** 66 betreten; **~ sth** 120 *(Wettbewerb usw.:)* an etw teilnehmen
entertaining 87 unterhaltsam
entertainment 37 Unterhaltung
entire 52T ganze/r/s, vollständig
entirely 59 völlig, vollständig
entrance 88T Eintritt, Einlass
entrepreneur 61 Unternehmer/in
entry 27 Eintrag, Beitrag
equal(ly) 35 gleich
equality 147 Gleichheit, Gleichberechtigung,
Gleichbehandlung
equipment 32 Ausrüstung, Ausstattung,
Geräte; **piece of ~** 63T Gerät
errand, to run ~s 65V Besorgungen machen
error, administrative ~ 237 Verwaltungs-
irrtum
especially 30T besonders, insbesondere
essential 159 wesentlich, unerlässlich
esteem, self-~ 216 Selbstachtung, Selbst-
wertgefühl
to **estimate** 96 schätzen
ethnicity 168 ethnische Zugehörigkeit
eve, New Year's E~ 129 Silvester
even though 35 obwohl
event 34 Veranstaltung; **103T** Ereignis
eventually 133 schließlich, am Ende
evidence 122 Indizien, Hinweise; to **provide ~**
147 Beweise liefern
exaggerated 74T übertrieben
exam, school-leaving ~ 133 Abschlussprüfung

to **examine** 19F, 46 untersuchen
example, to set an ~ 41 ein Beispiel geben
except for 60 außer, abgesehen von
exception (to sth) 10 Ausnahme (von etw)
to **exchange** 33 austauschen;
180 umtauschen
exchange 16 Austausch; **hospitality ~** 83
Aufenthalt bei einer Gastfamilie; **exchange,
school ~** 30T Schüleraustausch; **~ student**
34 Austauschschüler/in
exciting 30 aufregend, spannend
exercise, to do ~ 52 trainieren, sich fit halten;
~ bike 31 Trainingsfahrrad, Heimtrainer
to **exert** 131 *(Einfluss usw.)* ausüben
exhausted 142T erschöpft
to **exhibit** 126 ausstellen
exhibition 126 Ausstellung, Messe
exhibitor 126 Aussteller/in
to **expand sth** 76 etw erweitern,
etw ausweiten
expense 83 Kosten, Ausgabe(n),
Aufwendung(en)
experience 40 Erlebnis, Erfahrung; **work ~**
100 Praktikum
to **experience sth** 74T etw erleben,
etw erfahren
expert 48 Fachmann/-frau, Experte/-in
expiry date 181 Ablaufdatum
explanation 79 Erklärung, Erläuterung
explicit 78 klar, unverblümt
exploitation 151F Ausbeutung
exploration 151F Erforschung, Entdeckung
to **explore** 83 erkunden
to **express** 50 ausdrücken, äußern
expression, facial ~ 230 Mimik, Gesichts-
ausdruck
extended 93 erweitert
extra 22 zusätzliche/r/s
extract 125 Auszug, Ausschnitt
extracurricular 52T außerhalb des Stunden-
plans, außerschulisch
eye, to turn a blind ~ to sth 101T bei etw ein
Auge zudrücken; **~-catching** 92 prägnant,
auffallend, ins Auge springend; **~ contact**
114 Blickkontakt
eyewitness 147 Augenzeuge/-in

F

to **face sth** 17 mit etw konfrontiert sein/
werden, einer Sache gegenüberstehen
face-to-face 44 persönlich, unter vier
Augen
facilities *pl* 9 Einrichtung(en), Ausstattung
factor 68 Faktor
to **fail** 108 *(Prüfung)* nicht bestehen, durch-
fallen; **~ to do sth** 29F versäumen, etw zu
tun; es nicht schaffen, etw zu tun;
168 nicht in der Lage sein, etw zu tun
failure, mechanical ~ 174 technisches
Versagen, Motorschaden
fair, trade ~ 126 (Branchen-/Handels-)
Messe
to **fall: ~ in love with sb/sth** 63T sich in
jdn/etw verlieben
fame 37 Ruhm
familiar, to be ~ with sth 93 mit etw vertraut sein, etw kennen
family, blended ~ 93 Patchworkfamilie;
nuclear ~ 93 Kernfamilie, Kleinfamilie;
single-parent ~ 93 Einelternfamilie; to
start a ~ 174 eine Familie gründen
fantasy 7 Phantasie-; **~ world** 159 Traum-
welt, Phantasiewelt

far, so ~ 30 bislang
farm machinery 174 Landmaschinen
farmhand 124 Landarbeiter/in
farming 138 Landwirtschaft; **animal ~** 17 Tierhaltung
fashion 37 Mode; to **go out of ~** 143T aus der Mode kommen
to **fasten one's seat belt** 110T sich anschnallen
to **fast-forward** 116 vorspulen, springen
fat, low in ~ 214 fettarm
fatal outcome 147 tödlicher Ausgang
fault, sth is sb's ~ 51 jd ist schuld an etw
favour, to be in ~ of sth 149 etw befürworten
fear 145 Angst
to **feature sth** 37 über etw berichten, (Story) bringen
federal 106 Bundes-
to **feed** 16 ernähren; 130 füttern; **~ one's addiction** 51 sich Stoff besorgen
to **feel: ~ comfortable** 79 sich wohlfühlen; **~ confident** 159 sich sicher fühlen; **~ left out** 77 sich übergangen/ausgeschlossen fühlen
feeling 62 Gefühl, Ansicht, Meinung
fellow student 48 Mitschüler/in
festival 113F, 129 Fest, Festtag
to **fight back** 37 sich verteidigen, zurückschlagen
figure 69 Zahl; 148 Persönlichkeit, Gestalt; 151F Figur; **sales ~s pl** 79 Verkaufszahlen, Umsatzzahlen
to **fill** 6 füllen; **~ in** 14 eintragen, ausfüllen
final 20T letzte/r/s; **semi-~** 30T Halbfinale
finally 19F schließlich, zuletzt
to **find** 143T feststellen; 168 befinden, entscheiden; **~ one's way around** 134 sich zurechtfinden; **~ one's way somewhere** 59 wohin gelangen
finding 80 Ergebnis
to **fire sb** 168 jdn entlassen, jdn feuern
fire, to catch ~ 166 Feuer fangen, in Brand geraten
firefighter AE 35 Feuerwehrmann
fireworks pl 125 Feuerwerk
first, at ~ 74T zunächst; **in the ~ place** 51 überhaupt, von vornherein; **~ aid** 49 Erste Hilfe
to **fit: ~ sth** 16 zu etw passen; **~ into sth** 106 sich in etw einfügen
fit, sth is a comfortable ~ 177 etw sitzt bequem
to **fix sth** 41T etw (Problem usw.) beheben; 107 etw reparieren, etw flicken
flash 125 Blitz(licht)
flat BE 83 Wohnung
flatmate 85 Mitbewohner/in
flatshare 150 Wohngemeinschaft
flexible 101T flexibel
flight 45 Flug; **~ of steps** 168 Treppe; **~ attendant** 7 Flugbegleiter/in
flirty 162T kokett
floor, shop ~ 180 Verkaufsfläche; **~ plan** 126 Grundriss, Übersichtsplan
flour 17 Mehl
flow chart 61 Flussdiagramm
fluent 159 (Sprache:) fließend
flyer 34 Handzettel, Broschüre
focus 94 Schwerpunkt, Hauptaugenmerk; 148 Brennpunkt, Mittelpunkt
to **focus (on sth)** 52T sich (auf etw) konzentrieren

folk, city ~ 124T Stadtmenschen, Städter
follow-up 48 Nachfassen
food: ~ hall 180 Lebensmittelabteilung; **~ production** 16 Nahrungsmittelproduktion
fool 63 Narr
foot 121 Fuß (ca. 30,5 cm); to **stamp one's feet** 121 mit den Füßen trampeln; to **step ~ in sth** 99 etw betreten
footage 147 Aufnahme(n), Filmmaterial
football: ~ practice 155 Fußballtraining
footpath 83 (Wander-)Weg, Pfad
force, police ~ 147 Polizei, Polizeiapparat
to **force** 139 zwingen; to **be ~ed to do sth** 18F gezwungen sein, etw zu tun
forefront, to bring sth to the ~ 147 etw öffentlich machen, etw in den Vordergrund stellen
foreground 151F Vordergrund
foreign 110 ausländisch, fremd; **~ language** 98T Fremdsprache
forest 17 Wald
fork 177 Gabel
forklift truck 166 Gabelstapler
to **form** 81 bilden
Formula One 127 Formel 1
fortunately 162T glücklicherweise, zum Glück
fossil fuel 41T fossiler Brennstoff
to **found** 32 gründen
foundation 35 Stiftung
to **freak out** 95 ausrasten, durchdrehen
free of charge 33T gebührenfrei, kostenlos
to **free up sth** 67 etw freimachen, etw entlasten
freedom 139F, 174 Freiheit
freezing 112 eiskalt
fridge 112 Kühlschrank
fried 22 gebraten, Brat-
friend, to make ~s 26 Freunde finden/gewinnen
to **frighten sb** 32 jdm Angst einjagen
frightening 123 beängstigend, erschreckend
front, in ~ of 8 vor
frozen lake 32 zugefrorener See
fuel, fossil ~ 41T fossiler Brennstoff
to **fulfil** 110T erfüllen
full 23 satt; **~-time** 176 Vollzeit-
to **fund** 156 finanzieren
fundraiser 152 Spendensammler/in
furious(ly) 125 wild, heftig
further 114 weiter, weitergehend; **~ education** 44 Weiterbildung
furthermore 101T außerdem, darüber hinaus

G

to **gain** 109 erwerben, erlangen; **~ sth from sth** 165 sich etw von etw versprechen, etw mit etw erreichen; **~ muscle** 104 Muskeln aufbauen
gambling 119 Glücksspiel
game, role-playing ~ 159 Rollenspiel
gap 23 Lücke
garbage 59 Müll, Abfall
gardener 177 Gärtner/in
gardening tool 177 Gartengerät
gate 130 Tor, Pforte
to **gather** 101T vermuten, sich etw denken; 147 sich versammeln; **~ sth** 80 etw sammeln, etw zusammentragen
gathering, social ~ 138 geselliges Beisammensein
gender 78 Geschlecht
generalization 54 Verallgemeinerung
generally 17 normalerweise, im Allgemeinen

generation 93 Generation
gentle 147 sanft
gentleman 44T Herr
genuine 37 echt, authentisch
to **get: ~ sth across** 41T etw vermitteln; **~ back to sb** 101T sich bei jdm melden; **~ by with sth** 63T mit etw auskommen; **~ on (with sb)** 134 (mit jdm) zurechtkommen; **~ on well with sb** 109 gut mit jdm auskommen; **~ ready** 28 sich fertigmachen, sich vorbereiten; **~ started** 6 loslegen, anfangen; **~ stuck** 167 hängen bleiben, sich verfangen; **~ used to sth** 112 sich an etw gewöhnen; **~ a life** 27 mit seinem Leben (endlich) etwas anfangen
giant 147 Riese
gig 37 (Rock-, Pop-, Jazz-)Konzert
to **give: ~ sth away** 60 etw verschenken; **~ up** 27 aufgeben; **~ sth up to sb** 148 jdm etw überlassen; **~ directions** 103T den Weg erklären; **~ reasons** 15 begründen; **~ thanks** 128 Dank sagen
glacier 184 Gletscher
glad, to be ~ 17 froh sein, sich freuen
glass, to raise your ~ 22 sein Glas erheben
glasses pl, safety ~ 166 Schutzbrille
global 16 global, weltumspannend; **~ warming** 17 Erderwärmung
globe 157 Welt, Erde, Globus
globetrotting 173 weltreisend
glove 33T Handschuh; **protective ~s pl** 166 Schutzhandschuhe
glue 58 Klebstoff
to **go: ~ along with sb** 30T mit jdm mitkommen/mitgehen; **~ on** 44T weitermachen, fortfahren; **~ crazy** 137T durchdrehen; **~ for walks** 65V spazieren gehen; to **let ~ (of sth)** 167 (etw) loslassen; **There you ~.** 23 Bitte sehr. Bitteschön.; **Off we ~.** 110T Los geht's!
goal: career ~ 161F berufliches Ziel; **~ line** 29F Tor(aus)linie
goods pl 61 Güter, Waren
to **govern** 138 regeln, bestimmen
government 32 Regierung
gown 137T Abendkleid
grade 52T Note
to **graduate** 147 den (Schul-/Universitäts-) Abschluss machen
graduation 89 Abschluss, Schulabschluss
to **grant** 109 gewähren
graph 80 Diagramm, Grafik
grass 177 Gras
grateful 37 dankbar
to **greet** 44 begrüßen
greeting 44 Begrüßung
to **grind sth** 59 etw zermahlen
groceries pl 66 Lebensmittel
grocery store 66 Lebensmittelladen
grounds pl 124T Anlage, Gelände
to **grow** 17 wachsen, zunehmen; **~ sth** 128 etw (Pflanzen usw.) anbauen; **~ out of sth** 74T aus etw entstehen; **~ up** 95 aufwachsen
growing 74T zunehmend, steigend
grown up 137T erwachsen
guard 166 Schutzhaube
to **guess: G~ what!** 159 Stell Dir vor! Wissen Sie was?
guest 7 Gast
to **guide** 101T leiten
guide 83 Reiseführer
guided tour 88T Führung
guideline 162T Richtlinie, Empfehlung

guild 159 Zunft, Gilde
gun 147 (Schuss-)Waffe
gunmen pl, **vigilante ~** 236 bewaffnete Milizen
guy 31 Typ, Kerl
gym 25 Fitness-Studio
gymnastics, to do ~ 29F turnen

H

habit 16 Gewohnheit
hairstyle 138 Frisur
halfway 116 auf halbem Wege, halbwegs; ~ **though sth** 121 mitten in etw, während etw
hall, food ~ 180 Lebensmittelabteilung
to **hand: ~ sth in** 55 etw abgeben
hand, on the other ~ 52T andererseits, allerdings; to **put one's ~ up for sth** 103T sich für etw melden; to **shake ~s** 44T die Hand geben, die Hände schütteln; to **take sth off sb's ~s** 59 jdm etw abnehmen
hand-painted 41T handgemalt
to **handle horses** 124T mit Pferden arbeiten
handout 46 Arbeitsblatt, Handzettel
to **hang out with sb** 26 mit jdm Zeit verbringen, mit jdm abhängen
to **happen** 20 geschehen, passieren, vor sich gehen; to **make sth ~** 20 dafür sorgen, dass etw geschieht; 103T etw verwirklichen, etw ermöglichen
happiness 154 Zufriedenheit, Glück
hardly 159 kaum; ~ **ever** 99 kaum, so gut wie nie
harmful 102T schädlich, nachteilig
harsh 76 scharf, streng, hart; 173 rau
harvest 128 Ernte
hazard 166 Gefahr
head: ~ of sales 79 Verkaufsleiter/in
to **head: ~ for sth** 22 sich auf den Weg zum/r … machen; ~ **east** 173 gen Osten aufbrechen; to **be ~ing for sth** 50 auf dem (besten) Weg zu etw sein
heading 16F Überschrift
headline 48 Überschrift
to **heal** 51 heilen, abheilen
health 20T Gesundheit; **mental ~** 52 geistige Gesundheit; ~ **and safety** 166 Arbeitsschutz, Arbeitssicherheit; ~ **insurance** 174 Krankenversicherung; ~ **issue** 37 Gesundheitsproblem
healthcare 172 Gesundheitswesen, Krankenversorgung
healthy 17 gesund
hearing loss 37 Schwerhörigkeit, Gehörverlust
heart: ~ attack 49 Herzinfarkt; **His ~ missed a beat.** 176 Dies ließ sein Herz höher schlagen.; **sb has sb's interests at ~** 229 jdm liegen jds Interessen am Herzen
heat 17 Wärme, Hitze
heating 140T Heizung
height 130 Höhe, Körpergröße; to **be scared of ~s** 121 nicht schwindelfrei sein, Höhenangst haben
helmet 166 Helm
helpful 40 nützlich, hilfreich
here: H~ you are. 23 Bitte sehr. Bitteschön.; **H~'s to …!** 22 (Trinkspruch:) Auf …!
hero 9 Held
to **hesitate** 101T zögern
hidden 48 verborgen, versteckt
higher education 161 Hochschulbildung
highlight 126 Höhepunkt
to **highlight** 41 hervorheben
highly 83 sehr

hike 86 Wanderung
to **hike** 89 wandern
hill 87 Hügel, Berg
hint 122F Hinweis, Tipp
to **hire: ~ sb** 168 jdn einstellen; ~ **sth** 137T etw mieten
to **hit** 33T schlagen, treffen; ~ **sb** 37 jdn anfahren
to **hitchhike** 86 per Anhalter fahren/reisen
to **hold: ~ sth out** 44T etw ausstrecken; ~ **the line** 152T (Telefon:) am Apparat bleiben
holder 140 Halter
holiday, public ~ 128 gesetzlicher Feiertag; **walking ~** 142T Wanderurlaub; **working ~** 83 Ferienpraktikum, Arbeitsurlaub; ~ **resort** 14 Urlaubsort, Ferienort
home town 177 Heimatstadt
homework 13 Hausaufgaben
honest 54 ehrlich, aufrichtig; **to be ~, …** 59 ehrlich gesagt …
honour 52T Ehre
to **hop on/off** 87 ein-/aussteigen
hopefully 134 hoffentlich
horizon 171 Horizont; to **broaden one's ~s** 99 den eigenen Horizont erweitern
horrible 83 schrecklich
horrified 98T entsetzt
horse, to handle ~s 124T mit Pferden arbeiten; ~ **riding** 119 Reiten; ~**-drawn vehicle** 138 Pferdefuhrwerk
horseback, to ride on ~ 124T reiten
hospitality 83 Bewirtung, Gastfreundschaft; ~ **exchange** 83 Aufenthalt bei einer Gastfamilie
host 71 Moderator/in (einer Sendung usw.); 83 Gastgeber/in
to **host sth** 157 etw (Veranstaltung usw.) ausrichten
household items pl 66 Haushaltsartikel
housekeeping 140 Hauswirtschaft
however 30T allerdings, aber, doch, jedoch, dagegen
hug, to give sb a ~ 164 jdn umarmen
to **hug sb** 162T jdn umarmen
human 20T Mensch
humour 54 Humor
to **hurry** 155 eilen; ~ **up** 12 sich beeilen
to **hurt** 88T wehtun, schmerzen, verletzen
hurtful 163 verletzend
hygienic 140T hygienisch

I

ice, to break the ~ 125 das Eis brechen, einander kennenlernen, miteinander ins Gespräch kommen; ~ **rink** 32 Eisbahn
to **ice skate** 29F eislaufen
iced tea 8 Eistee
idea: ~ (of sth) 46 Auffassung (von etw); to **get the wrong ~ (about sth)** 162 etw falsch verstehen
identical (to sb/sth) 177 identisch (mit jdm/etw)
identical twins pl 95 eineiige Zwillinge
to **identify** 15 identifizieren, (die Identität) feststellen; 77F ermitteln, bestimmen; ~ **with sb/sth** 42 sich mit jdm/etw identifizieren
identity 32 Identität; ~ **theft** 71 Identitätsdiebstahl
if: as ~ 55 als ob; to **act as ~** 98T so tun, als ob
to **ignore sth** 116 etw ignorieren
illness 114 Krankheit
illusion 87 Täuschung, Illusion

to **illustrate** 24 illustrieren
to **imagine sth** 76 sich etw vorstellen
immediately 130 sofort, unverzüglich
immigrant 128 Einwanderer/-in
impact 65 Auswirkung(en), Folgen, Einfluss; to **make an ~ (on sth)** 41T Wirkung haben
to **implant** 178 einpflanzen
impolite 165 unhöflich
to **import** 102 importieren, einführen
importance 26 Bedeutung, Wichtigkeit; to **place ~ on sth** 163 einer Sache Bedeutung beimessen, auf etw Wert legen
impossible 37 unmöglich; ~ **standards** pl 37 unerreichbare Maßstäbe
impressed 66 beeindruckt
impression 117 Eindruck; to **make an ~** 164 einen Eindruck hinterlassen
impressionable 37 leicht zu beeindrucken
to **improve** 24 verbessern, sich bessern
in itself 102T an sich
inactivity 121 Untätigkeit
inappropriate(ly) 162T unangemessen
incident 147 Vorfall
incinerator 59 Müllverbrennungsanlage
income 72 Einkommen
incompetent 165 unfähig, inkompetent
inconvenient 85 ungünstig gelegen, unpraktisch
incorrectly 51 unsachgemäß, falsch
to **increase** 173 zunehmen, sich steigern; ~ **sth** 52T etw steigern, etw erhöhen
increasing(ly) 74T zunehmend
incredible 172 unglaublich
independence 137 Unabhängigkeit
independent 83 unabhängig
indigenous 132 einheimisch, eingeboren; Ureinwohner/in, Eingeborene/r
individual 77 einzeln, individuell; 168 (selbstständige) Persönlichkeit, Individuum
individualist 162T individualistisch
induction 176 Einarbeitung
industrial accident 167 Arbeitsunfall
to **industrialize** 178 industrialisieren
industry 65 Branche; 148 Industrie
inequality 173 Ungleichheit
inexperienced 139 unerfahren
inferior 133 minderwertig
to **influence** 40 beeinflussen
influence (on sb/sth) 17 Einfluss, Auswirkung(en) (auf jdn/etw)
infographic 113 Infografik
to **inform (sb of sth)** 16 (jdn über etw) informieren
informative 87 aufschlussreich, informativ
ingredient 17 Zutat, Bestandteil
inhabitant 17 Einwohner, Bewohner
initial 78 erste/r/s
to **injure** 51 verletzen
injury 50 Verletzung
ink 167 Druckfarbe
insight (into sth) 107 Einblick(e) (in etw)
to **insist** 101T darauf bestehen
inspiration 77 Anregung(en), Inspiration
to **inspire** 37 anregen, inspirieren
instant 76 sofortig, unmittelbar
instead 31 stattdessen; ~ **of** 17 anstelle von, anstatt
to **instruct sb to do sth** 156 jdn anweisen, etw zu tun
instruction 124 Anleitung, Anweisung
instructor, ski ~ 172 Skilehrer/in
insurance 100 Versicherung; **health ~** 174 Krankenversicherung

to **integrate** 135 eingliedern, integrieren
to **intend to do sth** 60 die Absicht haben, etw zu tun; vorhaben, etw zu tun
intense 52T heftig, intensiv
intention (of doing sth) 98T Absicht (etw zu tun)
to **interact with sb** 147 mit jdm zu tun haben, mit jdm interagieren
interaction 138 Austausch, Interaktion
interested in sth 30T an etw interessiert
interesting 19 interessant
interethnic tension 145 Spannung(en) zwischen ethnischen Gruppen
intern 33 Praktikant/In
internship 42 Praktikum
to **interpret** 139 auslegen, interpretieren
to **interrupt** 162T unterbrechen
interstate *AE* 121 Autobahn, Fernstraße
to **interview sb** 114 mit jdm ein Vorstellungsgespräch führen
interview 114 Vorstellungsgespräch
interviewee 70 *Person, die interviewt wird*
interviewer 114 *Person, die ein Vorstellungsgespräch führt*
intimate 72 intim
intolerant, to be ~ of sb/sth 145 intolerant gegenüber jdm/etw sein
intravenous drip 50 Infusion
to **introduce** 32 einführen, vorstellen; **~ sb to sb** 7 jdn jdm vorstellen
introduction 41 *(Text:)* Einleitung
introductions *pl* 114 Vorstellung, Bekanntmachen
to **invent** 32 erfinden
to **invite sb to do sth** 44 jdn auffordern, etw zu tun
to **involve** 30T beinhalten, erfordern; **~ sb in sth** 41T jdn an etw beteiligen
involved, to get ~ with sb 40F mit jdm zu tun haben; to **get ~ with sth** 226 sich auf etw einlassen
inward 74 innere/r/s
iodine 17 Jod
iron 17 Eisen
irony 98T Ironie
island 14 Insel
islander 134 Insulaner/in, Inselbewohner/in
isolated 178 einzeln, vereinsamt
isolation 52T Vereinsamung
issue 16 Frage, Streitpunkt, Problem; **health ~** 37 Gesundheitsproblem
to **issue sth** 148 etw veröffentlichen, etw herausgeben
italics, in ~ 118 kursiv (gesetzt)
item 14 Gegenstand, Artikel, Ding, Sache; **fan ~** 219 Fanartikel; **household ~s** *pl* 66 Haushaltsartikel
itself, in ~ 102T an sich

J

jacket 64 Jacke, Jackett
jam 140 Marmelade
to **jam** 172 eine Jamsession machen, jammen
jealous 112 neidisch
Jewish 95 jüdisch
job, casual ~ 137T Gelegenheitsarbeit; **~ advertisement** 106 Stellenanzeige; **~ description** 107 Stellenbeschreibung; **~ interview** 114 Vorstellungsgespräch
to **join** 59 sich dazugesellen, dazukommen; **~ in** 33T mitmachen; **~ sth** 30T einer Sache beitreten, bei etw mitmachen; 41T sich einer Sache anschließen; **~ sb in doing**

sth 41T sich jdm bei etw anschließen, jdm bei etw zur Seite stehen
journey 28 Reise, Fahrt
to **judge** 116 zum Urteil kommen, der (begründeten) Meinung sein; **~ sb/sth** 40F jdn/etw bewerten, jdn/etw beurteilen
juice 22 Saft
to **jumble sth up** 18F, 48 etw durcheinanderwerfen
jump 33T Sprunghindernis
to **jump to conclusions** 74T voreilige Schlüsse ziehen
justice 147 Gerechtigkeit; **court of ~** 168 Gerichtshof

K

keen, to be ~ to do sth 109 etw unbedingt tun wollen
to **keep: ~ to sth** 155 sich an etw halten, bei etw bleiben; **~ up sth** 159 mit etw weitermachen; **~ sb safe** 124T auf jdn aufpassen, jdn beschützen
keycard 140 Schlüsselkarte
to **kick: ~ off** 124T starten, anfangen; **~ the ball** 29F den Ball treten/schießen; **~ a ball** 121 einen Ball schießen
kickoff 121 Start, Anfang, Anstoß
to **kill** 20T töten, umbringen
killing 149 Ermordung, Tötung
kind 28 Art; **~ of** 43V irgendwie
kind(ly) 121 nett, freundlich, liebenswürdig
kit, press ~ 156 Pressemappe
to **knock sb down** 121 jdn niederschlagen, jdn umhauen
to **know: to get to ~ sb** 82 jdn kennenlernen; to **let sb ~** 88T jdm Bescheid sagen
knowledge 22 Wissen, Kenntnisse; **previous ~** 230 Vorkenntnisse

L

label 139 Etikett, Bezeichnung
lack (of sth) 17 Mangel (an etw)
ladies' wear 180 Damenbekleidung
lake, frozen ~ 32 zugefrorener See
landfill 59 Mülldeponie
landline 101T Festnetzanschluss
landscape 83 Landschaft
language, body ~ 44T Körpersprache; **native ~** 159 Muttersprache; **official ~** 157 Amtssprache; **spoken ~** 12 gesprochene Sprache
large, runner at ~ 103T *etwa:* Laufbursche für besondere Aufgaben
largely 107 überwiegend, größtenteils
last but not least 17 zu guter Letzt, nicht zu vergessen
to **last long** 58 lang halten
lasting 102T dauerhaft
laugh 95 Lachen
to **launch sth** 37 etw *(Unternehmen usw.)* gründen; 37 etw starten
law 42 Gesetz(e), Recht
law enforcement 147 Polizei (und Justiz), Exekutive, Strafverfolgung
to **lay** 92 legen; **~ the table** 99 den Tisch decken
lazy 27 faul
to **lead** 20T führen, bringen; **~ the way** 59 führend sein, wegweisend sein
lead, to follow sb's ~ 238 jds Beispiel folgen
leader, team ~ 60 Teamleiter/in
least, at ~ 17 mindestens; **last but not ~** 17 zu guter Letzt, nicht zu vergessen

to **leave a message** 152T eine Nachricht hinterlassen
left: to feel ~ out 77 sich übergangen/ausgeschlossen fühlen; **~ over** 68 übrig (geblieben)
legal(ly) 128 gesetzlich
legumes *pl* 17 Hülsenfrüchte
leisure 70 Freizeit
to **lend** 12 leihen, borgen
length: ~ of service 107 Dienstzeit, Beschäftigungsdauer; **~ of stay** 89 Aufenthaltsdauer
lentil 17 Linse
to **let: ~ go (of sth)** 167 (etw) loslassen; **~ sb know** 88T jdm Bescheid sagen
letter, covering ~ 106 Anschreiben, Begleitschreiben
level 168 Niveau; **sea ~** 122 Meereshöhe; **A ~s** *pl BE* 142T Abitur; **on a personal ~** 41T persönlich, selbst
liberal(ly) 139 freizügig, liberal
library 56 Bibliothek
life, from all walks of ~ 41T aus allen Gesellschaftsschichten, aus allen Milieus; to **move on with one's ~** 96 seinen eigenen Weg gehen, das Vergangene hinter sich lassen; **way of ~** 108 Lebensweise, Lebensart; **~-support system** 48 Lebenserhaltungssystem
lifetime, in our ~ 43V zu unseren Lebzeiten; **of a ~** 110 einmalig
to **lift** 29F heben, hochheben
light 123 hell
likely 44T wahrscheinlich
limit 88T Beschränkung
line *AE* 88T Warteschlange; **goal ~** 29F Tor(aus)linie; **tag ~** 28 Bildunterschrift, Slogan; to **hold the ~** 152T *(Telefon:)* am Apparat bleiben
to **line the streets** 125 die Straße säumen, Spalier stehen
liquid 140T flüssig
liquor store *AE* 147 Spirituosenladen
literacy, computer ~ 107 Computerkenntnisse
literally, not ~ 112 nicht wirklich
littered, to be ~ with sth 60 mit etw übersät sein
living, to make a ~ from sth 71 seinen Lebensunterhalt mit etw verdienen
local 28 örtlich, lokal
location 85 Standort, Lage
to **lock** 86 verschließen, abschließen
to **log on (to sth)** 100 sich (in etw) einloggen
lonely 26 einsam
long, as ~ as 20T solange; **~-lasting** 58 langlebig
to **look: ~ after sb/sth** 103T sich um jdn/etw kümmern; **~ ahead** 171 nach vorne schauen; **~ sth up** 94 etw *(in einem Wörterbuch)* nachschlagen; **~ up to sb** 35 zu jdm aufsehen, jdn bewundern; **~ sight of sth** 177 etw aus den Augen verlieren; **~ weight** 27 abnehmen
loss, hearing ~ 37 Schwerhörigkeit, Gehörverlust; **weight ~** 37 Abnehmen
lost, to be ~ 12 sich verlaufen haben; **~ property** 103T Fundsachen
lottery, to win the ~ 184 im Lotto gewinnen
low, of ~ priority 236 unwichtig, unbedeutend; **~-cut top** 44T tief ausgeschnittenes Oberteil
love, to fall in ~ with sb/sth 63T sich in jdn/etw verlieben

luckily 37 glücklicherweise
lucky, to be ~ 67 Glück haben
lunch break 48 Mittagspause
lunchtime 88T Mittag
luxury 63 Luxus

M

machinery 166 Maschinen, Geräte; **farm ~** 174 Landmaschinen
magnitude 43V Größe
to **maintain sth** 182 etw instand halten, etw unterhalten
major 17 groß, bedeutend
majority 147 Mehrheit
to **make: ~ sb do sth** 11 jdn dazu bringen, etw zu tun; **~ up one's mind** 41T beschließen, (sich) entscheiden; to **be made up of sth** 37 aus etw bestehen
make-up artist 137T Visagist/in
to **manage** 141 zurechtkommen; **~ to do sh** 42 es schaffen, etw zu tun
management 101T Geschäftsleitung, Führungskräfte; **money ~** 137 Umgang mit Geld
manager 33 Leiter/in
manner 78 Art, Weise
manufacturer 58 Hersteller/in
map 34 Landkarte, Karte
mark 52T Note
married, to get ~ 111 heiraten
martial art 32 Kampfsport, Kampfkunst
match 29F, 30 Spiel, Partie
to **match: ~ sth (to sth)** 6 etw (einer Sache) zuordnen
mate 98T Kumpel, Freund; **team ~** 30T Mannschaftskamerad
maths 11 Mathe
matter 33T Sache, Angelegenheit; **no ~** 26 egal, ganz gleich
to **matter** 41T wichtig sein, von Belang sein
maturity 137 Reife
meal: Did you enjoy your ~? 23 Hat es Ihnen geschmeckt?
to **mean** 6 bedeuten; 43V meinen; **~ to do sth** 99 beabsichtigen, etw zu tun; etw tun wollen
meaning 60 Bedeutung
measurement 78 Maß
mechanic 124 Mechaniker/in; **motor ~** 172 Automechaniker/in
mechanical failure 174 technisches Versagen, Motorschaden
media pl; **~ studies** pl 134 Publizistik, Medienwissenschaft
medication 51 Arzneimittel
medicine 52 Medizin
to **melt sth down** 59 etw einschmelzen
member 30T Mitglied; **~ of staff** 111 Mitarbeiter/in
memo 101 Notiz, Vermerk, Kurzmitteilung
memory 90 Gedächtnis, Erinnerung
menswear 180 Herrenbekleidung
mental 27 geistig, mental; **~ health** 52 geistige Gesundheit
to **mention: Don't ~ it.** 152 Nichts zu danken.
menu 23 Speisekarte, Speiseplan
mess 60 Chaos, Sauerei
message, text ~ 69 SMS; to **leave a ~** 152T eine Nachricht hinterlassen; to **take a ~** 152 (Telefon:) jdm etw ausrichten
messenger 35 Botschafter/in
method 52 Methode, Verfahren; **~ of payment** 89 Zahlungsart, Zahlungsweise
midday 22 Mittag

middle-aged 177 mittleren Alters
to **mind** 54 etw dagegen haben
mind, to change one's ~ 63T seine Meinung ändern; to **make up one's ~** 41T beschließen, (sich) entscheiden; to **open the ~** 120 Denkanstöße vermitteln, den Geist öffnen; to **say what's on your ~** 162T sagen, was man denkt; **~-blowing** 43V irre, überwältigend
mineral 17 Mineral(stoff)
mining 150T Bergbau
minority 147 Minderheit
mint 150T Minze
mirror 68 Spiegel
miserable 67F (Wetter:) mies, grässlich
misfit, social ~ 159 Außenseiter, Sonderling
missing, sb is ~ sth 79 jdm fehlt etw
misunderstanding 78 Missverständnis
misuser 51 (Drogen-)Konsument/in
mixed 23 gemischt
mobile (phone) BE 8 Handy
model 126 Modell; **role ~** 33T Vorbild
moderate 77 gemäßigt, leicht
moisturizer 140 Feuchtigkeitscreme
moment, at the ~ 23 im Moment, gerade
monarch 87 Herrscher/in, Monarch/in
money, pocket ~ 13 Taschengeld; **prize ~** 124T Preisgeld; **~ management** 137 Umgang mit Geld; to **make ~** 124T Geld verdienen
monument 14 Denkmal
most recent 40F jüngste/r/s
mostly 31 hauptsächlich, meistens, überwiegend
mother tongue 109 Muttersprache
motivated 27 motiviert
motivating 30T motivierend
motor 174 Auto, Motor; **~ mechanic** 172 Automechaniker/in; **~ show** 126 Automobilmesse; **~ skills** pl 30T Motorik
motoring 127 Autofahren, Automobil-
to **move: ~ on (to sth)** 44T (mit etw) weitermachen; **~ on with one's life** 96 seinen eigenen Weg gehen, das Vergangene hinter sich lassen
movement 41T Bewegung
mugging 184 Raubüberfall (auf der Straße)
multilingual 159 mehrsprachig
murder 87 Mord
murderer, serial ~ 42 Serienmörder/in
muscle 13 Muskel; to **gain ~** 104 Muskeln aufbauen
muscly 118 muskulös
mushroom 150T Pilz
musician 71 Musiker/in
must, a ~ 44 ein Muss
mysterious(ly) 121 geheimnisvoll, rätselhaft
mystery 87 Rätsel, Geheimnis

N

to **name** 30 nennen; **you ~ it** 103T was auch immer, alles Mögliche
nation, United N~s pl 157 Vereinte Nationen
national: ~ anthem 121 Nationalhymne; **N~ Trust** 83 brit. Organisation für Denkmalpflege und Naturschutz
nationality 14 Staatsangehörigkeit, Nationalität
native 128 einheimisch; **~ American** 32 amerikanische/r Ureinwohner/in; **~ language** 159 Muttersprache; **~ speaker** 157 Muttersprachler/in
natural wonder 119 Naturwunder
neck 46 Hals

never 20 nie
nevertheless 101T trotzdem, dennoch
New Year's Eve 129 Silvester
news agency 179 Nachrichtenagentur
next to 6 neben
niece 162T Nichte
no matter 26 egal, ganz gleich
Nobel Peace Prize 35 Friedensnobelpreis
nomad 159 Nomade/-in
non-violent 147 gewaltlos, gewaltfrei
norm 162T Norm
normally 31 normalerweise
not: ~ literally 112 nicht wirklich; **~ quite** 121 nicht ganz; **~ unless** 144 nur (dann), wenn
note 22 Geldschein, Banknote
notice 24 Ankündigung, Mitteilung, Aushang, Hinweis; to **take ~ of sth** 166 etw beachten; **~ board** 56 Schwarzes Brett
nourishing 24 nahrhaft
now, right ~ 31 gerade (jetzt)
nowadays 30T heute, heutzutage
nuclear family 93 Kernfamilie, Kleinfamilie
nurse, registered ~ 172 examinierte/r Krankenpfleger/-schwester; **paediatric ~** 173 Kinderkrankenpfleger/-schwester
nursing 173 Krankenpflege
nutrient 20T Nährstoff
nutritionist 20T Ernährungswissenschaftler/in

O

obese 168 fettleibig
obesity 168 Fettleibigkeit
to **obey: ~ sth** 184 etw befolgen
obligation 50 Verpflichtung
obscure 147 (völlig) unbekannt
observer 147 Beobachter/in
obvious 108 klar (erkennbar), offensichtlich
obviously 101T natürlich, selbstverständlich
occasion, formal ~ 230 feierlicher Anlass; **social ~** 124T gesellschaftlicher Anlass; **on several ~s** 156 mehrfach
occasionally 104 gelegentlich, ab und zu
off, to be well/better ~ 83 gut/besser dran sein; **well-~** 95 wohlhabend; to **take time ~** 110 sich frei nehmen; **on and ~ the pitch** 30T auf und neben dem Spielfeld; to **take sth ~ sb's hands** 59 jdm etw abnehmen; **~ piste** 172 abseits der Piste, jenseits ausgetretener Pfade; **Off we go.** 110T Los geht's!
to **offend sb** 162T jdn beleidigen, jdn verletzen
to **offer** 33T bieten, anbieten
office, open-plan ~ 101T Großraumbüro
officer, police ~ 147 Polizist/in, Polizeibeamter/-in
official 100 offiziell; 156 (Sport:) Kampfrichter/in; **~ language** 157 Amtssprache
old-fashioned 125 altmodisch
old town 87 Altstadt
once 14 einmal; 61 sobald; **at ~** 49 auf einmal
one day 18, 229 eines Tages
one-way street 107 Einbahnstraße
only child 95 Einzelkind
to **open: ~ up** 74T sich öffnen; **~ the mind** 120 Denkanstöße vermitteln, den Geist öffnen
open: ~ day 158 Tag der offenen Tür; **~-minded** 134 aufgeschlossen, unvoreingenommen; **~-plan office** 101T Großraumbüro
opening ceremony 121 Eröffnungszeremonie

openness 98 Offenheit
opera, soap ~ 71 Seifenoper
to operate sth 166 etw *(Geräte)* bedienen;
  182 etw betreiben
opinion, in my ~ 20T meiner Meinung nach
opponent 32 Gegner/in
opportunity 34 Möglichkeit, Gelegenheit
to oppose sth 139 gegen etw sein, etw
  ablehnen
opposing 121 gegnerisch
opposite 16 gegenüber(liegend);
  85 gegenteilig, entgegengesetzt
option 17 Alternative, Möglichkeit
to order 15 bestellen
order 20 Reihenfolge; 79 Bestellung, Auftrag; 149 Ordnung; running ~ 103T Ablaufplan; to get sth in ~ 27 etw ordnen, etw
  auf die Reihe kriegen; in ~ to 16 um … zu
ordinary 74T gewöhnlich, normal
organizational 124T organisatorisch,
  Organisations-
organizing committee 103T Organisationskomitee
origin 128 Ursprung
original 163 eigene/r/s; ~(ly)
  144 ursprünglich
otherwise 53 sonst
out: ~ and about 88T unterwegs; to take
  time ~ 142T sich freinehmen
outback *AusE* 112 Hinterland, Busch
outcome, fatal ~ 147 tödlicher Ausgang
to outperform sb 125 jdn übertreffen
outsider 138 Außenstehende/r
outward 74 äußere/r/s
overall 24 Gesamt-, insgesamt
to overcome sth 37 etw überwinden
overdose 48 Überdosis
overnight 147 über Nacht
overseas 137T im/ins Ausland, in/nach
  Übersee
overview 51 Überblick
overweight 37 übergewichtig
own, to pay one's ~ way 137T alles selbst
  bezahlen
to own 64 besitzen
owner 103T Besitzer/in, Inhaber/in

P

packaging 140 Verpackung
packet 22 Packung, Tüte
paediatric nurse 173 Kinderkranken-
  pfleger/-in
pain, to be in ~ 51 Schmerzen haben;
  ~ reliever 50 Schmerzmittel
painkiller 51 Schmerzmittel
painted sign 125 handgemaltes Schild
pan 150T Topf, Pfanne
paper plate 177 Pappteller
paragraph 16 *(Text:)* Absatz
paramedic 48 Rettungssanitäter/in
parent, adoptive ~s *pl* 95 Adoptiveltern;
  set of ~s *pl* 95 Elternpaar; single ~ 93
  Alleinerziehende/r; single-~ family 93
  Einelternfamilie
parenthood 96 Elternschaft
parking space 10 Parkplatz
parliament 41T Parlament
to part 63 auseinandergehen, (sich) trennen
part, to take ~ in sth 16 an etw teilnehmen;
  ~-time 124 Teilzeit(-)
participant 101T Teilnehmer/in
to participate (in sth) 59 (bei etw) mitmachen, (an etw) teilnehmen

particular 20 spezielle/r/s, bestimmt;
  sth in ~ 180 etw Spezielles
particularly 17 besonders, insbesondere
pass 137T Monatskarte, Zeitkarte
to pass 52T *(Prüfung)* bestehen; ~ sb 177
  jdn überholen, an jdm vorbeigehen; ~ sth
  down to sb 66 etw an jdn weiterreichen;
  ~ sth on 136 etw weitergeben
passage, rite of ~ 137 Initiation(sritus),
  Erwachsenwerden
passenger 116 Fahrgast
passion 159 Leidenschaft
passionate(ly) 32 leidenschaftlich
past sth 24 an etw vorbei
patch of land 124 (kleines) Stück Land
path, career ~ 134 (beruflicher) Werde-
  gang, Laufbahn
patient(ly) 116 geduldig
patrol, on ~ 147 auf Streife
pay 110T Lohn, Bezahlung
to pay: ~ attention to sth 31 auf etw
  achten, etw beachten; ~ one's own way
  137T alles selbst bezahlen
payment, method of ~ 89 Zahlungsart,
  Zahlungsweise
peace 35 Frieden; Nobel P~ Prize 35
  Friedensnobelpreis
peaceful(ly) 148 friedlich
pedagogical staff 107 Lehrpersonal
pedestrian 116 Fußgänger/in
peer pressure 131 sozialer Druck
percentage 59 Anteil, Prozentsatz
to perform 52T *(in einer Prüfung usw.)*
  abschneiden; ~ sth 32 etw aufführen, etw
  spielen; 169 etw *(Tätigkeit usw.)* ausführen,
  etw durchführen
performer 103T Künstler/in, Darsteller/in
period: ~ (of time) 48 Zeitabschnitt, Zeit,
  Phase; trial ~ 176 Probezeit
permanent 176 unbefristet; ~(ly) 172
  dauerhaft
permission 50 Erlaubnis
permit, work ~ 110 Arbeitserlaubnis
person, in ~ 121 persönlich, selbst
personal 7 persönlich, privat; on a ~ level
  41T persönlich, selbst
personality 37 Persönlichkeit
to persuade sb 20 jdn überzeugen, jdn
  überreden
persuasive 161F überzeugend, schlagkräftig
petition 37 Petition
phone, to pick up the ~ 88T ans Telefon
  gehen; ~ duty 152 Telefondienst
phone-in 142 *Sendung mit Hörerbeteiligung
  per Telefon*
physical 52T körperlich, physisch
piano 9 Klavier
to pick: ~ sth out 177 etw aussuchen,
  etw auswählen; ~ sth up 60 etw aufheben;
  ~ up the phone 88T ans Telefon gehen
pickled 150T (sauer) eingelegt
pie chart 80 Tortendiagramm
piece: ~ of advice 98 Rat; ~ of equipment
  63T Gerät
pile 60 Stapel, Haufen
pilgrimage 108 Pilgerreise
to pin 24 (mit einer Nadel) anheften
piste 184 Skipiste; off ~ 172 abseits der
  Piste, jenseits ausgetretener Pfade
pitch 30 (Spiel-)Feld, (Fußball-)Platz;
  football ~ 217 Fußballfeld, Fußballplatz;
  on and off the ~ 30T auf und neben dem
  Spielfeld

place, in the first ~ 51 überhaupt, von
  vornherein
to place importance on sth 163 einer
  Sache Bedeutung beimessen, auf etw Wert
  legen
placemat 77 Tischset
plan, floor ~ 126 Grundriss, Übersichtsplan;
  open-~ office 101T Großraumbüro
plant 20T Pflanze; 61 Werk, Fabrik;
  printing ~ 166 Großdruckerei
to plant 83 pflanzen
plantation 32 Plantage
plastic, used ~ 59 Altplastik
plate 99 Teller; paper ~ 177 Pappteller
platform 26 Plattform
playground 48 Spielplatz
pleasant 54 angenehm
to please sb 26 jdm einen Gefallen tun,
  jdm gefallen
pleasure 103T Vergnügen
pocket money 13 Taschengeld
pod 176 Gondel, Kapsel
point, decimal ~ 78 Dezimalpunkt; ~ of view
  149 Perspektive, Blickwinkel; up to a ~
  74T bis zu einem gewissen Grad; to make a ~
  33T ein Argument vorbringen; to score a ~
  130 einen Punkt erzielen; there's no/little
  ~ in doing sth 59 es hat keinen/wenig
  Sinn, etw zu tun; What's the ~? 102T Was
  soll das? Was hat das für einen Sinn?
to point out sth 37 auf etw hinweisen
police: ~ department *AE* 147 Polizeibehörde;
  ~ force 147 Polizei, Polizeiapparat; ~ officer
  147 Polizist/in, Polizeibeamter/-in
policy: ~ (on sth) 100 Richtlinie(n) (für etw),
  Politik, Vorgehensweise
polite 54 höflich
politeness 162T Höflichkeit
politician 41T Politiker/in
to pollute 59 verschmutzen
pollution 58 (Umwelt-)Verschmutzung
to ponder sth 65 über etw nachdenken,
  etw erwägen
pool table 56 Billardtisch
poor choices *pl* 147 falsche Entscheidungen
popular 30T beliebt
populated, densely ~ 178 dicht besiedelt
population 17 Bevölkerung
pork 20T Schweinefleisch
position 106 Stelle, Stellung, Position
positivity 40 positive Einstellung
possibility 89F Möglichkeit
post, goal ~ 217 Torpfosten; ~ code 181
  Postleitzahl
postage 181 Porto, Versandkosten
postal, Universal P~ Union 157 Weltpostverein
pound 33T Pfund
poverty 43V Armut
power 140 Strom; 147 Macht, Einfluss;
  will-~ 217 Willenskraft
practice 74 Praxis; 140 Praktik, Verhaltens-
  weise, Maßnahme; football ~ 155 Fußballtraining; in ~ 148 praktisch, in der Praxis
to practise 6 üben; ~ sth 32 etw ausüben
precise 34 genau, präzise
prediction 108 Voraussage, Vorhersage
pregnant 172 schwanger
preparation 150 Vorbereitung
to prepare 16 (sich) vorbereiten
prepared, to be ~ to do sth 44T bereit sein,
  etw zu tun
to prescribe sth 51 etw verschreiben

prescription 50 (ärztliches) Rezept; rezept-pflichtig

present 12 Geschenk; 164 anwesend

to **present: ~ (sth to sb)** 24 (etw jdm) vorstellen, (etw jdm) präsentieren; **~ sth** 37 etw (Sendung usw.) moderieren; **~ difficulties** 98 Schwierigkeiten darstellen, mit Schwierig-keiten verbunden sein

presenter 37 Moderator/in

to **preserve** 144 bewahren

president 147 Präsident

press 126 Presse; **printing ~** 167 Druck-maschine; **~ kit** 156 Pressemappe

pressure 28 Druck; **peer ~** 131 sozialer Druck

pretzel 22 Brezel

to **prevent** 101T verhindern

price 24 Preis

primary school 116 Grundschule

to **print** 140 drucken

print 19 gedruckt, Druck-; **~ run** 167 Auflage

printer 64 Drucker

printing: ~ plant 166 Großdruckerei; **~ press** 167 Druckmaschine; **~ works** 167 Druckerei

prison 32 Gefängnis

privilege 95 Privileg

privileged 52T privilegiert

prize 120 Preis, Gewinn; **Nobel Peace P~** 35 Friedensnobelpreis; **~ money** 124T Preisgeld

procedure 167 Vorgang; **safety ~s** pl 166 Sicherheitsmaßnahmen, Sicherheits-bestimmungen

to **process sth** 156 etw bearbeiten

procession 124T Festzug, Umzug

to **produce sth** 23 etw produzieren, etw erstellen

production, food ~ 16 Nahrungsmittel-produktion

profession 45 Beruf

professional 105 beruflich; 134 professio-nell; 124T Profi

to **profile** 159 porträtieren

progress 27 Fortschritt(e), Entwicklung, Vorankommen

to **promote sth** 33 etw begünstigen, etw fördern; 37 für etw werben, für etw Werbung machen

promotion 37 Werbung

prompt 104 Stichwort

to **pronounce** 6 aussprechen

proper(ly) 140T richtig, ordentlich

property, lost ~ 103T Fundsachen

proportion 37 Anteil

prospects pl, **career ~** 159 Berufsaussichten

protection 168 Schutz

protective 177 schützend, Schutz-; **~ clothing** 166 Schutzkleidung; **~ gloves** pl 166 Schutzhandschuhe

protectors pl, **ear ~** 166 Gehörschutz

protein 16 Eiweiß, Protein(e)

to **protest** 41T protestieren, demonstrieren

protest 41T Protest, Demonstration

proud (of sb/sth) 37 stolz (auf jdn/etw)

to **prove (sth to sb)** 124T (jdm etw) bewei-sen, (jdm etw) nachweisen

to **provide** 26 liefern, bieten, zur Verfügung stellen; **~ evidence** 147 Beweise liefern

provided 102T vorausgesetzt, dass

provocative 161F provokant, provozierend

proxy 176 Stellvertreter/in, stellvertretend

psychological 52T psychologisch

pub 22 Kneipe, Gasthaus

public 41 Öffentlichkeit; **~ holiday** 128 gesetzlicher Feiertag; **~ transport** 134 öffentliche Verkehrsmittel; **in ~** 38 in der Öffentlichkeit

publicity 71 öffentliche Aufmerksamkeit, Werbung

to **pull** 167 ziehen; **~ sth down** 166 etw herunterziehen

pumpkin 128 Kürbis

punctual 162F pünktlich

punctuality 162T Pünktlichkeit

to **purchase** 58 kaufen

purchase 62 Kauf, Einkauf

pure 122 pur, rein

to **put: ~ sth aside** 180 etw zurücklegen; **~ in sth** 60 etw (Zeit, Energie usw.) inves-tieren; **~ sth up** 140 etw aufhängen; **~ sb through** 152T (Telefon:) jdn durchstellen; **~ one's hand up for sth** 103T sich für etw melden; **~ out the word** 102T die Nachricht verbreiten

puzzle 87 Rätsel

Q

qualification 110T Abschluss, Ausbildung

qualified, to be ~ 168 eine Ausbildung haben, einen Abschluss haben

quality 106 Eigenschaft

quantity 52T Menge

question mark 96 Fragezeichen

questionnaire 80 Fragebogen

to **queue** 130 sich (in einer Warteschlange) anstellen

queue BE 88 Warteschlange

quite, not ~ 121 nicht ganz

quotation 161 Zitat

quote 155 Zitat

R

race 145 Rasse; 156 Rennen

racial 148 Rassen-

racing 127 Rennen, Renn-

racism 147 Rassismus

racist 148 Rassist/in

radio advertisment 102T Werbespot (im Radio)

rail 137T Bahn, Eisenbahn

railway 42 Eisenbahn

rainy 116 regnerisch

to **raise: ~ awareness** 65 Bewusstsein schaf-fen; **~ your glass** 22 sein Glas erheben

ramp 33T Rampe

range 168 Bereich; **wide ~** 234 breites Spektrum

to **rank** 24 einstufen, (nach Rang) ordnen

ranking list 33 Rangliste

rapid(ly) 17 schnell, rasch, rapide

rarely 21 selten, kaum

rather than 136 anstatt

rating 85 Bewertung

to **reach** 56 erreichen

realistic 159 realistisch

to **realize: sb ~s sth** 40F, 71 jdm wird/ist etw klar, jdm wird/ist etw bewusst

reason, to give ~s 15 begründen

to **receive** 36 erhalten, bekommen

recent, most ~ 40F jüngste/r/s

recently 59 in letzter Zeit, neulich

reception 101T Empfang(sbereich), Rezeption

receptionist 7 Empfangsmitarbeiter/in, Rezeptionist/in

recipe 18F, 99 (Koch-)Rezept

to **recommend** 23 empfehlen

recommendation 86 Empfehlung

to **record** 27 aufzeichnen, aufnehmen, protokollieren

record 28 Aufzeichnung(en), Protokoll; **criminal ~** 236 Vorstrafen

to **recover** 37 sich erholen

recruiter 106 einstellendes Unternehmen, Personalvermittler/in

red blood cells pl 20 rote Blutkörperchen

to **redesign** 77 umgestalten, neu konzipieren

to **refer to sth** 151F sich auf etw beziehen, auf etw verweisen

referee 109 Referenzgeber/in

to **reflect** 95 widerspiegeln, wiedergeben

refugee 109 Flüchtling

to **refuse to do sth** 148 sich weigern, etw zu tun

to **register** 126 sich anmelden

registered nurse 172 examinierte/r Krankenpfleger/-schwester

registration 126 Anmeldung

to **regret** 86 bedauern, bereuen

regularly 58 regelmäßig

to **regulate** 101T regeln

regulations pl, **safety ~** 7 Sicherheits-vorschriften, -vorkehrungen

to **relate to sth** 137 mit etw zu tun haben, mit etw in einem Verhältnis stehen

relationship 37 Beziehung, Verhältnis

relatively 95 vergleichsweise, relativ

relaxed 71 locker, entspannt

to **release** 71 veröffentlichen

to **relieve stress** 47 Stress abbauen

relieved 88 erleichtert

reliever, pain ~ 50 Schmerzmittel

religious 17 religiös, Religions-

to **rely on sb** 124T auf jdn angewiesen sein

to **remain** 75 bleiben

to **remind sb that …** 66, 221 jdn daran erinnern, dass …

remote 132 abgelegen

to **remove: ~ sth** 53 etw entfernen; **~ sth** 147 etw wegbringen; **~ sb from sb** 135 jdn jdm wegnehmen; **~ sth from sth** 140 etw aus etw nehmen

to **renovate** 116 renovieren

rent 83 Miete

to **rent** 83 mieten

to **repair** 83 reparieren

to **replace** 50 ersetzen, austauschen

reply 40 Antwort, Erwiderung

to **reply** 176 antworten, entgegnen

report 48 Reportage, Bericht

to **report: ~ back to sb** 8 jdm berichten, jdm Bericht erstatten; **~ on sth** 41T über etw berichten

to **represent** 41 vertreten, repräsentieren

representative 115 Vertreter/in, Repräsen-tant/in; **service ~** 238 Kundenbetreuer/in, Kundendienstmitarbeiter/in

request (for sth) 79 Bitte (um etw)

to **request sth** 71 um etw bitten, sich etw wünschen

to **require sth** 89F, 140 etw benötigen, etw wünschen

research 34 Recherche, Nachforschungen

to **research sth** 34 etw recherchieren, Nachforschungen über etw anstellen

to **reserve** 89 reservieren

reserved 95 zurückhaltend, reserviert

resident 176 Bewohner, Einwohner

to **resolve** 147 *(Problem usw.:)* lösen
resort 82 Ferienort; **holiday ~** 14 Urlaubsort, Ferienort
resources *pl* 17 Rohstoffe, Ressourcen
to **respect** 33T respektieren, achten
respectful 162T respektvoll
respective 95 jeweilige/r/s
to **respond** 14 antworten
to **respond to sth** 74T auf etw reagieren
response 74 Reaktion, Antwort
responsibility 103T Verantwortung; 125 Zuständigkeit, Aufgabe; **sense of ~** 137 Verantwortungsgefühl
responsible 41T verantwortungsbewusst, verantwortungsvoll; 135 verantwortlich, zuständig
to **restrict** 101T einschränken, beschränken
retail 181 Einzelhandel
to **retain sth** 178 etw behalten
to **rethink sth** 16 etw überdenken
reunification 129 Wiedervereinigung
to **reunite sb/sth with sb** 103T jdn/etw mit jdm wieder zusammenbringen
review 85 Rezension, Kritik
rewarding 103T erfüllend, befriedigend
to **rewrite** 85 umformulieren, neu schreiben
to **ride: ~ a bike** 29F Fahrrad fahren; **~ on horseback** 124T reiten
ride 127 Fahrt
rider 124T Reiter/in
riding, horse ~ 119 Reiten
right now 31 gerade (jetzt)
rights *pl* 35 Rechte; **civil ~** 148 Bürgerrechte
to **rinse sth** 99 etw (mit Wasser) abspülen
riot 147 Aufstand, Aufruhr, Unruhe
rising 17 steigend
risk, to be at ~ 50 gefährdet sein; to **put sb at ~** 49 jdn gefährden, jdn in Gefahr bringen
rite of passage 137 Initiation(sritus), Erwachsenwerden
river 14 Fluss
road, on the ~ 173 unterwegs; **~ trip** 184 Autoreise
to **rob** 147 ausrauben, überfallen; **~ sb** 173 jdn bestehlen; **~ sb of sth** 43V jdn einer Sache berauben
robber 173 Räuber/in
robbery 147 Überfall, Raub
robot 176 Roboter; **manufacturing ~** 238 Fertigungsroboter
robotic 177 Roboter-
rock climbing 119 Klettern
role 23 Rolle; 38 Funktion; **~ model** 33T Vorbild
role-playing game 159 Rollenspiel
roller 167 Walze
romantic 124T romantisch
rooftop garden 177 Dachgarten
root 32 Wurzel
rough 33 grob, rau
route, bus ~ 85 Buslinie
routine 147 routinemäßig, Routine-
rude 54 unverschämt, unhöflich
to **ruin** 67T ruinieren
rule 9 Regel, Vorschrift
run 26 Lauf; **print ~** 167 Auflage
to **run: ~ sth** 73 etw betreiben, etw führen; **~ out of sth** 99 etw nicht mehr haben; **sb ~s out of sth** 51 jdm wird etw knapp, jd hat etw nicht mehr; **~ errands** 65V Besorgungen machen
runner 26 Läufer/in; **~ at large** 103T *etwa:* Laufbursche für besondere Aufgaben

running order 103T Ablaufplan
to **rush** 121 eilen

S

sacred 65V heilig
sadly 51 leider
safe 72 sicher, unbedenklich, ungefährlich; to **keep sb ~** 124T auf jdn aufpassen, jdn beschützen
safety 49 Sicherheit; **health and ~** 166 Arbeitsschutz, Arbeitssicherheit; **workplace ~** 167 Sicherheit am Arbeitsplatz; **~ glasses** *pl* 166 Schutzbrille; **~ procedures** *pl* 166 Sicherheitsmaßnahmen, Sicherheitsbestimmungen; **~ regulations** *pl* 7 Sicherheitsvorschriften, -vorkehrungen; **~ sign** 166 Sicherzeitszeichen, Warnzeichen
to **sail** 182 segeln
sail 182 Segel
sailing ship 151F, 182 Segelschiff
sailor 182 Matrose/-in, Segler/in
sales: ~ figures *pl* 79 Verkaufszahlen, Umsatzzahlen; **head of ~** 79 Verkaufsleiter/in; **~ tax** *AE* 66 Mehrwertsteuer
saltwater 134 Salzwasser
salutation 79 *(Brief:)* Anrede
sanctuary 113F Schutzgebiet, (Tier-)Pflegestation
sanitation 43V Abwasserkanalisation, Frischwasserversorgung
satisfaction 41T Zufriedenheit, Genugtuung
saturated fats *pl* 17 gesättigte Fette/Fettsäuren
to **save** 19F, 35 retten; 63T *(Geld usw.)* sparen; **~ sb/sth from sth** 59 jdn/etw vor etw bewahren
savings *pl* 65 Ersparnisse
to **say what's on your mind** 162T sagen, was man denkt
saying 63 Sprichwort
to **scare sb** 125 jdn erschrecken, jdm Angst einjagen
scared, to be ~ of heights 121 nicht schwindelfrei sein, Höhenangst haben
scary 87 gruselig, unheimlich
scene 149 Ort, Tatort; **behind the ~s** 103T hinter den Kulissen
scheme 118 Programm, Maßnahmen
scholarship 133 Stipendium
school, primary ~ 116 Grundschule; **~ exchange** 30T Schüleraustausch; **~ leaving certificate** 109 Schulabgangszeugnis; **~-leaving exam** 133 Abschlussprüfung; to **drop out of ~** 51 die Schule abbrechen
scientist 17 (Natur-)Wissenschaftler/in
scissors *pl* 10 Schere
scooter 11 Tretroller, Motorroller
score 52T Punktzahl, Ergebnis
to **score** 121 einen Punkt machen, ein Tor erzielen; **~ a point** 130 einen Punkt erzielen; **~ a try** 29F *(Rugby:)* einen Versuch erzielen
screen 69 Bildschirm
sea: ~ level 122 Meereshöhe
seagull 60 Möwe
seaside 83 Küste
season 112 Jahreszeit; 121 Saison
seat 38 Sitz, Platz; **collapsible ~** 37 Klappsitz; to **take one's ~** 49 seinen Platz einnehmen
seating 37 Bestuhlung
seaweed 17 Seetang

secure 73F sicher
security, food ~ 234 Nahrungsmittelsicherheit
to **seek** 74 suchen
segregation 147 Rassentrennung
to **select** 89 auswählen
selection 67T Auswahl, Angebot
self 74 Selbst; **~-confident** 38 selbstbewusst
semi-final 30T Halbfinale
to **send** 12 schicken, senden
senior 137T älter, höherrangig
sense, common ~ 103T gesunder Menschenverstand; **~ of belonging** 131 Zugehörigkeitsgefühl; **~ of responsibility** 137 Verantwortungsgefühl; to **make ~** 116 vernünftig sein, einleuchten
sensible(-ly) 103 vernünftig
sensitive, to be ~ towards sb/sth 107 für jdn/etw Verständnis haben, verständnisvoll mit jdm/etw umgehen
sentence 10 Satz
to **separate** 95 trennen
separate(ly) 30T getrennt, separat, einzeln
serial murderer 42 Serienmörder/in
serious 50 ernst, ernsthaft; to **take sb/sth ~ly** 54 jdn/etw ernst nehmen
to **serve: ~ as sth** 41 als etw dienen; **~ sb** 22 jdn bedienen
server 177 Servierer/in
service 22 Bedienung, Service; 176 Dienstleistung; **counselling ~** 51 Beratungsdienst; **length of ~** 107 Dienstzeit, Beschäftigungsdauer
serving 17 Portion
session, training ~ 44 Schulungseinheit
to **set, ~ off** 174 losfahren; **~ up sth** 94 etw einrichten, etw gründen; **~ up a tent** 89 ein Zelt aufschlagen; **~ an example** 41 ein Beispiel geben; **~ the course of sth** 52T die Weichen für etw stellen
set of parents 95 Elternpaar
to **settle: ~ down** 44T die Plätze einnehmen, zur Ruhe kommen; **~ down** 117 Fuß fassen, sich eingewöhnen; **~ into sth** 98T sich an etw gewöhnen, sich in etw einleben
settler 128 Siedler/in, Kolonist/in
several, on ~ occasions 156 mehrfach
severe 77 schwer, ernst
to **sew** 115 nähen
sex 30T Geschlecht; **same-~** 228 gleichgeschlechtlich
sexual 139 sexuell
to **shadow sb** 67 mit jdm *(zur Einarbeitung)* mitlaufen
to **shake** 173 zittern; **~shake hands** 44T die Hand geben, die Hände schütteln
to **shame** 36 beschämen
to **share** 33 teilen; **~ sth** 41T über etw *(vor Publikum)* sprechen; 96 sich etw teilen
shared 95 gemeinsam
shark 174 Hai
sheep, sheep 10 Schaf, Schafe
sheet 66 Bettlaken; **~ (of paper)** 77 Blatt (Papier)
shelf, shelves 9 Regal, Regale; to **stock a ~** 66 eine Regal befüllen
shift, cultural ~ 238 Kulturwandel; **policy ~** 236 Politikwandel
to **shine** 86 scheinen
shock, electric ~ 166 Stromschlag
shocked 43V schockiert

337

to **shoot: ~ sb** 146 jdn anschießen, jdn erschießen; **~ sb dead** 147 jdm erschießen

shooting 147 Erschießung

to **shop for sth** 21 etw (ein)kaufen

shop: ~ assistant 180 Verkäufer/in; **~ floor** 180 Verkaufsfläche

shopkeeper 116 Ladenbesitzer/in

shore; shores pl 136V Küste, Ufer; Land

short, to be ~ on sth 6 zu wenig von etw haben

to **shorten** 112 verkürzen, abkürzen

show 37 (Radio-, TV-)Sendung, (TV-)Serie; **motor ~** 126 Automobilmesse

to **show sb around** 82 jdn herumführen

shut 128 geschlossen

to **shut down** 167 abschalten

shy 38 schüchtern

siblings pl 137 Geschwister

sidewalk AE 147 Bürgersteig, Gehweg

sight 88 Sehenswürdigkeit; **in ~** 116 in Sicht; to **lose ~ of sth** 177 etw aus den Augen verlieren

sign 130 Hinweisschild

sign, safety ~ 166 Sicherzeitszeichen, Warnzeichen; **painted ~** 125 handgemaltes Schild

sign-off 79 (Brief, Telefonat usw.:) Schluss, Verabschiedung

significant 137 bedeutend

to **silence** 100 (Handy) stummschalten

silent, on ~ 101T stummgeschaltet

similar (to sb/sth) 41 (jdm/einer Sache) ähnlich

similarity 145 Ähnlichkeit

since 86 weil

sincerely, Yours ~ 109 Mit freundlichen Grüßen

to **sing along** 173 mitsingen

singing 163 Gesang

single: ~ parent 93 Alleinerziehende/r; **~-parent family** 93 Einelternfamilie

site, building ~ 159 Baustelle

situated, to be ~ 66 liegen

to **sketch** 92 skizzieren

sketch 180 Skizze

ski instructor 172 Skilehrer/in

skiing 119 Skifahren

skill 16 Fähigkeit, Fertigkeit, Kompetenz; 30T Geschicklichkeit; **circus ~s** pl 71 Zirkuskünste, Akrobatik; **motor ~s** pl 30T Motorik; **people ~s** pl 217 soziale Kompetenz

skillful 30T geschickt, erfahren, gut

to **skim** 58 (Text) überfliegen

skin 74T Haut

skinny 37 mager, dürr

skyscraper 176 Wolkenkratzer

slave 32 Sklave/Sklavin

slavery 32 Sklaverei

to **sleep** 9 schlafen

slice 18 (Kuchen-)Stück

slightly 55 leicht, ein wenig

slim 38 schlank

slimming product 38 Schlankheitsmittel

to **slow down** 6 langsamer sprechen

smart(ly) 44T (Kleidung:) schick, elegant

to **smell** 140T riechen, stinken

smell 150T Geruch, Gestank

smooth(ly) 44T reibungslos, glatt

snake 174 Schlange

so: ~ far 30 bislang; **~ that** 37 damit

soaking wet 86 klatschnass

soap, bar of ~ 141 Stück Seife; **~ opera** 71 Seifenoper

sociable 83 gesellig, umgänglich

social 26 gesellig, sozial; **~ gathering** 138 geselliges Beisammensein; **~ media** pl 26 soziale Medien; **~ misfit** 159 Außenseiter, Sonderling; **~ occasion** 124T gesellschaftlicher Anlass

socializing 158 Geselligkeit

society 37 Gesellschaft

to **soften** 54 mildern, abschwächen

sole 157 alleinig, einzig

solution 77 Lösung

solvable 43V lösbar

to **solve** 43V lösen

sometime 23 irgendwann, (demnächst) einmal

somewhat 55 etwas, irgendwie

soon, as ~ as 86 sobald

to **sort: ~ sth into sth** 39 etw in etw einsortieren; **~ out sth** 103T etw klären, etw regeln

sound 10 Laut, Klang

to **sound** 17 klingen

source 16 Quelle

soya 20T Soja

space, parking ~ 10 Parkplatz; **wide open ~s** pl 124 weites Land, Weiten; **~ of time** 49 Zeitspanne

to **spare sth** 87 etw übrig haben

to **speak: ~ out against sb** 30T sich (öffentlich) gegen jdn aussprechen, jdn kritisieren; **~ up** 6 lauter sprechen; **Speaking.** 152 (Telefon:) Am Apparat.

speaker, native ~ 157 Muttersprachler/in

special deal 126 Sonderangebot

spectacular 124T eindrucksvoll, spektakulär

spectator 122 Zuschauer/in; **~ sport** 33 Publikumssport

to **speculate** 119 mutmaßen, spekulieren

speculation 149 Mutmaßung(en), Vermutung(en)

speech 33 Vortrag, Rede; **~ bubble** 11 Sprechblase

speed 121 Geschwindigkeit; **data ~** 224 Datengeschwindigkeit

spelling alphabet 90 Buchstabieralphabet

to **spend** 13 (Zeit) verbringen; 61 (Geld) ausgeben

spending 102T Ausgabe(n), Geldausgeben

spicy 150T würzig, scharf

spirit, in good ~s 103T guter Dinge, gut gelaunt

to **split up** 31 sich trennen

spokesman 41T Sprecher

spokesperson 41T Sprecher/in

sport, to do ~ 25 Sport treiben

sportswear 59 Sportbekleidung

sporty 154 sportlich

to **spread; ~ awareness about sth** 37 Bewusstsein für etw schaffen

stadium 120 Stadion

staff 88T Personal; **pedagogical ~** 107 Lehrpersonal; **member of ~** 111 Mitarbeiter/in

stage 41T Bühne

stall 124T (Markt-)Stand

to **stamp one's feet** 121 mit den Füßen trampeln

standard, impossible ~s pl 37 unerreichbare Maßstäbe; **~ English** 112 hochsprachliches Englisch

star 85 Stern

to **star in a show** 37 in einer Serie mitspielen

to **start a family** 174 eine Familie gründen

to **start off** 6 anfangen

starter 24 Vorspeise

state 14 Staat; 28F Zustand

to **state sth** 51 etw erklären, etw sagen, etw feststellen

statement 6 Aussage, Aussagesatz

statistics 50 Statistik(en)

stay 83 Aufenthalt; **length of ~** 89 Aufenthaltsdauer

steep 87 steil

step 26 Schritt; **flight of ~s** 168 Treppe

to **step: ~ on sb/sth** 124T auf jdn/etw treten; **~ out of sth** 177 aus etw steigen, aus etw treten; **~ foot in sth** 99 etw betreten

stereotype 159 Klischee

steward 103T Ordner/in

stick 32 Stock

to **stick to sth** 114 sich an etw halten

to **stock a shelf** 66 eine Regal befüllen

stolen 133 geraubt, gestohlen

to **stop: ~ sth** 37 etw verhindern; **~ sb from doing sth** 29F jdn daran hindern, etw zu tun

store 63T Laden, Geschäft; **convenience ~** 147 Laden um die Ecke, Spätkauf; **department ~** 180 Kaufhaus; **grocery ~** 66 Lebensmittelladen; **liquor ~** AE 147 (konzessionierter) Spirituosenladen

storey 176 Stockwerk

strait 135 Meerenge, Straße

stranger 46 Fremde/r, Unbekannte/r

strategy 159 Strategie

street, one-way ~ 107 Einbahnstraße; to **line the ~s** 125 die Straße säumen, Spalier stehen; to **take to the ~s** 147 auf die Straße gehen (um zu demonstrieren)

strength 137 Stärke, Kraft

to **strengthen** 32 stärken

stressful 47 anstrengend, stressig

to **stretch** 66 sich erstrecken

strict(ly) 101T streng

strike 41T Streik

to **strike** 41T streiken

structure 46 Aufbau

to **structure sth** 46 etw strukturieren

struggle 107 Kampf

to **struggle with sth** 52T mit etw zu kämpfen haben; mit etw ringen

student 9 Schüler/in, Student/in; **exchange ~** 34 Austauschschüler/in; **fellow ~** 48 Mitschüler/in

studies pl 52T Studium, hier: Schule; **media ~** 134 Publizistik, Medienwissenschaft

study 51 Untersuchung, Studie; **case ~** 167 Fallstudie

to **study** 52 lernen; **~ sth** 17 sich etw genau ansehen

stuff 60 Sachen, Zeug

style 54 Stil, Art

sub-heading 16 Zwischenüberschrift

subscriber 71 Abonnent/in

substitute 50 Ersatz, Ersetzung

suburb 147 Vorort

to **succeed** 145 Erfolg haben

success 52T Erfolg; to **make a ~ of sth** 116 etw zum Erfolg führen, etw gelingt

successful 41 erfolgreich

sudden 122 plötzlich, jäh, überraschend

to **suffer: ~ sth** 50 etw erleiden; **~ from sth** 20 an etw (Krankheit usw.) leiden

to **suggest** 26 vorschlagen; 151F andeuten, nahelegen

suggestion 16 Vorschlag

suicide 52T Selbstmord

suitable 26 geeignet
sum, total ~ 181 Gesamtbetrag
to sum: to ~ up 26 zusammenfassend
to summarize 82 zusammenfassen
summary 28 Zusammenfassung
sunburned, to get ~ 103 sich einen
  Sonnenbrand holen
supervisor 101 (direkte/r) Vorgesetzte/r
to supply sth 109 etw zur Verfügung stellen
to support 122 (Argument) untermauern,
  stützen; **~ sth** 41T etw unterstützen;
  ~ sb 40 jdm helfen, jdn unterstützen
support 52T Hilfe, Unterstützung; **life-~
  system** 48 Lebenserhaltungssystem
supportive 75 hilfsbereit, unterstützend
to suppose 88T annehmen, glauben
supposed, to be ~ to do sth 32 etw
  (eigentlich) tun sollen
sure, to make ~ 33 dafür sorgen, sicher-
  stellen; **for ~** 234 ganz bestimmt; **That's
  for ~.** 173 Na klar! So viel steht fest.
surgery 50 Operation
surprised 66 überrascht, erstaunt
surrounded 87 umgeben
surrounding area 108 Umland, Umgebung
surroundings pl 85 Umgebung
survey 77 Umfrage
to survive 16 überleben
to suspect 95 vermuten
suspect 149 Verdächtige/r
suspicious, to be ~ of sb 145 jdm gegenüber misstrauisch sein
sustainability 58 Nachhaltigkeit
sustainable 17 nachhaltig
to swap 57 tauschen, austauschen
to swear 98T fluchen
swear word 98T Schimpfwort
sweater 66 Pullover
to switch: ~ off 47 abschalten; 102T ausschalten, ausmachen; **~ to sth** 51 auf etw
  umsteigen, auf etw umstellen
sympathetic 74 mitfühlend, verständnisvoll
sympathy 74T Mitgefühl, Mitleid
symptom 77 Symptom, Anzeichen
system 49 Organismus; **life-support ~**
  48 Lebenserhaltungssystem
systemic 147 systembedingt

T

table, pool ~ 56 Billardtisch; **to lay the ~** 99
  den Tisch decken
tablet 51 Tablette
taboo 52T Tabu
tactful 164 taktvoll
tag line 28 Bildunterschrift, Slogan
take (on sth) 74T Sicht (auf etw), Meinung
  (zu etw)
to take: ~ sth on 95 etw übernehmen, etw
  annehmen; **~ up** 176 (Platz, Raum) einnehmen; **~ part in sth** 16 an etw teilnehmen;
  ~ to the streets 147 auf die Straße gehen
  (um zu demonstrieren); **~ turns to do
  sth** 6 etw abwechselnd tun
tale, tall ~s pl 137T abenteuerliche
  Geschichten
talented 41 begabt, talentiert
talk 58 Vortrag; **to engage in small ~ with
  sb** 67 mit jdm ins Plaudern kommen
talkative 176 gesprächig
tall tales pl 137T abenteuerliche Geschichten
tanned 118 sonnengebräunt, braun
target group 24 Zielgruppe
task 16 Aufgabe

taste 20T Geschmack; 124T Kostprobe,
  Vorgeschmack; **to cater for all ~s** 126 für
  jeden Geschmack etw bieten
to taste (of sth) 15 (nach etw) schmecken
tasty 23 schmackhaft, lecker
tattoo artist 137T Tätowierer/in
tax 66 Steuer; **sales ~** AE 66 Mehrwertsteuer
team: ~ leader 60 Teamleiter/in; **~ mate**
  30T Mannschaftskamerad
to team up with sb 59 sich mit jdm zusam-
  mentun, mit jdm zusammenarbeiten
technician 143T Techniker/in
technological 63T technologisch, technisch
technology 16 Technologie, Technik
temporary 110T befristet
to tend to do sth 98T dazu neigen,
  etw zu tun
tension, interethnic ~ 145 Spannung(en)
  zwischen ethnischen Gruppen
tent 82 Zelt; **to set up a ~** 89 ein Zelt
  aufschlagen
term 74T Begriff
terrible 42 furchtbar
terrifying 121 entsetzlich, furchteinflößend
territory 134 Gebiet, Territorium
to test, ~ drive 126 probefahren
testimony 161F Aussage, Erfahrungsbericht
to text 98 eine SMS senden, simsen
text (message) 69 SMS
that, so ~ 37 damit
theft, identity ~ 71 Identitätsdiebstahl
theoretical 162T theoretisch, spekulativ
theory, in ~ 147 theoretisch
thief, thieves 184 Dieb, Diebe
thinking 76 Denkweise, Denken
though, even ~ 35 obwohl
thought 31 Gedanke
threat (to sb/sth) 41T Gefahr, Bedrohung
  (für jdn/etw)
thrill 177 Nervenkitzel, Kick
thrilling 33 aufregend, spannend, mitreißend
throughout … 106 in ganz …
to throw sb off 125 jdn abwerfen
thunder 121 Donner
to thunder 173 donnern
to tidy (up) 156 aufräumen, saubermachen
tight-knit 134 eng verbunden
time, in ~ 51 rechtzeitig; **on ~** 114 pünktlich; **at the same ~** 49 gleichzeitig; **by the ~**
  86 wenn, als; **period of ~** 48 Zeitabschnitt,
  Zeit, Phase; **space of ~** 49 Zeitspanne;
  waste of ~ 64 Zeitverschwendung; **full-~**
  176 Vollzeit-; **part-~** 124 Teilzeit(-); to
  take ~ off 110 sich freinehmen; **to take ~
  out** 142T sich freinehmen; **sb has a hard ~
  doing sth** 168 jdm fällt es schwer, etw zu tun
timekeeping 134 Pünktlichkeit
timetable 13 Fahrplan, Zeitplan
tiny 134 klein, winzig
tip 22 Trinkgeld
to tip sb 66 jdm ein Trinkgeld geben
title 16F, 37 Titel
titled 37 mit dem Titel
toiletries pl 140 Kosmetikartikel
to tolerate 138 dulden, tolerieren
ton 61 Tonne; **a ~ of** 63T jede Menge; **~s
  of …** 165 jede Menge …, tonnenweise …
tongue, mother ~ 109 Muttersprache
tool, gardening ~ 177 Gartengerät
tooth, teeth 10 Zahn, Zähne
top, low-cut ~ 44T tief ausgeschnittenes
  Oberteil; **on ~ of sth** 134 zusätzlich zu etw

total 49 Gesamt-, Gesamtmenge/-betrag;
  ~ sum 181 Gesamtbetrag
to touch 44T berühren; **~ down the
  ball** 29F (Rugby:) den Ball niederlegen
touch, to keep in ~ 96 in Verbindung bleiben
touchy-feely 95 körperbetont, emotional
tough 52 hart
to tour 172 (Land usw.) bereisen
towards the end 110T gegen Ende
towel 66 Handtuch
town, home ~ 177 Heimatstadt; **old ~** 87
  Altstadt; **twin ~** 44 Partnerstadt; **~ council**
  44T Stadtrat, Stadtverwaltung
toxic 37 giftig, (äußerst) schädlich
to trade 102 Handel treiben, handeln
trade 157 Handel; **~ fair** 126 (Branchen-/
  Handels-)Messe
to train for sth 45 eine Ausbildung zu etw
  machen
trainer 44 Dozent/in, Ausbilder/in
trainers pl BE 58 Turnschuhe, Sportschuhe
training, vocational ~ 44 Berufsausbildung;
  ~ session 44 Schulungseinheit
to translate 11 übersetzen
translation 16 Übersetzung
translator 177 Übersetzer/in
transport, public ~ 134 öffentliche Verkehrsmittel
trash 60 Müll, Abfall
travel guide 83 Reiseführer
traveller 83 Reisende/r
treadmill 31 Laufband
to treat 35 behandeln
treat 121 Vergnügen, Leckerbissen
treatment 37 Behandlung; **course of ~** 50
  Therapie, Behandlung
trial period 176 Probezeit
tribal 144 Stammes-
tribe 136 Stamm
trivial 165 banal, belanglos
trolley 8 Wagen
trolley 66 Einkaufswagen
truck 60 Lastwagen; **forklift ~** 166 Gabelstapler
true, to make a dream come ~ 116 sich
  einen Traum erfüllen
truly 173 wirklich, echt
trust 77 Stiftung; **National T~** 83 brit. Organisation für Denkmalpflege und Naturschutz
to try sth on 68 etw anprobieren
try, to score a ~ 29F (Rugby:) einen Versuch
  erzielen
tune 70 Lied, Song
turkey 128 Truthahn
to turn: ~ 16 138 16 werden; **~ up** 28
  kommen, auftauchen; **~ out** 121 sich
  herausstellen; 123 sich entwickeln, laufen;
  ~ out to be sb/sth 42 zu jdm/etw werden, sich als jd/etw herausstellen; **~ to sth**
  147 zu etw werden, sich zu etw entwickeln;
  ~ sth into sth 74T etw zu etw machen,
  etw aus etw machen; **~ sth off** 100 etw
  ausschalten; **~ a blind eye to sth** 101T bei
  etw ein Auge zudrücken; **~ bad** 88T sich
  verschlechtern, (Wetter:) umschlagen
turn, to be sb's ~ 30T an der Reihe sein,
  dran sein; **to take ~s to do sth** 6 etw
  abwechselnd tun
tutor 52T Nachhilfelehrer/in
tutoring 140 Nachhilfe
twice 17 zweimal
twin 95 Zwilling; **identical ~s** pl 95 eineiige
  Zwillinge; **~ town** 44 Partnerstadt

U

ugly 85 hässlich
unarmed 147 unbewaffnet
uncertain 78 unsicher, ungewiss
uncomfortable 85 unbequem, unkomfortabel
uncountable 12 unzählbar
to **underestimate** 168 unterschätzen
to **undergird** 43V untermauern
to **undergo sth** 137 sich einer Sache unterziehen, etw mitmachen
underprivileged 35 benachteiligt, unterprivilegiert
underscore 90 Unterstrich
understanding 137 Verständnis
unedited 37 unbearbeitet
unexpected 103T unvorhergesehen
unfair 74T ungerecht, unfair
unfiltered 38 ungefiltert
unfortunately 121 leider
to **unfriend sb** 163 *(soziale Medien:)* jdn als Freund löschen
unfriendly 85 unfreundlich
unhappiness 74 Elend, Traurigkeit
unhealthy 38 ungesund
union, Universal Postal U~ 157 Weltpostverein
unique 137T einzigartig
to **unite** 81 sich vereinigen
United Nations *pl* 157 Vereinte Nationen
unity 136V Einheit, Zusammengehörigkeit
universal 176 allgemein, universell; **U~ Postal Union** 157 Weltpostverein
university, to get into ~ 52T einen Studienplatz erhalten
unless 90 außer wenn, es sei denn; **not ~** 144 nur (dann), wenn
unlike sth 177 anders als etw
unlikely 63T unwahrscheinlich
unnecessary 101T unnötig
unpredictable 124T unberechenbar
unsociable 159 kontaktarm, menschenscheu
unsure 58 unsicher
unusual 16 ungewöhnlich
unwelcoming 162T abweisend
up: ~ close 173 aus nächster Nähe; **~ to a point** 74T bis zu einem gewissen Grad
to **update** 181T aktualisieren, auf den neuesten Stand bringen
to **upload** 76 hochladen
upset 162T aufgebracht, verärgert; to **get ~** 98T sich aufregen, sich ärgern
urban 124 städtisch, Stadt-
use, to make ~ of sth 143T etw verwenden, etw nutzen
used, to be ~ to sth 141 etw gewohnt sein; **~ plastic** 59 Altplastik
usual, as ~ 59 wie üblich

V

vacancy 55 *(Hotel:)* freies Zimmer
vacant 148 *(Stelle:)* unbesetzt
vague 74 vage, diffus
valley 116 Tal
valuable 76 wertvoll
value 41T Wert
to **value** 134 schätzen, wertschätzen
van, camper ~ 82 Wohnmobil
varied 103 abwechslungsreich
variety 20 Vielfalt, (große) Auswahl, Abwechslung
various 37 verschiedene/r/s
vast 62F, 124 gewaltig, riesig

vehicle 126 Fahrzeug; **horse-drawn ~** 138 Pferdefuhrwerk
venue 36 Veranstaltungsort
vest 156 Laufshirt
via 95 mittels, über, per
victim 147 Opfer
view 46 Ansicht, Meinung; 87 Aussicht; **point of ~** 149, 219 Perspektive
violence 33T Gewalt
violent 121 brutal, gewalttätig; **non-~** 147 gewaltlos, gewaltfrei
viral, to go ~ 41T sich rasant (im Internet) verbreiten
virtual 71 virtuell
visa 110 Visum; **work ~** 118 Arbeitsvisum
to **visit** 162T zu Besuch sein
visitor 44 Besucher/in
vocational education 133 berufliche Bildung
vocational training 44 Berufsausbildung
voice call 69 Sprachanruf
voicemail 87 Mailbox
voluntary: ~ service 106 Freiwilligendienst; **~ work** 109 Freiwilligenarbeit
volunteer 51 (freiwillige/r) Helfer/in; **~ work** 51 ehrenamtliche Tätigkeit
to **vote** 34, 137 abstimmen, wählen
vowel 9 Vokal

W

wage 176 Lohn
to **wait: I can't ~!** 88T Ich kann es kaum erwarten!
waiter 7 Kellner
to **walk: ~ by** 177 vorbeilaufen, vorübergehen
walk, from all ~s of life 41T aus allen Gesellschaftsschichten, aus allen Milieus; to **go for ~s** 65V spazieren gehen
walking: ~ aids *pl* 37 Gehhilfe(n); **~ holiday** 142T Wanderurlaub
wallet 12 Brieftasche, (Herren-)Portemonnaie
to **warm: ~ to sb** 95 sich für jdn erwärmen; **~ up** 17 sich erwärmen, sich erhitzen
warming, global ~ 17 Erderwärmung
warmth 118 Wärme
to **warn** 70 (auf etw) hinweisen, warnen; **~ sb of sth** 51 jdn vor etw warnen
warning 101T Verwarnung, Abmahnung
to **wash: ~ up sth** 59 etw anspülen; **~ the dishes** 156 (Geschirr) spülen
to **waste** 52T verschwenden, vergeuden
waste 58 Müll, Abfall; **~ of time** 64 Zeitverschwendung
watch 182 Wache, Wachmannschaft
to **watch out** 98T vorsichtig sein, aufpassen
water polo 29F Wasserball
way: ~ of life 108 Lebensweise, Lebensart; **by the ~** 99 übrigens; **in a ~** 133 sozusagen, in gewisser Weise; **this ~** 23 hier entlang; to **change one's ~s** 20T seine Gewohnheiten ändern; to **find one's ~ around** 134 sich zurechtfinden; to **find one's ~ somewhere** 59 wohin gelangen; to **lead the ~** 59 führend sein, wegweisend sein; to **pay one's own ~** 137T alles selbst bezahlen; **one-~ street** 107 Einbahnstraße
weakness 42 Schwäche
wealth, distribution of ~ 102T Wohlstandsverteilung
wear 59 Abnutzung, Verschleiß; to **get all the ~ out of sth** 59 etw benutzen, bis es nicht mehr geht; **ladies' ~** 180 Damenbekleidung
wearer 137T Träger/in

wedding, ~ ring 167 Ehering
weekday 13 Wochentag, Werktag
to **weigh** 37 wiegen
weight 27 Gewicht; **~ loss** 37 Abnehmen; to **lose ~** 27 abnehmen
weird 18 verrückt, schräg, seltsam
welcome: You're ~. 124T Bitte (sehr). Gern geschehen.
welcoming 163 freundlich, gastfreundlich
well: ~-being 52T Wohlbefinden; **~-off** 95 wohlhabend; **It's just as ~ that …** 174 Da ist es gut, dass …
wet 140 feucht, nass; **soaking ~** 86 klatschnass
wheelchair 25 Rollstuhl
whenever 173 immer wenn, wann immer
while 9 während; 173 solange; 88T Weile
wide: ~ open spaces *pl* 124 weites Land, Weiten
to **widen** 174 erweitern
will, against sb's ~ 221 gegen jds Willen
willing, to be ~ to do sth 33 bereit/willens sein, etw zu tun
win 30T Sieg
to **win: ~ a contract** 65 einen Auftrag erhalten, den Zuschlag erhalten; **~ the lottery** 184 im Lotto gewinnen
to **wind down** 47 abspannen, sich entspannen, runterkommen
winner 26 Gewinner/in, Sieger/in
wisdom 137 Weisheit, Lebenserfahrung
wolf, wolves 178 Wolf, Wölfe
to **wonder** 54 sich fragen
wonder, natural ~ 119 Naturwunder
word, to put out the ~ 102T die Nachricht verbreiten
to **work: ~ out** 123 sich entwickeln, laufen; **~ sth out** 88T etw herausfinden
work: ~ experience 100 Praktikum; **~ permit** 110 Arbeitserlaubnis; **~ visa** 118 Arbeitsvisum; **~ class** 147 Arbeiterklasse; **~ holiday** 83 Ferienpraktikum, Arbeitsurlaub
worker, white-collar ~ 222 Büroangestellte/r
workplace 166 Arbeitsplatz; **~ safety** 167 Sicherheit am Arbeitsplatz
works, printing ~ 167 Druckerei
workshop 44 Werkstatt
world cup 30T Weltpokal, Weltmeisterschaft
worldview 76 Weltsicht, Weltbild
worn out 59 abgenutzt, *(Schuhe:)* ausgelatscht
worried 13 besorgt, beunruhigt
to **worry about sth** 49 sich um etw Sorgen machen, sich über etw Gedanken machen
worrying 147 beunruhigend
to **write up sth** 24 etw formulieren, etw ausarbeiten
writer 76 Schriftsteller/in
wrong, to get the ~ idea (about sth) 162 etw falsch verstehen
wrong, to go ~ 147 schiefgehen, aus dem Ruder laufen

Y

youngster 33T Jugendliche/r
Yours sincerely 109 Mit freundlichen Grüßen
youth centre 32 Jugendzentrum

Z

zip 65 Reißverschluss
to **zoom off** 177 davonsausen

be	was/were	been	sein
beat	beat	beaten	schlagen, besiegen
become	became	become	werden
begin	began	begun	anfangen, beginnen
break	broke	broken	brechen
bring	brought	brought	bringen
build	built	built	bauen
burn	burnt/burned	burnt/burned	(ver)brennen
buy	bought	bought	kaufen
catch	caught	caught	fangen
choose	chose	chosen	(aus)wählen
come	came	come	kommen
cut	cut	cut	schneiden
do	did	done	tun, machen
draw	drew	drawn	zeichnen
dream	dreamt/dreamed	dreamt/dreamed	träumen
drink	drank	drunk	trinken
drive	drove	driven	(Auto) fahren
eat	ate	eaten	essen
fall	fell	fallen	fallen
feed	fed	fed	füttern, ernähren
feel	felt	felt	(sich) fühlen, empfinden
fight	fought	fought	kämpfen
find	found	found	finden
fit	fit/fitted	fitted	passen, sitzen; anbringen
fly	flew	flown	fliegen
forget	forgot	forgotten	vergessen
get	got	got (AE gotten)	bekommen
give	gave	given	geben, schenken
go	went	gone	gehen, fahren
grow	grew	grown	wachsen
hang	hung	hung	hängen
have	had	had	haben
hear	heard	heard	hören
hide	hid	hidden	(sich) verstecken
hit	hit	hit	schlagen
hold	held	held	halten, festhalten
keep	kept	kept	behalten
know	knew	known	kennen, wissen
lay	laid	laid	legen
learn	learnt/learned	learnt/learned	lernen
leave	left	left	abfahren, verlassen, weggehen
let	let	let	lassen
lie	lay	lain	liegen
light	lit	lit	anzünden, beleuchten, anmachen

Irregular verbs

lose	lost	lost	*verlieren*
make	made	made	*machen*
mean	meant	meant	*meinen, bedeuten*
meet	met	met	*treffen, kennen lernen*
pay	paid	paid	*bezahlen*
put	put	put	*setzen, stellen, legen*
quit	quit/quitted	quit/quitted	*verlassen, aufhören*
read	read	read	*lesen*
ride	rode	ridden	*reiten, fahren*
rise	rose	risen	*(an)steigen*
run	ran	run	*laufen, rennen*
say	said	said	*sagen*
see	saw	seen	*sehen*
sell	sold	sold	*verkaufen*
send	sent	sent	*senden, schicken*
set	set	set	*setzen, stellen*
show	showed	shown	*zeigen*
shut	shut	shut	*schließen*
sing	sang	sung	*singen*
sit	sat	sat	*sitzen*
sleep	slept	slept	*schlafen*
smell	smelt/smelled	smelt/smelled	*riechen*
speak	spoke	spoken	*sprechen*
spell	spelt/spelled	spelt/spelled	*buchstabieren*
spend	spent	spent	*ausgeben, verbringen*
stand	stood	stood	*stehen*
steal	stole	stolen	*stehlen*
swim	swam	swum	*schwimmen*
take	took	taken	*nehmen*
teach	taught	taught	*unterrichten, beibringen*
tell	told	told	*sagen, erzählen*
think	thought	thought	*denken*
throw	threw	thrown	*werfen*
understand	understood	understood	*verstehen*
wake	woke	woken	*aufwachen, aufwecken*
wear	wore	worn	*tragen*
win	won	won	*gewinnen*
write	wrote	written	*schreiben*

Allgemeiner Hinweis zu den in diesem Lehrwerk abgebildeten Personen:
Soweit in diesem Lehrwerk Personen fotografisch abgebildet sind und ihnen von der Redaktion fiktive Namen, Berufe, Dialoge und Ähnliches zugeordnet oder diese Personen in bestimmte Kontexte gesetzt werden, dienen diese Zuordnungen und Darstellungen ausschließlich der Veranschaulichung und dem besseren Verständnis des Inhalts.

Umschlag: (Cover) stock.adobe.com / Cybrain; stock.adobe.com / Kzenon; stock.adobe.com / con-trastwerkstatt; stock.adobe.com / Robert Kneschke; stock.adobe.com / Bojan; Shutterstock / wavebreakmedia; stock.adobe.com / contrastwerkstatt; stock.adobe.com / pictworks; stock.adobe.com / goodluz; stock.adobe.com / contrastwerkstatt; *(Karten)* CV/Carlos Borrell Eikö-ter

S. 7: *(1)* stock.adobe.com / Rido; *(2)* stock.adobe.com / michaeljung; *(3)* stock.adobe.com / Milissenta; *(4)* stock.adobe.com / Kalim; **S. 8:** CV / Nicole Rademacher; **S. 9:** Shutterstock.com / Redshinestudio; **S. 10:** CV / Nicole Rademacher; **S. 11:** CV / Nicole Rademacher; **S. 12:** CV / Nicole Rademacher; **S. 13:** CV / Nicole Rademacher; **S. 14:** *(1)* stock.adobe.com / olenatur; *(2)* Shutterstock.com / Jaro68; *(3)* Shutterstock.com / Baturina Yuliya; *(4)* Shutterstock.com / Fotografie-Kuhlmann; **S. 15:** *(1)* stock.adobe.com / uwimages; *(2)* stock.adobe.com / al62; *(3)* Shutterstock.com / Anastasia_Panait; *(4)* stock.adobe.com / travelphotos; *(5)* stock.adobe.com / alotofpeople; *(6)* stock.adobe.com / Jenifoto; **S. 17:** stock.adobe.com / inguaribile; **S. 19:** Shutter-stock.com / Great Divide Photography; **S. 20:** *(1)* stock.adobe.com / ponomarencko; *(2)* stock.adobe.com / sumnersgraphicsinc; **S. 22:** Shutterstock.com / Andreea Tudor; **S. 25:** *(1)* stock.adobe.com / lzf; *(2)* Shutterstock.com / ostill; *(3)* Shutterstock.com / Sergey Nivens; *(4)* Shutterstock.com / Dusan Petkovic; *(5)* Shutterstock.com / pio3; *(6)* Shutterstock.com / iko; *(7)* Shutterstock.com / pio3; *(8)* Shutterstock.com / Eugene Onischenko; **S. 26:** stock.adobe.com / Gstudio Group; **S. 27:** *(1)* stock.adobe.com / the_lightwriter; *(2)* Shutterstock.com / BaLL LunLa; **S. 28:** *(1)* stock.adobe.com / the_lightwriter; *(2)* Shutterstock.com / Ross Petukhov; **S. 29:** *(1)* Shutterstock.com / ShutteCreat; *(2)* Shutterstock.com / vectorfusionart; **S. 30:** Shutterstock.com / wavebreakmedia; **S. 31:** Shutterstock.com / Thisislove; **S. 32:** *(1)* Shutterstock.com / sainthorant daniel; *(2)* Shutterstock.com / Andrey Yurlov; *(3)* Shutterstock.com / Cool_photo; *(4)* Shutterstock.com / Yash Keswani; *(5)* Shutterstock.com / Dani Llao Calvet; **S. 33:** *(1)* Shutterstock.com / MSSA; *(2)* Shutterstock.com / shurkin_son; **S. 34:** Shutterstock.com / matimix; **S. 35:** *(Yousafzai)* Imago Stock & People GmbH / Pacific Press Agency; *(Neuer)* Imago Sportfotodienst GmbH / Sven Simon; *(King)* Bridgeman Images / AGIP; *(Firefighter)* stock.adobe.com / gwimages; *(Mum)* stock.adobe.com / Sunny studio; *(Grandad)* Shutterstock.com / Catalin Petolea; *(Hintergr.)* Shutterstock.com / -strizh-; **S. 37:** Shutterstock.com / Rawpixel.com; **S. 38:** Shutterstock.com / Ronnie Chua; **S. 39:** CV / Nicole Rademacher; **S. 40:** mauritius images / alamy stock photo / Stills Press; **S. 41:** akg-images / TT NEWS AGENCY; **S. 42:** Shutterstock.com / Thinglass; **S. 43:** Shutterstock.com / kenary820; **S. 44:** *(1)* stock.adobe.com / Ilyes Laszlo; *(2)* stock.adobe.com / leungchopan; **S. 47:** *(1)* Shutterstock.com / lassedesignen; *(2)* Shutterstock.com / Diego Cervo; *(3)* Shutterstock.com / Barnaby Chambers; *(4)* Shutterstock.com / Mladen Zivkovic; *(5)* Shutterstock.com / Eric Eric; *(6)* Shutterstock.com / Pressmaster; *(7)* Shutterstock.com / sezer66; **S. 48:** Shutterstock.com / Zerbor; **S. 49:** *(1)* Shutterstock.com / Brendan Howard; *(2)* stock.adobe.com / Cigdem; **S. 52:** Shutterstock.com / Tom Wang; **S. 54:** Shutterstock.com / TheCreativeMill; **S. 55:** Shutterstock.com / Ljupco Smokovski; **S. 57:** *(1)* stock.adobe.com / Monkey Business; *(2)* mauritius images / alamy stock photo / D / Gruffydd Thomas; *(3)* stock.adobe.com / Kzenon; *(4)* stock.adobe.com / beeboys; *(5)* stock.adobe.com / WavebreakmediaMicro; *(6)* stock.adobe.com / daviles; *(7)* Shutterstock.com / YIUCHEUNG; *(8)* Shutterstock.com / Rishiken; **S. 58:** Shutterstock.com / cris-ti180884; **S. 59:** *(1)* Shutter-stock.com / maradon 333; *(2)* Shutterstock.com / Liu zishan; *(3)* Shutterstock.com / Katrevich Valeriy; **S. 63:** *(1)* Shutterstock.com / namtipStudio; *(2)* Shutterstock.com / vilax; *(3)* Shutterstock.com / Kiselev Andrey Valerevich; **S. 64:** CV / Nicole Rademacher; **S. 65:** Shutterstock.com / OksanaOO; **S. 67:** Shutterstock.com / Dean Drobot; **S. 68:** Shutterstock.com / Syuzann; **S. 69:** (ob.) stock.adobe.com / canbedone; *(1)* Shutterstock.com / Luna Vandoorne; *(2)* stock.adobe.com / Olaf Speier; (3) Shutterstock.com / Syda Productions; *(4)* Shutterstock.com / YAKOBCHUK VIACHESLAV; *(5)* stock.adobe.com / DragonImages; **S. 70:** *(A/Mozialla)* stock.adobe.com / alessandradesole; *(A/TessaJune)* stock.adobe.com / Mat Hayward; *(A/Diogenes)* stock.adobe.com / yellowpaul; *(B/Songbird)* Shutterstock.com / Eugenio Marongiu; *(B/OliverD)* stock.adobe.com / kues1; *(B/TessaJune)* Shutterstock.com / Lia Koltyrina; *(emojis)* Shutterstock.com / JosepPerianes; *(icons)* Shutterstock.com / Vasya Kobelev; **S. 71:** *(1)* Shutterstock.com / carlos castilla; *(2)* stock.adobe.com / Alex White; **S. 73:** Shutterstock.com / Aa Amie; **S. 74:** Shutterstock.com / conrado; **S. 75:** Shutterstock.com / Rawpixel.com; **S. 77:** CV / Oxana Rödel; **S. 81:** *(ob./a–d)* Shutterstock.com / okili77; *(un./a)* Shutterstock.com / Gavin Ritchie; *(un./b)* stock.adobe.com / chrisdorney; *(un./c)* Shutterstock.com / JeniFoto; *(un./d)* Shutter-stock.com / Ruth Black; *(un./e)* dpa Picture-Alliance / PA Wire / empics; (un./f) mauritius images / alamy stock photo / Findlay; **S. 82:** *(a)* Shutterstock.com / satit sewtiw; *(b)* Shutterstock.com / Dmitry Naumov; *(c)* Shutterstock.com / Dragon Images; *(d)* Shutterstock.com / shutter_o; *(e)* Shutterstock.com / Aleksey Stemmer; *(un. li.)* Shutterstock.com / Syda Productions; *(un. re)* Shutterstock.com / Phovoir; **S. 83:** Shutterstock.com / esfera; **S. 84:** Shutterstock.com / Shaiith; **S. 86:** *(1)* Shutterstock.com / Lekcha; *(2)* Shutterstock.com / Uber Images; *(3)* stock.adobe.com / Kybele; *(4)* stock.adobe.com / imageegami; *(5)* Shutterstock.com / Billion Photos; **S. 87:** *(1)* Shutterstock.com / David Ionut; *(2)* Shutterstock.com / Evannovostro; *(3)* Shutterstock.com / Mariusz S. Jurgielewicz; *(4)* Shutter-stock.com / Daxiao Productions; *(5)* mauritius images / alamy stock photo / Paul Bagot; *(6)* stock.adobe.com / sonyakamoz; **S. 88:** Shutterstock.com / Stuart Jenner; **S. 92:** Shutterstock.com / JosepPerianes; **S. 93:** *(1)* Shutterstock.com / Fotoluminate LLC; *(2)* Shutterstock.com / Halfpoint; *(3)* stock.adobe.com / ricardoferrando; *(4)* Shutterstock.com / Billion Photos; *(5)* Shutterstock.com / Monkey Business Images; *(6)* stock.adobe.com / Fotolia365; **S. 94:** stock.adobe.com / yupachingping; **S. 95:** Shutterstock.com / create jobs 51; **S. 97:** Shutterstock.com / Doglikehorse; **S. 98:** Shutterstock.com / Monkey Business Images; **S. 100:** CV / Nicole Rademacher; **S. 102:** Shutterstock.com / Beykov Maksim; **S. 103:** Shutterstock.com / melis; **S. 105:** *(1)* Shutterstock.com / ded pixto; *(2)* Shutterstock.com / Nestor Rizhniak; *(3)* Shutterstock.com / michaeljung; *(4)* stock.adobe.com / JackF; *(5)* Shutterstock.com / wavebreakmedia; *(6)* Shutterstock.com / Photodiem; *(7)* Shutterstock.com / Ikonoklast Fotografie; *(8)* Shutterstock.com / quinky;

Quellenverzeichnis

S. 107: *(1)* Shutterstock.com / szefei; *(2)* Shutterstock.com / vepar5; *(3)* Shutterstock.com / Sokolenko; **S. 109:** Shutterstock.com / ArtFamily; **S. 110:** *(un. ll.)* Shutterstock.com / Khongtham; *(ob. re.)* Shutterstock.com / Franco Volpato; *(un. re.)* Shutterstock.com / SamJonah; **S. 113:** *(2)* stock.adobe.com / Luap Vision; *(1)* Shutterstock.com / E3D; **S. 114:** Shutterstock.com / Anna Klepatckaya; **S. 115:** *(1)* Shutterstock.com / Dipak Shelare; *(2)* Shutterstock.com / wavebreak-media; *(3)* stock.adobe.com / Antonioguillem; **S. 116:** Shutterstock.com / Joe Kirby Photography; **S. 117:** Shutterstock.com / Undivided; **S. 119:** *(1)* Shutterstock.com / Bob Pool; *(2)* Shutter-stock.com / margaret.wiktor; *(3)* Shutterstock.com / Barbara Tripp; *(4)* Shutterstock.com / f11photo; *(5)* Shutterstock.com / Jacob Haskew; *(6)* Shutterstock.com / Nicholas Courtney; *(7)* Shutterstock.com / PSboom; **S. 120:** *(1)* stock.adobe.com / Tomasz Zajda; *(2)* Shutterstock.com / Vasyl Shulga; *(3)* Shutterstock.com / Monkey Business Images; **S. 121:** stock.adobe.com / Billion-Photos.com; **S. 122:** Shutterstock.com / JoeSAPhotos; **S. 123:** *(1)* Shutterstock.com / DJP3tros; *(2)* Shutterstock.com / kosmos111; **S. 124:** Shutterstock.com / SNEHIT PHOTO; **S. 125:** Shutterstock.com / Jackson Stock Photography; **S. 126:** stock.adobe.com / pincasso; **S. 129:** *(1)* Shutterstock.com / Zurijeta; *(2)* Shutterstock.com / S.Borisov; *(3)* Shutterstock.com / lisheng2121; *(4)* Shutterstock.com / niroworld; *(5)* Shutterstock.com / Frank Gaertner; *(6)* Shutterstock.com / nnattalli; **S. 131:** *(1)* Shutterstock.com / Evgeny Atamanenko; *(2)* Shutterstock.com / Dean Drobot; *(3)* Shutterstock.com / Rawpixel.com; *(4)* Shutterstock.com / Willy Barton; *(5)* Shutterstock.com / Billion Photos; *(6)* Shutterstock.com / nopporn; *(7)* Shutterstock.com / Chip-munk131; **S. 132:** *(1)* Shutterstock.com / Taras Vyshnya; *(2)* mauritius images / alamy stock photo / Ashley Cooper; *(3)* Shutterstock.com / JJFarq; *(4)* Shutterstock.com / AJR_photo; *(5)* Shutterstock.com / GagliardiPhotography; *(6)* Shutterstock.com / simez78; *(7)* mauritius images / alamy stock photo / Mimmo Lobefaro; **S. 133:** Shutterstock.com/TheMumins; **S. 135:** Shutterstock.com / Marcell Faber; **S. 136:** Shutterstock.com / Soloviova Liudmyla; **S. 137:** *(1)* Shutterstock.com / Jtn pictures; *(2)* Shutterstock.com / Serlena Bessonova; *(3)* Shutterstock.com / Rocketclips, Inc.; **S. 138:** Shutterstock.com / hutch photography; **S. 139:** Shutterstock.com / Dan Thornberg; **S. 140:** *(a)* stock.adobe.com / Scanrail; *(d)* stock.adobe.com / tanawatbig; *(c)* Imago Stock & People GmbH / blickwinkel; *(e)* Shut-terstock.com / Stockforlife; **S. 142:** Shutterstock.com / Ollyy; **S. 143:** Shutterstock.com / Rawpixel.com; **S. 145:** *(1)* stock.adobe.com / marino; *(2)* stock.adobe.com / Joshua Resnick; *(3)* stock.adobe.com / stokkete; *(4 / ob.)* Shutterstock.com / anna karwowska; *(4 / un.)* CV / Oxana Rödel; *(5)* stock.adobe.com / ink drop; *(6)* stock.adobe.com / Rafael Ben-Ari; *(7)* stock.adobe.com / Robert Kneschke; *(8)* stock.adobe.com / Cylonphoto; **S. 146:** CV / Timo Grubing; **S. 149:** Shutterstock.com / Jacob Lund; **S. 150:** stock.adobe.com / mihail39; **S. 151:** Cartoonstock / Mark Lynch; **S. 152:** stock.adobe.com / Gajus; **S. 155:** *(1)* stock.adobe.com / moloko88; *(2)* stock.adobe.com / chronicler; *(3)* Shutterstock.com / Milkovasa; *(4)* Shutterstock.com / HQuality; **S. 157:** *(a–d)* Shutterstock.com / Filip Bjorkman; **S. 158:** *(1)* Shutterstock.com / F8 studio; *(2)* Shutterstock.com / Syda Productions; *(3)* Shutterstock.com / Phovoir; *(4)* Shutterstock.com / michaeljung; **S. 159:** stock.adobe.com / Melpomene; **S. 160:** Shutterstock.com / Fabrik Bilder; **S. 162:** *(1)* Shutterstock.com / STUDIO GRAND WEB; *(2)* Shutterstock.com / pathdoc; **S. 163:** *(1)* Shutterstock.com / Anton_dios; *(2)* Shutterstock.com / Marko Rupena; *(3)* Shutterstock.com / Milles Studio; **S. 166:** *(ob.)* stock.adobe.com / bartsadowski; *(1, 4, 5)* Shutterstock.com / Barry Barnes; *(2)* stock.adobe.com / alona_s; *(3)* stock.adobe.com / nazar12; *(6)* stock.adobe.com / alona_s; *(7)* stock.adobe.com / teracreonte; *(8)* stock.adobe.com / Barry Barnes; **S. 167:** *(1)* stock.adobe.com / Kybele; *(2)* Shutter-stock.com / zefart; *(3)* stock.adobe.com / zefart; **S. 171:** *(1)* Shutterstock.com / Peshkova; *(2)* Shutterstock.com / Syda Productions; *(3)* stock.adobe.com / Hemant; *(4)* stock.adobe.com / BillionPhotos.com; *(5)* Shutterstock.com / 1000 Words; *(6)* stock.adobe.com / lenets_tan; *(7)* stock.adobe.com / pressmaster; *(8)* Shutterstock.com / Ditty_about_summer; *(9)* Shutterstock.com / Roman Samborskyi; **S. 172:** *(1)* stock.adobe.com / hanack; *(2)* Shutterstock.com / Dean Drobot; *(3)* Shutterstock.com / Josu Ozkaritz; **S. 173:** *(1)* Shutterstock.com / Sunny Whale; *(2)* Shutterstock.com / PlusONE; *(3)* Shutterstock.com / Miceking; *(4)* Shutterstock.com / Aureliy; **S. 174:** *(1)* Shutterstock.com / NatalyaOst; *(2)* Shutterstock.com / Ollyy; **S. 176:** stock.adobe.com / Algol; **S. 178:** Shutterstock.com / Nat-o-Nat; **S. 179:** *(1)* Shutterstock.com / Nejron Photo; *(2)* Shutterstock.com / puhhha; **S. 180:** *(1)* Shutter-stock.com / Dasha Petrenko; *(2)* Shutterstock.com / A and N photography; *(3)* Shutterstock.com / sabarwal; *(4)* Shutterstock.com / Iakov Filimonov; *(5)* Shutterstock.com / Dragon Images; *(6)* Shutterstock.com / mimagephotography; *(7)* stock.adobe.com / Alex Ishchenko; *(8)* Shutterstock.com / Sergey Ryzhov; **S. 181:** Shutterstock.com / Dean Drobot; **S. 183:** *(1)* Shutterstock.com / Tom Wang; *(2)* Shutterstock.com / oneinchpunch; *(3)* Shutterstock.com / Stefanovic Mina; *(4)* Shutterstock.com / benjaminec; *(5)* Shut-terstock.com / Africa Studio; *(6)* Shutterstock.com / Artashes; *(7)* Shutterstock.com / ImageFlow; *(8)* Shutterstock.com / biletski-yevgeniy.com; **S. 209:** *(1)* Shutterstock.com / KawaiiS; *(2)* Shutterstock.com / cocoo; *(3)* Shutterstock.com / nito; *(4)* Shutterstock.com / Kwangmoozaa; *(5)* Shutterstock.com / Tero Vesalainen; *(6)* Shutterstock.com / 5 second Studio; *(e-book reader)* Shutterstock.com / Erlo Brown; *(tablet)* Shutterstock.com / Peshkova; *(whiteboard)* Shutterstock.com / Gorodenkoff; (laptop) Shutterstock.com / Savanevich Viktar; *(printer)* Shutterstock.com / Nerthuz; **S. 210:** *(1)* Shutterstock.com / Debra James; *(2)* Shutterstock.com / ChameleonsEye; *(3)* Shutterstock.com / Jodie Johnson; *(4)* Shutterstock.com / Benny Marty; *(5)* Shutterstock.com / Yatra; *(6)* Shut-terstock.com / eo Tang; *(7)* Shutterstock.com / OSORIOartist; *(8)* Shutterstock.com / Marek Bidziski; *(9)* Shutterstock.com / studio-stoks; *(10)* Shutterstock.com / Olivier Le Moal; *(11)* Shutterstock.com / Tupungato; *(12)* Shutterstock.com / Krakenimages.com; **S. 211:** AFPTV / A. Buthier, N. Larson; **S. 212:** AFPTV / B. Logan / Wei Lan / E. Malykhina; **S. 213:** AFPTV / AFP / Glenda Kwek; **S. 214:** *(ob.)* stock.adobe.com / markobe; *(un. li.)* stock.adobe.com / viperagp; *(un. re.)* Shutterstock.com / Arturs Budkevics; **S. 216:** Shutterstock.com / Monkey Business Images; **S. 219:** Shutterstock.com / sirtravelalot; **S. 220:** Shutterstock.com / Mauro Carli; **S. 222:** Shutterstock.com / courage007; **S. 226:** *(1)* Shutterstock.com / Songquan Deng; *(2)* Shutterstock.com / Paul Seftel; **S. 229:** Shutterstock.com / Joanna Dorota; **S. 231:** Shutterstock.com / Thomas Amby; **S. 233:** CV / D'avila Illustration Agency; **S. 237:** Shutterstock.com / Photo_Grapher; **S. 239:** Shutterstock.com / Rawpixel.com